D0161230

The T.A.T., the C.A.T., and the S.A.T. in Clinical Use

ALSO BY LEOPOLD BELLAK

Dementia Praecox: The Past Decade's Work and Present Status: A Review and Evaluation. New York: Grune & Stratton, 1948.*

Projective Psychology: Clinical Approaches to the Total Personality (editor and contributor; with Lawrence Abt). New York: Alfred A. Knopf, 1950, paperback, Grove Press, 1959.*‡

Manic-Depressive Psychosis and Allied Disorders. New York: Grune & Stratton, 1952.

The Psychology of Physical Illness: Psychiatry Applied to Medicine, Surgery and the Specialties (editor and contributor). New York: Grune & Stratton, 1952; London: Churchill, 1953.†

Schizophrenia: A Review of the Syndrome (editor and contributor, with P. K. Benedict). New York: Logos Press; now distributed by Grune & Stratton, 1958.*†

Contemporary European Psychiatry (editor). New York: Grove Press, hardcover and paperback, 1961.

A Handbook of Community Psychiatry and Community Mental Health (editor and contributor). New York: Grune & Stratton, 1964.

Emergency Psychotherapy and Brief Psychotherapy (with Leonard Small). New York: Grune & Stratton, 1965.†§

The Broad Scope of Psychoanalysis: Selected Papers of Leopold Bellak, ed. Donald P. Spence. New York: Grune & Stratton, 1967.

The Schizophrenic Syndrome (editor, with Laurence Loeb). New York: Grune & Stratton, 1969.

Progress in Community Mental Health, Vol. I (editor and contributor, with Harvey H. Barten). New York: Grune & Stratton, 1969 (Vol. II, 1971; Vol. III, 1975).

The Porcupine Dilemma. New York: Citadel Press, 1970; Tokyo: Diamond Publishing Company, 1974.§†

Ego Functions in Schizophrenics, Neurotics, and Normals (with Marvin Hurvich and Helen Gediman). New York: John Wiley & Sons, 1973.☐

A Concise Handbook of Community Psychiatry and Community Mental Health (editor and contributor). New York: Grune & Stratton, 1974.

The Best Years of Your Life. A Guide to the Art and Science of Aging. New York: Atheneum, 1975.§•

Overload: The New Human Condition. New York: Behavioral Publications, 1975.

Geriatric Psychiatry: A Handbook for Psychiatrists and Primary Care Physicians (editor and contributor with Toksoz B. Karasu). New York: Grune & Stratton, 1976.

Emergency Psychotherapy and Brief Psychotherapy, with Leonard Small. New York and Larchmont: Grune and Stratton and C.P.S., Inc. 1978.

The Disorders of the Schizophrenic Syndrome, editor and contributor. New York: Basic Books, 1979.☐

Psychiatric Aspects of Minimal Brain Dysfunction in Adults (editor and contributor). New York: Grune & Stratton, 1979.

Specialized Techniques in Individual Psychotherapy, editor and contributor with Tokusz B. Karasu. New York: Brunner/Mazel, 1980.☐

Crises and Special Problems in Psychoanalysis and Psychotherapy, with Eleanor P. Faithorn. New York: Brunner/Mazel, 1980.☐

Reading Faces, with Samm Sinclair Baker. New York: Holt, Rinehart & Winston; paperback, Bantam Press, 1981.

Handbook of Intensive Brief and Emergency Psychotherapy, with Helen Siegel. Larchmont, NY: C.P.S., Inc., Box 83, 1984.☐

The Broad Scope of Ego Function Assessment, with Lisa A. Goldsmith. New York: John Wiley & Sons, 1984.

Handbook of Intensive Brief and Emergency Psychotherapy, with David M. Abrams and Ruby Ackermann-Engel. Larchmont, NY: C.P.S., Inc., Box 83, 1992.

Psychoanalysis as a Science. Boston: Allyn and Bacon, 1993.

Confrontation in Vienna. Larchmont, NY: C.P.S., Inc., 1993.

ALSO BY DAVID M. ABRAMS

The Folkstories of Children. (Brian Sutton-Smith with D. M. Abrams, G. J. Botvin et al.). Philadelphia: University of Pennsylvania Press, 1981.

Handbook of Intensive Brief and Emergency Psychotherapy. (Leopold Bellak with D. M. Abrams and R. Ackermann-Engel). Larchmont, NY: C.P.S., Inc., 1992.

---

*Selection of the Basic Book Club, † Also published in Spanish, ‡ Also published in Italian, § Also published in German, ☐ Selection of the Macmillan Book Club, • Also published in Japanese.

The Thematic Apperception Test, The Children's Apperception Test, and
The Senior Apperception Technique in Clinical Use

SIXTH EDITION

LEOPOLD BELLAK, M.D.

Emeritus Professor of Psychiatry,
Albert Einstein College of Medicine/Montefiore Medical Center
Clinical Professor of Psychology,
Postdoctoral Program in Psychotherapy,
New York University

DAVID M. ABRAMS, Ph.D.

Clinical Associate Professor in Clinical Psychology
Doctoral Program in Clinical Psychology,
City University of New York
Doctoral Program in School Psychology,
Ferkauf Graduate School of Yeshiva University

ALLYN AND BACON
Boston   London   Toronto   Sydney   Tokyo   Singapore

Nihil est in intellectu quid non antea fuerit in sensibus.
Hume

Esse est percipi.
Berkeley

Allyn & Bacon
A Viacom Company
Needham Heights, MA 02194

Internet: www.abacon.com
America Online: keyword: College Online

Library of Congress Cataloging-in-Publication Data
Bellak, Leopold
    The Thematic Apperception Test, the Children's Apperception Test, and the Senior Apperception Technique in clinical use / Leopold Bellak and David M. Abrams. —6th ed.
        p.   cm.
    Includes bibliographical references and index.
    ISBN 0-205-18999-7
    1. Thematic Apperception Test.   2. Children's Apperception Test.
3. Senior Apperception Technique.   I. Abrams, David M.   II. Title.
RC473.T48B45   1996   96-29032
155.2′844—dc20   CIP

Printed in the United States of America
10   9   8   7   6   5   00

CONTENTS

v

CHAPTER 20
GENDER AND MULTICULTURAL ASSESSMENT WITH
THEMATIC TESTS

CHAPTER 21
THE PSYCHODIAGNOSTIC TEST REPORT BLANK

PREFACE

It is now over six decades since the first publication on the Thematic Apperception Test by Morgan and Murray (1935) and over four decades since Leopold Bellak published the first edition of this book in 1954. Leopold Bellak and Sonya Sorel Bellak developed the Children's Apperception Test (C.A.T.), the Children's Apperception Test-Human Figures (C.A.T.-H.), the Children's Apperception Test-Supplement (C.A.T.-S.) for children, and the Senior Apperception Technique (S.A.T.) for elderly individuals. Thematic tests are now mainstays in the standard battery of psychological tests employed by nearly every psychologist who conducts a psychological evaluation.

The many new advances in the research and clinical use of thematic tests have contributed to major revisions in this book over the last six editions. In the past, many psychologists have been unsure as to the value of the T.A.T. in diagnostic assessment, since past practices have been characterized by inadequate methods of administration that elicit only sparse descriptions of T.A.T. cards, choosing different cards for different test takers based on which cards "pull" for material that resembles the test taker's personality, and interpreting the stories based only on "an impressionistic summary of themes." This sixth edition presents a clear and scientifically consistent approach to the T.A.T. with a standard method of administration, a standard T.A.T. sequence of 10 cards (which can be supplemented by cards that "pull" for specific material), and a standard method of scoring. This is the same concept that Bellak utilizes with the C.A.T. and C.A.T.-H., which can be supplemented by other cards from the C.A.T.-S., and the S.A.T., which can be supplemented by other cards after the standard sequence is administered.

Another development in thematic testing is a multidimensional assessment approach, which is part of the Bellak Scoring System. Originally, thematic tests were considered only personality tests; today, the contemporary psychologist utilizes an entire group of tests in the psychological test battery to evaluate all the different dimensions of cognitive-intellectual functioning, neuropsychological or learning disability assessment, creative thinking, and social-emotional functioning. Intelligence tests are no longer considered only cognitive-intellectual measures. The Bender Gestalt test is no longer considered only a neuropsychological screening instrument, and the T.A.T. and the Rorschach are no longer employed only as personality, projective tests.

Psychologists use intelligence tests to evaluate intellectual functioning; however, test behavior and other aspects of the intelligence test also reveal many aspects of the test taker's personality. The Bender Gestalt is primarily employed for screening perceptual-motor neuropsychological functioning; however, specific evaluation of line pressure, spacing of designs, and size of designs also reveal a lot about personality characteristics. Thematic tests are primarily windows into the inner feelings, conflicts, defense and coping mechanisms, interpersonal relations, and other personality factors of the test taker. Psychologists also utilize them to obtain a sample of language usage, evaluate the level of logical thinking in the organization of story elements into a coherent whole, and evaluate other aspects of cognitive, intellectual, and neuropsychological functioning of the test taker. (See the updated Chapter 13 on neuropsychological assessment with thematic tests and the two case examples of individuals with attention deficit disorder).

Murray's (1943a) *Thematic Apperception Test Manual,* which is published with the test pictures, is no longer employed in clinical use of the T.A.T. Leopold Bellak worked with Murray during the development of the T.A.T. and developed an interpretative system that includes part of Murray's scoring approach within a more comprehensive and practical scoring system. Thus, this book has become the primary manual for administering and interpreting the T.A.T., and, of course, the C.A.T. and the S.A.T. The last six decades of extensive research and clinical use of these tests have set in motion a process of continuous revision and updating of the text in order to provide for a comprehensive and current coverage of the main uses of these tests in contemporary practice. What was once the relatively slim volume of the first edition of this book has now grown into a substantial book in order to provide an overall review of the clinical use and research with the T.A.T. and related methods and to show the clinician how to administer thematic tests in a standardized manner and how best to score the T.A.T. protocol from a clinical standpoint.

The primary purpose of this book is to improve the psychologist's ability to utilize the T.A.T., C.A.T., and S.A.T. in making clinical diagnoses and facilitating the psychotherapeutic process. Since the senior author is a long-standing exponent of Freud's ego psychology and its related object relations and self-psychology approaches, this book also includes an introduction to the history and theory of the psychoanalytic, or psychodynamic, approach to projective testing in Chapter 2. This chapter, entitled "Theoretical Foundations for Projective Testing," shows how pivotal this perspective is in the history of projective tests and why Murray and others employ the term *apperception* in the names of most of the thematic tests. The book also provides as comprehensive a review of research with thematic tests as possible in order to assist students and researchers undertaking their own research. However, our main aim is for this book to serve as a practical handbook for the working clinician to consult on aspects of testing different age groups, individuals of different gender and cultures, and different clinical disorders.

The chief goals in this book are the following:

1. To provide an explanation of the theoretical bases for thematic tests in particular and projective tests in general
2. To provide a comprehensive, up-to-date introduction to thematic tests in clinical use
3. To provide a comprehensive review of the clinical and research literature on thematic tests
4. To present the background on the varieties of administration of the T.A.T. in the field and the rationale for following a standard "set" T.A.T. administration

5. To provide a clear introduction to the Bellak Diagnostic Scoring System for thematic tests
6. To provide an understanding of how the Bellak Interpretive System facilitates assessment of different pyschiatric disorders
7. To provide an introduction as to how thematic tests may be utilized in the treatment process
8. To provide a review of the important gender and cultural issues in utilizing thematic tests in research and psychological evaluation.

For the sixth edition, we have added two pivotally important and related new chapters: Chapter 1, which gives an introduction to the projective hypothesis and the main sections and issues in the clinical use of thematic tests, and Chapter 20, which reviews the many attempts to develop gender-specific and culture-specific thematic tests. The majority of this past literature has been limited to adapting Murray's original T.A.T. pictures primarily by making pictures that portray people, background settings, and situations familiar to the particular culture. In today's multicultural society, we emphasize that the contemporary clinical use of thematic tests also needs to take into consideration the test taker's primary language and cultural belief framework, the existence of test norms for the thematic test being employed for the test taker's particular culture, and the gender and cultural context of the testing situation (i.e., whether the tester is male, the test taker female, the tester of mainstream culture, the test taker of a minority culture, etc.).

The ends of Chapters 1 and 20 come back to our beginning issue of the projective hypothesis as to what makes for the most meaningful and revealing projective test—pictures that are clearly similar to the individual being tested, pictures that are slightly ambiguous or that portray individuals slightly different from the test taker, culturally familiar everyday situations, or situations that portray universally powerful human situations? In this continuing debate on the importance of gender and cultural sensitivity in psychological testing, we emphasize that the value of culturally specific T.A.T. cards should not overshadow the equally important value of a standardized T.A.T. administration, comprehensive categories of interpretation, norms for different ages and different psychiatric disorders, and more quantitative test analyses in order to bring the T.A.T. to the level of Exner's (1994) more quantitative approach for scoring the Rorschach. This book emphasizes that the last six decades of research and clinical use of thematic tests have brought professionals much closer to a more standardized and scientific approach to the use of these tests in clinical practice. The establishment of age, gender, and cultural norms for individuals with different clinical disorders make it possible for the psychologist to administer a standard T.A.T. card sequence with individuals of widely different cultures and to supplement the standard T.A.T. sequence with gender-specific and culture-specific cards, if these are available.

Other highlights of this new edition are major revisions of the extension of the Bellak Scoring System to the lively interdisciplinary field of the study of narrative and life history (Chapter 10), guidelines have been added for the assessment of adolescents with the T.A.T. (Chapter 7), and substantial updating of the chapter on the S.A.T., which now includes new test pictures (Chapter 19). Chapter 19 describes the critical role of thematic tests in the important, developing field of social gerontology or geriatic psychology, and it provides a clinical case example utilizing the 1996 revised S.A.T. pictures. The entire book has been completely revised and updated to include references that (1) are more comprehensive, to include the most significant publications from the entire span of six decades of thematic test research; and (2) cover the important and exciting new research in the last decade.

Several individuals have contributed significantly to this book over the years. Drs. Leonard Small and M. Brewster Smith read the first edition of the book and made many helpful suggestions. Lynn Lustbader helped with literature review and Ann Noll helped with editorial suggestions with the second edition. Caroline Birenbaum helped edit the third edition. Dr. Susan Berger helped with the fourth edition, and Lorin Perits, Mylan Jaixen, Deborah Reinke, and Lynda Griffiths assisted with the fifth edition. For the sixth edition, Jane Slater contributed many insights, translated the manuscript among several different word-processing formats, handled the considerable international correspondences, kept track of new citations, and provided editing and proofreading. Her monumental efforts to help bring the text into the computer age were indispensable.

A wonderful highlight of this new edition is the revised 1996 S.A.T. pictures that were redrawn by artist Violet La Mont, to whom we are very grateful for her fine and careful work. Marina Livshits of the clinical psychology department of Yeshiva University in New York City assisted in administering the new, revised S.A.T. pictures and assisted with the literature review. Michael Hiam helped prepare the bibliography to meet A.P.A. style and contributed important clinical and editorial suggestions. Special thanks also to Emilito Osorno, Yvonne Prempeh, Helen Marsh, Madeleine Seifter Abrams, and Jonathan and Rebecca Abrams for their assistance.

At Allyn and Bacon, we are indebted to our main editor, Mylan Jaixen, for his editorial direction and many creative ideas; his assistant, Susan Hutchinson; and Lynda Griffiths of TKM Productions for valuable copyediting. We would also like to thank the three reviewers who contributed many useful suggestions for this revision: Scott D. Churchill, University of Dallas; Steven Kubacki, University of Wyoming; and Sharon Shindelman, Board of Cooperative Educational Services in Yorktown Heights, New York.

Finally, Marlene Kolbert, as Leo Bellak's administrative assistant, has had a major role in this book, as she has had in the previous editions. She has also contributed in many invaluable ways over the last decades as the manager of C.P.S., Inc., which publishes the C.A.T., C.A.T.-H., C.A.T.-S., S.A.T., the Bellak Short Form for scoring thematic tests, Ego Function Scoring Blanks, handbooks, and other books.[1]

---

[1]A list of these tests and publications may be obtained by writing C.P.S., Inc., Box 83, Larchmont, NY 10538, or by calling or faxing a request to (914) 833-1633.

ABOUT THE AUTHORS

Leopold Bellak, M.A., M.D.[1]

Most psychologists know Leopold Bellak as the inventor of the C.A.T., C.A.T.-H, and S.A.T., who worked with Henry Murray at Harvard University from 1940 to 1942 prior to the publication of the T.A.T. (Murray, 1943) and who published one of the first and best experimental research studies on Freud's concept of projection using the T.A.T. (Bellak, 1944), a paper successfully replicated nearly 50 years later by Cramer (1991b). Other inventions in the field of assessment are the scoring template that is placed over the Coding and Digit Symbol subtests in the Wechsler intelligence tests and the *dysphorimeter,* a simple sound-clicking device useful in research on depression, anxiety, pain, and other dysphoric states (Bellak et al., 1989).

Born in Vienna, Austria, on June 22, 1916, Bellak attended medical school at the University of Vienna and studied psychoanalysis in Sigmund Freud's last years in Vienna from 1935 to 1938. When Hitler's forces marched into Vienna on March 13, 1938, he was arrested and imprisoned by the Nazi Secret Service. American psychoanalyst, Dorothy Tiffany Burlingham, arranged for Bellak's release, and he was able to emigrate to the United States, where he completed an M.A. in psychology at Boston University in 1939 and an M.A. in psychology at Harvard University in 1942. He completed all requirements for the Ph.D. in psychology, except the dissertation, prior to completing his M.D. at New York Medical College in 1944 and his internship and residency in psychiatry at St. Elizabeth's Hospital in Washington, D.C. He completed psychoanalytic training after an additional four years at the New York Psychoanalytic Institute in 1950.

Therefore, Bellak has the highest level of training in the fields of clinical psychology, psychiatry, and psychoanalysis. He is a licensed psychologist in the state of New York and a Diplomate in Clinical Psychology from the American Board of Examiners in Professional Psychology. He is similarly licensed in medicine and psychiatry and certified in psychoanalysis from the American Psychoanalytic Association. Bellak has held many teaching appointments in psychology at City College of New York, the New School for Social Research, Columbia University, and New York University, and in psychiatry at New York Medical College, George Washington University, and Albert Einstein College of Medicine.

Bellak published his first book, *Dementia Praecox,* in 1948, which brought a systems orientation to the diagnosis of schizophrenia and opened it up to be viewed

---

[1] Written by David M. Abrams.

not as a single entity but as including several subtypes. He later (1952, 1958, 1969, 1973, 1979) published five additional books on this systems approach to schizophrenia, affective, and related disorders. Along the same lines, he (1979) contributed one of the first books on the diagnosis of attention deficit disorder in adults, continuing to bring a systems perspective to this disorder (1983, 1984, 1986) and a subtype analysis with his identification of "ADD psychosis" (1994).

Since Bellak studied psychoanalysis during Freud's last years in Vienna, he brought to Harvard University in the early 1940s the latest thinking in psychoanalysis based on Freud's (1920, 1923) more sophisticated theory of ego psychology. Most U.S. mental health practitioners and academic psychologists at that time knew Freud primarily from his book, *The Interpretation of Dreams* (1900), and primarily applied Freud's first libido theory, which views the libido, or sexual drive, as the main motivator of human experience. Murray's approach to the T.A.T. was primarily influenced by Freud's libido or drive theory and that of other early psychoanalysts, such as Alfred Adler's emphasis on the aggressive drive and the power motive, Otto Rank's emphasis on the creative drive, and Carl Jung's emphasis on self-realization and other motivators. Murray broadened the early psychoanalytic drive notions to a hierarchy of internal "needs" and environmental "presses." Bellak, on the other hand, chose as his doctoral dissertation the aforementioned experimental study of the ego defense of projection on the T.A.T. (1944), wrote the first paper on how ego defense mechanisms are seen on thematic tests (1950), and developed an ego psychology scoring system for the T.A.T. (1947 and this text).

Bellak is equally well known in the fields of psychoanalysis and psychiatric diagnosis for his identification and clarification of 12 *ego functions*, which has become a major component of diagnostic evaluation by all mental health practitioners, particularly psychiatrists, when they conduct a psychiatric evaluation to evaluate a patient for admission to an inpatient hospital, as part of treatment planning for psychotherapy, and prior to prescribing medication. He (1973) published a major research study on schizophrenics, neurotics, and normals, which established his ego function assessment as an invaluable tool in clinical assessment that has been used by many other researchers and clinicians (Bellak & Goldsmith, 1984) and that Bellak (1989) further clarified in his popular *Handbook of Ego Function Assessment*.

Bellak's ego function assessment is as important in the fields of social work and psychiatric evaluation as the current book on the T.A.T. is in psychology. Bellak's 12 ego functions are an established part of what is known in mental health as *the Mental Status*. There is not a psychiatrist today who would make a diagnosis of a patient without utilizing Bellak's ego functions, such as reality testing, judgment, sense of reality, object relations, defensive functioning, stimulus barrier, synthetic function, or the level of the individual's adaptive functioning. Bellak is especially appreciated for this ability to translate contemporary mental health concepts into methods of assessment that are clear, direct, and practical. He has developed simple scoring forms that facilitate scoring a T.A.T. (Bellak, 1947, and this text), writing up the overall psychological report (*The Psychodiagnostic Test Report Blank*, 1965), and conducting a Mental Status evaluation in psychiatry and other fields (Bellak, 1989).

Undoubtedly, his training in clinical and research psychology, psychiatry, and psychoanalysis helped him apply an interdisciplinary, systems approach to several different fields simultaneously. Hence, the editor of an early collection of Bellak's papers entitled the book *The Broad Scope of Psychoanalysis* (Spence, 1967), which Bellak (1993) further demonstrates in his presentation of experimental research on psychoanalytic concepts and of the psychoanalytic treatment process in *Psychoanalysis as a Science.*

When he was Chief of Psychiatry at Elmhurst Hospital in New York City, Bellak established the first 24-hour emergency psychiatry service. His continued contributions in emergency psychiatry, crisis intervention, and community mental health include 11 full-length books (Bellak, 1964, 1965, 1969, 1972, 1974, 1975, 1978, 1980, 1984, 1987, 1992). Another field in which he is one of the major pioneers is social gerontology, geropsychology, or geriatric psychiatry, to which he (1975) contributed the first handbook for the general public and one of the first handbooks in geriatric psychiatry (Bellak & Karasu, 1976). Both lend increased authority to his development of the Senior Apperception Technique (S.A.T.).

Bellak is the author of over 37 popular, technical, and research books; over 200 published papers and other unpublished psychological tests, inventions, unpublished papers; and an unpublished play about the inventor of dynamite, Alfred Nobel. The autobiography of his youth, *Confrontation in Vienna* (Bellak, 1993), "a compelling account of the worst sides of Viennese prejudice and barbarity" (Roazen, 1996), provides a dramatic contrast to the many later decades of open-minded and endlessly creative contributions to clinical psychology, psychiatry, and psychoanalysis. His unusual practice and high level of leadership of three active professions caused the psychologist-psychoanalyst Erich Fromm to say, when he first met him, "Oh, I know the other Bellak."

Among his many honors are the Annual Merit Award from the New York Society of Clinical Psychologists in 1964, the Frieda Fromm Reichmann Award by the American Academy of Psychoanalysis for outstanding contributions toward a better understanding schizophrenia in 1981; the Bruno Klopfer Award from the Society for Projective Assessment in 1990; the Award for Distinguished Professional Contributions to Knowledge from the American Psychological Association in 1993, and an honorary doctorate in psychology, the Honoris Causa, from the University of Paris in 1996.

David M. Abrams, Ph.D.[2]

David M. Abrams has collaborated with Bellak since 1980–1983, when Bellak was his supervisor in the Postdoctoral Training Program in Psychoanalysis and Psychotherapy of New York University's Department of Clinical Psychology. Abrams (1977) had earlier applied an ego psychology and folklore analysis to children's narrative fantasies in his doctoral dissertation at Columbia University under Professor Brian Sutton-Smith, an expert in the developmental psychology of children's expressive behavior (such as storytelling, symbolic play, games, and humor), and Professor Rosalea Schonbar, an expert in clinical psychology research on dream narratives.

---

[2] Written by Leopold Bellak.

Abrams coauthored with Sutton-Smith (1981) and others, *The Folkstories of Children,* a book that helped establish the growing, new interdisciplinary field of narrative studies in children and adults. For the 1986 fourth edition of this book, Abrams coauthored three chapters with Bellak on a new way to score object relations on thematic tests, the use of thematic tests in the assessment of borderline and narcissistic disorders, and neuropsychological indicators on thematic tests. The latter chapter presented the first thematic test protocols of the then-not-well-accepted diagnosis of attention deficit disorder (ADD) in children and adults, which has now become the "diagnosis of the 90's." Abrams also coauthored with Bellak and Ruby Ackermann-Engel a book in 1992 entitled *Handbook of Intensive Brief and Emergency Psychotherapy.*

Among his own pioneering papers is one on the intensive treatment of a profoundly deaf girl (Abrams, 1991), dream interpretation (Abrams, 1992) and the first case presentations of thematic test protocols of children and adolescents with a primary diagnosis of the not-yet-well-accepted diagnosis for children of narcissistic disorder (Abrams, 1993, 1995, in press).

Abrams has broad experience in the field from personality assessment to neuropsychology, crisis and early intervention, and a long-standing commitment to community mental health with profoundly deaf and poverty populations. He is qualified in both adult psychoanalysis and child psychoanalysis and is a member of the Association for Child Psychoanalysis. Over the last several years, he has been researching and writing a book on Herbert Graf (1903–1972), the inventive opera stage director who was the subject of Freud's (1909) famous case known as "Little Hans" (a 4-year-old boy who was afraid of horses), and working on a handbook on treatment planning.

From his doctoral dissertation and 13 years as Chief Psychologist at the Center for Preventive Psychiatry, White Plains, New York, to later work as Clinic Director, East New York Diagnostic and Treatment Center; Lexington Center for Mental Health Services; Associate Clinical Professor in the Doctoral Program in Clinical Psychology at City University; the Doctoral Program in School Psychology of Yeshiva University; and the Institute of Child, Adolescent, and Families Studies in New York City, he has perhaps administered and supervised more thematic tests than many psychologists of his generation. Abrams approaches clinical work as a creative collaboration with patients to help them discover their own cure, which brings unique insight and prescience to his psychological test evaluation and psychotherapy with children, adolescents, and adults.

CHAPTER 1

INTRODUCTION

The Projective Hypothesis

In the field of psychological testing, intelligence tests such as the Wechsler I.Q. tests and achievement tests such as the Wide Range Achievement Test are often referred to as *cognitive tests*. Personality assessment instruments such as the House-Tree-Person Drawing Test (H-T-P), Kinetic-Family-Drawing Test (K-F-D), Rorschach, and Thematic Apperception Test (T.A.T.) are often referred to as *projective tests*.

The term *projective test* goes back to Sigmund Freud's (1900) conception of *projection*, defined as a psychological mechanism by which an individual "projects" inner feelings onto the external world, then imagines these feelings are being expressed by the outside world toward oneself. For example, a 4-year-old boy is angry at a babysitter who left for another job. He projects this anger onto the babysitter and now believes that the babysitter took another job because "she hates me!" Similarly, when an individual has a dream, draws a picture, or makes up a story, this form of imaginary self-expression may be considered a "projection" onto the dream, drawing, or story of the individual's own inner thoughts, feelings, and conflicts. Cognitive tests generally ask for only one response and are more specific; they are a fact-based way of eliciting what an individual knows about the world and how he or she thinks and solves intellectual, logical problems. Projective tests do not have any correct answers; they are considered to be less structured, more open ended, and more creative, and the individual is freer to express inner feelings and reveal his or her basic personality orientation.

A tradition in projective tests is that the more unstructured and more ambiguous the stimulus, the more an individual may express her or his deepest inner wishes, anxieties, and conflicts. If the psychologist asks an individual to "draw a person," the individual may express a deeper feeling about the self-image than if the request is to "draw yourself." Similarly, the Rorschach set of inkblot pictures has the vagueness of looking at clouds that allows everyone to see many different things in them.

Some argue that intelligence tests also can be interpreted as projective tests in the sense that the Vocabulary and Comprehension subtests of the Wechsler I.Q. tests can be seen as *word association tests;* that is, the individual's particular choice of words may contain projections of inner feelings and conflicts as well as the attempt to find the best answer to the questions. Similarly, the Rorschach also presents a perceptual and logical problem for the individual to solve by structuring the inkblot into a logically organized Whole (W) response.

When Henry Murray (1943a) and his associates developed the Thematic

Apperception Test (T.A.T.), they predominantly had pictures of white, middle-class individuals in different situations, a couple of pictures of working-class and poor people, a dragon near a mountain, an imaginary-looking man in a graveyard, and a pastoral scene of a small lake. They also had different card sequences recommended for women, girls, men, and boys. Murray's idea was that, depending on the individual's age and sex, he or she should be given the sequence that primarily depicted individuals of the same age and gender in order for the individual to feel most comfortable in revealing her or his deepest feelings. Some of the individuals were drawn in order to make the particular gender of the individual *ambiguous,* so that individuals of both genders could utilize the same pictures.

This gave birth to numerous adaptations of the original T.A.T. cards for different ethnic groups, cultures, and countries. Such adaptations were based on the same hypothesis that an individual will feel freest to express inner feelings if he or she is asked to make up stories to pictures that show individuals as the central figures who most resemble the storyteller's age, gender, ethnicity, socioeconomic status, and culture.

Since the T.A.T. elicits a group of fantasy narratives, it is probably the projective test most similar to a dream, which Sigmund Freud (1900) believed was the "royal road to the unconscious." For that reason, perhaps, Freud's famous biographer, Ernest Jones, wrote to Murray to tell him that he believed that the T.A.T. provided the best bridge between Freud's psychoanalysis and academic psychology (Robinson, 1992, p. 413). Freud believed that all dreams have disguised meanings beneath the most obvious surface meaning of the story of the dream. The figure that most resembles the dreamer in a dream may be said to be what is closest to the individual's "conscious awareness," whereas the figures least resembling the dreamer may express deeper, more "unconscious" feelings about the self (Abrams, 1992).

An exciting, developing area in T.A.T. research in the last two decades, called *interpersonal object relations,* has as one of its basic assumptions that every figure in a dream or T.A.T. story is an aspect of the self on some level. This approach then looks at the level of interpersonal object relations in a T.A.T. as a way of assessing how an individual being tested conceptualizes his or her relations with others. Bellak (1947, 1950a, 1950b, 1950c, 1950d, 1954a) has frequently pointed out that one of the T.A.T.'s major strengths is that it provides a way to assess a person's relationship with others by examining the relationships among the figures in the T.A.T. stories; "relations to others" has always been one of Bellak's main scoring categories. For the Fourth edition of this book, Abrams and Bellak (1986) published a more specific approach to scoring this dimension of interpersonal object relations, which is the currently updated Chapter 11.

Other object relations scoring approaches were published by Thomas and Dudeck (1985) and Westen (1991b). Certain psychiatric disorders—such as schizophrenia and borderline and narcissistic personality disorders—have as one of their major symptoms an impairment in the ability to relate well with other people. Hence, it is important for the clinician to make a very careful and thorough evaluation of this interpersonal relations dimension in a psychological assessment. For that reason, we provide a case example of an actively psychotic man's T.A.T.

in Chapter 11. We have also updated Chapter 12 to reflect the exciting new developments from the fields of ego psychology, object relations theory, and self-psychology on the use of thematic tests with individuals who have borderline and narcissistic disorders.

Freud's projective hypothesis was also the basis of Bellak and Bellak's (1949) Children's Apperception Test (C.A.T.), which does not consist of pictures of children but of little animals in different situations. The C.A.T. has become the most popular thematic apperception test for children from 3 to about 11 or 12 years of age. This follows the assumption that an individual may feel more comfortable to project feelings about his or her self-image onto a figure drawing if the individual is first asked to "draw a person" rather than "draw yourself." Therefore, one argument is that T.A.T. pictures that are not obviously similar to the individual being tested may help the individual to feel "freer" to express deeper feelings about the individual's internal identity. Blum (1950) also developed a thematic apperception test for children featuring a little dog named "Blacky"; hence, this test is known as The Blacky Pictures. The C.A.T. has been published in 11 different countries and has become the main thematic test used by school psychologists, by clinicial psychologists, and in a plethora of important research studies. Bellak and Bellak (1965) developed a human version of the C.A.T. called the C.A.T.-H., which is useful for children from 11 or 12 years to 14 or 15 years, if the children are still preadolescent before the age when the T.A.T. would be preferable. Chapters 14 through 18 present the C.A.T. and C.A.T.-H. and their clinical and research tradition.

A fascinating question related to the projective hypothesis is: Why do preschool and elementary school-aged children prefer making up stories to the animal pictures of the C.A.T. to making up stories to pictures of children in the same situations on the T.A.T. or C.A.T.-H.? This topic will be discussed in Chapters 14 and 15.

Another area of exciting, developing T.A.T. research during the past two decades is the literature on gender and multicultural assessment that appears to disagree with presenting individuals being tested with pictures that are ambiguous or somewhat dissimilar to the individual's gender, ethnicity, socioeconomic status, and culture (Abel, 1973, Dana, 1993). Just as it is obviously culturally biased to evaluate an individual's level of intelligence based on I.Q. tests developed and normed for white, middle-class individuals, this research tradition argues that personality assessment also should not be conducted with culturally biased test materials. This assumption has spawned many adaptations of the T.A.T. and C.A.T. for different cultures, which have a huge literature dating from the 1940s to the present. Early research on the Thompson (1949) modification of the T.A.T. for African Americans found that African Americans were as comfortable and told as revealing stories to the Thompson T.A.T. as they did to Murray's T.A.T.

The main aim of the majority of cultural adaptations of the T.A.T., the C.A.T., and C.A.T.-H. is to have people and backgrounds that are culturally specific for different cultures. Some of the better cultural adaptations, such as the TEMAS (Costantino, Malgady, & Vazquez, 1981) of the C.A.T.-H. for elementary school-aged urban poor and working class Hispanic American children, attempt to have culturally specific people and backgrounds as well as the depiction of culturally specific situations. The C.A.T.'s depiction of young animals has made this test a universally appealing projective test stimuli for children of widely different cultures, which may make the C.A.T. a more useful clinical and research instrument than the TEMAS with children of the Hispanic American urban culture, since the C.A.T. is basically independent of culture specificity.

A drawback of many of these T.A.T. adaptations is that the pictures of *people, backgrounds, and situations* are not always as revealing and powerful as those of Murray's original cards. Murray and his colleagues worked for over nine years, trying out hundreds of different pictures, redrawing pictures to have a coherence of style, and trying out different sizes to pictures, from the first paper by Morgan and Murray (1935) to the current version of the T.A.T. (Murray, 1943a). It is also interesting that Murray had two versions—the first series of everyday situations and the second series of more dramatic situations—and different pictures for males, females, young boys, and young girls. However, over the years, clinicians have found a combination of pictures that they use with both males and females that are primarily from the first everyday series.

Another important point regarding the question of gender and cultural adaptation of the T.A.T. and C.A.T. is that there has now been over six decades of research on the T.A.T. and over four decades of research on the C.A.T. Thus, there is a background of age norms and norms for individuals with different personality orientations and psychiatric conditions. In attempting to meet questions of gender and cultural bias regarding these instruments, it is important to consider carefully the down side of discarding this long history of research and clinical experience in favor of more contemporary and more culturally specific pictures of the moment. A solution proposed in Chapter 4 of this book is to administer a basic set of 10 T.A.T. cards in the same order, independent of the gender and culture of the individual tested, so that there is a standardized stimulus for all individuals given the test. After that, other T.A.T. cards in Murray's series or culturally specific cards developed by others could be employed by the researcher or clinician. In this way, the T.A.T. will continue to build on a standardized research tradition, which will pave the way for the level of quantitative, computer program scoring of the Rorschach scoring system of Exner (1994).

When Abrams and Bellak (1986) wrote Chapter 13 on "Neuropsychological Assessment with Thematic Tests," attention deficit disorder (ADD) was only beginning to be used as a diagnosis by mental health professionals. Earlier, when it was called "minimal brain dysfunction," Bellak (1979) was one of the pioneers in leading the way for ADD to be recognized as a viable diagnosis in adults at the time. Bellak contributed several papers on ADD in adults. In fact, his (1994) paper for the lifetime award from the American Psychological Association presented his identification of ADD psychosis as a particular subtype of schizophrenia that calls for specific psychiatric medication and psychotherapeutic intervention. Chapter 13 has been updated to incorporate these important developments on neuropsychological indicators on thematic tests, as well as these new developments on ADD psychosis and attention deficit disorder, which is currently recognized as one of the major psychiatric diagnoses in children and adults.

A new feature of this sixth edition is the publication of revised pictures for the

Senior Apperception Technique (S.A.T.) for elderly individuals. The normal life span for people throughout the world has been steadily increasing. The world's population of those over 65 years of age is rapidly becoming so large that psychologists are increasingly being asked to evaluate elderly individuals in a number of different contexts. The increasing population of elderly individuals has given rise to new fields, such as gerontological psychiatry, for which Bellak was one of the pioneers. Bellak (1975) wrote one of the first general handbooks on aging for the lay public and one of the first handbooks in the new field of geriatric psychiatry (Bellak & Karasu, 1976). Thematic tests also were the foundation for the classic research in the new field of social gerontology (Neugarten & Guttmann, 1968; Maddox, 1994). While the S.A.T. pictures of Bellak and Bellak (1973) have been the mainstay of many researchers and clinicians working with the elderly, the pictures were redrawn by Violet Lamont in 1996, the same artist who drew the pictures for the C.A.T. Research and clinical experience with these new S.A.T. pictures find that the increased detail and artistic style similar to the C.A.T. and T.A.T. make the revised S.A.T. a much more successful projective test with an elderly population. Chapter 19 has been totally rewritten to reflect the important developments of gerontological psychology—or *geropsychology*—and the exciting use of the S.A.T. and revised S.A.T. of 1996.

The reader is invited to consider the following important questions about what makes for the most revealing and useful thematic apperception tests in research and clinical use:

1. Should Murray's (1943a) pictures be redrawn to be more up to date, showing people and backgrounds more in tune with contemporary fashion, rather than continuing to administer Murray's pictures from the 1930s and 1940s?
2. Should the people and backgrounds in Murray's pictures be redrawn to be culturally specific for testing individuals from other than white, middle-class U.S. culture and society?
3. Should totally different pictures than Murray's be developed that depict individuals of the same age, gender, and culture as the person being tested?
4. Should clinicians continue to use a small group of different T.A.T. cards for specific clinical problems (such as cards 1, 3BM, and 13MF for possibly depressed individuals)? Or should a standard set of the same 10 T.A.T. cards be administered in the same order for all individuals, independent of their possible clinical disorder?
5. Should a projective instrument provide the person being tested with a little psychological distance and ambiguity? Or should it be an immediately recognizable picture of a person in an everyday situation that looks very similar to the person being tested?
6. Is Murray's second series of "more dramatic situations" as revealing or more revealing than his first series of "everyday situations"?
7. Which are more revealing psychologically projective tests: (a) T.A.T. cards that depict a central character of the same general age, gender, and culture as the individual being tested, (b) T.A.T. cards that depict people from a past era of society, (c) T.A.T. cards that depict people of a slightly different culture and

background or even gender as the individual being tested, or (d) C.A.T. cards that depict animals?

8. Is the T.A.T. an appropriate instrument for young children? What are its main drawbacks as an instrument used with this age group?

9. Is the S.A.T. a more appropriate instrument with elderly individuals than the T.A.T.?

10. If the T.A.T., C.A.T., and S.A.T. are too open to gender and cultural bias, should the contemporary psychologist avoid using them altogether in favor of more ambiguous, more culture-independent stimuli, such as the Rorschach?

11. Are thematic apperception tests the best projective tests for evaluating interpersonal object relations?

12. What do thematic apperception tests offer that other projective tests do not?

Description of the T.A.T.

The Thematic Apperception Test (T.A.T.) of Murray (1943a) consists of 31 pictures of people in different solitary and social situations. There is a specific sequence of cards for girls, women, boys, and men that have, as the central figure, an individual of the same sex and general age group as the individual who is being tested. There are some common cards used for all ages and sexes and one blank card. The individual is asked simply to "make up a story" to each picture. The first half of the stories are considered to be pictures of everyday events; the second group is considered to be more dramatic, more similar to the deeper world of the dreamlife. In Murray's *need-press* method of scoring the stories, the psychologist makes an inventory of the numerous "needs" of the hero of each story and an inventory of contrasting requirements or forces from the environment that "press" on the hero. An example is the hero loves a woman, but she hates him. Hence, there is a "*need* for love or affiliation" met by a "*press* of hate or rejection."

Murray (1938) developed a theory of personality called *personology* that consists of a large variety of these need-press dichotomies. His system lists *needs* for abasement, achievement, aggression, acquisition, autonomy, creation, deference, destruction, dominance, intraggression, nurturance, passivity, and succorance. His list of *presses* include affiliation, aggression, dominance, nurturance, lack, loss, and physical injury. In Murray's (1943a) method of scoring the T.A.T., each story is analyzed according to all these needs and presses, each of which receive a weighted score. A hierarchy of the relationship of the needs to each other is also obtained with such concepts of Murray's as need-conflict, need-subsidiation, and need-fusion. For example, if a hero wants to buy a restaurant with the notion of giving people better and more healthful food and at the same time enriching himself by means of this public service, we would speak of a *fusion* of the hero's need for nurturance and acquisition. On the other hand, the hero may want to buy the restaurant because he expects it to be a good source of income that he needs to take care of his family. In this case, we would say that his need for acquisition (of money) is *subsidiary* to his need for nurturance; namely, he wants to acquire money in order to be able to take care of his family. By means of these two concepts, whole hierarchies of motivation can be recognized in the T.A.T.

Nearly a dozen such schemes of categories provide a quantitative need-press rank ordering along with a page for recording more general clinical impressions. Although Murray's (1943a) *Thematic Apperception Test Manual* is sold with every copy of the T.A.T. plates, his method of scoring never became a popular method of scoring the T.A.T., since learning to score these need-press dichotomies is very difficult and each T.A.T. scoring takes nearly four hours to complete.

A more comprehensive and practical method of scoring the T.A.T. is that of Leopold Bellak, who came to work with Murray at Harvard University after Bellak emigrated from studying psychoanalysis in Vienna, Austria, in 1938. Bellak proposed an early method of scoring the T.A.T. in 1941 (with Murray's encouragement) that included a shorter inventory of the hero's needs with key categories of the later "ego psychology" approach of Sigmund Freud (1920, 1923). For example, categories included conception of the world, relationship to others (now called interpersonal object relations), aggression, main conflicts, defense mechanisms, ego functions, and superego functioning (Bellak & Murray, 1941). Bellak (1947) further developed his system of analysis, which was published by the Psychological Corporation as the *Bellak TAT Blank, Analysis Sheets, and Guide to the Interpretation of the TAT.* (The interested reader will find this early scoring scheme in Abt and Bellak [1950, p. 196]). Bellak (1954b) later expanded on his method of T.A.T. analysis in the first major textbook on the T.A.T., which was the first edition of this book.

Bellak's system consists of 10 categories of analysis: (1) main theme; (2) self-functioning of the hero; (3) main needs and drives of hero; (4) conception of the world; (5) interpersonal object relations; (6) main conflicts; (7) nature of fears, insecurities and anxieties; (8) main defense and coping mechanisms; (9) superego functioning; and (10) general ego functions. Each story is scored quickly for each category on a fold-out form called the Bellak (1947) T.A.T. Short Form. This is a clinical way of thinking about the T.A.T. of an individual, rather than a quantitative scoring method. However, different dimensions can be scored in a quantitative manner, as was demonstrated for general ego functions in Bellak, Hurvich, and Gediman (1973) and Bellak and Goldsmith (1984). The clinician quickly jots down notes about each of the 10 categories for each story on the Short Form and then works across all stories for each category to make some general comments about the individual tested on each category. For example, the clinician will look at his or her notes for the defense mechanisms seen in all the stories in order to make a general listing or commentary about the individual's main defenses at the end of this category. Finally, the clinician works downward over all 10 categories in order to come to a general commentary on the personality organization as expressed on the overall T.A.T. protocol.

History of the T.A.T., C.A.T., and S.A.T.

When he developed the T.A.T., Murray was a professor of psychology at Harvard University at a time when the psychoanalysis of Sigmund Freud was being translated into English and being brought to the United States by students of Freud's, such as Murray's young graduate student, Leopold Bellak. The most famous work of Sigmund Freud (1900) is his *Interpretation of Dreams* in which Freud shows that dreams have two layers of meaning: the *manifest content* that consists of the "surface" everyday meaning of the dream's story and the *latent content* that consists of the often disguised, underlying unconscious meaning of the dream. For Freud, the primary motivation of most dreams was a disguised, unconscious, sexual or "libidinal" wish. An example is a woman who dreams of going to a musical concert and sitting next to a man, who asks her in the dream for the directions to go to a restaurant after the concert. In the dream, she answers that she does not know any good restaurants in the entire city. The manifest content is the basic facts of the dream, as a story of being asked a question that the dreamer cannot answer, which could mean that the woman has an anxiety about what she knows about the world. The latent content might be that she is attracted to the man and wants him to ask her to go to a restaurant with him after the concert and perhaps later to make love.

The first theory of Freud's psychoanalysis was called the *libido theory,* because he first believed that the primary motivation of all of human behavior was related to the sexual or libidinal drive. A *drive* is defined as a motivating force within the personality similar to a primary need, such as the need for hunger and sleep. In 1900, Freud thought that the sexual drive was the primary motivating force within the personality. Toward the end of his life, Freud (1920, 1923) changed his theory to what he called *ego psychology,* which broadened his view of human motivation to include a loving libidinal drive as well as an aggressive drive, called the *Id,* an internal conscience as to what is right and wrong, called the *Superego;* and an internal organizing force that attempts to maintain a balance within the personality, called the *ego.* The *ego* itself includes the functions of perception, memory, symbolic thinking, and the defense and coping mechanisms with which the individual attempts to manage the sexual and aggressive impulses from the id and the conflicting internalized moral imperatives of the superego.

An *ego psychology* view of the previously mentioned dream example is that the woman has an underlying id wish of going out with the man, which is the unconscious libidinal meaning of the man asking her for directions to go to a restaurant after the concert they are attending. Her answer that she does not know any good restaurants in the entire city is her moral sense from her internal conscience superego that she should not allow her loving impulses to be expressed so freely as to agree to go to a restaurant and perhaps later make love to a man she has just met. The ego comes in to defend against these "unconscious" desires and conflicts by distancing their meaning from her conscious awareness in the form of a dream that does not state anything about wanting to go out with this man, let alone make love to him. The defense mechanism is repression or denial to push this underlying id impulse or wish into the unconscious, and the defense mechanism of projection, which takes the unconscious wish and projects it into a disguised story in the form of a dream.

Freud (1900) proposed that the unconscious meaning of a dream can be discovered by *free associating* to each element in the dream. One can ask oneself what comes to mind about this man in the dream? What did he look like? What about the man's question about restaurants and the woman's answer that she did not know any good restaurants and so on. A therapist can help a patient understand her or his unconscious anxieties, wishes, conflicts, and feelings by working in this way on dreams that the patient reports during psychotherapy. On the other hand, Freud showed in his *Interpretation of Dreams* (1900) that anyone can work his or her way toward understanding deeper, unconscious meanings of personal dreams by free association to parts of the dream by oneself, as Freud did with many examples of his own dreams.

When Murray and his colleague, Christiana Morgan, published the first paper on the T.A.T., they argued that the T.A.T. was a kind of brief, inexpensive alternative to psychoanalytic therapy, especially for young people. They stated that it is "an effective means of disclosing a subject's regnant preoccupations and some of the unconscious trends that underlie them"(1935). Among the many different methods Murray had developed at the Harvard Psychological Clinic, the T.A.T. yielded what they felt was "the best understanding of the deeper layers of personality" (Morgan & Murray, 1935, pp. 8–12). Since a T.A.T. story is a personal narrative similar to a dream that might be reported by a patient to a psychotherapist, the T.A.T. lends itself very nicely to similar methods of analysis as in Freud's *Interpretation of Dreams*.

As we will present later in the book, one of the first scoring steps in Bellak's system is to do an analysis of the main theme of each story in which the clinician begins with a descriptive level and moves to an interpretative level, to a diagnostic level, and then to an elaborative level. One way of looking at this is that the *descriptive level* is the "manifest content" of the story, or a short digest of what is stated on the surface of the basic plot. It is what could also be called *experience-near* analysis (i.e., what the person who is administering the test actually experiences as she or he hears the words spoken by the individual being tested). Then the clinician proceeds to an *interpretative level* of underlying psychological meaning, which is proceeding to the latent content of the story. Next, one moves to a *diagnostic level* statement according to one's understanding of the storyteller's possible personality orientation, psychiatric symptoms, or clinical disorder. Finally, the *elaborative level* allows for some free association to let oneself go and see if one associates to some other type of meaning to the story (Abrams, 1993a, 1995).

An important biography of Murray, entitled *Love's Story Told: A Life of Henry A. Murray* by Forrest Robinson (1992), shows how Murray's background made him an ideal individual to develop a major personality test that could lend itself to a comprehensive personality diagnostic assessment for working clinicians based on the main dimensions of research on the psychology of personality in academic psychology. Often, interdisciplinary thinkers have training in a different field from their chosen profession, and innovative theorists occasionally bring a new perspective to their chosen field by not having been trained in the established tradition of this field. Sigmund Freud was a physician with extensive experience in medical research and neurology, but he had little, if any, direct training in the field of psychiatry. Jean Piaget worked with Alfred Binet on pioneering research on the beginnings of intelligence testing, but his formal degree was in biology—not psychology. Henry Murray was a physician who did a fellowship in biochemistry and who qualified in surgery. He became a literary authority on Herman Melville, became attracted to the psychoanalytic theories of Freud and Carl Jung, and cofounded the Harvard Psychological Clinic. His background and reading was always eclectic, broad, and interdisciplinary.

At the Harvard Psychological Clinic, Murray experimented with a number of different methods with which to study human imagination and human personality organization. One of his students and colleagues, Cecilia Roberts (who married historian Crane Brinton), is said to have returned home one night to find that her son had created stories to different pictures in a magazine. When she reported this to Murray, he and Christiana Morgan, one of his assistants who had considerable artistic ability, set out to collect a number of different pictures of paintings in museums, advertisements in magazines, pictures for movies, and other sources. Morgan and Samuel Thal then redrew these items in order to have a consistent style of presentation (Douglas, 1993). One of the most interesting sources for the T.A.T. pictures is the picture of the child prodigy violin virtuoso, Yehudi Menuhin, sitting at a desk in front of his violin, which became the picture for card 1. The current set of 31 pictures is the third version of this test, following a suggestion by psychologist Frederick Wyatt to double the size of the pictures to increase the power of the pictures to elicit personal psychological identifications. Wesley Morgan (1995) has an interesting paper that details the history of each of the current T.A.T. cards.

To Murray's broad, humanistic mind, Freud's theory of unconscious sexual and aggressive drives oversimplified the multifaceted complexity of human motivation. He found Freud's "contribution to man's conceptualized knowledge of himself" as "the greatest since the works of Aristotle"(Murray, 1959, p. 37), but at the same time, he felt that Freud's view of human nature was too one-sided. Murray stated that Freud's early libido theory was much too circumscribed and limited, as if the "libido has digested all the needs contributing to self-preservation, self-regard, and self-advancement, together with a host of others, and rebaptized them in the name of Sex; and that sex itself is never given either its profound evolutionary status or its interpersonally creative status" (Murray, 1959, p. 37). For that reason, Murray emphasized in the *T.A.T Manual* that his need-press approach provides a way of scoring the T.A.T., so "a psychologist can use these variables without subscribing to any particular theory of drives" (Murray, 1943a, p. 9).

On the other hand, Murray had a period of supervision under psychoanalyst Hanns Sachs, whose understanding of patients Murray found to be outstanding. "Time and time again," Murray noted, Sachs "could predict my patients' trends several days or even weeks before they were exhibited. A theory that can do this is valuable" (Murray, 1940, p. 156). Perhaps largely because of his profound respect for the clinical utility of psychodynamic theory and his broad albeit ambivalent feelings about psychoanalysis, Bellak feels that Murray never seemed to view what Bellak brought to T.A.T. as a threat to what Murray had contributed. Therefore, Bellak and Murray (1941) collaborated on Bellak's first attempt to outline a T.A.T. scoring approach based on the Freud's later ego psychology. Murray and Bellak remained friends until Murray's death in 1988 at the age of 95 years.

In 1948, art historian-psychoanalyst Ernst Kris suggested to Bellak that children might feel freer to identify with pictures of young animals in different situations than pictures of actual children. Freud's (1909) most famous child case, the case of Little Hans, revolved around a 4-year-old boy who was afraid to travel outside his house for fear a horse would bite him. Freud showed how the little boy had first identified his parents with horses and later in the treatment identified himself as a young horse. Therefore, Bellak and his wife, artist Sonya Sorel, set out much like Murray and Christiana Morgan before them—to create a series of different pictures of animals in different situations in order to determine which pictures would be most evocative in clinical use with children. The final set of 10 cards was then drawn by the gifted artist, Violet Lamont. This test has since enjoyed international popularity, being published in 11 countries.

In 1973, Bellak and Sonya Sorel Bellak worked in the same way to develop a set of pictures appropriate for clinical use with an elderly population. The S.A.T. was then published, which has been used successfully for over two decades. The S.A.T.'s situations have been found to be clinically powerful stimuli to elicit issues of primary concern to elderly individuals. However, it increasingly became apparent that the test would be even more successful as an assessment device if the pictures were redrawn in a style as richly detailed and evocative as that used in the C.A.T. and T.A.T. pictures. Therefore, the S.A.T. pictures have been redrawn by Violet Lamont, artist of the pictures for the C.A.T. These revised pictures are newly published in the current edition of this book and have been found to be much more profound stimuli than the original S.A.T. pictures. They are already being utilized with interesting results in cross-cultural studies in the United States, Brazil, France, and Spain.

Six Decades of T.A.T. Research

The beginnings of T.A.T. research in the 1940s and 1950s tended to focus a great deal of attention on the study of sexual and aggressive drives in T.A.T. protocols of different groups of people influenced by Freud's first libido theory and on studies of selected parts of Murray's need-press approach. These consisted of the research direction of McClelland and colleagues (1953), McClelland (1955), and McClelland and Steele (1973) on the need for achievement; and of Atkinson, Hyns, and Veroff (1954) and Shipley and Veroff (1952) on the need for affiliation.

Research on aspects of the Bellak scoring system developed most prominently in the late 1950s, 1960s, and 1970s, influenced by Freud's later ego psychology theory. There was work on Bellak's scoring dimension of the *main hero* (Friedman, 1957b); *significant conflicts* (Abrams, 1977; Epstein, 1962); *nature of anxieties* (Mandler, Lindzey, & Crouch, 1957; Stamps & Teevan, 1974); *main defenses* (Blum, 1964; Cramer & Carter, 1978; Dias, 1976; Haworth, 1963; Heath, 1958; Heilbrun, 1977; *superego and moral judgment* (Kohlberg, 1969; Shore, Massimo, & Mack, 1964); and *general ego functions* (Bachrach & Peterson, 1976; Born, 1975; Dies, 1968; Dudek, 1975; Johnson & Kilmann, 1975; Morval, 1977; Pine & Holt, 1960; Stolorow, 1973; Weissman, 1964; Wyatt, 1958).

In the decades of the 1980s and 1990s, contemporary psychodynamic theory has developed in three primary areas with parallel developments in T.A.T. research: (1) the analysis of internal conflict expressed in drive-defense constellations developed within mainstream psychoanalysis; (2) the British so-called object relations school developed Freud's ego function of "interpersonal object relations" into a primary approach to treatment, and (3) Kohut (1971, 1977) developed Freud's early work on narcissism and the ego function of the capacity for self and object representation.

Consequently, this book and Bellak's Comprehensive Scoring System have further emphasized these three important developments. Most notably, the work within mainstream ego psychology on defense and ego analysis by Joseph Sandler, Charles Brenner, and Paul Gray can be seen in the valuable scoring system for defense mechanisms on the T.A.T. by Cramer (1991a). The development of the British Object Relations School of psychoanalysis is best represented in T.A.T. research in the object relations scoring systems of McAdams (1980), Thomas and Dudeck (1985), and the promising work of Westen and colleagues (Berends et al., 1990; Leigh, 1992; Westen et al., 1990a, 1990b, 1991b). The Kohut direction of self-psychology or the study of normal and pathological narcissism has not resulted in any development in T.A.T. scoring. However, pioneering adult T.A.T. case presentations of narcissistic patients have been published by Françoise Brelet-Foulard, who has also published under the name of Françoise Brelet (1981, 1983, 1986) in France, Shulman and Ferguson (1988) and Shulman, McGarthy, and Ferguson, (1988) in the United States, and narcissistic child and adolescent C.A.T. and T.A.T. case presentations by Abrams (1993a, 1995, in press).

Related to the area of interpersonal object relations is the major therapy field of family therapy, which has contributed T.A.T. family studies by Ferreira and Winter (1965), Ferreira, Winter, and Poindexter (1966), Minuchin and associates (1967), Richardson and Partridge (1982), Werner, Stabenau, and Pollin (1970), and Winter and Ferreira (1969, 1970). Perhaps the most important application of the family systems perspective to T.A.T. research is the communication deviance scoring approach first published by Jones (1977), which has continued to be developed in a host of valuable research publications (Doane et al., 1989; Doane & Mintz, 1987; Goldstein, 1985; Karon & Widener, 1994; Miklowitz et al., 1986, 1991; Rund, 1989; Sharav, 1991, Velligan et al., 1990).

Given the fact that the three pivotal approaches to psychotherapy are psychoanalytic therapy, family therapy, and behavior therapy, we have long awaited a contribution to T.A.T. research and clinical diagnosis from the field of behavior therapy. Finally, there has appeared the well-conducted research papers on the personal problem-solving T.A.T. scoring approach of George Ronan and colleagues (Ronan, Colavito, & Hammontree, 1993; Ronan, Date, & Weisbrod, 1995), which is an important new development in the field.

Other developments in the last two decades of T.A.T. research have been the extension of T.A.T. into diagnostic studies of borderline disorders (Rogoff, 1985; Rosoff, 1988; Westen et al., 1990a, 1990b), the aforementioned work on narcissistic disorders (Abrams, 1993, 1995; Brelet, 1981, 1983, 1986; Brelet-Foulard, 1994, 1995; Harder, 1979; Shulman & Ferguson, 1988), attention deficit disorder (Abrams & Bellak, 1986, Costantino, Malgady, & Vazquez, 1988), mental retardation (Hurley & Sovner, 1985), substance abuse (Cabal Bravo et al., 1990, Fassino et al., 1992), and trauma (Henderson, 1990; Hoffman & Kuperman, 1990; Ornduff et al., 1994; Ornduff & Kelsey, 1996; Stovall & Craig, 1990).

Bellak and Exner

As the T.A.T., C.A.T., and S.A.T. move into the twenty-first century, the Bellak scoring approach will further strengthen its quantitative, empirical foundation in the manner of Exner's (1994) Comprehensive System for the Rorschach. Bellak's system resembles that of Exner's, since both scoring systems are based on the major clinical and research dimensions of their respective tests in contemporary clinical practice and academic research psychology.

Moreover, after more than six decades of research on the T.A.T. (since the first publication on the T.A.T. in 1935 by Morgan and Murray), there is now a strong foundation for understanding the major personality dimensions expressed on the T.A.T. necessary for diagnostic evaluation. There is solid research literature on how individuals with different psychiatric disorders behave on this test and there is an ever-increasing literature on how individuals of different ages, gender, and culture express themselves on thematic tests. From 11 research studies in 1941, the current textbook has close to 800 T.A.T. research studies in its bibliography, with increasing numbers being reported each year throughout the world.

Several important large-scale studies have attempted to develop empirical scoring approaches to the T.A.T. (Avila Espada, 1990; Neman, Neman, & Sells, 1974; Zubin, Evon, & Schumer, 1965) in which a large number of quantitative scoring variables with good inter-rater reliability are scored on a large normative sample. However, these approaches did not also test the same quantitative scoring variables with different clinical groups in order to compare what is typical for "normal" individuals of the same age with what is typical for individuals with different psychiatric disorders. Exner, on the other hand, has established statistical age norms and norms for different psychiatric disorders on the Rorschach with hundreds of empirical studies using the same set of quantitative scoring variables. Another valuable aspect of his approach is his computer program, which a psychologist may use to input the individual's scores. The scores can then be compared against the normative data from Exner's age group and clinical subgroup studies and a set of clinical hypotheses of "subjective probability" outlined by Exner from his own expert clinical experience and that of other Rorschach specialists. The end product is a printout of a narrative assessment of the individual's main personality characteristics and probable psychiatric disorder(s).

Bellak's Comprehensive System by contrast, is a more *clinical* approach. The different dimensions of his system are not *quantitative,* as in Exner's approach. They constitute a way of addressing the important dimensions of personality organization, such as identifying the individual's anxieties and different ways the individual attempts to defend against these anxieties with different defense mechanisms. Bellak's scoring dimensions are a way of reminding oneself which are the important dimensions of the personality, so that the psychologist does not forget to address some of the significant areas. For example, when a clinician works with a patient in psychotherapy who reports a dream, the clinician may choose to discuss one or two dimensions of the dream that appear to communicate a pressing, current issue in the treatment. If a recently divorced woman is struggling with her relationship with her ex-husband and dreams of the ex-husband having a car accident, the therapist and patient may choose to focus on the dream's expression of the woman's anger at the ex-husband for leaving her (perhaps symbolized in the dream by traveling in a car). Bellak's system helps the psychologist consider the *main theme,* such as the ex-husband leaving and having a car accident; a *main need,* such as the woman expressing anger at the husband for leaving; and other dimensions, such as the *superego* aspect of the ex-husband perhaps being punished severely for leaving the woman by having the car accident.

Some of Bellak's scoring categories have quasi-quantitative scoring dimensions, such as number of figures and number of objects introduced in a story. Also, the user is able to rate the adequacy of superego functioning in a story according to three levels if the superego is appropriate or innappropriate, or three levels of ego integration in a story if the plot is complete, incomplete, or inappropriate.

Bellak's system helps the psychologist run quickly through these 10 basic dimensions of personality dimension for each story in order to come to an overall summary as to how the individual's personality is organized. If only one dimension is known—for example, that most of the stories deal with the *main theme* of a woman being angry with a man for leaving—nothing else is yet known about how the woman attempts to defend against these feelings (defense mechanisms); if she has any other main needs and other anxieties other than fear of someone leaving her; her overall view of the world (conception of the world); the level of her interpersonal object relations; what her main conflicts are; how adaptive her coping mechanisms are and other ego functions; and how her superego functions to help monitor her desire to express antisocial feelings (such as wishing her ex-husband would have a car accident). If the psychologist identifies from repeated themes on the T.A.T. that a woman seems to have a need to express angry feelings toward her ex-husband, yet she is unaware of those feelings, her psychotherapy will be benefited. However, an overall view of how her personality is organized is of considerably more benefit from a clinical standpoint. For example, if the psychologist also knows that the woman has good ego functioning to control her antisocial wish for her ex-husband to have a car accident and adequate superego control that would not permit her to act on such antisocial feelings, the psychologist will have a better understanding of the woman's likelihood to act or not to act out these feelings.

Similarly, in the case of identifying suicidal ideation in T.A.T. stories, the psychologist needs to address the evidence of suicidal feelings on several T.A.T. stories, how the individual attempts to defend against these feelings being expressed in reality, and the level of superego functioning as to whether the individual appears to feel she or he should be punished severely for these feelings or past actions. If a man draws a head cut off from the rest of a body or without the hands attached to the arms at the wrist on the Draw-a-Person Test, it may suggest suicidal feelings. A next step is for the psychologist to look for evidence of lack of ego control or impulsivity indicators, such as uneven dots, overlapping designs, or very largely drawn figures on the Bender Gestalt Test. The Bellak system helps the psychologist consider how these different personality dimensions are expressed and related together on the T.A.T., which can later be checked and corroborated with similar indicators on other tests in the psychological test battery.

A Basic Set of T.A.T. Cards for Males and Females

In previous editions of this book, we have criticized the sloppy practice of a psychologist only using a few cards chosen primarily for which cards seem to "pull" the most for personality aspects the clinician senses may be at issue with an individual being tested. Typically, if the individual appears depressed in slow-moving test behavior and lack of motivation on previous tests, the psychologist, becoming tired at this point in the test battery, may decide only to administer for the T.A.T. card 1 (a boy sitting at a desk looking passively at a violin on the desk), card 3BM (a man or woman sitting on the floor resting his or her head against a couch with a revolver on the floor), and card 13MF (a man standing with downcast head buried in his arm, behind him a woman is lying in bed as if asleep or dead). This practice has undoubtedly developed because Murray's original instruction to administer 10 cards the first day and then another 10 the following day made the T.A.T. administration too time consuming.

Therefore, we advocate the use of the same basic set of 10 T.A.T. cards for males and females to be administered in the same order: Cards 1, 2, 3BM, 4, 6BM, 7GF, 8BM, 9GF, 10, and 13MF. If clinicians want to administer other "favorite" cards that are not included in this basic set, they can do so after first administering the basic set. The recommendation of the basic set is based on numerous polls of which cards are most frequently administered by psychologists, by our own clinical experience, and the importance of a balance between male-designed and female-designed cards. Standardized administration of this gender-balanced T.A.T. basic set facilitates the kind of sequence analysis possible on the Rorschach and helps to move the clinical use of the T.A.T. closer to the standard for Rorschach administration set by Exner.

By utilizing a basic set of 10 T.A.T. cards administered in the same order, which can be supplemented by other T.A.T. cards, it is also possible to bring the 10 Bellak scoring categories to a more quantitative level. Moreover, since the majority of quantitative research on the T.A.T. has studied variables that fit under Bellak's 10 major categories, it may soon be possible to follow the example of Exner's quantitative scoring of the Rorschach to be able to input quantitative scoring data for the T.A.T. In this way, the clinician's scoring of the T.A.T. will be improved and a research corroboration will be provided for the clinical analysis of the stories according to the major personality dimensions of contemporary psychology and mental health practice.

CHAPTER 2

THEORETICAL FOUNDATIONS FOR PROJECTIVE TESTING

During World War II, the personnel needs of the Armed Forces constituted a tremendous task and challenge. Young men with little training had to become clinical psychology experts in weeks, and older ones with experience and training in the laboratory and in academic settings also had to become clinical specialists. This pressure of circumstances produced many new projective techniques and led to their acceptance as gospel, even when the "oldest" were almost entirely invalidated and poorly understood.

The Thematic Apperception Test was developed during this fertile period during World War II and shortly thereafter by Professor Henry Murray with the assistance of Christiana Morgan and other colleagues at the Harvard Psychological Clinic. The fascinating historical story of Murray's work with Christiana Morgan and others during this formative period of the T.A.T. is profiled in the biography by Robinson (1992), *Love's Story Told: A Life of Henry A. Murray*. While Murray developed what he called a need-press approach to scoring the T.A.T., his student, Leopold Bellak, worked with him to develop a scoring approach based on the ego psychology of Sigmund Freud (1920, 1923). This state of affairs paralleled the development of intelligence testing during World War I. After the periods of pressure that both wars produced to develop intellectual and personality assessment instruments, this heightened phase of pioneering innovation was followed by more careful scrutiny and empirical investigations of the tools themselves.

Consider the large number of Rorschach research papers after World War II on the nature of the Color and Achromatic Color response (Lazarus, 1949; Meyer, 1951; Rockwell et al., 1948; Siipola, 1950), the statistical normative studies on adults by Hertz (1970), developmental norms from childhood to adulthood on the Rorshach by Louise Bates Ames and colleagues at the Yale Child Center (Ames, 1961; Ames et al., 1961), and a wealth of other empirical studies that paved the way for the major breakthrough in a systematic structural scoring for the Rorschach by Exner (1974, 1986, 1994).

This book shows that the T.A.T. has a similar history. On the one hand, there have been many empirical investigations of individual dimensions of the T.A.T., such as word length, word frequency tables, and aspects of test behavior, which we refer to in this book as "research studies of thematic tests." On the other hand, there have been many different scoring systems similar to those of Murray and Bellak that provide the clinician with a way to address the key personality dimensions of the individual tested.

Following the discovery of the T.A.T., we have seen these two areas increasingly converge. The majority of empirical research studies of individual characteristics of thematic tests have essentially researched different needs in Murray's system—such as need for achievement, the need for affiliation, and the need for power—and different aspects of the original ten scoring categories of Bellak's system, such as Cramer's (1991a) important work on defense mechanisms and Westen's (1991a, 1991b) work on interpersonal object relations. As the reader we see, the Bellak scoring system provides a comprehensive diagnostic scoring for thematic tests, since it includes the major personality components that have also been the predominant areas of empirical research.

The Psychology of Projective Techniques in General and the T.A.T. in Particular

The requirements for validity and usefulness in projective techniques can be seen as twofold: Projective methods are expected to perform as tools of both nomothetic and idiographic sciences. Formulated by Windleband (1904) and notably elaborated by Allport and Vernon (1937), *nomothetic science* is concerned with general lawfulness (e.g., in physics, chemistry, etc.) and *idiographic science* is concerned with understanding one particular event (e.g., of a historical nature, such as what led to the unique event of the storming of the Bastille). The main efforts in U.S. psychology are directed toward making projective methods the tools of nomothetic science; the basic Rorschach scores (Exner, 1994; Judson, 1963), the development of signs (Hertz, 1970; Piotrowski, 1950), and the work with group Rorschachs (Harrower, 1950; Munroe, 1951) bear testimony to that trend. The purpose—extremely valuable and, in part, carried over from brass-instrument laboratory concepts of the "average" person and from statistical psychometrics— is to arrive at criteria that are applicable to groups of people or to syndromes. When these signs are encountered, they are helpful in assigning a given person to a given group. For instance, Mr. Jones perceives in such a way that he must be considered a schizophrenic, a criminal, or an engineer. Idiographically speaking, one would be satisfied to describe Mr. Jones as a unique person who perceives configurations in a certain way and tends to control his impulses under given circumstances, generally constituting a uniqueness of functioning that will not be exactly duplicated by any other individual.

Some projective methods undoubtedly lend themselves more readily to the nomothetic approach than others. Perhaps the generalization can be made that the expressive methods and those scoring schemes primarily predicated on formal characteristics lend themselves better to valid generalizations than those concerned primarily with content. Surely the Rorschach is relatively easier to harness lawfully than the T.A.T. (which has remained one of the most idiographic of all instruments). From a clinical standpoint, in fact, one might choose testing procedures according to whether one wants nomothetic or idiographic information. The nomothetic approach, to be sure, is extremely valuable and necessary. The failures and limitations of projective methods as nomothetic instruments are the main impetus for further research and attempts at better conceptualization. The problem is often discussed as the difficulty of making inferences from test data to behavior. Naturally, if a psychiatrist wants to know if someone is suicidal or of criminal inclination, the psychologist is expected to be able to report whether the signs and dynamics of suicide or criminality in the person's projective data imply whether the person is likely to act on her or his destructive impulses. Similarly, the personnel executive will want to know from the psychologist if an individual will make a good officer in reality, not in fantasy!

It is quite possible, however, for a technique to fail idiographically. When psychological testing is done prior to an extensive psychotherapy, psychotherapists occasionally discover that while the major components of personality functioning were addressed by the psychologist who conducted the testing, the psychotherapy process may later uncover other areas not covered in the psychological test report. Thus, while nomothetic performance can best be checked statistically, idiographic performance can probably best be investigated by a study of records against data from an intensive course of treatment, which may be said to be the most idiographic of all studies.

The failures and limitations of projective techniques have often been related to a lack of consistent conceptualization (Bellak, 1993a; Cattell, 1951; Exner, 1994; Rapaport, 1947). When Frank (1939) coined the term *projective methods* (or *projective tests*), it was certainly the most appropriate at that time, but it has proved to be a misleading term. *Projection,* taken from Freud, was generally formulated in U.S. psychology (Bellak & Chassan, 1964) as a defense mechanism in the service of the ego, designed to avoid awareness of unacceptable wishes, thoughts, and impulses, accomplishing its task by ascribing such undesirable *subjective* phenomena to the *objective* world. For example, a 5-year-old girl has a dream of a monster angrily attacking her after she was angry with an adult the day before the dream. Here, she is projecting her own anger at the adult into the figure of a scary monster being angry at her. Projection has this type of boomerang effect of displacing one's inner thoughts and feelings onto someone else, who one then imagines is having these thoughts and feelings. This meaning of projection was primarily taken from Freud's discussion of paranoia in the case of Schreber (Freud, 1943), who projected his own thoughts and feelings onto other people as well as onto inanimate objects.

The T.A.T., Rorschach, House-Tree-Person Drawing Test, Kinetic-Family-Drawing Test, and the Sentence Completion Test are considered projective tests in the sense that the individual is thought to project his or her main conflicts, thoughts, and feelings into these tests. The story told to a T.A.T. card, such as the little girl's dream of a scary monster, is thought to be a projection of the individual's own thoughts and feelings.

Only belatedly did some workers in the field (Bell, 1948; Bellak, 1944) become aware that Freud (1938) saw projection in a much broader sense as a general perceptual process, whereby *all contemporary meaningful perception is predicated on and organized by the memory traces of all previous perceptions.* This broader concept, formulated by Bellak (Bellak & Brower, 1951) as *apperceptive distortion,* might possibly serve as a more useful frame of reference for some of the so-called projective methods. This is the meaning of the term *apperception* in the Thematic Apperception Test. The basic assumption of an individual's T.A.T. protocol is that the individual tends to distort some of what she or he perceives in each picture, because of her or his own personality dynamics.

An attempt at a breakdown of the processes involved in all the tests currently considered "projective" led to five categories of study (Bellak & Brower, 1951): (1) content, (2) expressive data, (3) Gestalt formation, (4) body image, and (5) a study of choices.[1]

1. *Methods based upon the study of content.* Here, we are concerned with *what* the patient says. The T.A.T. and the Make A Picture Story (M.A.P.S.) Test are the best examples. To a certain extent, the Rorschach inquiry and finger-painting method also belong here.

2. *Study of expressive, structural aspects.* The main inquiry is directed toward *how* the subject says or does something. Here, we refer to techniques like the Mira, Mosaic, Rorschach, and graphology, which belong to the subsemantic levels of myoneural functioning insofar as these are valid procedures for the understanding of personality factors and structure.

3. *Gestalt functions.* These are exemplified in the Bender Gestalt, the Mosaic, and again in the Rorschach. In the T.A.T., this function enters only rarely, to any extent when the subject is unable to apperceive the picture as a whole or when he or she leaves the stimulus altogether.

4. *Body image or self-image.* The Figure Drawing Test is primarily predicated on this approach. It also enters into the Rorschach when, for example, the subject identifies with puppets, and in the T.A.T. when the subject sees the hero as crippled (picture 3BM), or sees the violin as broken and/or "dead" (picture 1), or identifies with an athlete (picture 17BM).

5. *Methods of preference.* The Szondi, as a test of an individual's unconscious identifications, is based on a system of selective choices as personality indicators. Color choice in finger painting, selection of figures in doll play (as well as in the M.A.P.S.), and so on, also come under this category.

It is apparent that all five organismic aspects enter into every one of the projective methods in varying degrees.

The problem is to find a consistent body of theory under which five such divergent aspects of psychologic functioning can be subsumed. All these variables—fantasy content as in the T.A.T.; perceptual organization as in the Rorschach; ability to see Gestalten as in the Bender; self-perception and motor expression as in the Figure Drawing Test, the Mira test, or graphology; and recognition and the making of choices as in the Szondi—are functions of the ego and resultants of its interaction with inner drives, which are internal impulses, thoughts, and feelings that motivate or drive the individual in certain directions.

The answer—a broad enough roof to cover the house of projective testing—

---

[1] See "Toward a General Psychology of Thematic Apperception Tests" in this chapter for further elaboration.

lies in contemporary psychodynamic personality theory. Projective techniques, similar to early psychoanalysis, have primarily been steeped in Freud's (1900) first theory called the libido therapy, which was primarily concerned with the libidinal or sexual impulses or drives and their expression. In this view, the majority of dreams were thought of as projections of the dreamer's own unconscious sexual wishes. Psychoanalysis made its major step forward when it turned from being solely a psychology of the unconscious drives to a study of the interaction of these drives with the ego, superego, and the outside world (Anna Freud, 1936). Murray's need-press theory of personality was an attempt to broaden the conception of *drives* to a large variety of basic *needs*, which are thought to motivate and drive the individual (such as a need for achievement), and forces that *press* on the individual from the outside world.

Contemporary personality theories—such as interpersonal object relations, self-psychology, and family systems theory—provide further understanding for a comprehensive theory of personality functioning. Since the foundation of contemporary personality theory is ego psychology, we will discuss how its basic assumptions relate specifically to the T.A.T.

The Role of the Ego in Imaginative Production

In order to study the participation of the ego in imaginative productions, we need first to review briefly the psychoanalytic concept of the nature and functions of the ego, most succinctly formulated by Hartmann (1950) and discussed by Bellak (1993a), particularly from the standpoint of ego strength.

The ego is that aspect of personality that:

1. Organizes and controls motility and perception.
2. Serves as a protective barrier against excessive and internal stimuli (see number 6).
3. Tests reality and engages in trial action (Freud's concept of thinking) and sends out danger signals (anxiety).
4. Has organizing and self-regulating functions that include mediating between ego and superego and id on the one side, and reality and all the variables on the other. This includes frustration tolerance, capacity for detour behavior, and all that is comprised under defenses.
5. Has some autonomous functions that include abilities, intelligence, and an unspecified number of inherited characteristics, possibly including ego strength.
6. Has the capacity for self-exclusion. Not only must the well-functioning ego be able to repress (i.e., exclude) disturbing id (and superego) impulses for the sake of good organismic functioning (e.g., a driver must not be unduly distracted by a pretty girl or feel unreasonably compelled to avoid a mud hole) but it must also be able to exclude some or nearly all of its own functions. Hartmann (1951) and Kris (1950), who described the ego's capacity for self-exclusion and regression in the service of the ego (one of the last discovered and most important functions), have pointed out that it is necessary that cog-

nitive ego functions be excluded in order to be able to fall asleep. For instance, a person who is driven by undue anxiety of nocuous stimuli to maintain his or her cognitive functions will keep his muscles tense, hear the clock ticking, see the light flashing, feel the blanket pressing, and so on. Under certain circumstances, the withdrawal of the cognitive functions can be subjective experiences (hypnagogue phenomena, especially Silberer's [1951] functional phenomenon).

Our projective tests, their strength and limitations, now need exploration in the light of these ego functions. The amount of ego participation in various productions, and the type of ego function involved, differ from method to method and from case to case. The ego participates in varying degrees in imaginative productions in a way that suggests a continuum from minimal to maximal participation, in the following sequence: dream, hypnagogue phenomena, preconscious fantasy, daydream, free association, artistic productions, test behavior on projective techniques, and problem solving.

The Dream
One could consider Freud's description of "dreamwork" (condensation, symbolization, displacement, and secondary elaboration) as defensive efforts of the ego. (The theory of the ego had not yet been developed when *The Interpretation of Dreams* was written.) Some patients may recount a number of dreams experienced in one night, or four or five different parts of one dream, manifestly connected or not. Dream analysis demonstrates that all dreams or dream parts have the same content; sometimes the first one may be the most undisguised statement, and the subsequent ones may be more and more covered up. At other times, *sequence analysis* will reveal the opposite—a decrease of defensive distortion of underlying latent content—and other times, there may be a fluctuation back and forth. This greatly resembles phenomena observed in T.A.T. productions (Bellak, 1952e; Cramer, 1991a). Patients' particular constellations of defense mechanisms are often expressed in their dreams.

However, for the most part, the dream is predominantly a primary process and shows less ego participation than any other mental phenomenon, except possibly psychotic productions. This is related to the problem of the diagnostic value of dreams, in terms of identification of nosological syndromes from dreams. Most mental health professionals hold that one cannot diagnose a psychosis from the manifest dream content (i.e., the dreams of psychotics are not manifestly differentiable from those of nonpsychotics). Piotrowski (1952) pointed out that there are typical dreams of psychotics. This involves the assumption that there may be more or less pure "primary processes" in dreams and thus, by implication, better or less well-functioning defenses in the dream. In advanced or chronic psychotics, there may be such a decided lack of any dreamwork as to be manifestly different. Mental health professionals, in part, agree with this position when they differentiate children's dreams from those of adults as being manifestly more primitive and more directly wish fulfilling. Similarly, if, in a clinical situation, a patient should recount an openly incestuous dream before the analytic process had loosened the defenses, a psychoanalyst would at least carefully consider this lack of defensive dreamwork as a possible indication of psychosis.

Hypnagogue Phenomena

Hypnagogue phenomena[2] are associated with the process of falling asleep. Described particularly by Silberer (1951) as autosymbolic phenomena, and by Isakower (1938), these phenomena are predicated on partially existing cognitive ego functions: a subjective awareness of the process of falling asleep, of the withdrawal of the cognitive functions, and of external cathexis. The most frequent type of experience is having a door shut or a window screen closed, sudden darkness indicating the closing of the eyes or the narrowing of the visual perception. Actually, such phenomena occur primarily when the process of falling asleep is disturbed, either in a situation where one should stay awake and thus struggles against falling asleep, or where anxiety disturbs the smooth self-exclusion of the ego. An even more widespread phenomenon of this type, which may also be considered a hypnagogue phenomenon, is that of having fallen asleep and waking with a start upon the sensation of falling. This phenomenon is due to a disturbance in the smooth self-exclusion of the ego functions concerned with muscular control and awareness.

Preconscious Fantasy

Preconscious fantasies are processes that are not conscious at the time but can easily be made conscious on effort. They were most extensively described by Varendonck (1931) and occur particularly while some monotonous or semiautomatic task is being performed. Frequently, upon some additional stimulus, one may "snap out of it" and suddenly become aware of the fantasies that have lived a nearly autonomous life. Such fantasies may have started as regular daydreams, or may have developed in tangential relation to some internal or environmental stimulus that

---

[2] The distinction between hypnagogue phenomena, preconscious fantasies, and daydreaming is not an entirely clear one, nor is there agreement on the definition. Silberer (1951) stated that the autosymbolic phenomena comes about in a transitional state between waking and sleeping, in the presence of a struggle between the two states (he did not conceptualize in terms of the ego.) He gives the following example: He was trying to think through some philosophical problem, part of which began to elude him, while he was nearly falling asleep. Suddenly, he had some dreamlike experience in which he requested some information from a secretary who morosely disregards him. He had symbolized and concretized his quest for enlightenment as met by his sleepiness. In response to an internal stimulus, a preconscious fantasy developed antonomously that could be made conscious and brought in relation to a conscious process.

On the other hand, much of what Varendonck (1931) reported as preconscious fantasy also took place in the process of falling asleep. Rapaport (1951) believes that Verendonck spoke of preconscious fantasies when he really meant daydreams. At any rate, we wish to differentiate preconscious fantasies by their quality of being *ego alien*, similar to mild obsessive phenomena, as compared with such fantasy as *ego syntonic*, and for which I prefer the term *daydream*. It is, however, entirely possible for a person at one time to run the entire continuum from hypnagogue thinking to preconsious thinking, daydreaming, and problem solving, all possibly related to the same problem. Kris (1950), in a discussion of preconscious mental processes, has discussed this continuum and its relation to the creative process and its metapsychologic implications.

may be recognized as related by subjects who have learned to introspect. People in psychotherapy, people who are deeply preoccupied, and prepsychotics may experience an abundance of such fantasies that are, to a certain extent an ego function (inasmuch as they are in some relationship to environmental or originally conscious stimuli) and can be made conscious upon effort.

Daydream

To a considerable extent, daydreams are under the control of the ego. Many people will reach for ready-made daydreams that they think of routinely in frustrating situations. Others will keep their daydreams within some limits of reality. Indeed, controlled daydreams may be the forerunners and concomitants of problem-solving behavior (e.g., a person who daydreams of success and in this process hits on a workable formula).

Free Association

The patient who is asked to free associate in the clinical situation is asked to perform a complex task: to let his mind run freely (i.e., to decrease the controlling function of his ego), and at the same time, or in brief succession, to increase the cognitive function of the ego concerned with self-awareness. It is the nature of this complex task, of an *oscillating* function or ability of the ego to change from self-exclusion to control, that makes free association so difficult for some patients. Notably, obsessive-compulsives find it difficult to "let go" and thus report a dearth of ideas. In these cases, rigidity is in direct contrast to the flexibility of ego functions necessary for free associating. Frequently, their ability really to free associate coincides with the time of their cure. Some other patients, possibly hysterics more than others, may find it difficult to keep enough distance to do a good job with the observing function (The tasks for the ego become even more complex when a third function becomes necessary; aside from "letting go" and observing, insight presupposes the ability to see new configurations.) (Bellak, 1961, 1993a; Bellak & Goldsmith, 1984).

The process of free association can be explained in a more lucid way by reformulating the concept of self-exclusion of the ego or, better, of adaptive regression in the service of the ego (Bellak, 1961). As it involves free association, it involves a relative reduction of certain adaptive functions, one of which is a reduction of secondary process qualities of thinking and an emergence of primary process thinking and unconscious content. The first phase of the process is succeeded or overlapped by an increase in adaptive and synthetic ego functioning. In this way, insight emerges, partly due to oscillation from regression of specific ego functions to an increase in others.

The regressive phase consists of two aspects: the temporal regression of ego functions to levels characteristic of earlier ages and the topological regression from mainly conscious functioning to functioning at the preconscious and unconscious levels. The topological regression of certain ego functions, frequently simultaneously, involves a temporal regression of these ego functions and often a regression in the libidinal zones and modes. In the process of free association, metapsychological problems other than the topological are involved; these are the structural, dynamic, genetic, and energetic (Bellak, 1993a).

Artistic Creation

This process, similar to free association, also necessitates both the ability of self-exclusion of the ego and the rapid change to cognitive critical awareness. Ernst Kris has pointed out that only in the presence of intact ego functions (regression in the service of the ego) can one speak of art (an accentuated form of *communication of experiences* in distinction to the productions of advanced psychotics). In the case of many borderline or ambulatory psychotics who are artists, there is still enough ego function left so that one can consider their productions as truly artistic.

Projective Techniques

In a procedure such as the T.A.T., the person is again asked to perform a complex task. We ask the individual to let his or her mind run freely—that is, to induce some self-exclusion of the ego. Then we continue our instructions to the effect that he or she is to tell a story about the picture, tell us about what is going on, what led up to the situation, and what the outcome will be. We ask the subject to adhere to the stimulus and to maintain a set consistent with our formula. As in free association and artistic production, performance on the T.A.T. and other projective techniques presupposes an oscillating function of the ego. The overly rigid patient will not be able to decrease the control and will give only descriptive data and meager data altogether; the patient with insufficient ego control will leave the stimulus and leave the task.

The "letting go" gives us the drive content thus far primarily studied in projective methods. By observing the oscillating functions and the defenses against the underlying impulse or drive material, we may infer ego strength and may often observe drive content that does not appear prima facie. The following stories may illustrate the point.

9BM: Group of four men who are running away from something—something the fellow on the left is looking for. Probably they've broken out of confinement. The position—the way they're lying doesn't seem to indicate they're under any great stress or tension. They could just as well be four hunters. The fellow on the left could be watching for whatever they're hunting, duck or game of any sort. Little siesta after working on any kind of on-location job.

This response of an adolescent boy really consists of at least three stories: They are running away from something, possibly escaping confinement; then (a much more innocuous story than the first) they are merely hunting; and (even more innocuous), finally, the aggressive connotation of hunting is given up and the picture becomes one of utmost peace and passivity—siesta.

Thus, we see one way of meeting, with obsessive elaboration, the threat of (one's own) aggression. It is by such study that fine features of defense and character may be discovered. From the ellipse or the omission, or from the sequence of defenses, we may learn the content. A study of the equilibrium of impulse and defense or drive and control is the most useful method of investigation. Similarly, in the Rorschach, one studies the ego's ability to perceive, to organize, to perform complex tasks (see later discussion of color shock), and to control anxiety, aggression, and sexual impulses.

In the Figure Drawing Test, graphology, and the Mira test, one studies the motor executive functions of the ego. In the Bender Gestalt Test, and to a certain extent in the other tests, the ability to perceive figure and ground properly and the capacity to interpret well are studied (see discussion of signs). In the Szondi, a system of selective choices is the basis for personality indicators. The nature of the choices involved is a matter of disagreement, but there can be no doubt that the activity of choosing between alternatives is always, to a certain extent, influenced by the ego; this holds true cognitively and conatively.[3]

Projective Responses as Products and Indicators of Creativity

There are four central factors in making inferences from projective responses as creative products that are different from those operant in other creative acts. First, the unconscious and preconscious conditions needed in artistic and scientific creativity often require a (conscious) mental set to create that may not be available in objective settings. Second, whereas the creative process generally attains the emergent level only in its own course, in projective testing, the administrator commands the subject to create. Similarly, in interpreting projective protocols, it is assumed that creativity is composed of continually operant variables of personality whenever it is present. This is not valid for all creative people; creativity may by cyclic. (See item 4 under "Possible Means of Increasing Productivity of T.A.T. Material by an Ego Psychological Approach" later in this chapter.) The third difficulty in inferring general creative ability from projective tests is based on the fact that the creative product is the resultant of many factors, including situational factors, the nature of the stimulus, and so on. The fourth problem in making inferences about creativity is due to the fact that the personality syndromes are not the same at different times, and that the degree of variability over a period of time is a highly significant personality index. Consideration of these four problems leads to the conclusion that it may be impossible to ascertain creative potential with standard tests (Bellak, 1958).

The Latent and the Manifest

The ability to relate *to and from the latent to the manifest* (behavioral) level—from the projective test data to actual behavior—has often been considered the crucial problem of projective testing. This is not true for clinical practice, since, in this situation, the psychologist should not be called on to make blind diagnoses. A good therapist would never interpret a dream from the manifest content without know-

---

[3] *Problem Solving* as an imaginative production is the type of activity involving more ego participation than any of the others. There, reality testing and adaptation, with all the resources of the ego, are involved. Nevertheless, even in this situation, a certain ability for self-exclusion of the ego may he helpful. Cases in which a solution to a difficult problem comes to one just prior to falling asleep, or even apparently during sleep, are not infrequent. The capacity for insight—to see new wholes—presupposes some flexibility of the perceived boundaries of existing wholes.

ing the life situation, the day's residue, and the like. Similarly, a psychologist should only interpret unconscious data as a complement of behavioral data. One can learn the most from a combination of both levels: If a man's T.A.T. drips with blood and gore and he turns out to be a Casper Milquetoast behaviorally, one can make inferences as to the nature of his conflicts and tensions.

There are, however, certain situations in which therapists are legitimately called on to make inferences from the latent to the manifest. Examples include theoretical, experimental purposes; clinical situations such as the prediction of criminal behavior and suicide; and problems such as personnel selection.

The ego must be considered the *intervening variable between the latent and the manifest level.* A study of ego functions in relation to drive may permit one to see that aggressive impulses are or are not permitted to break through. This can be illustrated by the following story of an obsessive patient given in response to picture 17BM:

> The man shown here is a circus performer and has been one for many years. His ambition has always been to be a solo performer instead of part of a trapeze trio. Until now he has not had the opportunity. In tonight's performance he will save a fellow trouper from a serious accident and as a reward for his bravery will be given the chance to do his act alone.

One may formulate the following: This person wants to be in the limelight and do away with the competitors; this thought is not permitted expression. Instead of the aggressive thought, the hero gives help in an accident—that is, the aggression is impersonalized, the helpfulness appears manifestly, and the original goal is given as a reward. In other words, the sequence of the story demonstrates this subject's use of reaction formation in avoiding expression of manifest aggression. Sometimes, a picture of the entire defensive nature of the character structure reveals itself clearly in the T.A.T.

A relationship among drive and superego and ego may permit one to prognosticate suicide. Stories in which the punishment far exceeds the crime, and in which the punishment is immediate and severe (or cruel), are consistent in our experience with real suicidal danger.

The adequacy of the hero in dealing with the task that the subject himself has constructed is an excellent criterion of ego strength. The more adequate the hero and the more appropriate, realistic, and happy the outcome, the safer the inference that one is dealing with a person who will bring other tasks to a good completion. One is not now considering specific aspects of ego strength needed for specific jobs; the ego strength required of a research scientist is concerned with ability for detour behavior and so on, as compared with the abilities required of a combat officer (e.g., capacity for anxiety tolerance and the ability to libidinize anxiety).

Further Problems an Ego Psychology of Projective Techniques May Answer

Barren Records

The problem of barren records has been mentioned before in connection with one of the ways in which a projective technique may fail. Murray (1951c) speaks of "chaff" needing to be separated from the "wheat" in T.A.T. stories. We are not in agreement with this formulation. To speak of chaff is reminiscent of the days when psychoanalysts still saw resistance as a nasty way in which patients behaved and something they had to overcome. With the analysis of the ego, the analyst has learned a great deal from the analysis of the resistance. The analyst learns, in fact, how the ego and the defenses are structured, which was not possible to learn without also understanding the resistances. Similarly, analysis of the chaff, of what is considered barren, will give much information about the defenses of the ego, as in the earlier examples. From the standpoint of determinism as an essential axiom of psychological science, every psychological performance—and thus every utterance—must be meaningfully related to the total structure of personality. It is true that, practically and clinically speaking, it will usually not be worthwhile or possible to investigate each detail.

In patients whom we have treated for as long as three years, and whose T.A.T.s and other projective data we also have, we have had occasion to compare production in treatment and on the tests. For all practical purposes, the generalization can be made that the defenses used in the clinical situation and on the projective techniques were identical: Those who use avoidance, denial, and isolation, and who gave barren records, also tended to spend hours on the couch reporting apparently meaningless data that had to be interpreted and could become meaningful only by inferring the basic issue about which they were.

Considerable experimental studies have supported the fact, long known in clinical practice, that avoidance of aggressive responses to aggressive stimuli is indicative of a great deal of aggression (Bellak, 1950a; Kaplan, 1967; Kornadt, 1982; Megargee, 1967; Megargee & Hokanson, 1970; Tachibana et al., 1984).

Inconsistent Result

In certain cases, failure to obtain test data that one could expect to find may be understandable in terms of ego psychology. For instance, in lobotomized or topectomized patients, various projective techniques and other tests may fail to show any deficit behavior. Lobotomies, in particular, and topectomies, to some extent, are still blind procedures neurologically and, particularly, psychologically speaking. The results and effects differ widely from case to case, sometimes strengthening and sometimes weakening the ego. When the surgical procedure somehow interferes with the "drive push" of the patient, the ego may be secondarily strengthened and none of its integrating functions impaired in such a way that a disturbance in the ego function would manifest itself in psychological test behavior. In other words, the failure of tests to reveal expected pathology incident to the surgical trauma is due to the fact that none of the ego functions involved in test behavior were involved in the trauma.

Signs

Organic signs are symptoms of ego defect in situations in which the organic lesion involves ego functions. The reliability and validity of organic signs will be greatly improved if they will be expected only in such lesions that are likely to involve the ego functions tested in a particular procedure.

Other inconsistencies in test results may consist not only of not finding what "ought" to be there but also, not infrequently, of finding data that "ought not" to be there, in the sense of indicating much more pathology than can be accounted for. For example, if more than 50 percent of the students of a city high school show schizophrenic signs on the Rorschach, *there is obviously something wrong with the signs.*

Signs are a result of the pressure for nomothetic data in the search for the "average" person and the hunted deviant. Many of them are arrived at simply by the use of faulty generalizations by the factor-analysis hunters. Schizophrenia being the most fashionable diagnosis, faulty diagnosis of this syndrome probably constitutes the majority of all misdiagnosis. It is safe to say that the less experienced the psychiatrist or psychologist, the more often she or he will make the diagnosis of schizophrenia, notwithstanding the fact that she or he will sometimes miss it when it does exist. The main problem seems to be that the so-called signs of schizophrenia are almost all signals of disturbances of the ego, such as poor control, poor reality testing, and so on. Although ego weakness is a primary factor in schizophrenia and other disorders (Bellak, 1952b), it must be remembered that it is not the sole criterion (cathexis also playing a role) and that other conditions of ego weakness may obtain the same ego indicators. Adolescents notably have weak egos, and many phenomena in adolescence would have to be interpreted as schizophrenia in other age groups (which makes the diagnosis of the real adolescent schizophrenic one of the most difficult). By the same token, an artist who has learned to exclude his or her ego functions in creative situations may "let go" in the testing situation to the point of giving signs of ego weakness that may be inappropriately interpreted as schizophrenic. Eron (1948) has shown that what was reported as schizophrenic in T.A.T.s by Rapaport (1946) could frequently be found in nonschizophrenics of all kinds, including people who are considered "normal."

Another group that is frequently inappropriately diagnosed as schizophrenic on the basis of signs is the mentally deficient. These subjects also have a defect of the ego, which often manifests itself in poor control, poor perception of reality, and even paranoid interpretation of an environment that they have every reason to fear and suspect of "putting something over" on them. It is not useful to mistake their intellectual deficit state for a psychosis.

Color Shock

Color shock is one of the most interesting and most embattled signs of the Rorschach. Siipola (1950) has done important work on this phenomenon. She has contended that when color and form suggest divergent concepts, there may be three different ways of dealing with the situation. The normal individual may be able to achieve an integration nevertheless (an object first suggesting a bear by shape but being green in color may be quickly seen as a chameleon); the neurotic may be stymied and "shocked" into silence by the conceptual conflict; and the psychotic may have judgment impaired to the point where he or she cheerfully gives the response, "green grass bear." It is Siipola's contention that color shock occurs only where form and color clash, and that it constitutes a response to a more difficult task. We would go further and say that this is best stated in terms of ego psychology—namely, that the normal ego is strong enough to achieve a difficult integration, the neurotic's ego is too weak to accomplish this, and the judgment functions of the psychotic ego are so impaired that he or she easily combines form and color inappropriately. In line with what was said about caution in the interpretation of signs, it must be pointed out that a nonrepresentational artist, accustomed to decreasing ego functions without being psychotic, might well not hesitate to say "green grass bear," and that a psychoanalyzed subject may equate the testing situation with the analytic situation and induce a similar ego-excluding "set" that might permit the same "green grass bear" response.

Conscious Control and Faking

Superseding questionnaires and rating scales, projective psychologists like to think of themselves as real scientists and of their instruments as practically foolproof. All the more disturbing to them, therefore, are reports of successful conscious control and faking on the Rorschach, the T.A.T., and other tests (Holmes, 1974; Lindzey, 1952; Orpen, 1978). Such faking can be understood and restricted to its limitations by understanding the productions from an ego point of view. To the extent to which conscious attitudes and conscious ego control can be introduced, the subject may alter the record to a relatively small degree in one direction or another, concerning such variables as overall "wholesomeness." Particularly with regard to Weisskopf and Dieppa's (1951) work with the T.A.T., it must be remembered that only a few pictures were used, and the most difficult task for the subject would be to fake *consistently* over the whole series of pictures. Furthermore, an analysis of the defenses would probably reveal the basic structure of the character, no matter how much faking the subject endeavored to engage in. Naturally, such characteristics, which, though under the control of the ego, are not under its conscious control and not on the semantic level, are unlikely to be affected at all.

Possible Means of Increasing Productivity of T.A.T. Material by an Ego Psychological Approach

If relative "barrenness" of records is the chief complaint of psychologists, we may be able to suggest a number of ways to increase productivity:

1. *An analysis of the defenses* as they appear in the T.A.T. record has already been discussed at some length as a means of increasing the yield, which has been reviewed in detail in books on the thematic apperception tests and defenses by Brody and Siegel (1992), Cramer (1991a), and Dias (1976). If barrenness is the result of overly increased ego control, for example, a number of measures capable of decreasing ego control must then increase the productivity. This could be accomplished by:
2. *Providing stronger stimuli.* If the stimuli have more affective pull, the ego will find it more difficult to control the affect. In the T.A.T., this coincides with the need for better pictures—primarily a wider range of stimuli to facilitate study of apperceptive distortions of situations not currently provided for in the existing set. A recent example is the Senior Apperception Test (S.A.T.), which now has new, improved drawings that are able to elicit richer fantasy responses (Bellak & Bellak, 1996).

3. Any other form of *increase of pressure* might also increase productivity. Stein's (1949) use of tachistoscope exposure is one way in which this might be done, the shorter exposure time causing more tensions and increasing the ambiguity (see item 4). Both this approach and the one of stronger stimuli might prove a double-edged sword: Although this might decrease the ego control in some subjects, others might freeze up even more. It is helpful to utilize the standard approach first, and only if this has failed and if there are no other contraindications (such as excessive anxiety) will it be economical to increase the pressure.

4. *Increasing ambiguity* has been attempted by Weisskopf (1950a) and Weisskopf and Lynn (1953) with the T.A.T. and the Children's Apperception Test (C.A.T.). Presenting tracings of the usual pictures and interrupting the outlines to make less good Gestalten may—up to a point—increase productivity to some extent. Murray's (1951c) modification in presenting the pictures for only 30 seconds and then removing them also increases ambiguity and prevents excessive descriptive clinging to the stimulus.

    Other studies indicate that cards that are medium ambiguous are best for projection (Epstein, 1966, Kaplan, 1969, 1970). Murstein (1965d) suggested that pictures most useful for thematic production are those that are clearly structured as to who is in the picture but relatively ambiguous as to what is going on. Such cards are medium ambiguous. Many studies have indicated that highly ambiguous cards are least useful for personality assessment (Kaplan, 1967; Kenny, 1961). Lazarus (1953) and Kaplan (1970) have noted that, because of high ambiguity of stimuli in projective tests, the lack of expression of certain needs (i.e., aggression) could be due either to lack of arousal value of the stimulus or to ego defenses against the related impulses.

5. *Physiological means* of weakening the ego, such as barbiturates or alcohol, have worked well at times.

6. A *stress inquiry* in the form of a request for controlled associations to any of the stories, and particularly to any specific concrete references in them (after all the stories have been told), may be a useful means of increasing the data of otherwise barren records.

7. Finally, if a certain test fails to give the necessary data, *use another test*. Some psychologists utilize a variable series of different tests, rather than a standard battery of a core of the same tests for all individuals of the same age group. This is reminiscent of the shotgun prescriptions of prescientific medicine. The doctor puts dozens of ingredients into every prescription in the hope that, if one would not help, another might. Clearly, a psychological test should be fitted to the needs. If one needs content of the psychodynamics, one should use the apperceptive tests; if one wants an assay of ego strength and generally quantitative indicators, one should use the formal expressive tests. But if, for example, aggression is not meaningfully expressed in the T.A.T., it may be very useful to study figure drawings. The verbal expression of aggression may be successfully controlled when its muscular expression is clearly seen in heavy line pressure of the human figure or other drawings. Often enough, the problem can be stated in a generalization—namely, that when one fails to obtain data on the semantic level, tests probing the subsemantic

area may produce information. There is good reason, on the other hand, not to leave out the semantic tests routinely, since they can elicit much more detailed, more subtle information than can safely be inferred from the organizational subsemantic methods of personality appraisal.

Apperceptive Distortion: A Theory Concerning Content of Responses as Seen Particularly in the T.A.T.

The preceding section discussed the general framework of ego psychological theory of projective techniques and the various dimensions of tests subsumed under that term. Since we wish to describe the T.A.T. particularly, and the T.A.T. is characterized as primarily a test of content, we will now address, more specifically, psychological theory concerning *what* the patient says.

Certain theories concerning adaptive and expressive formal test behavior are necessary. It will require special parts of a general ego psychological theory of personality (to be postulated and verified) to determine why outgoing movements on Mira's test should be associated with outgoing, aggressive personalities, or why extensor movements in the Rorschach should be associated with healthy, active striving. Why a preference for Dd in the Rorschach should be related to obsessive-compulsive tendencies might well be satisfactorily explained by psychoanalytic hypothesis. Why color should play a special role may need psychological hypotheses additional to those of Exner (1994), Siipola (1950), and others. However, projection in its original sense—namely, as referring to content of perception—is our special concern.

The term *projection* was first introduced by Freud (1940a) as early as 1894 in his paper, "The Anxiety Neurosis," in which he said: "The psyche develops the neurosis of anxiety when it feels itself unequal to the task of mastering [*sexual*] excitation arising endogenously. That is to say, it acts as if it had projected this excitation into the outer world."

In 1896, in a paper, "On the Defense Neuropsychoses" (Freud, 1940d), elaborating further on projection, Freud stated more explicitly that projection is a process of ascribing one's own drives, feelings, and sentiments to other people or to the outside world as a defensive process that permits one to be unaware of these "undesirable" phenomena in oneself. Still further elaboration of the concept occurs in his paper on the case of Schreber (Freud, 1943) in connection with paranoia. In brief, the paranoiac has certain homosexual tendencies that he transforms under the pressure of his superego from "I love him" to "I hate him," a reaction formation. He then projects this hatred onto or ascribes to the former love object, who has become the persecutor. The ascription of hatred presumably takes place because emergence into consciousness and realization of the hatred is prohibited by the superego, and because an externalized danger is more readily dealt with than an internal one. The superego inhibits expression of the hatred because it morally disapproves of it.

Although projection thus originated in connection with psychosis and neuroses, it was later applied by Freud to other forms of behavior—for example, as the main mechanism in the formation of religious belief as set forth in *The Future of an Illusion* (1940) and in *Totem and Taboo* (1938). Even in this cultural context, projection was still seen as a defensive process against anxiety. Freud originally considered repression the only defense mechanism; at present, at least 10 mechanisms are mentioned in the psychoanalytic literature. Although projection is firmly established as one of the most important defensive processes, relatively little work has been done on it. Sears (1943) stated: "Probably the most inadequately defined term in all psychoanalytic theory is projection." There is a long list of papers on projection, however, particularly clinical psychoanalytic and some academic ones.

The definition of *projection* as a defense mechanism was more than adequate until a crucial point arose in connection with attempts at the experimental investigation of the phenomena in one of the earliest studies on the T.A.T. (Bellak, 1944), which was later successfully replicated by Cramer (1991b). The *first experiment* consisted of provoking a number of subjects and giving them pictures of the T.A.T. under controlled conditions. In the *second experiment,* the subjects were given the posthypnotic order to feel aggression (without being directly aware of it) while telling stories about the pictures. In both instances, the subjects behaved according to the hypothesis of projection and produced a significant increase of aggression, as compared with their responses of the pictures when they had not been made to feel aggressive first. Similarly, when the subjects were under posthypnotic orders and were told that they were extremely depressed and unhappy, it was found that they projected these sentiments into their stories. Up to this point, there was no need to change the concept of projection as the ascription to the outside world of sentiments that are unacceptable to the ego.

When the experiment was varied, however, and the posthypnotic order was given to the subjects that they should feel very elated, it was found that elation, too, was projected into the stories given to the T.A.T. pictures. At this point, it occurred to us that this could not possibly be subsumed under the concept of projection as a defense mechanism, since there was obviously no particular need for the ego to guard against the "disruptive" effects of joy. Such a case can be hypothesized, for example, when joy is inappropriate, as in the death of a person toward whom ambivalence is felt. Such was not the case, however, in the experiment. Therefore, it was necessary to examine further the concept of projective phenomena and to suggest a reexamination of underlying processes.

As so often happens, it was found on careful rereading of Freud (following a reference by Ernst Kris) that Freud had anticipated our present trend of thought. He said in *Totem and Taboo:*

> But projection is not specially created for the purpose of defense, it also comes into being *where there are no conflicts.* The projection of inner perceptions to the outside is a primitive mechanism which, for instance, also influences our sense-perceptions, so that it normally has the greatest share, in shaping our outer world. Under conditions that have not yet been sufficiently determined, even inner perceptions of ideational and emotional processes are projected outwardly, like sense perceptions, and are used to shape the outer world, whereas they ought to remain in the inner world. . . . (1938, p. 857)

The thing which *we, just like primitive man, project in outer reality,* can hardly be anything else but the recognition of a state in which a given thing is present to the senses and to consciousness, next to which another state exists in which the thing is latent, but can reappear, that is to say, *the coexistence of perception and memory, or, to generalize it, the existence of unconscious psychic processes next to conscious ones.* (p. 879)

This thought of Freud's, not further elaborated on nor systematically expressed anywhere and stated without any of the sophistication of modern semantics, contains everything necessary for a consistent theory of projection and general perception.

Freud's main assumption is that *memories of percepts influence perception of contemporary stimuli.*[4] The interpretation of the T.A.T. is, indeed, based on such an assumption. A subject's past perception of her own father influences her perception of father figures in T.A.T. pictures, and this constitutes a valid and reliable sample of her usual perception of father figures. Clinical experience, as well as experimental investigation, has borne out this point. Our own experiments have shown that the behavior of the experimenter can bring out sentiments that originally were probably related to the father figure. While these sentiments had a demonstrable but temporary overall influence on the perception of stimuli—individual differences were maintained according to the genetically determined structure of the personality.

It seems, then, that percept memories influence the perception of contemporary stimuli—and not only for the narrowly defined purpose of defense, as stated in the original definition of projection. One is compelled to assume that all present perception is influenced by past perception, and that, indeed, the nature of the perceptions and their interaction with each other constitutes the field of the psychology of personality.[5]

It is necessary to describe the nature of these perceptual processes and later to attempt to formulate a psychoanalytic or more general psychology of personality based on these conceptions. Projection as a variant of perception has indeed become an integral part of the psychology of personality (see below).

Apperception and Apperceptive Distortion

To use the term *projection* for general perceptual processes does not seem useful in view of the history of the concept and its present clinical applications. On the other hand, *perception* has been so definitely linked with a system of psychology that has not been concerned with the *whole* personality that we hesitate to use it any further in the context of dynamic psychology. Although terminology is certainly not a matter of primary importance here, the term *apperception* should be used hence-

---

[4] Herbart antedates Freud on this idea (see p. 16 of Runes, 1955).

[5] This theory, in its broadest implications—name, that perception is subjective and is the primary datum of all psychology—is, of course, not original with Freud. Hume's *"Nihil est in intellectu quid non antea fuerit in sensibus"* is virtually a perceptual theory of personality, though not meant that way. Similarly, philosophical idealism, such as Schopenhauer's *Die Welt als Will and Vorstellung* and Kant's transcendental state, represent a similar position.

forth. We speak of apperception as an organism's (dynamically) meaningfully interpretation of a perception, following the definition by C. P. Herbart in his *Psychologie als Wissenschaft* (Part 111, Section 1, Chapter 5, p. 15) as quoted in Dagobert D. Runes, editor of the *Dictionary of Philosophy:* "Apperception (latin, *ad* plus *percipere* to perceive) in psychology: *The process by which new experience is assimilated to and transformed by the residuum of past experience of any individual to form a new whole. The residuum of past experience is called apperceptive mass.*"

This definition and the use of the term *apperception* permit us to suggest, purely for the purpose of a working hypothesis, that there can be a hypothetical process of noninterpreted perception, and that every subjective interpretation constitutes a dynamically meaningful *apperceptive distortion.*[6] Conversely, we can also establish, operationally, a condition of nearly pure cognitive "objective" perception in which a majority of subjects agree on the exact definition of a stimulus. For instance, the majority of subjects agree that picture 1 of the T.A.T. shows a boy sitting in front of a violin. Thus, this perception can be established as a norm. Anyone who, for instance, describes this picture as a boy at a lake (as one schizophrenic patient did) distorts the stimulus situation apperceptively. If we let any of our subjects go on to further description of the stimulus, however, we find that each one of them interprets the stimulus differently, such as a happy boy, a sad boy, an ambitious boy, or a boy urged on by his parents. Therefore, we must state that purely cognitive perception remains a hypothesis, and that every person distorts apperceptively, the distortions differing only in degree.

In the clinical use of the T.A.T., it becomes quite clear that one deals with apperceptive distortions of varying degrees. The subject is frequently unaware of any subjective significance in the story he or she tells. In clinical practice, it has been found that simply asking the subject to read over his or her typed-out story may often give the individual sufficient distance from the situation to perceive that the gross aspects of it refer to himself or herself. Only after considerable psychotherapy, however, is the subject able to see his or her more latent drives, and he or she may never be able to "see" the least acceptable of the subjective distortions, on the presence of which any number of independent observers might agree. It may be permissible, then, to introduce a number of terms for apperceptive distortion of varying degree for purposes of identification and communication.[7]

Forms of Apperceptive Distortion

Inverted Projection

It is suggested that the term *projection* be reserved for the greatest degree of apperceptive distortion, such as paranoid delusions. Its opposite pole would be, hy-

---

[6] We might add that, as long as the formation of a new configuration results in a commonly agreed upon "apperception," we may call it just that (e.g., the apperception of a certain wooden structure as a "table"). If there is any disagreement on the nature of an apperception, somebody must be engaged in apperceptive distortion.

[7] It must be understood that these various forms of apperceptive distortion do not necessarily exist in pure form and frequently patently coexist with each other.

pothetically, a completely objective perception. Projection was originally described in clinical psychoanalysis as pertaining to psychoses, in particular, and to certain neurotic defenses, generally, and to some "normal" maturational processes. In the case of true projection, one is dealing not only with an ascription of feelings and sentiments that remain unconscious, in the service of defense, but that are unacceptable to the ego and are therefore ascribed to objects of the outside world. In addition, they *cannot be made conscious* except by special prolonged therapeutic techniques. This concept covers the phenomenon observed in a paranoid that can be essentially stated as the change from the unconscious "I love him" to the conscious "He hates me." True projection in this case is actually a very complex process, probably involving the following four steps: (1) "I love him" (a homosexual object)—an unacceptable id drive; (2) reaction formation—"I hate him"; (3) the aggression is also unacceptable and is repressed; and (4) finally, the percept is changed to "He hates me." Only the last step usually reaches consciousness.

That process might well be called *inverted projection,* as contrasted with simple projection (discussed next). The first step in the process usually involves the operation of another defense mechanism: reaction formation. It is sufficient to say here that, in the case of the paranoid, "I hate him" is approved, whereas "I love him" (homosexually) is socially disapproved and was learned early by him in relation to his father as a dangerous impulse. Therefore, in this case, "I hate him" extinguishes and replaces the loving sentiment. Thus, in inverted projection, one really deals first with the process of reaction formation and then with an apperceptive distortion that results in the ascription of the subjective sentiment to the outside world as a simple projection.[8]

Simple Projection

The mechanism of simple projection is not necessarily of clinical significance; it is a frequent everyday occurrence and has been well described in the following joke:

> Joe Smith wants to borrow Jim Jones's lawn mower. As he walks across his own lawn, he thinks of how he will ask Jones for the lawn mower. But then he thinks: "Jones will say that the last time I borrowed something from him I gave it back dirty." Then Joe answers him in fantasy by replying that it was in the same condition in which he had received it. Then Jones replies in fantasy by saying that Joe will probably damage Jones's fence as he lifts the mower over. Whereupon Joe replies . . . and so the fantasy argument continues. When Joe finally arrives at Jim's house, Jim stands on the porch and says cheerily, "Hello, Joe, what can I do for you?" and Joe responds angrily, "You can keep your damn lawn mower!"

Broken down, this story means the following: Joe wants something but recalls a previous rebuff. He has learned (from parents, siblings, etc.) that the request may not be granted. This makes him angry. He then perceives Jim as angry with him, and his response to the imagined aggression is: "I hate Jim because Jim hates me."

In greater detail, this process can be seen as follows: Joe wants something

---

[8] See Murray's (1938) concepts, p. 38.

from Jim. This brings up the image of asking something from another contemporary—his brother, for example—who is seen as jealous and would angrily refuse in such a situation. Thus, the process might simply be: The image of Jim is apperceptively distorted by the percept memory of the brother, a case of inappropriate transfer of learning. We will attempt to explain later why Joe does not relearn if reality proves his original conception wrong. The empirical fact is established that such neurotic behavior does not usually change except under psychotherapy.

Joe differs from the paranoid not only by the lesser rigidity with which he adheres to his projections but also by less frequency and less exclusiveness as well as the smaller degree of lack of awareness, or inability to become aware of how patently subjective and "absurd" is the distortion. The following process is certainly not infrequent: Ann arrives late for work on Monday morning and believes, incorrectly, that her supervisor looks angrily at her later in the day. This is spoken of as "a guilty conscience"—that is, Ann behaves as though the supervisor knew that she had come late, when, in reality, the supervisor may not know it at all. This means that Ann sees in the supervisor the anger that she has come to expect in such a situation. This behavior can then be understood again as a simple (associative) distortion through transfer of learning, or in more complex situations, the influence of previous images on present ones.

Sensitization

If the preceding case of a subject's coming late to work is modified so that there is a situation in which the supervisor feels a very slight degree of anger at the latecomer, a new phenomenon may be observed. Some subjects may not observe the anger at all and thus not react to it, whereas others may observe it and react to it. In the latter case, one will find that these subjects are the ones who tend to perceive anger even at times when it does not objectively exist. This is a well-known clinical fact and has been spoken of as the "sensitivity" of neurotics. Instead of the creation of an objectively nonexistent percept, one is now dealing with a *more sensitive perception of existing stimuli*.[9] The hypothesis of sensitization merely means that an object that fits a preformed pattern is more easily perceived than one that does not fit the preformed pattern. This is a widely accepted fact, for example, in the perceptual problems of reading, wherein previously learned words are much more easily perceived by their pattern than by their spelling.

Sensitization is also the process that took place in an early experiment by Levine, Chein, and Murphy (1943). When these experimenters first starved a number of subjects and then fleetingly showed them pictures in which, among other things, were depicted objects of food, they found two processes: (1) When starved, the subjects saw food in the fleeting pictures, even if there was none, and (2) the subjects correctly perceived actual pictures of food more frequently when starved. Apparently, in such a state of deprivation, there is an increased cognitive efficiency of the ego in recognizing objects that might obviate its deprivation, and also a sim-

---

[9] A very similar process has been described by Eduardo Weiss as *objectivation*.

ple compensatory fantasy of wish fulfillment that the authors call *autistic perception*. Thus, the organism is equipped for both reality adjustment and substitutive gratification where real gratification does not exist. This is really an increase in the efficiency of the ego's function in response to an emergency—a more accurate perception of food in the state of starvation. This process can also be subsumed under our concept of sensitization, since food images are recalled by the starvation and real food stimuli are more easily perceived.

An experiment by Bruner and Postman (1954) may possibly also follow the same principle. The authors had their subjects adjust a variable circular patch of light to match in size a circular disk held in the palm. The perceptual judgments were made under the influence of varying degrees of shock and during a recovery period. Results during shock did not vary markedly. During the postshock period, however, the deviations of perceived size from actual size became very marked. The authors tentatively proposed a theory of selective vigilance. In terms of this theory, the organism makes its most accurate discriminations under conditions of stress. When tensions are released, expansiveness prevails and more errors are likely to occur. We may make the additional hypothesis that the tension results immediately in a greater awareness of the image in memory, and more acute judgments of equality of size between the percept memory of the disk and the light patch are made.

The concept of the *mote-beam mechanism* of Ichheiser (1947) may also be subsumed under the concept of sensitization. Ichheiser proposed to speak of the mote-beam mechanism in cases of distortion of social perception when one is exaggeratedly aware of the presence of an undesirable trait in a minority group, although one is unaware of the same trait within oneself. In other words, that there is a sensitization of awareness (coexistent with unawareness of the process itself and of the existence of the trait within oneself, as inherent in any defensive mechanism) owing to one's own unconsciously operating selectivity and apperceptive distortion.

Autistic Perception

Whether the perception of desired food objects in the state of starvation among stimuli that do not objectively represent food objects constitutes a form of simple projection or is a process that should be described as distinct from it depends on rather fine points. Both Sanford (1936) and Levine and colleagues (1943) have demonstrated the process experimentally. One may see that the increased need for food leads to a recall of food objects, and that these percept memories distort apperceptively any contemporary percept. The only argument that can be advanced for a difference from simple projection is that one deals here with simple basic drives that lead to simple gratifying distortions rather than to the more complex situations possible in simple projection.

Externalization

Inverted projection, simple projection, and sensitization are processes of which the subject is ordinarily unaware, and decreasingly so in the order mentioned. It is correspondingly difficult to make anyone aware of the processes in himself or herself. On the other hand, every clinician has had the experience of a subject relating a story about one of the T.A.T. pictures similar to this: "This is a mother looking into the room to see if Johnny has finished his homework, and she scolds him for being tardy." On looking over the stories in the inquiry, the subject may spontaneously say: "I guess that really was the way it was with my mother and myself, though I did not realize it when I told you the story."

In psychoanalytic language, one may say that the process of storytelling was preconscious; it was not conscious while it was going on but could easily have been made so. This implies a slightly repressed pattern of images that had an organizing effect that could be easily recalled. The term *externalization* is suggested for such a phenomenon purely for the facilitation of the clinical description of a frequently occurring process (Cramer, 1991a; Sandler, 1985).

Murray (1951b) has formulated a number of hypotheses concerning projection that need mention here. In the first place, he chose to differentiate between *cognitive projection* (actual misbeliefs of what he calls the Freudian type) and *imaginative projection*, which he believes is what therapists deal with in projective techniques. Murray feels that when therapists ask patients to imagine something, the process involved deserves differentiation from the clinical concept of projection. This seems a good idea to keep in mind for distinguishing the severity of disturbance as it appears in the protocol, but probably does not merit a theoretical differentiation. There are many patients who, when shown the T.A.T., believe that they are functioning cognitively and that their response corresponds to the actual content of the pictures. At best, one might say that the degree of ego participation or voluntary exclusion of its reality testing functions varies in the case of response to projective techniques. However, Murray very usefully differentiated between *supplementary projection* and *complementary projection*. He reserved the first term for projection of self-constituents—that is, for the distortion of external objects by one's own needs, drives, wishes, and fears. He would speak of complementary projection as the projection of what he called figure-constituents, which he defined as "the tendencies and qualities that characterize the figures (imaged objects) that people the subject's stream of thought and with which he interacts in fantasy. For the most part these are images of significant objects (father, mother, siblings, friends, enemies) with whom the subject has been intimately related. . . . In short, subjects are apt to ascribe self-constituents to one character (say, the hero) of the story, and figure-constituents to other characters." In other words, Murray's concern centered primarily on the definition of subtypes of projection predicated on the *specific content* of the projection, whereas our discussion so far has been primarily concerned with the *degree of severity or complexity* or relative unconsciousness of distortion. It may be profitable to combine the two points of view.

The problem of *degree* of distortion was also investigated by Weisskopf. Weisskopf wondered how well the T.A.T. pictures lend themselves to projection (by eliciting more than purely cognitive perception). Weisskopf developed a "transcendence index" as a quantitative measure of this factor. Subjects were instructed to describe each of the T.A.T. pictures rather than to tell a story about it. In order to obtain the transcendence index of a picture, the number of comments about the picture that went beyond pure description were counted. The transcendence index of the picture is the mean number of such comments per subject. Pictures with high transcendence indices make impersonal observation difficult and lure the subject away from the prescribed objective path of the instructions, forcing him or her to project. Weisskopf found that the pictures that had high transcendence indices were those lending themselves to interpretation in terms of parent/child relationships or in terms of heterosexual relationships between contemporaries.

Purely Cognitive Perception and Other Aspects of the Stimulus Response Relationship

Pure perception is the hypothetical process against which one measures apperceptive distortion of a subjective type, or it is the subjective, operationally defined agreement on the meaning of a stimulus with which other interpretations are compared. It supplies the end point of a continuum upon which all responses vary. Inasmuch as behavior is considered by general consent to be rational and appropriate to a given situation, one may speak of *adaptive behavior* to the "objective" stimulus, as discussed next.

In Bellak's earlier experiments, it was found that aggression could be induced in subjects and that this aggression was "projected" into their stories in accordance with the projection hypothesis. It was further found that certain pictures are more often responded to with stories of aggression, even under normal circumstances, if the experimenter does nothing beyond simply requesting a story about the pictures. Also, those pictures that, by their very nature, suggested aggression lent themselves much more readily to projection of aggression than others not suggesting aggression by their content.

It seems that the first fact (e.g., that a picture showing a huddled figure and a pistol leads to more stories of aggression than a picture of a peaceful country scene) is nothing more than what common sense would lead one to expect. In psychological language, this simply means that *the response is, in part, a function of the stimulus.* In terms of apperceptive psychology, it means that a majority of subjects agree on some basic apperception of a stimulus and that this agreement represents the operational definition of the "objective" nature of the stimulus. Behavior consistent with these "objective" reality aspects of the stimulus has been called *adaptive behavior* by Allport and Vernon (1942). In card 1 of the T.A.T., for example, the subjects adapt themselves to the fact that the picture shows a violin. Several hypotheses may be formulated:

1. The degree of adaptive behavior varies conversely with the degree of exactness of the definition of the stimulus. T.A.T. pictures and the Rorschach test inkblots are purposely relatively unstructured in order to produce as many apperceptively distorted responses as possible. On the other hand, if one of the pictures of the Stanford-Binet Test (the one depicting a fight between a white man and Native Americans) is presented, the situation is well enough defined to elicit the same response from the majority of children between the ages of 10 and 12.

2. The exact degree of adaptation is determined also by the *Aufgabe,* or set. If the subject is asked to describe the picture, there is more adaptive behavior than if he or she is asked to tell a story about it. In the latter case, the subject tends to disregard many objective aspects of the stimulus. If an air-raid siren is sounded, the subject's behavior is likely to differ greatly if he or she knows about air raids, expects to hear sirens, and knows what to do in such a situation. He or she will differ from the individual who does not know the significance of the sound, and who may interpret the noise as anything from the trumpet of the Day of Judgment to the announcement of a stoppage of work, and behave accordingly.

3. The nature of the perceiving organism also determines the ratio of adaptive versus projective behavior, as previously discussed. The experiment of Levine, Chein, and Murphy (1943) demonstrated sensitization, and we have found that people distort apperceptively in varying degrees. Even the same person may react altogether differently to a stimulus when awakened from sleep than when wide awake.

Other aspects of the subject's production—for example, that given in response to T.A.T. pictures—have been more simply discussed in an earlier paper (Bellak, 1944), which refers to what Allport has termed *expressive behavior.*

By *expressive aspects* of behavior, we mean, for example, that if a variety of artists are exposed to the same conditions, one would not expect the same creative productions. There would be individual differences expressed in the way the artists made their strokes with their brushes or with their chisels; there would be differences in the colors they preferred and differences in arrangement and distribution of space. In other words, certain predominantly myoneural characteristics, as Mira (1940) calls them, would determine some features of their product.

Expressive behavior is of a different nature from both adaptation and apperceptive distortion. Given a fixed ratio of adaptation and apperceptive distortion in a subject's response to either Stanford-Binet picture, individuals may still vary in their styles and in their organization. One may use long sentences with many adjectives; another may use short sentences with pregnant phrases of strictly logical sequence. If individuals write their responses, they may vary as to upper and lower length in spacing. If they speak, they may differ in speed, pitch, and volume. All these are personal characteristics of a rather stable nature for every person. Similarly, the artist may chisel in small detail with precision or choose a less exacting form. He or she may arrange things either symmetrically or off center. And again, in response to the air-raid signal, a person may run, crouch, jump, walk, talk—and do each of these things in his or her own typical way.

If, then, adaptation and apperceptive distortion determine *what* one does and expression determines *how* one does it, it is needless to emphasize that one may always ask *how* one does *what* one does. Adaptive, apperceptive, and expressive behavior are always coexistent.

In the case of artistic production, for example, the ratio of adaptive to apperceptive material and to the expressive characteristics may vary, of course, from artist to artist and, to a certain extent, from one product to the other of the same artist. In a similar way, expressive behavior influences the T.A.T. productions, accounting for individual differences in style, sentence structure, verb-noun ratio

(Balken & Masserman, 1940; McGrew & Teglasi, 1990; Sells, Cox, & Chatman, 1967), and other linguistic and formal characteristics. Expressive features reveal, then, *how* one does something; adaptation and apperceptive distortion concern *what* one does.

The Basic Assumptions for Diagnostic Inferences from the T.A.T. and Similar Methods

Basic Principles

A *diagnosis* is an heuristic hypothesis concerning (1) a variety of causal relationships (e.g., between the present and the past, between several discrete phenomena and a common base); (2) psychodynamics; and (3) structure (e.g., in the form of ego functions and general adaptiveness). In its broadest sense, analytically speaking, the concept of diagnosis involves a metapsychological formulation of the adaptive, genetic, dynamic, structural, economic, and topographical factors. A diagnostic hypothesis thus involves propositions concerning the etiology, treatment, and prognosis of the disease under consideration. A temporal statement should, therefore, depart from all diagnostic propositions to the extent that, when one is dealing with dynamic constellations, one is dealing only with quasistable configurations.

If one accepts an *organismic* view—that any part is a function of the whole—any aspect of human behavior can be used for "testing." A "test" can be considered a sample situation that permits inferences concerning the total personality.

In principle, asking a subject to stand on his or her head could be used as a testing situation, and inferences could be drawn concerning his or her personality. Similarly, in organic medicine, since the fingernails are undoubtedly a part of the bodily organism, a diagnosis could be made by inspection of the fingernails, as someone is said to have done. Presumably, with enough experience and detailed analysis, many conditions could be recognized by their reflection in the metabolic changes in fingernails.

Nevertheless, diagnosis in organic medicine is not made by inspection of the fingernails but by physical examination of the whole body and by such tests that tend to be most valid and economical as indicated for specific problems. A final diagnosis cannot be obtained without carefully integrating the various X-ray and laboratory findings with the clinical picture; diagnoses on laboratory evidence alone are often misleading. Similarly, in psychological diagnosis, test findings can never stand alone; they must be integrated with the total picture, whether the clinician is a psychiatrist, a psychologist, or a social worker. There is no slot-machine diagnosis possible—one cannot put in a coin and get out a diagnosis—either in medicine, in psychiatry, or in psychology. *Integration* of test results with other facets of the personality is an essential principle. Thus, it is preferable that test results be reported as follows: "The results are *consistent* with a diagnosis of. . . ."

Psychological determinism is another basic assumption that is absolutely essential to the interpretation of T.A.T. productions. The hypothesis of psychological determinism is regarded as a special case of the law of causality,[10] namely, that everything said or written as a response to some stimulus situation, like all other psychological productions, has a dynamic cause and meaning. The principle of *overdetermination* must be taken into account in this context since it insists that each part of the projected material may have more than one meaning, corresponding to different levels of personality organization. It is useful to recall, by way of example, that a story may be consciously taken from a movie recently seen and yet may be reported only because it reflects an important conflict of the subject on a preconscious level and also because it may, at the same time, have significant symbolic meaning on an unconscious level. Similarly, a given act may have several different unconscious meanings, each of them valid in relation to the whole personality.

Startling as this principle may appear at first to behaviorists, it must be pointed out that it holds in the physical sciences also. In physics, for instance, the flight of an object through the atmosphere is the result of a number of factors, such as its size, weight, and shape and the wind velocity. In present language, its final path is *overdetermined*. In a quite similar manner, a psychological act is the result of a number of different psychological processes. Saying that a psychological event may have several meanings simply indicates that it may be viewed as causally related to a number of different factors.

Another basic assumption is that of the *continuity* of at least the basic personality of one person. To use an analogy: If a river is sampled at various relatively close intervals, the chemical analysis of the content will be highly similar. Any pailful will be representative of the total content. Now, if a new tributary joins the river (as compared to a new situational or developmental factor in psychological sampling), it may, of course, add factors about which the assayer has to know in order to account for changes in content. A primarily genetic theory of personality, like psychoanalysis, maintains that the main contents of the stream will remain the primary matrix which, beyond a certain point, tributaries can only modify to a greater or lesser degree.

Some Common Assumptions

There are certain assumptions basic to the interpretation of the T.A.T. that are commonly held by most practitioners of this method. According to Lindzey (1952) these assumptions are the following:

In completing or structuring an incomplete or unstructured situation, the individual may reveal his own strivings, dispositions, and conflicts. Lindzey (1952) then lists five assumptions involved in determining revealing portions of stories:

1. In creating a story, the storyteller ordinarily identifies with one person in the drama, and the wishes, strivings, and conflicts of this imaginary person may reflect those of the storyteller.
2. The storyteller's dispositions, strivings, and conflicts are sometimes represented indirectly or symbolically.

---

[10] In the sense of a high probability, causality remains a useful concept despite the apparent exceptions in quantum mechanics.

3. All the stories are not of equal importance as diagnostic of the storyteller's impulses and conflicts. Certain crucial stories may provide a very large amount of valid diagnostic material, whereas others may supply little or none.
4. Themes that appear to have arisen directly out of the stimulus material are less apt to be significant than those that do not appear to have been directly determined by the stimulus material.
5. Recurrent themes are particularly apt to mirror the impulses and conflicts of the storyteller.

Lindzey (1952) then lists four assumptions involved in deriving inferences about other aspects of behavior from these revealing portions of fantasy material:

1. The stories may reflect not only the enduring dispositions and conflicts of the subject but also the conflicts and impulses that are momentarily aroused by some force in the immediate present (e.g., the test administration). (See Chapter 7, under the heading "The Influence of Contemporary Events on T.A.T. Stories.")
2. The stories may reflect events from the past that the subject has not personally experienced but has witnessed or observed (e.g., street scene, motion picture, story). It is assumed further that, although the subject has not experienced these events and is telling them as he or she observed them, the fact that he or she selects these events rather than others is in itself indicative of the subject's own impulses and conflicts.
3. The stories may reflect group membership or sociocultural determinants in addition to individual or personal determinants.
4. The dispositions and conflicts that may be inferred from the storyteller's creations are not always reflected directly in overt behavior or consciousness.

All of these points are discussed in various chapters of this book.

One major qualification to assumptions such as the preceding that needs to be recognized is that the cognitive style of the subject often determines whether and how his or her needs and conflicts will be expressed in thematic content. Klein (1954) has noted that cognitive controls function as delay mechanisms and need to be considered in the evaluation of behavior (e.g., projective test responses). This cognitive control approach is consonant with the current psychoanalytic trend of regarding ego processes as determinants of perception, rather than simple need states.

In line with this thesis are Holzman and Klein's (1969) comments concerning the importance of cognitive controls in perception, specifically in relation to the perceptual dysfunction in schizophrenia. Literature is accumulating on both cognitive styles and proprioceptive feedback disorders in the schizophrenic syndrome. Holzman has stated that the act of *perception,* defined as the transferring of physical stimulation into psychological information, can be broken down into its component phases of reception, registration, processing, and feedback. The perceiver, due to his or her particular personality organization, has a unique influence on the organizing and reorganizing of the percept at each of these successive stages as well as in the feedback function. Each individual's personality organization is based on his or her unique set of cognitive controls that are manifested in any disease process (i.e., through the level of perceptual functioning), including states of disorganization. These controls determine the nature of the individual's psychopathological organization.

Bases for Diagnostic Validity of the T.A.T. and Related Tests

Normative, Statistical Factors (Interindividual Factors)

Projective techniques have been a matter of much concern to academic psychologists because they cannot easily be made to conform to the usual methods of establishing reliability and validity.

The collection of norms of intelligence or achievement tests can follow a clear-cut pattern: A representative sample population is tested and the norms are established on a distribution curve. Any individual subsequently tested can then be compared to the sample population, and a specific point on the distribution curve may be assigned to him or her.

This type of procedure is difficult to follow with projective techniques. For one thing, it is almost impossible to find a sample representative of a large enough segment of the population. Although this may not be quite so difficult for the Rorschach, it is extremely difficult for a test such as the T.A.T.; the content of psychodynamics is infinitely more affected by the many cultural substructures in the United States than, for example, an intelligence test. New Yorkers of second-generation Irish, Italian, or Jewish background will differ markedly from each other, not to mention midwesterners or southerners, even if they are all matched for age, sex, intelligence, and economic level.

Further, even if such a normative approach were possible—or to the extent that it is possible—it is hardly very useful. As Rosenzweig and Fleming (1949) have pointed out, in projective techniques we are not only interested in the definitive value of the subject's standing with regard to group modes of behavior (what they call interindividual comparisons) but also, and primarily, in those aspects of the responses characteristic of this one individual. A statistical approach to projective techniques is of necessity to an atomistic approach, whereas the value of projective techniques lies in their molar approach to personality. Thus a breakdown of the responses robs the test results of much of their meaningfulness.

Sharkey and Ritzler (1985) review the general status of studies of the diagnostic validity of the T.A.T. They cite Renaud as having found few differences and Davison as being unable to find consistent differences between neurotics and schizophrenics. On the other hand, they cite Dana (1955, 1956a, 1956b, 1959a, 1959b) who found consistent differences between normals, neurotics and psychotics on measures of story organization. They are critical of the studies of Eron and associates (1950; Garfield & Eron, 1948; Ritter & Eron, 1952) for using measures of emotional tone, story outcome, and activity level to differentiate normals, neurotics and psychotics. They feel that the story content in response to T.A.T. stimuli is excessively determined by the stimulus characteristics. This is a critique difficult to understand, since many therapists have, for decades, found great individual differences in response to these stimuli (Lundy, 1985).

Lundy's comment regarding studies of reliability of the T.A.T. is that the standard psychometric test, coefficient alpha, is not an appropriate means of determining the reliability of the T.A.T., despite its wide usage. T.A.T. pictures are selected from a domain that is highly heterogeneous, and coefficient alpha is most reliable when determining the reliability of a test whose concern is homogeneous. In addition, the T.A.T. test-retest conclusions may be adversely affected by the standard instructions to write a "creative" story.

To a certain extent, any accumulation of statistical data concerning the T.A.T. may be helpful as a frame of reference, particularly in respect to formal characteristics. For example, it may be useful to accumulate thousands of samples to ascertain what percentage of males sees the figure in 3BM as male or what percentage sees the woman on the right in picture 2 as pregnant. If we were to discover, for instance, that only 10 percent of a large population tested sees the woman as pregnant, we would then hesitate to infer that not seeing her as pregnant signifies a meaningful scotoma; if 50 percent or more men see the figure in 3BM as a female, we would hesitate to consider such a response as even the merest suggestion of a feminine identification. Nevertheless, even knowing this, we might have to decide that it may mean feminine identification in some and not in others, depending on how much empathy with specifically feminine traits is revealed in making a woman the hero of the story. Even if 90 percent of all males do not mention the woman in picture 2 as pregnant, if someone describes her as slim and well proportioned, we would still have to interpret this as a denial of pregnancy. In other words, although we recommend accumulation of such data, the final interpretation must be from an idiographic approach. Each response must be evaluated in relation to all the other responses in the test.

Content Analysis

Content analysis is a method of counting the occurrence of certain words within a given context. One could, for instance, count all the words pertaining to aggression and love on a page of Dickens and a page of Hemingway. One might find that words connoting aggression occur much more often on the Hemingway page. One can apply the same technique counting the frequency of various words in transcripts of psychotherapeutic sessions utilizing apperceptive methods. Within certain limits of usefulness, relative frequency of certain words will tell one something about the narrator, if compared to frequency of the same words in other peoples' responses to the same stimuli. The technique therefore lends itself to a quantitative analysis of responses to apperceptive techniques.

Intratest Patterns

In essence, the T.A.T. deals with a series of social situations to which subjects are asked to respond. In interpreting the results, therapists are primarily interested in any repetitive patterns of behavior in dealing with these various situations. A response gains its meaningfulness in part from its relationship to the rest of the responses and in part from its relationship to similar responses to other situations.

For instance, if all stories end on a hopeless note, or if all females are seen as benign and nurturant, or if all males are seen as protective, a therapist feels entitled to make the inference that the repetitiveness of the apperceptions are related to a definite variable in the subject's personality. Thus, the repetitiveness itself, and any patterning within the test responses, becomes a criterion of reliability (and by implication, of validity) of the responses for the given individual, irrespective of any relationship to population scores. By this token (and the facts mentioned below), the responses of one individual to a stimulus may be considered interpretable as psychologically significant. We suggest calling this basis of validity the *intratest validity*. (Rosenzweig speaks of this as the *intraindividual comparison*, but we prefer to reserve this term for the following variable.)

Intraindividual Comparisons: Behavior Variables and "Fanstasy" Test Variables

In addition to the two comparisons mentioned by Rosenzweig and Fleming, it should be pointed out that a comparison between manifest behavior and fantasy behavior in the test responses is a valuable basis for inferences. For instance, if we learn that, behaviorally, someone is a Casper Milquetoast and all his stories are filled with blood and thunder, we may feel entitled to infer that there is a good deal of repressed aggression in the subject. Or if we deal with a manifestly boisterous and aggressive male and find a predominance of themes of passivity, we may make the inference that manifest behavior is in a defensive relationship to the latent variables. This factor again emphasizes the importance of a global approach to personality; in clinical practice, there is no place for experimentation. The psychologist should be informed of behavioral data, or final evaluation of test data should only be made by a clinician who has access to both the behavioral and test data.

Toward a General Psychology of Thematic Appercepion Tests

The predominant theoretical orientation to clinical diagnosis in psychology, psychiatry, social work, and the other allied mental health professions is that of psychoanalytic ego psychology. This is the reason why the psychoanalytic ego psychology point of view is emphasized in this book. However, the best illustration of the prominence of this perspective in mental diagnostic clinical practice is in the gradual addition of new axes to the American Psychiatric Association's *Diagnostic and Statistical Manual*, as it develops through its several different versions. The first axis is that of the primary, presenting disorder of the individual. The second axis is the predominant personality orientation, the third is the possible physical disorder, the fourth is the individual's level of environmental stressors, and the fifth is a global rating of adaptational functioning. The addition of other axes have been regularly proposed and discussed, such as the level of adaptational and defense mechanisms developed by Vaillant (1971, 1977).

As the reader will readily recognize from the preceding discussion in the chapter, the gradual addition of several axes of diagnosis represented in the *Diagnostic and Statistical Manual* follows Freud's (1915) recommendations to evaluate clinical data from "multiple points of view." The clinician not only considers a list of presenting symptoms but also evaluates these symptoms in relation to current and past stressors, the level of adaptation and defense mechanisms, degree of the superego, and other factors. It is this multiple perspective that is the basis of the Bellak *Long and Short Form* approach to thematic apperception test diagnosis, which we will present in this book.

We will discuss alternative methods of T.A.T. analysis that are built on other theoretical orientations to personality diagnosis, most notably that of interpersonal object relations (which some argue is a subfield of psychoanalytic ego psychology), family systems therapy, and cognitive-behavioral therapy. However, it is our belief that the majority of individual dimensions in these alternative thematic test-scoring schemes are already included within the multiple perspective of the Bellak system of 10 categories. Therefore, it would appear that clinical diagnosis and personality research are gradually developing from an individual "trait" analysis to an ego psychology and currently toward an increasingly more comprehensive general psychology of personality.

CHAPTER 3

CLINICAL USE
OF THE T.A.T.

The T.A.T. and Related Methods

The Thematic Apperception Test is a technique for the investigation of the dynamics of personality as it manifests itself in interpersonal relations and in the apperception or meaningful interpretation of the environment. In its present form, it consists of a series of 31 pictures. Testees are asked to tell stories about some of the pictures, thereby presumably revealing their personal, individual apperceptions of purposely ambiguous stimuli.

Although the T.A.T. was originally described by Morgan and Murray in 1935, Tomkins and Tomkins (1947) show that there were earlier attempts by psychologists and psychiatrists to elicit meaningful responses of individuals to pictures. These include Brittain, who published such an attempt in 1907; Libby, who used a procedure like that of Brittain with children in 1908; and Schwartz, who developed his Social Situation Test in 1932. None of these forerunners, however, attained the popularity of the T.A.T., which currently ranks second only to the Rorschach in projective tests. In fact, most surveys of psychological test usage show that the T.A.T. is among the top six tests used in the standard battery of psychological tests, consisting of a Wechsler intelligence test, the Wide Range Achievement Test, the Bender Gestalt Test, the Rorschach, and the Minnesota Multiphasic Personality Inventory (MMPI) (Archer et al., 1991; Craig & Horowitz, 1990; Goh, Teslow, & Fuller, 1981; Lubin & Larsen, 1984; McCully, 1965; Piotrowski & Keller, 1984; Thelan, Varble, & Johnson, 1968).

In the 1950s and 1960s, the T.A.T. and the Rorschach led all other tests in frequency of usage. The August 1953 *Newsletter* of the Division of Clinical and Abnormal Psychology stated that the Rorschach and the T.A.T. were the two most widely used tests. An A.P.A. report on the use of tests (*Report on Survey of Current Psychological Practice,* Supplement to *Newsletter,* Division of Clinical and Abnormal Psychology, A.P.A., Vol. 4, No. 5) indicated that the Rorschach and the T.A.T. were used to about the same extent, with the Rorschach being used somewhat more. The report stated: "In general the TAT runs the Rorschach test a close second . . . but is not as frequently considered 'very important' (62% for T.A.T. versus 85% for Rorschach)."

In the 1970s and early 1980s, Polyson, Norris, and Ott (1985) found a slight decline in T.A.T. research. However, surveys of test usage for the purposes of psychological evaluation conducted at the same time showed that the T.A.T. continued to rank in the top six or seven tests (Goh, Teslow, & Fuller, 1981; Lubin & Larsen, 1984; Piotrowski & Keller, 1984; Piotrowski, Sherry, & Keller, 1985). For example, Piotrowski and colleagues (1985) investigated test usage and practices of the membership of the Society for Personality Assessment (SPA). A questionnaire was sent to 400 potential respondents in 1984; 206 returned it. The results for SPA members with regard to the frequency of usage of various psychodiagnostic tests showed that of 35 techniques, the Wechsler scales were the most frequently used, followed by the Rorschach, the MMPI, and then the T.A.T. The C.A.T. was in ninth place, following the Bender Gestalt, Draw-a-Person, Sentence Completion (all kinds), and House-Tree-Person. If, however, one looks only for a test for children exclusively, then the C.A.T. ranks first, as the preceding tests are equally used with adults as with children.

The present T.A.T. pictures (Murray, 1943a) are the third set to be used since 1935. Aside from additions and omissions made since the first series was issued, the cards in the second and third series are distinguished by being twice the original size—a fact that probably facilitates the testee's rapport with the pictures.

Aside from the present wide use of the T.A.T., similar verbal and picture tests have been devised to meet the special problems presented by different cultures and particular age groups. These include the M.A.P.S. (Make A Picture Story Test) developed by Edwin S. Shneidman in 1947. It varies the T.A.T. material principally by separating the figures and the background, allowing the test taker to select and place his or her figures on depopulated backgrounds before telling his or her story. Thus, the test taker responds to a stimulus situation that he or she has partly created and he or she has the opportunity for using motor expressive acts in accomplishing the test task. The materials for the M.A.P.S. Test consist of 22 background pictures, which comprise both structured and unstructured (ambiguous) situations, and 67 figures—adults, children, minority group figures, silhouettes, and figures—with blank faces.

The Thompson (1949) Modification of the T.A.T. for African Americans is based on the assumption that it is easier for racial/ethnic groups to identify with figures of their own group than figures of white individuals. Accordingly, several of the original pictures have been adapted by substituting African American figures for the original white ones. Six of the original pictures have been used unchanged, and one has been omitted. The new drawings were made by V. A. Winslow, director of the Art Department of Dillard University, New Orleans, Louisiana.

In 1942, the U.S. Office of Indian Affairs and the Committee on Human Development of the University of Chicago inaugurated the Research on Indian Education. About 1,000 children from 6 to 18 years in 11 Papago, Zuni, Hopi, Navaho, and Sioux communities were studied. The T.A.T. used was a series of 12 pictures drawn by a Native American artist and representing people and social situations presumed to be within the everyday experience of all Native American children—a picture of two boys facing a man; two adults, one leading a horse; an adult woman with a baby in arms and with two other children seated before her; a group of children and adults around a grinding stone; several young men in dance regalia; and a landscape scene of fields, fences, dried animal bones, and the like. All the people in the pictures are Native Americans.

A modification of the T.A.T. was designed by Uma Chowdhury (1960a) of the Department of Anthropology, Indian Museum of Calcutta. The pictures were made from live models and imaginary pictures to suit Indian cultural patterns.

Another cultural modification of the T.A.T. was developed by Boris Iflund of the University of California for use on the University Expedition to South Africa. The same principle was employed—translating the dramatis personnae and the setting to South Africa. Another set of pictures was devised for the South Pacific Micronesian culture (Lessa & Spiegelmann, 1954). Several pictures from these different culture-specific T.A.T. adaptations can be found in Edgerton's (1971) book, *The Individual and Cultural Adaptation*. Chapter 20 of this book discusses research with these thematic tests and related clinical issues in gender and multicultural assessment.

There have been attempts to develop alternatives to Murray's T.A.T. for use in mainstream Western culture, such as the Apperception Picture Test (APT), which utilizes a Likert-type scale approach to measure aspects of the test taker's perceptions about each figure in each picture, such as rating whether a figure is "very unfriendly," "unfriendly," "neutral," "friendly," or "very friendly" (Holmstrom et al., 1992, 1994). A very interesting variation of the T.A.T. is the Object Relations Technique of Phillipson (1955), consisting of photographs of people in different situations, using various degrees of ambiguity and clarity. The Iowa Picture Interpretation Test is a multiple-choice variation of Murray's T.A.T. (Hurley, 1955; Johnston, 1957). Another intriguing variation of the T.A.T. is Stone's (1953) Auditory Apperception Test (AAT), which asks people to make up stories to the presentation of different sounds.

The basic conception of a projective method for diagnosing group properties was developed at the Research Center for Group Dynamics by Horwitz and Cartwright (1951). The technique, involving a projective picture test with slightly modified T.A.T. instructions, was first employed at the National Training Laboratory for Group Development, at Bethel, Maine, in 1947. The way the interacting group phrases a relatively unstructured stimulus configuration, the kind of relationships it sees, and the feelings it deems relevant may provide important insights into the group's structure and internal processes. A set of five pictures was developed by Henry and Guetzkow (1951) to show up different aspects of group processes. They consist of: (1) a conference group—seven men assembled around a conference table; (2) a man standing in the doorway of a house; (3) two men facing each other; (4) an older woman and a younger man; and (5) an informal scene of four men in what looks somewhat like a club room.

It had long been felt that the T.A.T. was not particularly suitable for young children, so in 1949, Leopold Bellak and Sonya Sorel Bellak developed the Children's Apperception Test (C.A.T.) consisting of pictures of animals in different situations for use with children between the ages of 3 and 10.[1] Blum (1950) similarly developed The Blacky Pictures of a little dog in different family situations to be used with young children. Costantino, Malgady, and Vazquez (1981) developed

---

[1] See Chapter 13 on the C.A.T.

the TEMAS, which features pictures in color of urban African American and Hispanic children. Since Thompson and Bachrach (1951) and Semeonoff (1976) found that using chromatic T.A.T. pictures appeared to increase the level of emotional reactions, as established for the Color and ColorForm Rorschach cards, Costantino and associates (1981) developed a picture story test for urban minority children using colored paintings, which is a good projective test alternative for African American and Hispanic urban elementary school-aged children.

Another variation of the C.A.T. is the School Apperception Test (SAM), consisting of pictures of children in school settings (Solomon & Starr, 1968). A similar group of thematic test pictures of school situations was developed in France (Nathan, 1966). These pictures are useful in obtaining information as to a child's different school-related conflicts and overall level of socialization.

Symonds's (1948, 1949) Picture Story Test was designed for the study of adolescent boys and girls. It consists of 20 pictures divided into set A and set B, both of which may be used on successive days, or set B may be used alone. These pictures are designed to facilitate the projection of problems typical of the adolescent, such as leaving home, coming home late at night, social-sexual rivalry around dating, concern about the future (in a picture showing a young boy and girl cónsulting a fortune teller), a girl looking at her new self in the mirror, a boy apparently suffering from *Weltschmerz* (sorrows of the world), pictures concerned with delinquency and jail, and other situations.

A further variation on the T.A.T. theme (though developed earlier and independently) is the Four-Picture Test designed by D. J. van Lennep and Houwink (1948). The task here is not to tell four separate stories but to tell a single story in which all four pictures appear. The first picture shows two people together, the second shows one person alone, the third represents being socially alone (a figure leaning against a lamppost in a dark street), and the fourth signifies being together with others in a group (the scene is of two tennis players with others watching). Lennerlof (1967) developed a variation of the T.A.T. showing people in industrial work situations, which he calls the Industrial Thematic Apperception Test. Independently at the same time, two thematic tests were developed for elderly individuals depicting elderly individuals in different situations—the Gerontological Apperception Test of Wolk and Wolk (1971) and the Senior Apperception Technique of Bellak and Bellak (1973, 1996), which is presented in Chapter 19.

Indications for Use of the T.A.T.

The T.A.T. is a complex test which, even in the hands of the most experienced practitioner and when used in an abbreviated form, takes considerable time and effort in administration and interpretation. Even though the test can be group- or self-administered, any systematic interpretation will still take at least half an hour per record, and often longer.

Aside from the economic aspects, it is in the nature of the T.A.T. to deal with the subtle, dynamic factors of the personality that will be the subject of investigation only under specific circumstances. Perhaps a comparison of the psychological examination and the physical examination is in order. There are routine physical examinations by inspection, auscultation, and percussion, possibly by taking the blood pressure. A more complex examination may include urine examination, fluoroscopy, and a blood count. Chest X-rays have become routine, but X-rays of other parts of the body, tests of body chemistry, basal metabolism, and the like, are requested only when there are stringent differential diagnostic reasons, or a particularly careful evaluation is necessary for especially stressful tasks or prior to undergoing major surgery.

Similarly, for ordinary purposes, paper and pencil tests of ability, intelligence, and achievement may suffice for routine examinations of students, employees, and so on. However, if one is called on to do a special selection for highly demanding tasks—such as those of pilots, special government personnel, or chief executives—if differential diagnosis is indicated, or if the patient is about to undergo a major form of psychotherapy, then more complex procedures such as a T.A.T. are indicated, and deserve the time and effort investigated.

The question, of course, remains as to which of the major tests should be used when a complex psychodiagnostic task is to be performed. One popular answer to that problem is to use batteries of projective tests. This approach undeniably has some merit. For reasons that are only partly understood, one test may show problems that the other tests do not, even though, in principle, it should illustrate the same problem. However, the principle of "the more, the better" should not apply. The unnecessary use of whole batteries has bogged down personality testing more than necessary. One principle in assorting batteries should certainly be that the tests included tap the personality structure and dynamics by different means (e.g., a verbal test such as the T.A.T. should be combined with an expressive test such as the Figure Drawing Test).

The indications for using the T.A.T. can be stated even more specifically: The T.A.T. is a content test. More than any other test in use at present, it shows the actual dynamics of interpersonal relationships. There is the Kinetic-Family-Drawing Test, which asks the subject to "draw your family doing something." The various spatial elevations, the sizes of the figures, and the differences in line pressure provide insight into how the drawer views the role relationships and power structure of the family—who is more important in the family, who is more important to the drawer, and so on. Degrees of closeness among family members may be glimpsed by examining which family members are drawn closer to which other family members, and other issues, such as rivalry, may be visually communicated by the drawer showing two siblings playing a competitive game or other similar activity. The T.A.T. is a much richer vehicle for examining the test taker's interpersonal dynamics within the family and in relations with others. It provides a way to corroborate hypotheses about family dynamics suggested by the Kinetic-Family-Drawing Test and it provides an indepth view of the test taker's level of interpersonal object relations, which is one of the most important dimensions to assess from the standpoint of psychotherapy (see Chapter 11).

The T.A.T. is also the best vehicle for revealing an individual's basic fears, anxieties, and insecurities and defense and coping mechanisms employed to deal with these fears, anxieties, and insecurities. Schafer's (1954) book, *Psychoanalytic*

Interpretation of Rorschach Testing, is a classic treatise on how to diagnose affect/defense constellations on the Rorschach. However, Exner's (1994) Comprehensive System does not adequately include the same level of diagnostic assessment of these very important dimensions. It is most important to know the test taker's main anxieties and concerns and how the test taker attempts to defend against or to cope with these issues. Test behavior provides a glimpse of defenses by the way the test taker sits, sits back away from an "unpleasant" card, and answers too quickly or pauses rather too long. But T.A.T. stories with adequate action sequences provide excellent vehicles for analyzing how the test taker may approach an area of conflict or concern, such as interpersonal intimacy presented in card 10, and how the test taker attempts to deal with it. The juxtaposition of actions in narrative that is unique to the T.A.T. is what facilitates the assessment of the relationship of psychological problem areas, anxieties, and conflicts and defense and coping mechanisms. The important work of Cramer (1991a) in this area is described in Chapter 9.

The Rorschach test is invaluable as a formal, percept-analytic technique, since it reveals better than any other test available the formal, expressive nature of thought processes and those of emotional organization. By this token, it reveals patterns that are more or less typical for certain psychiatric syndromes or disease processes, particularly those of severe psychopathology. The content analysis of the Rorschach test, although it has its natural limitations, has not been utilized to the extent it deserves in the majority of present methods of interpretation.

By the very nature of the pictures, the T.A.T. also gives basic data on the test taker's relationship to male or female authority figures, to contemporaries of both sexes, and frequently suggests the gender in certain family relationships, which is basically only hinted at on the Rorschach. For example, the Rorschach card 4 shows a large, looming figure, which may provide some hints as to how the test taker may view certain aspects of her or his own father. But the T.A.T. actually shows pictures of different family relationships, which provide a vehicle for corroborating these hypotheses from the Rorschach. The T.A.T. may not so clearly indicate the intensity of fears as does the Rorschach, but it tells the nature of them—fear of lack of support or fear of attack by males in specific situations—and it shows the hierarchy of needs and the structure of the compromises among id, ego, and superego.

The T.A.T. and the Rorschach corroborate aspects of clinical assessment. They are not competitive or mutually exclusive techniques. It is very misleading to make an assessment of an aspect of someone's personality from only one indicator on only one test. The customary practice in psychological testing is to employ a standard battery of several different tests and to examine "patterns of response" across these different tests. If a child in the middle of a custody battle between the parents drew herself or himself closer to one parent than to the other, the psychologist would not want to state in the report that the child therefore feels closer to this parent and should remain with this parent after the divorce is finalized. Forensic child custody evaluations in the past used to attempt to assess which parent is the primary "psychological parent," as if any child only has a psychological need for only one parent. Contemporary practice considers one indicator on one test a "hypothesis," and looks for corroborating evidence of this hypothesis elsewhere on the same test and across the entire standard test battery.

Standard Administrative Procedure for the T.A.T.

As in every testing situation, the test taker should be put at ease and a proper noncommittal rapport established. The test taker is seated in a chair. Usually, it is desirable to have the test administrator seated *behind and to the side* of the test taker so that he or she cannot see the examiner but so that the examiner may have full view of the patient's facial expressions. This position may have to be modified with suspicious and otherwise disturbed patients and with children.

The instructions for administration of the T.A.T., as suggested by Murray, are as follows: *Form A* (suitable for adolescents and adults of average intelligence and sophistication): "This is a test of imagination, one form of intelligence. I am going to show you some pictures, one at a time; and your task will be to make up as dramatic a story as you can for each. Tell what has led up to the event shown in the picture, describe what is happening at the moment, what the characters are feeling and thinking, and then give the outcome. Speak your thoughts as they come to your mind. Do you understand? Since you have 50 minutes for 10 pictures, you can devote about five minutes to each story. Here is the first picture." *Form B* (suitable for children, adults of little education, and psychotics): "This is a storytelling test. I have some pictures here that I am going to show you, and for each picture I want you to make up a story. Tell what has happened before and what is happening now. Say what the people are feeling and thinking and how it will come out. You can make up any kind of story you please. Do you understand? Well, then, here's the first picture. You have five minutes to make up a story. See how well you can do."

The exact wording of these instructions may be altered to suit the age, intelligence, personality, and circumstances of the test taker. It may be better not to say at the start, "This is an opportunity for free imagination," as an instruction of this sort sometimes evokes the suspicion in the test taker that the examiner intends to interpret the content of his free associations (as in psychoanalysis). Such a suspicion may severely check the spontaneity of one's thought.

The instructions recommended in this book are, in essence, identical, except we omit "This is a test of imagination, one form of intelligence" since it seems inappropriate in the clinical setting; also, we often add: "Let yourself go freely." Then one may have to answer, in a nondirective way, any questions the test taker may ask. It is permissible and even helpful to make some encouraging remark at the end of the first story. Otherwise, it is better for the examiner to say nothing for the rest of the time, unless the test taker has become too involved in a long, rambling story. At such times, one may remind the test taker that what is wanted is a story about what goes on, what leads up to it, and what the outcome will be. If the test taker remains entirely on the descriptive level, or tells only very brief stories, it is useful to remind him or her that what is needed is a story of what is going on, what people are feeling and thinking, what happened before, and what the outcome may be.

Self-Administration

The standard procedure is for the test taker to tell each story orally and for the examiner to record the responses by hand or by means of a recording device.

It is economical in many cases to give the selected cards to the test taker with written or oral instructions, emphasizing that each picture should be looked at one at a time, and then to write the stories on plain paper in the office or at home. It is helpful to let the test taker know that she or he is expected to write about 300 words per story as spontaneously as possible. The following instructions may be typed on the front inside cover of the set that is given to the test taker for self-administration:

Instructions for Self-Administration
1. Please write a story about each picture in this folder.
2. Do not look at the pictures before you are ready to write.
3. Look at one picture at a time only, in the order given, and write as dramatic a story as you can about each. Tell what has led up to the event shown in the picture, describe what is happening at the moment, what the characters are thinking and feeling, and then give the outcome. Write your thoughts as they come to your mind.
4. It should not be necessary to spend more than about seven minutes per story, although you may spend more time if you wish.
5. Write about 300 words per story, or about one typing-paper page if you write in longhand. If at all possible, please type the longhand story later, without changes, in duplicate, double-spaced, one story per page.
6. Please number the stories as you go along, and then put your name on the front sheet.

The obvious advantage of this time-saving procedure is somewhat offset by such disadvantages as a possible loss of spontaneity by the test taker, the inability to control the length of the stories, and the lack of opportunity to intervene if the test taker begins to show lack of cooperation in responding. Nevertheless, in psychiatric and psychological office practice, the self-administration method has proven quite satisfactory.

Again, for practical reasons, it has increasingly become the custom to use a standardized sequence of 10 pictures (see Chapter 4). After administering the standard sequence, the clinician may then select other cards that seem most indicated, most likely to illuminate the details of presumably existent problems of the patient. A discussion of the special usefulness of each picture and the special features of personality it is likely to elicit is presented in Chapter 4. This is particularly true when the T.A.T. is used as part of a clinical practice, where one is likely to know a few things about the test taker prior to testing and the practitioner can permit oneself as much flexibility as one wishes in obtaining material for one's own use.

Group Administration

Group administration of the T.A.T. continues to be a popular method of obtaining T.A.T. stories for the purposes of research. Typically, the pictures are projected on a screen and the research participants are given the same instructions as for individual administration, but are asked to write their stories down. Many of Cramer's (1991a) well-done studies of defense mechanisms in T.A.T. studies were obtained through this group administration approach—an approach first reported by Clark (1944). Clark (1944) collected 852 stories from a wide group of individuals ranging in age from 16 to 64, and basic themes for each picture were selected. Then, 50 college students were shown T.A.T. pictures projected on a screen, given a list of the basic themes for each card, and asked to check the story that most nearly represented their idea of the picture portrayed. The same students were also given a modified form of the usual T.A.T. in which they were asked to write original stories. Clark found a substantial relationship between results obtained by both methods, but the relationships were higher when the clinical form was administered first. She concluded that the group projection test merits further study as a possible screening device when the usual administration is not feasible. Other group administration T.A.T. studies are those of Lindzey and Silverman (1959) and Murstein (1972), whose T.A.T. norms for college students provide norms for written stories to a group-administered T.A.T. This is obviously different from the T.A.T. obtained by a psychologist in the usual testing situation in which the individual relates a story for each card and the psychologist writes down the responses.

Comparative studies of different methods of T.A.T. administration are those of Baty and Dreger (1975), Eron and Ritter (1951a), and Garfield, Blek, and Melker (1952). Eron and Ritter (1951a) investigated possible differences between T.A.T.s administered orally-individually and those obtained in a group where everybody wrote his or her own stories. Using two groups of 30 students each, they found that oral stories were longer, but that the quality and amount of thematic content were identical. The written stories had a somewhat happier tone and seemed to evoke more flippancy. However, the authors felt that because of the similarity of thematic content, the written stories elicited much the same material.

Inquiry

Contrary to statements by other authors, such as Rapaport (1946), it is most important that the inquiry be conducted only *after all the stories have been told*—not following each story. Otherwise, the clinician's inquiry questions may influence subsequent T.A.T. responses and preconscious material may become conscious and interfere with the rest of the test responses. The inquiry may actually become a free association process and part of a psychotherapeutic situation (see Chapter 8).

Clearly, the T.A.T. inquiry becomes more useful, as the psychologist gains increasing experience in interpretation and knows what to ask for. As a routine, one inquires for free associations or thoughts concerning all places, dates, proper names of persons, and any other specific or unusual information given by the test taker (Becache, 1987). Bruno Bettelheim (1947), the celebrated psychologist, contributed a creative discussion of the conduct of the inquiry after obtaining T.A.T. stories in which he suggests the value of asking test takers to provide their own ideas and impressions about the possible psychological meaning of their stories. Luborsky (1953) also illustrates the value of self-interpretation with the T.A.T.

One way of doing a self-interpretation of the T.A.T. is to have a session with the test taker after all the tests have been administered, but before the test report is written up and the final results are provided. In this session, the psychologist provides preliminary results of the cognitive and achievement tests and then goes over the raw data of the projective tests, asking the test taker what thoughts and feelings could be communicated by each test. For example, when each T.A.T. picture is shown and the examiner reads back the responses, the test taker attempts to interpret what each story may communicate about underlying psychological issues conflicts, the test taker's overall personality, and personal interests.

This clinical approach resembles working with a patient's dream in psychotherapy. Toward the beginning of treatment, the therapist may be more active in asking patients to free associate to different aspects in the dream, to think about what events during the previous day could have influenced the themes in the dream (what Freud called the "day residue"), and to ask them about how the situation in the dream may relate to aspects in the their current lives and relationships with friends, family, and possibly with the therapist. As treatment becomes more of an active collaboration, patients increasingly take more initiative in choosing which aspects of the dream to explore through free association, and eventually they provide their own interpretations (Abrams, 1992).

Psychological testing is much more therapeutic when there is an active collaboration between the psychologist and the patient (in the case of testing an adult) or between the psychologist, the child, and the parents (when testing children and adolescents). When testing an adult or a child, the preliminary report could be sent to the parties most involved to read and think about prior to coming to meet with the psychologist for the final feedback session. This provides the test taker with more opportunity to react to the preliminary results, provide more of his or her own interpretations of the projective tests, and have more input into which interventions may be most helpful.

Psychological Problems of Test Administration

The administration of the T.A.T. is simple in manifest procedure, but it is intrinsically fairly complex. Undoubtedly, the relation between the tester and the testee is very important for the richness of the responses. Beginning students almost invariably complain that the stories they get are too short. Brevity need not be a serious drawback (Murray states in his manual that he considers 300 words as average per story); as the course continues, the protocols the students obtain become miraculously longer.

The tester/testee relationship has a certain resemblance in its problems to those of the transference situation in psychotherapy. The test taker comes for help; he or she may be frightened and not know what to expect. *Rapport* is a magic word—in this instance, it means the tester must appear interested but not overeager or the test taker may feel the enterprise is chiefly for the interest of the psychologist. The clinician should be friendly but not overfriendly, which may elicit heterosexual or homosexual panic in the patient. The best atmosphere is one in which the test taker feels that the two of them are working together seriously on something very important that will be of help and that will not be something threatening.

Having had the opportunity to get to know patients well over a long stretch of time in intensive psychotherapy makes it possible to learn a good deal about what test administration means to patients. One patient with an anxiety disorder with hysterical features provided unexpectedly poor stories when tested on the T.A.T. About two weeks later, she had a dream in which the therapist was sitting at a front desk of an advertising agency, as a clerk, and she was sitting as she had sat during the test administration with the same therapist. Her associations to the dream revealed that she felt that since the therapist worked in a clinic, the therapist could not be any good (just a clerk) and that she was there primarily as a guinea pig, and that the therapist would tell (advertise) all about her to medical students. Naturally, such a mental set, whether conscious or unconscious, does not permit good responses.

Another patient had an even more markedly negative dream concerning the test administration: She dreamed that the therapist was peeking into her bathroom while she was defecating. Her T.A.T. stories were very constricted. Generally, people do not respond with the first thought or story or impulse to any projective technique. When they do not tell the first thing that comes to mind and the response is given aloud, the defense operations become clearly apparent. However, it is very encouraging that the preferred substitute is nearly as informative as the suppressed response, and it reveals defenses in addition.[2]

These processes hold true for all the projective techniques, not just the T.A.T. For instance, Dr. Molly Harrower[3] asked one patient to draw whatever was most unpleasant to him (as part of her Most Unpleasant Concept Test), and he drew a crab. While free associating in the treatment situation with Bellak, the patient stated that actually his first idea had been "vagina." He associated by seeing the crab as a dangerous, cutting, castrating animal. In other words, instead of the object of the drive aim, the patient responded with a concept expressing his idea of punishment for the wish. Thus, the response may be seen as the result of the original impulse plus—or rather, substituted by—the superego representation. However, when the patient associated during the testing situation, the fuzziness of the crab's tentacles reminded him of pubic hair, thus constituting more of a breakthrough of the original idea.

If some individuals relate very short, meager stories, one may simply suggest that they could tell a longer story, or suggest that they try to let themselves go more, adding some reassuring words to this statement. Some individuals may tell poor stories regardless of how the test administration is carried out, and this is as diagnostic as any other form of behavior. In our clinical experience, hysterical individuals typically take more to the T.A.T. and obsessive-compulsive individuals to the Rorschach. This may also hold true for the choice of method by psychologists (i.e., more obsessive psychologists may prefer to work with the Rorschach). A number of artificial steps can be taken in an attempt to enrich the responses, such as Murray's[4] suggestion to show the test taker each card for only 10 seconds, after which the story is told, thus obviating description.

---

[2] In the treatment situation, test takers will often report what their first real response was that they had not given to the tester.

[3] Personal communication to Bellak.

[4] As reported in *The T.A.T. Newsletter,* 1952, 6, 152, p. 2.

CHAPTER 4

THE T.A.T. PICTURES AS STIMULI

Murray's (1943a) original plan for the T.A.T. administration was for 20 cards to be given to each subject, with a slightly different set given to females than to males. The first 10 are to be given one day, the second 10 on a subsequent day. The first 10 are more everyday-type scenes, whereas the second 10 are more bizarre, strange, and extraordinary. Going from the first to the second grouping is like going from the more mundane world of one's daydreams to the deeper, unconscious world of one's dreams and nightmares. The richness of such complete 20-card T.A.T. protocols can be seen in Schafer (1948).

The large number of tests in contemporary psychological test batteries makes it very time consuming to administer all 20 cards. This has led to a rather informal practice of some psychologists employing a smaller number of cards, which they choose based on an attempt to match their clinical impressions of the test taker's personality with T.A.T. cards that seem to feature themes and issues more typical of these particular types of personality. The term most often used for this practice is choosing cards for particular individuals that "pull" for their particular issues (i.e., "card pull"). For example, if the test taker appears depressed, the psychologist may administer cards 1, 3BM, or 13MF, since these cards are thought to "pull" for feelings of depression. If it appears to be a reactive depression to the death of a closely related person, card 15 or 12M may be given. Card 12M is also very valuable in eliciting a patient's attitudes toward therapy and therapist, thus providing clues as to the prognosis of psychotherapy. If an individual seems to have intimacy fears, 9BM, 10, 17BM, and 18BM may also be included.

One problem with administering a limited number of cards to "corroborate" a clinical impression from the test taker's test behavior and responses on previous tests is that one may not tend to gain any new information. Another problem is that one is not able to do a "sequential analysis," as one can do with the House-Tree-Person Drawing Test or the Rorschach. Sequential analysis is often very revealing as to an individual's areas of conflict and difficulty and ability to deal with these problem areas. As in the Rorschach when one deals with a card that stimulates a conflict response, such as regressing by giving a lower level of response on a "color shock" card, it is possible to assess the individual's capacity to "recover" from such a regression by organizing a higher-level, more adaptive response on a subsequent, less conflictual card.

A few researchers have utilized the full 20-card sequence (Avila Espada, 1983, 1985; Eron, 1950). However, it is more common for researchers to employ only a handful of T.A.T. cards, as in the example of McClelland and colleagues' (1953) studies of need for achievement, Cramer's (1991a) research program on defense mechanisms, or Ronan's (Ronan, Colavito, & Hammontree, 1993; Ronan, Date, & Weisbrod, 1995) cognitive-behavioral studies of problem solving. While many research studies have used similar cards, others have recognized the value of establishing a standard T.A.T. sequence of 8 to 10 cards, as in the 9 cards of the Bender Gestalt Test, 10 cards for the Rorschach, or 10 cards for the C.A.T. Hartman (1970) surveyed 90 psychologists, asking them to rank order their most frequently employed T.A.T. cards. The rank order from the most frequent to less frequent was: 13MF, 1, 6BM, 4, 7BM, 2, 3BM, 10, 12M, and 8BM. A drawback of Hartman's basic set is that the cards are all cards for males.

Chusmir (1983) pointed out that a T.A.T. sequence that is gender balanced is preferable to a gender-specific sequence, because it provides the test taker with an opportunity for "psychological distance" with those cards featuring the opposite gender. Other studies of the most popular core group of T.A.T. cards show a parallel grouping to that of Hartman (Cooper, 1981; Irvin & Woude, 1971; Newmark & Flouranzano, 1973). Psychologists have increasingly adopted the practice of employing a basic set of 10 cards administered in the same order to males and females, which are chosen based on these surveys of what is considered the essential core T.A.T. cards, the recommendations in tests such as the current one, and including the most popular cards developed by Murray for both males and females (cards 1, 2, 4, 10, and 13MF).

Standard Sequence of 10 T.A.T. Cards

This has led to a gradual consensus on the following gender-balanced T.A.T. sequence recommended to be administered to both males and females in the same exact order:

1, 2, 3BM, 4, 6BM, 7GF, 8BM, 9GF, 10, and 13MF

If the clinician has other "favorite" cards not on this list or wants to give certain cards that "pull for" or elucidate specific problems, such as marital conflict or suicide, then these cards may be given *after* first administering the standard sequence of 10 cards. These 10 pictures appear to illuminate powerful emotions and basic human relationships, as well as make it possible to compute statistics for the 10 scoring categories and 12 ego functions of the Bellak T.A.T. Blank and Analysis Sheet. The number of the total 10 cards that show the defense of denial, for example, can be reported similar to reporting the number of shape rotation errors on the Bender Gestalt Test (Koppitz, 1963) or of Whole responses on the Rorschach (Exner, 1994; Klopfer & Kelly, 1942; Schafer, 1948). Cognitive scoring of narrative form and thematic content scoring may then be derived for the T.A.T. similar to Rorschach structure and content systems of analysis, and sequential and other response patterns may then be mathematically computed in the manner of the Rorschach ratios.

For those clinicians who wish to administer a gender-specific T.A.T. sequence, the most common practice has been to administer the following sequence for females: 1, 2, 3BM, 4, 6GF, 7GF, 9GF, 10, 11, and 13MF. For a male-specific T.A.T. sequence, the following is recommended: 1, 2, 3BM, 4, 6BM, 7BM, 8BM, 10, 12M, and 13MF. However, the gender-balanced T.A.T. sequence recommended above is preferable for the reasons stated earlier, as well as consistency with the gender-balanced sequence of the C.A.T. and S.A.T.

No doubt there are many areas of life not as fully suggested by the T.A.T. pictures as one might wish. For this reason, modifications for other age groups—such as Symonds's M.A.P.S. and Bellak's C.A.T., C.A.T.-H., and S.A.T.—were designed. Murstein (1965a, 1965b, 1965c, 1965d) discusses the general area of thematic modifications, some of which can also be added after the standard set of 10 cards are administered. A major weakness of the T.A.T. is that there are not sufficient experimentally derived performance standards for "normals" and for various diagnostic groups, although much work has been carried out to provide evidence of modal performance for members of various groups. It is hoped, therefore, that with the increasing use of this standard set of 10 cards, it will become possible to computerize the scoring categories of the Bellak Long and Short Form in a manner similar to Exner's (1994) comprehensive system for Rorschach analysis. The T.A.T. may then find its proper place on a more rigorous and scientific empirical foundation.

Typical Themes Elicited by the Standard T.A.T. Sequence

Picture 1

A young boy is contemplating a violin that rests on a table in front of him.

This is the single most valuable picture in the T.A.T., insofar as such a statement can be made. If permitted only one picture, this would be the best choice for an attempt to make statements about the total personality. One great value of this picture lies in the fact that it is a good start to the testing situation. It is nonthreatening and induces a feeling of reverie in adults and adolescents.

As to themes, this picture usually leads to an easy identification of the test taker with the boy and brings out *the relationship toward the parental figures*. That is, it usually becomes quite apparent whether the parents were perceived as aggressive, domineering, helpful, understanding, or protective. Aside from learning about the test taker's relationship to her or his parents, one may also gain insight into the type of relationship with each parent. Frequently, we obtain themes on the conflict between autonomy and compliance with authority in all its wide variations and different patterns. For example, the boy may try to escape the parental commands to practice the violin by playing in the street, but then he finally feels that he ought to go in and play the violin, or he may run away from home. Or the hero may be described as not obeying his parents and doing what he wants. Later on, he experiences failure because he did not obey them. Thus, one may display guilt feelings about one's autonomy, while in other cases, all may go well after one has broken away. Hence, this card is especially successfully employed with adolescents.

Another need this card frequently brings out is that of *achievement*. It is particularly important to see how the success is achieved, whether just on a fantasy level or on a reality level.

Finally, many subjects give *symbolic sexual responses* to this card. The play on the strings of the violin, the play with the fiddle, frequently become symbolic stories of repetitive self-soothing behavior, such as masturbation; and castration fears in boys and men often emerge when one relates in a story that the strings have been broken. The relationship between bow and violin may also be seen as that of a male and a female. Mastery of the violin frequently constitutes a fusion of sexual and achievement drives—to be able to fiddle as well or better than the father.

Aggression may also be expressed, with and without sexual connotations, in breaking the violin or bow. Superego anxiety may express itself in stories in which the boy is said to be blind, which could be, from a psychodynamic view, an expression of castration fears related to voyeuristic wishes.

The *body image* or, in a wider sense, the *self-image* is frequently significantly illuminated in this picture. Most often, the violin, and sometimes the bow, serve in this capacity; although the image of the boy may do so, too. There may be references to the violin's having a crack, or being dead inside and mute, revealing a sense of not functioning well, of being muted. Reference to "deadness" usually indicates feelings of very severe emotional impoverishment to an extent that compels one to consider schizophrenia in the differential diagnosis. The figure of the boy is sometimes seen as crippled, also suggesting a literally warped body image.

Obsessive preoccupations may become apparent when the test taker is much concerned with the notepaper, or the mussiness of the hair, or a black speck present in most of the reproductions of the pictures. In these instances, it is referred to as dirt. Frequently, the violin, as lying beneath, is identified as a female and the bow as a male, and the whole story about playing the violin may then be seen as sexual activity. *Neuropsychologically,* picture 1 is particularly useful. For years, it has been an amazing experience to find that there are a good number of subjects with adequate eyesight, of average intelligence, and who are nonpsychotic, who *do not recognize the violin,* to judge by their spontaneous stories. Inquiry will often lead them to recognize it correctly. It is not entirely clear why this occurs. In none of the cases in our experience has there been valid reason to suspect that cultural factors might have been involved. Some individuals who have difficulty with attention, such as those with attention deficit disorder, may tend not to recognize the violin.

Picture 2

Country scene: In the foreground is a young woman with books in her hand; in the background, a man is working in the fields and an older woman is looking on.

This picture usually offers excellent indications of the subject's *family relations.* Even males usually identify with the central figure of a young girl, because it is so definitely the figure in the foreground. Again, varying themes of autonomy from the family versus compliance with the conservative, backward existence are extremely frequent. These themes show the type of divergence between the test taker and the family. Oedipal themes and sibling rivalry also appear in full bloom.

Most useful for our purposes is the test taker's handling of the woman lean-ing against the tree, who is often seen as pregnant. A great deal of information can be obtained from the manner in which the subject handles apperception of *preg-nancy*. It may be completely ignored or it may lead to highly informative notions about it in all ages.

The figure of the man may illuminate heterosexual and homosexual attitudes: Men may overly admire his musculature, for example.

In this picture, which contains a relatively large number of objects, obsessive-compulsive subjects may comment on small details such as the lake in the back-ground and the tiny figure in the background among others, in a way that virtually permits the diagnosis of *compulsive tendencies*. Sometimes, most of the remarks con-cern the horse, possibly a regressive and avoidance phenomenon. Similarly defen-sive may be obsessive preoccupation with the small details or complaints that the furrows are not straight. Again, stories to this picture are frequently removed in time and place, as a form of removal from one's own conflicts.

The way in which the relationship of the two women to the man is discussed—whether as a farmhand run by the woman, or as a father, husband, or brother—adds a good deal of information about the test taker's conception *role of the sexes*.

Picture 3BM

On the floor against a couch is the huddled form of a boy with his head bowed on his right arm. Beside him on the floor is a revolver.

This also belongs to the group of most useful pictures. As already mentioned, this card may be used for females too—they identify with the figure readily enough, manifestly seeing a woman, or identifying latently. Normative data on the percent-age of men seeing it as a man may be most useful for future research. Empirically speaking, most men see the huddled figure as a man; if it is seen by men as a female figure, this may be considered a point to keep in mind—not to make the diagnosis but to keep in mind factors of possible latent *homosexuality*, which may be confirmed if more suggestive evidence appears in other pictures. How the object on the left is perceived often gives a great deal of information about problems concerning ag-gression. Officially, this object is described as a gun. Some individuals may recog-nize it as a gun; it is interesting to observe the manner of handling the aggression—whether it is used as extra-aggression (e.g., somebody else is being shot by the hero) or whether it is used as intra-aggression (the hero is being shot or he commits sui-cide). If it leads to extra-aggression, it will be interesting to see what happens to the hero. Whether he is punished severely or whether he escapes is a kind of protocol that indicates the strength of the superego of the subject.

On the other hand, some clue is desired as to what leads to the depressive pat-tern that finally results in suicide. It is obvious that this picture is especially useful with *depressed patients*. The pistol may be turned into a toy pistol and thus rendered harmless. This may indicate denial, but it is important to find out by checking the consistency with other stories whether it is a superficial escape from reality enter-ing into the story or whether this corresponds to the fact that one is simply dealing with a healthy person who has neither excessive intra- nor extra-aggression. Again, a person who has to repress latent aggressiveness may completely deny the presence of the gun by omitting reference to it, seeing it as a hole in the floor, as a cigarette case, or not seeing it at all. Sometimes, a great conflict around aggression, particularly when it has led to a compulsive pattern, will manifest itself by the test taker's hemming and hawing for a considerable time over what the object may be.

Here, again, the body image may become illuminated: The figure may be seen as crippled, extremely ill, and the like.

The mere fact that a story concerns suicide has, in itself, no prognostic significance. Only if such a story coincides with a great deal of latent intra-aggression, a severe superego, and a great deal of aggression should suicide be considered as a serious possibility.

Picture 4

A woman is clutching the shoulders of a man whose face and body are averted as if he were trying to pull away from her.

This picture elicits a great variety of needs and sentiments in regard to *male/female relationships*. Themes of infidelity are often found, and the male attitude toward the role of women may appear. She may be a protector who tries to keep him from rushing into something poorly thought out or one who tries to hold onto him by being overly possessive, dependent, or clinging. Similarly, a woman's attitude toward men as persons who may have been aggressive toward her becomes apparent.

Another object of interest is the picture of the semi-nude in the background, which is perceived by more than two-thirds of the test takers. If it is not perceived or discussed at all, it may be a clue to the fact that there is a *sexual problem*. On the other hand, it may be seen as a poster or as an actual figure in the background, prompting themes of *triangular jealousy*. Whether the difference in depth perception involved in seeing it as a poster or as a living person may be considered a differential criterion of value is not clear at this point. There is a possibility that there is a defensive element in seeing it as a poster.

Picture 6BM

A short elderly woman stands with her back turned to a tall young man. The latter is looking downward with a perplexed expression.

This is an indispensable picture for males, reflecting all the problems of *mother/son relationships* and all their derivatives in relation to wives and other women. Oedipal themes are frequent. The stories given to this picture run such a complete range of this fundamental problem that only a monograph could do it justice. The downward-cast heads of the two figures often elicit feelings of loss, such as the son bringing the news to the mother than the father has died.

Picture 7GF

An older woman is sitting on a sofa close beside a girl, speaking or reading to her. The girl, who holds a doll on her lap, is looking away.

This picture will bring out the relationship between *mother and child in females*. It may encourage negative attitudes toward the mother, because of the fact that the girl is looking off into the distance rather than at the mother. The doll, in turn, may reflect the test taker's attitude toward *expectancy of children*. Often, the theme concerns the mother telling a fairy tale, and very instructive data may be in this theme within a theme.

Picture 8BM

An adolescent boy faces the front of the picture. The barrel of a rifle is visible at one side, and in the background is the dim scene of a surgical operation, like a reverie image.

This is a very useful picture. Male test takers usually identify with the boy in the foreground. The *aggression-essential themes* that may be developed center on either someone being shot and now being operated on (in the background) or on stories of *ambition*—the boy dreaming of becoming a doctor, for example. The operation scene may elicit a fear of being mutilated while passive. Whether the rifle at the left is recognized or not, and what is made of it, are problems similar to those of the pistol in 3BM. The way in which the figures are described—for example, the attitude toward the doctor as an older person or toward the person being operated on—if seen as a paternal figure, frequently gives clues as to the oedipal relationship.

This picture may be fairly difficult to cope with for some people, since it taxes the synthetic integrative capacity. Most often, it is made into a dream or a daydream of success as a surgeon or of the perpetrator of a shooting. One way of distancing oneself is to ascribe the scene to something that happened long ago. Also, the event may be described as an accident of someone else's. In those people, who tend to deny aggression, the gun may be simply ignored. The clinical inference that avoidance of mentioning the weapon in this or other T.A.T. pictures may mean particularly severe latent hostility has frequently been attacked as "damned if you do and damned if you don't" by academic psychologists. However, this fact has been verified experimentally by Eriksen (1951).

Picture 9GF

A young woman with a magazine and a purse in her hand looks from behind a tree at another young woman in a party dress running along a beach.

This is an invaluable picture in getting a notion of the *woman-to-woman feeling*, particularly for bringing out sister rivalry or daughter/mother hostility. It is very important in cases in which one suspects *depression and suicidal tendencies*, since frequently in such circumstances the girl below is made into someone who, in a panic, runs into the sea. Again, suspiciousness, at the least, may be brought out by the fact that stories sometimes raise discussions as to why this one person is watching the other maliciously. This factor may, at times, be strong enough to warrant the *consideration of paranoia*. Men are frequently introduced in stories to this picture, often in romantic or aggressive connotations. A male is frequently introduced into the story as a sexual attacker from whom one woman flees, while the other comes to her rescue. On the other hand, one often obtains stories of one woman or the other or both running to greet a long-lost lover arriving by ship. One may be jealous of the other's relative success in love relations.

Picture 10

One person's head is against another person's shoulder.

The gender of the two individuals is rather ambiguous, as in card 3BM. For those who see the figures as a man and a woman, it may bring out the level of intimacy the test taker may experience in relationship with one of the opposite gender. If it is interpreted as an embrace between two males by a male test taker or an embrace between two women by a woman test taker, it may suggest *latent homosexuality* or actual homosexual activity. If it is described as a man and a woman by either males or females, it will be interesting to observe whether it is made a story of arrival or departure, reflecting in the departure theme latent hostile needs.

Picture 13MF

A young man is standing with his downcast head buried in his arm. Behind him is the figure of a woman lying in bed.

This is an excellent picture for disclosing *sexual conflicts in both men and women*. In very inhibited subjects, this may virtually lead to "sex shock," which will find expression in the stories. In females, it may elicit fears of being raped, attacked, or otherwise abused by men. In males, it will often bring out guilt feelings about sexual activity and will easily show the disgust of homosexuals. Feeling between husband and wife may be projected. Not unusual are stories of *economic deprivation* in response to this picture, and *oral tendencies* will frequently appear in discussion of the breasts. Again, since this is one of the pictures containing a relatively great amount of detail, *obsessive-compulsives* will easily be recognized by their concern with details.

Typical Themes Elicited by the Other T.A.T. Cards

Picture 3GF

A young woman is standing with downcast head, her face covered with her right hand. Her left arm is stretched forward against a wooden door.

This is a picture that may also bring out *depressive* feelings. Frequently, however, it has been found more useful with females to use 3BM, with which they easily identify, as stated earlier.

Picture 5

A middle-aged woman is standing on the threshold of a half-opened door looking into a room.

This is often interpreted as the *mother who may be watching* different activities. At times, this becomes a symbolic story of fear of observed masturbation, or the mother appears as benevolently interested in how the child is, or she may be seen as reprimanding the subject for being up late. *Voyeuristic material* is quite frequent and may actually lead to disguised stories of the *primal scene*. Again, *fear of attack,* particularly in female subjects, is often reflected in a story of burglary, whereas in males it may lead to *rescue fantasies,* in the psychoanalytic sense.

Picture 6GF

A young woman sitting on the edge of a sofa looks back over her shoulder at an older man with a pipe in his mouth who seems to be addressing her.

This is really meant to be a counterpart of 6BM to reflect the *relationship of females to the father,* probably because of the apparently relatively slight age difference. However, the man is usually, at least manifestly, not seen as the father image but rather as a contemporary, who may thereupon be invested with any number of qualities, from those of an aggressor, a seducer, or a proposer of marriage. Frequently, this man is made into an uncle, who probably represents the picture of an idealized father, as is so often done in folklore, as in the instance of Uncle Sam or Uncle Czar. All in all, the picture is not a particularly useful one.

Picture 7BM

A gray-haired man is looking at a younger man who is sullenly staring into space.

This picture of an old man and a young man is helpful in bringing out *the father/son relationship* and all its derivatives (in males) in the form of attitudes to male authority.

Picture 8GF

A young woman sits with her chin in her hand looking off into space.

Almost any theme may be produced to this picture, usually of a shallow, contemplative nature. The card is not particularly useful.

Picture 9BM

Four men in overalls are lying on the grass taking it easy.

This is another important picture for disclosing *contemporary, man-to-man relationships.* It may, for one thing, offer a general indication of social relationships—namely, with which of the figures the test taker is identified. In extremes, the test taker may identify with someone outside the group, who looks askance at the group or he may be part of it or even the center. Again, *homosexual feelings or fears* may become apparent in stories to this picture. *Social prejudices* may be brought to light here, as in stories of homeless individuals.

Picture 11

A road skirting a deep chasm between high cliffs. On the road in the distance are obscure figures. Protruding from the rocky wall on one side are the tong head and neck of a dragon.

Picture 11 is particularly useful because it operates on a more disguised plane and puts many people off guard; although it may frighten others. Here, many *infantile or primitive fears* emerge, since the animals permit projection of such emotions. If a person has *fears of attack,* this is a most useful picture, since it may expose the fine features of the fears of being attacked, as for example, by the phallic symbol of the dragon. Stories of *oral aggression* are also frequent. This picture offers good clues to the mood of the test taker, whether or not one escapes and, if so, how.

Anxiety, in common with other psychopathologic symptoms, is often expressed in content changing with cultural factors. For example, in the Middle Ages, hallucinations were primarily thought of as the undue influence of the devil and other supernatural forces. In the early twentieth century, electricity and, later, radio waves entered into hallucinatory and delusional content, as in a paranoid individual who felt that radar was being used on him. Similarly, fear of destruction is frequently elicited by this picture in stories about an atomic holocaust leaving everything desolate in its wake. When such stories refer to everything being dead, it may indicate an intrapsychic state consistent with very severe emotional impoverishment.

Picture 12M

A young man is lying on a couch with his eyes closed. Leaning over him is the gaunt form of an elderly man, his hand stretched out above the face of the reclining figure.

This is a most important picture for indicating the qualities of the *relationship of a younger man to an older man,* particularly regarding *passive homosexual fears* and fears of being under the domination of superior figures.

Stories to this picture may reveal whether passivity is ego syntonic or greatly feared; sometimes, the man in the upright position is seen as helpful, administering aid, giving comfort, and no anxiety is expressed. At other times, he is seen as exerting an evil influence (e.g., by hypnosis) or as attacking or having attacked a helpless victim.

Rapaport (1946) has stated that this picture may prognosticate therapeutic success. Insofar as complete, unthreatening passivity may make therapy much more difficult, this may be correct. As to the stories revealing positive or negative feelings toward the therapist, it must be remembered that the mere fact of an initial positive or negative transference is not of therapeutic significance.

Stories to this picture may indeed nicely reflect the relationship to the therapist, inasmuch as the couch and supine position may be unconsciously related to the psychoanalytic treatment situation or the generally dependent attitude of the patient. Such stories lend themselves particularly well to direct use in therapy, as vehicles for insight and interpretation. The following example illustrates this point:

This can't have too many stories. He's either dead or being hypnotized. If dead, the person with his hand raised over him is doing a rather uncommon thing. Trying to practice some kind of witchcraft. The other man has his knee raised, so he doesn't look too dead. Reclining on a small bed of some sort. Not too dead. Probably just waiting for some kind of black magic from the other fellow. If he's sick, they're trying to remove whatever his sickness is. If he's dead, this fellow is trying to perform whatever they do to dead men, so that he will be acceptable to wherever he's going, if he's going anywhere. This picture seems more abnormal than any of the others. It's so terribly abnormal that I don't see how anybody could tell anything but a terribly abnormal story—not even a story but to keep on going and not necessarily ever to have to finish. I'm struck by this and shocked. The hypnotizing, or black magic.

Picture 12F

A portrait of a young woman. A weird old woman with a shawl over her head is grimacing in the background.

This may bring out *conceptions of mother figures,* but, in all, it is not a picture that is particularly useful. Frequently, the evil mother figure is made the hero of a story in the guise of a mother-in-law. To appreciate this tendency, it must be understood that mothers-in-law are often the recipients of the negative emotions felt toward one's own mother. One may be aware only of positive feelings toward one's mother and readily project all the negative feelings onto the less holy figure of the mother-in-law. This is responsible for the position of the mother-in-law in so many cartoons and jokes.

Picture 12BG

A rowboat is drawn up on the bank of a woodland stream. There are no human figures in the picture.

This picture is meant, as the initials indicate, for boys and girl, but it has not proven very useful. The fact that none of the T.A.T. pictures was useful often enough with children below the age of 10 prompted Bellak's development of the Children's Apperception Test.

This picture has not been found too helpful in any specific case, except in *suicidal* or very *depressed subjects.* It may, then, elicit stories of someone having jumped or fallen out of the boat.

Picture 13B

A little boy is sitting on the doorstep of a log cabin.

To a lesser degree, this is not unlike the boy with a violin picture of Card 1 in prompting *stories of childhood* and may be of some use with young boys, although not markedly. It may induce reverie in adults in much the same way as the violin picture.

Picture 13G

A little girl is climbing a winding flight of stairs.

This picture has not been found to be especially useful thus far in our experience.

Picture 14

The silhouette of a man (or woman) against a bright window. The rest of the picture is totally black.

This silhouette may be a most useful figure. For one thing, it is interesting to note the *gender identification* of the figure. It often brings out childhood *fears* in relation *to darkness.* Again, this card may be very useful, when one suspects *suicidal tendencies,* which may be expressed in a story of jumping out of the window. Frequently, it may induce themes of simple contemplation and reveal much of the philosophical rationalization of the subject. Occasionally, it may reveal *esthetic interests,* and wish-fulfillment stories may be offered. It may result in burglary stories, if someone is seen as coming into the window.

Picture 15

A gaunt man with clenched hands is standing among gravestones.

This picture of a figure in a graveyard is especially important if the test taker has had a *death in the immediate family* and the clinician wants to discover the test taker's sentiments regarding that death. It is also very useful in that it may disclose notions and *fears of death* in most people who are presented with this picture. *Depressive tendencies* manifest themselves clearly. What is clinically interesting and important, and may appear in response to this picture, is the fact that there are many different conceptions of death. Psychopathology may differ according to whether the idea of death is one of being violently hurt (castrated or anally hurt) or devoured; or whether the idea is concerned with being dead, as an acceptable or unacceptable fantasy of passivity of an oral nature, as Lewin (1950) in particular has pointed out. The most specific and unusual fear of death Bellak encountered existed in an agoraphobic patient where the exhibitionistic fantasy of lying stark naked on the undertaker's slab was particularly fear arousing. The aggressive and passive fantasies of death are probably represented in the religious dichotomy of heaven and hell. All these considerations are particularly important in those pictures concerned with suicidal possibilities.

Picture 16

This *blank card* is of extreme value with verbally gifted subjects, who may really let loose and project freely. If the test taker has given previous indications of difficulty in expressing fantasy material, however, the blank card is often of not of any real value. The instructions here are first to imagine a picture and then tell a story about it, producing something like superprojection (Wakefield, 1986).

Picture 17BM

A naked man is clinging to a rope. He is in the act of climbing up or down.

There are many useful aspects to this picture. There may be revelations of fears in the stories of escape from physical trauma, such as fire, or fleeing from someone. The latter often leads to disclosures concerning *oedipal fears,* particularly in young, socially immature adolescents, where this picture may actually be seen as someone fleeing from the king or the prince. Again, *homosexual feelings* are easily brought out, even by descriptive details. Not unusual are stories of a competitive nature, making this an athletic meet or the like. In males, there will often be an indication of their *body image*—whether or not they feel themselves to be muscular, for example.

It has been suggested that outgoing, active people tell stories of people climbing up, in distinction to others. This makes sense in terms of Mira's (1940) observations and those of other expressive studies.

Picture 17GF

A bridge over water. A female figure leans over the railing. In the background are tall buildings and small figures of men.

Here is another useful card when one suspects *suicidal tendencies in women,* since it opens the way for stories about jumping from a bridge. Otherwise, a great variety of stories may be told to 17GF, which is not one of the more useful cards, except for the one purpose just stated.

Picture 18BM

A man is clutched from behind by three hands. The figures of his antagonists are invisible.

This is another of the more important pictures for learning about, or verifying, any *anxiety, particularly in males.* Fears of attack, particularly of a homosexual nature, become most apparent. If a test taker has any anxiety at all, it is bound to come out in response to this picture. On the other hand, it can be made into something innocuous, such as a story of support, for example, of a man in an intoxicated condition being brought home by his friends. How the problem of supernumerary hands is handled is frequently of great interest insofar as the thought processes of the person are concerned. Sometimes, the story is made innocuous in somewhat the following way: "A man was out at a stag dinner and now, inebriated, is being helped home by his companions, who have ducked behind him to push him up the stairs. *Viribus unitis!*"

Hard-luck stories are often related to this picture, and, of course, one wants to know what a particular person thinks of or fears as hard luck.

Picture 18GF

A woman has her hands squeezed around the throat of another woman, whom she appears to be pushing backwards across the banister of a stairway.

This picture gives an excellent indication of how *aggression is handled by women.* It may be completely evaded by the denial that any aggressive act is taking place. Sometimes, stories of how one woman is helping another up the stairs or up from the floor are told in attempts to evade aggressive implications. *Mother/daughter conflicts* may also be highlighted.

Picture 19

A weird picture of cloud formations overhanging a snow-covered cabin in the country.

A picture sometimes useful with young adolescents, but otherwise not notable.

Picture 20

A dimly illuminated figure of a man (or woman) in the dead of night leaning against a lamppost.

The figure may be seen either as a man or as a woman. We do not have any definite indication of the differential implications of such gender identification. Women may present stories of fear of men or of the dark. Otherwise, fears may be brought out by either gender in making it a gangster story. Again, it may be made an entirely innocuous theme by a story of an evening's date.

Sequential Analysis of the Standard T.A.T. Sequence

The recommended sequence of 10 T.A.T. cards include 9 cards from the first series of so-called everyday situations (1, 2, 3BM, 4, 6BM, 7GF, 8BM, 9GF, and 10) and only one from the second series of more dramatic situations (13MF). This sequence is similar to that of the Rorschach, since it provides for a relatively easy beginning of a boy thinking about practicing the violin (1) and a young girl going off to school holding her books (2), but moves back-and-forth to more "dramatic" deeper conflict situations and more familiar "everyday situations." This facilitates a sequence analysis of the test taker's level of defensive reactions to different situations and capacity to "recover" and organize a higher level of response to subsequent cards. The level of defensive reaction is often a measure of the level of intensity of a conflict. For one source of insight into an individual's conflicts and to the intensity of these conflicts is often through evaluating the defenses organized to attempt to manage these conflicts (Freud, Anna, 1936). This is one of the main reasons that sequential analysis on the Rorschach and T.A.T. is so valuable in the process of psychological evaluation.

The first two Rorschach cards are black-and-white achromatic cards that similarly provide for a relatively easy association to butterflies, moths, and so forth. However, the second and third Rorschach cards add the new element of the color red, which many associate with blood or aggression. For those with conflicts around aggression or physical illness related to internal bleeding, the second card is experienced as providing "color shock." This conflictual situation is likely to bring about defense reactions of denying or blocking the red by not including it in one's associations to the cards or a regression in providing a fragmented or other lower-level response. The next four Rorschach cards return to the achromatic black-and-white situation, which provides the psychologist with an opportunity to evaluate if the individual has coping mechanisms with which to "recover" from the earlier conflictual "color shock" situation in order to be able to provide higher-level or integrated responses. The last three Rorschach cards, then, reintroduce color, but this time the amount of color progressively increases to the full panoply of card 10.

Another dimension of Rorschach sequence analysis is the type of common figures seen in the different cards. For example, some cards are associated with females, such as cards 3 and 7, and other cards are associated with males, such as cards 4 and 6. If one has considerable conflict around females, the associations may be more fragmented, lower-level responses. Or if one experiences males as aggressive and sadistic, the associations to the "male" cards may be to more primitive, sadistic animals or people, rather than to more benign and friendly figures. As with the color dimension, one may evaluate this individual's ability to "recover" from a conflict area on one card, when one approaches the task of associating to subsequent cards. Further dimensions for sequence analysis on the Rorschach are the ratios and other dimensions (Exner, 1994; Schafer, 1954).

After the first two family situations around achievement of a child in T.A.T. cards 1 and 2, the test taker is presented with card 3BM of the dejected person sitting on the floor with head against a couch and a revolver next to the figure prior to the more dramatic situation of a figure sitting on a floor with head on a couch and a revolver next to the figure. For an adult, the first two pictures help to take the individual back to a common situation of childhood regarding studying, practicing a skill, and going to school with common issues surrounding the child's relationship with the parents around schoolwork, achievement, growing up, and independence. These first two situations are also fraught with conflict, more for some than for others, but the conflict around achievement is a common issue for most all individuals in the world (McClelland et al., 1953).

The next card, 3BM, the individual with downcast head sitting on the floor next to a revolver, brings the test taker to the more primitive situation of an individual possibly contemplating a violent end to one's life. This is very similar to the "color shock" situation of cards 2 and 3 on the Rorschach, since it brings in a similar possible association to aggression to which the test taker may defend by not mentioning the revolver. The next card, 4, a woman holding onto the shoulder of a man, who is looking in another direction, provides for some relief from the primitive situation of card 3BM. This situation is a more familiar one of a couple perhaps having a disagreement over the man feeling a need to go do something elsewhere and the woman attempting to hold him back. Cards 6BM, of a man with head down next to a woman looking out a window, and 7GF, of a girl listening to a woman read her a story, are similarly more familiar everyday situations. Hence, the test taker may provide longer and more organized narratives to these three cards than may have been provided to card 3BM (which is parallel to the dimension of form level and level of integration of details into an organized Whole response on the Rorschach).

Card 8BM, a boy looking at the front with the two men appearing to operate on a man on a table with a rifle to the side, brings the test taker back to a deeper, more conflictual and more primitive situation of someone, possibly the boy's father, having been shot and being operated on in a primitive, perhaps military, setting. This may bring out primitive oedipal wishes of the boy for the death of the father or a bereavement issue of the test taker over the loss of a family member, who may have died from an illness. Card 9GF tends to bring the test taker back to the "surface" of more everyday reality of two peers, perhaps one jealous of the other, who may be more successful in a love relationship than the other, since it features two women, one watching the other walking along a beach. Card 10 may bring some relief from Card 9GF, since it shows two individuals very close to each other, perhaps in an intimate, love situation.

The closeness of Card 10 is then followed by Card 13MF, which shows a man with his arm against his forehead standing in front of a woman, who is supine with her breast somewhat exposed, as if he is feeling guilty over having slept with her or sad over her death. This last card is similar to the emotionality of the many-colored card 10 on the Rorschach and, as such, it is a fitting finale to the T.A.T.

Therefore, it is clear that Murray's first series that include cards 3BM and 8BM are not exclusively "everyday situations." Moreover, the moving back-and-forth from pictures featuring children, young adults, and older adults on the T.A.T. sequence encourages the test taker to bring out earlier conflicts in one's life, to confront deeper, more primitive types of conflicts, and then to move back up to the surface of more adult current reality. As mentioned earlier, the psychologist may wish to add two or three favorite cards not in this sequence or two or three cards that "pull" for specific conflict areas that appear germane to the main questions of the psychological evaluation or based on clinical impressions of the test taker gained from test behavior or previous tests. This standard T.A.T. sequence provides consistency with the standard sequence for the Bender Gestalt Test, House-Tree-Person Drawing Test, Rorschach, as well as for the Wechsler intelligence and other cognitive and achievement tests in the standard test battery. The standard T.A.T. sequence is also possible to administer, along with time for an inquiry, in about 30 to 45 minutes.

CHAPTER 5

REVIEW OF
SCORING APPROACHES
FOR THE T.A.T.

If one accepts the hypothesis of determinism of psychological behavior, it follows that deductions concerning the personality of an individual can be based on any kind of performance. Similarly, nearly any test can be analyzed for a great many different aspects and, since each dimension is by necessity a function of the test taker's personality, one is bound to have results. The crux of the matter is for tests to combine maximum applicability with maximum validity, reliability, and economy. By the same token, analytical variables or scoring categories that offer the most information with the least effort are needed.

Scoring categories are like fishnets. Large, coarse mesh nets will catch only a few very large fish, losing many medium-sized ones. Exceedingly fine-meshed nets will catch so many tiny organisms as to make it almost impossible to pull in the net and haul in a useful catch. Therefore, one must select the sort of net best adapted to the task at hand and the desired goal. For research purposes, a very finely meshed set of categories may be desirable. Having very few variables, or none at all, may leave one almost empty-handed. The ideal set of variables will be one that obtains enough information for clinical purposes without making the task overwhelming.

Before discussing different methods that have been applied to interpretation of the T.A.T., it is helpful to review the main working assumptions held by psychologists concerning the nature of psychological tests. Interpretations of T.A.T. responses, and the diagnostic inferences based on them, are most useful when the interpreter views such responses in the light of the broader framework provided by the following assumptions:

1. Psychological tests represent a way of securing behavior samples of the individual.
2. The individual's test responses are the end results of thought processes stimulated by test items. These end products are causally linked to the person's typical ego-organizing principles—that is, to the means used in selecting and organizing internal and external stimuli. Test responses should be differentiated from scores. Scores are "designed to facilitate intra- and inter-individual comparisons and, as such, are extremely useful in clinical testing," but "to rea-

son only in terms of the score, or even score patterns, is to do violence to the nature of the raw material" (Schafer, 1948).

3. Interpretation needs to take account of the context in which the test responses are made. For example, the meanings of similar formal test patterns may be different in different contexts.

4. A battery of tests is needed in order to obtain a good picture of the many dimensions of ego functioning. No one test is able to reach all the different levels of psychic functioning.

As we outlined in Chapter 1, Murray's (1943a) scoring system for the T.A.T. was based on the interest within academic psychology of the 1930s and 1940s in Freud's (1900) first theory of psychoanalysis called the *libido theory,* which conceptualizes human motivation as based on the sexual or libidinal drive. Freud (1920) added the aggressive drive in his book, *Beyond the Pleasure Principle,* and other members of the group of early Freudians, such as Alfred Adler, Carl Jung, and Otto Rank, added other drives, such as the power motive (Adler), self-realization (Jung), and the creative drive (Rank). Murray (1938) renamed these drives as *needs* and expanded the small list of needs from the early Freudians into a large group of needs from within the person and a corresponding list of presses acting on the individual from the environment. The group of needs becomes organized into a hierarchy of needs and the relationship of each person's hierarchy of needs and the contrasting presses from the environment are what define the person's behavior. Murray called this the *personology* theory of human personality.

This is applied to the T.A.T. in the following manner: The hero of a story loves a woman, but she hates him: need (for) love met by (press) hate. Every story is analyzed according to all needs and presses, and each need and press receives a weighted score. A rank-order system of the needs and presses is then tabulated. At the same time, the hierarchical relationship of the needs to each other is investigated, with such concepts of Murray's as *need-conflict, need-subsidiation,* and *need-fusion.* Nearly a dozen possible schemes of categories were developed by Murray and Bellak in 1941 at the Harvard Psychological Clinic. A test manual and a guide to the interpretation were designed based on an earlier one by White and Sanford (1941). Aside from a page for the recording of the quantitative need-press data, there is also a page for the recording of more molar qualitative data, not unlike some of the categories described in the recommendations for interpretation that indicated below.

The need-press scheme of interpretation still has many advantages for use in experiments in which detail is most important and time is no object. The method has not become at all popular clinically, however, since it is not easy to master the need concept, and it takes four to five hours to interpret 20 stories with this system. Therefore, a great number of attempts to interpret the T.A.T. have been developed. The majority of scoring systems have been either extensions of Murray's need-press approach, such as McClelland and colleagues' (1953) scoring system for need for achievement and Winter's (1973) scoring system for the power motive or extensions and variations on the scoring system of Bellak (1947 and this text). Some of the more interesting of these scoring systems are presented below.

Rotter (1947) suggests interpretating the T.A.T. in three steps:

1. The first step encompasses autobiographical quality; coherence; predominant mood; handling of sex; endings and their relationships to stories; repetition of themes; unusual wording; attitude toward the world; characteristics of central figure; typical methods of solving problems; and characters that can be identified with mother, father, daughter, son, and so on.
2. In the second step, five principles of interpretation are proposed: frequency of occurrence of an idea; unusualness (regarding plot, language, misrecognition); determination of identification; determination of cliches; and selecting alternate interpretations (decision between two possible interpretations).
3. The third step contains qualitative suggestions for the analysis of personality trends as the final step of interpretation.

In a later paper, Rotter and Jessor (1951) proceed in five steps:

1. The entire protocol is read for suggestive leads (mood, unusual plots, unique verbalizations, methods of solving problems, and frequency of specific themes) and for the formulation of tentative interpretations and questions to be investigated further.
2. Each story is analyzed for basic ideas and structural characteristics and is compared with plot norms.
3. Each story is considered as a unit in order to identify the characters, the conflicts, and the relationship; to decide whether the material is wishful, autobiographical, or superficial; and to select hypotheses on the basis of consistency.
4. All the stories are considered as one organized combined unit.
5. The interpretive hypotheses are integrated into a final summary evaluation, under five categories: familial attitudes; social and sexual attitudes; general (educational, vocational, etc.) attitudes; personality characteristics; and etiological implications.

Rapaport's (1947) interpretation is predicated on an examination of the cliché quality of the responses, and the subject's deviation from clichés serves as a baseline for orientation. In his "points of view" for scoring, Rapaport suggests two major classes:

1. Formal characteristics of story structure, of which there are three aspects:
   a. *Compliance with instruction* (omissions and distortions; misplacing of emphasis; dwelling on picture rather than on situation; introduction of figures and objects not pictured)
   b. *Consistency within the test taker's production* (inter-individual consistency, as shown by deviation in expressive and aggressive qualities, deviation from the usual significance of a particular picture, and deviation concerning language and narrative form; intraindividual consistency)
   c. Characteristics of verbalization
2. Formal characteristics of story content:
   a. *Tone of narrative*
   b. *Figures of story identifications and memory representations*

    c. *Strivings and attitudes*
    d. *Obstacles*

Henry (1947), in one of the most extensive and detailed scheme for analysis next to Murray's, distinguishes (1) *form characteristics* from (2) *content characteristics.*

1. *Form characteristics* are divided into six major categories, each of which has several subclasses:
   a. *Amount and kind of imaginal production* (length of story, amount and kind of introduced content; vividness, originality; rhythm and smoothness; variation in the consistency of all these factors)
   b. *Organizational qualities* (presence or absence of antecedents of story and of outcome; level of organization; coherence and logic; manner of approach to central concept; contribution of elaborations and of details; variation in the consistency of all these)
   c. *Acuity of concepts, observations, and their integration*
   d. *Language structure* (movement, action, qualifying, descriptive words, etc.)
   e. *Intraception-extraception*
   f. *Relation of story told to total thought content* (condensed, suppressed)
2. *Content characteristics:*
   a. *General tone* (positive and negative tone of language; passivity or aggressiveness of language; expressed or implied conflict; expressed or implied interpersonal harmonies or affiliative action and thought)
   b. *Positive content* (characters described in the story; interpersonal relations; action core of story)
   c. *Negative content* (what subject failed to say; what subject might have been expected to say)
   d. *Dynamic structure of content* (symbols, associations)

In the relation of the form and content characteristics, eight areas are considered: mental approach, creativity and imagination, behavioral approach, family dynamics, inner adjustment, emotional reactivity, sexual adjustment, and descriptive and interpretive summary.

Tomkins and Tomkins (1947), in a systematic attempt at a logically consistent analysis of fantasy, distinguished four major categories:

1. Vectors, comprising needs, or the quality of strivings "for," "against," under," "by," "away," from," and "of"
2. Levels, such as those of wishes and daydreams
3. Conditions that may be either external forces (Murray's press) or inner states, such as anxiety or depression (conditions do not refer to the goals of strivings but to given states the individual finds outside or inside himself or herself)
4. Qualities, such as intensity, contingency (certainty), and temporal considerations

The principle underlying this system of analysis is that each class can be related to any other class. One vector can be the object of any other vector (e.g., the wish to act).

The Tomkins method, which is primarily for training and research, comprises both scoring and interpretation. Each story is scored according to the previously mentioned four main categories: 10 vectors, 17 levels, 12 conditions, and 6 qualifiers. The interpretation utilizes three main approaches: canons of inference, such as Mill's methods (of agreement, difference, of concomitant variation, etc.) and additional methods (for the study of cause and effect involving two or more factors); level analysis (degree of variance, relative frequency, cause-effect relationships, and sequence analysis of levels) to study the relationship between overt and covert needs, the degree to which the subject is aware of his own wishes and behavior, and the nature of the conflict between repressed wish and repressing force; and diagnosis of personality, which includes relative importance of the family, love and sex, social relationships, and work.

Korchin's (1951) use of the Tomkins method is a variant of the previously mentioned approach. It is less formalized and therefore better adapted to clinical use. It examines the characteristics of the heroes, the more generalized meanings of the main themes, the outcomes, and the levels. It also analyzes the areas of family, social relationships, work, and so on.

Wyatt (1947) uses 15 variables for the analysis of the T.A.T.: (1) story description, (2) stimulus perception, (3) deviations from typical responses, (4) deviation from self, (5) time trend, (6) level of interpretation, (7) tone of story, (8) quality of telling, (9) focal figure, (10) other figures, (11) personal relationships, (12) striving, avoidances, (13) press, (14) outcome, and (15) thema.

Arnold's (1951) method of interpreting the T.A.T. emphasizes the content of the stories. Situations involving interpersonal relations—such as parent/child, heterosexual, and so on—are examined for the feelings and actions described. Thus, information is obtained about the subject's attitudes, conflicts, and dominant problems. The stories are also subjected to a brief "sequential" analysis in order to see whether there is a consistent development of the central theme. The five steps in this procedure are synopsis, situational analysis, analysis of attitudes (from the situational analysis), sequential analysis, and final integration.

Aron (1951) works on the level of manifest story content, deliberately leaving aside, for the most part, formal aspects of the performance. She uses the Murray-Sanford scheme of variables—need and press—with numerous changes intended to bring the scheme into close harmony with clinical approaches and psychoanalytic theory. Each need or press is recorded together with the characters who are the subject and object of the behavior, so that a given variable can be examined in relation to the context in which it is expressed. Also recorded are surface defenses, such as conflict, denial, rejection of behavior, fantasy, uncertainty, and so on; intensity of variables, which is expressed numerically; and outcomes. The results are analyzed in terms of the main features in variable scoring and in variable sequences.

Eron (1951b) uses a normative, statistical approach. Norms are based on all 20 T.A.T. cards for adult males administered in the original prescribed order. Stories are rated for emotional tone (from very sad to very happy) and for outcome (from complete failure to great success). Themes are noted according to a checklist of more than 100 themes classified as interpersonal, intrapersonal, and impersonal; disequilibrium (tension) and equilibrium. Any deviations from the task of making up a narrative and any distortions of the physical properties of the pictures, as well as certain other formal characteristics, are noted. The ratings are then compared with the norms. The basic data for this system are the frequency and unusualness of specific fantasy content. Interpretation of personality structure and content depends on the theoretical orientation of the interpreter and on the behavioral data from other sources.

Fine's (1951) method stresses primarily feelings and interpersonal relationships. It makes use of a checklist for scoring the presence or absence in each story of feelings (affection, anxiety, pain, etc.): interpersonal relations (moving toward, moving against, etc.) between specific types of persons (mother to child, man to woman, etc.); and the outcomes (favorable, unfavorable, or indeterminate). The interpretation is a sort of qualitative summary of the results.

Hartman (1951) uses a psychometric approach originally designed for research and aims at establishing quantitative norms as a basis for interpretation. It consists of the following steps:

1. Each story is rated on a five-point scale for 65 response categories covering thematic elements, feeling qualities, topics of reference, and formal response characteristics.
2. Numerical ratings on each category are totaled for all stories, and consistency and trend of ratings are noted.
3. From a list of over 40 personality variables, which previous research proved significantly correlated with certain response items, those personality variables are selected which are associated with each response category found important in the protocol.
4. Data thus obtained are integrated with other findings, to obtain a clinically meaningful personality picture.

The method used by Holt (1951) is a clinical approach in which the interpreter reads over the stories, jots down tentative hypotheses as she or he goes along, and integrates these notes into a final personality summary. There is not any formal scoring system, and the method may be described as intuitive. The theoretical bases are those of psychoanalytic theory and Murray's need-press formulations.

The system devised by Joel and Shapiro (1951) deals primarily with the functioning of the ego. First, interpersonal warmth and hostility and flight from such interpersonal feelings are translated into scoring symbols. Then the sequence of these interactions is analyzed, and finally the interpretation provides a picture of the process of coping with the social environment.

In Klebanoff's (1951) method, intended primarily for research, the content of the stories is tallied on a checklist according to overtly stated themes grouped under such categories as loss of life, aggression, internal stress, and positive themes. Profiles of absolute and percentage frequencies for each theme and each category are then analyzed. Interpretation is based on that analysis.

Lasaga (1951) uses a clinical method intended to discover the psychodynamic causes of neurotic and psychotic disturbances and to be an aid in psychotherapy. It focuses attention on the patient's main conflicts and emphasizes the fact that conflicts may be disguised by a process of symbolic substitution. The actual procedure consists of the following: reading the record for general impressions; underlining phrases that express the main idea or important aspects of the main idea; summarizing each story in terms of the main idea; finding clues for discovering the key conflicts; studying anomalies among the ideas or among reaction times; taking into consideration "basic data" about the patient; and knitting all these impressions together into a summary evaluation.

Sargent (1953) has devised two methods. The Sargent Insight Test Scoring Method was originally developed for scoring written responses to the author's Insight Test, but is also applicable to the T.A.T. Affects (A) are scored under 12 categories (pleasure, aggression, etc.) and three expressive modes (action, manifest, and latent feeling expression); defense activities (D) are scored under three categories (evaluations, elaborations, and qualifications). Maladjustment (M) scores, based on the use of the first person pronouns, irrelevant feeling expressions, and "subjectivism," are also obtained. The A/D ratio and the A-D-A/D pattern are evaluated and interpreted in terms of established norms, together with qualitative interpretation of the content.

The Cox-Sargent T.A.T. Normative Scoring Method is designed as a research tool for analyzing the normative aspects of responses to individual T.A.T. pictures. It uses the following main categories: feelings (frustration, anxiety, etc.); heroes (man, girl, etc.); needs (security, conformity, etc.); threats (guilt, death, etc.); actions to meet need or evade threat (negative, evasive, etc.); and outcomes (success, failure, etc.).

Symonds's (1951) method utilizes impressions derived from careful readings of the protocol as a whole, rather than from the separate stories. The data extracted from the stories are classified largely in terms of themes (aggression, love, punishment, anxiety, defenses, moral standards, conflicts, guilt, depression, forms of sublimation, etc.) and relationships (to parents, siblings, teachers, etc.). The final write-up attempts to synthesize the themes of primary importance and to indicate the dynamic relationships among them.

White (1951) devised a "value analysis" method, wherein the manifest content is rewritten in terms of 50 value words that represent motivating forces. In addition, the notations indicate whose point of view is considered, so as to shed light on the storyteller's identification, and also indicate the terms in which the characters are described, in order to get at the storyteller's social perception. The data are treated quantitatively by tallying. A frustration/satisfaction ratio is obtained from the frequencies of the positive and negative values. The overall interpretation "depends on the clinical insight and disciplined imagination of the analyst."

Piotrowski (1950) does not offer any systematized, formal method of approach to the T.A.T., but he lists nine rules of interpretation, as follows:

1. Proceed on the assumption that T.A.T. stories reflect with much greater freedom and with much less distortion the test taker's activities and attitudes than they reflect the actual individuals toward whom the test taker's activities are directed and toward whom the test taker assumes the attitudes are manifested in the T.A.T.

2. When interpreting T.A.T. stories, proceed on the assumption that every figure in the T.A.T. stories expresses some aspect of the test taker's personality.

3. The more acceptable an intended action (drive) is to the consciousness of the test taker, the greater the similarity between the test taker and the T.A.T. figure to whom the drive is attributed.

4. Bear in mind that the degree of generalization of your conclusions affects their validity. The more specific the conclusions, the more difficult it is to confirm and the more easy it is to invalidate them by facts. The more general and more restrained the conclusions, the more likely they are to be valid.

5. Take into consideration the possibility that the stories may not reflect genuine drives but superficial and stereotyped attitudes developed by the test taker in order to hide specific personality traits.

6. Proceed on the assumption that the stories frequently reflect what the test taker thinks and feels about persons represented by the T.A.T. figures (i.e., about the old and the young, the male and the female persons). Of course, the T.A.T. could disclose the test taker's ideas about those old, young, male, and female persons who play important roles in the test taker's life rather than the test taker's ideas about old, young, male, or female persons, as such.

7. The more varied and the more incompatible the drives in a person's stories, the greater the possibility of poor personality integration, of great inner tension, of fear that the unacceptable drives will undermine self-control and will prompt the test taker to act contrary to one's self-interest. The greater the diversity of the T.A.T. drives, the greater the test taker's indecisiveness and anxiety.

8. The chances of a T.A.T. thema being manifested in the test taker's overt behavior are positively correlated with the frequency of the thema's appearance in the T.A.T., with the consistency of the total T.A.T. record (absence of incompatible themas), and with the emotional intensity accompanying the expression of the thema.

9. Employ all formal rules that have been proven valuable in the study of creative associative power. Theses rules are not specific to the T.A.T. and refer to a variety of formal aspects of the T.A.T. performance: uneven pace in the production of the stories, long and variable pauses, marked differences in the number and elaboration of ideas elicited by some pictures as compared with those prompted by other pictures, disregarding of picture details which usually produce comments, farfetched and bizarre notions, sudden or gradual increase or decrease of ideas, and so on.

McClelland (McClelland et al., 1953), addressing himself to *achievement motivation* exclusively, has devised a measure of this motive as it is expressed in imaginative stories, particularly the T.A.T. First, the scorer must determine whether the story contains any reference to an achievement goal that would justify scoring the subcategories as achievement related. Stories are scored for such Achievement Imagery (A.I.) only when at least one of three criteria, all of which deal with manifestation by a story character of "competition with a standard of excellence," is met. The scoring subcategories are:

1. *Stated need for achievement (N).* Someone in the story states the desire to reach an achievement goal.

2. *Instrumental activity.* (I+, I?, I−). Indicates whether the outcome of the instrumental activity is successful, doubtful, or unsuccessful.

3. *Anticipatory goal states (Ga+, Ga−).* Someone in the story anticipates goal attainment or frustration and failure.

4. *Obstacles or blocks.* Stories are scored for obstacles when the progress of goal-directed activity is blocked or hindered by a personal obstacle (Bp) or environmental obstacle (Bw).

5. *Nurturant press (Nup).* Forces in the story, personal in source, that aid the character who is involved in ongoing achievement-related activity, are scored as nurturant press.

6. *Affective states (G+, G−).* Affective states associated with goal attainment, active mastery, or frustration of the achievement-directed activity are scored G.

7. *Achievement thema (Ach Th).* Achievement thema is scored when the achievement imagery is elaborated so that it becomes the central plot of the story.

The *n* achievement score for any individual is computed by combining indexes as follows: Unrelated imagery is scored −1, doubtful achievement imagery is scored 0, and A.I. is scored +1. If a story is scored for A.I., the subcategories are scored. Each subcategory is scored only once per story and given a weight of +1. An achievement score for each story is obtained by summing algebraically the category scores for that story. The *n* achievement score for the subject is the total of scores obtained on all the stories.

Pine (1960) devised a manual for rating *drive content* in T.A.T. stories. Dual significance is posited in the use of drive content in these themes; absence of such content implies a pervasive, rigid, and fragile system of ego defenses, whereas at the other extreme there are two possibilities: (1) a weakening of ego control over impulses, such that results are maladaptive, or (2) drive energies have been neutralized, so that they can be used in productive mental activity. The present manual provides a method for rating libidinal and aggressive drive material in the manifest content of stories, and also describes a procedure for rating the degree to which drive content is integrated into the theme (effectiveness of such integration is considered an index of ego control). Three ratings are obtained for integration of drive content, based on three types of drive content that are distinguished: thematic, incidental, and nonappropriate. Three ratings are also arrived at for three levels of directness of expression of drive content; these levels are direct (unsocialized, direct-socialized) and indirect (disguised or weak).

Shentoub of the Université Reneé Descartes in Paris has developed a very detailed checklist scoring system for the T.A.T., which she has applied in numerous papers on the T.A.T. (Shentoub, 1972–1973, 1973, 1981; Shentoub & Debray, 1969) and two books (Shentoub, 1987; Shentoub et al., 1990). One of her students, Françoise Brelet-Foulard (1986, 1987, 1990), also published a book utilizing Shentoub's scoring approach in a comparison of narcissistic, borderline, and depressed patients. Si Moussi (1990) also utilizes Shentoub's approach in his book on use of the T.A.T. in Algeria. Shentoub's checklist contains over 50 scoring items, such as "presence of unusual details," "precise numbers," "abrupt change of direction of a story," "introduction of figures not in the picture," "fabulation far from the picture," "theatrical quality," "digressions," "hesitation on the sex of different figures," "tendency to refuse cards," "accent on the everyday, factual, actual, or the concrete," "accent on sensual qualities," "motoric agitation," "demanding behavior towards the examiner," "confusion of objects," "disorganization of temporal sequence," "vague, indeterminate discourse," or "short associations." Some of her checklist items are similar to Bellak's Short and Long Form, such as her listing of various defenses of "intellectualization" or "projection." But Shentoub does not appear to organize her checklist along the lines of contemporary psychoanalytic thinking in the manner of the Bellak scoring system.

In her scoring approach, Shentoub and her colleagues move from this checklist inventory of items in the manifest level of the content of a T.A.T. story and compare these items to certain common underlying latent content themes, such as considering the T.A.T. card 2 as the "oedipal triangle." Although this lends a more speculative dimension to her method of analysis, many of her checklist items are useful. Moreover, her scoring manual (Shentoub et al., 1990) and particularly the book of Brelet (1986) are notable for the richness of their clinical examples.

Ronan (Ronan et al., 1993, 1995) developed what he calls the *Personal Problem-Solving Scoring (PPSS)* approach, which appears to be the first application of the approach of cognitive-behavioral therapy to the T.A.T. The T.A.T. cards are conceptualized as presenting the test taker with different social and personal problems. The stories obtained are scored according to four subscales of problem solving:

1. *General orientation of the story.* This includes how challenging the hero views the situation, the level of emotional distress that is conveyed, the level of problem-solving confidence, the degree of personal control, and whether the hero adopts an approach or avoidance style. This dimension is a measure of the test taker's general orientation to the area of personal problem solving.
2. *Design of the story.* This includes the components of story integration, levels of distorted thinking, and formulating a story with a past, present, and future. This dimension is a measure of the process of problem formulation.
3. *Generation of story solutions.* This includes assessing the number of problem-focused responses that reflect instrumental acts, emotion-focused responses that reflect alternatives designed to alter one's thinking about an event, and the number of alternative story solutions. This dimension measures the test taker's flexibility and creativity in being able to consider different possible solutions to a problem, which increase the possibility of finding an optimal solution, and the individual's cognitive capacity for causal means-end thinking.
4. *Story resolution.* This includes the degree to which positive aspects of the story resolution outweigh the negative, the likelihood of maximizing both short- and long-term goals, and the time and energy required to bring about problem resolution. This dimension is a measure of the individual's decision making and the stages of verification in the cognitive-behavioral model of problem solving (Dobson & Block, 1988; D'Zurilla & Goldfried, 1971; D'Zurilla & Nezu, 1990; Heppner, 1988; Nezu & Ronan, 1985, 1988; Spivack, Platt, & Shure, 1976).

Ronan has done studies with the standard Murray (1943a) administration simply to "make up a story" and a modification in which he informs the test taker: "This is a problem-solving task. I have some pictures I am going to show you. For each picture, identify the main character and describe what his or her problem might be. Write a story about the problem. Be sure to note how the problem developed, what is happening now, how the problem will be resolved, and what the outcome might be. Say what the main character and the other people in the story are thinking and feeling. The type of problem situation you develop is up to you." Ronan reports that this alternative instruction make the T.A.T. stories much easier to score according to his problem-solving system.

The three major schools of psychotherapy are psychoanalytic, cognitive-behavioral, and family therapy. The school of psychoanalytic therapy has predominated the field of projective test assessment with the rare exception of Exner's (1994) Rorschach scoring system and a few others. Sobel (1981) points out that the majority of research from the cognitive-behavioral perspective has utilized paper-and-pencil measures. Therefore, this cognitive-behavioral problem-solving T.A.T. system of Ronan is a very valuable contribution to the projective test literature.

Family therapy has contributed a few interesting scoring systems. Most notably, there is the especially useful method for a modified, quantitative content analysis of T.A.T. stories of the entire families of schizophrenics, delinquents, and normals described by Stabenau and colleagues (1965), and a scoring manual developed by Werner, Stabenau, and Pollin (1970). Other schemes for scoring T.A.T.'s of different members of a family are those of Ferreira and Winter (1965), Ferreira, Winter, and Poindexter (1966), Fisher and Fisher (1960), McPherson (1974), Minuchin et al. (1967), Richardson and Partridge (1982), Winget, Gleser, and Clements, (1969), Winter and Ferreira (1969, 1970), and Winter, Ferreira, and Olson (1965, 1966).

A very important T.A.T. scoring approach from the standpoint of family systems therapy is that of *Communication Deviance (CD)* developed by Singer and Wynne (1966) and Jones (1977). This scoring approach derives from the pioneering work of Bateson and colleagues (1956), who suggest that a great deal of the pathological behavior in schizophrenia may be based on the parent transmitting conflicting, illogical, and unclear messages to the child, who then responds with the type of illogic, misperception of reality, peculiar verbalizations, and disruptive behavior typical in schizophrenic disorders. In this view, many of the "thought disorder" difficulties in schizophrenia are considered to be fostered by a child-rearing environment in which the parents do not clearly initiate and maintain a shared focus of clear attention in their communication with the child. This is a *psychogenic* theory of the etiology of schizophrenic behavior, since it hypothesizes that much of the symptoms in the disorder derive from communication problems in the family, rather than being primarily based on biological factors.

It could be argued that miscommunication styles between a parent and a child born with a biologically based schizophrenic disorder may develop miscommunication styles that are significantly influenced by the parent's frustrations in not being able to communicate logically and clearly with the child. This is not unlike the older theories of autism based on the concept that the parents were lacking in the capacity to make eye contact and to verbalize clearly with others. The pain and rejection experienced by parents of an autistic child may gradually engender a tendency to give up trying to get the child to look at them and communicate directly together.

Whether or not one believes that miscommunication styles are the primary cause of schizophrenia, the theory provides a focus of clear attention for assessment and treatment of schizophrenic individuals, particularly from the perspective of family therapy. The family therapy approach is, then, to meet with the family together, help them identify patterns of miscommunication, and help them develop a more direct, less confused method of communicating with each other. Projective tests, such as the Rorschach and T.A.T. are useful in diagnosing characteristic patterns of miscommunication at the beginning phase of treatment. The Communication Deviance scoring system of Singer and Wynne (1966) and Jones (1977) is based on the following four areas:

1. *Closure problems.* Fragments of words or phrases, unintelligible passages in a story, parts of a story are left for the listener to provide the meaning, a story is left hanging, presence of contradictions, lack of integration of picture elements, "I don't know" uncertainty type of endings, and so on.
2. *Disruptive behavior.* Interruptions of the task, peculiar set toward the task, questions about the task instructions after the story is begun, associations about self that are not part of the story, tangential replies to examiner questions.
3. *Peculiar perceptions and verbalizations.* A card is misperceived, idiosyncratic meaning is assigned to details, presence of odd phrasing and word usage, slips of the tongue, peculiar reasoning of any kind, repetition of words or phrases, incorrect abstract word usage.
4. *Additional formal characteristics.* An average is taken of reaction time from presentation of the card to beginning each story and an index is taken of story length.

This scoring system has generated many other interesting research studies on the relationship of communication deviance and schizophrenia (Karon & Widener, 1994), Miklowitz et al., 1986, 1991; Rund, 1989). Doane and associates (1989) conducted a cross-cultural study of communication deviance and schizophrenia in Mexican Americans and Anglo Americans. Longitudinal studies have been done with adolescents (Doane and Mintz, 1987) and in families over a 15-year period (Goldstein, 1985). This scoring system for the T.A.T. has also been employed in the assessment of adoptive parents (Sharav, 1991) and in a study of family problem-solving interaction (Velligan et al., 1990). The future of clinical and research use of the T.A.T. will undoubtedly bring about more integration among these three psychotherapy approaches of psychoanalytic, cognitive-behavioral, and family therapy.

The Bellak approach to T.A.T. interpretation provides for an integration of different therapeutic perspectives, since its categories of analysis include the major dimensions of contemporary personality assessment. Because it includes a category for Murray's needs, the important quantitative refinement of the need for achievement developed by McClelland and associates (1953) and the need for power developed by Winter (1973) may be included within the Bellak system. As we will present in Chapter 11, the valuable scoring schemes for interpersonal object relations developed by McAdams (1980), Thomas and Dudeck (1985), and Westen (1991b) are included in Bellak's category #5 of "Relation to Others" and in the ego function subcategory of "interpersonal object relations" of category #10 of "Integration of the Ego." Similarly, aspects of Ronan's important cognitive-behavioral problem-solving scoring system are addressed in Bellak's scoring categories of "significant conflicts," "main defenses against conflicts and fears," and "integration of the ego manifested in story outcome and solution." Aspects of the Communication Deviance family therapy scoring approach are addressed under Bellak's scoring category "integration of the ego manifested in thought processes revealed in characteristics of the plot and in different subcategories of ego functions of reality-testing, judgment, sense of reality, thought processes, defensive functions, autonomous functions, and synthetic functions."

The Bellak Scoring System, therefore, compares with that of Exner (1994) in providing for a comprehensive assessment of the major dimensions of psychological functioning and in being an approach that includes the other valuable research and clinical approaches of thematic apperception tests, rather than being an exclusive scoring approach that measures only one specific dimension from only one specific theoretical position. While based primarily on the perspective of contemporary psychoanalytic therapy, it is a broad-based, open system of assessment that addresses both the area of cognitive ego functioning and emotional personality functioning.

CHAPTER 6

THE BELLAK SCORING SYSTEM

T.A.T. responses have obviously been studied in many ways. The simplest procedure is the *inspection technique.* It is frequently helpful merely to read through the stories, treating them as meaningful psychological communications, and simply underlining anything that seems significant, specific, or unique. When an experienced examiner rereads the stories a second time, one can, almost without effort, find a repetitive pattern running through them, or one can find facets of different stories falling together into a meaningful whole. This method becomes easier the more experience one has with the T.A.T. and with the process of psychotherapy.

In psychotherapy (see Chapter 8), it may be particularly helpful to have patients hold one carbon copy of the T.A.T. stories, while the psychotherapist has another, and then have the patients free associate generally to the stories and make their own attempts at interpretation. Since the strength of the T.A.T. lies in its ability to elicit the content and dynamics of interpersonal relationships and the psychodynamic patterns, the Bellak Scoring System is primarily concerned with these dimensions and only to a small extent with the formal characteristics.

The main thing to remember in the interpretation of the T.A.T. is the following: *The T.A.T. pictures are best seen psychologically as a series of social situations and interpersonal relations.* Instead of responding to real people in real situations, the test taker is responding to people in the pictures, which the test taker imagines as certain social situations. When under less constraint of conventionality of reality, one's responses are more likely to depict inner feelings. This means it is possible to get at the contemporary patterns of the test taker's social behavior and often infer the genesis of these patterns. Interpretation is the process of finding a common denominator in the contemporary and genetic behavior patterns of a person (Bellak, 1993a).

Among other things, this definition of interpretation implies what cannot be too strongly emphasized, particularly for the beginner: A diagnostic statement should hardly ever be made that is based on data revealed in only one story. Impressions gleaned in one instance should only be considered to be a very tentative inference only, for which one must try to find corroboration in other stories or through some source of information external to the T.A.T. *A repetitive pattern is the best assurance that one does not deal with an artifact.*

Observation-Near and Observation-Distant Diagnosis

Psychoanalytic psychotherapy has, at times, suffered from the fact that one therapist may make one type of interpretation and another may make a divergent one. They may each be correct but be addressing themselves to different aspects of a patient's statement. It is, therefore, necessary to specify the level of abstraction one is addressing. "The patient is angry" would be an observation-near diagnosis. To say that some object representations are in conflict with some self-representations would be an observation-distant inference, involving structural concepts and internalization (e.g., of parental figures whose images interact conflictually with internalized images of oneself), which then produced anger. The chances for error and disagreements are much higher with such observation-distant conclusions.

Similar problems occur in T.A.T. interpretations. It may hold true that the less experienced a clinician, the "wilder" may be the interpretation. A major attempt to avoid wild interpretations is made by way of the *T.A.T. Analysis Blank.* This holds true especially for the breakdown of the theme into *descriptive, interpretive,* and *diagnostic* versions. The descriptive theme is the one nearest to observation, whereas the diagnostic and symbolic levels are quite observation-distant. Keeping these concepts in mind should further help avoid wild interpretations. The following story of a 15-year-old boy may serve as an example:

Story 1

He doesn't obviously want to play the violin. He's a little mad, because his mom [told] him to play the violin, right? But he can't get that note. So he's a little mad and frustrated. So he wants to give up. But I think he's going to stick to it. *What will the outcome be?* He'll stick to it. (Sings "stick to it" to himself).

Descriptive Level.   The boy does not want to play the violin because his mother told him to, but he feels frustrated that he cannot do it. He wants to give up, but also stick to it, and eventually sticks to it.

Interpretive Level.   If one is told to do something by a maternal figure, one gets angry and also frustrated that one cannot perform the task. Eventually, one sticks to it.

Diagnostic Level.   Reacts with anger to maternal figures. There is a conflict between disobeying and wishing to be able to do it, and eventually the boy conforms and succeeds.

This story reveals that the young man telling it has a conflict with maternal figures, but resolves the conflict by succeeding in his effort. The story tells one that this 15-year-old is rebellious against his mother, but that his own need for achievement makes him succeed in his tasks (broadly speaking, his growing up).

Story 2

Three different things to this. Doesn't look too good. Three people probably don't know each other. This girl goes to school, and she's thinking of what she might have left at home. This guy's too busy to know about anything, because he's trying to hit this horse. The lady's off nowhere. She doesn't know that she's doing it, either. She's just looking out yonder. So they all look like they're doing separate things.

Descriptive Level.   This card is usually considered to reflect family relations. The descriptive level is that three people do different things and do not even know each other. The girl might have left something at home. The guy uses business to stay uninvolved. He hits a horse. The female figure is "off" and does not know what she is doing, either.

Interpretive Level.   If a family of three is together, they remain utterly uninvolved with each other, though not without conflict. The girl thinks she might have left something at home. The guy uses overactivity for denial and directs his anger at the horse. The maternal figure is also off nowhere.

Diagnostic Level.   A family without any contact with each other, which the narrator regrets ("She might have left something at home"). The mother figure is described as "off nowhere." Her pregnancy is ignored. This is obviously a 15-year-old who feels a great deal of isolation within the family (which makes him angry) and wishes it were not so. He displaces his anger onto other things, as in hitting a horse.

The example demonstrates the ease with which one may distill considerable information by a careful progression from observation-near data to more abstract observation-distant ones.

Aside from this descriptive diagnosis, it is important to see that these two stories alone—and the rest of the stories not reported here and further insight—are a valuable guide to planning psychotherapy. The first picture of rebelliousness and poor performance in school becomes more hopeful therapeutically, as one sees the patient is frustrated and wants to do better and expresses perseverance. The second picture makes quite clear for anyone that he feels a lack of relationship in the family and that one will have to deal with the lack of warmth and relationship in the family, possibly with family therapy supplementing individual therapy.

These simple stories demonstrate again that even a superficial study of the stories—the observation-near data—can be extremely useful for the therapist. This young man was seen in consultation because of learning difficulties. He is so restless that he has been dismissed from several schools and has been arrested several times for minor misdemeanors. He lives with his mother and her boyfriend in comfort but in emotional isolation. At the same time, he appears manifestly outgoing, friendly, and dynamic. He denies any anger, but is very difficult to live with. Subsequent responses to the T.A.T. and neuropsychological testing led to the diagnosis of attention-deficit disorder.

The Bellak T.A.T. Analysis Blank

Chapter 1 outlines how the history of the Bellak Scoring System began as a collaboration between Bellak and his professor, Murray, in 1941. Bellak added to Murray's category of "needs of the hero" and "environmental presses" several scoring categories from Freud's (1923) later theory of ego psychology, such as analyzing defense mechanisms, anxieties, conflicts, and superego functioning. Bellak's (1947) scoring system and his analysis blanks were published by Psychological Corporation, as the *Bellak T.A.T. Blank and Analysis Sheet* (Figure 6–1).[1] The system is simple enough to be most easily mastered, to serve as a guide and frame of reference, and to make it possible to glean the most important data of a complete 10-story T.A.T. in about half an hour.

How to Use the T.A.T. Analysis Blank[2]

The Bellak T.A.T. Blank consists of a six-page folder plus separate recording and analysis sheets, of which one page from the folder is duplicated. On the cover of the folder, one records the personal data of the client and, when the analysis is complete, one writes a Final Report.

Assume that the examiner wishes to secure 10 stories from a client and that the examiner is going to write down these stories as the client tells them. The first story will be written on page 2 of the T.A.T. Blank; the second story will be written on the back of an analysis sheet. Story 3 is recorded on the back of another analysis sheet, and so on, until the 10 stories have been recorded. The examiner now has the 10 stories recorded, one on the inside cover of the blank and nine on the back of separate analysis sheets. If these are placed in order, printed side up, and laid on top of page 3 in the T.A.T. Blank, the examiner will note that when each sheet is turned over, there is an Analysis Sheet opposite the corresponding story. The Analysis Sheet for story 1 is on the front side of the paper on which story 2 is written, the Analysis Sheet for story 2 is on the front side of the sheet on which story 3 is written, and so forth. The analysis of story 10 (or the last story, if more or fewer stories are used) will be made on the Analysis Sheet that is printed as page 3 of the six-page Blank.

After the stories have been analyzed in this fashion, the examiner can write a summary of each of the stories in the space provided on page 4. (If more than 10 stories are used, more summaries can be written on the back of page 4.) It is best to write these summaries after all the stories have been analyzed, because the summary is one of the stages of formally integrating the content of the analysis of each separate story. When the summary sheet has been completed on page 4, one is pre-

---

[1] We are indebted to the Psychological Corporation of New York City for permitting the production here of material that they originally published as the Bellak T.A.T. Blank, Analysis Sheets, and Guide to the interpretation of the T.A.T.

[2] Revised, 1973, and published by The Psychological Corporation, 55 Academic Court, San Antonio, Texas 78204.

Name _____ Story No. _____ (TAT Picture No. _____

1. **Main theme (descriptive, interpretive, diagnostic):**

2. **Main hero:** age _____ sex _____ vocation _____
   interests _____ traits _____ abilities _____
   adequacy ($\checkmark$, $\checkmark\checkmark$, $\checkmark\checkmark\checkmark$) _____ body image and/or self-image _____

3. **Main needs and drives of hero:**
   a) behavioral needs of hero (as in story): _____
   _____

   dynamic inference: _____
   b) figures, objects, or circumstances *introduced:* _____
   _____

   implying need for or to: _____
   _____

   c) figures, objects, or circumstances *omitted:* _____
   _____

   implying need for or to: _____
   _____

4. **Conception of environment (world) as:** _____

5. **Parental figures**   (m ____ , f ____) are seen as _____ and subject's reaction is _____
   Contemp. figures (m ____ , f ____) are seen as _____ and subject's reaction is _____
   Junior figures   (m ____ , f ____) are seen as _____ and subject's reaction is _____

6. **Significant conflicts:** _____
   _____

7. **Nature of anxieties:** ($\checkmark$)
   of physical harm and/or punishment _____ of illness or injury _____
   of disapproval _____ of deprivation _____
   of lack or loss of love _____ of being devoured _____
   of being deserted _____ of being overpowered and helpless _____
   other _____

8. **Main defenses against conflicts and fears:** ($\checkmark$)
   repression _____ reaction-formation _____ rationalization _____ isolation _____
   regression _____ introjection _____ denial _____ undoing _____ splitting _____
   projective identification _____ other _____

9. **Adequacy of superego as manifested by "punishment" for "crime" being:** ($\checkmark$, $\checkmark\checkmark$, $\checkmark\checkmark\checkmark$)
   appropriate _____ inappropriate _____
   too severe (also indicated by immediacy of punishment) _____
   inconsistent _____ too lenient _____
   also: _____
   delayed initial response or pauses _____
   stammer _____ other manifestations of superego interference _____

10. **Integration of the ego, manifesting itself in:** ($\checkmark$, $\checkmark\checkmark$, $\checkmark\checkmark\checkmark$) (see also ego function rating scale on page 6 of Blank)
    adequacy of hero _____ outcome: happy _____ unhappy _____
                                                realistic _____ unrealistic _____
                                    solution: adequate _____ inadequate _____
    thought processes as revealed by plot being: ($\checkmark$, $\checkmark\checkmark$, $\checkmark\checkmark\checkmark$)
    structured _____ unstructured _____ stereotyped _____ original _____ appropriate _____
    rational _____ bizarre _____ complete _____ incomplete _____ inappropriate _____

Intelligence: ($\checkmark$) superior _____ above average _____ average _____ below average _____ defective _____

Analysis Sheet for Use with the Bellak TAT Blank (Revised)

Figure 6–1   Analysis Sheet for Use with the Bellak T.A.T. Blank

pared to write the Final Report. It will be noted that by folding the Blank, the space for the final report and the summary page may be exposed side by side.

When the task is done, the loose sheets may be stapled in the folder for safe-keeping, and the final report appears on the cover for convenient reference.

As noted earlier, some psychologists prefer to have individuals write the stories themselves. Since individuals should not have access to the outline on the analysis sheet, they should write their stories on plain 8½ by 11 paper. If the stories are so short that there are several on a sheet, they can be cut up and either pasted or clipped to the back of the separate analysis sheets so that the final arrangement will be the same as if the examiner had written on the back of the analysis sheets.

For some items on the analysis sheet, appropriate information from the story must be written in, using whatever short phrase or key word will most facilitate the analytic process. For others, indicated on the Blank by ($\sqrt{}$), a system of checks is suggested. A single check ($\sqrt{}$) may be used to indicate the mere presence of a given attitude, conflict, or the like. A double check ($\sqrt{}\sqrt{}$) or triple check ($\sqrt{}\sqrt{}\sqrt{}$) may be used to indicate increasing levels of importance to be assigned to the given item in summarizing the story. It is hoped that this approach to quantification will further research studies of inter-examiner reliability of interpretation in addition to increasing the flexibility of the analysis form. Blank spaces are provided for adding categories or ideas not given in the outline. Despite the increasing use of the more popular Short Form of the Blank, the Long Form is still highly useful, especially for training and research.

Scoring Categories (10 Variables)

The following suggestions for the use and interpretation of the individual scoring categories of the T.A.T. Blank may be helpful.

1. The Main Theme

The main theme is best understood as an attempt to restate the gist of the story. (It must be remembered that one T.A.T. story may actually have more than one basic theme.) Since beginners in the use of the test tend to go off on a tangent most often in an interpretation of the main theme, a breakdown of the main theme into five levels is recommended.[3] This breakdown of the main theme is an important teaching device. In essence, the student is guided to make *sound inferences in the*

---

[3] For the beginner, it is most helpful to force oneself to go through all five levels. However, it may not be necessary to put them all down in writing. The descriptive level, in particular, is a crutch; it may suffice just to state the theme at this level in one's mind. The interpretive level might be recorded on each analysis sheet, and the diagnostic, or higher, level may be the basis for the summary statement. These levels are primarily a learning device. Once one is experienced, the interpretive and diagnostic levels should be enough, just using the blanks for summaries.

transition from primary data to diagnostic formulation. In that process, one automatically proceeds from observation-near inferences to the more ambitious, but also more risky, observation-distant conclusions. This procedure should protect one against wild interpretations. The five levels are:

1. The *descriptive* level: On this level the theme should be a plain restatement of the summarized meaning of the story, a finding of the common trend restated in an abbreviated form and simple words.
2. The *interpretive* level: State the general meaning of the story.
3. The *diagnostic* level: State possibly expressed psychological problems.
4. The *symbolic* level: State possible symbols with psychological meanings.
5. The *elaborative* level: State any free associations to story elements.

The example of the following story may help (6BM):

This is a young successful engineer. He is the only son in his family; his father is dead, and his mother is very close to him. He is in the oil business and he has been offered a contract to go overseas to the East Indies. He has signed the contract and is about to leave. He obtains her farewell and they part heartbroken. After a while she feels very lonesome and decides to follow her son to the East Indies. It is wartime and somehow she obtains passage on a ship to the island on which her son is. An enemy submarine sinks her ship and she perishes. Her son had not heard about her intentions but had independently planned to visit her as a surprise. He decides to return home for a surprise. The ship on which he had obtained passage is taking the same route his mother had taken. At the exact spot where his mother perishes, another enemy submarine attacks and he perishes also.

The theme on a *descriptive* level could be briefly restated as: A son lives alone with his beloved mother and leaves her—when they both try to rejoin each other, they die on the same spot. On an *interpretive* level, one may go a step further and put the meaning in a generalized form, assuming a meaning beyond the story.

The patient believes that if one[4] permits oneself (incestual) fantasies, such as living with the mother, then both parties die. On a *diagnostic* level, one transforms these impressions into a definitive statements: This man has incestuous problems and oedipal conflicts that cause him severe guilt feelings. On a *symbolic* level, one may choose to interpret symbols according to psychoanalytic hypotheses; extreme parsimony and caution must be strongly recommended since this level takes one relatively farthest away from hard facts. In our example one might, for instance, possibly want to interpret the torpedoes as paternal phallic symbols that endanger and destroy both mother and son for their illicit attempted get-together. On an *elaborative* level, the psychologist provides elaborations and free associations to such specific data as: "East Indies," "engineer," to any proper names or dates, and any other associations he or she can give.

---

[4] The interpretive level can nearly always be stated as a generalized conditional clause introduced by "If one . . . ."

2. The Main Hero[5]

The main hero of the story is the one who is most spoken of, whose feelings and subjective notions are most discussed, and, in general, the figure with whom the narrator seems to identify himself or herself. In case of doubt, the figure resembling the patient most closely in age, sex, and other characteristics should be considered the main hero. At times, a man may identify himself with a female "main hero"; if this occurs repeatedly, it *might* be considered a sign of latent homosexuality (depending on the total picture). While practically all young men identify in picture 2 with the young girl in the foreground, only some (there is disagreement regarding the percentage) consider the figure in picture 3BM a female. Vocation, interest, traits, abilities, and adequacy as well as body image of the main hero frequently depict qualities or desired qualities of the patient.

By *adequacy* of the hero, we mean his ability to carry through tasks under external and internal difficulties in a socially, morally, intellectually, and emotionally acceptable manner. The adequacy of the hero frequently conforms to a pattern throughout the stories and is often in a direct relationship to the ego strength of the patient.

It should also be mentioned here that, at times, there may be more than one hero in a story. The patient may use a second figure with whom to identify herself or himself, aside from the clearly recognizable hero. This happens rather rarely; usually it involves a figure introduced but not present in the picture itself, and concerns drives and sentiments that are even more objectionable to the person than the ones pertaining to the main hero. (Other devices for emphatically trying to dissociate oneself from a story are to place it far away geographically and/or temporally (e.g., placing a story in Russia in the Middle Ages.)

The *body image* concept was originally created by Schilder (1925), who stated: "The image of the human body means the picture of our own body which we form in our mind . . . the way in which the body appears to ourselves." This concept reveals itself particularly clearly in the violin picture (picture 1), but also in 3BM and in the rope picture (17BM). In picture 1, one may learn about the subject's conception of his or her own body either in the discussion of the boy or often in the treatment of the violin. This instrument seems to become identified with the hero, and may be described as broken or empty, and dead and falling apart. Particularly in this latter case, the reference transcends the body image and really becomes a matter of self-image—including the emotional tone and the subject's conception of his role in the world. (Sometimes the violin is identified with the female body, the bow constituting the male.) Similarly, 3BM and 17BM lend themselves to the characterization of the conception of body and self and the social role.

---

[5] Some of the following variables were used by Bellak in an earlier mimeographed scoring blank Bellak designed while at the Harvard Psychological Clinic in 1940–42. Thus, a great and not easily specified extent of information and stimulation concerning these variables was received from Dr. H. A. Murray, Dr. R. W. White, and indirectly from Dr. R. N. Sanford who, with Dr. White, had written a mimeographed guide to the T.A.T. which served as the major stimulus for systematic attempts of interpretation. We wish to express our gratitude to these and other members of the staff of the Harvard Psychological Clinic.

3. Main Needs and Drives of the Hero

Experience in teaching the T.A.T. has shown that the inquiry concerning the hero's needs produces three types of data that are frequently confused to the detriment of the accuracy of the observations.

Behavioral Needs.   The behavioral needs of the hero constitute the rock-bottom data: If the hero is extremely aggressive in the story, attacking and hurting a number of people as the theme unfolds, it is worth recording. It is, of course, useful to remember that the behavioral needs of the hero *may* be the behavioral needs of the person, but prima facie they are only the fantasy needs of the person.

The problem of the relationship of *latent needs* in the T.A.T. to overt behavior is an important one. The interpreter of T.A.T. stories often must decide whether a need expressed pertains strictly to the fantasy level or reality; for example, the need for aggression or for achievement. The psychologist should have available a maximum of clinical and biographical data about the patient. The clinical situation is not one concerned with testing the validity of the instrument. Problems of the validity of the T.A.T. are dealt with in experiments and must be decided there. If one has sufficient information about the patient, then the T.A.T. stories must be seen as complementary to the behavioral data obtained. For instance, if the subject is shy and retiring and the stories are full of aggression and guilt feelings about the figures, the implications are obvious. On the other hand, there are certain indications from intratest situations that permit one to make assumptions about the manifest or latent needs expressed in the T.A.T. For example, in stories of achievement, it is extremely important to notice whether they follow the *deus ex machina* mechanism (simple wish fulfillment) or are actually accomplished piece by piece and suggest much more that they correspond to a behavioral need for achievement.

It was R. N. Sanford (1943) who pointed out some important rules concerning the relationship between fantasy needs and behavioral needs. He suggested that there are certain needs that are usually high in fantasy and low in behavior—namely, those needs that are usually prohibited and inhibited by cultural pressure from overt manifestation. These are mainly the needs for acquisition, aggression, autonomy, and sexual activity, the wish to be taken care of, and the need for harm avoidance. However, some needs may find little manifest expression in fantasy but may find much expression in manifest behavior because of reality demands—for example, the needs for order, for avoiding social blame, for learning. Again, there is a class of needs that may be high both in fantasy and in behavior, indicating that, while these needs are permitted and encouraged socially, they may yet be sufficiently frustrated to require particular gratification on the fantasy level (especially needs for achievement, friendship, and dominance).

Dynamic Inference.   If a person (hero) is frequently very nurturant and supportive to a number of other figures, one may have reason to suspect that these figures are secondary or tertiary identification figures for the person, and that the nurturance shown is indicative of a profoundly succorant, demanding attitude on the part of the hero, an attitude that he or she wards off in this way. Or one may have indications that the person who avoids all reference to aggression does so because of a great deal of aggression, which he or she has to keep under control by denying all of it (an inference permitted only if there is supportive evidence).

Figures, Objects, or Circumstances Introduced.   A person who introduces weapons of one sort or another in a number of stories (even without using them in the context) or who has food as an integral part (even without eating it) may be tentatively judged on such evidence as having a need for aggression or oral gratification, respectively. Similarly, the introduction of such figures as punisher, pursuer, benefactor, and the like, or such circumstances as injustice, deprivation, and so on, may be interpreted with due regard to the rest of the record.

Figures, Objects, or Circumstances Omitted.   If a subject omits reference to the gun in 3BM and to the rifle in 8BM, or does not see the one woman in 18GF choking the other, one may infer a need to repress aggression—or a need to repress sexual stimuli if the semi-nude in the background of picture 4 is ignored, or if 13MF is seen as entirely devoid of sexual references. The inference can only be tentative until we have a large enough sample to achieve a statistical basis for what the expectations are when a certain object is introduced or omitted, so as to be reasonably accurate in judging when a person deviates from the norm.

4. The Conception of the Environment (World)

This concept is a complex mixture of unconscious self-perception and apperceptive distortion of stimuli by memory images of the past. The more consistent a picture of the environment appears in the T.A.T. stories, the more reason we have to consider it an important constituent of the person's personality and a useful clue to his or her reactions in everyday life. Usually, descriptive terms will suffice, such as *succorant, hostile, exploiting, friendly, dangerous,* and so forth.

5. Figures Seen as . . .

The T.A.T. is primarily an instrument that permits a study of the apperceptive distortions of the social relationships and the dynamic factors basic to them. Therefore, an exhaustive study of the hero's attitudes to parental, contemporary, and younger or inferior persons is an integral part of our scheme. This method permits recording these apperceptions and the person's reactions to his or her perception—that is, each picture allows the person to create a situation that can best be understood as a problem ("Tell me what is going on") which he or she then has to proceed to solve ("And tell me what the outcome will be"), thus baring his or her ability to come to compromise formations with personal needs; in other words, to show one's defenses. For instance, if a person chooses to perceive female figures in the T.A.T. as aggressive, then it is worthwhile for us to determine how he or she proceeds to react to these creatures of one's fancy, whether with withdrawal, counteraggression, intellectualization, or other forms of behavior.

6. Significant Conflicts

When we study the significant conflicts of an individual, we not only want to know the nature of the conflict but also the defenses which the person uses against it. It is important, in designating which drive or force is in conflict with the superego, to specify in a word or two the resultant behavior: e.g., if the conflict is between superego and aggression, it may be that the person reacts with *shyness*. Here, one has an excellent opportunity for a study of the character structure and the prognosis of the person. Sometimes, the conflict may not be between the superego and such drives as aggression, acquisition, or sexual desires, but between two drives such as achievement and pleasure or autonomy and compliance.

7. Nature of Anxieties

The importance of determining the main anxieties hardly needs emphasizing. Again, it will be valuable to note the defenses in this context, whether they take the form of passivity, flight, aggression, orality, or those mentioned next.

8. Main Defenses against Conflicts and Fears

The T.A.T. should not be studied exclusively for need content, but should, in addition, be examined for the defenses against these needs. Such a study of defenses will often offer more information in that the needs may appear less clearly than the defenses against them; on the other hand, the defensive structure may be more closely related to manifest behavior. By studying drives and defenses, the T.A.T. often permits a clear-cut appraisal of the character structure of the person. It is also valuable to study the molar aspects of the stories. For instance, some people choose obsessive defenses against a disturbing picture content; they may produce four or five themes, each very short and descriptive, manifestly different but dynamically identical. Sometimes a succession of themes to one and the same picture shows the person's attempts to deal with a disturbing conflict; successive stories may become more and more innocuous, showing an increase in the defenses. On the other hand, each successive theme may permit more expression of the forbidden desire or need.

9. Adequacy of Superego as Manifested by "Punishment" for "Crime"

The relationship of the nature of the punishment to the severity of the offense gives one an excellent insight into the severity of the superego; a psychopath's hero may consistently receive no punishment in stories of murder, with no more than a slight suggestion that he may have learned a lesson for later life; whereas a neurotic may have stories in which the hero is accidentally or intentionally killed or mangled or dies of illness following the slightest infraction or expression of aggression. On the other hand, a nonintegrated superego, sometimes too severe and sometimes too lenient, is also frequently met in neurotics.

10. Integration of the Ego

This is, of course, an important variable to learn about; it reveals how well a person is to function. It tells to what extent he or she is able to compromise between needs and the demands of reality on the one hand, and the commands of superego on the other. The adequacy of the hero in dealing with the problems he or she is confronted with in the pictures, and his or her own apperception of it, reveals what the therapist wants to know in this respect.

Here, one is interested in some formal charcteristics: Is the person able to tell appropriate stories that constitute a certain amount of cognizance of the adaptive aspects of the stimulus, or does he or she leave the stimulus completely and tell a story with no manifest relation to the picture because he or she is not well enough to perceive reality or too preoccupied with personal problems to keep them out, whether pertinent or not? Does she or he find rescue and salvation from the anxiety pertaining to the test by giving very stereotyped responses, or is the individual well enough and intelligent enough to be creative and give more or less original stories? Having produced a plot, can the person attain a solution of the conflicts in the story and within himself or herself which is adequate, complete and realistic, or do his or her thought processes become unstructured or even bizarre under the impact of the problem?

These observations permit an appraisal of what really constitutes ego strength, often contributing a great deal to facilitating possible classification of the patient in one of the nosological categories, in addition to the dynamic diagnosis which the content variables supply as the main contribution of the T.A.T.

Here, too, belong such considerations *as the distance of the subject from his or her story;* for instance, if the setting of the story is far away or long ago, or if the hero is merely an onlooker, or if it is reported as a scene from a movie, or if emotional situations are told in a sarcastic tone and embellished with *sotto voce* remarks, all these factors usually imply an attempt to isolate oneself from the emotional content of the story as a defense mechanism. On the other hand, if a person immediately involves himself or herself personally in the story and says, "That is just what happened to me . . . ," it may mean a loss of distance and implies a very narcissistic preoccupation with the self.

From a formal standpoint, it is useful to consider that telling stories about the pictures is a task which the person must perform. We may judge the person's adequacy, ego strength, and other variables from the standpoint of his or her ability and way of meeting the task.

Clinical interest in *ego functions* has steadily increased. Therefore, a specific ego function assessment scale is provided on page 6 of the T.A.T. Blank. This scale is predicated on detailed definitions and extensive research reported elsewhere (Bellak, 1993a). When ego functions were studied by interview, psychological tests, and laboratory methods, it turned out somewhat surprisingly that ratings derived from the T.A.T. by several raters correlated more highly than those for the

Rorschach, WAIS, Figure Drawings, and the Bender-Gestalt Test (Arnold, 1951, p. 331). Ego functions may be assessed from the T.A.T. stories themselves and entered on the rating scale. If desired, highest may be drawn to connect the ratings (see the figure below). One may also wish to assess ego functions from the test behavior. It is suggested that this be recorded and reported separately in the space beneath the scale on page 6.

The 12 ego functions may be briefly defined as follows:

I. Reality Testing

The ability to differentiate between inner and outer stimuli involves continuous selective scanning and matching contemporary percepts against past percepts and ideas. Social contexts and norms will always be relevant in assessing reality testing.

Inner-reality testing is included in this scale. It is reflected here in the degree to which the person is in touch with the inner self. Stated another way, this implies psychological-mindedness" or "reflective awareness" (e.g., of the implications of the T.A.T. stories).

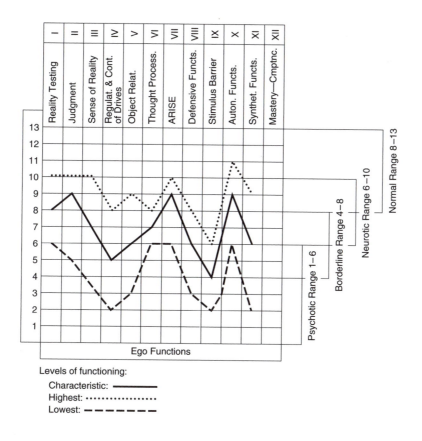

II. Judgment

Ratings for judgment are based on data indicating comprehension and appraisais of hypothetical and real situations, and the person's evaluations of the consequences of action or other behavior related to these situations, as the person creates them here.

III. Sense of Reality of the World and of the Self

This scale assesses disturbances in the sense of one's self, as it relates to the outside world. It also assays the sense of reality or unreality of the world. For instance, some T.A.T. stories include talk about ghostly creatures and unreal half-worlds!

IV. Regulation and Control of Drives, Affects, and Impulses

This function refers to the extent to which delaying and controlling mechanisms allow drive derivatives to be expressed in a modulated and adaptive way, characterized, optimally, by neither under- nor overcontrol.

V. Object Relations

Optimal relationships are relatively free of maladaptive elements suggesting patterns of interaction that were more appropriate to childhood situations than to the present ones. The most pathological extreme would be essentially an absence of relationships with any people; next would be present relations based on early fixations, unresolved conflicts, and very hostile sadomasochistic relationships. Optimal relations would be the most mature, relatively free of distortions, and gratifying to adult libidinai, aggressive, and ego needs. For picture 1 of the T.A.T., a story in which a violinist plays with pleasure before an empty Carnegie Hall, suggests a great deal of narcissism.

VI. Thought Processes

Disturbances in formal characteristics of logical thinking, as well as the interference of primary process material need to be rated.

VII. ARISE

Adaptive regression in the service of the ego (ARISE) refers to the ability of the ego to initiate a partial, temporary, and controlled lowering of its own functions (keep in mind here the component factors of the eleven ego functions) in the furtherance of its interests (i.e., promoting adaptation). Such regressions result in a relatively free, but controlled, play of the primary process. This ego function can be particularly well observed from the way in which the person is able to deal with the T.A.T. as a creative task.

VIII. Defensive Functioning

Defenses protect preconscious and conscious organizations from the intrusions of id derivatives, unconscious ego, and superego tendencies. They aid adaptation by controlling the emergence of anxiety-arousing, or other dysphoric psychic content, such as ego-alien instinctual wishes and affects (including depression), which conflict with reality demands. Excessive defensiveness is of course also mal-adaptive. A notation—whether excessive or defective—is useful.

IX. Stimulus Barrier

Both thresholds and responses to stimuli contribute to adaptation by the organism's potential for responding to high, average, or low sensory input, so that optimal homeostasis (as well as adaptation) is maintained. Stimulus barrier determines, in part, how resilient a person is or how he or she readapts after the stress and impingements are no longer present. A story of a mother who can't stand the yelling of her child and how it affects her would be very informative here.

X. Autonomous Functioning

Intrusion of conflict, ideation, affect, and/or impulse upon functioning is a major criterion for determining impairment of either the primary or the secondary autonomy.

The basic apparatuses and functiuons of primary autonomy are:

perception	memory	language
intentionality	hearing	productivity
concentration	vision	motor development
attention	speech	and expression

XI. Synthetic-Integrative Functioning

This ego function fulfills one of the major tasks of the ego as defined by Freud, in terms of reconciling the often conflicting demands of the id, superego, and outside world, as well as the incongruities within the ego. We focus on the reconciling of areas that are in conflict and also on the extent of relating together areas that are not in conflict.

XII. Mastery-Competence

Raters must score competence and sense of competence separately, since a number of different relationships between the two are possible: (1) they may be congruent, (2) actual performance may exceed the sense of competence, and (3) sense of competence may exceed mastery-competence.

The Summary and Final Report

After all the stories have been analyzed, the main data obtained from each should be noted down in the appropriate space on page 4. When the summary page is studied after the analysis of all the stories has been completed, a repetitive pattern in the person's responses ordinarily becomes quite clear.[6]

---

[6] Experienced T.A.T. workers, having become familiar with our method, may wish to use only the T.A.T. Blank, using the middle page for a guide to record relevant data on the summary sheet rather than actually filling in the details on 10 analysis sheets.

The final report can be written in full view of the summary page. It is suggested that the form of the final report follow the sequence of the 10 categories on the analysis sheet. The main themes, the second and third variables, permit a description of the *unconscious structure and needs* of the person, while the fourth and fifth variables show us his or her *conception of the world and of significant figures* around him or her. Categories six, seven, eight, nine, and ten may actually be used as headings for statements concerning the respective dimensions of personality.

The form of the final report will depend, of course, to a great extent on the person for whom it is intended. It is, however, strongly advised that empty phrases and erroneous inferences be avoided by the following procedure: The first half of the report may consist of general abstract statements concerning the person, following the outline above; a second part of the report should then consist of specific, concrete documentation by excerpts from stories or by specific references to stories from which the main abstract statements have been derived.

This arrangement is particularly useful in instances in which the psychologist reports as part of a team to psychiatrists and to social workers who may not have the time or the experience to read the stories themselves, and for whom a purely abstract statement will not be sufficiently meaningful.[7]

If a diagnosis must be offered, or if one wishes to state one, we suggest that the following formula be used: "The data represented in the T.A.T. are consistent with the diagnosis of . . . ." This expresses our belief that the T.A.T. is not primarily a diagnostic test (diagnostic in the sense of labeling nosologically—of course it is diagnostic of dynamic and structural variables) and also that, preferably, no diagnosis should ever be made on the basis of a single test, or better, never on test evidence alone without additional information provided by a clinical interview.

The Short Form of the Bellak T.A.T. and C.A.T. Blank[8]

The short form of the original Blank has been published mainly for clinical convenience. While it uses practially the same variables as the earlier Blank, it consists only of a three-page form that folds into a single 8 ½ by 11 sheet, with the summarized facts on the front. When the Blank is unfolded, each of the variables can be recorded in the appropriate boxes for all 10 stories and summarized consecutively under the same headings at the extreme right. The writing of the final report can be simplified by having the summary sheet opened out in full view. It should be noted that the 10 major variables or categories are used primarily as a frame of reference; not all aspects will be relevant to every story and, occasionally, details not included in the Blank will occur and have to be recorded.

The principal function of the Blank is to further facilitate the transition from concrete primary data to the inferential summary and final diagnosis by having all three pages unfolded in front of one. Also the Short Form is easier to handle. In its

---

[7] We are indebted to S. Sorel Bellak for suggestions and constructive criticism of the revision of this T.A.T. Blank and Manual.

[8] Published by C.P.S. Inc., P. O. Box 83, Larchmont, New York. For examples of the use of the Short Form, see Case 3, the analysis of Somerset Maugham's short stories (Chapter 10), and Chapter 16.

new revised version, it shows a shift to more interest in ego psychology in that the revised form lists 12 ego functions. These are to be gauged—as many of them and as well as possible—as a further indication of adaptive capacity. A detailed account of these ego functions can be found in Bellak and Loeb's *The Schizophrenic Syndrome* (1969), in *Ego Functions in Schizophrenics, Neurotics, and Normals,* and in a paper called "A Systematic Study of Ego Functions" (Bellak, Hurvich, & Gediman, 1973).

Briefly, they can be described as follows:[9]

Reatity Testing.   The major factors are (a) the distinction between inner and outer stimuli; (b) accuracy of perception (includes orientation to time and place and interpretation of external events); (c) accuracy of inner reality testing (psychological mindedness and awareness of inner states).

Judgment.   (a) Awareness of likely consequences of intended behavior (anticipating probable dangers, legal culpabilities, social censure, disapproval, or inappropriateness); (b) extent to which manifest behavior reflects the awareness of these likely consequences.

Sense of Reality of the World and of the Self.   The component factors are (a) the extent to which external events are experienced as real and as being embedded in a familiar context (degree of derealization, déjà vu, trance-like states); (b) the extent to which the body (or parts of it) and its functioning and one's behavior are experienced as familiar, unobtrusive, and as belonging to (or emanating from) the individual; (c) the degree to which the person has developed individuality, uniqueness, and a sense of self and self-esteem; (d) the degree to which the person's self-representations are separated from his or her object representations.

Regulation and Control of Drives, Affects, and Impulses.   (a) The directness of impulse expression (ranging from primitive acting out through neurotic acting out to relatively indirect forms of behavioral expression); (b) the effectiveness of delay and control, the degree of frustration tolerance, and the extent to which drive derivatives are channeled through ideation, affective expression, and manifest behavior.

Object (or Interpersonal) Relations.   The components are (a) the degree and kind of relatedness to others and investment in them (taking account of withdrawal trends, narcissistic self-concern, narcissistic object choice or mutuality); (b) the extent to which present relationships are adaptively or maladaptively influenced by or patterned on older ones and serve present, mature aims rather than past immature aims; (c) the degree to which the person perceives others as separate entities rather than as extensions of himself or herself; (d) the extent to which he or she can maintain object constancy (i.e., sustain relationships over long periods of time and tolerate both the physical absence of the object and frustration, anxiety, and hostility related to the object).

---

[9] The material from here to Section G is reprinted from Bellak, Hurvich, and Gediman (1973) by permission.

Thought Processes. The components are (a) the adequacy of processes that adaptively guide and sustain thought (attention, concentration, anticipation, concept formation, memory, language); (b) the relative primary-secondary process influences on thought (extent to which thinking is unrealistic, illogical, and/or loose).

Adaptive Regression in the Service of the Ego. (a) First phase of an oscillating process: relaxation of perceptual and conceptual acuity (and other ego controls) with a concomitant increase in awareness of previously preconscious and unconscious contents; (b) second phase of the oscillating process: the induction of new configurations which increase adaptive potentials as a result of creative integrations.

Defensive Functioning. (a) Degree to which defensive components adaptively or maladaptively affect ideation and behavior; (b) extent to which these defenses have succeeded or failed (degree of emergence of anxiety, depression, and/or other dysphoric affects, indicating weakness of defensive operations).

Stimulus Barrier. The component factors are (a) threshold for, sensitivity to, or awareness of stimuli impinging upon various sensory modalities (primarily external, but including pain); (b) nature of response to various levels of sensory stimulation in terms of the extent of disorganization, avoidance, withdrawal, or active coping mechanisms employed to deal with them.

Autonomous Functioning. The components are (a) degree of freedom from impairment of apparatuses of primary autonomy (functional disturbances of sight, hearing, intention, language, memory, learning, or motor function); (b) degree of or freedom from impairment of secondary autonomy (disturbances in habit patterns, learned complex skills, work routines, hobbies, and interests).

Synthetic-Integrative Functioning. (a) Degree of reconciliation or integration of discrepant or potentially contradictory attitudes, values, affects, behavior, and self representations; (b) degree of *active* relating together and integrating of psychic and behavioral events, whether contradictory or not.

Mastery-Competence. (a) Competence, the person's performance in relation to his existing capacity to interact with and master his environment; (b) sense of competence, the person's expectation of success, or the subjective side of actual performance (how well he believes he can do).

Case Illustrations[10]

Following are some examples of analyzed T.A.T. records.[11] An attempt has been made to present them as closely as possible to the actual use of the T.A.T.

---

[10] In the first two cases, the Long Form is used; in the third case, the Short Form is used.

[11] These records are by no means exhaustively analyzed, as anyone will recognize. To do so would not be practical here. Indeed, a whole monograph could be written about each T.A.T. record! Different styles of writing the final report are used to illustrate various possibilities.

Blank Analysis Sheets. Since the format of this book is smaller than the actual size of the blank, these pages must of necessity be rather crowded. Another limitation is that the running commentary of a classroom is not easily approximated. The clinical notes are meant to take the place of classroom remarks—enlarging on one aspect or another which might easily appear arbitrary. For instance, in story 1 of John Doe, blindness is scored both as a defense (namely, a form of denial of the voyeurism which is also expressed in the story itself by the person's failure to recognize the violin) and again as a form of punishment. Psychological acts are overdetermined. Fear of blindness, especially in children, must be regarded clinically both as a wish not to have to see (for instance, primal scene events), and also as a fear of being punished for wanting to look. Seeing is sometimes experienced as something active, (i.e., the glaring stare of the hypnotist), or as something passive, by the person into whose eyes someone is staring forcefully. The eye may thus serve either as a male or a female sexual symbol. Frequently during psychoanalytic sessions related to the topic of masturbation, patients will rub their eyes and transitory symptoms of compulsive eye rubbing are not uncommon. This usually constitutes a masturbatory equivalent.

The clinical notes accompanying each story are kept to a minimum and where possible printed on the same page as the story itself, as an editorial convenience. *They are not an essential part of the clinical record, but are appended here for didactic purposes.* Similarly, under clinical conditions, the descriptive theme need not be written out at all; the instructions are to write the *interpretive* theme under "Main Theme" on the Analysis Sheet, and to write the diagnostic level of the theme on the Summary Page. *However, for didactic reasons, we are reproducing here the descriptive, interpretive, and diagnostic theme* below each story to show how the final diagnostic level is arrived at by easy stages from the actual story as given by the person. Then, just to keep the record straight, we also reproduce the interpretive theme on the Analysis Blank and the diagnostic theme level on the Summary Page, where they belong in the actual clinical record.

Thus, the scheme as used here will often be repetitive in the interests of greater clarity.

Case 1

The first case we present is one of "blind" diagnosis—that is, the T.A.T. was administered by someone else in a neuropsychiatric hospital and sent to us as the protocol of "John Doe," male, age 25, single.[12] These stories are, on the whole, quite poor, thematically speaking, and as unsuitable for our type of analysis as could easily be found; we include them to show how much one can derive from the scheme even under poor story conditions.

Although at the time of analyzing the material we knew nothing about this man except his age and sex, we are now including a condensed version of the summary evaluation of John Doe made by the mental hygiene psychotherapist:

---

[12] Courtesy of Edwin S. Shneidman et al., *Thematic Test Analysis,* New York, Grune & Stratton, 1951. Since this T.A.T. interpretation was part of a research project, there was no objection to a blind diagnosis.

The patient is a tall, slender young man of 25 who gives the impression of boyishness. He seems suspicious, indecisive, and unable to relax. There seem to be considerable effeminate mannerisms in his behavior. He had never been able to make secure object relationships. He was very fearful and withdrawn from early childhood. Some of his guilt in relation to his sexual drives, masturbation, and probably also in relation to incestuous feelings toward a seductive mother. There seems to be considerable guilt in relation to his own hostility. He has established some defenses against this through obsessions, but his defenses are cracking. The patient seemed obsessed with thoughts about death, homocide, and suicide. There were depersonalization, many ideas of reference, and a considerable amount of hostile fantasy. It is felt that this patient is a paranoid schizophrenic who is still able to maintain control over his hostile and destructive impulses, although his control is very tenuous. As long as he can live a withdrawn and sheltered life, perhaps he can continue to function outside a hospital; however, in the face of frustration he may become actively psychotic with homicidal and suicidal impulses.

Following is a case reproduced as in the actual T.A.T. Blank, which means that the final report appears on what would be the first page of the blank, so that whoever the report is intended for can read the essentials at one glance. The reader is advised first to go through the stories and then to turn back to the final report. Further on in this book, this case is analyzed in terms of object relations.

BELLAK T A T BLANK

For Recording and Analyzing Thematic Apperception Test Stories

Name __John Doe_____ Sex _M_ Age _25_ Date _____

Education _____ Occupation _____

Referred by_____ Analysis by _____

FINAL REPORT

General:

This is an extremely disturbed man: he conceives of himself as ill, incapacitated, mutilated, feels depressed, fearful, and dead inside.

He is exceedingly ambivalent toward both father and mother figures; his oedipal problems are entirely unresolved: he has a tremendous attachment to the mother, whom he sees as dangerous at the same time. He sees the father as cold, hostile, and inadequate.

The patient has tremendous guilt feelings concerning both sexual and aggressive impulses (which appear fused). He frequently identifies with a female figure. He also has conflicts concerning exhibitionistic and voyeuristic tendencies, possibly related to urethral difficulties.

His thought processes appear disturbed, tending toward the bizarre. There are data consistent with cosmic delusions and hallucinations.

The total picture is consistent with a schizophrenic disorder, with potential paranoid and hebephrenic coloring. Suicidal risk is considerable. Homicidal risk should be considered. Sexual criminality, including overt homosexuality, is a possibility.

Specific:

Illness and mutilation appear in stories 1, 7BM; also in 12M, 14, and 16 (not reproduced here). Depression, fear, and guilt are apparent in every story, usually related to sex, such as prostitution in 7BM, adultery in 4, sex and murder in 6BM; sex and disgust also appear in 13MF, murder and stealing in 14 (the last two stories not reproduced here). Homosexuality is suggested by female identification.

Blindness occurs in story 1, great notoriety in 3BM, stage acting in 6BM; not looking in 13MF and photography in 14 (the latter two are not reproduced here). These themes are consistent with voyeurism and exhibitionism.

Water occurs in story 1, fire in 4, slightly suggestive of urethral problems.

Conflict with parental figures appears in story 1, the female figure is seen as dangerous and seductive in 4, mother seen as dangerous in 6BM, father as cold in 7BM, as inadequate in 7BM (was also sick) and in 13B (not reproduced), and is fought symbolically in 14 (also not reproduced here).

Thought processes appear most clearly to be disturbed and bizarre in stories 1, 6BM, and 16 (not reproduced here).

Printed in U.S.A.   Published by THE PSYCHOLOGICAL CORPORATION. New York, New York 10017   73-262AS

Note: The above represents one form of writing the final report, the general statements being separated from the specific concrete references they are based on. The reports for Case 2 and Case 3 show other possibilities.

1: This child is sick in bed. He has been given sheet music to study, but instead of the music he has come across a novel that interests him more than the music. It is probably an adventure story. He evidently does not fear the chance that his parents will find him thus occupied as he seems quite at ease. He seems to be quite a studious type and perhaps regrets missing school, but he seems quite occupied with the adventure in the story. Adventure has something to do with ocean or water. He is not too happy, though not too sad. His eyes are somewhat blank—coincidence of reading a book without any eyes or knowing what is in the book without reading it. He disregards the music and falls asleep reading the book.

Descriptive theme	Interpretive theme	Diagnostic level
A sick child is	(If one) is a sick child	Feels a child, sick, poor body image.
told to study music (ignores fiddle) and	told to work (ignores fiddle),	Feels coerced. Mechanism of denial—re masturbation?
prefers adventure story to studying,	prefers pleasure reading (concerning water) to studying,	Resists authority by withdrawal into fantasy; urethral interests, exhibitionism?
feels not happy, not sad,	without affect,	Anhedonia? Depersonalization?
unafraid of punishment,	unafraid of punishment,	(Fear of punishment), severe superego; denial.
reads without eyes or knows what is in book without reading,	can see without eyes and is omniscient,	Bizarre ideas of magic; severe superego, castration, omnipotence.
falls asleep.	falls asleep.	Withdrawal, passivity.

Clinical notes

The concept of the body image as sick, and merely a child, emerges here, supplemented by the idea of being blind later in the story, probably indicating poor concept patient has of himself, and at the same time probably indicating some intrapsychic awareness of (mental) illness which one finds in patients who seem consciously unaware of being psychotic.

Ignores fiddle altogether: rare in adults, usually signifying disturbance re violin playing as sexual symbol, particularly masturbatory.

Instead of studying, prefers fantasy: resistant to parents; unable to study, or unwilling.

Fantasy concerns water, ocean: since this is an entirely personal introduction by the subject, wonder if related to enuresis, urethral complex, and premature ejaculation as sexual disturbance, aside from actual urinary disturbances.

Unafraid of punishment: negation probably means "I wish I were not afraid" (actually quite afraid), as pointed out by Freud (denial).

Not happy, not sad: anhedonia, underlying depression—mechanism of denial.

Name_____ Story No.____1____ (TAT Picture No.____1____)

1. **Main theme:** (Interpretive) (If one is) a sick child, told to study music (ignores fiddle), prefers an adventure story concerning water, feels not happy, not sad, unafraid of punishment, possibly reading without eyes or knowing what is in book without reading it, falls asleep.

2. **Main hero:** age _child_ sex _male_ vocation _student_ ⌐not happy, not sad.
   interests _reading_ traits _studious, unafraid,_ abilities _reading book without eyes_
   adequacy (√, √√, √√√) _O ?_ body image and/or self-image _ill in bed; blank eyes—no eyes_

3. **Main needs of hero:**
   a) behavioral needs of hero (as in story): _Reads adventure story instead of studying music;_
      falls asleep.
      dynamic inference: _resistant to parents; passivity; withdrawal; prefers fantasy concerning_
   b) figures, objects, or circumstances *introduced*: _parents, book, water, school_   _urethral_
                                                                                        problems
      implying need for or to: _illness; to defy parents and withdraw into_   _to study._
      fantasy. Preoccupation with and awareness of illness.
   c) figures, objects, or circumstances *omitted*: _violin, bow_

      implying need for or to: _Guilt re masturbation_

4. **Conception of environment (world) as:** _coercive, rejecting_

5. **Parental figures** (m _√_, f _√_) are seen as _coercive-_ and subject's reaction is _escape into fantasy_
   Contemp. figures (m____, f____) are seen as _rejecting_ and subject's reaction is_____
   Junior figures (m____, f____) are seen as_____ and subject's reaction is_____

6. **Significant conflicts:** _Compliance-autonomy; achievement-pleasure; activity-passivity._

7. **Nature of anxieties:** (√)
   of physical harm and/or punishment_____ of illness or injury _√_
   of disapproval_____ of deprivation _√_
   of lack or loss of love_____ of being devoured_____
   of being deserted_____ of being overpowered and helpless_____
   other_____

8. **Main defenses against conflicts and fears:** (√)
   repression_____ reaction-formation_____ rationalization_____ isolation_____
   regression_____ introjection_____ denial _√_ undoing_____ splitting_____
   projective identification_____ other _withdrawal delusional omnipotence_

9. **Severity of superego as manifested by :** (√)   ⌐of voyeurism) sometimes also a form of castration.
   punishment for "crime" _Blind (as punishment)_ immediate_____ just_____ too severe_____
                                              delayed_____ unjust_____ too lenient _____
   inhibitions_____ stammer_____ delayed initial response or pauses_____

10. **Integration of the ego, manifesting itself in:** (√, √√, √√√)
    adequacy of hero _O ?_ outcome: happy_____ unhappy_____
                                     realistic_____ unrealistic _√_
                              solution: adequate_____ inadequate_____
    thought processes as revealed by plot being: (√, √√, √√√)
    structured_____ unstructured _√_ stereotyped_____ original_____ appropriate_____
    rational_____ bizarre _√_ complete _√_ incomplete_____ inappropriate_____

Intelligence: (√) superior_____ above average_____ average _√_ below average_____ defective_____

Analysis Sheet for Use with the Bellak TAT Blank

S1-119AS The Psychological Corporation

Note: A slightly revised version of variables 9 and 10 of the above blank, to be published as before by The Psychological Corporation, is in process. The changes are identical with those appearing in the revised Short Form.

Reading without eyes: bizarre statement; being blind is often punishment for voyeurism (related to exhibitionism) and often consistent with very great masturbatory guilt.

Knows what is in book without reading it: bizarre statement; implies telepathic notions, superhuman power, possibly related to cosmic delusions.

Falling asleep: resolves conflict situation (disobeying parents) by withdrawal.

Story is far removed from stimulus, poorly structured, bizarre, consistent with severe thought disturbance; flat mood consistent with schizophrenia.

3BM: This is a girl in a cell and she has been jailed because she was found guilty of prostitution. She is in this position in the picture because she is very ashamed, not because of being arrested, because she is quite familiar with the police, but because of the fact that her picture and a newspaper write-up was being sensationally spread across the country. She knew that her sister, who was a nun, would suffer from it, and it made her feel very badly because she, at one time, had a chance and an opportunity to follow her elder sister's example but it was too late now. She grabs a concealed knife from under her blouse and stabs herself.

Descriptive theme	*Interpretive theme*	*Diagnostic level*
A girl is jailed for prostitution;	(If a) girl is guilty of prostitution she is jailed;	Great guilt over sex; feminine identification.
is ashamed not for arrest (because she is quite familiar with police) but because of newspaper publicity which would hurt her sister, a nun. Once she could have followed her sister's example but it is too late now.	is ashamed of the publicity and the hurting of sister whom she should emulate in being a nun,	Severe superego concerning also exhibitionism and ambivalence to sibling seen as pure.
Kills herself with knife.	and kills herself.	Intra-aggression.

Clinical notes

Subject apparently considers sex as dirty, in speaking of prostitution here. Apparently feels like an habitual criminal, since he says he is quite accustomed to jail. His fear of the introduced theme of publicity is quite consistent as the exhibitionistic counterpart of the voyeurism in story 1.

Hero identifies with female in this story. This by itself is so frequent in this picture that it can only be considered a most tentative datum. However, this is such a vivid identification and sounds so convincing that it appears to portray something significant.

Name_____ Story No.____2_____ (TAT Picture No. _3BM____)

1. **Main theme:** (Interpretive) (If a) girl is guilty of prostitution she is jailed; is ashamed of the publicity and the hurting of sister whom she should emulate in being a nun, and kills herself.

2. **Main hero:** age _young_ sex _female_ vocation _prostitute_____
   interests _none noted_____ traits _guilty re sex_ abilities _none noted_____
   adequacy (√, √√, √√√) _0 ?_ body image and/or self-image _feminine identification?_
3. **Main needs of hero:**   outcast—criminal—sexually immoral.
   a) behavioral needs of hero (as in story): _Kills self because sister would suffer from her actions._

      dynamic inference: _depression—guilt over sex—suicidal tendencies? aggression against mother_
   b) figures, objects, or circumstances *introduced:* _sister—publicity—suicide_____

      implying need for or to: _exhibitionism and ambivalence to sibling (or mother) seen as pure___

   c) figures, objects, or circumstances *omitted:* _object usually seen as pistol is made into a knife_
      (_significance not clear—weakening aggression?_)
      implying need for or to:_____

4. **Conception of environment (world) as:** _punishing—shaming—reproving_____

5. **Parental figures** (m___, f___) are seen as_____ and subject's reaction is_____
   Contemp. figures (m___, f _√_) are seen as _pure___ and subject's reaction is _ambivalence___
   Junior figures (m___, f___) are seen as_____ and subject's reaction is_____
6. **Significant conflicts:** _guilt concerning sex_____

7. **Nature of anxieties:** (√)
   of physical harm and/or punishment_____ of illness or injury_____
   of disapproval _√_____ of deprivation_____
   of lack or loss of love _√_____ of being devoured_____
   of being deserted_____ of being overpowered and helpless_____
   other_____

8. **Main defenses against conflicts and fears:** (√)
   repression_____ reaction-formation_____ rationalization_____ isolation_____
   regression_____ introjection_____ denial_____ undoing_____ splitting_____
   projective identification_____ other _projection; identification with aggressor._

9. **Severity of superego as manifested by :** (√)
   punishment for "crime"_____ immediate _√___ just_____ too severe _√___
                                   delayed_____ unjust_____ too lenient_____
   inhibitions_____ stammer_____ delayed initial response or pauses_____

10. **Integration of the ego, manifesting itself in:** (√, √√, √√√)
    adequacy of hero _0 ?_____ outcome: happy_____ unhappy _√√√___
                                            realistic_____ unrealistic_____
                                   solution: adequate_____ inadequate _√√√_
    thought processes as revealed by plot being: (√, √√, √√√)
    structured_____ unstructured_____ stereotyped_____ original_____ appropriate_____
    rational_____ bizarre_____ complete _√___ incomplete_____ inappropriate _√___
Intelligence: (√) superior_____ above average_____ average_____ below average_____ defective_____

Analysis Sheet for Use with the Bellak TAT Blank

                              S1-119AS The Psychological Corporation

4: The girl in the picture is half-caste. She is in love with the man who is going to leave her and return to his wife. They have spent quite some time together in intimacy. She is pleading with him to stay with her or help figure some way to plan for the coming of the child she is going to bear. She is in poor circumstances financially, and he tells her she should make arrangements to conclude the birth and thus everything would iron out because he is definitely determined to leave as the affair in his mind is at an end. She is very broken up by it. She pleads for him to spend one more night, which he agrees to, and in the middle of the night she sets fire to the house, thus solving the problems of all concerned.

Descriptive theme	Interpretive theme	Diagnostic level
A half-caste girl has had a love affair with a man who has impregnated her and now plans to leave her to return to his wife.	(If one) commits adultery, one is "half-caste" (inferior); will be rejected, poorly off,	Sexual guilt; social prejudice; punishment is rejection, poverty.
In their last night together she sets a fire and kills them both.	will kill oneself and lover by fire.	Has intra- and extra-aggressivity; urethral complex (identifies with girl again); but may also say: women are bad, do this sort of bad thing; endanger one (in secondary identification).

Clinical notes

The reference to the half-caste is intentionally reworded, "If one commits adultery, one is a half-caste," making a causal connection where there had been mere juxtaposition. This is consistent with psychoanalytic practice (e.g., in dream interpretation concerning unconscious modes of thought). The theme is a typical triangular oedipal one; the subject here again identifies with a female in an even more significant way, since here he could easily identify with a male figure.

The introduction of fire again ties in with the urethral aspects of the use of water in the first story, aside from the fact that it connotes uncontrolled emotion. The occurrence of bizarre and unrealistic outcomes, in the presence of structured plots and thought processes, is probably a diagnostic sign of a latent psychotic who can still address himself to a task in an ordinary way even though the pathology underneath is extreme.

Name_____ Story No. __3__ (TAT Picture No. __4__)

1. Main theme: (Interpretive) (If one) commits adultery, one is "half-caste" (inferior); will be rejected, poorly off, will kill oneself and lover by fire.

2. **Main hero:** age _young adult_ sex __F__ vocation _none noted_
   interests _none noted_ traits _half-caste, poor_ abilities _guilty re sex—pregnant_
   adequacy (√, √√, √√√) _O ?_ body image and/or self-image _strong feminine identification; feels rejected—pregnant._

3. **Main needs of hero:**
   a) behavioral needs of hero (as in story): _love and support_

   dynamic inference: _fear of abandonment and rejection_
   b) figures, objects, or circumstances *introduced:* _pregnancy—setting fire to house_

   implying need for or to: _intra- and extra-aggression very strong—possibility of suicidal and homicidal impulses; unconscious fear of impregnation._
   c) figures, objects, or circumstances *omitted:* _half-nude female figure_

   implying need for or to: _sexual guilt—scotoma repression_

4. **Conception of environment (world) as:** _hostile and rejecting_

5. **Parental figures** (m____, f____) are seen as_____ and subject's reaction is_____
   Contemp. figures (m_√_, f____) are seen as _rejecting_ and subject's reaction is _guilt; depression; ag-_
   Junior figures (m____, f____) are seen as_____ and subject's reaction is_____ _gression_

6. **Significant conflicts:** _sexual guilt; intra- and extra-aggressivity; urethral complex_

7. **Nature of anxieties: (√)**
   of physical harm and/or punishment __√__ of illness or injury_____
   of disapproval __√__ of deprivation __√__
   of lack or loss of love __√__ of being devoured_____
   of being deserted __√__ of being overpowered and helpless_____
   other_____

8. **Main defenses against conflicts and fears: (√)**
   repression __√__ reaction-formation_____ rationalization_____ isolation_____
   regression_____ introjection_____ denial_____ undoing_____ splitting_____
   projective identification_____ other _projection_

9. **Severity of superego as manifested by : (√)**
   punishment for "crime"_____ immediate_____ just_____ too severe __√__
   delayed_____ unjust_____ too lenient_____
   inhibitions_____ stammer_____ delayed initial response or pauses_____

10. **Integration of the ego, manifesting itself in: (√, √√, √√√)**
    adequacy of hero _O ?_ outcome: happy_____ unhappy __√√√__
    realistic_____ unrealistic __√√√__
    solution: adequate_____ inadequate __√√__
    thought processes as revealed by plot being: (√, √√, √√√)
    structured __√__ unstructured_____ stereotyped_____ original_____ appropriate_____
    rational_____ bizarre_____ complete __√__ incomplete_____ inappropriate_____

Intelligence: (√) superior_____ above average_____ average_____ below average_____ defective_____

Analysis Sheet for Use with the Bellak TAT Blank

S1-119AS The Psychological Corporation

6BM: This is a scene in a play. The two characters are on the stage; one is a famous elderly actress, who has a son about the age of the young man appearing opposite her. The dialogue in the play has suddenly taken on a new meaning for her. She sees now that the play, which was written by her son, has an entirely different meaning in this scene in the picture. The boy is telling the mother that he has just committed a murder. She understands now that this was her son's way of conveying to her the terrifying fact that that is actually what had happened. In the play, as her son had written it, the climax comes when the mother calls the police. But the famous actress decides to put her own climax into action after the play is over. She calls her son and says, "The climax of your play will have to be changed." She says, "I think the audience will prefer this one," so here she draws a revolver and shoots him. (*What kind of murder was it?*) Oh, a girl. Motive primarily to do with sexual. She had been unfaithful.

Descriptive theme	*Interpretive theme*	*Diagnostic level*
In a play written by her son an elderly actress suddenly understands that he has killed a girl	If a man kills a girl because she has been unfaithful to him	Aggression fused with sex. Exhibitionism and symbolism.
for being unfaithful to him.	and mother finds out in a play,	Triangular oedipal situation—feels rejected by girl.
Thereupon she kills him.	symbolically the mother will kill him.	Mother seen as phalllic, aggressive, dangerous.

Clinical notes

The value of the theme construction is particularly obvious in this story, though cluttered with confusing descriptive detail. The aggressive sexual wishes of the subject toward the maternal figure and the fear of counteraggression by the mother figure become crystal clear. The "sudden understanding" is a typical experience in schizophrenics with paranoid tendencies, as so well described by Sullivan (1940). The patient is in a panic because of many different impulses and apperceptive distortions, finds a new configuration which gives him a measure of stability and a channeling of his fears and aggression—the paranoid constellation. The fact, too, that the information is conveyed symbolically is highly suggestive of a schizophrenic process.

The actor is probably another identification figure for the subject, who attempts at first to keep some distance between himself and the mother in having someone else play opposite her.

Name_____ Story No. ___4___ (TAT Picture No. ___6BM___)

1. **Main theme:** (Interpretative) (If a) man kills a girl because she was unfaithful to him, the mother will kill him.

2. **Main hero:** age _adult_ sex __M__ vocation _playwright_____
   interests _writing_____ traits _none noted____ abilities _none noted_____
   adequacy (√, √√, √√√) _0 ?___ body image and/or self-image _not noted_____

3. **Main needs of hero:**
   a) behavioral needs of hero (as in story): _to punish (kill) girl who was unfaithful to him._
   _____
   dynamic inference: _oedipal theme; feeling of being rejected; aggressive conception of sex._
   b) figures, objects, or circumstances *introduced*: _actor; audience; police; gun; girl he killed._
   _____
   implying need for or to: _punishment for oedipal guilt feelings; aggression; need for exhibitionism._
   _____
   c) figures, objects, or circumstances *omitted*: _none_____
   _____
   implying need for or to:_____

4. **Conception of environment (world) as:** _hostile; punishing_ —and rejecting_____

5. **Parental figures** (m____, f_√_) are seen as _punishing_ and subject's reaction is _aggression_____
   Contemp. figures (m____, f_√_) are seen as _rejecting_ and subject's reaction is _aggression_____
   Junior figures (m___, f___) are seen as _____ and subject's reaction is_____

6. **Significant conflicts:** _____
   _____

7. **Nature of anxieties:** (√)
   of physical harm and/or punishment ____√_____ of illness or injury___√_____
   of disapproval _____√_____ of deprivation_____
   of lack or loss of love _____√_____ of being devoured_____
   of being deserted _____ of being overpowered and helpless_____
   other_____

8. **Main defenses against conflicts and fears:** (√)
   repression_____ reaction-formation_____ rationalization_____ isolation_____
   regression_____ introjection_____ denial_____ undoing_____ splitting_____
   projective identification_____ other _projection_____

9. **Severity of superego as manifested by :** (√)
   punishment for "crime" _____ immediate___√_____ just_____ too severe_____
   _____ delayed_____ unjust_____ too lenient _____
   inhibitions_____ stammer_____ delayed initial response or pauses_____

10. **Integration of the ego, manifesting itself in:** (√, √√, √√√)
    adequacy of hero ____0 ?_____ outcome: happy_____ unhappy___√√√_____
    _____ realistic_____ unrealistic _√√√_____
    _____ solution: adequate _____ inadequate _____
    thought processes as revealed by plot being: (√, √√, √√√)
    structured __√√__ unstructured_____ stereotyped_____ original_____ appropriate_____
    rational_____ bizarre___√√_____ complete _____ incomplete_____ inappropriate_____

Intelligence: (√) superior_____ above average_____ average_____ below average_____ defective_____

Analysis Sheet for Use with the Bellak TAT Blank

S1-119AS The Psychological Corporation

7BM: This would be a man and his son. The son is very depressed over his health. The father is telling him that as a young man he too had the same illness, and that it can be cured if the son has the will to cure it. The father tells the young man that he himself alone can cure it. The son believes that there is no hope, but replies that he will go away for a little while and think it over. The father replies, "You are not doing a favor to me by saying it. I am thinking about your getting well for the simple reason that you have a wife and children to support, and in the event of your being bedridden, the responsibility for your family will be put entirely upon your mother and me." The young man finally concludes that he will take his wife and family with him and try to make things go better in a healthier climate. *(What kind of illness did he have?)* T.B. *(Did he get better?)* No, I don't think he does. After a few years he dies and the children are old enough to support mother or perhaps he left insurance. Never contacted father again. No correspondence. After not having heard from each other for a long time, the old man dies and leaves the children a large estate. This is his way of having repented.

Descriptive theme	*Interpretive theme*	*Diagnostic level*
A young man suffers from T.B.,	If one is sick with T.B.	Feels sick. T.B. is castration.
and father tells him he used to have it too	and father had the same illness,	Father also seen as previously sick, castrated.
and that the son will have to cure himself so that his wife and children will not burden father.	father selfishly rejects one.	Feels rejected by father. Father seen as cold, narcissistic.
Son removes himself, angry at father, Both die, father leaving money to children.	One is angry at father. One dies, and father dies too, repenting too late. Wants father to feels sorry about not having been nicer to him.	Aggression toward father. Oral wishes toward father.

Clinical notes

In several years of clinical work with tuberculars, we find that the fantasies of having T.B. are most frequently either those of being invaded (phallically) by the T.B. germs, particularly in an impregnation fantasy, and having holes made in one (i.e., being castrated, particularly in connection with hemorrhages [Bellak, 1952c]). The fact that the father has also had the illness suggests that patient tended to think of the father also as castrated and weak. Since the father was an identification figure, this may have influenced the subject's emotional growth. T.B. may also mean venereal disease here.

Name_____ Story No.___5____ (TAT Picture No. ___7BM___)

1. **Main theme:** (Interpretive) (If one) is sick with T.B. and father had the same illness, father selfishly rejects one. One is angry at father. One dies and father dies too, repenting too late. Wants father to feel sorry about not having been nicer to one.

2. **Main hero:** age _adult_ sex __M__ vocation _none noted_
   interests_ none noted_ traits_depressed; ill_ abilities _none noted_
   adequacy (√, √√, √√√)_O ?_ body image and/or self-image _ill with T.B.; helpless_

3. **Main needs of hero:**
   a) behavioral needs of hero (as in story): _Help and support because of being ill_

   dynamic inference: _feels weak, helpless, debilitated, oral needs_
   b) figures, objects, or circumstances *introduced:* _wife, mother, children, illness, death, money_

   implying need for or to: _heterosexual needs—wanting care from parents—fear of illness and death_

   c) figures, objects, or circumstances *omitted:*_____

   implying need for or to:_____

4. **Conception of environment (world) as:** _cold, hostile, uncaring_

5. **Parental figures** (m___, f_√_) are seen as _cold, spec-_ and subject's reaction is_withdrawal, anger_
   Contemp. figures (m___, f___) are seen as ___ulating_ and subject's reaction is_____
   Junior figures (m___, f___) are seen as_____ and subject's reaction is_____

6. **Significant conflicts:** _Bodily concern (T.B.—full of holes? or is it syphilis?) Strong dependency_
   needs. Aggression toward father.

7. **Nature of anxieties:** (√)
   of physical harm and/or punishment_____ of illness or injury___√___
   of disapproval_____ of deprivation___√_____
   of lack or loss of love___√_____ of being devoured_____
   of being deserted___√_____ of being overpowered and helpless_____
   other_of death_

8. **Main defenses against conflicts and fears:** (√)
   repression_____ reaction-formation_____ rationalization_____ isolation_____
   regression_____ introjection_____ denial_____ undoing_____ splitting_____
   projective identification_____ other _projection, withdrawal_

9. **Severity of superego as manifested by :** (√)
   punishment for "crime"_____ immediate_____ just_____ too severe___√____
   delayed_____ unjust_____ too lenient_____
   inhibitions_____ stammer_____ delayed initial response or pauses_____
   sees himself as fatally ill, possibly dies because of anger at father.

10. **Integration of the ego, manifesting itself in:** (√, √√, √√√)
    adequacy of hero___O ?_____ outcome: happy_____ unhappy___√√√___
    realistic_____ unrealistic_____
    solution: adequate _____ inadequate ___√_____
    thought processes as revealed by plot being: (√, √√, √√√)
    structured ___√___ unstructured_____ stereotyped_____ original___√___ appropriate_____
    rational_____ bizarre_____ complete_____ incomplete_____ inappropriate ___√___

Intelligence: (√) superior_____ above average_____ average_____ below average_____ defective_____

Analysis Sheet for Use with the Bellak TAT Blank

S1-119AS The Psychological Corporation

Summary
Record themes and summarize other significant data for each story.

1. Feels a child, sick, poor body image. Feels coerced by parents. Mechanism of denial—re: masturbation? Resists authority by withdrawal into fantasy; urethral interests, exhibitionism (?), anhedonia (?). Delusional omnipotence (knowing what is in book without reading it)—severe thought disturbance and flat mood consistent with schizophrenia.

2. Great guilt over sex; feminine identification. Severe superego concerning also exhibitionism and ambivalence to sibling (or mother) seen as pure. Intra-aggression. Self-image: outcast, criminal.

3. Sexual guilt; social prejudice; punishment is rejection, poverty. Intra- and extra-aggressivity. Urethral complex. Identifies with girl again, but may also say: women are bad, do this sort of thing, endanger one (in secondary identification). Possibility of suicidal and homicidal impulses. Unconscious fear of impregnation.

4. Aggression fused with sex. Triangular oedipal situation—feels rejected by girl. Mother seen as phallic, aggressive, dangerous. "Sudden understanding" consistent with paranoid schizophrenic process.

5. Feels ill and helpless with T.B.—full of holes? or syphilis? Father also seen as previously sick (castrated). Feels rejected by father. Father seen as cold, narcissistic. Aggression toward father. Oral wishes toward father. Sees self as fatally ill, disturbed body image.

6.

7.

8.

9.

10.

Ego function assessment from TAT data:

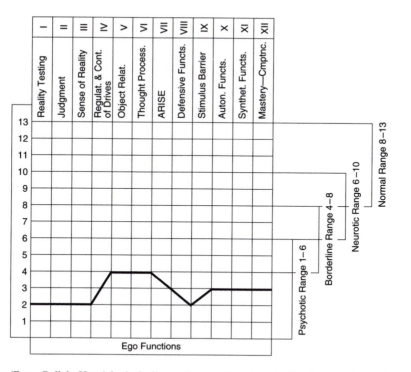

(From Bellak, Hurvich, & Gediman, *Ego functions in schizophrenics, neurotics, and normals.* Copyright © 1973, by C. P. S., Inc. Reprinted by permission of John Wiley & Sons, Inc.)

Ego functions observed during test administration:

Case 2

Following are stories given by a young man in his middle twenties.[13] We have chosen a few for illustration. At the time of the administration of the T.A.T. he was in a prison hospital. He had gone AWOL from the armed forces because he found it impossible to urinate in the presence of others, and others were always present in the latrines. When he was picked up by M.P.s, he made an inadequate gesture at aggression and was thereupon shot in the abdomen. These few data may suffice to highlight the dynamic material revealed with regard to homosexual problems, problems of voyeurism and exhibitionism, and the handling of the problem of aggression; the subject was just aggressive enough to invite almost suicidal counteraggression on the part of the armed military police. He was intelligent and industrious and came from immigrant stock.

The T.A.T. was not administered by the writer, and unfortunately, story 1, the boy with the violin, was not included.

---

[13] We are indebted to Dr. Blaise Pasquarelli for this material.

BELLAK T A T BLANK

For Recording and Analyzing Thematic Apperception Test Stories

Name _____ Sex _Male_ Age __26__ Date _____

Education __high school_____ Occupation __Army private_____

Referred by_____ Analysis by _____

FINAL REPORT

Choosing just a few of the stories of the subject, one sees his pervasive feeling of inadequacy of his fear of being overpowered running through nearly all the themes. He sees himself either as a woman (#2, 3BM) or as too small (14). When he has aggressive or sexual desires he thinks of himself as bad, inadequate (#13 MF and 18BM).

His needs appear as a need for autonomy (2, 7BM, 14), achievement, and an oedipal type of competitiveness allied to the partial sexual components of voyeurism and exhibitionism.

His conception of the world is one of deprivation (2, 3BM, 14, 18BM), of being overpowered and harmed (2, 7BM), actually representing an image of his parents whom he tries in vain to stand up to.

His main conflicts center around autonomy versus compliance, activity-passivity, and achievement-inadequacy, and he shows a great deal of anxiety of being overpowered and injured. His main defenses are emotional isolation, projection, and attempts at sublimation by intellectualization.

His superego is extremely severe, leading to intra-aggression particularly concerning incestuous sexual wishes.

The integration of the ego is inadequate in that the hero hardly ever succeeds, is usually unhappy, and frequently suicidal. The subject appears to be of above average intelligence.

Impulse control of aggressive and intra-aggressive drives seems so poor that one must consider him potentially suicidal and homicidal, particularly in homosexual panic. The record is consistent with that of a borderline schizophrenic with paranoid features.

Printed in U.S.A.   Published by THE PSYCHOLOGICAL CORPORATION. New York, New York 10017   73-262AS

Note: In this final report, abstract statements are interspersed with brief references to relevant stories. This procedure may be profitable enlarged, giving the condensed theme or part of the story as an illustration for the abstract statement.

2: What the hell could have happened before in this picture? I don't know . . . (resistance). . . . I would say that this here girl has just come from school and that she has something on her mind which she wants to ask her parents. . . . That's her father and mother in the background—her father on the plow, and her mother leaning up against the tree. She has been brought up very strictly, and her parents probably are of European stock but . . . they are immigrants. She is being held down and doesn't live the normal life that a normal girl should. She is very intelligent and a good student. She probably has just graduated and wants to ask her parents . . . or rather wants to talk . . . she wants to go to college and she doesn't feel that her parents will approve it. Whether or not, she probably has assumed that when she has finished high school that that is as far as a girl should have to go, and what she is thinking now is that she should get married and settle down on the farm the way they did. . . . Her father is a successful farmer who can afford to send her to college . . . but will refuse to do so. This girl is very passionate . . . emotional . . . and unless she is alllowed to go to college she will probably develop some physical ailment (snicker). . . . But that her father refuses in the end to send her to college whereas . . . strike out whereas. . . . They find her a . . . suitor who they think will be suitable for her, and plan to have her married. . . . Is this too long? . . . The father is willing to bestow a portion of his land and the money and materials for a home which they can build on the land. . . . (Long pause.) She is very unhappy, or rather let's say that they become married and she is very unhappy. She refuses to have any children . . . because she doesn't want to bring them up in this backward atmosphere, knowing that her parents will try to bring up her children as they brought her up. Her husband is similar to her father in his attitude towards education and how to bring up a child. . . . He insists that she bear him a child and in time attempts to use physical force to throw a fear into her so that she will do what he will ask of her. She becomes hysterical and ends it all by committing suicide. . . . That's all!

Descriptive theme	*Interpretive theme*	*Diagnostic level*
A very strictly brought-up girl wants to go to college,	(If one) is a young, strictly brought-up girl and wants to be autonomous,	Feels strictly brought up; need for autonomy, achievement.
but is afraid that her parents will be against it	the parents are against it	Parents seen as restricting, coercive.
and will marry her against her will, which makes her sick and unhappy.	and force one into a submissive situation to which one responds by unhappiness, (mental)-illness.	Feels unhappy, mentally ill, fearful of sexual aggression.
When her husband, who resembles her father, uses physical force to impregnate her,	When threatened with male sexual aggression (by paternal figure),	Fear of pregnancy, of male sexual aggression. Identifies men too much with father.
she becomes hysterical and commits suicide.	one commits suicide.	Suicidal tendencies.

Clinical notes

Father and contemporary males (husband) are completely equated in this story, in which the subject identifies so vividly with the female figure. There is some awareness of mental disturbance.

Name_____ Story No.____1_____ (TAT Picture No.___2____)

1. Main theme: (Interpretive) If one is a young, strictly brought up girl and wants to be autonomous, the parents are against it and force one into a submissive situation to which one responds by unhappiness and (mental) illness. When threatened with male aggression one commits suicide.

2. **Main hero:** age _young adult_ sex ___F___ vocation _student_____
   interests _education_____ traits _autonomy_____ abilities _intelligent_____
   adequacy (√, √√, √√√) ___√___ body image and/or self-image _feminine; helpless_____

3. **Main needs of hero:**
   a) behavioral needs of hero (as in story): _Education; autonomy; to do better than parents_____

   dynamic inference: _curiosity; feeling of helplessness toward parents; competition with parents._
   b) figures, objects, or circumstances *introduced*: _college; money; pregnancy; suicide._____

   implying need for or to: _intellectual achievement; suicidal tendencies; fear of impregnation._____

   c) figures, objects, or circumstances *omitted*: _pregnancy of the older woman leaning against the tree_ _is not mentioned in the story._
   implying need for or to: _fear of pregnancy._____

4. **Conception of environment (world) as:** _coercive; depriving; aggressive._____

5. **Parental figures** (m _√_ , f _√_) are seen as ___above___ and subject's reaction is _attempt at autonomy;_
   Contemp. figures (m ___ , f ___) are seen as _____ and subject's reaction is_____ _intra-_
   Junior figures   (m ___ , f ___) are seen as _____ and subject's reaction is_____ _aggression_

6. **Significant conflicts:** _Between autonomy and compliance; extra-aggression and intra-aggression._

7. **Nature of anxieties: (√)**
   of physical harm and/or punishment _____√_____ of illness or injury_____
   of disapproval _____ of deprivation_____
   of lack or loss of love _____ of being devoured_____
   of being deserted _____ of being overpowered and helpless___√_____
   other _strong homosexual fears_____

8. **Main defenses against conflicts and fears: (√)**
   repression_____ reaction-formation_____ rationalization_____ isolation____√_____
   regression_____√_____ introjection_____ denial_____ undoing_____ splitting_____
   projective identification_____ other _projection intellectualization_____

9. **Severity of superego as manifested by : (√)**
   punishment for "crime" _____ immediate___√___ just_____ too severe___√_____
                                                 delayed_____ unjust_____ too lenient _____
   inhibitions_____ stammer_____ delayed initial response or pauses_____

10. **Integration of the ego, manifesting itself in:** (√, √√, √√√)
    adequacy of hero_____√_____ outcome: happy_____ unhappy___√_____
                                                    realistic____√_____ unrealistic_____
                                            solution: adequate _____ inadequate __√_____
    thought processes as revealed by plot being: (√, √√, √√√)
    structured ___√___ unstructured_____ stereotyped _____ original_____ appropriate_____
    rational _____ bizarre_____ complete ____√_____ incomplete_____ inappropriate_____

Intelligence: (√) superior _____ above average __√__ average _____ below average _____ defective _____

Analysis Sheet for Use with the Bellak TAT Blank

S1-119AS The Psychological Corporation

3BM: Well, I would say that this was a young girl who . . . is in love with a young man. . . . And they had some disagreement, and in this picture she has committed suicide. . . so she is dead (snicker). I would say that the man distrusted her, or believed that she was unfaithful to him. . . . Oh yeah . . . you might add in there what happened to her fiancé. That after she committed suicide, that he was so stricken with grief that he, in turn, committed suicide. . . . That is a pistol by her on the floor. . . . I would say that she shot herself through the head. . . . That's all. . . . The awkward position she is in would indicate that . . . she would not just be sitting there, or laying there like that. . . . I would say her fiancé committed suicide the same way. I can't think of anything else to say. . . . I would say it is a woman because it looks feminine . . . a little wide through the hips . . . the long hair . . . the large bust . . . large legs. . . . That's all.

Descriptive theme	*Interpretive theme*	*Diagnostic level*
Two people are in love with each other, have a disagreement because the man distrusts her faithfulness.	(If one) has a love affair, one cannot trust the faithfulness of the loved one.	Sexual needs; distinct triangular oedipal theme; jealousy.
She commits suicide, and then he commits suicide too.	This leads to disagreement and intra- and extra-aggression.	Intra- and extra-aggression.

Clinical notes

Probably both are identification figures for the hero, since in the last few lines subject feels the need to give reasons for the feminine identification of the depicted figure.

Name_____ Story No.____2_____ (TAT Picture No.____3BM____)

1. Main theme: (Interpretive) (If one) has a love affair one cannot trust the faithfulness of the loved one. This leads to disagreement and intra- and extra-aggression.

2. **Main hero:** age _young adult_ sex___F___ vocation _none noted_____
interests_ none noted_____ traits _none noted___ abilities _none noted_____
adequacy (√, √√, √√√)___O___ body image and/or self-image _feminine_____

3. **Main needs of hero:**
   a) behavioral needs of hero (as in story): _to be loved; aggression_____

   dynamic inference: _need to be loved; fear of aggression; oedipal involvement_____
   b) figures, objects, or circumstances _introduced:_ _competitive males_____

   implying need for or to: _homosexual interests_____

   c) figures, objects, or circumstances _omitted:_____

   implying need for or to:_____

4. **Conception of environment (world) as:** _untrustworthy_____
5. **Parental figures** (m____, f____) are seen as ⌐untrustworthy⌐ and subject's reaction is_____
   Contemp. figures (m_√_, f_√_) are seen as _competitive;_ and subject's reaction is _aggression and intra-_
   Junior figures   (m____, f____) are seen as_____ and subject's reaction is_____ _aggression_
6. **Significant conflicts:** _Between need for love and fear of aggression; feeling of inadequacy_____

7. **Nature of anxieties:** (√)
   of physical harm and/or punishment_____ of illness or injury_____
   of disapproval _____ of deprivation_____√_____
   of lack or loss of love _____√_____ of being devoured_____
   of being deserted_____ of being overpowered and helpless_____
   other _strong homosexual fears_____

8. **Main defenses against conflicts and fears:** (√)
   repression_____ reaction-formation_____ rationalization_____ isolation____√_____
   regression_____ introjection_____ denial_____ undoing_____ splitting_____
   projective identification_____ other_____

9. **Severity of superego as manifested by :** (√)
   punishment for "crime" _____ immediate___√___ just_____ too severe___√_____
                                             delayed_____ unjust_____ too lenient _____
   inhibitions_____ stammer_____ delayed initial response or pauses_____

10. **Integration of the ego, manifesting itself in:** (√, √√, √√√)
    adequacy of hero_____ outcome: happy_____ unhappy____√√√___
                                                          realistic_____ unrealistic_____
                                              solution: adequate _____ inadequate __√√√__
    thought processes as revealed by plot being: (√, √√, √√√)
    structured ___√√__ unstructured_____ stereotyped_____ original_____ appropriate_____
    rational_____ bizarre_____ complete ___√√___ incomplete_____ inappropriate_____

Intelligence: (√) superior_____ above average_____ average__√___ below average_____ defective_____

Analysis Sheet for Use with the Bellak TAT Blank

S1-119AS The Psychological Corporation

7BM: In this picture I would say that the younger person is a student who is . . . who is holding some political theories and he is fanatical about them. . . . That the older person is probably, I would say, his father, or professor, or teacher, or whatever you want to call him. . . . I would say that it is his father. . . . His father is telling him to give up his wild ideas about the government, but he refuses to give in. . . . The student is in favor of radical changes in society due to some ideals he is holding. . . . The son will probably . . . well here . . . because of his political views will wind up in prison, or become killed . . . in some public forum somewheres where he is trying to arouse the masses more or less. . . . (Long pause.) But anyways, in the end he will learn that he should have listened to his father. . . . That's all. . . . I would say that he is just a reformer, that's all. . . . I would say he is against capital . . . don't know, I think this is silly myself . . . (snicker).

Descriptive theme	*Interpretive theme*	*Diagnostic level*
A young student has radical ideas	If one has aggressive ideas against authority,	Aggression against authority, particularly male figures.
and will wind up in prison or be killed for them, repenting that he did not follow his father's advice to give up such ideas. It's all silly.	one is severely punished and repentant. Should comply with father figure. Tries to laugh it off.	Severe superego. Need for compliance with males. Rationalization, isolation.

Clinical notes

This story illustrates nicely that it is not merely psychoanalytic imagination which considers the government as a parental figure or, in this case, a paternal one, since the subject equates them easily, suggesting that the source of his political ideas also has a parental origin. Again, the snickering is probably used for defensive purposes to dispel the tension.

Name_____ Story No.____3____ (TAT Picture No.__7BM__)

1. **Main theme:** (<u>Interpretive</u>) If one has aggressive ideas against authority one is severely punished and repentant.

2. **Main hero:** age <u>young adult</u> sex___M___ vocation <u>student–agitator</u>_____
   interests <u>rebellion</u>_____ traits <u>wild</u>_____ abilities <u>none noted</u>_____
   adequacy (√, √√, √√√)__√√__ body image and/or self-image <u>unsuccessful radical</u>_____

3. **Main needs of hero:**
   a) behavioral needs of hero (as in story): <u>aggression; revolt against father</u>_____
   _____
   dynamic inference: <u>fear of paternal figures</u>_____
   b) figures, objects, or circumstances *introduced*: <u>government; jail</u>_____
   _____
   implying need for or to: <u>concern with authority; severe superego</u>_____
   _____
   c) figures, objects, or circumstances *omitted*:_____
   _____
   implying need for or to:_____

4. **Conception of environment (world) as:** <u>overpowering; punishing; harmful</u>_____
   _____ advising; punishing
5. **Parental figures** (m____, f_√_) are seen as <u>powerful;</u> and subject's reaction is <u>rebellion; repentance</u>
   Contemp. figures (m____, f____) are seen as_____ and subject's reaction is_____
   Junior figures (m____, f____) are seen as_____ and subject's reaction is_____
6. **Significant conflicts:** <u>between autonomy fused with aggression and compliance</u>_____
   _____

7. **Nature of anxieties:** (√)
   of physical harm and/or punishment____√____ of illness or injury_____
   of disapproval_____ of deprivation_____
   of lack or loss of love_____ of being devoured_____
   of being deserted_____ of being overpowered and helpless__√____
   other_____

8. **Main defenses against conflicts and fears:** (√)
   repression_____ reaction-formation_____ rationalization_____ isolation__√____
   regression_____ introjection_____ denial_____ undoing_____ splitting_____
   projective identification_____ other <u>identification with enemy</u>_____

9. **Severity of superego as manifested by** : (√)
   punishment for "crime"_____ immediate__√__ just_____ too severe__√____
   _____ delayed_____ unjust_____ too lenient_____
   inhibitions_____ stammer_____ delayed initial response or pauses_____

10. **Integration of the ego, manifesting itself in:** (√, √√, √√√)
    adequacy of hero_____√√_____ outcome: happy_____ unhappy____√√√____
    _____ realistic____√____ unrealistic_____
    _____ solution: adequate_____ inadequate____√√____
    thought processes as revealed by plot being: (√, √√, √√√)
    structured__√__ unstructured_____ stereotyped_____ original_____ appropriate_____
    rational_____ bizarre_____ complete__√__ incomplete____ inappropriate_____
Intelligence: (√) superior_____ above average__√__ average_____ below average_____ defective_____

Analysis Sheet for Use with the Bellak TAT Blank

S1-119AS The Psychological Corporation

13MF: This is a young man who is going to the local university . . . a student. . . . He is very moralistic . . . that is, very virtuous . . . having a highly developed sense of what is right and what is wrong. He is also very religious. . . . He has been brought up very strictly and believes that one of the greatest sins that man can commit is to have sexual intercourse with a woman out of wedlock. . . . One evening, at a party, for some unknown reason, having taken too many drinks and feeling slightly lightheaded, he became very intimate with one of the girls present. He . . . his animal instincts came to the fore and he abandoned all his ideas of virtue, etc. He took this woman up to his room and went to bed with her. The next morning, after becoming sober and having regained his virtuous sense . . . or whatever you want to call it . . . he looked over and saw this woman beside him in utter nakedness. He was filled with anger, and wild . . . let's see (murmurs to himself). . . and bitter passion at what he had done. A profound hatred swelled up in his chest for this woman that lay next to him. He ordered . . . she by this time had become awake . . . and he ordered her to leave his room. . . . She, not understanding what has brought this attitude of his about, believed that he was joking, and refused to leave in a jocular manner. . . . This man could think of nothing but to clear himself of this sin he had committed . . . cleanse himself of this sin. . . . And as this woman lay there laughing, and being overcome with his guilt, he seized her by the throat and strangled her. . . . Rising from the bed, and putting on his clothes, he became . . . he realized his predicament. He not only had committed a sin . . . a moral sin . . . but he had committed a greater sin by taking her life. . . . He gazed down as she lay there at her statuesque stillness and was filled with remorse. Remembering a few days earlier . . . that a few days earlier he had bought a bottle of iodine, and which was now in the cabinet of the washroom, he went there and gulped down its contents (laughs) and consequently died. That was the end of that. . . . I just said that he strangled her because she was laying in bed next to him, and that was the easiest thing he could have done, by reaching over and grasping her neck.

Descriptive theme	*Interpretive theme*	*Diagnostic level*
A virtuous, moralistic, religious, strictly brought up student, who considers sexual intercourse a great sin, takes too many drinks and is intimate with a girl.	If one is extremely moralistic, one considers sex a great sin which can only be committed under the influence of liquor.	Feels extremely moralistic. Severe superego. Strong guilt feelings about sex. Need for liquor. Strong oral needs. Rationalizes.
Later he is very angry at her, tells her to leave, and when she refuses, strangles her.	Thereafter one is angry at the woman, kills her	Projects (anger) on the woman. Impulse-ridden (it was the easiest thing he could have done).
Filled with remorse, he kills himself by swallowing poison.	and oneself, remorsefully in turn, by swallowing poison.	Strong intra-aggression. Oral needs.

Clinical notes

This story repeats both the orality and the fear of degeneration, as well as the strict superego. When tendencies recur several times in a story, such as oral needs in relation to drinking liquor, and again in the method of suicide, it can usually be considered an indication of the intensity of the problem.

Name_____ Story No.____4_____ (TAT Picture No.___13MF____)

1. **Main theme:** (Interpretive) If one is extremely moralistic, one considers sex a great sin which can only be committed under the influence of liquor. Thereafter one is angry at the woman, kills her and oneself, remorsefully in turn, by swallowing poison.

2. **Main hero:** age _young adult_ sex ___M___ vocation _student_____
   interests _religion_____ traits _virtuous_____ abilities _none noted_____
   adequacy (√, √√, √√√)___0___ body image and/or self-image _moralistic; degenerate_____

3. **Main needs of hero:**
   a) behavioral needs of hero (as in story): _drinking; women; aggression; intra-aggression.___
   _____
   dynamic inference: _oral needs; severe superego; strong aggression_____
   b) figures, objects, or circumstances _introduced:_ _liquor; iodine_____
   _____
   implying need for or to: _oral needs_____
   _____
   c) figures, objects, or circumstances _omitted:_____
   _____
   implying need for or to:_____
   _____

4. **Conception of environment (world) as:** _tempting_____

5. **Parental figures** (m____, f____) are seen as_____ and subject's reaction is_____
   Contemp. figures (m____, f_√_) are seen as _licentious_ and subject's reaction is _anger_____
   Junior figures (m____, f____) are seen as_____ and subject's reaction is_____

6. **Significant conflicts:** _between need for sex and superego; extra- and intra-aggression_____
   _____

7. **Nature of anxieties:** (√)
   of physical harm and/or punishment_____ of illness or injury_____
   of disapproval _____ of deprivation_____
   of lack or loss of love _____ of being devoured_____
   of being deserted _____ of being overpowered and helpless_____
   other _of sexual and oral temptation_____

8. **Main defenses against conflicts and fears:** (√)
   repression_____ reaction-formation_____ rationalization___√___ isolation___√___
   regression_____ introjection_____ denial_____ undoing_____ splitting_____
   projective identification_____ other _projection_____

9. **Severity of superego as manifested by :** (√)
   punishment for "crime" _____ immediate___√___ just_____ too severe___√___
   _____ delayed_____ unjust_____ too lenient _____
   inhibitions_____ stammer_____ delayed initial response or pauses _____

10. **Integration of the ego, manifesting itself in:** (√, √√, √√√)
    adequacy of hero_____ outcome: happy_____ unhappy____√√√_____
    _____ realistic_____ unrealistic_____
    _____ solution: adequate _____ inadequate ___√√√____
    thought processes as revealed by plot being: (√, √√, √√√)
    structured ___√___ unstructured_____ stereotyped_____ original_____ appropriate_____
    rational_____ bizarre_____ complete ___√___ incomplete_____ inappropriate_____

Intelligence: (√) superior_____ above average_____ average_____ below average_____ defective_____

Analysis Sheet for Use with the Bellak TAT Blank

S1-119AS The Psychological Corporation

The most ominous feature of this story is the afterthought that he strangled her because "this was the easiest thing he could have done." Together with the re- alistic detail and the obsessiveness, it suggests that homicidal impulses are not far from the surface in this man.

14: Well, I'd say that this takes place in Paris, just for the heck of it. . . . That the pa- pers have announced that there will be a . . . I would say that there will be . . . there will be meteors shooting across the sky on this date. This here person is a man . . . is watch- ing . . . shall we say astral displays. . . . The room he is in is his bedroom and he has put the light out to make it easier for him to see what is going on. . . . He watches for about 15 minutes, closes the window, puts the light on, and gets undressed and goes to bed. . . . And that's the end of that! . . . (resistance). . . . The way the window opened up, I always imag- ined that windows like that were to be seen in Paris. . . . I would say that before he went to the windows he was laying on the bed, reading a book, until the time came around at which time the newspapers said that meteors would be seen shooting across the sky. . . . I would say that he is more or less of an amateur astronomer and that he has a great interest in the universe and . . . let's say . . . maybe we can make something out of this after all . . . that he is working on some small job which has no future . . . that he has always been interested in astronomy, but due to the fact that his parents did not have the resources with which to send him to school, that he could not further his education in that field . . . (resistance) . . . . He has some knowledge of the stars, and this display fascinates him and only makes him yearn for that education he might have had . . . that's all!

Descriptive theme	*Interpretive theme*	*Diagnostic level*
A young man in a bedroom in Paris at night is watching meteors appearing according to sched- ule and feels small in comparison.	If one watches big things at night ap- pearing according to schedule, one feels small in comparison	Patient has wit- nessed primal scene frequently and has felt insignificant in relation to his father,
This makes him yearn for education which the parents were too poor to give him.	and feels that par- ents should have given one more (ed- ucation).	and blames his parents for not having equipped him better genitally. Information and education are given phallic significance as a powerful tool.

Clinical notes

Paris probably means sex, as in the minds of so many. The meteors probably represent a big phallus. The reference to putting the light out to make it easier to see may well relate to the fact that patient would watch what was going on between parents when it got dark. The window is probably a reference to the female sexual organ and expresses the patient's notion that such (sexual) things would only go on in other dirty places, not in the parental home. He already knows what is going to happen from past experience (the newspaper) and feels himself but an amateur working in a small job (penis) and that it is his parents' fault that they did not equip him better.

Name_____ Story No.___5___ (TAT Picture No. ___14___)

1. **Main theme:** (*Interpretive*) *If one watches big things at night appearing according to schedule, one feels small in comparison, and feels that parents should give one more (education).*

2. **Main hero:** age *young adult* sex ___M___ vocation *amateur astronomer* _____
   interests *astronomy, education* traits *curiosity* ____ abilities *none noted* _____
   adequacy (√, √√, √√√)___✓___ body image and/or self-image *small; not having enough*

3. **Main needs of hero:**
   a) behavioral needs of hero (as in story): *to watch; to acquire an education* _____

      dynamic inference: *voyeurism; exhibitionism; sexual problems; urethral problems; to be powerful*
   b) figures, objects, or circumstances *introduced:* *Paris; meteors; parents; newspaper* _____

      implying need for or to: *sex; problem in relation to parents; voyeurism (newspaper); interested in phallus (meteors).*
   c) figures, objects, or circumstances *omitted:*_____

      implying need for or to:_____

4. **Conception of environment (world) as:** *big; fascinating; depriving* _____

5. **Parental figures** (m _✓_ , f _✓_) are seen as *depriving* and subject's reaction is *yearning* _____
   Contemp. figures (m___, f___) are seen as_____ and subject's reaction is_____
   Junior figures   (m___, f___) are seen as_____ and subject's reaction is_____

6. **Significant conflicts:** *Between need for achievement and feeling of inadequacy* _____

7. **Nature of anxieties:** (√)
   of physical harm and/or punishment_____ of illness or injury_____
   of disapproval _____ of deprivation_____
   of lack or loss of love _____ of being devoured_____
   of being deserted _____ of being overpowered and helpless_____
   other *of being too small* _____

8. **Main defenses against conflicts and fears:** (√)
   repression_____ reaction-formation___✓___ rationalization___✓___ isolation_____
   regression_____ introjection_____ denial_____ undoing_____ splitting_____
   projective identification_____ other *projection* _____

9. **Severity of superego as manifested by :** (√) *not noted*
   punishment for "crime" _____ immediate_____ just_____ too severe_____
                                           delayed_____ unjust_____ too lenient_____
   inhibitions_____ stammer_____ delayed initial response or pauses_____

10. **Integration of the ego, manifesting itself in:** (√, √√, √√√)
    adequacy of hero_____✓_____ outcome: happy___✓___ unhappy_____
                                                    realistic___✓___ unrealistic_____
                                     solution: adequate ___✓___ inadequate _____
    thought processes as revealed by plot being: (√, √√, √√√)
    structured ___✓___ unstructured_____ stereotyped_____ original_____ appropriate_____
    rational ___✓___ bizarre_____ complete ___✓___ incomplete_____ inappropriate_____

Intelligence: (√) superior_____ above average ___✓___ average_____ below average_____ defective_____

Analysis Sheet for Use with the Bellak TAT Blank

S1-119AS The Psychological Corporation

18BM: This is a young man and he was formerly a successful lawyer. Then due to his bad habits . . . such as women and liquor . . . he began to . . . let's see . . . his talents began to . . . degenerate. Uh . . . He is married and his wife is beginning to turn against him. On this particular night he has . . . he is in a barroom and has become quite intoxicated. It is time for the . . . business to close and the bartender is helping him on with his coat. The man is stupified and doesn't know what is happening. The bartender, not caring what happens to him, escorts him to the door and leads him out to the street . . . where he drunkenly walks, not knowing where is going, and finally winds up sprawled out on the sidewalk where he is picked up by the police and spends the night in the city jail . . . (snickers). His wife, knowing that he is in jail . . . that is, having been informed that he is in the city jail, but refuses to pay his fine, or to aid him in any way whatever . . . (laughs). He becomes melancholy, and when he is finally let out of jail . . . knowing that he is . . . where are we? . . . let out of the jail? . . . knowing that he has been overcome by his niggardly condition, he decides to depart . . . to desert his wife and the city that he is in, and decides to go to another city to begin life anew. . . . That's the end of that!

Descriptive theme	*Interpretive theme*	*Diagnostic level*
A formerly successful young lawyer degenerates because of bad habits (women and liquor),	If one indulges in bad habits such as liquor and women, one degenerates,	Feels himself a degenerate because of interest in liquor and women.
and his wife turns against him. He is intoxicated in a bar, and an uncaring bartender sends him out	is rejected by one's wife and others,	Feels rejected by male and female figures.
and he is put in jail.	punished,	Severe superego.
His wife refuses to aid him, and he leaves the city to start life anew.	becomes depressed, withdraws, but starts anew.	Depression, withdrawal, counteraction. Oral needs.

Clinical notes

"Bad habits" refer most frequently to masturbation and resultant guilt. This story shows at least a spark of health, in that the hero tries to begin life anew, although it is not told in any convincing detail.

Name_____ Story No.___6___ (TAT Picture No.___18BM___)

1. **Main theme:** (Interpretive) If one indulges in bad habits such as liquor and women, one degenerates, is rejected by one's wife and others, is punished, becomes depressed, withdraws, but starts life anew.

2. **Main hero:** age _young adult_ sex __M__ vocation _lawyer_ ⌐ _with women_
   interests _law, women, liquor_ traits _drinking; goes_ abilities _____
   adequacy (√, √√, √√√)___√___ body image and/or self-image _degenerate_

3. **Main needs of hero:**
   a) behavioral needs of hero (as in story): _drinking; relations with women; counter-action._

      dynamic inference: _oral needs and some defensive counter-action to passivity._
   b) figures, objects, or circumstances *introduced*: _wife; other women; liquor; jail._

      implying need for or to: _oral needs and severe superego._

   c) figures, objects, or circumstances *omitted*: _____

      implying need for or to: _____

4. **Conception of environment (world) as:** _rejecting; uncaring; hostile_

5. **Parental figures** (m___, f___) are seen as _____ and subject's reaction is_____
   Contemp. figures (m_√_, f_√_) are seen as _rejecting_ and subject's reaction is _depression; withdrawal;_
   Junior figures (m___, f___) are seen as _____ and subject's reaction is_____ _counter acting_

6. **Significant conflicts:** _Between passivity and counter-action._
                                    Sex and superego

7. **Nature of anxieties:** (√)
   of physical harm and/or punishment _____ of illness or injury_____
   of disapproval ___√___ of deprivation_____
   of lack or loss of love ___√___ of being devoured_____
   of being deserted ___√___ of being overpowered and helpless_____
   other _of loss of control_

8. **Main defenses against conflicts and fears:** (√)
   repression_____ reaction-formation___√___ rationalization_____ isolation_____
   regression_____ introjection_____ denial_____ undoing_____ splitting_____
   projective identification_____ other _projection_

9. **Severity of superego as manifested by** : (√) not noted
   punishment for "crime" _____ immediate_____ just_____ too severe___√___
                                                delayed_____ unjust_____ too lenient_____
   inhibitions_____ stammer_____ delayed initial response or pauses_____

10. **Integration of the ego, manifesting itself in:** (√, √√, √√√)
    adequacy of hero_____√_____ outcome: happy_____ unhappy_____
                                                      realistic___√___ unrealistic_____
                                            solution: adequate___√___ inadequate_____
    thought processes as revealed by plot being: (√, √√, √√√)
    structured __√√__ unstructured_____ stereotyped_____ original_____ appropriate___√___
    rational ___√___ bizarre_____ complete_____ incomplete_____ inappropriate_____

Intelligence: (√) superior_____ above average___√___ average_____ below average_____ defective_____

Analysis Sheet for Use with the Bellak TAT Blank

S1-119AS The Psychological Corporation

Summary
Record themes and summarize other significant data for each story.

1. Feels strictly brought up; need for autonomy, achievement. Feminine identification—feels helpless. Fear of pregnancy. Suicidal tendencies. Strong homosexual fears. Extra- and intra-aggression. Parents seen as restrictive, coercive. Feels unhappy, physically ill.

2. Sexual needs; distinct triangular oedipal theme; jealousy. Intra- and extra-aggression. Homosexual interests. Severe superego.

3. Aggression against authority, particularly male figures. Severe superego.

4. Feels extremely moralistic. Severe superego. Strong guilt feelings about sex. Need for liquor. Strong oral needs. Rationalizes. Projects (anger) on the woman. Impulse-ridden (it was the easiest thing he could have done). Strong intra-aggression. Oral needs.

5. Patient has frequently witnessed primal scene and has felt insignificant in relation to his father, and blames his parents for not having equipped him better genitally. Information and education are given phallic significance as a powerful tool. Voyeurism. Conflict between need for achievement and feeling of inadequacy.

6. Feels himself a degenerate because of interest in liquor and women. Feels rejected by male and female figures. Severe superego. Depression, withdrawal, counteraction. Oral needs.

7.

8.

9.

10.

Ego function assessment from TAT data:

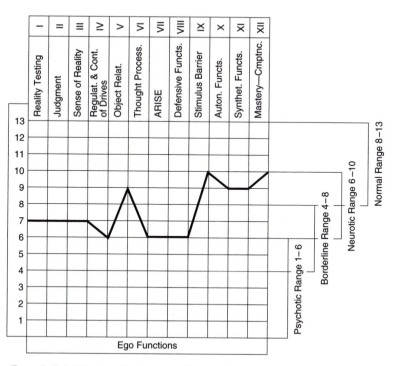

(From Bellak, Hurvich, & Gediman, *Ego functions in schizophrenics, neurotics, and normals.* Copyright © 1973, by C. P. S., Inc. Reprinted by permission of John Wiley & Sons, Inc.)

Ego functions observed during test administration:

Case 3

E.O. is a married man of 25 who came with marital difficulties as his chief complaint. He and his wife were of different religions, although this did not enter into the problems except for some difficulties with the in-laws on both sides. Both families, however, were several thousand miles away. The subject had suffered from depressive episodes of borderline nature and also from premature ejaculation. He had no specific complaints against his wife except that she was not a very good sexual partner, but he did have serious questions concerning his preference for another girl. It became clear dynamically that the other girl was probably a representation of a sister two years older than he and, in the long run, an image of his mother. Together with his ambivalence toward his wife went considerable jealousy (apparently unfounded) concerning her feelings toward other, usually older, men. At times the relationship to the wife was a clearly competitive one, with him equipping her in his fantasy with masculine features. She was in the entertainment field and he was a professional athlete.

The patient responded favorably to a 6-months' course of psychotherapy. Final diagnosis: cyclothymic personality with some tendency towards a borderline manic-depressive syndrome and pronounced narcissistic features.

For Case 3 we are using the Short Form (see also Chapter 16). The Short Form, as mentioned, is especially useful for the working clinicians. They are likely to make themselves brief notes in their personal shorthand, for which the space provided will usually suffice. In print, for public consumption, it is impossible to put all the necessary observations into the boxes. Therefore, the diagnostic theme also appears below each story, and only token references to it show in the boxes of the Blank.

The same limitations of printing versus personal notes limit the utilization of the other spaces in the Blank.

For the didactic purposes of this book, we are also reproducing the individual pages of the Long Form to allow the space necessary for printing some of the comments which might otherwise be personal abbreviations. Furthermore, also for didactic reasons, we chose some stories which by their richness allow more than an average of observations.

For those whose personal style runs counter to the small space provided in the Short Form, the Long Form remains the ideal record.

Note: All three final reports have been kept fairly brief in the interest of conciseness and because experience has shown that much longer reports are found objectionable by psychiatrists and others. Some T.A.T. workers may prefer a more rigid organization of the final report, under the specific headings referred to under "summary," namely, unconscious structure and needs of subject, conception of world and of significant figures, significant conflicts, nature of anxieties, main defenses against conflicts and fears, severity (and integration) of superego, integration of ego, diagnostic impression (this record is consistent with . . .).

SHORT FORM
BELLAK T.A.T. and C.A.T. BLANK
For Recording and Analyzing Thematic Apperception Test and Children's Apperception Test

Name _____ E. O. _____ Sex __M__ Age _25_ Date _____

Education _____ High School _____ Occupation Professional Athlete, m. s. w. d. (circle one)

Referred by _____ Analysis by _____

After having obtained the stories analyze each story by using the variables on the left of Page 2. Not every story will furnish information regarding each variable: the variables are presented as a frame of reference to help avoid overlooking some dimension.

When all ten stories have been analyzed it is easy to check each variable from left to right for all ten stories and record an integrated summary on page 4 under the appropriate headings. That way a final picture is obtained almost immediately.

Then, keeping Page 4 folded out, the Final Report: Diagnostic Impressions and Recommendations can be written on Page 1 by reference to Page 4. Page 5 gives available space for any other notations. The stories then can be stapled inside the blank against page 5.

FINAL REPORT: Diagnostic Impressions and Recommendations

The main problems of the patient are a low self-esteem and in seeing himself as an object of deprivation and aggression, as seen in stories 2, 13MF, and 18BM. He has a need to express his aggression, but there is a strong conflict in this regard and he frequently turns the aggression against himself (as in 18BM).

His oral needs are very pronounced, manifesting themselves in a need for acquisition of money and fame (1, 2, 13MF). He sees the paternal figure as aggressive and depriving. Contemporary male figures are seen as competitive, and there is a strong homosexual interest in them. Maternal figures are seen with considerable ambivalence and guilt over his aggressive feelings toward them, and also with strong oral demands toward them.

His main conflicts center around activity-passivity, the expression of aggression, and the expression of his oral demands. He shows distinct fears of physical harm and loss of love.

His main defenses are reaction formation (stories 2, 6BM, 13MF, 17BM, and 18BM) and denial (1, 6BM, and 18BM). He has an extremely severe superego.

This man's extreme narcissism is highlighted in stories 1 and 17BM. His only real need for people seems to be in their capacity as an audience. His exhibitionistic needs thus seem considerably stronger than his heterosexual needs (this is particularly clear in story 17BM, where he states that his interest is not in the girls per se but merely in their admiration of his prowess). Certainly his strong oedipal attachment impairs his heterosexual adjustment quite severely.

Ego strength is of such a nature as to enable him to tell structured, rational stories with, on the whole, perfectly adequate solutions. He deals well enough with reality problems but employs many pathogenic defense mechanisms in order to achieve some equilibrium, especially denial. He appears to be of above average intelligence with a great deal of verbal facility (approaching the verbose), inspiration, and considerable superficial affect.

The dynamic and ego psychological picture is consistent with an affective disorder without manifest psychosis.

The combination of orality, low self-esteem, and aggression against himself suggests some feelings of depersonalization, but they do not appear marked enough to constitute serious suicidal problems.

Dynamic psychotherapy centering on the problems highlighted above should offer very good chances for considerable improvement and some structural changes.

	Story No. 1	Story No. 2

1. **Main Theme:** (diagnostic level: if descriptive and interpretative levels are desired, use a scratch sheet or page 5)

> Story No. 1: Picture 1 Dissatisfied with life. Fantasizes.
> Story No. 2: Picture 2 Wants to do better than family.

2. **Main hero:** age *10-11* sex *M* vocation *musical genius* abilities_____ interests____ traits____ body image *boy feeling empty* adequacy (√, √√,√√√) and/or self-image *(violin as his image)*

> Story No. 1: Adequate on manifest level. √√√
> Story No. 2: Female 19. Student

3. **Main needs and drives of hero:**
   a) behavioral needs of hero (as in story): *to be a genius* implying: *a great musician, to be famous*

> Story No. 1: Feeling of failure, of emptiness.
> Story No. 2: Need for autonomy. Oral needs. Money

   b) figures, objects, or circumstances *introduced*: *unseen instruments, money, fame* implying need for or to: *fantasy gratification, artistic striving, need for financial and other success*

> Story No. 2: Success. Succorance. Reassurance.

   c) figures, objects, or circumstances *omitted*: *people playing the instruments, or even an audience* implying need for or to: *narcissistic gratification*

> Story No. 2: Pregnancy of older woman. Repression of sexual themes

4. **Conception of environment (world) as:** *mere backdrop for his needs*

> Story No. 2: Poor, but giving opportunity

5. a) **Parental figures** (m____, f____) are seen as_____ and subject's reaction to a is_____

> Story No. 2: Restrictive

   b) **Contemp. figures** (m____, f____) are seen as_____ and subject's reaction to b is_____

   c) **Junior figures** (m____, f____) are seen as_____ and subject's reaction to c is_____

> Story No. 2: Between nurturance and succorance

6. **Significant conflicts:** *between reality and fantasy, between strong affect, need for achievement and affection and their denial*

> Story No. 2: Contradiction of "eking out" and plentiful food

7. **Nature of anxieties:** (√)
   of physical harm and/or punishment _____
   of disapproval_____
   of lack or loss of love_____ of illness or injury_____
   of being deserted_____ of deprivation_____
   of being overpowered and helpless_____
   of being devoured_____ other *of emptiness*

8. **Main defenses against conflicts and fears:** (√)   *some secondary*
   repression_____ reaction-formation *withdrawal from people*
   regression __√__ denial __√__ introjection_____
   isolation_____ undoing_____
   rationalization_____ other *excessive fantasy*
   projective identification_____ splitting_____

> Story No. 1: Mentions "no people." Doesn't realize he is wealthy and famous.
> Story No. 2: Reaction-formation. Denial.

9. **Adequacy of superego as manifested by "punishment" for "crime" being:** ( )
   appropriate_____ inappropriate_____
   too severe (also indicated by immediacy of punishment)_____
   inconsistent_____ too lenient_____
   also:_____
   delayed initial response or pauses_____
   stammer_____ other manifestations of superego interference_____

10. **Integration of the ego, manifesting itself in:** (√, √√,√√√)
    Hero: adequate __√√√__ inadequate_____
    outcome: happy __√√√__ unhappy_____
    realistic_____ unrealistic __√√√__
    drive control_____
    thought processes as revealed by plot being: (√, √√,√√√)
    stereotyped_____ original *imaginative* appropriate   √
    complete __√__ incomplete_____ inappropriate_____
    syncretic_____ concrete_____ contaminated_____
    Intelligence *superior*
    Maturation level *immature*

> Story No. 2: Adequacy √√√ Happy √√√ Realistic √√√
> Story No. 1: Thought processes intact. Good intelligence
> Story No. 2: Thought processes appropriate and structured Superior intelligence

Story No. 3	Story No. 4	Story No. 5	Story No. 6	Story No. 7	Story No. 8
6BM Attachment to mother conflicting with marital adjustment.	13MF Feels deprived orally.	17BM Body narcissism. Exhibitionism.	18BM Need for verbal aggression.		
Young, indecisive male.	Male student.	Male athlete. Seen as skinny and funny.	Young male. Labor leader.		
To please mother and wife. Dependence on female.	For education to help wife make money	Exhibitionism. Competitiveness.	To speak truth. Sway people. Further justice.		
Problems with wife. Fear of phallus.	Implying: curiosity, nurturance. Acquisition. Poverty. Illness.	Second man. Girl.	Implying strict conscience. Wife, workers, beating. Masochism.		
			Aggression to mother. Problem with male authority.		
Pressuring. Demanding.	Depriving. Non-supporting.	Audience	Punishing. Exploiting. Aggressive.		
Mother-nagging, poor, omnipotent, aggressive.	Dead. Remorse shown.	Contemporary figures seen as competitive.	Parents seen as aggressive. Revolt.		
Anger. Remorse. Passivity.			Contemporary figures seen as passive-aggressive.		
			Reaction: aggressive-passive		
Between mother and wife. Aggression to-ward female figures.	Between aggression and guilt toward female figure.	Being strong and capable or small and funny as means of gaining approbation.	Between passivity and aggression		
Aggression. Fantasies. Guilt over anger toward mother. Fear of disapproval. Loss of love.	Physical harm. Punishment. Deprivation. Being helpless and overpowered.	Fear of lack or loss of love.	Fear of physical harm and punishment and fear of being helpless and overpowered.		
Reaction-formation. Denial. Projection.	Reaction-formation. Rationalization. Projection.	Reaction-formation.	Reaction-formation. Denial.		
Immediate. Too severe.			Immediate. Too severe.		
Happy ✓ Realistic ✓	Unhappy ✓ Inadequate ✓	Realistic ✓ Unhappy ✓ Inadequate ✓	Happy ✓ Realistic ✓ Adequate ✓		
Thought processes complete.	Thought processes structured and complete.	Thought processes structured and complete.	Thought processes structured and complete.		

3

Story No. 9	Story No. 10	SUMMARY
		1–3. Unconscious structure and drives of subject (based on variables 1–3
		A markedly oral, passive person of low self-esteem and high aspirations who reacts with a mixture of exhibitionism and mostly (secondary) narcissistic withdrawal, with similarly alternating depressive and elated moods.
		4. Conception of world: As depriving, restrictive, aggressive. Wishes it to be his audience.
		5. Relationship to others: Need for anaclitic, oral relationships. Wants to be admired and may experience some alienation. Often quite narcissistic.
		6. Significant conflicts: Between passivity and activity. Desire to be taken care of and its denial. Between aggression and superego.
		7. Nature of anxieties: Of emptiness, of inadequacy, of failure, of deprivation, and of his own (oral) passivity and homosexual concerns.
		8. Main defenses used: Reaction-formation. Denial. Rationalization. Mood swings are result of relative weakness of defenses.
		9. Superego structure: Consistently severe.
		10. Integration and strength of ego: Thought processes intact. Defenses rather weak but not enough so as to impair reality testing or judgment. Autonomous functions good. Impulse control good enough to avoid acting out. Some creative ability. Little sense of competence, or self-esteem.

Ego function assessment from TAT data:

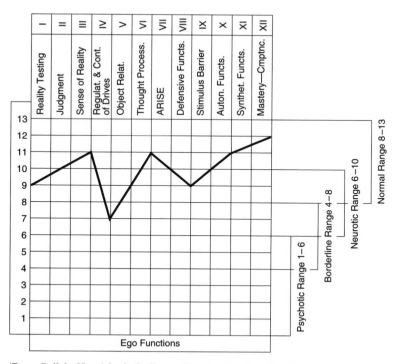

(From Bellak, Hurvich, & Gediman, *Ego functions in schizophrenics, neurotics, and normals.* Copyright © 1973, by C. P. S., Inc. Reprinted by permission of John Wiley & Sons, Inc.)

Ego functions observed during test administrations:

Summary
Record themes and summarize other significant data for each story.

1. Feels like a 10 year old boy. Dissatisfied with his life. Feels own shallow affect (poor sexual performance? mild depersonalization?). Denies being temperamental. Switches from activity to grandiose fantasies of fame in a narcissistic way. Denies interest in money. Defenses; regression, denial.

2. Need for autonomy, self-improvement. Wants to do better than family. Family seen as restrictive, later proud of one's success. Need for success, including money. Wish-fulfillment fantasies, rescue fantasies re mother. Need for nurturance, oral needs. Defense: reaction-formation.

3. Has attachment to mother, conflicting with marital adjustment. Projects own aggression toward mother on wife, rationalizing. Mother seen as nagging, poor. Identifies himself with child. Guilt over anger toward mother. Fearful fantasies of aggression (fellatio). Mother seen as omnipotent. Can feel peaceful only if conflict between attachment to mother and wife (and ambivalence toward both) is resolved. Defenses: reaction-formation, denial.

4. Feels deprived orally. Aggression against wife. Projection. Unconscious guilt feelings. Need for acquisition (money), for security. Guilt. Defenses: reaction formation, rationalization, projection.

5. Great body narcissism; exhibitionism. Little heterosexual interest. Homosexual competitiveness. Great stress on being thought entertaining. Feeling of inadequacy. Defense: reaction-formation.

6. Need for aggression denied. Sees female figure (mother?) as being against aggression, against authority. Authority is seen as depriving (inviting aggression-masochism). Severe guilt feelings. Socially acceptable aggression permissible (after self-punishment). Defense: reaction-formation.

7.

8.

9.

10.

Story 1

1: This young lad of 10 or 11 years does not know that he is a genius of the music world to come—via his violin. He has been practicing a piece of music. This particular piece does not please him. He isn't temperamental—but he puts down his violin and stares at the music—it's emptiness—just a cute little melody—no feeling —no warmth—no excitement—just an empty melody. As he sits there—he starts—in his mind—to fix it up the way he feels it should have been written—and the melody is going through his head. The way he sees it, it's very sad, but beautifully so. . . . And as he goes further on . . . different instruments join in—and very soon he has a whole orchestra in the background with the violin crying out its sad and beautiful melody—he isn't even conscious of the fact that there aren't any *people* playing—just the music and the instruments! As he grows older—he makes a name for himself in the music field—and later on, he tires of playing and starts composing the music that is constantly in his head—he becomes famous but this doesn't move him particularly—he doesn't even realize that he is wealthy—music is his life, and he is happy, because he is doing what he wants.

Descriptive theme	*Interpretive theme*	*Diagnostic level*
A 10-year-old boy is dissatisfied with his music piece, which feels empty, not warm. Stops it (though not temperamental).	If a boy is dissatisfied with his status because life is empty, cold, unexciting,	Feels like a 10-year-old boy. Dissatisfied with his life. Feels own shallow affect (poor sexual performance?) Denies being temperamental.
Fantasies writing a better one (sad and beautiful); instruments (not people) join in.	fantasies of resounding effect (without social participation).	Switches from activity to grandiose fantasies of fame in a narcissistic way.
Becomes very famous, happy with music, uninterested in money.	He achieves fame and money, without caring for the latter.	Denies interest in money and recognition.

Clinical notes

It is questionable whether one is justified in identifying the self-image with that of a boy in view of the fact that the picture actually shows a boy. However, people frequently tell stories of an adult thinking back to boyhood, thus clearly thinking of themselves as adults, and making the consideration of boyish self-imaging tentatively possible.

The repeated reference to emptiness suggests this man's feeling of emptiness, probably involving some depersonalization. The different "instruments" might well refer to the proximity of people he needs to dispel this feeling, but at the same time the shallow, narcissistic relationship to them (they exist only as needfulfilling objects) is suggested by the fact that it turns out that only the instruments themselves, without people, are playing.

Story 2

2: This girl, about 19 years old, would probably be named Olga, of Ukranian parentage and stock. For generations her family has farmed this piece of land . . . just barely eking out an existence on this tired overused land. But food was plentiful, pure, and wholesome, and they were satisfied, all, until Olga grew up. She was the first in the family to get full schooling. At first the family thought it was useless to keep sending Olga to school, year after year—there was so much work to be done, and at 13 she was almost full grown—but Olga wanted to study and learn more. Finally they conceded, and four years later it was with pride that they watched their Olga graduate from the town school! It was indeed difficult to allow her to go to school all these years. Of course she helped after school hours, but that wasn't enough. And now, now Olga wanted to go to Normal School to become a teacher! This was ridiculous—but—finally, after Olga showed them how, in another two years, she would graduate and get a job earning a hundred dollars a month as a teacher, they gave in again. We see Olga coming from town—Normal School! It is almost sunset—and as she comes across the field, she sees her brother, stripped to the waist, tilling the land, and her mother, tired and with an aching back from seeding—resting for a moment—Olga sees this and turns away for a moment—she hates to see them slave, just to eat and sleep. . . . Soon, she thinks to herself, "I'll be earning money and we can buy a tractor—with automatic seeder . . . and there are many kinds of farm equipment that could make work easy, and do it quickly; maybe we'll buy the adjoining piece of land and start making a living instead of an existence." She walks over to her mother, takes the seeds from her, and starts seeding. . . . Her mother, now holding Olga's books, looks at her young educated daughter, who is bent over covering the seeds with the earth, and a light shines in her eyes, as she thinks, "Good, she is not spoiled, my daughter with her books—soon she'll finish and all will be well"—and turns to go down to the house to prepare the evening meal!

Descriptive theme	*Interpretive theme*	*Diagnostic level*
A girl of simple European stock wants to study and improve herself. Food important.	If a girl wants to do better than her family by studying (though having enough food?),	Need for autonomy, self-improvement. Wants to do better than family. Oral needs.
At first the family objects but then concedes and watches her succeed with pride.	the family first objects, then concedes, and is proud of her success.	Family seen as restrictive, later proud of one's success.
The girl sees the family toil, dreams of helping them, and actually relieves mother of work.	One feels sorry for the family, fantasies of helping them, and actually helps mother.	Need for success, including money. Wish-fulfillment fantasies, rescue fantasies re mother. Need for nurturance.
Mother is happy about her and prepares a meal.		Oral needs.

Clinical notes

It is frequent for males to identify with the female figure in this picture, so that this by itself does not permit any particular inference. The need for success and money is repeated here, this time without denial of the latter. But denial appears in the contradiction of "eking out" and plentiful food. The need for nurturance (Bellak, 1950a) may simply stand for need for succorance.

This is a rather verbose, lively story of cheerful mood, probably typical of the somewhat hypomanic mood the patient was in (as compared with the meager, constricted, brief, often merely descriptive stories of obsessive-compulsives, for instance). This story is also to a certain extent autobiographical in that the patient did come from immigrant stock and helped support his family.

Story 6BM

6BM: This is an old folks' home, and the young man is visiting his old mother. She was only to have stayed for a short while. Till he had moved his family to the new house. . . . Then, when he thought of bringing his mother to the new home . . . his wife had started talking. . . "Grandma was spoilin the kids . . . She kept everyone awake with her nerve-wracking cough, and she was very untidy, and made so much extra cleaning work around the house." . . . At first, the young man was shocked to hear his wife speak that way of his mother . . . he wouldn't think of letting her live in the old folks' home. . . while he had a new house with plenty of rooms in it . . . but . . . after a few weeks . . . he got used to hearing his wife speaking in this manner . . . and he wasn't shocked to hear the words, but he was still upset about his mother living in the old folks' home. . . . His wife was stubborn and insistent . . . there wasn't anything he could say or do that would change her mind, well . . . there wasn't much he could say now . . . he was tired . . . she kept yelling and making scenes. . . . So finally one day he went to see his mother . . . to tell her . . . the easiest way he could, that it was inconvenient for them . . . for her to live with them . . . After much hemming and hawing . . . he finally blurted out his case. . . . The mother is very hurt, she sees how difficult it is for her son, and for his sake tries to make it all sound very trivial . . . and actually she likes it at the home! . . . But the man can see through her kind but obvious front. And finally the mother starts talking . . . about how you bring children into the world . . . and no matter how much they love you . . . and no matter what they try to do for you, you always feel that you are unwanted . . . and yet . . . what can an old woman with no income do? The man is feeling very bad . . . his little old mother going through all this pain because his wife didn't want to clean an extra room! He is disgusted with himself for not being man enough to make his wife take his mother in . . . and at the same time he is angry with his mother for making it so difficult for him.

Well, time wore on. The grandma would come to the house Sundays . . . play with the kids . . . enjoy their laughter and their tears. Stay for Sunday dinner, and around about eight . . . the son would drive her to the home.

About six months after the above incident . . . on a Sunday . . . they were having fish for dinner . . . when suddenly . . . one of the children started coughing and spluttering . . . everyone started pounding him on the back . . . the young mother started getting hysterical . . . and the father kept yelling. "He's got a bone stuck in his throat." . . . The child started getting blue in the face. The grandma ran into the kitchen . . . went to the bread box . . . took a piece of stale bread back to the choking child, put a good-sized piece of stale bread in his mouth . . . told him to chew it a couple of times, and then swallow . . . no matter how difficult. . . . The child by this time was almost unconscious but, hearing its grandmother's calm voice it did as it was bid . . . and the bread forced the bone down . . . and the child was all right, 'cept for fright. . . . The young mother looked at the man . . . who was her husband . . . and said. . . . "If it weren't for your mother's old-fashioned remedies . . . we might have lost our son. I could feel what it was like. I know how she must feel . . . living away from you . . . us . . . now! I think I can manage to clean one more room . . . !" So, the grandma moved back.

Descriptive theme	*Interpretive theme*	*Diagnostic level*
There is a conflict between hero's mother and wife. Hero gives in to wife, and mother has to move to old folks' home.	If there is a conflict in one's loyalties to mother and wife, one reluctantly gives in to wife	Has attachment to mother conflicting with marital adjustment. Projects aggression toward mother on wife, rationalizing.
Mother feels son is ungrateful. He doesn't dare stand up to wife and is angry at mother.	and rejects mother, who complains about it.	Mother seen as nagging, poor. Identifies himself with child. Guilt over anger toward mother.
When mother saves life of grandchild when it has a bone stuck in its throat, wife and mother make peace.	If there is trouble with the child (who has object stuck in throat), mother helps. If mother and wife can be reconciled, all is well.	Fearful fantasies of aggression (fellatio). Mother seen as omnipotent. Can feel peaceful only if conflict between attachment to mother and wife (and ambivalence toward both) is resolved.

Clinical notes

This story is most illuminating with regard to the subject's chief complaint of marital problems. Obviously, he is as ambivalent toward his wife as toward his mother and denies both. His relationship to the latter interferes with his relationship to the former. In his oedipal wishfulness, the father is out of the picture. Probably as a punishment both for his oedipal wishes and also because he conceives of the mother as a somewhat phallic woman, the phallus gets stuck in his throat. Making this happen to his own child removes the full impact from himself.

The story of the bone is not unlike the apocryphal story of the origin of the Adam's apple—the forbidden (sexual) fruit getting stuck (Bellak, 1942). It implies a breast-phallus equation. The Kleinian school would speak of the "bad breast." The child is a secondary identification figure. The solution of the conflict between the two women by the bone incident, and the solution by the bread, are somewhat of the nature of a *deus ex machina* solution.

Story 13MF

13MF: This scene takes place in a small room of a tenement house. Very poor people . . . young—students. The betterment of the mind means so much to them. They have starved to go to the university. . . . Sometimes working at nights . . . so . . . they can afford to go to school in the day. They have known each other since childhood, and as they grew older, married and, having much in common, lived happily though precariously, sometimes not having enough for food, most of the time dressed very poorly. This winter was very cold . . . the girl's coat was very thin . . . and somehow she must have caught a cold. . . . The boy, her young husband, finds her in bed shivering. . . . "What's the matter?" he asks. "Guess I caught a bit of a chill," she answers. He feels her brow and she is very hot! He becomes alarmed and says, "I'll go get a doctor!" . . . "I'll be all right, don't bother." . . . He sits by her side, and talks to her, to keep her company . . . besides, he has no money for a doctor! After a while he notices that she hasn't said anything for quite some time . . . he shakes her, but she is unconscious . . . he becomes frantic, and runs out to find some doctor, but the doctor down the street is not in his office . . . and he runs back to the room. The girl has pushed the covers partly off of her, in her fever, and her full round breasts are exposed . . . he leans down to talk to her . . . he sees . . . she is not breathing . . . ! So quickly life goes . . . he doesn't know how long he has been sitting by the small bed . . . he gets up . . . and calls the police . . . ! Heartbroken . . . he is determined . . . "To hell with education! Money is what counts! If we had had money . . . she wouldn't have died!" . . . He leaves school . . . goes into the world . . . amasses a fortune after a time . . . but, he has not peace of mind . . . money can't buy that!

Descriptive theme	Interpretive theme	Diagnostic level
A poor starving girl dies because husband cannot afford a doctor.	If one is poor, one has to let one's wife die,	Feels deprived orally. Aggression against wife. Projection.
He calls police.	calls the police,	Unconscious guilt feelings.
Heartbroken, he makes much money without peace of mind.	makes much money, is disturbed.	Need for acquisition (money), for security. Guilt.

Clinical notes

Again, the acquisitive needs, denied in the first story, come out here strongly, very often feelings of material deprivation stand for a feeling of being deprived of love. In this story reference to starvation clearly refers to oral deprivation.

The unconscious guilt feelings over unconscious aggression are demonstrated by his calling the police.

Story 17BM

17BM: The boy or young man on the rope is a gymnast . . . takes great pride in his muscles and ability. . . . Today some girls came in to see the men working out . . . and this particular boy was doing everything to appear the hero and strong man in their eyes . . . not that he cared particularly to meet the girls . . . it's just that he wanted them to see that he is the best around. While he is doing all this showing off . . . a small, thin chap with glasses . . . and a portfolio joins the girls, and they all turn eyes on the muscular young man. He smiles to himself and he takes a running leap at the hanging rope and shinnies up like Tarzan, and starts doing all sorts of difficult feats, one-arm planches, dislocations, and so on, for about five minutes, and then he looks at the group that were watching him, and sees that they (the girls) are laughing at the little fellow, who is trying to lift a huge weight . . . and being very funny about it. The muscular one comes down the rope, watching as he descends. "Why should they choose to look and laugh with the skinny, scholarly chap, when I was being so sensational!"

Descriptive theme	*Interpretive theme*	*Diagnostic level*
A young man with great pride in his muscles and ability shows off to girls to impress them as being best.	If one shows off with great pride in one's body, it is narcissistic more than heterosexual.	Great body narcissism; exhibitionism. Little heterosexual interest.
At the same time a thin scholarly fellow makes them laugh, and the muscular one feels the other is stealing the show.	The girls may prefer a funny scholarly chap.	Homosexual competitiveness. Great stress on being thought entertaining. Feeling of inadequacy.

Clinical notes

This story probably reflects a double identification, in that inquiry revealed that the subject thinks of himself both as muscular and, on the other hand, as too little. The other stories, too, show his need to be considered scholarly. His actual appearance was that of a small, inoffensive man, whereas he was a professional athlete. This theme is also related to competition with a brother three years older and has much to do with the patient's homosexual competitiveness with other men rather than genuine heterosexual interest. This man sees people primarily as an audience. His only object cathexis is an anaclitic one. The laughter which the second identification figure arouses was one of the patient's most important conscious needs (getting the laughs).

Story 18BM

18BM: His wife always said . . . "You can't step on peoples' toes . . . and not expect to get hurt yourself!" And he would answer, "If telling the truth . . . if honesty is stepping on peoples' toes, then I damn well am going to step on plenty of toes!"

This afternoon . . . during the lunch hour in the factory . . . he had a bunch of the workers gathered round him . . . and was explaining to them . . . the way the economic system worked. How they . . . the workers were browbeaten . . . how the people with money . . . made more money by making them work like slaves . . . for little more than slave money. That the worker had no chance for security in his old age . . . working conditions weren't even good. . . . Look at the way they had accidents, because the power machines didn't have protection screens around them . . . the bad lighting, etc. . . . etc. . . . One of the foremen overheard this and went to the boss' office . . . and told what he had heard.

That night, as he was walking down the dark street that led to his house . . . a car drove alongside, and some men jumped out . . . something hit him on the head . . . he was dazed by the blow . . . then he was hustled into the car . . . driven out to the country and beaten up. It was four o'clock in the morning by the time he got home . . . sick and sore in his body. . . . He knew why he was beaten up. . . .

The next day, although it was an effort for him to go to work . . . he went . . . his face all swollen . . . his body sore and wracked with pain. . . . His fellows started asking him questions . . . and he said . . . "You all know me. I have no enemies. I think I am well liked . . . yet last night coming from work . . . I was set upon by some thugs . . . thoroughly beaten . . . and apparently left for dead. It couldn't have been thieves . . . because they didn't try to take anything from me . . . and they kept shouting as they were kicking and punching me 'This oughta teach you to keep your mouth shut . . . you lousy communist!' . . . You see, it was for what I have been speaking to you about that I was beat up! . . . I must of said some very true things for them to try and shut me up . . . !" The workers asked . . . "What are we going to do?" . . . and he answered . . . "What they have done to ME is not of great importance . . . but WHY they have done it is! So, we must organize . . . a union . . . and force them to our demands!"

The workers organized . . . and started making small demands at first . . . until they forced the bosses into making their shop . . . clean . . . safe . . . and better wages. This showed the way . . . and very soon the other shops followed . . . and at least now, the workers live like humans. . . .

Descriptive theme	*Interpretive theme*	*Diagnostic level*
A man tells workers they are being abused, even though wife says this might lead to harm to himself.	If one is verbally aggressive against authority against a female's advice	Need for verbal aggression. Sees female figure (mother?) as being against aggression against authority.
Someone informs on him and he is severely beaten.	one is severely harmed by agents of the authority.	Authority is seen as depriving (inviting aggression—masochism). Severe guilt feelings.
Thereupon he leads the men to organize a union.	but then leads men to successful modified counteraggression.	Socially acceptable aggression permissable (after self-punishment).

Clinical notes

The female figure is certainly unexpectedly introduced here. The exploiting authority is probably an image of the parents. The whole story shows this man's problem with aggression, his turning it against himself, and his ability to express it only in a modified form after he has been punished.

CHAPTER 7

SOME CLINICAL AND OTHER SPECIAL PROBLEMS OF THE T.A.T.

On Diagnostic Groups

The T.A.T. facilitates assessing the 10 different categories of personality functioning of Bellak's Scoring System, as well as contributing to the assessment of verbal language, neuropsychological, and other dimensions. Although it is clear that no single test is ever sufficient in making an overall psychological evaluation, there is a question whether it is possible to diagnose psychiatric disorders from the T.A.T. alone.

Some individuals may reveal deep pathology, such as a suicidal level of depression, on most of the stories of the T.A.T., while their Rorschach, projective drawings, and other tests may appear fairly intact. Other individuals may not show any severe pathology on the majority of T.A.T. stories, but reveal deeper issues on only one or two stories. Our assumption is that the less structured and more ambiguous the test stimuli, such as the Rorschach inkblots, the more people are able to let go and reveal their deepest levels of psychopathology. If a patient is schizophrenic, the assumption is that the more structured stimulus of the T.A.T. will tend to show more ego structure, while the less structured Rorschach will reveal the patient's poor reality testing, poor level of self-object differentiation, and breakthrough of poorly controlled primary process sexual and aggressive impules.

Generally, an individual's T.A.T. protocol will show a higher degree of ego control and ego integration than will the Rorshcach. If one has a very good, ego-enhancing day when the Rorschach is administered and a very upsetting experience when the T.A.T. is administered, we expect that the test given on the very bad day will show a lower level of ego functioning. Similarly, we expect an intellectually gifted schizophrenic woman to show a higher level of functioning on cognitive intelligence tests than she might reveal in a series of her dreams. In making a diagnostic evaluation, it is important to consider the level of structure of the different tests, the situational factors surrounding the times the tests were administered, and if there are a number of corroborating indicators of a particular dynamic or only a limited number.

Pam and Rivera (1995) have presented a very thought-provoking and moving exception to these basic assumptions. After administering a psychological evaluation of a man who was hospitalized on a psychiatric ward, the psychologists recommended that he not be released in the near future, which led him to commit suicide. The patient's severe degree of dangerous aggressive imagery on the T.A.T. was the primary basis for their recommendation. The two authors have many years of experience in psychology internship training and their paper is an important teaching case on the issues of having sufficient data on psychological tests upon which to base one's diagnosis, the psychologist's responsibility to make difficult recommendations, when there are clear signs that the patient's and other individuals' safety is involved, and the importance of reexamining one's actions when there have been tragic outcomes in a patient's care.

All too frequently, the opposite situation is the case. It is more typical for a psychologist to have administered a T.A.T. toward the beginning of a lengthy treatment process, where core problems and conflicts become very clear in the treatment process that may not have appeared with such clarity in the beginning T.A.T. protocol. For instance, the entire treatment of one male patient of 20 years old centered to an unusual degree around one focal sadomasochistic fantasy. That fantasy existed when the patient was 5 years old, with him in the passive role. He was healthy enough to switch to a more active, masculine role by the time he was age 12, but the fantasy was, in essence, the same (instead of being kidnapped, he became the kidnapper). In the course of nearly three years of intensive psychotherapy, the treatment process managed to identify the most detailed features of the fantasy and various pictorial aspects could be identified with specific places, dates, and occurrences of several years of his life. This fantasy has layers like the trunk of a tree. Nevertheless, only a glimmer of this fantasy occurred in the man's T.A.T.

The intensive treatment, of course, did not merely consist of working on this one fantasy. On the contrary, the fantasy was pieced together only in the midst of all sorts of other more or less relevant material. And the T.A.T., of course, showed his anxieties, and that he used avoidance as a main defense mechanism; this very fact led to the suspicion, on first studying the T.A.T., that there must be more there than appeared in the stories.

It may be that the mechanism of denial is particularly pernicious to securing projective data. This is, of course, the mechanism of choice in manics, and therefore many of our examples come primarily from that group, although not exclusively. (The previously mentioned patient had a character disorder, and most patients referred to here were seen in private practice, while they were carrying on gainful activities and were certainly not psychotic.)

When the mechanism of avoidance is used, the T.A.T. material may be long and apparently very rich, yet it will defy analysis. This is, of course, the experience with any form of output of *manics* or *hypomanics*. Fortunately, at least one story usually turns out to contain the real core, while the others have such an overgrowth of defense that it requires very special pains and an awareness of the centrifugal nature of the material to be able to use it. With manics and other predominantly oral character disorders, a most useful story may be one told to picture 11. The theme of devouring, which this Boecklin picture suggests, contains precisely the stimulus to which this group respond. The defenses revealed by the T.A.T. are identical with those appearing in free associations and in dreams. Those patients who give the most frustrating T.A.T. stories may spend hours on seemingly irrelevant material and recount long, involved dreams more suitable for Hollywood scenarios than for analysis.

However, the T.A.T. is very useful in revealing an individual's underlying psychodynamics. It shows the ambivalence, the exhibitionism, and the fear of aggression in *agoraphobics,* as well as the figures against whom the aggression is directed. A posteriori, one may identify all the component parts that belong to the diagnostic picture. An exception may be the quantitative aspects; as in dreams and fantasies, it is difficult to appraise the strength of the variables involved, and it is difficult to predict whether they are strong enough to turn up as manifest syndrome formation. The study of defenses, however, may be more possible. There have been a number of records, particularly of the C.A.T., where one may successfully predict *anorexia* as a clinical syndrome, although at times only a detailed consideration of the defenses permit us to differentiate between overeating and anorexia.

These observations are entirely in agreement with the excellent theoretical formulations that Sargent (1953) presents in her pyramid of diagnostic inference (Figures 7–1 and 7–2). She states that after a consideration of the raw data of the tests comes a level of generalization; then a second inferential level of theoretical interpretation; and only then a third (abstract) inference as to the classificatory diagnosis. She demonstrates the overlapping of the two levels of inference for two (or more) diagnostic labels.

It is clear that the identifying features of psychodynamics and character structure are revealed in the T.A.T. Within limits, one can often make statements about the diagnostic group to which a patient belongs from a T.A.T. protocol.

Not infrequently, one will notice that *obsessive-compulsives* give their attention to small details in the pictures, and they will often respond with more than one story to a picture. We may also find that the storyteller stays distant and expresses sarcastic attitudes toward the hero, remaining emotionally isolated himself or herself (Finn, 1951). In *hysterics and hypomanics,* on the other hand, we find a great deal of affect and a lively identification with the hero.

Manics will often indicate strong tendencies of oral incorporation; very many references to food and getting things may appear (although this is, of course, not pathognomonic at all). Again, in *depressed patients,* suicidal themes, a depressed overall mood, and self-depreciation, along with other signs of a very strong superego, may be apparent (Shneidman & Farberom, 1958; Valentine & Robin, 1950b).

Following is the story of a manic-depressive girl in remission, illustrating the oral tendencies with three references to eating in a brief story. The picture (11) frequently elicits reference to food; stories of attack are often integrated with this theme:

> This picture takes place in Texas about 5,000 years from now. Civilization is extinct. An atom bomb has killed everyone, and the whole earth is beginning again. The remains of civilization are the Spanish arch in the right lower corner. On the top are a few birds looking for food. There's a mountain on the left side, and from a cave a sort of snake-bodied, duck-footed animal is wiggling out. He's going to strike the birds, eat them, and then go merrily on his way looking for more food.

In the T.A.T. stories of *psychopaths,* one usually finds little punishment for any aggressive act engaged in by the hero in the story, evidence of a weakly integrated

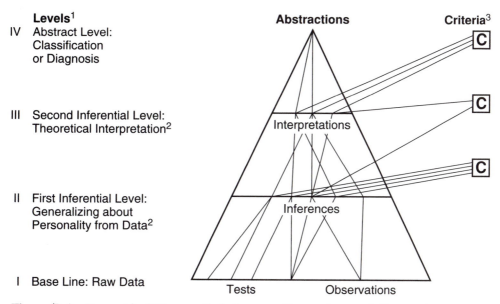

Figure 7–1 Pyramid of Diagnostic Inference, Reasoning, and Abstraction

Source: H. Sargent, *The Insight Test* (New York: Grune & Stratton, 1953). Reproduced by permission.

[1]Level I. Test scores, patterns, scatter, quantitative and qualitative signs (perceptual distortions, peculiar associations, content, over- or underresponse, etc.).

Level II. Identifying characteristics: overalert, complaint, rigid, naive, anxious, disoriented, etc.

Level III. Postulated mechanisms and processes such as projection, repression, regression, denial, isolation, introjection, etc.

Level IV. Categories such as neurosis, psychosis, schizophrenia, hysteria, obsessive-compulsive; "good" or "poor" candidates for profession, employment, etc.

[2]Intrinsic validity established by convergence of independent judgments.

[3]External validity established by pre- or postdiction of events or conditions from tests and observations checked against criteria (C). Sample criteria: life history, course of illness, progress in therapy, vocational adjustment, experimental behavior, etc.

superego (see stories of Streicher later in this chapter). Several other studies have noted similar T.A.T. characteristics of psychopathic defective criminals (Kutash, 1943) and of juvenile delinquents (Megargee, 1966a, 1966b; Purcell, 1956; Young, 1956).

There are other cases where we would like to be able to make real inferences—for instance, if the potentiality (or actuality in the past) of antisocial acts exist—and we wish to help predict future behavior. One such case occurred when the senior author (Bellak) was asked to help determine whether a young boy should be released from an institution. He had killed a small child, apparently in some sexual excitement. Institutionalized, he was a model inmate on a behavioral level—bland, noncommittal, and inaccessible to psychotherapy. At the time of commitment and again when he came up for disposition at the end of a year, he was given the T.A.T. and other tests by the staff for help in understanding his problems. When none of the tests threw any light on the psychodynamics of the crime, he was referred to the senior author for the administration of a T.A.T. under the influence of intravenous

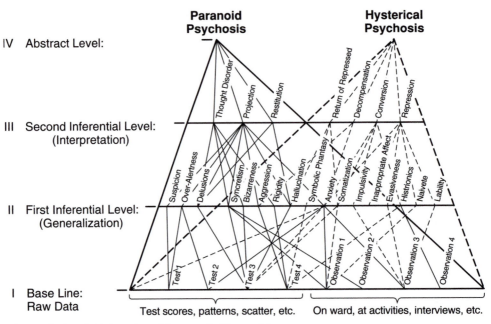

Figure 7–2 Overlapping Diagnostic Pyramids

Source: H. Sargent, *The Insight Test* (New York: Grune & Stratton, 1953). Reproduced by permission.

Solid lines represent, for one case, the derivation of inference from raw data, interpretation from inference patterns, and abstraction from interpretations subsumed under the finally selected label. Dotted lines represent the same sequence for a second case. Note that a single first-level inference (e.g., anxiety) may be based on data from several tests and/or observations and that a single test score may lead to more than one inference (e.g., test 3, perhaps the Rorschach). The interpretation that projective defenses are operating derives from not one but several inferred characteristics. Likewise, the diagnosis of paranoid schizophrenia or hysterical psychosis depends on a combination of theoretical interpretations or conceptualized processes.

Amytal Sodium. After the intravenous administration of 7½ grams of Amytal Sodium and 1½ grams of Nembutal orally, a marked psychomotor effect of the drugs was noted: general relaxation, drowsiness, slurring of speech, and occasionally such lack of motor control and sleepiness that the T.A.T. cards dropped out of the young boy's hands. Despite the action of the drugs, the boy gave 15 stories that, in no single instance, revealed any primary pathological evidence in the theme itself that would have permitted one to pick out his T.A.T. as belonging to a noticeably disturbed person.

However, although it was impossible from his T.A.T. stories to predict his actual behavior, small breakthroughs of original impulses came to light. For instance, he made one slip of the tongue in the following story to picture 8BM:

These two boys have gone out hunting. They shot a lot of boys—I mean, animals, and decided to split up to get more pheasants. They agreed to meet at 8:30 at night to count the game and to go home. This boy was standing in the bushes. Twenty feet from him he heard something move. He goes to look at what he caught and finds his friend and rushes him to the doctor. The doctor says the boy will be all right, and in the end the boy gets OK and forgives him for what he did.

The slip betrays the apparently original aggressive impulse that becomes absorbed in a perfectly acceptable hunting story, then breaks through again in the boy's injury. An inquiry into the small detail of 8:30 at night revealed that that was the time for lights out at the institution and strongly suggested that it was at this time that his fantasies were permitted to emerge. Similarly, he started his story to picture 1 by saying:

This boy does not like to practice his trumpet—I mean he likes to play his violin.

He changes a negative response immediately to a positive one. The story he gave to picture 15 is as follows:

An undertaker; he is very sad because he is putting to rest all these people. He goes out one night and looks with remorse at all the work he has done. He tries to find out how he can undo his work. He can do nothing about it.

In this story, the undertaker behaves as if he had killed all the people he buried, revealing the original aggressive impulse only by what would otherwise be incongruent guilt feelings.

There are other T.A.T.s of murderers that present similar problems. A woman who had previously attempted to kill her sleeping children by stabbing told the following story to 3BM:[1]

Is this a girl? I think it's a girl; she seems to be crying; leaning against a bed. At her feet I think there's a gun. Well, it looks as though she had planned to use the gun and instead of doing so had fallen asleep. (?) Probably planned to shoot someone with it. (?) Well, a neighbor perhaps that she didn't like. (?) No one would know that but herself—can't imagine what reason you'd have for it except disliking them, maybe. I don't think anything will happen. She'll have changed her mind by the time she's more rested.

Although, like all this woman's stories, the content is innocuous in that nothing actually occurs, and it would be impossible to make any concrete predictions as to her behavior, certain things do emerge. The effect in this story is grossly inappropriate: a girl who had planned to shoot someone falls asleep instead. An active impulse is easily replaced by a passive one. There appears to be not particularly strong reason for the planned shooting of the neighbor except a vaguely expressed dislike. The story she tells to 13MF is in some ways reminiscent of those of the boy murderer:

There's a picture of a young lady in bed and a man standing with his arms across his eyes; seems to be walking away from the bed. Seems to me the lady has died and he is remorseful; seems he is in a shock state of remorse over her death. (?) Nothing to indicate it wasn't from natural causes. (?) Husband; he'll have to go on alone.

Although the woman in the picture died from natural causes, the husband is in a "shock state of remorse" over her death. (This resembles the undertaker in the previous story who is remorseful over the people he has buried.) In this story, there seems to be a clearer aggressive impulse and its denial.

---

[1] Courtesy of Ms. B. Guttman, of the Psychology Department, Queens General Hospital, N.Y.

Psychiatric Differentiation

Although attempts at psychiatric differentiation with use of the T.A.T. have been unsatisfactory in general, a good deal of recent work has supported our contention that various diagnostic groups differ clearly in certain of their ways of responding to thematic stimuli. In a study of psychoneurotics, Foulds (1953) found that *hysterics* started stories more quickly than depressives and told longer stories at a quicker pace. *Depressives* produced more illness themes to picture 3GF than hysterics, who produced more themes involving quarrels. Davison (1953) has described differences among certain diagnostic groups in the terms of the kinds of interaction described in their stories. He concluded that *anxiety reactives* produced a significantly greater number of themes of "man moving toward man, the depressive reactives of man moving toward woman, the hebephrenic schizophrenics of man moving against man, and the catatonic schizophrenics of no relationship between man and woman."

There have been only a few studies of thematic test characteristics of individuals who are *mentally retarded* (Hurley & Sovner, 1985; Montague, Jensen, & Wepman, 1973; Upadhyaya & Sinha, 1974). They mostly focus on the tendency to use concrete description of the picture stimulus, inflexible stereotyped narratives, and a paucity of words. Chapter 12 discusses thematic test studies of *borderline patients* (Brelet, 1986), Rogoff (1985), and Western (1991a, 1991b) and of *narcissistic patients* (Abrams, 1993a, 1995; Brelet, 1981, 1983, 1986, 1994; Harder, 1979; Shulman & Ferguson, 1988; Shulman, McGarthy, & Ferguson, 1988). Chapter 13 discusses thematic test characteristics of children and adults with *attention deficit disorder* (Abrams & Bellak, 1986 edition of this text; Costantino et al., 1991).

An important area of thematic test research is that of *psychological trauma studies*. From Haworth's (1964b) important study of the thematic test characteristics in children who suffered the death of a parent, the emphasis in later research has been primarily on thematic test characteristics of children and adolescents who have been the victims of child neglect, physical abuse, or sexual abuse (Henderson, 1990; Hoffman & Kuperman, 1990; Kalaita, 1980; Miller & Veltkamp, 1989; Ornduff et al., 1994; Ornduff & Kelsey, 1966; Stovall & Craig, 1990).

The T.A.T. with Schizophrenics

Theoretical stress on the role of power concerns underlying paranoid symptomatology led Wolowitz and Shorkey (1966) to study power themes in the T.A.T. stories of *paranoid schizophrenics* and other psychiatric patients. Paranoids' stories contained significantly more power imagery than those of the nonparanoids. Subdividing the nonparanoids into different diagnostic categories, it was found that paranoids were most highly differentiated, in terms of a greater number of power themes, from patients classified as anxiety neurotics, psychophysiological reactions, and nonparanoid schizophrenics.

Karon's (1963) hypothesis, drawn from clinical experience—that mothers of schizophrenics are unable to meet the needs of their children and use the children to meet their own needs by manipulating their behavior—has been analyzed by means of the T.A.T. Mitchell (1968) has demonstrated that mothers of schizophrenic children can be differentiated significantly from mothers of normal children on the basis of T.A.T. responses. The criteria used for the successful differentiation supported Karon's (1963) hypothesis; if there was an interaction between a dominant and dependent individual and the dominant individual did not meet the specified needs of the dependent individual or met his or her own needs at the expense of the dependent individual, the story was scored pathogenic. Most mothers of schizophrenic children received higher pathogenic scores than control mothers.

Contrary to findings by Rapaport (1946), and in partial agreement with Eron's report (1948), schizophrenia does not appear to be easily diagnosed as such from the T.A.T. We are speaking here of the *ambulatory schizophrenics* one sees as they come to private offices. Rapaport's signs probably hold true primarily for hospitalized schizophrenics, where there is such manifest pathology that one would hardly need a T.A.T. to make the diagnosis. However, in a considerable percentage of even ambulatory schizophrenics, one may find ample indications of the severe disturbance in the T.A.T. stories. These indications may be either stories of bizarre content that did not appear in ordinary communication, such as John Doe's reference to "reading without eyes" in his story to picture 1 in Chapters 6 and 11, or very blatant symbolic expressions suggesting a closeness of the unconscious to conscious awareness far beyond the ordinary. *Thought disturbances* may become apparent in T.A.T. stories, when they are not discernible in conversation or in interviews. Certain signs may also be considered as suggestive, but not conclusive, indicators—for instance, reference to deadness (e.g., with regard to the violin in story 1, and ruins and destruction in story 11). This type of response suggests a reflection of intrapsychic consciousness of lack of affect severe enough to be consistent with the diagnosis of schizophrenia. Other studies of T.A.T. characteristics of schizophrenics is the tendency to avoid the nuclear family (Alkire, Brunse, & Houlihan, 1974), the family research of Werner and colleagues (1970), the case presentation of Piotrowski (1950), and the study of changes in T.A.T. stories at different points in treatment (Goldman & Greenblatt, 1955).

One may, however, find these signs or criteria in the records of adolescents or artists who are not schizophrenic insofar as one can determine. Following are good examples of stories given by a latent schizophrenic artist who was referred for somatic complaints. After fairly short-term psychotherapy, this man is now able to lead a happy and productive life. Since he is an artist, the grossly bizarre nature of his stories was influenced by his lack of conventionality and, possibly, a somewhat tongue-in-cheek attitude. Here is his story to picture 7BM, which he entitled, "Don't Kiss Me Any More":

Papa, your moustache, with its horrid, dirty color, feels unpleasant against my cheek when you kiss me. In fact, I feel uncomfortable when you come too near. Why don't you embrace a bush, it has the same texture? And don't give me your old philosopher's look, your philosophy is not objective enough, it's only based upon your own shortcomings and frustration, which all hark back to the fact that you were abnormally kind to your mother. And so Papa takes the son's advice and goes in the backyard to a bush, but finds that it is his own father.

Following is his story to picture 11:

Liberatus has just flown from the womb which hangs lazily on the castle ramparts, swinging in the breeze. He dashes over the bridge pursued by three horrible mammoth turkeys, with beaks lined with alligator teeth. The bridge expanse between them crumbles, dashing the turkeys against the rocks below. Temporarily safe, he looks back at the womb and it now appears as a tremendous tongue with four webbed feet. But his safety is temporary, for his supposed refuge ahead is the City, gleaming not from the sun but from heavy phosphorus powder, which having been put layer on layer on the outside of the building, appears sponge-like, and when viewed closely is not glamorous but dusty and deadish. The heroic view of the city from this distance is indeed deceptive.

The subject reported many dreams just like this story. His story to picture 12M follows:

The son with his sensuous upper lip drawn up, his feet languidly held apart, and his hand close to his genitals, seems to be in the midst of a very pleasant dream. The old man motions and chants, believing he has induced this dream and sleepy state. As the old man turns, one sees that he has no facial features. He wants the young man to awaken now, so he can suck some of his youth from him, vampirish or something like that. The old man feels that then perhaps he will have a face again. But when the young man finally gets up, he kicks the old man down and walks away.

An absence of facial features is another schizophrenic sign.

Story 13MF:

The young woman stands nude on the model stand. But she is without detail, no facial features, no teats, no fingernails. The artist first paints small circles on her breasts of a very beautiful color, a wonderful coral, like the color in some shells he brought from Acapulco. But as he paints in more details, she becomes less, rather than more, lifelike and finally falls down flat as if she were an unsupported mannequin. The artists feels very tired and sick in the stomach; all this work for nothing. He goes out into the streets and sees all his fellow mannequins mechanically moving about.

An indication of emotional impoverishment consistent with schizophrenia may be seen in the "mechanically moving about."

Story 17BM:

Mike Jensen is climbing the thousand-foot rope that leads, though he does not know it, to Hell. He pauses on his ascent in the arena, as he notices a woman sitting in the second balcony, feet wide apart. Why is man always attracted to frustrating glimpses of women's thighs and hairy organs, when women happen to be a bit indecorous in the way they sit? Needless frustration, must train oneself not to be diverted by such things; the only worthwhile thing is the whole salami.

So upward he goes again, but he slips when he unexpectedly comes to some thorns interwoven in the rope. And as he slips down the rope at a terrific speed, he is split in half, as he lands in the sawdust of the arena, he appears as two sides of a cow, newly delivered to the butcher, and waiting to be put in the icebox.

But some people like warm meat; and just as spectators break from the bleachers to uproot the football goals, many people with grotesque ape-like faces rush to rip at the red-purple meat.

The utter cruelty and bizarreness are again very suggestive and a strong indication of a schizophrenic process. An example of thought disturbances in the T.A.T. of another latent schizophrenic is the following story to 17BM:

The man is climbing up the rope. There is a crowd chasing him. He is viewing something. Might be looking out to sea. Looking for a boat to come in. He'd be one of the men to bring in the cargo. He's alongside of the building. People are chasing him because he is on the side of a building. He is in a hurry—he is in a funny position. People are mad at him—has no clothes on. Walking around the streets naked. He is some character in history. Brutus. He wouldn't be looking for a boat after all—just fleeing from the crowd. They are after him. He took their money—he wants to get rich all of a sudden and retire. He gets away—does not look worried. Gets on top of the building. Gets on the road and gets away. He has no money with him—so he gets away somehow without the money.

In this story one may see some incoherence, some non sequiturs: "People are chasing him because he is on the side of the building."

Another example of a schizophrenic who, in the course of time, made a serious suicidal attempt, may be seen in the following stories:

Story 1:

. . . Broken violin . . . sick boy . . . unhappy boy . . . lonely boy . . . Outcome should be successful . . . could be competent violinist. May I ask, is there a time on this? *(None)* . . . *(What led up to?)* Well, he may have lost his mother—or his father. . . . Either of which may have been violinists. . . . Is that enough? . . . The alternate is suicide. . . . That's a problem which he will have to face himself.

Story 3BM:

(Long initial pause) It appears like—appears that this picture represents—a deformed person—possibly a hunchback . . . depressed and—contemplating what to do about his dilemma . . . As in the first picture, this problem is unresolved. I mean by that—it could be successful in that an adjustment can be made to his deformity . . . or . . . the alternate course of action. (Returns picture.) *(Which would be?)* Suicide.

The "broken violin" and the "deformed hunchback" suggest extreme disturbances of self-image. The mention of suicide in a relatively inappropriate context forecasts the future development.

Adolescents

The T.A.T. stories of adolescents deal with stage-related developmental conflicts of separation versus individuation, dependency versus independence needs, loyalty to the peer group versus the desire to be unique, and the struggle with emerging feelings of sexuality (Bachtold, 1977; Brody & Siegel, 1992; Cooper, 1977; Dana, 1986; Henry & Farley, 1959a, 1959b; Megargee, 1966a, 1966b; Neman, Neman, & Sells, 1974; Oz, Tari, & Fine, 1992; Porter, 1990; Sheikh & Twerski, 1974; Teglasi, 1993). The full-length book clinical presentations of T.A.T.'s of adolescents in Brody and Siegel (1992) and Teglasi (1993) are especially recommended for the in-depth discussion of typical adolescent characteristics on the T.A.T. The one drawback of Teglasi's interesting book is that she confines her use of thematic tests to the T.A.T., even with young children, while Brody and Siegel's important developmental study more appropriately employs the C.A.T. with the same research participants when they were children and the T.A.T. during their adolescence.

The majority of the adolescent T.A.T. studies stress the typical reemergence of the preschool conflict of separation/individuation and oedipal conflicts, as in the following story of a 13-year-old boy to picture 5:

(Long pause) I am trying to figure the thing out. Well, she could be either calling a member of the family or investigating a noise she's heard in this room. The light's on. Looks to me like she's showing a little bit of the element of surprise. She's surprised. A little bit of fright mingled in with this. Surprise and fright mingled in. As if maybe she heard a burglar downstairs in the house. The way it's drawn she's tensed up in a way. As if ready for sudden action. Might be that there's a burglar in the house. She's calling somebody in the house. She could be calling one of the children or her husband. Or she heard this noise, came downstairs, found this burglar in the house. Doesn't quite know what to do. Been taken by surprise. Doesn't know whether the burglar will kill her or not—like most people who own their own homes, and burglars enter. Don't know whether the burglar will kill you or not. Most burglars carry guns or a blackjack to knock you out. Burglar overpowers her and takes valuables, or her husband comes down and overpowers the burglar.

In saying, "She could be calling one of the children or her husband," he really asks whether he or the father would be the rescuer of the mother; also either the father or he could probably be the burglar. Judging by associations to the story in the last two lines, we have a choice of his being the burglar and taking the valuables or the father coming down and overpowering him. This story represents variations on the classical rescue fantasies. It also illustrates the most frequent dynamics behind burglar fears, and makes use of the classical symbolism of robbery of valuables from a woman as a representation of sexual drives.

Similarly, story 11 of another adolescent boy of age 18 shows the paranoid-like fear of the father figure who has always "bested him":

. . . Some surrealistic painter's idea of a fleeing individual chased by a number of goblin-like monsters led on by another person, possibly it's—a—sna—possible escape of this man being chased will be of no avail. He's just going on and on into everlasting nightmare. . . . By the appearance of the. . . . Man's touch has been around here . . . through the bridge, road. Must be a nightmare, then, of some human—because in the dream man's influence has shown itself in the bridge and the road. Possibly the dreamer is seeing himself chased into an eternity that there was no hope to escape from. Perhaps he was just fooling himself that getting away from these things for a while would make him safe. I suppose he hasn't given up life or thoughts of a better life because he hasn't given up running away from these evil things. Maybe the man behind these ghoul-like things is a person he fears or hates—some strong emotion between him and that man. Feels that he's been persecuted all his life by this man and has spent his whole life running away. Possibly this man driving the beasts has bested him in business deals or in the choice of a mate. . . . he's always had the upper hand. On the other hand, it may be his own reflection on himself that he—during his life has persecuted some individual and—a—is repenting or seeing himself as a chased individual sees himself. The man whose mind is reflected in being the pursuer, he may because of his dastardly deeds be a washout or disintegrate because he feels sorry for the other man. And the other man, after seeing himself in actual life being treated the same way he is, in his dreams, probably finally gave up trying to escape some relationship that will never end; just continue on till he dies; just gave up all hope.

Another case of an adolescent girl (Bellak, Levinger, & Lipsky, 1950) permits us to demonstrate the value of the T.A.T. for studying small developmental changes in a personality. A 16 ½-year-old girl was seen in a social agency and given a T.A.T., a Wechsler-Bellevue Intelligence Test, the Goodenough Drawing Test, and the Bender Gestalt Test. At that time, the girl was found to be an essentially normal adolescent with a compliant attitude toward a mother seen as benevolent, though somewhat domineering.

Eight months later, the girl returned to the social agency because of a minor emotional problem. At that time, a psychiatric interview substantiated the impressions gained from the various tests. However, since the girl had suffered quite a traumatic experience since the administration of the test, a second T.A.T. was administered by a different examiner to ascertain whether there were any new dynamic developments. It was noted in the psychiatric interview that the girl now described the mother as somewhat more domineering—the description may have had some basis in fact, related to the mother's entering into the menopause.

The first and second T.A.T.s were compared; they were then shown, independently, to two psychiatrists and to three classes on the T.A.T. that the senior author was conducting. These classes contained 110 students, most of whom had acquired a Ph.D. and many of whom were practicing clinical psychologists. In all cases, the two T.A.T. records were shown for blind comparison; the judges were told that these were T.A.T. records of the same person, given on two different occasions. They were not told which test was given when, nor what happened in between. The results were unanimous; the second record was identified as having been given later and was thought by the judges to have been administered after psychotherapy. They pointed out changes in the direction of maturation in the second record.

It must be emphasized that the subject had not received any psychotherapy and that the changes noted by the judges confirmed our personal impression of this girl's spontaneous emotional growth over a critical eight-month period, as reflected in the difference in the two T.A.T. records. The slight emotional disturbance for which the girl returned to the agency seems to have been incidental to this developmental process and disappeared promptly.

Following are four stories from each of the two T.A.T.'s administered, which are representative of the changes discussed.

Picture 1, boy with violin:

First record of T.A.T. See a boy at the fiddle; doesn't look very happy; seems to be sad. Don't think he wants to play fiddle, though mother must want him to. I think mother wants him to for his education; wants him some day to be a violinist, but he doesn't want to by looks of this.

Second record of T.A.T. This is a boy looking at a violin. There is a sheet of music. He is thinking if he can play or not. I imagine he likes to play. He asked his mother for a violin and is thinking about it now. He played and became great. He looks very interested in it.

In the first record, one sees the hero compliant to the mother, unwillingly and unhappily. In the second record, there is an independent striving, interest, the mother seen as giving. The tone is happier, though self-criticism has entered in it.

Picture 14, silhouette at window:

First record. Picture of fellow looking at stars or moon; must be thinking of someone he loves, or perhaps his mother; likes to be with her; seems lonesome; might be far away from home somewhere. That's all.

Second record. This is a boy looking out of a window. It's dark out. He is looking at the stars and sky. He is thinking of his future; of opening up a business—or what he's going to do. He is thinking of his girl and home, and is peaceful. Maybe he got what he wanted, a happy life today, a happy home.

The first record shows dependence on mother, longing and lonesomeness.

The second record shows a very similar story, but the hero is peaceful, planning for the future, with independence and heterosexual gratification (even though the hero is still a male).

Picture 17GF, a girl on bridge.

First record. This picture looks as if by the river and men are working there. Girl leaning over bridge and she must be dreaming that someday her boyfriend, off to war, and someday he would come home. That's about all. *(What sort of girl is she?)* Looks to be nice, sits home and waits, wouldn't go out with other fellows; she must love him very much.

Second record. This is a river scene, down South. I'd say a girl is on a bridge. It's a nice day and men are working. She's dreaming; looking out on water.[2] Must have someone on seas—husband, or boyfriend and she's longing to have him near her and see him again, to have him safe. He comes home and she sees him once more and they're happy.

Again, the two stories are extremely similar. But in the first record, it all stays on the fantasy level, and there is no resolution. In the second record, a happy solution of the same problem is permitted on the reality level.

Picture 20, man by lamp post:

First record. Man by a light; seems to be waiting for someone; seems to be impatient; seems to be waiting for fiancee and they can't see each other. Waiting for another man. The reason he may not be able to see his fiancee, for mother forbids it. *(Why?)* She may not like him and so they have to meet on corners. *(Why doesn't the mother like him?)* Bad disposition or different faith. *(How does the girl feel about this?)* Girl likes him very much and doesn't care what the mother says, but she doesn't want to hurt mother so sees him on the side. *(What is the outcome?)* In the end, she realized that he is bad for her and listens to her mother.

Second record. He is waiting for his girl to come down. She is someone he loves. Her mother may not approve of him and they have to meet outside. They love each other deeply. They meet on street corners. In the end her mother realized that they love each other and grants their wish that they want to be married. Her mother disapproves of him because he might be of a different faith, might not have job, or be of a different class than she.

In the first record, mother is seen as a barrier to the hero's psychosexual adjustment and the girl complies with her mother's wishes, which she identifies with her own advantage. In the second record, the mother is still seen as disapproving but her approval is no longer essential for the hero, who is more autonomous now, and, by implication, more attached to the heterosexual object than to the mother. Here, the mother subsequently grants her approval, and the person has thus achieved a synthesis.

The Influence of Contemporary Events on the T.A.T. Stories

Bellak's (1944) doctoral dissertation study under Murray at Harvard dealt with the experimental situation of artificially introducing aggression in subjects by provoking them or giving them posthypnotic orders to feel aggressive. Therefore, when these subjects were asked to give stories to the T.A.T. pictures, it became ap-

---

[2] Any reference to water or fire in T.A.T. (or C.A.T.) stories suggests a history of enuresis. Empirically, this correlation has thus far been 100 percent in cases where inquiry was possible.

parent that they would project some of the aggression into the stories. Split-half comparisons between five stories told under these circumstances and five stories told without induced aggression, however, showed that the main personality characteristics persisted despite the artificial situation that was introduced. To a large extent, the subjects would differ in their manner of handling the problem of aggression, expressing it either as extra-aggression or intra-aggression, or reacting with guilt feelings, and so on. This study was successfully replicated nearly a half century later by Cramer (1991b).

On another occasion in a similar manner, Bellak (1944) studied depressive feelings and joyfulness induced by means of hypnosis. Again, the effect on the T.A.T. stories was such as to leave the essential personality structure intact. In an experiment by Coleman (1947), an attempt was made to gauge the effects of a pleasurable, optimistic movie on the T.A.T. stories of children. Of all the stories obtained from the 37 children tested both before and after the movie showing, only one story (out of a total of 370) seemed clearly to reflect the content of the film. A grim real-life situation provided us with another more reliable opportunity to study the effect of current experience on T.A.T. stories. Julius Streicher and Alfred Rosenberg were given T.A.T.s in Nuremberg prison at the time of their trials. The tests were given in German and then translated as carefully as possible.[3] Both men were in prison at the time, after the failure of what to them was a life's work, awaiting a nearly certain death at the gallows. Since their T.A.T.s have no specific outstanding merit in and by themselves, for the sake of brevity only a few illustrative stories will be presented from each record.

Streicher[4]

Julius Streicher probably deserved more than any other top-ranking Nazi the clinical diagnosis of psychopathy (in the sense of a person with an undeveloped superego). His newspaper, *Der Stuermer*, was full of perverse, pornographic literature and pictures. He pulled out men's beards and engaged personally in whippings and other expressions of sadism and uninhibited impulses. His intelligence was the lowest of all the Nazis tested at Nuremberg. Below are presented four of his T.A.T. stories.

3BM: Kurt Heinz is the only son of the manufacturer Grundher. Just as the proverb says, "one child is a misfortune," so it turned out to be in this case. All of Kurt Heinz's wishes were fulfilled both by his father and his mother. There was nothing denied him. He was both Mama's and Papa's boy—but an unfortunate child. Although his father told him: "Kurt Heinz, never take the revolver I have in my night table," the spoiled child did what he had secretly decided to do. While the father and mother were going walking, he took the revolver

---

[3] The tests were given by Dr. G. M. Gilbert (1947), in his official capacity as Army Prison Psychologist at Nuremberg; he reported on his experiences elsewhere. We are greatly indebted to Dr. Gilbert for making these T.A.T. records available.

[4] Reprinted by permission of the *Journal of Projective Techniques*.

out of the bedroom, and said to his friend Lothar: "Stand against the wall, I'll put an apple on your head and I'll play William Tell. Stand against the wall. You will see, nothing will happen. I'll shoot the apple off your head." Kurt Heinz suddenly realized the consequences of disobedience. Greatly disturbed and repentant, he waits for the return of his parents with the determination to tell his father: "Father, you were right when you warned me. I have learned enough from this moment to last me a lifetime. Father, I promise you, you will never have any more trouble with me."

4: He is an artist. His model is sitting half naked on the sofa. Suddenly, the door opens and his girlfriend surprises him in his studio, having just returned from a vacation and surprised him in this intimate episode in the studio. "Why do you do this to me?" she says to him. "Didn't you promise to think only of me, when I left you? Didn't you say, when you kissed me good-bye, that I am the only girl in your heart? Speak, why do you turn away? Can't you look me in the eye any more?" His eyes turned far away and he said: "I did not want to be unfaithful to you; I fought against it—but some demon in me caused me to forget for a moment—only for a moment. We'll talk about this later. Go now. Leave me alone with the girl. I'll talk to her and explain how this came about and why it had to be this way." After the model left, the young painter knocked on the door of the adjoining room and said: "Now we can talk." He looked at her with a penetrating look, as if to say, "We don't have to talk—you understood me when you left." She gave him both hands, and said to him, "My dear friend, I feel that I have not lost you. You are alive in me, and will always be in me. Your love excuses the moment you forgot me." *(Now let loose and tell me what you really think.)* Of course, she is a mulatto; the artist is a fine type, with bright eyes and blond hair, is surprised by his mulatto lover at the moment that a blonde, blue-eyed Nordic girl came to pose for him. The mulatto makes accusations that he is two-timing her with the blonde. He is silent—if he were to talk, he would say, "I loved you only with lust. There is blood in you which prevents me from possessing your soul. Blood attracts blood. My true love belongs to the blonde girl, with whom I wanted to enjoy this hour."

5: The woman opens the door and says to her snoring husband: "Come on, the food is on the table." But the man says: "As long as I am eating, please stay in the kitchen, because when I see that face of yours I lose my appetite."

8BM: There was a duel. The two men had fought over a woman. Two doctors are busy trying to get the bullet out of the wounded one's body. The victor turns away from the operation and looks thoughtfully into the distance. He knows that he was the guilty one and his bullet had apparently killed an innocent man. He is thinking about it—self-accusations about the injustice of fate in this duel. He says with bitterness: "It's a terrible thing that I, the guilty one, am victorious, and the innocent one, who had a right to kill me, had to lose his life."

Streicher's story to picture 3BM shows the hero engaged in a forbidden aggressive act—endangering his friend with a pistol. It is unclear from the story whether he actually wounds or kills his friend. If the latter, the story is certainly remarkably shallow with regard to punishment. Even if the implication is that he only used the forbidden pistol without causing physical harm, the repentance is shallow and without punishment (e.g., even a disciplinary measure by the father). In this, the theme differs markedly from similar stories of neurotics or well-adjusted people, who may express various forms of retribution or remorse; the hero might be punished by the parents or by the police or court, or the hero might be considering suicide and might even think of a variety of ways of apologizing and attempting to console the victim.

Story 8BM shows a similar theme. Against the background of an oedipal theme, the hero appears guilty and yet, in the duel, is permitted to kill the innocent man without punishment or consequence except some very superficial verbalization in the form of a monologue. We have found in past experience (Bellak, 1952e) that the relationship between a crime committed in the stories of the T.A.T. and the punishment meted out to the guilty one by the subject is an excellent measure of the strength of the superego. The more severe the punishment in relation to the crime, the more severe a superego we deal with, and vice versa. In the case of Streicher, we can certainly say that the punishment is much less than to be expected by any civilized mores and thus can conclude that he hardly suffered from a severely controlling superego.

Similarly, in stories 4 and 5, we can observe the aggressive, unkind, primitive attitude toward women and the utter lack of feelings; he uses a glib rationalization for his unfaithfulness by ascribing it to some demon within him—a not infrequent mechanism in young children (particularly postencephalitic ones). His attitude toward women in story 4 leaves room for speculation about his possibly identifying Jews with them—seeing them as an inferior race—and its ultimate relationship to his feelings about his mother, but this is outside our present frame of reference.

Rosenberg

Alfred Rosenberg was the original theoretician, or rather, the mythologist, of the Nazi party, of Aryanism and racialism. He emphasized the cultural values of early Germanism, urged a return to the pre-Christian religious cults, and a love for unadulterated nature. In conflict with other Nazi leaders, he fell into disgrace years before the final debacle. Below are seven of his T.A.T. stories.

3BM: This is a woman who has had little happiness in her life and had no pleasure in her work. She has fallen in love with an adventurer, full of fantastic hopes. She clung to this last hope of her womanly existence and sacrificed all her savings to him. When the lover began to notice that her money was becoming exhausted, he began to desert her until she finally realized one day that he had left her completely. When she realized this, her last hope was lost and she just collapsed. This moment is represented in the picture. It shows a woman who is not beautifully built, with ugly hands and fingernails, crying on the sofa. She is middle-aged and has no further hopes.

7BM: In a popular restaurant, a carefree young man gets acquainted with a man of the world. The old man sees a new victim in the young man. He introduces the young man into a circle of young adventurers and adventuresses. In the course of time, the young man drinks and gambles his fortune away so that he finally must tell the old man that he is no longer in a position to continue this wild life. At this moment, the friendship of the old man ceases and he considers whether to leave him for good or to advise him to get money by underhanded means. The picture shows the scheming old man and the disillusioned young man at this moment.

9BM: An adventurous youth gets tired of his home. The peaceful existence in his mother's home has become boring. He decides to go bumming and see life in the raw. On the way home, he runs into a vagabond party. A Negro who has run away from his boss and other similar characters are looking for jobs with little work and good pay. The young man joins this trio; they do some work on farms along the way and the young man notices that each time they leave a place, they take something with them. But that was not what he left his home for. He finally decides that adventuring doesn't have to be combined with stealing and such things. On a hot afternoon, all four lie down on the grass for a rest. . . . The three tramps fall asleep and our young man now has time to look them over. He decides that they are rather brutal company with whom he could not live very long. He gets up slowly as they lie there snoring and decides to look for better company for his adventurous spirit.

10: A loving mother notices how her daughter has become gradually estranged from her. All her admonitions to be careful in her selection of friends are laughingly rejected. The estrangement between mother and daughter becomes greater and greater. The daughter trusts herself entirely to her lover and ignores all warnings from her mother. One day, the daughter realized that her friend has left town without saying a word. She learns from her friend that he does not intend to return but has left for a foreign country. Betrayed in all her hopes, she returns to her mother. The latter receives her with understanding and love. This is the moment of the expression of motherly love, with an attempt to show that the daughter intends to be more careful in the future.

12M: In a little town there lived an old man who had all kinds of mysterious magnetic and telepathic powers. It was said that he could often, though not always, produce cures by this means. One day he is asked for help by a worried mother. She tells him of her son who has recently become somewhat mentally disturbed. He suffered from attacks of mental depression. Little incidents appear to him like the persecution of bitter enemies and he has become quite sick and desperate. The old man follows the woman to her son. He sits at his bed, listens to the young man's stories, and then strokes him gently on the temples. At the same time, he explains all these incidents in a calm manner and in a short time the boy falls asleep. The next day, he wakes up refreshed and after some further visits the anxiety actually disappears and he can again associate freely with his friends.

17BM: The acrobat is pulling himself up for his trapeze act. At the other side of the circus he sees an old colleague doing a new stunt. He holds still for a while and watches this new stunt. His attitude is half wonder and half jealousy. He grasps his rope more tightly and says to himself, after watching a while, that he could never perform such a stunt with all his strength. Thus depressed, he climbs down again and refuses to perform any stunts that day.

19: A schoolboy had many friends who were artistically talented. One was musical; another had written some stories. And so the boy was also inspired to take up some form of art. He tried painting. Since he could not succeed in spite of all efforts, he took lessons from a well-known painter, in order to be able to compete with friends. He pursued this study with great interest and, just as his friends indulged in fantasy on the piano, he wanted to make pictorial compositions. He painted clouds and waves. But when he finished a painting like that and showed it to his friends, he got only a storm of laughter. It was evident that, without talent, even painting was a book with seven seals. That was probably the story of the man who painted this picture.

In story 3BM, Rosenberg identifies with a girl who has fallen in love with an adventurer who promptly deserts the girl and leaves her depressed.

Story 10 is a repetition of this theme, with the one addition that the mother is left by a hapless girl who, however, returns to the understanding maternal care after having been left by the faithless man. Story 7BM is only a slight variation of the theme in that a young man comes under the spell of a ruthless adventurer who is about to desert the youngster as soon as he has been fully exploited. In story 9BM, the hero leaves what is specified as his *mother's* home, for bad company, with which he soon becomes disenchanted.

In these stories it appears that Rosenberg identifies himself with a girl, or a young man, seduced and exploited and betrayed by a figure that one must strongly suspect of representing Hitler himself. Aside from the feminine-homosexual relationship of Rosenberg to Hitler, which these stories suggest, it becomes apparent that our subject had a strong mother fixation. A tone of depression and hopelessness can be noted throughout all responses. The bad company that the hero gets into in 9BM probably represents the Nazi party, for the plundering and brutality of which our subject expressed belated disdain.

Story 12M again shows the general tone of depression, with awareness of a mental disturbance in the hero, and a wishful ending. This is the only story in which a male figure is seen as benign; it must be pointed out, though, that even here the male is helpful only through the instrumentality and care of the mother. Story 17BM also shows hopelessness and depression in a competition that may well refer to the higher star of Joseph Goebbels. Story 19 speaks of a young man who tries to learn from a well-know painter in vain. It is most likely a repetition of the themes of the earlier stories, Hitler being the house painter and erstwhile illustrator of picture postcards who achieved quite some notoriety. The bitter criticism, at the same time, against the unsuccessful painter we may surmise to be directed against Hitler himself, in a not unusual condensation of the theme and the main identification figures.

Streicher appeared in the T.A.T. as a man of great physical and verbal aggressiveness and with primitively lustful and despising attitude toward women. At the same time, he showed an absence of superego functioning consistent with the diagnosis of psychopathy. Rosenberg appeared markedly depressed. He seems to have had a passive homosexual attachment to Hitler, identifying himself twice as a girl in this relationship. He also reveals a strong fixation on his mother.

Both men were in jail, expecting to be hanged, with all their desires and hopes doomed. Even so, our brief and simple analysis of their T.A.T. records shows widely differing personalities despite the overwhelming contemporary situational factors to which both were equally exposed at the time of the administration of the T.A.T. The stories not published are consistent with this statement except for the fact that some depressive overtones also appear in some stories of Streicher, although mostly as superficial religious speculations.

These T.A.T.s, then, we believe, throw some light on the much-discussed point of the possible invalidating influence of contemporary situational factors on the overall validity of the T.A.T. While the current mood of depression enters into the stories of both men, there is nevertheless evidence to show that clearly different personalities emerge; the essential character structure revealed is consistent with the historically known facts about these two men, and may be taken to represent the more stable, permanent, and significant features of their makeup. Thus, the influence of contemporary situational factors does not seem to affect the validity of the T.A.T. as a method of clearly demonstrating the essential dynamics of personality. Furthermore, these two T.A.T. records confirm previous work (Bellak, 1950c) which showed that such current experiences as experimentally provoked anger or depression (Bellak, 1944) did not disadvantageously affect the fundamental validity of the personality structure revealed in the T.A.T.

The Problem of Overt and Latent Needs in the T.A.T.[5]

The interpreter of T.A.T. stories is frequently presented with the necessity of deciding whether a need expressed pertains strictly to the fantasy level or might be

---

[5] See Chapter 2.

expressed in reality—for example, the need for aggression or for achievement. The psychologist should have available a maximum of clinical and biographical data about the patient. It must be kept in mind that the clinical situation is not one concerned with testing the validity of the instrument. Problems of the validity of the T.A.T. are dealt with in experiments and must be decided there. If one has sufficient information on the patient, then the T.A.T. stories must be seen as complementary to the behavioral data obtained. For example, if the subject is unduly shy and retiring and the stories are full of aggression and guilt feelings, the dynamic implications are obvious.

On the other hand, there are certain indications from intra-test situations that permit us to make assumptions about the manifest or latent needs expressed in the T.A.T. For instance, in stories of achievement, it is extremely important to notice whether they follow the *deus ex machina* mechanism or are actually accomplished piece by piece, suggesting much more that they correspond to a behavioral need for achievement.

It was R. N. Sanford who pointed out some important rules concerning the relationship between fantasy needs and behavioral needs. He suggested that there are certain needs that are usually high in fantasy and low in behavior—namely, those needs that are usually prohibited and inhibited by cultural pressure from overt manifestation. These are mainly the needs of acquisition, aggression, autonomy, and sexual activity; the wish to be taken care of; and the need for harm avoidance— the last two suffering more cultural repression in men. On the other hand, some needs may find little manifest expression in fantasy but much expression in manifest behavior because of reality demands, such as the need for order, for avoiding social blame, for learning. Again, there is a class of needs that may be high both in fantasy and in behavior, indicating that, while these needs are permitted and encouraged socially, they may yet be sufficiently frustrated to need particular gratification of the fantasy level. To these belong especially the needs for achievement, for friendship, and for dominance.

The study of the defenses as a means of linking the latent and the manifest is of signal importance (see Chapters 6 and 9). Again, it must be emphasized that the T.A.T. should be used to complement behavioral data; only in specific instances is it necessary or desirable to use the T.A.T. for the prediction of overt behavior. For these cases—personnel studies, appraisal of suicidal tendencies, or likelihood of overt extra-aggression—the internal evidence of drive versus defense must be weighted apart form manifest behavior.

Psychosomatic Disorders and Thematic Tests

There has been a considerable upsurge of the interest in the use of apperceptive techniques for exploring psychosomatic disorders (Cabras et al., 1983; Blumenthal et al., 1985; Hoffman & Kuperman, 1990; Silva, 1985; Viberg et al., 1987). This may be a time for cross-fertilization of all the fields concerned with psychodynamics and it may behoove physicians and pediatricians to acquaint themselves with treatments of the apperceptive techniques, certainly in simple ways more accessible than the Rorschach to anybody who can make any dynamic inference.

Distorted notions of illness and medical procedures may be illuminated in simple projective techniques, and thus make the patient more accessible and cooperative. This plays a specific role in liaison psychiatry—where the task is to understand the patient in his or her illness very promptly and arrive at useful insights very promptly.

In a study by Silva (1985), the Rorschach and the T.A.T. of two groups diagnosed with duodenal ulcer were compared. The initial aim of the paper was to verify if the Rorschach and the T.A.T. could discriminate between the group whose ulcers healed after one month of treatment and the group whose ulcers did not heal or had reappeared. Factor analysis of the correspondent results suggested that the Rorschach tends to discriminate between them and the T.A.T. does not.

In the same paper, a sample of responses characteristic of boys and girls to the C.A.T.-H were studied. The stories told to C.A.T.-H by 50 boys and 50 girls, from 6 to 10 years old, were analyzed in reference to apperceptive and thematic data. Significant differences of such data in boys and girls were found in each of the 10 cards, and occasionally consistent in more than 1 card. The assumption of sex-related patterns of response was discussed.

Aaron (1967) was able to determine several personality differences between asthmatic, allergic, and normal children using T.A.T. responses. Some of the obtained differences were: Asthmatics showed significantly more hostility than normals on a measure of hostility relating to card 3; asthmatics showed significantly more disturbance with the parent of the opposite sex than did normals, but none with the parent of the same sex; and asthmatics and allergics both indicated general feelings of loneliness and rejection by the parents significantly more than did normals.

Other studies of thematic tests of individuals with somatic conditions include that of Cabras and associates (1983) of *ulcerative colitis* patients, Blumenthal, Lane, and Williams (1985) of *cardiac patients,* Greenbaum and colleagues (1953) of *physically handicapped children,* Holden (1947) of *children with cerebral palsy,* and Viberg, Blennow, and Polski (1987) of *epileptic adolescents.* Valuable research on T.A.T. characteristics of *substance abusers* is Brelet (1988) on alcoholics, Cabal Bravo and colleagues (1990) on heroin addicts, and Fassino and associates (1992) on the image of the self and the environment in substance abusers. A related study by Volhardt and associates (1986) finds signs of *alexithymia* in patients with *rheumatoid arthritis,* which is the tendency to blunt the expression of affect.

CHAPTER 8

USE OF THE T.A.T.
IN PSYCHOTHERAPY

Special Therapeutic Uses of the T.A.T.[1]

Test responses are forms of behavior of the patient, like any other forms of behavior except that the responses are made to standard stimuli and thus permit controlled comparisons from one person to another. Furthermore, the content that appears in psychological tests may demonstrate fantasies and psychodynamics, which even a skilled psychoanalyst will not anticipate or suspect after many months of psychoanalysis. Many years ago, a training analyst permitted the senior author to administer the T.A.T. to a patient of his who volunteered to participate in the investigation. The analyst agreed that the T.A.T. pictures brought out important features that had not become clear during almost a year of psychoanalysis. Ethel Tumen Kardiner, in an unpublished study, was able to demonstrate experimentally with the cooperation of a number of psychoanalysts and their patients that the T.A.T. could successfully illustrate the psychodynamics that had become clear only after prolonged analysis. From the standpoint of planning treatment, it is useful to obtain as much advance information as possible.

The T.A.T. is of particular value as a vehicle of the psychotherapeutic process itself, especially in cases where therapy must of necessity be short term, in emergency situations (self-endangering or extremely crippling depressions, or acute anxiety), or in social agency settings, clinics, and the like (Araoz, 1972; Bellak et al., 1992; Hoffman & Kuperman, 1990; Meyer, 1951). Bellak, Pasquarelli, and Braverman (1949), Meyer (1951), and Rosenzweig (1948) have suggested ways the T.A.T. may be employed with patients in regular individual psychotherapy. Araoz (1972) showed how it may be useful in marital therapy. Hoffman and Kuperman (1990) suggested how a discussion with patients in psychotherapy of repetitive themes in T.A.T. cards may be useful in pointing to a history of trauma, and Bellak, Abrams, and Ackermann-Engel (1992) outlined steps in utilizing thematic tests to obtain a quick view of psychodynamic issues in brief and emergency psychotherapy.

The type of patient encountered in any of the preceding situations is frequently quite naive about psychotherapy and entirely unaccustomed to the thought processes involved in it. Patients may consider their complaints to be organic or en-

---

[1] The T.A.T. may be especially useful in Emergency Psychotherapy and Brief Psychotherapy (see additional references, Bellak & Small, 1965, and Bellak, Abrams, & Ackermann-Engel, 1992).

vironmentally caused, since they are quite unused to any degree of objective intro-spection.

In such cases, one very important use of the T.A.T. is to help patients *gain some "distance" from themselves* and to establish the *psychotherapeutic attitude*. Adolescents, for instance, may come completely isolating all feeling, intellectualizing, and, in essence, saying that they are coming only because their parent wants them to. After creating T.A.T. stories, they can be asked what they think of them. They often reply that these are stories about the pictures and have nothing to do with them. The first step, then, is to tell them that we have heard very many stories about these pictures and that their responses differ from others we have heard before. To illustrate this to them, we can give them a number of themes, quite different from their own, to several pictures. This fact of being different often makes a strong impression; the entering wedge has been supplied. *Part of their behavior has become ego alien instead of ego syntonic.*

We can now proceed to wonder *why* their stories are the way they are rather than the way some other people's stories are. Some very contrasting stories may be chosen to tell them. For instance, an emotionally isolating adolescent boy may have told stories that actually show a good deal of despair and anxiety. We may read someone else's less disturbed stories (if this seems necessary) and ask him what the difference is between his stories and the others. Now, *insight* may slowly emerge, and he may say that his stories show some unhappiness. We may then ask why that should be. If necessary, we may point out the specific circumstances of unhappiness in the stories—namely, loneliness, fear of failure and incompetence, and so on. A preferable approach is to hand the patient several of his own stories and ask him to play psychologist and tell the therapist what the two of them seem to have in common. This way, the patient may actually learn to look for common denominators in his behavior, and the process of *working through* may be started. By asking the patient to tell whatever else the stories bring to his mind introduces the patient to the concept of *free association*.

Often, a central problem can be approached in this way, which may otherwise be almost unapproachable except in very long-term therapy. For instance, an ex-tuberculous patient was referred to the senior author in a social agency. He was well recovered but still retained considerable secondary gains from his past illness. It was extremely urgent that he help support his family again. He had been in the theater, and many of his difficulties stemmed from the fact that he still wanted to pursue a theatrical career rather than a presumably steadier and more attainable means of livelihood. He was, to some degree, aware of the unreasonableness of his attitude, but felt unable to react differently—his heart was in the theater.

Among a number of instructive T.A.T. stories, the one to 17BM proved most useful for the occupational problem. The patient's story was as follows (the italics in this and other stories are the authors'):

A circus performer on a rope. There is a security on the rope that indicates that he has had much practice. He does not seem young though his physical appearance is that of a young man. There is a kind of satisfaction on his face, which makes me believe that his work is his greatest satisfaction. He knows he's good at this, if nothing else. *He enjoys doing this spectacular work, for at other times he is lonely and passes unnoticed. To hear the audience marvel at his dexterity is compensation for his personal unhappiness.*

In associating to this story, the patient related that he had always liked to be admired. As a boy, he felt very much overshadowed by an older and very brilliant sister. Slowly, it emerged that he was a very good singer. His family came to marvel at his voice, and he was the center of the party when he sang. He finally felt less in the shadow. Then one day his voice started changing and his claim to admiration and love vanished, which caused him to be most depressed. Not long thereafter, he had occasion to participate in a school theatrical production, and thus the transition was made to a theatrical ambition and new approbation.

Now we could discuss things. Here, we had the dynamic core of this man's obsession with a profession he could not afford to follow. We could discuss his feelings of loneliness and inferiority, which he felt were assuaged when he was in the limelight. Naturally, no miracles were achieved; the T.A.T. is not a magic wand. All the principles of psychotherapy must be observed. But this story served as a starting point for two or three sessions, which helped the man change enough to find gainful employment and maintain it. For the two succeeding years, he was a steady supporter of his family for the first time in his life.

All test data may be useful when tied in to interpretations by the therapist. When one patient discussed the difficulties with which his wife threatened him, it facilitated matters greatly to show him his Figure Drawing Test, in which he had depicted the figure of the woman as a powerful Amazon while the male figure was much smaller and weaker. On seeing the pictures, he was struck by the fact that he tended to see women as stronger and himself as weak.

In another case, a Rorschach response was useful after many months of psychotherapy, when the patient described her feelings of compliance: She had to do everything to please others, and she lacked a feeling of identity, always fitting herself into a role consonant with what the environment demanded of her. A "dressmaker's dummy," who will wear any clothes and comply inanimately, was the Rorschach response describing her feelings.

In a patient who uses isolation as a main defense and who maintains an attitude of false unconcern, one may find it expedient to point out the recurrence of a hopeless, depressed tone and content in the stories. For instance, the 15-year-old boy whose stories 1 and 2 were mentioned in Chapter 6 also told the following stories.
3BM:

Looks like a female in *great despair.* Just had a great tragedy befall her. Gadget at her knee seems to be a collapsed knife or keys or something like that. The *tragedy* could be anything. Dead parents, or husband—running away—or a horrible misfortune like that. She does seem to be a little deformed. (*Author's note:* Self-image—deformed, crippled, etc.) Can't put my finger on it but—could be a deformed person pondering and weeping over her misfortune. I see less in this picture than in most of the others.

This is followed by a story to picture 13B:

Some perspective there. Looks as though the picture were taken from the top of the door. Seems to be a rather recent picture, of the past 75 years. Modern dungarees. He wouldn't be a pioneer. House is put together with nails; a kind of Tobacco Road. Boy is just staring at this photographer, who is a very unusual, a very new thing in his life. Seems to be looking at him with a little wonder, apprehension, tiny bit of fear. At first hand, I would have said he was a Kentucky mountaineer but the fact that the cabin seems to be in a dusty, sandy place—so—dust bowl, Oklahoma. The house is handmade, very old. The interior of the house seems to be *very dark and that would be the most revealing thing about him. And that's rather obscure.* The family is *very, very poor.* He is *jealous, envious* of the big owners and bankers that come around to check up on the sharecroppers' lives. Probably sees very few people like himself. Works with his father—will hold the same position as his father *without ever having a chance to have enjoyed himself.* Multitude of brothers and sisters just like himself, though. Doesn't look like he's too happy a child in the picture. Seems to stem from his *bewilderment* and his environment, which isn't a very enjoyable picture. The *lack of anything about him* seems to show that he's very alone or very . . . (pause) . . . empty.

In story 2, the hero feels isolated, alone, and angry. In 3BM, the hero is in great despair and deformed, and in 13B, the hero belongs to the suppressed and underprivileged. Yet, this boy presented a manifestly bland personal picture, denying any need for help and psychotherapy (for which his parents had referred him). The stories, however, offer a *wealth of other material* which, in due course, one may come to utilize as well (see Chapter 6).

In the case of another patient who was referred for scholastic difficulties in college, the opening story immediately reveals how he compares himself unfavorably with his successful parents, on the one hand, and the conflict between immediate enjoyment and investment in work for the future on the other hand. To picture 1, the patient said:

George's *family is talented.* His father and mother both have played before royalty. George is now eight years old and has been taking violin lessons for nearly a year. Today, after George has completed his practice session, he is reflecting on the months he has spent with his music *while his friends have been enjoying themselves* with less intellectual pursuits. *He is wondering if he will benefit enough* from the coming years of study to make it worthwhile. He has been told that he is very talented and, after all, his environment is ideal. Perhaps he will become a virtuoso comparable to his idols. His young mind unable to look any further into the future, George puts his violin in its case with reverence. He will now go out in the sunshine and tomorrow he will practice with renewed vigor.

Another patient, a 52-year-old man, gave the following story to picture 1:

The violin belongs to the boy's father. Now his father is dead. The boy is thinking of the times his father invited some other musicians in for a home concert as he often did. His mother played the piano and all the friends brought their instruments—a flute, a cello, an oboe, a French horn. They would play far into the night—but the boy would listen from his bed and seek to catch the clear strains of the violin played by his father. One night the party was most gay—they played waltz tunes from Vienna and Hungarian dances. The boy heard the laughter and gay talk between pieces. Then they played the most beautiful waltz of all—the Blue Danube. In the final beautiful movement as the waltz neared its climax, the boy heard the string on his father's violin break. Then all the playing stopped and the boy heard no sound—then a wail, low and prolonged, from his mother. He rushed down from his room. When the string broke, his father's heart had stopped. He was dead.

This story probably reflects a biographical detail of listening to "the parents making music"—presumably overhearing an intercourse scene. The boy feels isolated and competitive. Intercourse is probably conceived of as dangerous on the one hand; on the other hand, the father's death represents a wish and leaves the boy the inheritor of the violin. The T.A.T. was given some time after psychotherapy had started and probably reflects some transference phenomena, since the Viennese music is probably a reference to the therapist (senior author).

These examples may illustrate the direct use of one psychological test—the T.A.T.—as a vehicle for communication from patient to therapist as a basis for insight for both, and as providing a pattern for interpretation and working through, providing economy in all these processes in cases where economy is indicated, for external or internal reasons.

Another therapeutic function of the T.A.T. has been noted by Holzberg (1963). He conceptualizes resistance to change in psychotherapy in terms of the patients' anxiety about adaptive regression. Holzberg's point is that projective techniques, such as the T.A.T., can play a significant role in overcoming such anxiety so that therapy can commence or continue. He regards the projective test experience as providing a chance to experience adaptive regression; thus, such test experience can overcome resistance to treatment by permitting the patient to practice regression under controlled conditions. Resistance in two patients noted by Holzberg was diminished in this way.

A rather unique use of the T.A.T. cards was made by Seymour Hoffman and Nili Kuperman (1990). They jointly treated a 13-year-old boy by using indirect therapeutic intervention that focused on the patient's responses to the T.A.T. cards. Rather than just exploring the content of the boy's story (which related directly to the traumatic event he had inadequately suppressed), they attempted to positively alter his perception of the story. To begin, the co-therapists each wrote their own stories to the same T.A.T. cards, each from a contrasting perspective. The psychologist, Hoffman, wrote of the central character's id and rigid superego aspects, which included his maladaptive coping mechanisms. The social worker, Kuperman, emphasized the positive and healthy aspects of the hero's ego in the story. Three consecutive sessions were held to discuss 8 of the 12 stories with the boy. The therapists first read the patient's story and then presented each of theirs in turn. The three then had an open dialogue to determine whose version of the story seemed the most accurate. During this discussion, a good amount of material was presented and the social worker's view mainly held up over the psychologist's.

The Systematic Use of the T.A.T. in Relation to the Basic Steps of Psychotherapy

In psychoanalytic therapy, one can speak *schematically* of four basic processes (which often overlap and coexist): communication, interpretation, insight, and working through.

Communication

The patient communicates with the therapist by means of verbal expressions.[2] Through these, the therapist learns of the patient's behavior in a great many situations and finds a number of common denominators in the patient's behavioral patterns. The T.A.T. responses may serve as such communication.

---

[2] This is not the only means of communication. The patient imparts information also by posture, facial expression, and so on.

Interpretation

When the therapist has become acquainted with a number of life situations of the patient, the therapist may perceive a certain common denominator in the behavioral patterns and point it out to the patient in such doses as seem to be suitable at various times.

1. *Horizontal study.* The therapist may find a common denominator among the behavior patterns and interpersonal relationships of the patient's contemporary life situation. This process may be regarded as a horizontal study of patterns.

2. *Vertical study.* Sooner or later, it will be possible to trace, by free association or otherwise, the historical development of these patterns in the life history of the patient, leading to a more or less definitely defined early set. This part of the therapeutic investigation may be seen as the vertical study of life patterns. Frequently, it is necessary to point out both the vertical and the horizontal common denominators of the patient's current behavior in order to lead to a solution of the problems.

3. *Relationship to the therapist.* As a special case of current life situations of the horizontal pattern in its relation to the earlier historical ones, the relationship to the therapist may be discussed specifically in what is known in psychoanalysis as *analysis of the transference situation.*

Interpretation, then, means that the therapist points out to the patient the common denominators in the behavioral patterns, horizontally, vertically, and in special relation to the therapist. In all three instances, the therapist finds that the patient suffers from apperceptive distortions of life situations. Interpretation really consists of pointing out the *common denominators of the apperceptive distortions* and, in certain cases, demonstrating the relationships of earlier life situations to percept memories in which these apperceptive distortions arose. The process involves the analysis of the present complex apperception into the parts that came to constitute the whole.

A brief example may be helpful here. A young man may come in with the presenting problem of vague anxiety attacks. It may develop that these apparently puzzling attacks typically occur when the patient is in contact with a strict authority figure who produces hostility in him. After this horizontal pattern has appeared, at one time or another a vertical one may also be found: The patient had a more or less specific relationship to his father (as becomes clear in the T.A.T., for instance), who originally produced these feelings of hostility in him with resulting anxiety. Further study will reveal a whole history of relationships to similar authorities prior to the current situation, and a similar attitude will be expressed to the therapist.

Insight

Insight development is the next step in the therapeutic process. The term *insight* is abused almost as much as the term *psychotherapy*. Frequently, the term *insight* is used to mean simply that the patient is aware of being mentally ill. This is most often used in the discussion of psychotics, usually implying no more than just that.

In the context of dynamic psychotherapy, insight must have this specific meaning—
*the patient's ability to see the relationship between a given symptom and the previously un-
conscious apperceptive distortions underlying the symptom.* More strictly speaking, we define *insight* as the patient's apperception (i.e., meaningful perception) of the
common denominators of behavior as pointed out by the therapist. The problem is
seen in a new light and handled differently from then on. This process may be analyzed into two parts:

1. *Intellectual insight.* Patients can see the interrelationship of their different
horizontal and vertical patterns; they can see them as special cases of a general class
or, in Gestalt language, they learn by insight and experience closure. The pieces of
isolated happenings become a memory whole, and a repatterning and relearning
takes place.

2. *Emotional insight.* The patient reproduces the affect pertaining to the intellectual insight—relief, anxiety, guilt, happiness, and the like.

If the intellectual insight alone is produced, limited or no therapeutic result
may be achieved, because emotional repatterning is an essential of the therapeutic
process, be it conceived of as a regular libidinal-metapsychologic process or as a
learning process in conventional academic psychological terms. The affect must be
part of the Gestalt of a therapeutic experience.

Working Through

The next step in therapy consists of the working through of the new insight:

1. *Intellectually.* The patient now applies what has been learned to pertain to
a few situations, as pointed out by the therapist, to a number of other situations to
which the same general denominator applies. If it has been pointed out that a pattern of apperceptive distortion exists as applying to a woman's present employer,
her teacher, her therapist, and her father, she may now remember situations involving an uncle, an elder brother, or others as having been reacted to similarly.

2. *Therapeutically (emotionally).* In the therapeutic situation, the patient must
experience the preceding situations with real feelings, and also reproduce the feelings in relation to the therapist, and work them through.

3. *Behaviorally.* Outside the therapeutic session, the patient goes on meeting
the situations discussed and new ones similar to the ones scrutinized. While in real
situations, she is aware of the insight recently gained. Under the influence of her
new "mental set," she reacts differently to a progressive extent to these situations in
the corrective direction suggested by the analysis of the situation. New problems
arising are reanalyzed and the problem is worked out by persistent adjustment and
readjustment between mental set and reality.

While the process of insight and the purely intellectual aspects of working
through are best understood in terms of perceptual learning theory, the therapeutic and behavioral working through are actually best seen as a matter of condition-
ing and reconditioning, as well as a problem in which trial and error and reward
and punishment lead to the final best result.

The T.A.T. is an excellent, tailor-made way of studying both the horizontal and the genetic patterns that are revealed, particularly by the more psychologically naive subjects, who are often not aware of the implications of their stories. Valuable insight and cooperation are frequently gained when the patient discovers, to his surprise, that he has unwittingly reproduced some of his most important problems.

Combs (1946) has demonstrated that there is an abundance of autobiographical material revealed in the T.A.T. that should enable the therapist to study some of the vertical patterns in the person's behavior.

For the clinical use of the T.A.T. in therapeutic practice, one may either take down the stories oneself or use recording devices. In this situation, we have found it advantageous to have the patient *write down the stories herself or himself* either in the office or at home. It will quickly appear to any therapist at all conversant with dynamics that the T.A.T. practically always mirrors some or all of the basic problems, conflicts, and sentiments of the individual. Thus, it can be used not only by therapists for their own insights into their patients' psychodynamics but it can also be given to them for them to work on, in the same way as any of their other productions.

To summarize
1. The T.A.T. can be used as a vehicle with any kind of psychotherapy. It is especially indicated in brief psychoanalytic psychotherapy because it reveals the situations that need discussing. One may select those pictures that are most apt to bring out the problems of a specific patient, where time is of the essence for external or internal reasons (Bellak et al., 1992).

2. The T.A.T. may be a useful vehicle when the patient has a special difficulty in free associating or in communicating generally because of lack of familiarity with the psychotherapeutic process, inhibitions, specific resistances (when protracted resistance is not analytically useful), and so on.

When using the T.A.T. in the actual psychotherapeutic session, it is advised to wait for a time at the beginning of the session before presenting the story or stories to the patient. During that time, one may find out if there is anything more acute and specific the patient may have in mind that is more urgent than the material in the T.A.T. If there is nothing acute, and particularly if the patient has difficulty in starting or quickly runs out of material, it is a good time to take up the T.A.T.

It is expedient to stop the interpretations of the T.A.T. material some time before the end of the session. This will allow the patient an opportunity either to bring up more distantly related material that was evoked or to discuss current problems that he or she did not remember before.

The technique of analyzing and interpreting the stories for the patient varies. There should be two copies of each story. The method of choice in handling each story is to let patients read it and elaborate on it if they can, then to discuss it and free associate to it. After all associations have been made, the therapist steps in and discusses all the material again, with analysis and interpretations, as indicated. One or several stories may thus be taken up during each session, and therapy proceeds according to patterns revealed in the T.A.T. stories.

Another method is to use the stories only when the patient has difficulty in free associating or when one or several of the stories contain the same pattern currently revealed by the patient's associations. Again, patients should be allowed to read a copy of their own productions. Often, they will see the pattern of their own accord and be able to interpret the story and their revelations, thus acquiring insight in the most desirable manner. If they fail to do this, the therapist can try to help them do so or analyze and interpret the material for them.

In handling the T.A.T. stories, the therapist should consider the material as similar to a *dream* or *fantasy* and analyze it on that basis. The story and its analysis may be presented to patients as though it were their dream or fantasy, or it may be taken up as an almost direct statement of biographical material or emotional content connected to behavior patterns.

The T.A.T. is helpful in facilitating the establishment of the "psychotherapeutic attitude," when patients find it hard to relate data of any value. In psychotherapy, we are, in essence, asking patients to stand off and observe themselves, to report to us what they observe, and to collaborate with us with a part of themselves. This is a difficult task, especially for the less sophisticated individuals. When we ask them to read over their own stories, they may say that they simply described the pictures. We can then tell them of other stories and interpretations that have been given to the same pictures. This usually has a marked effect on them: It may introduce them for the first time to a *subjectivity* of their thought processes, and they may now be more willing and able to stand off and observe themselves. This process may be facilitated if, on rereading their stories, they are spontaneously impressed by how much of the content refers to themselves, or if we have occasion to *point out certain repetitive patterns* to them.

The use of the T.A.T. does not obviate the fact that all the principles of careful psychotherapy must be observed: One should start with the more acceptable aspects, not upset the patient unduly, not interpret things that the patient is not ready for. No one inexperienced with psychotherapy should use the T.A.T. in therapy.

Use of the T.A.T. in Group Psychotherapy Programs

Brief mention should be made of observations that have indicated the usefulness of the T.A.T. in selection of group therapy candidates and in evaluating behavior in group therapy programs. Ullmann (1957) has noted that significant correlations were obtained in his investigation between T.A.T. scores of neuropsychiatric patients and group therapy scale predictions, as well as between T.A.T. scores and a hospital status criterion. The fact that T.A.T. cards are concerned with interpersonal relationships apparently affords the best explanation for their suitability as a potential method of selecting group therapy patients. Fairweather and colleagues (1960) have employed the T.A.T. to compare the relative effectiveness of psychotherapeutic programs. The test diagnosis interaction was significant; group therapy and control groups indicated more positive T.A.T. changes for nonpsychotics than for psychotics, and individual therapy was superior in terms of T.A.T. change when given to long-term psychotics.

The ability of the T.A.T. to describe patients' behavior in psychotherapy has thus received some validation; the test can be used by the psychotherapist as one measure of evaluation of the patient's progress. Several authors have reported valuable results in the use of the T.A.T. an an outcome measure in psychotherapy research (Coche & Sillitti, 1983; Dymond, 1954; Frank & Gunderson, 1990; Goldman & Greenblatt, 1955).

Diagnostic Aspects in Relation to Therapy[3]

Psychological tests have much the same relationship to psychotherapy as clinical pathological tests and X-rays have to general medicine. Like a medical doctor, the psychotherapist should have a basic knowledge of testing procedures in order to be able to request the *appropiate* one, and should understand the basic meaning well enough to be able to integrate the test results with the additional data. As in general medicine, the therapist should not blindly rely on the test results, nor should an exact diagnostic answer to every problem be expected. It is the clinician's job to make a careful clinical evaluation and to integrate all the factors. No test can be a substitute for clinical knowledge and acumen. It is inappropriate for the psychotherapist to expect an answer to all his or her problems from the psychologist, and for the psychologist to offer definitive statements without knowing the clinical situation. It is preferable to express test results in the form that they are "consistent with" such and such a disorder (i.e., "This patient's record is consistent with a sado-masochistic character disorder").

Psychological tests may be helpful in diagnosis, if diagnosis does not imply simply attaching labels to a patient, but rather implies gauging liabilities and assets. If diagnosis involves therapeutic planning and prognostication, the great significance of the tests is obvious.

If one restricts oneself to the projective personality tests, then it seems that they can be divided into two kinds: those concerned essentially with testing formal quantitative aspects (which appear to test primarily degrees of ego strength) and those which reveal content (psychodynamics). Of the first category, the Rorschach is the main representative; of the second, the T.A.T. It should be kept in mind that this division is somewhat arbitrary, in that the Rorschach may elicit some indications of interpersonal relations and the T.A.T. offers some ego strength indicators.

From the standpoint of therapy, the quantitative indicators may permit one to gauge the amount of strain and stress to which a patient may be safely exposed by interpretations and transference tensions; the content tests supply the substance of the pesonality itself, like dreams and fantasies made to order.

The quantitative indicators are predicated on the probing of subsemantic levels, by studying neuromuscular expressions (e.g., in a figure drawing) or perceptual patterns (e.g., in the Rorschach). Thus, they may reveal motivations that are unconscious in the sense of never having had any verbal representations. A break-

---

[3] Diagnostic aspects are discussed throughout the book. Here, we merely wish to emphasize a few considerations with regard to therapy.

through of aggressive impulses due to a brain defect may often be covered up verbally, while it will manifest itself myoneurally (e.g., in a drawing). The content tests reveal particularly well matters that are unconscious in the psychoanalytic sense.

More detailed principles of classification of what is usually subsumed under projective tests might be helpful for the clinical selection of proper tests for therapeutic purposes. These suggestions will indicate only the *primary* useful aspects of certain tests and will not ignore the fact that each test contributes on several levels.

Available techniques may be grouped under five headings:

1. *Methods based on the study of content:* The T.A.T., C.A.T., and S.A.T
2. *Study of expressive, perceptual, structural aspects:* Mira, Mosaic, Rorschach, and projective drawings
3. *Gestalt functions:* Bender Gestalt, Mosaic, Rorschach
4. *Body-image or self-image:* Figure Drawing, T.A.T., Rorschach
5. *Methods of preference:* Szondi

It is apparent that all five organismic aspects enter into every one of the projective methods, although in varying degrees. One may keep these categories in mind for the selection of techniques for each individual problem of diagnosis and therapy—either for the purpose of arranging a rounded battery or for selecting the one test for a specific clinical need. The five variables may be used for a systematic inquiry into the test results of any one technique.

A more general classification scheme, relevant to the choice of tests for therapeutic purposes, derives from the *levels hypothesis,* which has generally been interpreted as meaning that the less the structure of the test, the deeper the level of personality being tapped. For example, Stone and Dellis (1960) found that the Wechsler-Bellevue, Forer Sentence Completion Test, T.A.T., Rorschach, and Draw-A-Person Test reached successively lower, or more primitive, impulse control systems in their subjects. In a similar vein, Theiner (1962) noted greater frequency of acceptable needs expressed in response to a relatively structured test (Rotter Incomplete Sentence Test), and greater frequency of unacceptable needs on the T.A.T. (less structured).

Again, it is feasible that this "levels" principle can be used either toward the selection of a specific test in order to obtain specific kinds of information or toward the selection of several tests to secure a more global picture of the individual.

Some Contraindications to the Use of Psychological Tests

A brief statement is in order concerning *contraindications for psychological tests,* for whatever purpose they may be used. Meyer (1951) has published a paper on this topic. He showed particular concern with the effect of the prospect of testing on the patient (in terms of keeping or breaking appointments) and with how testing affects the continuation of therapy. By examining extensive clinical records, he found that testing does not generally have an adverse effect. However, he suggested seven contraindications to testing in order to avoid disturbing consequences:

1. Acute psychosis, incipient psychosis, or acute anxiety states
2. Extreme difficulty in establishing relationships (where adjustment to an additional person would be an undue burden)
3. Likelihood that the patient will interpret referral for testing as disinterest on the part of the therapist
4. Likelihood that referral will be interpreted as evidence of incompetence of the therapist
5. A specific fear of "test" situations in life and a tendency to run away from them
6. The possibility that testing material might stimulate more material than seems desirible at the time (incipient psychosis?)
7. Indication that the therapeutic situation at the time of referral seems to make testing inadvisable, whereas it might be advisable at a later, more suitable date

These points seems to comprise the most careful consideration published thus far on the entire subject of the testing situation from the point of view of the patient/therapist relationship.

We have frequently used the T.A.T. ourselves with patients in acute anxiety states and severe depressions without any untoward effects. Judgment must be used in all cases, and if extra precautions are taken to create a nontraumatic atmosphere, tests may still be very useful. In fact, in many acute conditions, when patients are otherwise unable to profit by communications, the T.A.T. and other tests may be easier for them to deal with and may help them focus on the very core of their problems.

CHAPTER 9

REVIEW OF LITERATURE RELEVANT TO INTERPRETATION OF THE T.A.T.

Stimulus Value of the T.A.T.

It has long been recognized that, in order to properly interpret thematic responses, it is of primary importance to take into account the influence of the stimulus itself in determining the response. There have been studies of stimulus factors in specific cards, such as the level of conflict and depression responses to Card 12BG (Boekholt, 1987), factors determining the gender of the figure in T.A.T. Card 3BM (Dungan & Holmes, 1982; Holmes & Dungan, 1981), and a long tradition of research on relative degrees of ambiguity in different cards (Epstein, 1966; Kaplan, 1967, 1969, 1970; Kenny & Bijou, 1953; Murstein, 1964, 1965b). Goldfried and Zax (1965) took the position that in evaluating T.A.T. themes, it is necessary to make interpretations *only* with regard to the stimulus value of the specific card. They obtained ratings of all the T.A.T. cards on 10 bipolar adjectival scales, such as happy/sad. The ratings indicated that the cards vary a good deal as to their ambiguity—that is, the number of scales that consistently describe the picture. It was also observed that the stimulus properties of some cards are such that it is likely they will "pull" negatively toned stories. Specifically, it was found that for certain cards (e.g., 2 and 5), the stimulus pull is weak enough to assume that the story reflects the inner state of the test taker; on the other hand, for pictures such as 4 and 13MF, the stimulus properties of the card are likely to be more responsible for the resultant story than are the test taker's inner needs.

A few other studies have been reported that investigated the effect of stimulus properties on the expression of specific needs or personality variables. Lubin (1960) tested the effects of T.A.T. cards whose stimulus properties elicit the expression of either sex or aggression. The significant effect of the stimulus properties of cards of sexual and aggressive expression was interpreted as indicating that certain dimensions (Kagan, 1959) of the T.A.T. response are determined by stimulus configurations. Murstein (1962) studied the projection of hostility on the T.A.T. as a function of stimulus, background, and personality variables. The stimulus properties of the cards used accounted for more than half of the total variance. Murstein concluded that the results provide evidence that the stimulus is definitely the most important determinant of the content of a T.A.T. response.

Another possible way in which the stimulus properties may influence responses has been investigated in studies that have dealt with the effects of similarity between the test taker and certain characteristics of the T.A.T. figures. Weisskopf-Joelson and colleagues (1953) hypothesized that physical similarity between the test taker and the central T.A.T. figure would affect the amount of projection, but their findings indicated that increasing similarity did not yield statistically significant increases in either amount of projection or in the diagnostic value of the stimuli. Thompson (1949), using the African American T.A.T. that he devised, found that African Americans produced more when the T.A.T. used African Americans than they did with the traditional T.A.T. Other research, though, has questioned this result (Korchin et al., 1950; Riess et al., 1950). Weisskopf (1950b) has refuted Murray's (1943a) hypothesis that males project more when the central figure is male rather than female. Finally, Weisskopf and Dunlevy (1952) found no effect on amount of projection when pictures of physically normal, obese, and crippled figures were shown to the respective test-taker groups. After reviewing these findings, Weisskopf-Joelson and colleagues (1953) suggested that differences in the similarity dimension may cause qualitative changes in projection rather than quantitative, and specifically that decreasing similarity should lead to increased projection of ego alien materials.

Hunt and Smith (1960) studied the constraining effects on responses to thematic projective material of structural elements involving shared cultural meanings. It was hypothesized that patterns such as those depicted in the T.A.T. are likely to include a variety of cultural and subcultural symbols that can act so as to evoke responses mediated by shared cultural meanings and given independently of any effects of individual personality. By comparing a modified T.A.T. card with the original, it was shown that variations in component features of the cards produced notable differences in sociocultural classifications that were likely to affect their use (e.g., differences in the test taker's perceptions).

Sample Variables

Illustrative examples of the possible influences of certain sample variables on thematic responses are contained in the following studies. Sex differences in fantasy patterns have been found by May (1966), who deduced from clinically oriented studies the types of sequences to be expected in men's and in women's fantasies. In women's fantasies, it was hypothesized that the following would be reflected the sequence in feminine masochism: suffering followed by joy, failure followed by success. Fantasies of men were expected to reflect the pattern of ascension followed by descension, the syndrome of the male's attempt at ascension and later fear of falling. These hypotheses were strongly supported by May's study with the T.A.T. in that, in terms of sequence of action and feeling, women's stories showed movement from more "negative" emotion and experience to more "positive" emotion and experience, whereas with men this direction of movement was reversed. Men tended to see any decline or fall as total and final, while the possibility of resurgence was implicit in the female pattern. A second finding was that stories written by women tended to include, more often than those of men, phenomena such as dreams, fantasy, and prayer—elements that signify that women are more likely to tolerate, and make use of, shifts in level of psychic functioning

Tooley (1967) examined the expressive styles of three age groups of women, adolescents, late adolescents (18 to 22 years), and adults, as reflected in T.A.T. themes, in order to obtain a description of the defensive and adaptive modes peculiar to late adolescence. Themes written for card 2, which has shown its relevance to late adolescent problems (Henry, 1956), and card 18GF, chosen to maximize affective arousal so that defensive techniques could be seen, were judged according to the criteria of "flamboyant," "impersonal," and "constricted." Late adolescents were judged to be flamboyant in writing style significantly less often than the other two age groups, and impersonal significantly more often. The expressive style of late adolescents was described as moderate in emotional tone and heavily characterized by intellectualizing defenses—a style that facilitates the handling of developmental tasks of late adolescence and that indicates a defensive structure specific to that developmental period. This kind of study points to the potential usefulness of the T.A.T. in studying developmental differences.

Rubin (1964) compared the T.A.T. stories of two I.Q. groups: seventh- and eighth-grade girls of high I.Q. (M = 124), and seventh- and eighth-grade girls of low I.Q. (M = 78). With respect to data uncorrected for the effects of verbal productivity or socioeconomic status, there was a tendency for the high I.Q. group to use more achievement, dominance, and affiliation themes in their stories than the low I.Q. group; there was no difference between the two groups in number of rejection, seclusion, or dependency themes expressed; and the high I.Q. group used a greater total number of themes in their stories. In general, differences in the incidence of specific themes or total number of themes did exist between the two groups, but such differences were found to be associated with either verbal productivity, socioeconomic status, or both. When the effects of socioeconomic status were held constant, differences continued between the measures of achievement and dominance themes in the two groups, although differences on the measures of affiliation and total number of themes disappeared. One of the findings is contrary to past research done by Rosen (1958) and by Veroff and colleagues (1953), who found that incidence of achievement themes in T.A.T. stories is related to socioeconomic status. Present findings indicate that the incidence of achievement themes is more closely related to I.Q. than to socioeconomic status.

Thematic expression has been found to vary along the dimensions of so many variables that it is not surprising to learn that thematic drive expression has been studied in relation to different occupational groups. Levine (1969) compared the T.A.T. performances of mathematicians, creative writers, and physicians by means of Pine's (1960) system for rating amount, integration, and directness of drive expression, and also in terms of expression of affect. Writers were most expressive, followed by mathematicians and then physicians. Mathematicians tended toward relatively high use of direct, socialized forms of drive content, whereas physicians were characterized by indirect, disguised forms more than the other groups. These emphases appeared to serve defensive and integrative functions. Writers showed no emphasis on either direct or indirect expression. Intergroup differences that were obtained indicated the existence of relationships between occupations and characteristic patterns of regulating drives and affects. The study also demonstrated the reliability of Pine's system, which evidently taps dimensions of personality not necessarily relevant to psychopathology but that reflect characterological differences significant in major life adaptations.

The studies that have been concerned with possible race differences in thematic responses have led to somewhat less than definitive conclusions, mainly because of variations in the number and kind of related variables that have been experimentally controlled and in the type of differences being evaluated. Mussen (1953) compared the T.A.T. responses of African American and white lower-class boys and found that African Americans perceived the general environment as more hostile. Aggression expressed by African Americans was more verbal and less physical; African Americans expressed less need for achievement and fewer themes of accomplishment, and whites suffered more feelings of rejection in personal relationships, particularly in the case of the mother. Mussen concluded that many differences exist among the African American and white cultures not attributable to differences in class structure. Megaree's (1966a) conclusions about this problem area are somewhat different, although he is concerned more with personality differences than cultural ones, as manifested in the T.A.T. He compared the scores of lower-class white and African American male juvenile delinquents on the T.A.T. and two other projective tests and found no differences on T.A.T. scores. The two groups had been matched on I.Q. It was noted that these results were consistent with those of other studies previously reported in the literature that also matched African American and white samples on I.Q.; earlier studies that had not matched I.Q.s reported more projective test differences. For example, Veroff and colleagues (1953) did not match for I.Q. and found a high proportion of significant differences. Megaree's concluding opinion was that projective test differences should not be used to make inferences about basic racial personality structure unless careful matching on other variables has been achieved. The present study indicates that white norms are applicable to African American test takers of equivalent I.Q. in custodial settings.

Johnson and Sikes (1965) investigated subcultural differences in thematic responses. They compared the T.A.T. responses of African American, Mexican American, and Anglo male psychiatric patients, whose ages, educational backgrounds, and occupational levels were quite similar. Diagnostically, the subgroups were almost equal. Using themes of achievement on card 1 as the measure of achievement concern, a tendency was found for Mexican American and African American groups to show more achievement. These themes also included the subcategory of frustration, which appeared more often in African American and Mexican American stories than in Anglo stories. Large differences were found for the family unity dimension, as shown in card 2 themes. The Mexican American group had the most consistent view of the family as unified, whereas the African Americans were lowest in this category. Responses to the mother/son card (6BM) showed significant differences. For Mexican Americans, the scene was one of a son leaving his mother, both viewed as being sad, whereas African Americans tended to see the mother as rejecting and a situation of conflict. The father/son card elicited significant differences also, with African Americans and Anglos responding similarly, and Mexican Americans seeing a father giving his son advice and the son taking it. Johnson and Sikes concluded that it may be in the measurement of the relative strengths of interpersonal identifications that projective tests can be most useful in the formulation of culture and personality theories. These issues of cultural differences in thematic tests are discussed in greater detail in Chapter 20.

Aggression and Hostility

Considerable research has focused on the dimensions of aggression and hostility as they are manifested in T.A.T. responses (Benton, 1983; Fiester & Siipola, 1972; Gluck, 1955; Kagan, 1956, 1958, 1959; Kornadt, 1982; Matranga, 1976; Megargee, 1967; Megargee & Cook, 1967; Megargee & Hokanson, 1970; Mormont, 1988; Pam & Rivera, 1995; Pollack & Gilligan, 1982; Tachibana et al., 1984). The study of Megargee and Cook (1967) was one of the first to demonstrate that aggressive fantasy on the T.A.T. is directly related to overt acting out of aggression. Mormont (1988) pointed out that 20 years of further research on this topic continue to support Megargee and Cook's basic finding.

James and Mosher (1967) emphasized the relevance of the stimulus situation. They related thematic aggression, which was elicited by thematic stimuli of high- and low-stimulus relevance, to the aggressive behavior of a group of Boy Scouts. Thematic aggression to high "pull" cards was related significantly to physically aggressive behavior, but thematic aggression to low "pull" cards was not. There was no relationship between self-reported hostility/guilt and fighting behavior; nor was any relationship obtained between hostility/guilt and thematic aggression elicited by cards of high stimulus relevance. Hostility/guilt was significantly negatively correlated with aggressive stories told to cards with little aggressive stimulus relevance. It was hypothesized that, when pictures are not suggestive of aggression, perhaps only people who are low in guilt over hostility are able to accept the responsibility for producing aggressive themes. The relationships obtained between thematic aggression and fighting behavior in adolescent boys support Kagan's (1959) position. Kagan has stated that "unambiguous pictures are the best stimuli for yielding indicants of behavioral aggression." The results of the present study imply that to maximize prediction for thematic cards one must use stimuli that are quite similar to the relevant behavior.

Megargee (1967) studied hostility on the T.A.T. as a function of defensive inhibition and the stimulus situation. He hypothesized that there would be significant differences in the aggressive imagery of inhibited and uninhibited test takers when T.A.T. cards or instructions strongly suggested an aggressive response, but not when experimental conditions did not suggest hostile themes. The following findings held true for women but not for male test takers: Less inhibited people had higher hostility scores than the more inhibited; instructions to give hostile stories resulted in higher hostility scores than did neutral instructions; the higher the aggressive pull of the cards, the higher were the obtained hostility scores; and finally, the major hypothesis, noted above, was confirmed, but for women only. Partial support was thus found for the hypothesis that variations in aggressive imagery in response to stimulus conditions that are likely to elicit aggression reflect differences in inhibition level. Since the present study used group administration, the obtained sex difference could be an artefact of sex differences in response to group T.A.T.'s, such as were found by Lindzey and Silverman (1959).

Reznikoff and Dollin (1961) investigated the concept that persons rated high on a social desirability (SD) scale would avoid expression of aggression on the T.A.T., which the authors considered socially undesirable. Test takers were grouped according to their Edwards SD scale score and given T.A.T. cards that were later scored for overt, covert, and total hostility. SD groups could not be differentiated with regard to mean score on any hostility variables, although significant differences were obtained for all variables with regard to stimulus pull of the cards. Further analysis did indicate that high SD test takers were more likely than others to use covert hostility rather than overt. This is consistent with the idea that people with high SD are not likely to express aggressive feelings directly. It is Murstein's (1963b) opinion that personality sets such as the SD do not really affect the themes obtained with strongly structured cards such as those that compose the T.A.T.

Hafner and Kaplan (1960) conducted a methodologically sound hostility content analysis of the Rorschach and T.A.T. and compared the hostility dimension on the two tests. The constructed scales were applied to the Rorschach and T.A.T. protocols of a group of psychiatric patients. For the Rorschach, correlations between overt and weighted scale scores, covert and weighted scale scores, and overt and covert scales were all positive and significant. The same results were obtained for the T.A.T. hostility scales except that the correlation between overt and covert scales was significantly negative. Correlations between the Rorschach and T.A.T. weighted scale scores, overt scale scores, and covert scale scores were all nonsignificant. Since for the T.A.T., overt and covert scale scores were highly related to weighted scores, but not to the same degree as for the Rorschach, and since T.A.T. overt and covert scale scores were negatively related as well, it was concluded that the T.A.T. was more sensitive to individual differences in regard to the overt/covert dimensions of hostility than was the Rorschach. An interesting study was conducted by Winter and colleagues (1966) using the Hafner-Kaplan scoring system (1960). T.A.T. stories were produced conjointly by three-member families: 50 families with normal children (Nor), 44 with emotionally maladjusted children (Mal), 16 with schizophrenic children (Scz), and 16 with delinquent children (Del). The Nor and Scz groups produced stories low both in weighted hostility and overt hostility, stories of Mal groups were high in both variables, and the Del families scored high in weighted hostility but close to the normals in overt hostility. The deviation of the Scz families' responses from the kind expected from clinical experience led the authors to suggest that their hostility is either so far removed from the level of explicit expression that it is conveyed in highly subtle ways or that the families avoid expression of emotional antagonism. No hypotheses were proposed in explanation of the unexpected responses from the Del groups. It was deduced, in general, that the basic value systems of the Mal, Del, and Scz groups are equally abnormal, but the mode of expression of hostility differs. In addition to the information about the expression of hostility contributed by this study, it should be noted that research such as this can result in effective use of the family T.A.T. as a diagnostic instrument as well as effective use of the T.A.T. in assessing family pathology.

In a series of well-conducted studies of the relationship between simple T.A.T. aggression and overt aggression, Murstein (1963a, 1963b, 1965a, 1965b, 1968; Murstein et al., 1961) concluded that there is little correspondence between the two with typical samples of adults, adolescents, and children. On the other hand, he stated that for both adults and children, persons with histories of overt hostility are relatively easily differentiated by thematic aggression. The following studies are representative of those that have been conducted using the T.A.T. with test takers who have such histories of overt hostility. Stone (1956) studied army prisoners who had committed nonviolent crimes, or deserted, or murdered, or intended to kill someone. The assaultive group projected significantly more hostility than the combined nonassaultive groups in their T.A.T. responses. Purcell (1956) classified army trainees into three groups varying in antisocial behavior. Of the 15 comparisons made between any two of the three groups, 12 indicated highly significant differences. Antisocial men responded with more aggression themes than other groups, and their hostility expression was more direct. Punishment depicted was often of the external kind, while nonantisocial people manifested more frequent internal punishment than external.

Mussen and Naylor (1954) were inspired in their research by Sanford and colleagues' (1943) finding that expression of high aggressive needs in the T.A.T. was correlated with low overt aggression, with a middle-class sample. Mussen and Naylor predicted that with lower-class test takers, high fantasy aggression would be overtly expressed, since in lower-class environments aggressive behavior is not punished. They tested preadolescent and adolescent delinquent lower-class boys with the T.A.T., and found that, among these boys, those who manifested high aggressive needs on the T.A.T. showed more aggressive behavior than those with low fantasy aggressive needs. A second result was that boys who showed much punishment press relative to aggressive needs in their stories showed less overt aggression than those who had low punishment press relative to aggressive needs. This relationship was less marked than the first was. Third, when high expression of aggressive needs was paired with a low ratio of anticipation of punishment to aggressive needs, a high amount of overt aggression was generally found, and vice versa. This study was offered as evidence of the validity of T.A.T. inferences concerning aggressive needs, although the conclusions were limited to the social class and age levels studied.

A study that confirmed Mussen and Naylor's (1954) general finding but whose scope was somewhat broader was conducted by Weissman (1964). Four matched groups of adolescents participated. They were identified as (1) aggressive acting-out institutionalized test takers, (2) less aggressive acting-out institutionalized test takers, (3) nonacting-out high school boys, and (4) aggressive acting-out high school boys. T.A.T. stories were compared on several hypothesized dimensions deemed relevant to aggressive acting-out behavior. The following three dimensions manifested significant and consistent differences: (1) The number of aggressive stories was viewed as most likely to be useful as an indicator of aggressive overt behavior when groups being compared are distinctly different with respect to aggression. Weissman suggested that T.A.T. fantasies of aggressive adolescents, when compared to adults', are more closely related to characteristic behavioral patterns than to conflicts resulting from artificially induced drive states, such as reported by other studies. (2) Aggressive boys were more likely to tell aggressive stories to nonaggressive cards than were nonaggressive test takers. (3) Reaction time was the single best predictor of aggressive overt behavior for all groups. Other studies include that of Shalit (1970) on the relationship between environmental hostility and hostility on thematic tests and Tachibana and associates (1984) aggression and catharthis in Japan.

A major controversy in the field is whether the acting out of serious aggression can be predicted by mental health practitioners. Megargee and Cook's (1967) finding that aggressive fantasy on the T.A.T. is directly related to overt acting out of aggression is illustrated in a thought-provoking clinical case presentation by Pam and Rivera (1995). The case reported by Pam and Rivera is a man, who was tested during his psychiatric hospitalization. The T.A.T. specifically contained many projective indicators of serious aggressive, acting-out tendencies, which led the two psychologist authors to recommend that the patient not be discharged. When the patient was informed of this decision, he committed suicide. Ten years after this tragic outcome, the authors took a second look at the T.A.T. protocol and considered whether their decision on the basis of this T.A.T. protocol was the correct clinical decision. The paper presents the full T.A.T. protocol, so that the reader can also analyze the test results and decide if the authors were, in fact, justified in their clinical recommendations.

In view of Klein's (1987) controversial argument that projective tests are too subjective to be clinically useful, the courageous paper of Pam and Rivera (1995) is a wonderful teaching device for all clinicians employing the T.A.T., since it orients the reader to important ethical and clinical responsibilities facing psychologists who work in psychiatric hospital situations. Jo-Ann Rivera was a staff psychologist and Al Pam was her supervisor at the time of the psychological testing. The authors provide a very valuable picture of some of the difficult emotional reactions such extreme indicators of dangerous aggression may elicit in a psychologist, who obtains a T.A.T. protocol of this nature, and the process of carefully examining such a serious case in supervision in terms of the overall quality of care, when a clinical service has an incident of suicide. This case is a very powerful example of the most useful finding on the relationship of aggressive fantasy to the possibility of overt acting out of aggression by Megargee (1970)—cards that have a high pull for aggression, such as Card 13MF, indicate poor inhibition of aggressive acting out, and cards that have a low pull, such as Cards 6BM and 7GF, indicate self-instigation of aggressive acting out.

Motivation and Apperception

The effects of several needs on the content of thematic stories, and the conditions that appear to determine whether or not these needs will be manifested in test takers' responses, have become the focal point of interest for many investigators (Atkinson, 1964; Byrne et al., 1963; Blumenthal et al., 1985; Campus, 1976; Chusmir, 1985; Heckausen, 1967; Maddi et al., 1965; McAdams, 1980; Spangler, 1992; Winter, 1973). The previous review of literature that has dealt with aggression represents only one area within the more general field that will presently be surveyed. The achievement motive has been extensively studied by McClelland and colleagues (1953). They have determined that the occurrence of achievement in a thematic story is a joint function of three variables: (1) cues in the everyday environment and in the relatively autonomous thought processes of the individual, (2) specific cues introduced through the experiment, and (3) controllable cues in the specific picture. According to McClelland, when achievement imagery is part of the thematic story, it can be concluded that the individual is motivated to achieve and not indicating wish-fulfilling fantasy.

McArthur (1953) reexamined the effects of need achievement on the content of T.A.T. stories and hypothesized that self-projection accounts for all such effects. This hypothesis inherently questioned the list of eight effects of increasing the test taker's need achievement that had previously been proposed by McClelland, who had considered four possibilities as to the description of the relationship between the test takers and the traits of the characters in his story. These were self-projection, contrast projection, complementary projection, and instrumental projection. McArthur stated that four of McClelland's proposed effects (more mastery tales, hero states need for mastery, hero wishes for mastery, and more mastery images) should hold true, while the other four (failure by the hero, actions to overcome failure, press hostile to mastery, and anxiety about mastery) merely represent artifacts of McClelland's design. This hypothesis was tested against a group of academic overachievers, and the results suggested that the concept of self-projection does explain most of the achievement content of T.A.T. stories.

An interesting study was conducted by Orso (1969), in which he compared the effects of achievement and affiliation arousal on the need for achievement (nAch). As determined from T.A.T. responses, it was found that male nAch scores were not significantly affected by achievement or affiliation arousal, whereas female nAch scores increased significantly after affiliation arousal and decreased significantly after achievement arousal. These sex differences were discussed in terms of differences between the male and female roles in society insofar as there are discrepant meanings of achievement for men and for women.

Several studies have sought to provide an index of the strength of the affiliation motive in T.A.T. stories (Atkinson et al., 1954; Byrne et al., 1963; Carrigan & Julian, 1966; Orso, 1969; Rosenfeld & Franklin, 1966; Shipley & Veroff, 1952). Shipley and Veroff (1952), for example, used "separation imagery" as the criterion for designating affiliation-related stories. The results did not differentiate between aroused and control conditions. The scoring procedures used by Atkinson and colleagues (1954) represent a more general definition of affiliation than those used in the earlier study, in which the definition of affiliation imagery was limited to separation anxiety. In the study by Atkinson and associates, affiliation imagery was scored when the story indicated concern in one or more of the characters over establishing, maintaining, or restoring a positive affective relationship with another person. Affiliation motive arousal in some test takers was achieved by administering a sociometric test to them before the T.A.T. The low motivation control condition was a college classroom. The success of the scoring system and of the method of motive arousal was indicated by the significant difference obtained between the two conditions for their median n affiliation scores.

The relationships between the need for dependency and the T.A.T. and interview measures of dependent behavior were investigated by Kagan and Mussen (1956) and Fitzgerald (1958). Fitzgerald based his research on Rotter's formula (1960)—that need potential is a function of freedom of movement (FM) and need value (NV). Fitzgerald hypothesized that projective responses represent symbolic ways of obtaining gratification, and that frequency of response would be greatest when FM was low and NV high, thus creating a conflict situation. The finding was that projection of dependency on the T.A.T. was significantly related to conflict but not related to interview ratings of dependency. It was inferred that, at least for dependency, the T.A.T. is not a direct medium for the expression of need but is instead related to ego functions (e.g., conflict).

Thematic sexual responses have been investigated in relation to experimentally induced drive and inhibition (Clark, 1952; Clark & Strivzer, 1961; Cuenca & Salvatierra, 1981; Davids & DeVault, 1960; Epstein & Smith, 1957; Martin, 1964; Pine, 1959, 1960; Ruth & Mosatche, 1985; Strivzer, 1961). Clark (1952) found that men shown pictures of nude women projected less sexual imagery than controls, whereas Strivzer (1961), in a comparable study demonstrating the influence of drive on apperception, found that arousal increased sexual imagery. The factor that seems to have determined these conflicting results is that Clark's upper-class test takers were probably more inhibited than the lower-class test takers who participated in Strivzer's study. Thematic responses to some degree depend on the individual's personal evaluation of the situation.

The research conducted by Davids and DeVault (1960) explicitly investigated the relations between personality and perception that were implicitly suggested in the two previously described studies. The T.A.T. and Draw-A-Person Test (D.A.P.T.) were included in a battery of psychological tests given to pregnant women. The sample was subdivided into a "normal" group and an "abnormal" group on the basis of hospital records of childbirth experiences. As predicted, a significantly greater proportion of women in the normal group perceived pregnant women in the T.A.T., particularly a pregnant woman in card 2, and drew female pictures on the D.A.P.T. Davids and DeVault noted that the finding in regard to selective perception in response to T.A.T. stimuli is relevant to the area known as "personality and perception," in which concern is directed to the influences of motivational factors on selection in perceptual organization. In the present study, working with a real-life condition with specific physiological correlates, definite relations between motivation and perception were obtained. Compared to many women who have taken the T.A.T., the pregnant women in this study manifested a much greater likelihood of selectively perceiving pregnant women in the stimuli.

Spangler (1992) and Dana (1968, 1972, 1985, 1993) reported that the majority of the research that has employed thematic techniques to assess human needs has focused specifically on the needs for achievement, affiliation, hostility, sex, and power. This large body of research suggests that the most relevant variables for clinical practice are card cue value, test-taker variables, examiner variables, and arousal conditions. These variables interact with each other and affect the expression of any need in thematic content.

Cue Value

Crude sortings of thematic stimuli for degrees of card pull for any one need have been frequent. While criteria for achievement cards of high and low cue value have been established, cue content for achievement should also be varied for similarity to work experience (Veroff et al., 1953), race (Cowen & Goldberg, 1967), and sex (Veroff et al., 1953). Low cue-value pictures (Veroff et al., 1953) and early use of low cue-value stimuli are valid need measures, where as high cue-value pictures may measure guilt, at least for sex and hostility (Epstein, 1962). Murstein (1963a) has suggested the use of medium or low cue-value cards following strong arousal by instructions. Such cards are clear in regard to identification of hero but ambiguous as to what is happening in the picture.

Test-Taker Variables

Dana (1968, 1972, 1985, 1993) identified these two major classes: (1) relatively permanent conditions that directly affect the intensity of need states (sex, race, religion, social class, education, intelligence, values, parental conditions, and family behaviors); and (2) transitory internal states that influence the expression of need states, generally by inhibition of scores (anxiety, conflict, defenses, guilt, and self-concept conditions). Not all the conditions of either class have the same effects across need states. The following data are relevant to the first class of variables. The sex of the test taker is more relevant to nAch than to nAff. Whenever there is a differential definition by sex of what constitutes any need state, the thematic stimuli and arousal conditions must be varied in accord. Normative data from a sample of both sexes for nAch, nAff, and nPower have shown the contributions of age, education, family income, occupation, and race (Veroff et al., 1953), although test-taker variables had only limited effects. Rosen (1961) showed the interactive effects on nAch of social class, family size, birth order, and age of mother. Nuttal (1964) determined that although race (African American) is relevant to nAch scores, the geographic region of childhood experience has as large an influence. It has also been demonstrated that religion influences nAch, with Jews, Catholics, and Protestants, respectively, obtaining decreasing scores in a national sample (Veroff et al., 1953). One finding relevant to the second class of test-taker conditions was that, for nAch, all measures showed that anxiety or conflict over fears of possible failure served to inhibit or distort achievement scores (Sampson, 1963).

Examiner Variables

Bernstein (1956) has shown that the sheer presence of an examiner and individual differences between examiners influence the expression of affect on the T.A.T. Broverman and colleagues (1960) have pointed out that there are definite differences, at least for nAch, between individual and group administration due to the more immediate influence of the examiner on individual administrations. Sexual imagery and nSex scores are also affected by examiners or social settings

(Martin, 1964). In conclusion, Dana (1968, 1972, 1985, 1993) suggested that future research relevant to clinical assessment should include these issues: (1) simultaneous measurement of needs, (2) assessment of anxiety and conflict relative to each need by independent indices and/or by intraindividual comparison of need scores from neutral and aroused conditions, (3) control of both classes of test-taker conditions, (4) recognition of examiner influences, and (5) consensus on methods for measuring needs.

In the German language, two books dealing with the T.A.T. are in the form of slim volumes. Seifert (1984), in a paperback illuminatingly called *Der Charakter und Seine Geschichten (The Character and Its Stories)*, developed a schema with four subgroups: Complaint, the Gelebte Methode, Style of Life, and Problems of Construction. These apparently refer to an attempt at systemization of the complaint and the actual behavior of the patient. The difficulties of translation reflect the difficulties of conceptualization. The four subdiagnoses resemble in part the subdiagnostic level of Bellak's T.A.T. Blank, where he speaks of a descriptive level of the stories, the interpretive, and the diagnostic level as an attempt to project the progression from primary data to observation-distant diagnoses. In other respects, Seifert proceeds along the lines of classical psychoanalysis in arriving at psychodiagnostic data.

A book by Revers and Allesch (1985) called *Handbuch zum Thematischen Gestaltungstest* concerns itself primarily with the Thematic Gestaltungs Test, a series of 20 pictures designed to supplement the T.A.T. pictures. The volume addresses itself frankly to the clinical practitioner, with a few critical asides to academic psychologists. The interpretation, though following some schemata of the author's own, is basically a psychoanalytic one.

Study of Character and Defenses in the T.A.T.

A very important area of research has been the study of defense and coping mechanisms in thematic tests, which began in Bellak's earliest T.A.T. papers (1944, 1947, 1950). As Schafer (1954) demonstrated in his profound explication of defense mechanisms on the Rorschach, Bellak's early papers and the scoring category on defenses in his Short Form have been enriched by many later studies of defenses on thematic tests (Blum, 1964; Brody & Siegel, 1992; Bush et al., 1969; Cramer, 1991a, Dies, 1976; Haworth, 1963; Heath, 1958; Heilbrun, 1977; Kimura, 1983; Lazarus, 1961). A valuable effort in developing a scoring form for the C.A.T. for adaptational mechanisms is that of Haworth (1963), which is included in the Bellak's manual for scoring and interpreting the C.A.T. (see Chapter 15).

The books by Dies (1976) and Cramer (1991a) on defenses in the T.A.T. are also important additions to this research tradition. A problem with the work of Dies is that the particular way of scoring individual defenses is not clearly spelled out in the book. Cramer's work, on the other hand, sets a high standard for clearly defining the T.A.T. scoring for defense and submitting her scoring method to several reliability and validity studies (Cramer, 1979, 1983, 1991a, 1991b; Cramer & Blatt, 1990; Cramer & Carter, 1978; Cramer et al., 1988). The only drawback of her work is that, unfortunately, she has only studied the three defenses of denial, projection, and identification. Hibbard and colleagues (1994) compared 40 undergraduate college students with 29 successive admissions to an acute psychiatric ward of a VA hospital on Cramer's Defense Mechanism Manual for the T.A.T. They found that the psychiatric patients used more primtive types of defense (more denial and projection) in their T.A.T. stories, whereas the college students used more of the higher-level defense of identification. This study provides further validation of Cramer's scoring approach for defense mechanisms.

Defense mechanisms can be defined as methods employed by an individual in order to manage fears, anxieties, and insecurities. For example, if a child gets bitten by a dog, the child may decide to avoid going near dogs for a period of time. The defense, in this case, is termed *withdrawal* or *avoidance*. If the child continues to avoid dogs over a long period of time, the defensive avoidance of the fear of being bitten by a dog once again may harden into a habitual avoidance of dogs and later transfered to a generalized avoidance of all larger animals. As the habitual avoidance becomes more "second nature,"—that is, as it becomes more ingrained in one's daily behavior of avoiding larger animals and perhaps also assertive people— the defensive avoidance may be said to have "hardened" into becoming part of the individual's character. In other words, the individual now has what may be called an *avoidant personality disorder.*

The word *character* in the English language can be roughly equated with moral traits: One speaks of a good character and a bad character, and of character witnesses (who testify to one's good moral character). The word *character* in German is not exactly identical with but roughly corresponds to the American usage of the term *personality.*

However, in U.S. psychoanalysis, psychiatry, and psychology, the term *character neurosis* is generally accepted and does not clearly relate either to character or neurosis. A *character neurosis* is a disorder of which the afflicted is usually unaware, although it is apparent to persons in his or her environment. It consists of character traits that are ego syntonic for the person having them. They usually cause the person no complaint or concern, and are often the object of pride and affection on the part of their owner. However, by directly bringing him or her into conflict or unpleasant contact with environmental forces, the character traits may produce hardship and discomfort. Probably the most frequently mentioned subspecialty of this disorder is the obsessive/compulsive character neurosis in which a person isolates his or her emotions very well (too well), is apparently unaffected by what goes on around him or her or manages to appear well controlled and smooth, and is often thought of as machine-like in efficiency, orderliness, lack of spontaneity and real warmth, and so forth.

The diagnostic counterpart of a character neurosis is the *psychoneurosis,* in which the person suffers from test symptoms that appear more or less ego alien. It has become axiomatic that there is scarcely a psychoneurosis without some character neurosis, and that there is hardly a character neurosis that does not show some psychoneurotic features under pressure or under some psychoanalytic scrutiny. Nevertheless, the distinction is a very useful one, although it may be only quantitative.

Having neurotic character traits can probably most easily be conceptualized as a syndrome of defenses functioning well enough to avoid direct and open drive conflict at the cost of impoverishment of other ego functions. The impoverished ego functions may be those of spontaneity (e.g., in the case of obsessive rigidity) or those of reality testing (as in the case of extensive rationalizations, such as are involved in systematic political, ethnic, or scientific bias) or in the inability to learn from past experiences (e.g., in the "success neurosis," which will be discussed later).

The justification for this discussion of psychopathology lies in the fact that the T.A.T. may be an excellent means for the analysis of such character problems. Not infrequently, a single story may clearly set forth the central theme of a person's life—an often pernicious theme and one of which the one afflicted may be entirely unconscious. The following story told to picture 1 clearly illustrates such a pernicious theme:

At the age of 9, Karl was intrigued by the wonderful tones of his father's violin. Whenever Karl's father played, Karl would watch and listen and dream. After one such performance, Karl's father asked him to put the violin back in its case. Karl was placing the violin on the table when he just sat back and stared at the instrument. It was at this moment that Karl realized that he must be a violinist like his father. Staring at the violin, Karl suddenly closed his eyes and dreamed, as most children do, of some years later, when he would stand on a pedestal in the Great Palace of Vienna. It was his premiere as a soloist with a great orchestra. He was shaking, nervous, and afraid, yet intent. Intent on fulfilling his ambition. The noise of the impatient audience, the shouting of the stage hands in the adjustment of props and lights, the tuning of the various instruments, all helped to create his nervousness. Then, without further delay, the curtain opened, the audience became dead silent, the conductor knocked his baton repeatedly on the stand, raised it a final time, and on the drop, Karl began to play. A sweet Viennese waltz, combined with the pleasures of his heart and soul, poured from his violin. The music ended, the audience rose to its feet and acclaimed Karl as a great interpreter of his country's music. The music of his father. Taking the customary bow in the recognition of his appreciation, Karl suddenly fell from the pedestal. He never awoke from his dream, you see, Karl was dead. The shock of visualizing such a success was too much for his ailing heart to bear. Thus, the music world lost a promising musician because of a violin, an ambition, and a dream.

Freud coined a term, *Schicksalsneurose,* which can only be poorly translated as "fate neurosis." It is sometimes spoken of as a success neurosis, with a more limited meaning. It could also be called the "Schlemiehl syndrome" to describe a person for whom everything seems to go wrong, through no apparent fault of his or her own—fate always seems to play the person a dirty trick. The term *success neurosis* is more properly reserved for those cases where the attainment of success produces anxiety, depression, and other symptoms. Both disorders have in common a deep masochistic disturbance.

The story just quoted can probably be easily analyzed for its main features by anyone conversant with psychopathology: Karl tries to fiddle as well as his father. When he permits himself this attainment, even in a dream, he dies for it. This must be viewed as a theme of competition with the father (probably on an oedipal level) and the punishment commensurate with the crime of wanting to replace the father. The analysis of the story was corroborated by the man's therapist, who reported that he had suffered from repeated uncanny failures in his life. Hence, it is possible to guess that the main content of this person's character neurosis is almost entirely accounted for in this story.

Another individual told the following story to picture 11:

> Two men have come to kill the dragon. When the dragon appears, spouting flames that light up the area, one man flees in terror, while the other, equally afraid, hides from the terrifying animal by turning away from it but is unable to flee.
> This dragon has been the scourge of a country, devastating the land by scorching it with his breath whenever it walks abroad. Two strangers who visit this country are told of this danger to the community and volunteer to kill this menace.
> The man who has remained behind finds soon that the heat and light disappear and turning around comes face to face with the dragon, who no longer is terrifying. The dragon speaks of his loneliness because all run from him. He wants to be able to have contact with people but realizes they are frightened of him. He is very happy that this man has stayed and asks what it is that makes everyone run from him. The man tells him of the destruction the dragon leaves behind him. The dragon then understands this but also knows that his breathing flame is a part of him that he does not know how to change. He promises that he will not in the future wander around as he has done but remain hidden in the rocks where he will not do injury, and the man returns to the village to tell the people what happened. The people run him out. They are divided between those who do not believe him and those who believe him but blame him for not having taken this opportunity to kill the dragon, since they are sure the dragon will not keep his promise. However, the dragon does, and as the community again is able in time to build up its wealth, the people make pilgrimages to the mountain to leave thank-you offerings to the dragon.

It is most regrettable that Alfred Adler had to renounce all of psychoanalysis in order to feel that his contribution was secure; it is equally regrettable that psychoanalysis has not adopted some of his terms (e.g., "style of life"). Many character neuroses can most easily be described in terms of a defensive style of life, geared to neurotic goals, and blindly repetitive. For instance, in the case of the story just quoted, the patient clearly identified with the would-be monster who really wanted to be loved and appreciated. The patient felt monstrous inside because of his hostility. Orally deprived, the patient had often described himself as feeling like a puppy—inappropriately over friendly to strangers, yet at the same time holding himself aloof from any real emotional involvement. He often antagonized people deeply without being aware of it and left himself open to being hurt by his expectation of being loved by everyone. In the story, he is not only the monster but also the victim (who wants to be) befriended by the monster. Such a style of life finally led to enough realistic repercussions to bring him into treatment.

A different problem is depicted in the stories of a brilliant young scientist, who suffered conflicts between his allegiance to the ways of his parents and new ideas (superimposed on earlier conflicts). This is his story to picture 1:

> A youngster has been called in from play by his mother to practice his violin lessons. He is annoyed and sulking over it. He is thinking of all the activities he would prefer to be carrying on. But he is a talented and sensitive child. Soon he will get over his annoyance and will take the instrument into his hands and practice. He will begin to enjoy his lessons.

This story shows a conflict between autonomy and compliance, which is resolved in favor of compliance. The most significant aspect of this story is that the compliance becomes ego syntonic: He will begin to enjoy his lessons.

The other stories show that this process of psychoneurosis into character neurosis was not quite successful. Following is his story to picture 3BM:

The peasant boy has just been told by his father that he may not go to the big city to study sculpting and carving. He is needed to help on the farm. The family is poor and cannot pay for hired labor. The boy has gone into his own room and, unable to control himself, leans against his cot and weeps. His carving knife lies on the floor. But in time he will forget and accommodate himself to the limited ways and aspirations of the peasant. The weight of frustration will make him somewhat irritable, impatient, dulled, unaspiring, and uninspiring.

To picture 9BM, he tells the following:

Four hoboes relaxing. They have just finished their improvised lunch, prior to which they had relaxed, prior to which they had breakfasted, prior to which they relaxed. On completing their noon nap, they will be on their way, planning the evening meal so they may again relax. They have accepted tedium as their lot and made peace with it. Tedium is the lot of so many of us; we differ only in that we have not reconciled to it. Within us weighs heavily the hope and longing for end and purpose.

And to picture 14:

He has spent several pained and fruitless hours twisting and turning in his bed, dissecting in his mind the two choices before him. Shall he hold onto the security of his present job, whose future is uncertain, or leap into the uncertainty of the present in the hope of achieving a greater certainty in the future? How difficult he finds it to renounce! He leaves his bed, goes to the window, and looks out among the pinpoints that dot, and the houses silhouetted against, the gradually lightening sky—as though they would offer him some aid in resolving his dilemma. He will return to his bed, his choice unmade, and will find a solution in his dreams.

These stories show the unresolved conflict, the intrapsychic awareness of the deadening process of repression and emotional isolation: tedium, dulled, uninspiring. Only irritability and impatience remain as a semblance of emotion, in what otherwise could best be characterized by Myerson's term, *anhedonia*. This anhedonia, this absence of any pleasurable sensation, is frequently the outcome of gross emotional impoverishment under the impact of obsessive/compulsive defenses, somewhat equivalent to a mild depression. The process depicted in the T.A.T. is incomplete. Had it gone on to its completion, the person would probably become somewhat peculiar, mild-mannered, gentle, and living up to one-tenth of his potential.

This study of the character really involves a study of the defenses. The study of the defenses is so intimately connected with the problems of personality that this topic had to be discussed extensively in the elaboration of the ego psychology of projective techniques and again in discussing the relationship of the overt to the latent. If this test-taker matter is once more taken up here for its own sake, it is because a strictly clinical discussion should be presented in its own context: This aspect of apperception is relatively the newest, least is known about it, and it is probably the most important.

According to Fenichel (1945), ego defenses may be divided into successful defenses, which bring about a cessation of that which is warded off, and unsuccessful defenses, which necessitate a repetition or perpetuation of the warding-off process to prevent the eruption of the warded-off impulses. Sublimation is a successful, not a pathogenic, defense. It is not characterized by a specific mechanism and is thus not very easily discernible in T.A.T. stories.

Denial is an exceedingly common defense. The tendency to deny painful sensations and facts is as old as the feeling of pain itself. The ability to deny unpleasant parts of reality is frequent, both in children and in adults, and we find many instances of this defense mechanism in T.A.T. stories.

One patient, in response to picture 2, described the woman ordinarily seen as pregnant as "slim, thin, and well proportioned." His mother's pregnancy with a younger sibling had played an important role, and pregnancy fantasies were at the root of his anxieties. Here, he simply denies the existence of pregnancy.

Denial of one's own aggressive impulses is another very frequent defense. The following story was told to picture 18GF by a woman who had attempted to kill her children:

> Looks like a mother holding a child at the foot of a staircase; might have been that the child fell down the staircase and the mother picked him up to see if he's hurt; looking him over very anxiously but I don't think he's hurt. The mother will be much relieved. (?) Tripped.

This picture is usually seen as a woman attempting to choke another. The test taker who told this story identified with the older (maternal) figure but felt compelled to deny any element of aggression in the situation.

Projection is one of the most archaic of the defense mechanisms. It belongs to that early stage in which everything pleasurable is experienced as belonging to the ego, while everything painful is experienced as being nonego.

In one sense, of course, the T.A.T. deals entirely with projection, and some degree of this particular defense mechanism is to be seen in every T.A.T. story. However, in certain stories this element is particularly strong. When figures are introduced that are not in the pictures, this element can be said to be at work. In a story such as the following (to picture 13MF), the dynamic content (apparently killing the girl and directing the aggression against her) suggests the use of projection by this test taker. (The fact that he seems partially aware of his own guilt feelings does not obviate the use of projection.) It is as if he might say, "True, it's my fault, but it's hers even more!"

> This is a young man who is going to the local university . . . a student. . . . He is very moralistic . . . that is, very virtuous . . . having a highly developed sense of what is right and what is wrong. He is also very religious. . . . He has been brought up very strictly and believes that one of the greatest sins that man can commit is to have sexual intercourse with a woman out of wedlock. . . . One evening, at a party, for some unknown reason, having taken too many drinks and feeling slightly lightheaded, be became very intimate with one of the girls present. He . . . his animal instincts came to the fore and he abandoned all his ideas of virtue, etc. He took this woman up to his room and went to bed with her. The next morning, after becoming sober and having regained his virtuous sense or whatever you want to call it . . . he looked over and saw this woman beside him in utter nakedness. He was filled with anger, and wild. Let's see (murmurs to himself) . . . and bitter passion at what he had done. A profound hatred swelled up in his chest for this woman that lay next to him. He ordered . . . she by this time had become awake . . . and he ordered her to leave his room. . . . She, not understanding what had brought this attitude of his about, believed that he was joking, and refused to leave in a jocular manner. This man could think of nothing but to clear himself of this sin he had committed . . . . cleanse himself of this sin. . . . And as this

woman lay there laughing, and being overcome with his guilt, he seized her by the throat and strangled her. Rising from the bed, and putting on his clothes, he became . . . he realized his predicament. He not only had committed a sin . . . a moral sin . . . but he had committed a greater sin by taking her life. . . . He gazed down as she lay there at her statuesque stillness and was filled with remorse. Remembering a few days earlier . . . that a few days earlier he had bought a bottle of iodine, and which was now in the cabinet of the washroom, he went there and gulped down its contents (laughs) and consequently died. That was the end of that. . . . I just said that he strangled her because she was laying in bed next to him, and that was the easiest thing he could have done, by reaching over and grasping her neck.

Repression is a relatively less archaic mechanism, a derivative of denial. It consists of an unconsciously purposeful forgetting or not becoming aware of internal impulses or external events that usually represent possible temptations or punishments for, or mere allusions to, objectionable instinctual demands. The purposeful exclusion of these facts from consciousness is intended to hinder their real effects as well as the pain on becoming aware of them. Sometimes, certain facts are remembered as such, but their connections, their significance, their emotional value, are repressed.

There are many neurotic attitudes that are obvious attempts to deny or to repress some impulse, or to defend the person against some instinctual danger. They are cramped and rigid attitudes, hindering the expression of contrary impulses, which sometimes nevertheless break through in various ways. The original opposite attitudes still exist in the unconscious; these secondary, conscious attitudes are called *reaction formations*.

Both the conscious and the original, unconscious attitude are apparent in the following story told to picture 17BM:

The man shown here is a circus performer and has been one for many years. His ambition has always been to be a solo performer instead of part of a trapeze trio. Until now he has not had the opportunity. In tonight's performance he will save a fellow trouper from a serious accident and as a reward for his bravery will be given the chance to do his act alone.

In this story, the act of bravery, saving the fellow trouper, is the reaction formation, or disguise, for the unconscious aggressive wishes against this person. It is somewhat reminiscent of the overprotective mother who constantly fusses over her child to hide from herself her basic (unconscious) lack of acceptance of the child.

Undoing is related to reaction formation. In reaction formation, an attitude is taken that contradicts the original one; in undoing, one more step is taken. Something positive is done which, actually or magically, is the opposite of something which, again actually or in imagination, has been done before. This mechanism can be most clearly observed in certain compulsive symptoms that are made up of two actions, the second of which is a direct reversal of the first. For example, a patient must first turn on the gas jet and then turn it off again. Obsessive elaboration is not uncommon in the stories of obsessive/compulsive patients. The following story was told to picture 13MF:

A man and woman who may be in a bedroom or living room with a cot. She may have been ill and had been put to bed. The man may have seen to her wants or he may be a doctor who had been with her a long time, especially through the night, and is now very tired. The woman may be sleeping or resting or may have died, and the man, her husband or doctor, has just gone through a long siege, or if the woman is his wife who died, he shows sorrow, or if he is just sick, he shows fear and is tired. It may be that homicide has been committed and the man shows remorse and realization of the gravity of his act. Or there may have been cohabitation, the woman undraped in bed, the man having dressed. Also, a husband getting up early in the morning to go to work, not quite awake, while his wife is still asleep.

In this case, at least four stories show a progression from a relatively innocuous apperception to breakthrough of plainly homicidal thoughts. Whether cohabitation is a further progression to an even worse crime in the mind of the test taker or whether it constitutes a renewed vigor of defenses that culminates in the utterly innocuous domestic scene could not be ascertained.

Another mechanism of defense prevalent in compulsion neuroses is *isolation.* Here, the patient has not forgotten his pathogenic traumata, but has lost trace of their connections and their emotional significance. The most important special case of this defense mechanism is the isolation of an idea from the emotional cathexis that originally was connected with it. The patient remains calm while discussing the most exciting events. The following story, told to picture 2, is an excellent example of isolation:

Very interesting picture. Is it a painting of some sort? The first idea that comes into my head is terribly Hollywoodish. *(The idea, not the picture.)* A man and a wife who work a farm and she looks as if her parents and forebears have also worked a farm. The girl in the foreground is the daughter who doesn't want to work the farm but who wants to lead a more intellectual life away from the burdens of the farm. The parents resent this. They seem to ignore her. She looks as if she's leaving them after an unsuccessful argument or discussion as to whether she's doing the right thing or not. I have no doubt she will leave them. The part where she's standing in the picture seems very rocky—whereas where the parents are standing seems very well worn. So we might say that her path may be uphill and that may be causing some of her parents' dissent. Well, the parents will continue in their way of life and the girl will continue on her rocky road and the way it always happens in Hollywood is that the girl always makes something of herself. *(How does it happen outside of Hollywood?)* It can be either way, but that's because I really don't care.

The last few words of the story—"I really don't care"—is the credo of the isolated person. By this defense mechanism, he has managed to detach himself from all his feelings. This detachment is also inherent in his opening words: "Very interesting picture." The whole story has a cold, detached, intellectualized feeling tone common to stories of test takers who use the mechanism of isolation. Isolation and overintellectualization usually go together. In fact, the normal prototype of isolation is the process of rational, logical thinking, which actually consists of the elimination of affective associations in the interest of objectivity. Compulsion neurotics, in their isolation activities, behave like caricatures of normal thinkers.

Whenever a person meets frustration, there is a tendency for him or her to long for earlier periods in life when experiences were more pleasant, and for earlier types of satisfaction that were more complete. The intensity of this tendency increases with two factors that are closely interrelated: the degree of hesitancy with which the individual accepts newer modes of satisfaction, and the degree to which he or she is fixated to earlier types. However, very intense and sudden disappointments and dangers may provoke *regressions* even in individuals without strong fixations.

Regression is much more common in children than in adults who are not psychotic, since the precondition for the use of regression as a mechanism of defense is a weakness of the ego organization. The following story was told by a 9-year-old boy in response to story 3 of the C.A.T.:

Well, this lion is troubled by mice. He's sitting there and doesn't know what to do about the mice. He's tried everything, so he calls the exterminator and the exterminator says, "The only thing to do is to blow the mice out," but the lion says, "I've tried that and lost three houses." "Why not make traps?" "But the mice have certain things that disconnect the traps and they always get the cheese." "Why not try poison, then?" "But that's impossible because the mice know it's poison and they'll never come out." Finally the lion decides he will move to Florida, but when he gets there he sees now . . . he's being troubled by worms coming through the floor. So finally he says, "I'll go back and live in the jungle where I belong."

This little boy was troubled by his younger sibling. First he tried aggression, then agression with the help of someone else (the therapist), then withdrawal (moving to Florida), and when that didn't help either, he regressed to infantile habits (the jungle).

The mechanism of *displacement* is employed when the anxiety aroused by a certain situation, person, or the like is displaced onto something else. There can be displacement of affect as well as displacement of object. In T.A.T. stories, this defense reveals itself by the use of far-distant times and places and by ascribing problems to people other than the hero, as well as by changing the nature of the anxiety. One test taker, of Jewish American stock, began his story to picture 4 as follows:

This seems to be taking place in some isolated place. Maybe a South Sea Island.

The same test taker started his story to picture 2 by saying:

This girl, about 19 years old, would probably be named Olga, of Ukranian parentage and stock.

Coping

A concept broader than the one of defense is the concept of coping. It offers a useful way of viewing the evaluation of the T.A.T. (and C.A.T. and S.A.T.). Being asked to tell stories to the pictures is to perform a task. How does the test taker go about coping with this task? How does he or she respond behaviorally? Is she confused, frightened, negativistic? Does the story constitute a good coping effort? Does the test taker achieve closure? Are there different ways in which closure is being achieved? Is the first attempt at a story the most successful and the following two increasingly disorganized by uncontrolled drives? Or is it the other way around and the stories show improved coping effort, suggesting a potential of dealing with problems that were found overtaxing initially? In a broad sense, all of human behavior—including dreams, neurotic and psychotic symptoms, and "normal" behavior—can be usefully viewed as attempts at coping. Vaillant (1971, 1977) discussed the adaptational coping mechanism of *sublimation,* when one expresses undesirable feelings, such as aggressive anger, in an adaptive vehicle of self-expression, such as assertive playing of music, expressive dancing, or painting. Other coping mechanisms, according to Vaillant, are *humor and wit* (e.g., when one is able to laugh at one's own areas of vulnerabilities), *anticipation,* (when one actively prepares for a difficult task expected to be confronted in the future) and *suppression* (when one actively puts a distressing thought or feeling out of one's immediate attention and consciousness in order to be able to go about one's activities, such as when one is mourning the death of a loved one, but has to put this temporarily out of one's mind during the day at one's place of work).

Vaillant has arranged about 30 different defense and coping mechanisms into a theoretical hierarchy of adaptational mechanisms. The hierarchy has four levels—psychotic defenses, immature defenses, neurotic defenses, and the above-noted coping mechanisms. The model is based on a continuum of mental health functioning from severe pathology to psychologically healthy adaptation. Anna Freud (1936) outlined a developmental model of defense and coping mechanisms, beginning with those that are typical at infancy (withdrawal, avoidance, denial), early childhood (identification with the aggressor, displacement, reveral of affect, clowning, affectualization), elementary school ages (repression, reaction formation, isolation of affect, intellectualization), to those of adolescence (rationalization, asceticism, altruistic surrender, passive aggressive acting out, etc.).

An important direction for future clinical use of thematic tests is to develop a clear way to score the full array of adaptational mechanisms of Vaillant's and Anna Freud's schemes with the same level of empirical specificity in Cramer's (1991a) work on projection, denial, and identification.

CHAPTER 10

THEMATIC ANALYSIS IN THE STUDY OF NARRATIVE AND LIFE HISTORY

The study of narrative has developed into an interdisciplinary field including psychology, sociology, political science, comparative literature, literary theory, folklore, anthropology, and many other fields (Cortazzi, 1993; Griffin, 1993; Mishler, 1995; Polkinghorne, 1988; Sarbin, 1986; Toolan, 1988; Young, 1987). The main focus is the study of different types of narrative behavior, which ranges from studies of traditional narratives of fairytales of different cultures (Child et al., 1958; Cramer, 1991a), myths, and children's storybooks (McClelland, 1961) to studies of the way narratives may function in the reporting of a rape (Abrams, 1991) or the chronology of a lynching (Griffin, 1993). From this perspective, the analysis of different forms of narrative behavior provides a framework for understanding a culture, an individual's identity, or the meaning of a significant experience.

Cain (1991) suggested that the telling of personal life histories of alcoholism in Alcoholics Anonymous provides a very important opportunity for acquisition of a sense of identity and self-understanding. The content of the life story and how the story is told are both equally important, as Roy Schafer (1958) emphasized in a rare and valuable early contribution on the T.A.T.

Anthropologists have often employed the method of learning about a particular culture by locating an articulate individual with whom to undertake an in-depth interview of the current way of life and personal life history. Other approaches in anthropology are to examine the relationship between the personal history of cultural informants and the anthropologist's manner of writing up these stories (Clifford & Marcus, 1986; Fabian, 1983; Geertz, 1988). Applying the tools of linguistics and literary structure analysis to examples of event structure models in ethnographic data is another application of the study of narrative to the field of anthropology (Corsaro & Heise, 1990) as well as to the field of sociology (Griffin, 1993).

Good examples of this broader, interdisciplinary study of narrative behavior is that of Ochs and Taylor (1989), who compare the narrative structure of stories families relate at dinner to detective stories; the cross-cultural comparison of newlywed stories by Veroff and associates (1993); or Michaels's (1981) research on different ways children relate personal stories during "sharing time" in day care and early school settings. Research on the structure and function of narrative was conducted by Abrams (1977), Miller and Moore (1989), Miller and colleagues (1990), and Sutton-Smith and colleagues (1981) in studies of how narratives are used by a culture as part of the socialization process. Studies of the structure and function of narrative in the psychotherapy process have been conducted by Spence (1982) and White and Epston (1990). One of the main organs of communication for this exciting interdisplinary field of narrative is the *Journal of Narrative Analysis and Life History*.

In this chapter, we provide an example how Bellak's Scoring System for the T.A.T. may be extended to the study of other forms of narrative behavior, such as dreams, folktales, narrative discourse in Alcoholic Anonymous meetings, or works of literature. Since the T.A.T. is a group of short stories, perhaps the best example we can provide is an analysis of several short stories of the author, Somerset Maugham. In this case, the artistic product serves as the primary data from which inferences about the personality of the writer are made with the help of the same outline that we used for T.A.T. stories.

Earlier, we touched on some of the differences between the creative process under ordinary circumstances and in response to T.A.T. or C.A.T. cards (see Chapter 2). We mentioned the difference in mental set, among other things. The creative end product in the case of a published literary effort and a T.A.T. story also vary widely, of course. The published story may be the result of innumerable rewritings and editing (from that standpoint, writers' first drafts may be the best source for analysis of their personality). Also, part of a writer's frame of reference is adaptive to the audience the writer wants to reach. Many writers may have developed a style adaptively and, to a considerable extent, consciously, and may even have made a concentrated effort to keep content referring to themselves personally out of their work.

Despite all these differences and caveats to be kept in mind, the end product, unless vitally affected by other than the author, is a product of one's personality, albeit modified by a variety of adaptive ego mechanisms. This product therefore basically lends itself to analysis as a personal document just as T.A.T. stories do, except that one has to allow for special complexities and possible difficulties in arriving at correct inferences with regard to unconscious motivation. (Incidentally, the analysis of political documents and speeches with regard to the personality of the author is also possible and may be extremely valuable in the future if the caveats about ghostwriters, editors, and the like are remembered.) Among writers, some always write essentially about themselves, and every story is their own story. Others attempt to keep themselves out and supposedly "think up" stories totally unrelated to their own experiences. Nevertheless, their product—in terms of choice of content and with regard to expressive and cognitive style, aside from its susceptibility to study by content analysis in the sense of counting the frequency of words, noun-verb ratio, and so on—remains uniquely theirs and therefore lends itself in principle to an analysis of their personality (Judson, 1963).

Somerset Maugham's stories fall somewhere between the two extremes of direct biography and self-exclusion. Manifestly, source material comes from all over the world—Europe, Russia, the Far East. However, Maugham's personality shines through all of them.

Thirty of Maugham's (1953) stories were selected randomly from two volumes, picked by the senior author's then 6-year-old daughter and by their numerical characteristics—1, 2, 11, 12, 21, 22. It will become quite clear that the themes and characteristics that become manifest in the selected stories have a great similarity to most of the rest of Maugham's writings, including his major work, *Of Human Bondage,* which is considered to be, in large part, autobiographical.

Somerset Maugham: Analysis of the Stories[1]

The first story, luckily enough, is "Rain"—luckily, because it is particularly widely known both as a movie as well as the original short story.

"Rain"

Descriptive Theme.   A zealous missionary, driven by great religious fervor, has always resisted the ordinary feelings of compassion, sex, and fear in his desire to rise above them for the sake of a stern religious morality. When he meets Sadie Thompson, a prostitute, he feels compelled to interfere with her activities in his efforts to save her soul (at the cost of great misery and actual danger to her). However, he finds himself increasingly attracted to her (note his dream of breast-like mountains, his remaining with her later and later into the night) and ultimately makes a sexual advance. He kills himself in consequence.

Interpretive Theme.   If emotions are very strong, especially sexual desire, and one tries to control them while in intense contact with a woman, control may be destroyed as well as oneself.

Diagnostic Level.   Presence of strong drives, aggressive and sexual. Attempted defenses are denial, repression, rationalization, withdrawal, and reaction formation. Adaptively tries to deal with his conflict by becoming a missionary. Fears loss of control over drives, especially sexual drive. Fears destruction by women. Concern about self-destruction; suicidal ideas are present.

These bald statements leave out many subtleties of the story. For the sake of economy, we will point out only a few of the other features. The theme of the missionary is not the only one. He is not the only hero; Sadie Thompson is another.

Descriptive Theme.   A prostitute is reduced to a fearful clinging wreck by a zealous missionary bent on saving her soul, but she rises contemptuously when his moral principles collapse and ordinary lust shows through.

Interpretive Theme.   If a lustful woman meets a zealously moral man, she is reduced to weakness, but she recovers her strength if the man appears prey to lust.

---

[1] Quotations on pages 207–215 from Maugham (1953) are reprinted by permission.

Diagnostic Level.   Woman is seen as lustful, seductive. Moral man is seen as strong. Man unable to control his desires is seen as contemptible by woman. Control is very important; its loss is contemptible.

Another subtheme is concerned with Dr. Macphail. One must consider him another identification figure for the author (of course, Maugham projects some of his own sentiments on all the figures). One may simply remark that the doctor appears compassionate, but tries to remain uninvolved to avoid the discomfort of too much emotion. He tries to accept with passivity the missionary, his own wife, and the world around him but finds himself uneasy. He engages in action in a desultory way (and with a good deal of conflict) only when he feels he can no longer avoid it.

The minor female characters in the story appear as controlling, either by their aggressive attitudes or by their moralistic ones. In fact, the most repetitive concern seems to be with emotions that could overcome one, especially with regard to women who tend to control.

One may anticipate some broader inferences here by pointing out that the waitress, Mildred, in *Of Human Bondage* is not too different from Sadie Thompson in her effect on the protagonist. Nor is the principle character, Philip, himself a doctor, too different from Dr. Macphail. It is common knowledge that Maugham was a medical school graduate.

"The Fall of Edward Barnard"

In a general sense, one may describe this story as a not so gentle mockery of American culture, especially as seen through the bourgeois pretensions of wealthy women and their effect on men.

Descriptive Theme.   Edward Barnard is a traditional and upstanding young Chicagoan. Just as soon as he saves enough money from his work in Tahiti, he plans to return home and marry the beautiful, cultured, controlling, and ambitious Isabel. However, he comes to enjoy the easy and simple life of the islands, particularly the companionship of a half-caste girl. Unlike Isabel, she puts him at ease.

Bateman Hunter, in love with Isabel, but friend to Edward also, is vaguely puzzled and distressed by Edward's change. He tries to persuade Edward to return home. When Edward renounces Isabel, Hunter himself returns to marry her. Isabel's dreams, as she embraces Hunter, are of business success, tea dances, and the look of distinction and solidity which horn-rimmed glasses will give her new fiancee.

Interpretive Theme.   If one is caught in the demands of petty bourgeois culture, as represented by controlling, ambitious women, one may find life much happier in an undemanding culture (which permits more passivity) and with simpler women (who are no threat and do not make one feel inferior). A selfless male friend helps out reliably.

Diagnostic Level.   An unease about cultural demands. Sees women of society as subtly controlling, demanding, ambitious. Sophisticated women of this kind produce feelings of unease, inferiority. Attempts solution of anxiety and conflict by withdrawal (geographic and psychological) and by turning to more primitive women and less demanding societies. Uses rationalization, emotional isolation, and withdrawal as defense. A male friend is seen as selfless and dependable. Since we know something of the author's actual life history, we can add that his travels to primitive countries were adaptive ways of dealing with his problems. Writing was another way of dealing with his conflicts. He described writing *Of Human Bondage* as a cathartic experience. His friendships with men were often lifelong, his heterosexual relations apparently either transitory or distant and tempestuous (Judson, 1963).

"The Yellow Streak"

Descriptive Theme.   Izzart, the handsome, English-educated son of a white father and half-caste mother, is constantly unnerved by the thought that someone will discover his mixed parentage. During a mission with Campion, a visitor to the Malayan Jungle, the men are involved in a boating accident. Izzart is so intent on saving his own life that he ignores Campion's pleas for help. Miraculously, both men survive. Campion is publicly silent about Izzart's part in the near catastrophe but, triggered by Izzart's fear and guilt, makes it privately plain to him that he attributes his cowardice to the "yellow streak"—the "tainted" blood.

Interpretive Theme.   If a man is "tainted" by a (racially) inferior woman (mother), he fears his inferiority (the yellow streak) will emerge to his shame and peril. His fear that others will recognize this inferiority constantly haunts him.

Diagnostic Level.   Feels inferior. Projects his feelings of inferiority on others. Inferiority is blamed on a woman, specifically his mother. Woman is seen as something inferior as well as source of embarrassment and shame. The main concern is one of controlling emotion, particularly fear.

"P & O"

Descriptive Theme.   Mrs. Hamlyn is returning alone to England from the tropics after 20 years of happy marriage. Her husband has fallen helplessly in love with another woman. She and her husband both viewed the intrusion of his new love as one would an illness—it is uncontrollable, and one must bow before it. On shipboard, she meets the vital and forward-looking Mr. Gallagher, a retired planter, who is going home to begin a new life. Mr. Gallagher has left behind his native wife, after making what he considered generous financial provision for her. This wife, however, has become incensed and cast a spell upon him. When Mr. Gallagher sickens and dies on board, to the consternation of the ship's doctor, apparently as a result of this spell, Mrs. Hamlyn's own anger evaporates, and she feels great compassion for the love that, like an unrestrainable force (a spell), befell her husband.

Interpretive Theme.   If love befalls one, it is like a sickness against which one is defenseless. If one fights a (native) woman's love, she will kill one. It is best to bow to uncontrollable emotions.

Diagnostic Level.   Fear of emotion, particularly of heterosexual love. Fear of being overwhelmed by love (for woman). Fear of being killed by hate of woman. Defense used is emotional isolation and sublimation into compassion.

This story also involves the complexities of the caste system in British society, observations on emotional callousness, and selfless relationship between simple men. Once again, a doctor (the ship's doctor—a sympathetic character) is cast into a hopeless conflict between passivity and activity.

"Mr. Harrington's Washing"

Descriptive Theme.   Mr. Harrington is the prototype of the proper Philadelphian. He has a strong set of morals and principles of behavior, which he takes with him into the upheaval of revolutionary Russia. There he comes in contact with Alexandra, "a mad Russian," who has had a powerful effect on all sorts of men and whom he significantly nicknames Delilah. Mediocre, resolute, stubborn, but rigidly sticking to his principles throughout, Harrington insists on getting his laundry before departing from unsafe Petrograd. Alexandra, who loyally accompanies him on this last mission, is attracted by a street crowd. Harrington, trailing behind her, is attacked and killed.

Interpretive Theme.   If one has a strong set of moral and behavioral patterns, one is helped through many difficult situations. But one may also be led into absurdity. If one gets tangled up with a woman, she is likely to cause one's misfortune and death even though her intentions are the best.

Diagnostic Level.   Conflict between conventional and less rigid behavior. Gentle mockery of bourgeois mind in unresolved conflict. Woman is seen as powerful and dangerous. Even when she means to be loyal and protective, she may be fatal.

"Footprints in the Jungle"

Descriptive Theme.   Bronson, a plantation man, takes Cartwright, temporarily down on his luck, into his home in order to lend him a helping hand. In time, Cartwright and Mrs. Bronson have a love affair, "swayed by turbulent passion." Although all three are basically decent people, Mrs. Bronson encourages her lover to kill her husband rather than risk discovery. The police chief learns of the crime, but there is insufficient evidence to bring the case to court. The new couple live on happily, since remorse for a crime does not seem to sit heavily if one can be absolutely sure one will not be found out.

Interpretive Theme.   If a woman comes between two men, she causes trouble and death. Sexual passion may be the motive for murder even though the people involved were, and remain, perfectly decent people. They may not even suffer remorse.

Diagnostic Level.   Sees women as causing trouble to men, as separating them, and as being fatal to them. There is the suggestion of an oedipal problem: one man must be killed for the other to get this woman. Passion is seen as overpowering, threatening to transcend control, specifically control of aggression. An uninte-grated superego condones murderous aggression as an uncontrollable force.

"A Friend in Need"

Descriptive Theme.   A seemingly pleasant, kind, middle-class sort of man is ap-proached by an irresponsible, happy-go-lucky acquaintance, who is in desperate need of a job. The former casually sends him to his death by proposing to him a dangerous swimming feat as the price for a job—a job which in fact he doesn't have to offer at all.

Interpretive Theme.   If one is happy-go-lucky, one may be prey to the most incon-gruous hostilities of one's fellow man. This is probably due to disapproval and envy of an easy way of life and implied success with women.

Diagnostic Level.   Fear of and desire for drifting, passivity. Sees people as incongru-ously and often casually cruel. This ascription of cruelty may be associated with con-cern over their envy and disapproval of easy-going ways and of success with women. The latter are felt as dangerous. There is fear of helplessness, guilt over sexual de-sires, and passivity, and a great deal of cruelty is projected on others.

"A Romantic Young Lady"

Descriptive Theme.   The beautiful daughter of a duchess falls in love with a poor young man who returns her affection. Her mother disapproves and begs for help from a countess who employs him as mule driver to her valuable and showy team. When the young man is made to choose between his beloved and his glamorous job, he chooses the latter.

Interpretive Theme.   If a man has to choose between a woman and an esteemed job (with animals), he rather callously chooses the job.

Diagnostic Level.   A sarcastic, low esteem is expressed for women. "There is not a pair of mules in the whole of Spain to come up to ours . . . one can get a wife any day of the week, but a place like this is found only once in a lifetime. I should be a fool to throw it up for a woman" (Maugham, 1953). So says the young man.

   A subtheme is also concerned with the fact that the duchess and countess, though rivals previously, get together in this adversity. The beautiful young woman is met many years later, settled down comfortably as the stout, flaunting widow of a diplomat.

"The Kite"

Descriptive Theme.   A young boy, in joint venture with his parents, learns to love fly-ing kites. As he grows older, this becomes the guiding passion of his and their lives. He meets a girl of whom his mother disapproves and, against her wishes, marries. His marriage is unhappy, his wife interferes with his kite flying, and in anger he leaves her and returns to his parents. In retribution, his wife smashes his best kite. He retaliates angrily by choosing prison to the alternative of paying her support.

Interpretive Theme.   If a young man who has lived happily with his parents gets involved with a woman of whom they disapprove, the new woman may make him unhappy, interfere with his freedom, destroy the things he loves. Feels tremendous anger toward her.

> You see, I don't know a thing about flying a kite. Perhaps it gives him a sense of power, as he watches it soaring towards the clouds and of mastery over the elements as he seems to bend the winds of heaven to his will. It may be that in some queer way, he identifies himself with the kite flying so free and so high above him, and it's as if it were an escape from the monotony of life. It may be that in some dim, confused way, it represents an ideal of freedom and adventure. And you know, when a man once gets bitten with the virus of the ideal not all the King's doctors and not all the King's surgeons can rid him of it. (Maugham, 1953)

These are the events commented upon by the narrator of the story.

Diagnostic Level.   Tends to see life with parents as peaceful in an infantile (sexually?) gratifying way. Woman is seen as making one unhappy, controlling one's life, interfering with infantile phallic pleasures and with man's freedom. Woman is seen as undermining his power. Conflict between monotony and adventurous, whimsical diversion. Woman is seen as plainly castrating, evil, controlling, interfering with narcissistic (sexual?) pleasures.

"The Happy Couple"

Descriptive Theme.   An apparently insignificant couple, in love with each other and warmly devoted to their baby, are found to have been the one-time doctor and female companion to an old lady they killed. Her inheritance enabled them to be married. At their trial, the jury found them not guilty despite overwhelming evidence, supposedly because of the fact that they had not had sexual intercourse during their long premarital relationship. The woman had been willing to commit murder to marry the man she loved, but not to have an illicit love affair.

Interpretive Theme.   People are not what they seem. They may appear to be very decent people and yet commit murder. If people control their sexual desire, anything may be forgiven them. People are very strange. Sometimes one person must be disposed of for others to find happiness.

Diagnostic Level.   Suspicious of people, of their deceptive appearances, of their complex natures that may conceal murderous aggression. The problem is of reconciling aggression and conscience. Unintegrated superego. Sex appears more prohibitive than aggression. Oedipal problem. Sees people as odd.

It is interesting to compare this story with "Footprints in the Jungle." In both instances one meets a quiet, pleasant, unobtrusive middle-aged couple, who have committed murder in order to live with one another. In both stories, the murderers escape punishment for their crimes and live happily (though somewhat furtively) ever after. Once again, in "The Happy Couple," a doctor is the protagonist and is under the sway of love for a woman.

Summary

Unconscious Structure and Drives (1–3)[2]

The author of these stories seems to have a continual struggle with his aggressive and sexual drives. He feels strongly that their control is vital. Death follows loss of control. The character structure that has resulted from his attempts to deal with these problems is one of emotional isolation and detachment. He is an onlooker, peering in from the outside with considerable puzzlement and much suspicion of the barely repressed feelings that lurk beneath the surface of his fellow men. And yet he is not without compassion. There seems to be a conflict between active participation in the demands of the world, especially those of bourgeois culture, and the giving in to passive desires, to the call of simpler living under more primitive circumstances. From the attempted resolution of this conflict arises the beachcomber, the wanderer; albeit in this case a highly sophisticated one. The self-image that results seems that of a mildly ineffective person, who feels rather like a leaf in the wind and is not at all aware of his own strong emotions, especially of cruelty toward women.

Conception of the World (4)
Puzzling, demanding, to be faced with wary eyes, full of surprises and overwhelming situations.

Relationship to Others (5)
Urbane, mildly compassionate, warily expectant, but uninvolved manifestly; latent, strongly aggressive, hostile feelings toward women, projected onto them. Sometimes there is aggression toward men, though often men are seen as dependable if not affected by women.

Significant Conflicts (6)
Control versus lack of control of aggression and sex. Conflict between activity and passivity, between conformity and nonconformity, between identification as a man and as a woman.

Nature of Anxieties (7)
To be dominated, constrained, controlled, especially by women. To kill or be killed in triangular conflicts. To be embarrassed. To lose control of aggressive or sexual drives.

Main Defenses (8)
Reaction formation, emotional isolation, repression, and withdrawal from object relations. Extensive projection of aggression and sexual desires. Very superficial object relations.

---

[2] Numbered headings correspond to those of the T.A.T. Blank.

Superego Structure (9)

An unintegrated superego; it is usually quite harsh, but occasionally, with a touch of cynicism or detachment, aggressive transgressions seem permissible, possibly more so than sexual ones.

Integration and Strength of Ego (10)

The well-constructed stories show an ego strong enough to attain some closure and to maintain control. However, control is attained at the cost of considerable emotional isolation, of constriction and stereotyping of experiences, and of tangential relations to people. The self-image is one of a good deal of ineffectualness, but identification with the role of an urbane, controlled Englishman serves adaptively to maintain adequate functioning, which is enhanced by a very high intelligence and vast experience with the world.

Final Report

The author seems to have a continuous struggle with aggressive and sexual impulses, feeling strongly that their control is literally vital, as seen in the stories "Rain," "The Happy Couple," and "Footprints in the Jungle."

The character structure that has resulted from his attempts to deal with these problems is one of some emotional isolation and detachment—an onlooker looking from the outside in, not without compassion, with considerable puzzlement and a good deal of suspicion of the barely repressed feelings that may lurk under the surface in his fellow man, as seen through the eyes of Dr. Macphail in "Rain," the narrator in "Mr. Harrington's Washing," and in the plot of "A Friend in Need."

There seems to be a conflict between active participation in the demands of the world, especially of the bourgeois culture, and the giving in to passive desires, generally, and the call of simpler living under more primitive circumstances, specifically, as in "The Fall of Edward Barnard" and "A Friend in Need."

The self-image that results seems that of a mildly ineffective person, who feels somewhat like a pebble pushed about by the tides (e.g., "The Fall of Edward Barnard" and Macphail in "Rain").

Women are seen as domineering and demanding, such as Isabel in "The Fall of Edward Barnard," the women in "Rain," the wife in "The Kite"; or as leading to disaster, such as Sadie Thompson in "Rain" and Delilah in "Mr. Harrington's Washing." Women are also often seen as causing a feeling of inadequacy, either as Edward Barnard had in relation to Isabel or as in the case of Izzart's mother in "The Yellow Streak." Apparently, the author uses his defenses so extensively that he is not aware of his own strong aggressive feelings, projected especially on women.

Continual conflicts between activity and passivity, conformity and nonconformity, and male and female identification are seen all throughout the stories, with fears of failure, embarrassment and shame and feelings of inadequacy constantly threatening to emerge.

When one is aware of some of the writer's life history, it becomes apparent that his defenses indeed necessitated a certain amount of constriction of his life to a rather restless, tangential relationship to people, traveling a good deal, almost by design—an onlooker who participates only vicariously via his notebook in stories which, as seen in the sample examined, center on a relatively narrow range of themes. He was nevertheless able to function by conforming with a character quite acceptable within the setting of the upper-crust Anglo-Saxon society—urbane, polished, knowledgeable, and, above all, not causing any difficulties by uncontrolled emotions. He was very sensitive and shy beneath this stiff-upper-lip front, and yet he was often involved in blood-curdling and sometimes cold-blooded cruelties, as in his work as an intelligence agent. His own account of his married life suggests something less than affectionate warmth.

One wonders if the attempt to control all emotion may be related to the fact that some critics have spoken of Maugham as a great craftsman, rather than a great artist, feeling apparently that his stories lacked depth and were too neatly packaged. Could this same problem, especially in relation to women, also be related to his marital difficulties and to the fact that he wandered the earth so restlessly and aloof?

Discussion

The external features and the geographical settings of Maugham's stories vary a great deal. If one compares him, for instance, with Tennessee Williams, it is obvious that he is not constricted with regard to milieu. Williams almost always chooses the setting of the American South. However, Maugham shares with Williams the constrictions of essential subject matter. Whether the adventures are in Malaya or India, Chicago or Petrograd, the theme and its treatment stay fairly constant. Control of the emotions, the difficulties people get themselves into if they do not control them, and especially the dangers to men in their feelings for women are the leitmotifs that govern his work. A certain aloof compassion goes hand in hand with urbanity. Stylistically, one always notes a form of prompt dispatch in the tightly organized plots. There is constriction and a measure of stereotype within the creative personality.

Freud, in his paper on the poet, mentioned perceptual selectivity with regard to the causal relationship between a writer's productions and his personality. In the case of Maugham, it seems that his stories are the result of such a selective viewing of life. They are the product of the forms of adaptation and defenses with which he tried to deal with his own life and his own emotional problems. There are some clues as to what these emotional problems may have been: suggestive relations among his feelings for women, the loss of his mother at an early age, his aggression and his stammer, his personal shyness, his marital difficulties, and his restless wanderings. However, these conjectures with regard to causal interrelations to the early life history are not of central concern and could not progress beyond the usual state of loose guesses on the basis of limited material. One is on safer ground if one limits oneself to inferences covering the relationship between literary production and the personality of the author.

One may speculate further: In what way may the kind of story analysis done here contribute to the understanding and critical analysis of literature? The systematic frame of reference for analysis of literary products may be generally useful for any author's work. The range and depth of a literary piece are often at the center of critical appraisal, and a T.A.T. type of analysis may well give a more reliable account than the customary free-style appraisal. Perhaps one of the reasons for widely differing critiques may be, at least in part, the lack of any base line of comparison. The type of psychological analysis presented here may well throw some interesting light on the relationship between an author's personality and his or her work.

CHAPTER 11

OBJECT RELATIONS ASSESSMENT WITH THE T.A.T., C.A.T., AND S.A.T.

Perspectives on Object Relations Theory

From its beginning in Bellak and Murray (1941) and Bellak (1947) Bellak's T.A.T. interpretive method included a central fifth category of *interpersonal object relations,* also called *Figures seen as,* where one examines the story characters as to how father figures, mother figures, peers or siblings, and subordinates are seen in relation to the central figure in the story. One examines the types of personality of each character and the quality of interaction with the hero. An early attempt to develop a whole scoring approach around this single dimension was the Object Relations Technique of Phillipson (1955), which consists of photographs of people in different situations with relative degrees of ambiguity. Bellak revised the T.A.T. Blank in 1973 to include 12 ego functions under the tenth category of "Integration of the ego," one ego function being that of *object relations.*

Since that period, there have been several specific assessment approaches to scoring aspects of this dimension. Truckenmiller and Schai (1979) developed a scoring approach for interpersonal relatedness. McAdams (1980) developed a thematic coding system for the intimacy motive. Thomas and Dudeck (1985) focused on the variable of "interpersonal affect." Abrams and Bellak (1986 edition of this chapter) presented a more specific approach to this dimension, looking at the different personalities of the "cast of characters" in each story and the specific types of relationship in each specifically stated or implied interaction between two or more characters.

The most detailed scoring approach for interpersonal object relations in the T.A.T. is that of Westen (1991b; Berends et al., 1990; Nigg et al., 1991; Westen et al., 1990a, 1990b). Westen's approach includes the four subcategories of (1) complexity of representations of people, which is also reported in the T.A.T. study of Leigh (1992); (2) a variation of Thomas and Dudeck's (1985) dimension of "interpersonal affect," which Westen calls "affect-tone of relationship paradigms"; (3) capacity for emotional investment in relationships and moral standards; and (4) the social cognition category of the understanding of social causality. Object relations focuses on the types and quality of social interaction as well as the way these experiences of interpersonal relations are internalized as mental "representations" of different individuals and different types of relationships. The four subscales of Westen's scoring approach are detailed here.

1. *Complexity of representations of people.* Internalized self and object representations become increasingly more separate and differentiated from each other throughout child development to adulthood. The child's capacity to mentally represent one's self-image and one's images of others also becomes increasingly more complex. Polar extreme feelings of "all good" and "all bad" self and object representations and extreme affect states of love and hate gradually become more differentiated and integrated as the child matures. Westen's subcategory examines the level of differentiation of story characters and the extent to which an individual can see the self and others as having stable, enduring, and multifaceted qualities and subjective experiences.

2. *Affect tone of relationship paradigms.* Social relations in infancy begin in pleasure pain states and, in optimum circumstances, develop within increasingly more positive, interpersonally related experiences. Westen's dimension looks at the types of interactions in the T.A.T. stories along a continuum from malevolent, painful interactions to those that are more benign, enriching, caring, and loving.

3. *Capacity for emotional investment in relationships and moral standards.* This dimension considers the extent to which individuals are treated as ends rather than as means and the extent to which events are experienced as need-fulfilling. This is the dimension of the capacity for empathy. Child development optimally proceeds from more narcissistic, self-centered relations based on meeting the child's basic needs and develops increasingly toward mutual love, respect, and concern for others. This scale also examines the extent to which relationships are experienced as meaningful and committed and the extent to which moral standards are developed and considered.

4. *Understanding of social causality.* As the child matures, there is an increasing understanding of the causes of actions, thoughts, and feelings within oneself and in others. The understanding of social causality becomes deeper, more complex, more abstract, accurate, and internal.

Westen's scoring approach has been used to differentiate borderlines, manic depressives, and normals (Westen et al., 1990a), borderline adolescents (Westen et al., 1990b), and sexually abused girls ranging in age from 5 to 16 years (Nigg et al., 1991; Ornduff et al., 1994). A very interesting study of Berends and colleagues (1990) used the four Westen scales to compare T.A.T. stories, interview data, and stories told to the Picture Arrangement subtest of the Wechsler intelligence scale. Westen's scales are difficult to learn and rather time consuming to score. The scales may become more useful in clinical assessment if they could be simplified to some degree, so that scoring could be easier and quicker. However, the scales have been found to be very useful in quantitative research.

The approach of interpersonal object relations developed out of Freud's psychoanalysis. Freud made that most concrete in his conception of the *superego* as being largely the result of internalized parental images expressing strictures and inhibitions. In *The Ego and the Id,* Freud (1923) showed how the superego is formed out of internalized identifications, primarily with the father for the oedipal-stage male child. And, in his paper on "Mourning and Melancholia," Freud (1917) suggested that one of the ways people become able to work through a mourning reaction over the death of a loved one is to develop an "inner image" or "introject" of the lost object.

Melanie Klein, W. R. D. Fairbairn (1954), and other members of the British school emphasized the importance of the earliest internalized objects. Klein (1948) developed a rather comprehensive picture of how a child gradually builds up inner images of family members that then make up the child's internal fantasies of what these and other people are like. These then influence how the child experiences and relates to other people in his or her actual daily life. For example, if the child has a father who is extremely aggressive, the child may tend to build up an inner image of father figures as extremely aggressive and frightening. Other men similar in age to the child's father may then be experienced as if they were all as aggressive and frightening as the child's own father. Another example illustrated in Klein's clinical sessions with children is the way a child develops an inner fantasy of the parents' relationship to each other. This could be an image of a loving parental couple or of a couple who always fight and argue with each other. This interpersonal relationship of a parental pair is represented intrapsychically in the child's inner world.

Sandler and Rosenblatt (1962) suggested the term *representational world* for the constellation of images of parents, siblings, relatives, and other significant individuals that exist in the child's internal, intrapsychic world. Another way of putting it is that the child's unconscious is not made up only of libidinal and aggressive drives and unconscious wishes. The unconscious is also made up of fantasy images of human beings that significantly influence the individual's everyday behavior.

The many different characters in the T.A.T. stories produced by an individual may, then, be viewed as a window into the variety of self and object representations that made up the individual's representational world. They are the cast of characters within the individual's experience of actual people from day to day.

The T.A.T. and its offspring, the C.A.T. and S.A.T., are suitable projective tests for the assessment of an individual's interpersonal and intrapersonal object relations. Since the individual is presented with a set of pictures of human beings or animals in social situations and asked to construct a fantasy story about each picture, the outcome of these tests provides rich material about the individual's ability to relate to others, his or her capacity for experiencing other people with an appreciation of their complexities, and the individual's manner of experiencing interpersonal relationships in his family, job situation, or circle of friendships. The T.A.T., C.A.T., and S.A.T. allow a deep view into an individual's level of interpersonal experiences, conflicts, and level of development and functioning.

An Object Relations Approach to T.A.T. Analysis

The method of analysis presented here is similar to the basic approach previously outlined in which object relations is viewed as one of the ego functions (Abrams, 1991, 1992; Bellak, 1993a). One of the functions of the ego is to internally represent in fantasy the individual's actual and imagined interpersonal experience. For T.A.T. analysis, the clinician begins by making an inventory of the cast of characters in each story with a note or two about the personality of each character, like the program notes one reads before seeing a play. The next step is to make an inventory of the interactions among the characters with a few notes characterizing the type of each interaction. It is then a simple step to write a short summary of the object relations in each story and then an overall summary at the end of the protocol.

A useful way of doing this is to set up separate columns for the "cast of characters" on the left and "type of personality" for each of these characters on the immediate right. Then one lists the different "social interactions" in the chronological order of the story on the left with a brief note on the "type of interaction" for each of these actions on the adjacent right side of the page. Often, it is helpful to list each action in the story under "social interaction," since many interactions are implied in a stated action, as the action of "throws a ball" may imply that someone else is these to "catch it." One then writes a brief summary of all these object relational issues in a paragraph underneath these object relations columns. In the "overall object relations summary" at the end of the protocol, it is important to consider personality characteristics of the "main characters" and the degree of differentiation between the main characters and the "secondary characters." Relationships between child and father figures, with mother figures, and with siblings, grandparents, and peers are all important considerations in this final summary.

To illustrate this method of analysis, we will present the T.A.T. protocols of two individuals, the first a neurotic early adolescent and the second an actively psychotic adult.

T.A.T. Protocol of a Neurotic Adolescent Boy

The following protocol is from a 13½-year-old boy, whose grades had gone down in the last year, and who was constantly getting into battles over completing homework assignments with his mother. He tended to withdraw into moody states of self-pity, and was often very demanding of expensive toys and other objects.

1: Once there was a boy and he was looking at his violin and thinking if he should play it. But he doesn't want to play it. But his Mom's going to make him and he's thinking about whether he should play it or not. He doesn't want to. *End?* His mother will make him play it for a year and then he gives it up. But they have a big fight over it. He's bigger than she is. So he wins the argument.

Cast of characters	Type of personality
Boy	Ambivalent, avoidant, argumentative, oppositional
Mom	Controlling, demanding, authoritarian

Social interactions	Type of interaction
Mother forces boy, who quits	Controlling, oppositional interaction

Summary

The story suggests this adolescent sees himself as locked in an oppositional battle with his mother, who is seen as demanding and controlling. The boy puts up with mother forcing him to play the violin for a year, then quits altogether. It may be that he tries to make deals (e.g., "I'll do it for only one year, then I'll quit"), so seems to be ambivalent over mother's demands, argumentative, and ultimately avoidant or withdrawing. The story ends with a wish that if he is bigger than mother, he could then prevail over her. The interpersonal object relation in this story seems to be that both of them relate in a controlling, oppositional manner.

2: This is a long time ago. This girl's sort of rich and she's being all snotty to this girl over here [on the right]. She just came from school and this guy back here is plowing with the horse. *Next?* Something. Nothing's going to change. *End?* Um, I think some day she's to go and get hurt [the one on the left] and she [on the right] will make fun of her, because she made fun of her all those years.

Cast of characters	*Type of personality*
Rich girl	Snotty, makes fun of others (implied)
Other less well-to-do girl	Victim of teasing, but later retaliates
Man plowing	No details given
Horse	No details given

Social interactions	*Type of interactions*
Snotty girl teases girl, who retaliates.	Other girl is first passive victim (implied), but later retaliates by teasing rich girl back (talion type of "eye for an eye" retribution)

Summary

Even though there are now three people in the picture, he again tells a story of a struggle between two people, in this case between the snotty girl who teases and her victim, the other girl, who ends up retaliating when the rich girl gets hurt. The opening statement that it happened "long ago" may be an attempt to distance himself from such ongoing struggles, or it could suggest that he is reporting something that happened a long time ago to him. The statement that "nothing's going to change" brings in depressive feelings of hopelessness, perhaps that he himself feels he will continue to be teased and hurt by peers. The retaliation at the end, then, may again be a wish to be able to retaliate in kind to hurtful peers. The style of interaction is one of uncaring, hurtful teasing and simple retaliation in kind.

3BM: What is this over here [points to gun-like object in picture)? They look like keys to me. This is an older girl, but she's crying because she can't get a car. She wants a car, but her Mom won't let her get one. At the end, her mother lets her get the car after a long time, after a lot of crying. Finally, the mother can't take it, so she lets her get the car.

Cast of characters	Type of personality
Older girl	Persistently demanding
Mom	First depriving, later acquiescing

Social interactions	Type of interactions
Demanding girl, depriving mother who later gives in out of annoyance	Demanding, depriving, acquiescing

Summary

This story is similar to that on card 1 with one person being demanding while the other resists but he later acquiesces. In the first, the boy resists mother's demand that he learn the violin, but later acquiesces and plays for one year. In this story, it is reversed. Now it is the child who demands a car. The parent resists but ends up giving it to her. The type of object relationship is one of demanding, oppositionalism, and acquiescing out of annoyance.

4: Ok. He's leaving. They had a fight and she doesn't want him to go. But he goes anyway. She's got long nails. A few years later, they bump into each other and get back together again. In a different place. Some other city or state. All is forgiven.

Cast of characters	Type of Personality
Boy	Argumentative, withdrawing
Girl	Demanding but forgiving

Social interactions	Type of interactions
Boy and girl fight over boy leaving	Demanding, withdrawing
Boy and girl get back together	Forgiving reconciliation

Summary

The theme of one person being demanding while the other is argumentative, resistive, and withdrawing is continued. The forgiving reconciliation suggests that he has a need to put a "happy ending" on many of his stories, which may be a reversal of affect to put on a happy face to cover over sad, angry, and other more uncomfortable feelings. It may also express a feeling that others leave him and he wishes for a happy, forgiving reconciliation.

6BM: This lady's worried about her son, who embezzled some money. She's looking out the window and she wants him to come back. He's the lawyer and he looks worried, too. Maybe he wants his money, too. The son goes to jail. Then he comes home and they're all happy and everything.

Cast of characters	Type of personality
Mother	Worried, lonely, object-longing
Son	Deprived, antisocial stealing
Lawyer	Demanding

Social interactions	Type of interactions
Son embezzles money	Demanding, antisocial
Son is punished (jailed).	Punishing, boxing-in, restricting
Lawyer wants his money	Demanding
Son and mother reconcile.	Happy, forgiving reconciliation

Summary

This is further expression of one person and the other wanting the other to return. That the son embezzled money suggests this boy may feel deprived and feel that something or someone was taken away from him, "stolen" from him. The idea of the mother wanting the boy to return may be a wish in this boy for his mother to want him, since he seems to be progressively picturing her as demanding, depriving, and withdrawing. The lawyer is demanding of money. The son is punished by being jailed. But again he ends it with a "happy ever after" wish-fulfillment type ending that may represent a defensive reversal of affect to cover up his angry, deprived feelings and feeling of being boxed in and punished by others, perhaps for being overly demanding.

7GF: This girl has her doll and her mother's reading a story and she's daydreaming and looking into space with her dolly in her hands. I think the story will be about some Prince and someday her dream will become true. She's imagining the story in her own version, and then that happens.

Cast of characters	Type of personality
Girl	Daydreaming, fantasizing, wishing
Mother	Intellectualized, fantasizing
Prince	No details given

Social interaction	Type of interaction
Mother reading to daughter	Intellectual, dreaming, withdrawing
Daughter daydreaming of Prince	Withdrawing into fantasy world

Summary

The story suggests this adolescent likes to withdraw from his mother into a fantasy world of marrying into a rich and powerful family, where all events end "happily ever after," everyone happily reconciles and all badness is forgiven. The story also suggests that he may see the mother as encouraging his withdrawal into fantasy away from the real world. The interpersonal object relation of mother and child is one of a rather distant, intellectualized, withdrawal into fantasy, rather than a genuine object-related and reality-oriented interaction.

8BM: Oh God. These are doctors back there and they're doing an operation. They're taking something out. And this kid's worried about his father, who's on the table. His father gets alright and the whole family's all happy he's still alive, 'cause in those days most of them weren't so successful. His was successful, so they're all happy.

Cast of characters	Type of personality
Doctors	Successfully lifesaving
Boy	Worried over potential loss of father
Father	Passively helped

Social interactions	Type of interactions
Doctors cure passive father	Helpful, life-saving
Boy worried over father's health	Caring or disguised anger?

Summary

The story may express an actual worry over the subject's father's physical health or it could be a reaction formation of overt concern to cover underlying angry, death fantasies towards the father, who is seen as passively helped. Again, there is the "happily ever after" type of ending where everything turns out happily successful. His comment that this operation was successful, but in "those days they weren't always so successful," may express a depressive feeling that it is rare for things to turn out totally successful and happy. The idea that the doctors cure the father by taking something out of him may express a feeling that psychotherapy could cure him if something inside him was taken out, perhaps helping him get rid of troubling thoughts.

9GF: It was a long time ago and they lived in a log cabin and the girl is sneaking out. But the mother is going to catch her and whip her. No, she writes down how many times the girl gets in trouble in those books she has and she shows' em to her every time she gets bad. But she's going to get older and still be immature when she's older; keep on sneaking out and getting hurt. But her mother's going to catch her each time and spank her.

Cast of characters	Type of personality
Girl	Withdrawing, gets in trouble
Mother	Pursuing, punishing

Social interactions	Type of interactions
Withdrawing child/pursuing parent	Approach avoidant, withdrawing
Naughty child/punishing parent	Possibly sadomasochistic interaction

Summary

This is further expression of the same theme of wanting to avoid and withdraw from mother's demanding pursuing and keeping track of all his misbehaviors. But this time, he does not end it with a happy wish-fulfillment. Instead, the pattern continues to be repeated of the misbehaving child sneaking out and the mother catching and spanking her. The child will still be immature, even when she is older. There may be a disguised wish in this boy for his mother to pursue and catch him. Perhaps he wants her to want to be with him and finds that he can get her to pursue and closely monitor him by doing bad things.

10: This is a priest kissing the guy coming to confess. No; a father giving blessing to his son going off to college. After that he comes back from college and they rejoice. I like happy endings.

Cast of characters	Type of personality
Priest	Giving forgiveness to sinner
Guy who is confessing	Guilty sinner that's committed a sin
Father	Accepting of son's independence
Son	Able to separate and return to parents

Social interactions	Type of interactions
Priest kisses sinner	Accepting, forgiving, saving
Father allows son to separate and return	Accepting of autonomy and return

Summary

The first association to this picture may be of one man kissing another, which may stir up homosexual fears in an early adolescent boy. So he turns it into a priest kissing a confessing man. But then retreats even more from this to make it into a father giving his son his blessing to leave home, perhaps to further distance from the idea of a man kissing another male. The conflict of autonomy versus dependency is typical of adolescence. So the idea of the father giving his okay for the son to leave home may suggest his perception that his father is more encouraging of his autonomy than what we have seen from his stories of his perception of his overinvolved and rather controlling mother. However, the rejoicing return from college as the "happy ending" may represent his reversal of affect wish-fulfillment covering over his inner conflictual feelings around independence/dependence. So this story may be a wish for his father to give his blessing for his growing up and leaving home.

13MF: Someone killed this guy and he's crying, 'cause he's the brother. The family grieves from then on. They're all sad and they go to her funeral and then . . . I don't know. They're all sad from then on and nothing's jolly or happy anymore. I can't make a happy ending for that one.

Cast of characters	Type of personality
Killer	Aggressive, homicidal
Dead male	No details given

| Brother | Grieving, sad, depressed |
| Other family members | No details given |

Social interactions	*Type of interaction*
Killer kills guy	Aggressive, homicidal
Man grieves for deceased brother	Grieving, sad, hopeless, depressed

Summary

Hypothesis of homosexual ideation is suggested by his making the person in the bed into a "guy," when the uncovered breasts clearly show the person to be female in the picture. As an adolescent just at the point of puberty, he may be defending against heterosexual feelings by making the story into one of only males. The grieving brother, who is forever sad and depressed, may express real feelings of loss for a sibling from whom he is separated or perhaps this represents underlying depressive feelings surrounding his real ability to grow up, become truly independent, and leave home with love in a good way, rather than separating and leaving out of anger as if someone has died.

Overall Object Relations Summary

The *main characters* are predominantly adolescents, who seem stuck in demanding, needy, oppositional battles with their controlling, demanding, and overinvolved mothers (stories 1, 3BM, 6BM, and 9GF) or who seem to be in an approach/avoidance conflict with a peer (stories 2, 4, and 13MF). The *secondary characters* of the mother figures are similarly seen as demanding and controlling, while the two stories that show father figures (8BM and 10) suggest that he sees the father as more helpful, accepting, and encouraging of independence and separateness. There is some suggestion that this is a daydreaming young adolescent, who is given to moodiness of sad, depressed feelings and who often withdraws into inner fantasies of happily-ever-after endings, when he is not locked in the more enmeshed oppositional battles with his mother. While there are not a lot of signs of differentiation between the adolescent characters and those of the mothers, the father figures seem to differ from the mothers in being more accepting of the two conflicting needs of autonomy and closeness in a young adolescent boy.

Analysis of the *social interactions* in his stories predominantly are those of an enmeshed, oppositional battle of wills between mother and adolescent and of the approach/avoidance pattern with a sibling or peer. Fathers and older males are seen as more helpful and encouraging of independence. Hence, this boy might at first do better with a male, rather than with a female therapist. Reversal of affect and reaction formation are very prevalent defense mechanisms, which he seems to utilize to put on a happy face to cover up underlying depressed and angry feelings and which help him retreat into wish-fulfilling fantasies away from the hard struggles of the everyday world. Overall, this boy's interpersonal object relations are age appropriate, as they center in the adolescent conflict between independence and dependence. The oppositional struggle with the mother and the tendency to see the father as more encouraging of autonomy is also typically seen in children at the dawn of adolescence, who are still very tied to dependency on the mother. Sex-role or homosexual/heterosexual conflict also tends to be age appropriate in early adolescents, whose chief conflict of identity versus role diffusion, as Erikson (1950) puts it, is also often seen in this area of sex-role gender and sexuality conflict. The diagnostic impression, therefore, seems to be adjustment disorder with mixed emotional oppositionalism, depressive mood, withdrawing, and approach/avoidant features. A short course of psychotherapy to assist him in these emotional adjustment difficulties is recommended and the prognosis of his accepting and being open to benefitting from psychotherapy is quite good.

T.A.T. Protocol of an Actively Psychotic Man

This is the case of "John Doe," male, age 25, and single, whose T.A.T. was previously described in Chapter 6, pages 107–121. The method of analysis is similar to the basic approach previously outlined in which object relations is viewed as one of the ego functions (Bellak, 1975, 1984). One of the functions of the ego is to internally represent in fantasy the individual's actual and imagined interpersonal experience. For T.A.T. analysis, the clinician begins by making an inventory of the cast of characters in each story with a note or two about the personality of each character, like the program notes one reads before seeing a play. The next step is to make an inventory of the interactions among the characters with a few notes characterizing the type of each interaction. It is then a simple step to write a short summary of the object relations in each story.

1: This child is sick in bed. He has been given sheet music to study, but instead of the music he has come across a novel that interests him more than the music. It is probably an adventure story. He evidently does not fear the chance that his parents will find him thus occupied as he seems quite at ease. He seems to be quite a studious type and perhaps regrets missing school, but he seems quite occupied with the adventure in the story. Adventure has something to do with ocean or water. He is not too happy, though not too sad. His eyes are somewhat blank—coincidence of reading a book without any eyes or knowing what is in the book without reading it. He disregards the music and falls asleep reading the book.

Cast of characters	Type of personality
Boy	Sick, withdrawn in bed, reads adventure novel instead of studying music, blank eyes, omnipotent (knows book's contents without having to read it)
Parents of boy	No details given
Classmates and teachers at school (implied)	No details given

Social interactions	Type of personality
Boy is given music to study	Passive receptive objective relation
Boy misses school	Object hunger evident

Boy reads novel about ocean or water (desire to regress to "womb," to mother as narcissistic gratifying object)	Passive receptive object relation

Summary

Sick, regressed, and passive/receptive self representation is given music to study, but instead withdraws into fantasy of regression to womb. Object representations seen as providing, but also as external superego figures to check up on him if he is practicing music. Story ends with regression to "womb" (ocean, water) resulting in merger with other (author of adventure novel) with symbiotic omniscience (ability to then know contents of book without reading it).

Sequence of story suggests withdrawing from reality-orientation of music study others gave him to work on into "womb" fantasy of psychotic level of merger of reading other's mind. Story suggests tendency to schizoid withdrawal from current reality of others as an adult (blank affect and inner fantasy life) and to regress to being a sick child or fetus, to be omnipotently cared for by the mother. Passive/aggressive anal level struggle for control seen in relation to parents, music, and school and statement of missing school are highest level of object relations noted. However, the fetal level of regression, somatization, idea of others attempting to control him, check up on him, and his knowing the book's contents without having to read it suggests a diagnosis of psychosis.

3BM: This is a girl in a cell and she has been jailed because she was found guilty of prostitution. She is in this position in the picture because she is very ashamed, not because of being arrested, because she is quite familiar with the police, but because of the fact that her picture and a newspaper write-up was being sensationally spread across the country. She knew that her sister, who was a nun, would suffer from it, and it made her feel very badly because she, at one time, had a chance and an opportunity to follow her elder sister's example but it was too late now. She grabs a concealed knife from under her blouse and stabs herself.

Casting of characters	Type of personality
Girl	"All bad," sexually promiscuous jailed for prostitution, and ashamed of national publicity (desire for grandiose level of exhibitionism)
Police	Superego representation that jail stops her from id discharge
Sister of girl (nun)	"All good," nun who suffers from problems of her sister

Social interactions	Type of interactions
Girl jailed by police with whom she is quite familiar	Police superego representation restricts and stops sexual drive discharge and exhibitionism of girl
Girl's sister, the nun, suffers due	"All good" self-representation suffers

to girl's	from threat of contamination by "all
badness	bad" self-representation, so "all bad"
	presentation must be killed off by
	suicide of bad girl prostitute

Summary

Primitive splitting between "all bad" sexual representation of girl prostitute and "all good" sexless self-representation of nun sister of girl. "All bad" self-representation may seek grandiose level of exhibitionism, while "all good" self-representation may suffer from such exposure and contamination. In order to preserve "all good" representation, solution offered is to kill off bad self by violent suicide. Since the patient is male, this could also be a homicidal desire to kill oedipal sexual mother, so as to preserve the need-fulfilling "all good" mother of infancy or fetal period.

4: The girl in the picture is half-caste. She is in love with the man who is going to leave her and return to his wife. They have spent quite some time together in intimacy. She is pleading with him to stay with her or help figure some way to plan for the coming of the child she is going to bear. She is in poor circumstances financially, and he tells her she should make arrangements to conclude the birth and thus everything would iron out because he is definitely determined to leave as the affair in his mind is at an end. She is very broken up by it. She pleads for him to spend one more night, which he agrees to, and in the middle of the night she sets fire to the house, thus solving the problems of all concerned.

Cast of characters	*Type of personality*
Girl	Poor, desperate about abandonment by man friend, pleading, suicidal, and homicidal
Man friend of girl	No details given
Unborn child	No details given

Social interactions	*Type of interactions*
Girl pleading with man not to abandon her and her her unborn child, so she kills all of them	Panicking at threat of abandonment, so aggressive impulses erupt (symbolized by fire) and killing
Man friend wants her to kill unborn child	Homicidal interaction
Fetus in womb	Passive receptive object relation

Summary

Poor, desperate, pregnant self-panics at threat of abandonment by father of baby and kills self and others, which may express merger wish through shared death. Abortion and setting fire to all of them may represent a desire to rid self of demanding, dependent fetus self representation. Theme of fetus in womb is now stated directly, where it was only implied in story 1.

Panic reaction to threat of abandonment, outbreak of homicidal and suicidal aggressive impulses, and regression to fetal or merged and fused state (united in death) further suggest primitive object relations with lack of self-object boundaries indicative of psychosis.

6BM: This is a scene in a play. The two characters are on the stage; one is a famous elderly actress, who has a son about the age of the young man appearing opposite her. The dialogue in the play has suddenly taken on a new meaning for her: She sees now that the play, which was written by her son, has an entirely different meaning in this scene in the picture. The boy is telling the mother that he has just committed a murder. She understands now that this was her son's way of conveying to her the terrifying fact that that is actually what had happened. In the play, as her son had written it, the climax comes when the mother calls the police. But the famous actress decides to put her own climax into action after the play is over. She calls her son and says, "The climax of your play will have to be changed," She says, "I think the audience will prefer this one," so here she draws a revolver and shoots him. *(What kind of murder was it?)* Oh, a girl. Motive primarily to do with sexual. She had been unfaithful.

Cast of characters	*Type of personality*
Famous elderly actress on stage	Exhibitionistic, homicidal (kills son to punish him for murder he committed)
Son of actress who wrote play about murder	Controls others (writes play they are in), homicidal, and is indirect (tells mother of his murder through his play she acts in)
Young man on stage same age as author of play	Twin fantasy? No details given
Police	No details given
Unfaithful girlfriend of play's author	Sexually unfaithful

Social interactions	*Type of interactions*
Actress feels son tells her of his crime indirectly and punishes him by killing	Manipulative and homicidal object relation (retaliatory)
Son writes play for mother and others to act in	Magically controls them
Young man in play	Passive, controlled by others
Girlfriend of play's author	Unfaithful to play's author

Summary

The idea of a scene in a play shows patient's desire for some distance from the primary process of earlier stories by isolation of affect defense. But this quickly breaks away, as author of play magically controls mother and others, is indirect (reappearance of passive/aggression of story 1), and has homicidal solution to girlfriend's being unfaithful to him (reappearance of homicidal retaliation for abandonment of story 4). "All bad" manipulative son is punished by mother killing him (reappearance of attempt to rid self of "all bad" self-representation by homicide as in stories 3BM and 4).

The magical control of others, homicidal aggression, and suggestion of twin theme in young man actor, who plays author of play, again shows the primitive level of the patient's object relations. Again we see attempt to rid himself of the bad, sexual, and homicidal part of the self.

7BM: This would be a man and his son. The son is very depressed over his health. The father is telling him that as a young man he too had the same illness, and that it can be cured if the son has the will to cure it. The father tells the young man that he himself alone can cure it. The son believes that there is no hope, but replies that he will go away for a little while and think it over. The father replies, "You are not doing a favor to me by saying that. I am thinking about your getting well for the simple reason that you have a wife and children to support, and in the event of your being bedridden, the responsibility for your family will be put entirely upon your mother and me." The young man finally concludes that he will take his wife and family with him and try to make things go better in a healthier climate. *(What kind of illness did he have?)* T.B. *(Did he get better?)* No, I don't think he does. After a few years he dies and the children are old enough to support mother or perhaps he left insurance. Never contacted father again. No correspondence. After not having heard from each other for a long time, the old man dies and leaves the children a large estate. This is his way of having repented.

Cast of characters	*Type of personality*
Father of son	Father identifies with son's illness
Mother of son	Mother will resent taking care of son's family
Son	Son is depressed over health, feels helpless, withdraws to healthier climate
Son's wife	Dependent, needing support, but ends up supporting mother?
Son's children	Children dependent, needing support

Social interactions	*Type of interactions*
Father tells son he had same illness and son should cure himself, so father and mother won't have to support son's wife and children	Father overidentifies (Patient's merger fantasies?) and relates by *telling* son what to do. Controlling of son and rejecting of him.
Children need support and later they support mother	Children dependent, but later reverse roles

Summary

Continuation of themes of bedridden dependence, threats of rejection responded to by someone dying in this case through somatization, schizoid withdrawal (to go off and *think*), and withdrawal and regression to womb (go to healthier climate). Primitive level of object relations, although this story shows more depression (oral dependency, turning aggression against the self, somatization, and object loss) than psychosis. Since this is the last story reported, it may mean that the patient is only capable of pulling himself out of psychosis to a level of severe depression. Narcissistic grandiosity is seen in comment that son can only cure himself alone.

Overall Object Relations Summary

The *main characters* in this man's T.A.T. stories are seen as sick, passive/aggressive, withdrawing, and regressively dependent (stories 1 and 7BM) or as sexually promiscuous and suicidal (3BM, 4, and 6BM). The *secondary characters* are very similar to the main characters. They tend to be controlling and rejecting (Parents in story 1, police in 3BM, boyfriend in 4, girlfriend in 6BM, and father and mother in 7BM), detached (sister in 3BM, father in 7BM), homicidal (mother in 6BM), or passive, withdrawing, and imitative (wife and children in 7BM).

The lack of much differentiation between the main and secondary characters suggests (1) lack of much self-object differentiation and (2) little evidence of development of repression. This is always important in object relations assessment on the T.A.T.—to look at the within group differences among the *main characters* and the differences between these two groups of story characters in order to get a clinical understanding of the level of self and object differentiation within the patient's internal representational world. The primitive splitting of the all good nun sister and all bad prostitute sister in story 3BM further corroborates that the patient has not developed much differentiation between self and other beyond primitive splitting and that he tends to defend by primitive splitting, rather than with higher more oedipal level defenses, such as repression, ambivalence, and other related defenses.

Analysis of the *social interactions* show that this man's object relations are very primitive. There is very little directly stated social interactions among any of the characters in his stories (1 and 3BM have the littlest interactions of all the stories). In story 4, the only stated interaction is in the pregnant girl's pleading with the father of her unborn baby not to leave her to return to his wife and her action of setting fire to the house killing him, herself, and the unborn baby. This tendency to react to threat of abandonment with panic and impulsive homicidal and suicidal aggression is a pre-oedipal response to anxiety, rather than the response of signal anxiety in individuals who have reached the oedipal and higher levels of development.

6BM has directly stated interactions of the son telling his mother he committed a murder, which now shows sequentially how the patient will follow the previous firesetting murder. The mother responds by shooting him (she abandons him and punishes him for his murder by killing him). The directly stated interactions in 7BM are the father telling the son to cure himself without anyone else's help including that of the father and mother. The son withdraws to a healthier climate with his wife and children, but later he dies and later the father dies. This shows a controlling and abandoning interaction by the father and a withdrawing somatization response of the son. Parallel action is seen in the son and family withdrawing together to the healthier climate and the son and father later dying. Withdrawal and imitative action is normal for a pre-oedipal age child. But the somatization response to parental abandonment by dying again shows the severe level of this man's depression.

Failure of reality testing is seen in "reading a book without any eyes" or knowing what is in the book without reading it in story 1; the prostitute who cannot reform, be forgiven, and become a nun in 3BM; the idea that the son can control his mother's reaction to his crime by having her act this idea out in a play he wrote in 6BM; and the idea that only he alone by himself can cure his tuberculosis in 7BM. This man's level of reality-testing, therefore, is not as actively fluid, loose, and grossly distorted as in individuals in the midst of active psychosis. Instead, we find subtle, indirect evidence of failure of reality-testing and delusional thinking in the above examples characteristic of latent schizophrenia or a psychotic condition currently in some state of remission.

Discussion of Implications of Object Relations

In object relations theory, three areas are useful in determining whether this patient is actively psychotic:

1. The level of self-object differentiation. The self-object differentiation of primitive splitting is a more borderline level of psychopathology that is more developed than the delusionally fusing self-object lack of boundaries in actively psychotic conditions. Which is his level?
2. The level of reality testing.
3. The level of acting out of sexual and aggressive impulses.

Clearly, in all these areas, this man's T.A.T. shows a psychotic condition. The lack of much difference between the main and secondary characters in his stories suggests little self-object differentiation and the reality-testing level shows delusional merger ideation. Finally, the level of acting out of sexual and aggressive impulses is extremely primitive with the imagery of prostitution, adultery, homicide, and suicide. The likelihood of acting out of these homicidal and suicidal ideations should be taken very seriously in treatment planning.

In sum, this man has a latent schizophrenic or psychotic depressive condition currently in remission with some presence of self-object differentiation and some reality testing. However, his acting out potential of suicidal and homicidal impulses is at an extremely dangerous level, particularly since he believes others want to control him, abandon, and murder him. The patient definitely does not have a borderline disorder, since his self-object differentiation, reality testing, and control of acting out impulsivity are not at the level of borderline patients. If the patient is not currently on a psychiatric inpatient service, on antipsychotic medication, and under active suicide and homicide watch, these interventions should be immediately put into effect.

Conclusion

This case example demonstrates an object relations analysis of a T.A.T. proto-col, which highlights an individual's self and object representations according to the approach of Kernberg (1976) and Volkan (1976). We have attempted to em-phasize the value of highlighting the cast of characters in the story with the type of personality of each character and of analyzing the types of social interactions among these story characters. The main characters can be viewed as the more con-scious self, while the other, secondary characters can be viewed as the part of the self that is less available to immediate awareness. The presence of primitive splitting seen in characters in the same story of opposite qualities and the level of reality-testing can be investigated in order to determine the pathological level of these object relations in the T.A.T. protocol.

Since object relations stems from Freud's ego function approach, the reader will note the similarity of this object relations analysis of this T.A.T. protocol with the earlier analysis of this case in order to illustrate the congruity of these two ap-proaches and the diagnostic agreement in interpretation of the T.A.T. in clinical practice.

CHAPTER 12

BORDERLINE AND NARCISSISTIC DISORDERS IN THE T.A.T., C.A.T., AND S.A.T.

Brief Overview of the Diagnostic Concept of Borderline and Narcissistic Disorders

Two very popular psychiatric diagnoses are the narcissistic personality disorder intensively studied by Heinz Kohut (1971, 1977), and the borderline personality disorder intensively studied by Otto Kernberg (1975, 1980). Other individuals made substantial contributions prior to, concurrent with, and subsequent to the contributions of Kohut and Kernberg. Their own prolific writings and those of a substantial number of disciples have stimulated several T.A.T. and C.A.T. studies (Abrams, 1993; Brelet, 1981, 1983, 1986; Harder, 1979; Rogoff, 1985; Rosoff, 1988; Westen et al., 1990a, 1990b).

The significant factor in both diagnoses is the identification of a psychiatric disorder that is characteristically pre-oedipal-level rather than oedipal-level neurotic disorder (obsessive/compulsive, hysterical, or phobic neurosis), but is possibly, except for brief episodes, not psychotic. Earlier, the term *borderline* referred to an individual at the border between psychotic and neurotic disorders. This could be a stable disposition or a labile one. It was Kernberg's contribution to insist that *borderline* designated a specific diagnostic entity with distinct criteria in terms of object relations and defenses and called for specific therapeutic management.

Narcissistic pathology was also earlier thought of as referring to a psychotic patient's withdrawal into a fantasy world of his or her own without a realistic relationship to the needs, perceptions, and existence of other people. However, narcissistic features could also be seen in a neurotic individual, as in someone who wants a circle of noncritical admirers or someone who marries a famous person. The dictionary defines *narcissism* as love of the self at the expense of love for others (as putting one's own needs above those of everyone else and a lack of empathy for and sensitivity to other people's feelings). This latter definition is the key factor in narcissistic personality disorder. In Kohut's theory, the development of narcissism follows a timetable of its own, similar to and parallel with Freud's original libidinal developmental schedule. From this theory it derives propositions concerning the treatment of narcissistic personality.

Neither Kohut's nor Kernberg's concepts are entirely accepted by psychoanalysts. The Kris study group (Abend, Porter, & Willick, 1983) on borderline conditions at the New York Psychoanalytic Institute did not find a circumscribed condition as defined by Kernberg and had doubts about the appropriateness and usefulness of his delineation. Psychoanalysis had usually accepted the coexistence of pre-oedipal and oedipal aspects in various admixtures and to varying degrees in virtually all neuroses and other conditions. Kohut's complex and rather idiosyncratic formulations have found similar critique. Nevertheless, the borderline concept as well as that of the narcissistic personality, without rigid definitions, have merit as heuristic hypotheses.

Diagnosis of psychotic process in psychological tests in general is well covered by Weiner (1966). Psychotic process on the T.A.T. is seen in the presence of direct sexual and aggressive themes, themes of persecution, characters magically transforming from one thing to another, themes of omnipotence, magical power, figures being part one thing and part another, juxtaposition of extremes (angels and devils, acts of murder and loving tenderness), ideas of reference (thinking one card is connected to another card previously given), disorientation and confusion as to person, place, and time, lack of clear body boundaries, and gross deviation from the stimulus. The more one sees these indicators on psychological tests, the greater the possibility that the individual is either actively psychotic, has a latent psychosis, or has psychotic features. The frequency of indicators helps decide the severity of the condition. (See also the discussion of schizophrenic T.A.T. indicators on pages 158–161.)

Another useful method was pioneered by Anna Freud (1965). Hers was a developmental approach to diagnosis, called the "Developmental Profile." The idea is to identify in the clinical material (social history, set of referring symptoms, therapy sessions, and psychological tests) the predominant level of development in the area of psychosexual phases (oral, anal, oedipal, latency, adolescence, etc.), aggression, interpersonal object relations, defense mechanisms, and other areas. A clinician who sees severely disturbed individuals for testing can begin with the item approach of looking for a large number of indicators of psychotic process and then consider a developmental diagnosis. Here, the key question is if the person tested is predominantly pre-oedipal (stuck on a level typical of a child from birth to age 3) or oedipal neurotic (3 years and above).

Salient Indicators of Pre-Oedipal- and Oedipal-Level Functioning

The following features are characteristic pre-oedipal versus oedipal diagnostic indicators:

1. Panic reaction when signal anxiety is appropriate.
2. Primitive splitting rather than ambivalence.
3. Denial and splitting as defenses, rather than repression to fend off awareness.
4. Part-object experience and part-object perception, rather than whole-object experience and whole-object perception.

5. Unstable internal object or lack of internal object, rather than stable, internalized object constancy (the ability to hold in one's mind an image of another person independent of being in the other person's presence).

6. Superego is split between extreme punitive "all bad" and libidinal "all good" images, rather than being flexible, reasonable, and appropriate, and in tune with society's ethical principles.

7. Affect states are extreme and "pure" forms of love, hate, fear, sadness, and joy, rather than a neutralized, modulated array of feelings and nuances of feelings in between.

8. Shame and humiliation is experienced rather than oedipal neurotic guilt.

9. Introjective/projective relatedness (Volkan, 1976) of self-object relatedness (Kohut, 1977) rather than identificatory relatedness or relating to others as independent, separate individuals.

10. Fragmentation and disintegration, rather than synthetic function (ability to organize experience and perception into integrated "Gestalt," or meaningful wholes).

11. Acting and reacting, rather than experiencing and acting with a presence of observing ego function (self-observation and self-monitoring).

12. Defenses of incorporation and introjection, rather than identification.

13. Immediate discharge of impulses in acting out, rather than delayed gratification.

T.A.T. indicators of these characteristics of pre-oedipal versus oedipal developmental stages are the following.

Panic anxiety rather than signal anxiety can be seen in characters in a story engaging in sudden, wild, frenetic, or repetitive actions in the face of danger or threat. A monster threatens and a small animal simply jumps up and down, runs, screams, or does an action over and over on the C.A.T. Or the smaller animal may simply "freeze," immobilized and overwhelmed with fear. A signal approach would be to mention a danger in the future and an attempt to plan, prepare, and cope with the danger, as in calling for help, building a fort, hiding, or working out a trap. In the chapter on neuropsychological assessment, we give the example of a child who symbolized the need for signal function by the need for the story figures to have a fire alarm to call the firemen to put out a fire in the kitchen.

Primitive splitting rather than ambivalence is the key feature for borderline pathology according to Kernberg (1976). He defines *primitive splitting* as the keeping apart of extreme affects of love and hate, extreme impulses of aggression and libido, and extreme images of the self and of other people (called self and object representations) that are characterized as "all good loving" and "all bad hating." One sees T.A.T. characters that are either angels or devils, good guys or totally evil ones, without evidence of story figures who are somewhat good and somewhat bad, who have more than one side to their personalities. Volkan (1976) speaks of such fantasies of borderline patients as being all in black and white, rather than in technicolor. Ambivalence is seen in the T.A.T. by such statements as "either this . . . or that." Splitting in narrative style would be something more like, "It's this. No, it is only that" or "She hates him and wants to kill him. He is the only one she loves."

Part-object rather than whole-object experience and perception is seen on the T.A.T. in splitting, as just discussed, where there is not a development of characters that have a combination of different feelings, traits, and activities, but a juxtaposition of good versus bad characters.

Object constancy is seen in the behavior when the toddler begins to be able to play alone, with the mother in the next room or having been left in the care of a babysitter. When the mother leaves, there is no longer the temper tantrum panic reaction to separation anxiety. The child can now realize that the mother still exists independent of the child's immediate perception of her. Prior to object constancy, the child experiences the separation as a death, "out of sight, out of mind." If the child doesn't see or hear his mother, then mother must be dead, hence the extreme level of panic and the extreme tantrums. The lack of object constancy can therefore be seen in T.A.T. stories as a theme of separation anxiety, upset shown when one figure leaves another. Right after leaving home, for example, the next action is falling and getting hurt (as in C.A.T. story 2 where one part figure lets go of the rope and the child on the other side falls and gets hurt, symbolizing separation from the parent), getting attacked by a storm or by a threatening figure, or getting sick. Object constancy could be seen in characters who leave others, who leave home, and can plan, use strategy, and use defenses to handle the dangers that occur in the future. Little Red Riding Hood telling the wolf along her path through the woods that she is going to grandma's house is an example in story form of maintaining an image in one's mind of the mother figure in the face of separation and threat.

Pre-oedipal superego is seen in T.A.T. stories of extreme punishment for mild transgression, as when a character is jailed or killed because he urinated on the floor or falls down a cliff and dies because he just "didn't look where he was going." A more oedipal, neurotic, or normal level of superego exists when the punishment fits the particular crime. The child spills his food on C.A.T. story 1 and the mother asks him to clean it up and not spill the next time. Or one character calls the other a name and then apologizes for it. Pre-oedipal children do not usually think to say, "I'm sorry," because their punishment for a crime is much more extreme than that, they feel as if they should be—or are going to be—severely beaten for what they did. A mere apology is not in their scheme of things due to the lack of development of an oedipal level of the superego. Pre-oedipal superego is often split between this very primitive, punitive, extreme punishment for extreme and even very mild infractions and extremely, magically good, all-forgiving godlike features. The child violates a taboo, such as stealing the giant's belongings in *Jack and the Beanstalk* and the primitive superego punishment is seen in the giant trying to eat and/or kill Jack. The all-good superego is seen in the ending, where Jack has the giant's magical belongings to share safely alone with his mother "happily ever after."

Extreme affect states rather than neutralized, modulated affect states are seen in T.A.T. stories in the use of extreme affect words, such as *hate, love, devastated,* or *ecstatic,* predominantly, rather than a range of gradations of affect words, such as *somewhat saddened, a little annoyed, interested, surprised but understanding,* and so on. This goes along with stories 2 (use of primitive splitting rather than ambivalence) and 4 (part-object rather than whole-object experience and perception).

Shame and humiliation rather than guilt is seen in stories where the antagonist ends up with his pants down in front of an audience, slipping on a banana peel, or publicly embarrassed in some way. While guilt is seen in characters expressing remorse over actions that caused harm to others, expressing sorrow over a missed opportunity due to doing something reckless or stupid, or expressing self-criticism or self-recrimination for actions they feel interfered with the happiness of other people. Egocentrism versus role-taking ability is related here in that the pre-oedipal individual becomes more upset over shame and humiliation and seeks to avoid doing things that will humiliate himself, while the oedipal individual is more concerned about the feelings of others and more guilty over causing hardship to others.

Introjective/projective rather than identifactory relatedness is seen in very young children relating to the mother as if they are an extension of the mother and as if the mother is an extension of them. The infant acts as if the mother is only there to feed and comfort him or should smile and laugh when he smiles and laughs. The toddler, when angry with the parent, may project this anger onto the parent and imagine the parent is a monster furious with the toddler. The young child treats the parent as a self-object, then, rather than as a separate individual with independent needs. The parent is treated as both part of the self and part of the other, part self and part the parent. This is seen in the T.A.T. in frequent changes of a character's identity, sex, changes of pronoun from singular to plural and back to singular, and magic transformations from one thing to another. The theme of eating up another or being eaten up on C.A.T. stories represents this oral incorporative, introjective attempt to obliterate the independent existence of the self and the other as separate individuals. The idea of one figure "reading another's mind" or having the exact same thought as the other at the same time is another example of this kind of symbiotic oneness characteristic of pre-oedipal individuals. This is seen in emphasis on symmetry or seeing "twin" context on Rorschach and also on T.A.T. as the theme of twins.

Fragmentation rather than synthetic function is seen on T.A.T. in stories that are disjointed, aimless, and lacking in a sequential organization towards a logical ending. The story may begin about a little chicken eating and abruptly switch to a baby sleeping in its bed as in a free association without a clear connection between the two themes.

Acting rather than acting with self-observation is seen on T.A.T. stories in which the characters simply do different things, while there is no attempt to reflect on meaning about the actions or the picture. The boy looks at the violin, tries to play it, then puts it down (on card 1) is an example of acting without self-observation. By contrast, having the boy thinking about what he should play, how long he should practice, if his parent is happy with his practicing, or comments about whether the picture reminds the storyteller of some of his own feelings, and so on, are examples of the observing function more characteristic of the oedipal level of development.

Finally, *defenses of incorporation and introjection rather than identification* are seen in stories where a figure experiences a separation or loss and reacts by eating up the other, being eaten up by the other, or imagining one is seeing a ghost of the deceased, rather than dealing with loss by doing something similar to the deceased person's former activities, such as taking up an activity that used to be the hobby of the deceased. *Acting out versus delayed gratification* is seen in eating right away, screaming for something he wants, demanding something immediately, rather than waiting. The constellation of pre-oedipal characteristics can be illustrated in C.A.T. protocols of children of preschool age, who are still predominantly on a pre-oedipal level. The first protocol is that of a girl 4½ years, whose father physically abused her.

C.A.T. Protocols Illustrating Pre-Oedipal- and Oedipal-Level Functioning

Card 1: There were three chickens pecking at the trees and then the tree falls down and then they'll have to get another tree.

Comment

Oral emphasis is stated (pecking the trees) and theme of impulsivity, fragmentation, and panic anxiety is suggested by the tree falling down, as if the child seeks oral supplies from the parent (symbolized by the tree) and the parent falls apart.

Card 2: A little, three little bears and they wanted to pull a rope to tie around a tree and then they tied another rope around a tree and then it will fall on the Daddy.

Comment

Some desire for body boundaries and for synthesis is perhaps symbolized by the pulling a rope around the tree (a boundary to hold the self together), but in the end the tree falls continuing the theme of impulsivity, fragmentation, and panic reactions of becoming helpless and overwhelmed in the face of stress, rather than being able to mobilize coping mechanisms. That the tree falls on the father may indicate her anger at the abusive father or express something about the parents "falling on" each other in a sexual or aggressive manner that was frightening to the child, as if the world were falling down.

Card 3: A big, big, fat Daddy lion and he killed a baby. A baby and then nothing happened. (She gets very excited and flings the card in the air.)

Comment

Stuttering is a typical anxiety reaction in young children, which perhaps occurred in this child when presented the lion and mouse picture that is often associated by children as a father and child. The lion "kills the baby," which indicates extreme aggressive impulsivity coming from her life experience and also intensified from her pre-oedipal tendency to project some of her anger onto others, so that she sees the other as even more threatening and angry. Flinging the card is again a panic response of acting out and immediately discharging her impulses, rather than being able to verbalize her feelings or mobilize other defense and coping mechanisms.

Card 4: Once upon a time there was kangaroos and they went in the forest and got lost. They went and then they got lost again.

Comment

Separation from the parents and loss is symbolized in this story, which states an oral level theme. Repetition in action is similar to stuttering, which indicates anxiety and acting out impulsivity, rather than acting with self-observation.

Card 5: Once upon a time there was a little crib and a baby. The baby wasn't sleeping, because it was his bedtime and he forgot to eat dinner.

Comment

Oral neediness is stated again indicating a pre-oedipal level of psychosexual development, rather than an oedipal level which would be expected from her current age of 4½ years.

Card 6: Once upon a time there was a little bear, little bears, and they wanted to eat frogs and then the frogs got hungry and they went into their place to eat the bears. They wanted to, but they couldn't do it.

Comment

This is an excellent example of the self-object or introjective/projective relatedness typical of pre-oedipal-level individuals. The larger figures (adults?) want to incorporate, merge with, fuse with, and introject the littler figures (children?) and the littler figures want to eat up and incorporate the larger figures (the frogs want to eat up the bears). Following the sequence of her C.A.T. stories shows that she attempts to defend against separation and loss by primitive oral incorporation fantasies (to eat up or be eaten by the other so that the two of them are joined together).

Card 7: That one! That's a funny one. I don't know. No story on that one.

Comment

This is a picture of the tiger attacking the monkey, which is first defended against by reversal of affect ("that's a funny one"), then denial ("I don't know"), and finally by avoidance and withdrawal ("No story on that one"). These are all typical pre-oedipal-level ego defenses, as opposed to more oedipal and higher level defenses of repression, reaction formation, rationalization, or sublimation, and so forth.

Card 8: Nothing about that one either. . . . Once upon a time there were four little monkeys. They were standing and the mother monkey said to the father monkey one, "I would like to go outside and play with the baby monkeys." And then nothing else. The father one said yes.

Comment

She starts with denial, avoidance, and withdrawal, but then manages to relate a mundane, everyday type of story. This type of trivializing is again a defense away from letting oneself go in free association and personally meaningful fantasy. It is similar to concrete description of the pictures. It may suggest a denial of parental criticism (the picture shows the mother monkey pointing her finger towards the child monkey next to her) and a desire for the mother to nurture and play with her without the abusive restrictions she experiences from her father in reality. The pause at the beginning can indicate denial or blocking defenses.

Card 9: Once upon a time there was a little, a mommy rabbit, and she was so sad that nobody was home with her and then she cried.

Comment

The affect of sadness to loss is expressed directly.

Card 10: Once upon a time there was two doggies. The baby doggy had to go outside and he went right there—he went in the toilet. The end.

Comment

We see a further denial of parental criticism in the failure to report the action in the picture on the card of a parent or adult dog spanking a puppy on its knee. The use of the word *suddenly* is typical of pre-oedipal-level thematic stories symbolizing the sudden outbreak of impulses, a panic reaction to stress. This story suggests the puppy first went to the bathroom where the puppy was when he suddenly had to go, which further expresses acting out impulsivity, rather than an ability to delay immediate gratification. But she then ends it with the puppy going to the bathroom in the appropriate place, a suggestion that she is able to move in the direction of oedipal-level development.

C.A.T. Summary

This girl of 4½ years should be within an oedipal, neurotic level of psychosocial development. Instead, the C.A.T. suggests that the life stress within the family (parental strife, father's physical abuse) contributed to her staying primarily at a pre-oedipal level more typical of a child of 1½ to 2½ years of age.

In terms of the pre-oedipal characteristics enumerated earlier in the chapter, her C.A.T. shows panic reaction rather than signal anxiety function (cards 1, 2, and 3 with falling trees and killing), impulsivity (cards 1, 2, 3, and 10 in stuttering, repeated actions, primitive actions, (use of "suddenly")), acting out rather than delayed gratification (card 10 with the going to the bathroom right where one is rather than in the toilet), dependency (card 2 with theme of rope tied to adult figure), themes of separation and loss (cards 4 and 8), regression to oral neediness (cards 1, 2, 5, 6 and 8), self-object relatedness rather than self and object independence (card 6 with the figures eating each other up), direct pure affect (cards 3 and 9), and pre-oedipal-level defense mechanisms of denial (cards 3, 7, and 8) reversal of affect (card 7), avoidance and withdrawal (cards 7 and 8), and blocking (card 8 with its pause).

The child might be diagnosed, then, as having an adjustment disorder with pre-oedipal fixation or regression secondary to the family stress and abuse.

Following is another typical pre-oedipal-level C.A.T. story to card 3 in a boy of 5 years of age, who is hyperactive.

Card 3: I'm not touching that one! This once upon a time is about a big lion that's sitting in his chair alone. He got up, went outside, scared all the people, ate one people, and real scary! You know what made him friendly?—a magic ball.

Comment

He first defends by avoidance and withdrawal (I'm not touching that one!"), then brings in the theme of oral incorporation (eating up people) and of panic anxiety (scaring everyone). Finally, he reaches for magical thinking in the magic ball that makes him friendly, which also suggests dependency upon the mother (perhaps symbolized by the round ball) and undoing (the scary one becomes magically friendly). This shows an ability in this child to respond to stress and anxiety with the mobilization of defenses, so this child is closer to an oedipal level of signal anxiety, rather than the predominantly pre-oedipal panic reaction to anxiety in the little girl of 4½ years above. But this boy's defenses are still pre-oedipal level defenses, rather than oedipal or higher ones.

The following is a story of a neurotic level child of 5 years, which shows what we would expect to see in a C.A.T. when a child is no longer on a pre-oedipal level, but has reached the oedipal level and by age 5 years is already well on the way to resolving and working it through on an age-appropriate level:

Card 7: Oh God! this is really scary. . . . OK, here I go. . . . Once upon a time there was a lion catching a monkey and the monkey was running away on his rope. Then he was climbing up the tree, and the lion was crying (he gestures a roar) like this, "Rhhhhh!" He sounded like my Dad laughin'. Every time I go "Whoo!" to my sister, she runs. She thinks it's a ghost, but it's only me. In the night, in the dark, I do it, when there's not the light.

Comment

He is able to verbalize his fear of this card with the picture of the tiger attacking the monkey, "This is really scary," which pre-oedipal-level individuals often do not do. They step back from the card, turn it over, refuse to do a story, or express a story only of aggressive actions of chase and escape. This boy then does retreat first to the pre-oedipal defense of avoidance and withdrawal (the monkey running away), but then comes back with a superb example of the typical oedipal level defense of identification with the aggressor. The boy identifies the tiger (lion here) with his father's loud laughing (a reversal of affect or reaction formation defense) and then tells us that he identifies with the father's roaring in scaring his sister. The father scares him, so he scares his sister, which shows oedipal identification with a quality of the father and a tendency to deal with aggressive threat by turning passive into active and becoming the threatening one to others, rather than remaining the helpless, panicked, passive recipient of threat from larger adults.

Specific Indicators of Borderline Pathology

In this chapter, we can only provide an introduction to this developmental type of T.A.T. and C.A.T. diagnosis. Abrams (1977) and Sutton-Smith and associates (1981) suggest further developmental analysis of narratives. What is important for this chapter is to first distinguish the T.A.T. or C.A.T. protocol from psychotic process by using the list of psychotic *indicators* we suggested earlier in the chapter and then move on to distinguish whether the protocol is predominantly pre-oedipal or predominantly oedipal or above in *developmental* level in ego functions, defenses, and object relations. If the protocol has numerous psychotic indicators and is predominantly pre-oedipal, a diagnosis of psychotic process is to be considered (along with psychotic indicators on the other projective tests). If there are only a few indicators of psychosis or no indicators of psychosis, but the protocol is predominantly pre-oedipal, then a diagnosis of borderline disorder could be considered (providing the patient is over 8 or 9 years of age and there are signs of borderline pathology on other psychological tests in the battery).

Borderline pathology is often identified with individuals whose level is predominantly pre-oedipal, but is not fundamentally psychotic. But one must also look for the following characteristics, as noted in the *DSM-IV* (APA, 1994):

1. Impulsivity or unpredictability in spending, sex, gambling, substance abuse, shoplifting, overeating, physically damaging acts (at least two of these)
2. A pattern of unstable and intense interpersonal relationships with marked shifts of attitude, idealization, devaluation, manipulation (consistently using others for one's needs)
3. Inappropriate, intense anger or lack of control of anger seen often in frequent temper tantrums
4. Identity disturbance manifested by uncertainty about several issues relating to identity, such as self-image, gender identity, long-term goals or career choice, friendship patterns, value, and loyalties
5. Affective instability: marked shifts from a normal mood to depression, irritability, or anxiety, usually lasting a few hours and only rarely more than a few days, with a return to normal mood
6. Intolerance of being alone seen in frantic efforts to avoid being alone (desperate calls to the therapist on Fridays before the weekend loneliness), depressed when alone
7. Physically self-damaging acts such as suicidal gestures, self-mutilation, recurrent accidents or physical figures; also periodic use of drugs, alcohol and overeating in the same manner
8. Chronic feelings of emptiness or boredom

T.A.T. Protocol Illustrating Borderline Disorders with Some Psychotic-Like Features

Adult Case of Borderline Disorder with Some Psychotic-Like Features

The following T.A.T. is from a 30-year-old woman, who had one hospitalization for a suicide gesture in which she took sleeping pills. This case nicely illustrates the presence of a few psychotic-like features within a developmental level that is predominantly pre-oedipal. Key characteristics of borderline disorder, as defined by DSM-IV, further substantiate the diagnostic impression that she is not fundamentally psychotic, but has a borderline disorder with mild psychotic-like features:

1: This little boy is, let me look closely. This is ambiguous. You'd have to be a genius to make what I'd like to about this picture. The boy is missing that, don't write that. Let's see. He just got this violin and he was told he had to play this musical instrument and he hates the violin. He just had a lesson and he's been practicing for hours and he's just taking a rest now, he hates the violin. I have two different endings—one's healthy and one's not. I don't know which one to go with. As he got older, one day he smashes that violin against the wall and broke it. Then another way of ending it, it is bothering him, so he practiced it so he could become a better player and he became a great violinist.

But there's a little piece down here which could be broken, so he's upset that his violin could be broken. Oh, no! That's because he doesn't know how to play it and he doesn't want to play it.

Comment

Primitive splitting is suggested by the juxtaposition of extremes—the "unhealthy ending" of smashing the violin against the wall and breaking it and the "healthy ending" of practicing and becoming a great violinist. In splitting, two opposite feelings or ideas are kept apart from each other. They could not be part of the same story, for example. So she makes two different endings. Splitting is also suggested by the juxtaposition of "genius" and the boy at the end who feels broken like the violin could be, "because he doesn't know how to play it (low self-esteem) and he doesn't want to play it (anal level oppositionalism)." Aggressive, angry impulsivity, grandiosity (great violinist, genius), and part-object perception ("little piece here") are borderline features.

2: Ah, this is the one I get stuck on, this picture. It doesn't make sense to me. Um, um . . . (pause) I'm much less anxious than I used to be when I talked about these pictures. This is a wierd picture. Um, ah (heaves a sigh). This daughter's going to school. She's, the bus is coming from the left, but she's looking toward the right. Her mother's standing up against the tree that doesn't belong in the picture, facing another direction. The brother is plowing the field beside a horse and they're all in different zones. Well, very soon after the girl leaves for school, the mother starts . . . what does the mother do? Um, the mother does work that she has to do in the house and the son plows and takes care of the animals and they have lunch.

Comment

Pre-oedipal, borderline characteristics are predominantly the sense of fragmentation, part-object, or splitting in the idea that the tree "doesn't belong in the picture" and that each family member is in a "different zone" and the notable separation anxiety, when presented with this picture of a girl appearing to be leaving for school or coming back from school to the family on the farm. She gets stuck, blocks, becomes vague, pauses, and heaves a sigh presumably at the idea of the "daughter's going to school" (all indicators of high anxiety).

3: (. . . she sighs). This girl goes to school for, um, disturbed people and she's just there now in the student common room, upset. Wait, I think there's scissors on the floor next to her. (She puts the card down.) She's upset because everyone's out that night and she's the only one there.

She goes to sleep early, she talks to a teacher, and then shortly after that, she flips out and leaves school. Could be a biography, but it's not. At the beginning, I was thinking she was pregnant and she was thinking she had to get an abortion and then there's another one where she kind of looks like a lesbian from the behind. I used to have pretty elaborate stories on these.

Comment

Anxiety over separation is clear from the beginning hesitation, sighing, filler sounds (ah, uh, um), and the content itself. The defenses of avoidance and withdrawal are noted in her putting the card down and the action in the story of "going to sleep," which is also an oral regression. Panic and fragmentation then is expressed in the next action of "flipping out," and "leaving school" is another form of avoidance, withdrawal, and regression. The negation form of denial comes in the statement, "Could be a biography (about herself), but it's not." Having an abortion may also continue the theme of separation anxiety and the idea of a "lesbian from the behind" expresses the possibility of sex-role identification confusion and identity disturbance often seen in borderline patients.

4: God!, these cards don't make much sense to me. (She holds the card up close.) This woman's husband just got home from work and . . . he, I can't tell if he's happy. He looks like he's rushing off to somewhere. He's going to run upstairs, because he heard that his daughter fell out of a tree today and the wife's just trying to tell him that it's not that bad. That she's sleeping, but he wants to rush right up there. They all come downstairs in an hour at the end and eat dinner and the little girl's a lot better.

Comment

"The meaninglessness" of the cards may illustrate her use of denial (blocking off immediate awareness) and possible splitting. Separation anxiety is suggested by the idea of coming home and "can't tell if he's happy" juxtaposed with the contrary idea that "He looks like he's rushing off to somewhere." Primitive splitting may be present here with this co-existence of opposite feelings and thoughts. The daughter's accident and sleeping after it show borderline features of self-damaging acts, impulsivity, and depressive withdrawal.

6GF: Who makes up these pictures, anyway? . . . (pause) . . . This woman's sitting on the couch and her husband just came back behind her to ask her what drink she wanted for dinner. They're waiting for company to arrive. That's it. . . . Later on, the company comes, they have a nice time, and have one too many drinks and just get very intellectual and on and on. There's sort of a debate going on and then the company leaves. The company sort of staggers out, crawls, and that's the night.

Comment

Pause suggests anxiety and blocking. Acting out impulsivity is suggested by having "too many drinks," possible defense intellectualization ("get very intellectual") and regression (crawling out). Some fragmentation of thoughts is evident by the fits and starts and disjointed ideas in the style of relating the story and in its overall narrative organization.

7GF: This mother's trying to talk to her daughter about, uh (long sigh) about her having to go into the hospital and her daughter's very upset. She can't even look at her and the daughter runs up to her room and spends the whole night there. She falls asleep, but the mother comes to say 'Goodnight' to make her feel better.

Comment

Theme of separation anxiety is repeated here (leaving the mother and going to the hospital), which is reacted to with defense of withdrawal (runs up to her room) and regression to sleep (falls asleep). But she only seems to feel better when separation is removed by the mother coming back to her.

8BM: How many are there? Well, ah, this boy is imagining what's happening behind him. These two men are cutting open his friend behind him. He often imagines things like that that scare him and sort of, he gets engrossed in these fantasies. He ruined the whole room. These men ruin the whole room. These men do it all. They shoot holes in the windows, knock out the walls, cut open this man's intestine. Take it out and leave him there and he's in pain. No anesthesia. These guys aren't doctors. This boy is just dreaming the whole thing up. It's just his fantasy. It didn't really happen. Well, he acts out sometimes and in drawings or what he writes. That's not me talking. I don't have thoughts like that, don't you think?

Comment

Acting out of aggressive impulses (ruining the whole room by shooting holes in walls, cutting open the man on the table) is defended against by displacement ("He ruined the whole room . . . these men ruin the room") and denial ("This boy is just dreaming the whole thing up. It's just his fantasy. It didn't really happen. . . . That's not me talking . . ."). The primitive and intense aggression and the pre-oedipal level of defenses against it are typical identifying features of the borderline disorder.

10: I don't understand this picture. I don't, I can't tell if it's two women or a man and a woman. They almost look alike. Like twins. Ah (she sighs), I don't know. These women are twins (she puts the card out at arm's length) and they were usually very close to each other here they're, they look very intimate with each other. Since they grew up as twins, they're always very physical with each other in a way, in a sisterly sense (she laughs embarrassingly) and here they haven't seen each other, because the funeral of a friend brought them together.

Comment

Sex-role confusion and the theme of twins (self-object merger) are further example of borderline disorder in this story. She also suggests the presence of primitive splitting in the juxtaposition of the theme of merger (twins and intimacy) with the opposite theme of death, loss, and separation (the funeral).

13MF: Ah, I don't like this one, either. They had a "one night stand" and they just picked each other up at a bar one night. Um, he's leaving after that, he has a hangover, and he's leaving. He's got all his clothes on. They never see each other again. He just leaves. Ah . . . I just thought of something else. She could be dead and he saw her and he's very upset. But why would she have no clothes on? Scratch that. Well, they weren't close before, but now he really cares about her, but she's dead.

Comment

Acting out impulsivity and the borderline experience of intense, short-lived interpersonal involvements are expressed in the idea of "one night stands," during which they meet, presumably have sexual relations, and "never see each other again"—an experience this patient has had frequently. Then she shifts the thought to extreme loss through death either because separation often feels like a total death to her (as in the previous story) or because her anger at separation stirs up extremely primitive and intense aggressive impulses. Denial is then evident in her desire to "scratch that."

Summary

The T.A.T. protocol reveals the key features of a borderline disorder with psychotic-like features with the frequency and primacy of primitive splitting (cards 1, 2, 10, and 13MF), denial (cards 3, 4, 8BM, and 13MF), and separation anxiety (cards 2, 3, 4, 6GF, 7GF, 10, and 13MF). Tremendous aggression, impulsivity, high anxiety, avoidance, withdrawal, regression and blocking are further identifying features.

Sex-role confusion is seen on card 3BM suggested by the lesbian themes and stated very directly on card 10, where she is not sure if they are a man and a woman and then moves on to make them twins. The borderline patient is also at the border in ego boundaries, so that the self is experienced as part-self and part-other and others are experienced as part-other and part of the self. The borderline fuses, separates, and refuses, back and forth. The borderline lacks cohesion of the self or ego integration and has unstable boundaries between the self and others. Therefore, at points of stress, the borderline's self becomes further fragmented, further disintegrated, and further split into part-object and part-self representations and there is a further tendency to merge and fuss with need-fulfilling objects. Separation anxiety is a key issue causing panic outbursts in which the inappropriate level of intense anger and aggression may appear psychotic to others. The borderline may attempt to frantically merge with the separating love object, so that a family member or boyfriend or girlfriend of a borderline individual feels overwhelmed by this overbearing demandingness. However, the borderline is often as terrified of closeness as he or she is of separation. So when the borderline begins to feel merged and intimate, he may begin to feel threatened with loss of the self, panic, and abruptly reject the love object so desperately desired. Because of these two deep fears of separation and of merger, the borderline's interpersonal relations are overly intense resembling the turbulent storms of conflicting needs for dependence and independence of toddlers and of adolescents.

These abrupt swings between intimacy to the point of twinship and extreme isolation in themes of death are seen in this T.A.T. protocol as we read from one story to the next. The borderline's interpersonal relations are also overly intense, because of the extreme "pure" expression of affect. The anger is a pure, deep anger, as is the sadness or love. Affects are unneutralized, unmodulated by the nuances seen in higher functioning individuals. So others feel intensely drawn to, involved with, and also rejected by borderline individuals. These extreme mood and feeling states also swing from one extreme to the other, so they are in a deep, almost suicidal depression one hour or day, in ecstatic joy the next, and later apparently calm and normal. When calm and normal, they complain of emptiness and boredom, which is really due to the schizoid-like operation of the defense of primitive denial and primitive splitting (a clouding over of immediate awareness).

The borderline individual may abruptly turn to self-damaging behavior, such as accidents, gambling, alcohol, or drug abuse, as a frantic attempt to feel alive again (after the schizoid emptiness and boredom has come upon him) or to calm the stimulus overload through drugs or alcohol (after the stimulating aspects of these behaviors have made him start to feel too alive and potentially out-of-control and fragmented). Because of this primitive splitting, mood swings, and swings between the schizoid emptiness level of denial and stimulus overload, the borderline individual typically is not consolidated enough to be an addictive personality, but uses drugs, alcohol, gambling and the lot in a fragmented and an intermittent manner.

A continuing debate in the literature is over what is the key issue in borderline pathology. Some feel it is separation anxiety and the lack of appropriate reaction to anxiety, rather than having developed a signal function to anxiety. Some feel it is due to a fragmented, split, or "unintegrated' ego that needs to develop further towards integration (Winnicott, 1965). Some feel it may be fundamentally influenced by organic factors, such as neuropsychological dysfunction in the area of perceptual, perceptual-motor, and motoric integration so that the individual has basic deficits in synthesizing functions and is thus prone to fragmentation and unorganized panic under stress. Others emphasize the predominant use of primitive splitting and related defenses, such as denial, idealization, devaluation, and projective identification, rather than repression and its related defenses of reaction formation, rationalization, intellectualization, and sublimation.

The reader will notice that these issues are the main characteristics of the pre-oedipal stage of development, which we listed earlier in this chapter. It is for that reason that Kernberg writes of the borderline disorder as the main disorder of pre-oedipally fixated individuals, who are not psychotic. He suggests that the disorder is due to a constitutional level of aggression that is higher than in normal individuals and to a failure to successfully resolve the rapprochement subphase of the separation-individuation process, when the child swings between intense separation and merger fears due to not having yet developed an inner image of the mother (object constancy).

Kohut (1971), on the other hand, viewed narcissistic personality disorder as the central pre-oedipal disorder. Consequently, for him, the borderline disorder is a subset of the narcissistic personality disorder. Abrams (1991) suggested that while the pre-oedipal splitting seen in borderline patients is often seen as deriving from a constitutional overabundance of the aggressive drive (Kernberg, 1975), it may also derive from actual experiences of disrupted merger and separation beginning in the first year of life with the significant caretaker and coming to a turbulent traumatic crisis in the rapprochement subphase of Mahler's (1968) separation-individuation process. Westen and colleagues (1990a, 1990b) suggest the same view.

Specific Indicators of Narcissistic Pathology

Since Kernberg views the borderline disorder as the central disorder of pre-oedipally fixated individuals, he views the narcissistic personality disorder and most other types of pre-oedipal pathology as a subset of the borderline disorder. Kohut (1971), on the other hand, views narcissistic personality disorder as the central pre-oedipal disorder. Consequently, for him, the borderline disorder is a subset of the narcissistic personality disorder. The characteristics of narcissistic pathology are similar to borderline pathology—difficulty in forming and maintaining relationships, little empathy for others' needs and feelings, grandiosity in unrealistic schemes, exaggerated self-regard, constant demandingness for attention, inappropriate idealization of certain hero figures, and intense envy of others. Extreme almost paranoid-like anger is often expressed, when the narcissistic person feels rejected or even mildly criticized, which is often referred to as *exquisite narcissistic vulnerability*. Also, there is an emotional aloofness at times and a sense of entitlement as the individual feels "splendidly isolated" from the common needs and world of other people. In the T.A.T. or C.A.T. protocols of narcissistically disordered individuals, one would expect to see the pre-oedipal characteristics we outlined earlier in this chapter, but without seeing the predominant borderline features of impulsivity, extreme mood swings, and indicators of fragmentation in storytelling style and content. The narcissistic patient is better organized and more stable. Brelet-Foulard (1986) gives an example of a T.A.T. protocol from an adult male, who sees himself as a hero on a grand theatrical stage putting on a "one-man show" without others, which masks underlying feelings of defectiveness and primary insecurity. The C.A.T. protocol below shows similar dynamics.

C.A.T. Protocol Illustrating Narcissistic Pathology

This protocol comes from an 8-year-old boy, very handsome, superb in sports, basically a straight-A student, but whose teacher and parents feel lacks a fundamental sensitivity to other people's feelings. If someone is upset over something, for example, he will appear cold and indifferent. He is a perfectionist in school, insisting on getting only straight As, and throwing temper tantrums if he receives any grade that is any less than an A. He is similarly totally intolerant of criticism of any kind and throws temper tantrums when disciplined, criticized, or any time anyone tells him he cannot have something he desires. When he is in one of his bad moods when he feels rejected or unappreciated, he is extremely disrespectful of others, calls them bad names, and says he does not want any part of them ever in his life anymore. At such times, it would appear that he projects outward onto others his own degraded self-image. The parents reported that most people who meet him at first fall in love with him due to his good looks, seeming outgoing and friendly personality, and lively vitality, but then can neither understand his temper outbursts nor his lack of feeling for them and others. This results in his currently not having even one close friend.

1: Sometime, in a little cabin, there are three birds eating their breakfast and a big, big shadow of a hen. *And then?* And then Babe Ruth came along and asked them if they'd pinch run for him in the World Series. And they said, "Yes." And then it was the World Series and they were pinch running. But they didn't know how to do it. And they got out. *Is that the end?* Yes.

Comment

Primitive splitting is suggested by the juxtaposition of the "little cabin" and the "big, big shadow of a hen." Lack of genuine, object-related contact with others is suggested by his referring to the larger figure as a "shadow of a hen," rather than speaking of this as a real mother chicken interacting with her children that most children his age tend to see on this card. A hypothesis is that he may experience his own mother as "shadowy," rather than being a real, concrete object with whom he can realistically interact. Grandiosity enters in his bringing in a famous baseball player, the legendary Babe Ruth, whom he has asking the little child figures of the baby chicks to substitute run for him, which is a grandiose wish for the little child figures to be able to do what a big baseball hero does, but even more so, he has them run instead of Babe Ruth doing the running. Defensively, this represents an omnipotent denial of the reality limitations of what a child can and cannot do. At the end, he reasserts reality-testing by saying that when it came to the World Series, the chicks didn't know how to pinch run for Babe Ruth, so they got out.

2: Once in the woods three bears were having a big tug-of-war and it was two against one. It seemed as if the person who only has two was winning. Although, the person, the two bears did fall in the mud. And that ended it. *Who were they, the different bears? What were they like?* Two very wimpy bears. They're all men bears.

Comment

Some difficulty in object-related interaction may be suggested by the vagueness again in this story about the different animals in the picture. The phrase "the person who only has two was winning" may suggest a lack of self-object differentiation and a wish to be symbiotically merged with another, in this case the picture shows a child with a parent figure on one side of the rope. When asked to identify the bears, he says the two are "very wimpy bears," but then adds that "they're all men bears." This may point to some underlying feelings of low self-esteem, which was first expressed in the first story of the little chicks, who blow their first big chance to participate in the World Series. Here they end up falling in the mud.

3: Once in a house, there was a house and there was a chair with an old lion in it smoking his pipe with a TV watching the World Series in 1986 (laughs). *And then?* Then he smokes his pipe so much that he starts to cough so he can't see a baseball game. So he falls to the floor, saying, "Hmm. This smells (laughs)."

Comment

This protocol was administered in June of 1989, three years after the New York Mets team had won the World Series in 1986. Usually, this card brings out the interaction of the little mouse looking and interacting with the lion. In his story, he perseverates on the theme of baseball's World Series, which has now come into each of his first three stories. The fact that the mouse is not mentioned and that the lion is "watching TV" may continue to express the sense that this boy feels aloof, on the sidelines of the world of others, merely an onlooker, rather than a true, object-related participant. This may also suggest that he does not experience much genuine involvement in his interaction with his own father. Primitive splitting is again suggested by the juxtaposition of the World Series theme with the old man, who smokes, can't see the TV, and ends by falling on the floor. The defense mechanism of reversal of affect is indicated by his laughing as he says that the old lion falls to the floor. So far, a distinct dynamic is his inner sense of low self-esteem, inability to do things successfully and to win, which he tries to defend against with omnipotent, grandiose denial, reversal of affect, and perhaps by keeping a distance from true emotional involvement with others.

4: God, this is hard. Once there were three kangaroos. One on her tricycle, one Mom bouncing, and one kangaroo in the Mom's pouch, and looks as though they're going on a picnic and here comes a house with its fire going and trees. *Happen?* They're going to eat their picnic food.

Comment

The opening "God, this is hard" suggest further feelings of personal inadequacy to which he may want to appeal for help to the omnipotent God. The figures in the picture get their oral needs met, since they are said to "eat their picnic food." But nothing else is given to this card. He is not able to go much beyond this simple description of the picture itself, which may again suggest some conflict with his own mother around whether or not he feels he can genuinely interact with her beyond the level of narcissistic need satisfaction of simply getting fed by her.

5: Once there was a house with two baby bears sleeping in a bed and the house had three windows, one giant bed, a night table with a lamp on it, and a staircase leading down to the door. *Anything happen next?* Through the night, a mysterious killer comes into their room wanting to kill them. But then the baby says, "I'm Superman!!! (he stands up yelling this out). He chops off the killer's head, and that was the end of Dan Quayle (laughs).

Comment

With this story, he brings in the idea that he may experience the world as suddenly and unpredictably threatening to him, threatening him with total annihilation in fact. He defends against the dangerous intruder with omnipotent, grandiose denial by having the baby jump up to turn into Superman. Superman kills the threatening killer, which he then turns into the current Vice President of the United States under George Bush, Dan Quayle, whom at the time of this C.A.T. was the butt of many jokes due to Quayle's apparent lack of competence. Therefore, this reiterates this boy's predominant dynamic of feeling basically inadequate underneath a cover of apparent good looks and seeming competence (one view of Dan Quayle).

6: Once in a cave there were one big bear and one little bear. There were lots of leaves in there. And suddenly came along a lion trying to rob all their money. So then the boy bear woke up and said, "Hey, you trying to steal my money?" So then the lion said, "Well, you make a good point there. But I still want your money." So then there was a big fight. But then the lion, he whipped her butt. And that was the end. And then Little Bear said, "What you do to Big Bear?" And then the lion said, "Oh, I just chopped off her butt."

Comment

He now begins this story by leaving out the third bear, which is often characteristic of pre-oedipally fixated individuals—they tend to see their interpersonal object relations as dyadic (mother/child), rather than the triadic (father/mother/child) relations of neurotic level individuals. That he feels threatened by others is suggested by the lion that comes along to rob them. The mother bear seems to take charge and tell the lion not to steal their money, but to go and get his own money. The lion seems to acquiesce by saying, "You make a good point there," but reiterates his threat to take the money. So the mother bear now threatens to kill the lion, who ends by beating up and killing the mother. He seems to see his parents as basically ineffectual against internal and external threats and he feels basically unprotected. Defensive reversal of affect is again seen in the lion responding to the father's opening retaliatory threat with "You make a good point there."

7: Once in a jungle there was a big tiger trying to kill a monkey. There were lots of vines and trees in this jungle and the monkey was trying to escape. But the tiger was too fast and ate up the monkey.

Comment

To this card showing a clearly threatening tiger, he can give only a short story where the monkey tries to escape, but ends getting eaten up by the tiger. This is further expression of the theme of feeling unprotected against an externally threatening world.

8: Once in a house with all monkeys, there was a picture of a monkey. And all the monkeys were sitting on a sofa and on a chair. And one was standing with what looks like an aunt monkey teaching him a lesson and two were drinking tea. And one was wearing a flower in her hair, one was wearing earrings and the monkey standing looks like he was going outside to play baseball. What happens next? Right when he was going outside to play baseball . . . um . . . he ran into . . . George Steinbrenner (at the time of this C.A.T., he was the owner of the New York Yankees baseball team, which had not done very well for several seasons). So he told George Steinbrenner, "Get lost, or else you're in trouble." So then George Steinbrenner said, "I can play baseball better than you!" So the monkey said, "Oh yeh! What about your stupid Yankees? How do you teach THEM to play?" And then George Steinbrenner says, "You make a point there. You're right. I do stink." *Is that the end?* Yeh.

Comment

On this card, he seems to recover and to bring back his defenses of intellectualization (listing all the figures and describing the details in the picture), isolation of affect (suggested by speaking of the "picture of a monkey" as if to distance himself from emotional interaction like the "shadow of a hen" in card 1), reversal of affect (the joking about George Steinbrenner), and identification with aggressor (George Steinbrenner tries to intimidate the child monkey, so the child monkey humiliates George Steinbrenner). Again the dynamic seems to be a famous individual who is supposed to have a lot of power, but whose competence underneath is shaky at best. Card 5 had Vice President Dan Quayle, this one has the former owner of the Yankees, George Steinbrenner, who often publicly acted very tough and controlling, yet never seemed to get his team to win on a very high level.

9: Hmm. Once in a house there was a room. Door slightly, I mean with a door opened with windows with curtains, and a mirror, and a night table, and a rabbit in the bed going to sleep. *Happen?* Um . . . She's going to dream that she's in rabbit land hopping, hopping, hopping. But here's a strange part of the story. Suddenly, her boss comes and says, "What you doing here?" Although her boss was a big fat guy, he didn't know how to do anything. He was just a lazy bum. So she just goes hopping along and she runs into an ice cream shop. So she buys ice cream and she tries to eat it. But instead of it melting, it melts her, and that's the end (laughs).

Comment

This powerful dynamic of underlying feelings of inadequacy beneath a cover of boastful grandiosity is again repeated in the figure of the lazy bum boss, who "although her boss was a big fat guy, he didn't know how to do anything." Underlying fearfulness is also expressed by the beginning of the door opening, while the child rabbit is going to sleep. While the boss who seems to threaten the child rabbit at first is ultimately seen as harmless, the child rabbit ends up melting away after eating an ice cream cone. Reversal of affect is again employed to defend against this unfortunate ending of the child rabbit, whose food seems to do her in in the end. This could again express a feeling that his mother and the nurturance she gives to him seems like a good dessert, but is cold and annihilating in the end.

10: Once up in a bathroom (laughs) there was two puppies. One looks like he wanted to go to the bathroom. And the other looks like he wanted to keep the other one from going to the bathroom. So it looks like she wanted to cut his toe nail. But it wasn't that, she just had to go to the bathroom, too. *Is that the end?* Yes.

Comment

The more common story to this card is of a child dog doing something wrong, such as drinking from the toilet bowl, so the parent dog gives it a spanking. To this scene, he instead leaves out the spanking, which may be an attempt to deny the punitive side of his mother that he seems to have expressed in other stories, particularly the previous one. He may wish to distance himself from this, so he changes it to the mother looking like she wanted to cut his toe nails, "but it wasn't that, she just had to go to the bathroom, too." It may look like the mother is punishing (or to him castrating), but she just wants to go to the bathroom as the child wants to keep the mother from going to the bathroom. Perhaps he sees himself and his mother or parents as in competition with each other over basic needs.

Summary

The overall picture is of a child with narcissistic pathology, who seems to feel very inadequate, unnurtured, unprotected, and threatened by a hostile and cold world. In such a world, people do not seem to be loving to each other and he does not appear to receive any genuine help and care from anyone. Other people threaten, boast, intimidate, and seem to give him unrealistic things to do that he feels totally inadequate attempting, such as Babe Ruth asking the baby chicks to pinch run for him in the World Series. In this type of world, everyone—the adult and the child figures—all seem to end up failing, falling in the mud, or melting away like cold ice cream.

As Kohut (1971, 1977, 1984) pointed out, the narcissistic individual feels cold, isolated, criticized, unloved, incompetent, and highly vulnerable to attack from others underneath. The main defense against these inferior feelings is to erect an omnipotent grandiose self to use as a cover and to remain splendidly isolated from others as if one does not have any need for anyone else. This child employs either fantasy omnipotent figures like Superman, real heroes like Babe Ruth, or real personnages like Dan Quayle or George Steinbrenner who have the veneer of power and success but who are not very successful and competent at what they are trying to do in actuality. While outgoing, lively, a straight-A student, and very handsome, this boy underneath feels rejected and empty. He seems to picture his parents as seemingly ineffectual, unprotecting, and unnurturing in any real way to him. There seems to be little differentiation of other people in his world, people are not distinct individuals with clear identities, but are shadowy, vague, caricaturish, and exaggerated characterizations, who strut about with large and noisy gestures but who basically seem dead inside. This child's C.A.T. is very similar to the dream of a narcissistically disordered adult described in Kohut (1984, pp. 17–18) in which an individual is inside a cold, icy heart and attempts to appeal to a shadowy figure for help, but to no avail. It is also reminiscent of Shakespeare (*Macbeth*, Act V, Scene V):

> *Life's but a walking shadow: a poor player,*
> *That struts and frets his hour upon the stage,*
> *And then is heard no more: it is a tale*
> *Told by an idiot, full of sound and fury,*
> *Signifying nothing.*

The T.A.T. protocol on pages 138–151 of a depressed man with significant narcissistic pathology shows many of the same above features.

CHAPTER 13

THE T.A.T., C.A.T., AND S.A.T. IN NEUROPSYCHOLOGICAL ASSESSMENT

Some General Remarks on Neuropsychological Assessment

An early view in psychological testing was that only intelligence and achievement tests measure cognitive functioning and only projective tests measure personality. When neurophysiological dysfunction was addressed, the Bender Gestalt was usually the only test examined, many psychological reports being limited to such single, general, and vague statements as "Organicity is evidenced (or ruled out) by the Bender."

However, with the advances of biological psychiatry (Bellak, 1979; Rutter, 1983; Wender & Klein, 1981), learning disability assessment (Bakker & Satz, 1970; Golden, 1978; Hynd & Cohen, 1983; Kirk, 1983; Knights & Bakker, 1976; Pirozzolo, 1979), and neuropsychology (Golden, 1979; Heilman & Valenstein, 1985; Herron, 1980; Kolb & Whishaw, 1980; Luria, 1973; Rourke et al., 1983; Russell et al., 1970), signs of possible organicity in perceptual, auditory, motor, language, verbal reasoning, and other domains were assessed across the entire range of tests in the psychological test battery. The Bender Gestalt test is now understood as one of the tests in the overall battery that specifically measures perceptual-motor functioning and its subdomains of directionality, left-right orientation, perceptual attention to small details, visual tracking and distractibility, perception of and short-term memory for visual gestalts to rule out apperceptive agnosia, and fine-motor integration. Signs of perceptual-motor dysfunction on the Bender are then compared with signs of similar dysfunction in the perceptual-motor subtests of the Wechsler Performance Scale, the Beery Test of Visual Integration, the Benton Test of Visual Retention, handwriting from a handwriting sample and on the spelling test of the Wide Range Achievement Test-Revised, and projective drawings. The overall result is a more specific, more finely tuned, and more comprehensive approach to psychological testing, so that, today, personality characteristics are also assessed on intelligence tests (Rapaport et al., 1970; Rothstein et al., 1988; Santostefano, 1978; Zimmerman and WooSam, 1973) and on the Bender (Brown, 1965; Hutt, 1969). Cognitive, neuropsychological characteristics are also beginning to be assessed on the projective tests of drawings, the Rorschach, and the T.A.T. (Costantino et al., 1991; Johnson, 1994; Lezak, 1983; Rothstein et al., 1988).

This chapter is a beginning sketch toward considering how neuropsychological characteristics may be expressed on the T.A.T., C.A.T., and S.A.T. After discussing Lezak's (1983) list of neuropsychological indicators on the T.A.T. and adding items from our own clinical experience, we will present two stories of a child and adult case with attention deficit disorder (ADD) as an illustration of a neuropsychological syndrome commonly seen in school and patient populations that was earlier referred to as minimal brain dysfunction (Bellak, 1979, 1985, 1994).

Since research on the cognitive structuring of narrative organization in thematic tests does not yet have as extensive a history as form level and other structure scoring on the Rorschach, this chapter should be considered a beginning sketch for future research in this exciting new area of possible neuropsychological dimensions on the T.A.T. Since the first publication of this chapter in the fourth edition of 1986, there have been some studies of neuropsychological indicators on thematic tests that support the list of indicators enumerated here. For example, Costantino and colleagues (1991) found that attention deficit disorder children tend to have more omissions of characters, objects, and events on the TEMAS, a chromatic apperception test for children, than their control group, and Johnson (1994) reports that Alzheimer patients tend to have a smaller number of words and to lose the instructional set.

In a comprehensive psychological testing assessment, the clinician looks to corroborate signs of difficulty on one test from signs of similar difficulty on as many other tests as possible. For example, an aggressively suicidal individual may see cutoff heads and wrists on the Rorschach; draw unattached heads and hands on human figure drawings; draw Bender designs very large with hard line pressure; and on Wechsler intelligence subtests have difficulty with the fragmentation of Object Assembly and Block Design (and perhaps also with the bright red color of the block design), with the missing elements of Picture Completion, and respond with suicidal ideation to Vocabulary subtest words and Comprehension subtest questions as if they were stimulus items on a word association or sentence completion personality test.

Similarly, an individual with the neuropsychological syndrome of ADD typically shows difficulty on Wechsler intelligence subtests measuring attention to small details (Picture Completion, Coding or Digit Symbol, Arithmetic, and Digit Span), visual tracking distractibility (Mazes), and part-to-whole integration of visual-motor gestalts (Object Assembly and Block Design). Scores on timed subtests are often lower than those on untimed subtests due to the distractibility and lack of sustained and efficient focusing and attention. The Bender and projective drawings often show a lack of integration of fine details, difficulty with representing geometric shapes and perspective, and maintaining the size and spacing consistency of Bender designs 1, 2, 3, and 5. Left-right orientation difficulty is often seen in shape rotations on the Bender and in wobbly or leaning house, tree, and human figure drawings, which may also lack secure baselines. The difficulty in perceptual synthesis on the Wechsler Object Assembly and Block Design subtests is commonly corroborated by a significant inability to provide well-integrated Whole (W) responses differentiated into an adequate number of small details (Hd, Ad, d) on the Rorschach. Without a comprehensive assessment approach, it would be easy to misdiagnose the relative lack of integrated Whole responses and the sudden break-through of sexual and aggressive associations in the Rorschachs of ADD individu-als—as if these individuals are more emotionally disturbed than they are in reality—rather than seeing them as predominantly suffering from a physical condition chiefly characterized by attentional, impulsive, and perceptual synthesis difficulties.

Just as perceptual form level (F score) is assessed on the Rorschach, the clin-ician can also gain a sense of form level on the T.A.T. by considering the degree to which each story has a well-connected beginning, middle, and end; a narrative con-sistency of one or two central characters; a logical organization of action sequences; language fluency; attention to salient details in the pictures; and appropriate gram-matical usage. In a series of developmental studies of children's narrative compe-tence, Sutton-Smith and colleagues (1981) investigated similar cognitive dimen-sions of story creating adapting scoring schemes from language development, Piaget's (1932) operations of logical thinking, literary criticism, and contemporary structural linguistics, which are most applicable towards a cognitive, neuropsycho-logical assessment of the T.A.T. In an attempt to coordinate psychodynamic and neuropsychological assessment, Rothstein and colleagues (1988) pointed out that the T.A.T. is useful, neuropsychologically, as a way to obtain a sample of sponta-neous language with which the clinician can assess such language dysfunctions as aphasia, dysnomia, aggramatism, and disordered syntax. It is also useful to ask a pa-tient to write out one T.A.T. or C.A.T. card in order to obtain a sample of written language that can be checked for the presence of grammatical, spelling, and other language difficulties (Walter Kass, personal communication).

Identifying Features of Neuropsychological Deficit in the T.A.T. and C.A.T. Responses

In a popular text on neuropsychological diagnosis, Lezak (1983) pointed out that "stories composed by brain injured patients possess the same response quali-ties that characterize organic Rorschach protocols." Following Piotrowski (1937) and Fogel (1967), Lezak lists the following characteristics:

1. Use of fewer words and ideas in relating stories. (Piotrowski [1937] calls this low R [low number of Rorschach responses]for the Rorschach test.)
2. Response times may be longer with several punctuating pauses (Piotrowski's T [response time] on Rorschach test).
3. Concrete description of the picture, rather than a free fantasy elaboration of one's own. Simple listing of items in the picture, such as table, chair, window, violin, and so on. (similar to Color Naming, Cn, on Rorschach.)
4. Tendency to provide a story that is trite with few characters and little action. (Piotrowski [1937] notes less M [less movement responses, M for Human Movement, FM for Animal Movement, and m for movement of inanimate objects].)
5. Presence of confusion, misinterpretations of items in the pictures, and con-fusion in the story theme (similar to Piotrowski's finding a low form [F] level

in the majority of Rorschach responses of those neurologically compromised).

6. Brain-damaged patients tend to give a few of the most common themes (few Popular [P] responses on Rorschach).

7. Perseveration of theme on several T.A.T. cards (Piotrowski's Rpt on Rorschach).

8. Automatic repetition of certain phrases or words (AP on Rorschach).

9. Inability to change an unsatisfactory response (Imp on Rorschach).

10. Expressions of self-doubt (Plx on Rorschach).

11. Inflexibility, concrete responses, catastrophic reactions, and difficulties in dealing with the picture as a whole.

To a lesser extent, individuals with attention deficit disorder or specific language influencing learning disabilities will also tend to show this constellation of characteristics in C.A.T. and T.A.T. stories. The senior author has long noted the failure to recognize the violin in a small subset of individuals on picture 1 of the T.A.T. A study by Chamson (1983) suggested that this is one of the most reliable indicators of ADD in the T.A.T. She compared 49 high school students classified as emotionally impaired. She administered the T.A.T. and visual contrast sensitivity tests. Fifteen percent of the A.D.D. population failed to see the violin, while none of the emotionally disturbed group misperceived it. The visual contrast sensitivity test yielded significant differences at the .01 level. It would also be constructive to compare these disorders with story form items of the Communication Deviance Scheme (see pages 86–87).

To the preceding list, we can also add the following additional characteristics from our own clinical experience:

1. Failing to report an obvious object in a picture that tends to be salient and organizing to most individuals without neuropsychological disorders (such as not mentioning the violin in T.A.T. card 1). This contrasts with the more psychogenic selective inattention, such as a child not mentioning that the dog is "spanking" the puppy on C.A.T. card 10, because of a desire to deny this perception out of one's own psychological conflicts around being punished. The individual with neurological dysfunction misses salient objects due to a deficit in attention and perceptual discrimination capacity. This can be measured specifically on the Bellak Scoring System in terms of noting the number of omissions of central and secondary characters.

2. Tendency to report a stereotyped story one has heard, read in a book, or seen on television, such as trying to turn C.A.T. card 1 into "Goldilocks and the Three Bears" or C.A.T. card 3 into "Old King Cole" or relating a movie plot to T.A.T. cards (similar to exclusive use of Popular [P] responses on Rorschach).

3. Inability to stick with one central character throughout. Individual may shift the story from being about one character, then change it to revolve around someone else. Children with attention deficit disorder tend to shift the C.A.T. story from being about a bear, to being about a lion, and the like, change the sex of the hero (he, she, he, etc.), and frequently change pronouns from he, it, us, you, and so on. This is also found on Rorschach content responses and is similar to the shift-

ing, distracted level of attention of these individuals in academic settings and in social interaction with others. Their minds seem to wander and not to focus and remain sustained.

4. Inability to develop a parallel plot ("Meanwhile, back at the ranch. . . ."). The ability to do this requires keeping one idea in the back of one's mind, while relating another idea, and then coordinating the two ideas together in a logical, integrated manner. A high development of this is seen in Russian novels or in the so-called family sagas of popular American literature.

5. Tendency not to bring the story to an ending, to a logical conclusion. The story, in effect, is left hanging. This is seen in ADD children's tendencies not to finish things they start in school, not to finish homework, and so on, and in the tendency of adults with ADD to frequently change jobs.

6. Breakthrough of primitive sexual and aggressive comments and ideas (similar to direct mention of "blood" to the perception of red color or the naming of shapes as sexual objects on the Rorschach). Without a developed synthetic function of coordinated, integrated perception, and of a level of organized repression, such individuals are very open to the sudden intrusion of very direct sexual and aggressive feelings and associations being immediate expressed. This is considered to be an ego function in psychoanalytic personality theory, which may also be influenced by physiological deficits in the capacity to form perceptions into meaningful gestalts mediated by the visual and brain functions.

7. Frequency of impulsive actions by characters in stories, which could also be described as characters engaged in acting-out behavior, such as spitting, kicking, hitting, biting, urinating, defecating, and so on. This is seen in ADD children's tendencies to be impulsive, to have outbursts, and to lash out suddenly at those bothering them.

8. Characters in the story do not appear to plan, prepare, or anticipate in advance of action. They do not think before acting. There is an absence of asking someone for advice, looking at a map, or reading a book to prepare for a future action. Characters simply act and react.

9. Noticeable lack of a coordinated action sequence. The Fogel and Lezak list speaks of little action. Here, we stress the absence of a chain of first one action, then another related action, then another, and on to a logical conclusion. Preschoolers typically give stories of one or two actions, elementary school children will provide a series of actions, and early adolescents may add a parallel action. Brain-damaged individuals or those with ADD or significant learning disabilities tend to give stories of no action, only a single action mentioned, or at the most, two actions.

10. One character may be described as dependent on another, clinging to another, or calling for help. This is due to need of such individuals for another person as a monitor of their impulsivity and as a guide to do what they feel they cannot do. Psychoanalytic theory calls this a need for an *auxiliary ego*. Separation anxiety may be present for this similar need (for an auxiliary ego) as a "container" of the individual's own impulsivity as well as for basic dependency behavior encouraged by a parent or due to the individual modeling dependency after a parent who is dependent.

11. Characters in stories described as trying to learn, trying to do things, but failing to do so successfully may reflect some aspect of ADD Adults on the T.A.T. card 1 may tell of a story about a boy trying to learn to play a violin, but after trying, he gives up, or fails to learn it. Within the stories, there may be an expression of a character having frequent accidents or falls, which is typical of ADD individuals with hyperactivity and intense impulsivity. Another frequent theme within a story is getting lost and being lost, something they often experience in life when trying to follow directions for driving somewhere. This involves their difficulty in paying attention to the one who gave them directions, paying attention to the road, and spatial difficulties in discriminating left from right, up from down.

12. Relative absence of characters working together in groups in a story. Generally, the action involves one or two. This is like the phases of early childhood play starting with solitary play, going to parallel play or imitating play (one child imitates what another does), going to turn taking (tag), and moving up to Cowboys and Indians, or Space Creatures, or the like. Individuals with serious neurophysiological deficits or disorders have difficulty organizing in groups, as they do planning in advance or even organizing their everyday routines.

13. Sudden outbursts of impulsivity in some individuals may be expressed in their thematic apperception stories as an action occurring quickly without warning. Children use *suddenly* or *all of a sudden* in their stories, while adults may have a character coming up from behind and startling another, as in story 6GF.

14. Individuals with hyperactive impulsivity may symbolize their need for a container of their feelings of sudden outbursts, wild abandon, and restless energy by story themes of a character returning home to his or her "house," returning to "mother," or drawing a "boundary line" or "frontier line" (lines that protect and "bound" one group of people from another). The idea of keeping American Indians on a reservation or poverty-stricken minority people in ghettoes, or nuclear power plants in rural, unpopulated areas simply may symbolize a need to keep wild impulses localized, structured, and safely contained. Keeping the dead in coffins buried in the earth is another symbolization of the need for a container for fears in some individuals' projective stories.

15. Left-right orientation difficulty in some individuals may be expressed by tending to report an object on the right side of a C.A.T. or T.A.T. picture as being on the left side or vice versa.[1]

The first T.A.T. (card 1) from an adult with significant ADD shows some of these above characteristics:

Once upon a time there was a little boy about 8 years old looking at something. Looks like a picture. But while he was looking, he was wondering about the future, more or less contemplating what the future would be like for him. He pictured himself having a family like the one he was in and since he was happy now, he figured he would always be happy. He was waiting to eat dinner one night, that's when he was looking at the picture of himself, his sister, and parents, and his dog. And as he was looking, he was thinking how happy he was and visualizing he would have the same kind of family himself. And as he was drifting off, his

---

[1] The authors are indebted to Dr. Perry Faithorn of New York, NY, for this valuable observation.

mother called him and said dinner was ready, and this sudden burst of reality snapped him out of the thoughts he was having.

Do you want to know my hidden thoughts? It reminds me of myself of when I was younger, dreams I had. But the mother calling is a good thing, snapping me into reality. Just being called for dinner is nothing bad in itself, but just a symbol of accepting reality.

Here, we see the tendency to wander off in thought, to become distracted. His mother snaps him back to reality, but he totally missed the object of the violin, which is generally a most salient, organizing object for most individuals for T.A.T. card 1. His mind drifts from the future to the past to the future, so that he is not grounded in the present reality. Teachers often describe such children as "in outer space," as never paying attention to what the teacher is trying to teach. While the story is long for an adult with ADD, we note that there are only two actions—looking at the picture and then hearing his mother call him to dinner. The action is not well coordinated and the subject fails to provide a logical ending to the story. There are few characters, only the boy and his mother, and the relationship seems to be one of dependency of the boy on the mother. The first action is really a description of the picture, which is repetitiously described for a long time until the second action of the mother calling him is introduced. There is very little action taking place in this T.A.T. story. Psychodynamically, we can speculate that while the mother of this adult may want to snap the individual into accepting reality and dealing better in the real world of everyday life, it is to come to dinner that is demanded, which could also express the mother's underlying desire to keep this adult dependent on her. (This adult, over age 34, lives at home.)

ADD In Children

Hyperactivity, impulsivity, and inattention in children has been widespread and was earlier described as "minimal brain damage" or "minimal brain dysfunction" (MBD). It is now referred to in the current *Diagnostic and Statistical Manual of Mental Disorders* of the American Psychiatry Association as "attention deficit disorder" (ADD), which is either "with hyperactivity" or "without hyperactivity." The typical symptoms are inattention (failing to finish things the person starts to do, seeming not to listen, becoming easily distracted, and not sticking to a play activity); impulsivity (acting before thinking, shifting excessively from one activity to another, not organizing work, needing a lot of supervision or for the teacher to be right next to the child when working, frequently calling out in class, and difficulty awaiting one's turn in games and group situations); and hyperactivity (running about or climbing on things excessively, difficulty sitting still or fidgeting excessively, difficulty staying seated, moving about excessively during sleep, and being always "on the go" as if "driven by a motor").

Boys are 10 times more apt to have this disorder than girls. Psychological testing usually looks for significant difference between nonverbal, perceptual-motor tests and the verbal tests that are typically much higher. The Wechsler Performance Scale IQ is usually 10 or more points lower than the Verbal Scale IQ and the Bender-Gestalt test usually has numerous errors of shape rotation, shape distortion, perseveration, overlaps, figure integration, and size consistency difficulty. These are all signs of both spatial, visual problems, difficulty in integration of visual and motor functioning, inattention, and impulsivity. Spatial integration difficulty can also be seen on the Rorschach in the failure to provide many Whole (W) gestalt responses with good differentiation into many details (Hd, Ad, d). Typically, the responses are not whole-object, but part-object responses. The subject sees the inkblot not as a whole gestalt (W), but as a part (D). Color Naming (Cn) is both a sign of concrete description of the inkblot picture and a sign of impulsivity. Projective drawings also have few details, poor integration of the details into organized wholes, and may also have poor perspective. The C.A.T. and T.A.T. are highly useful in further corroborating the diagnosis of A.D.D. by looking for some of the 26 characteristics listed at the beginning of the chapter.

C.A.T. Protocol Illustrating Attention Deficit Disorder

Lisa, age 6 years 9 months, was referred for testing due to school adjustment difficulties and hyperactivity. She has a poor attention span, is frequently switching her seat in class, and functions below grade level. Among several tests administered, the C.A.T. revealed the following:

C.A.T. Protocol

Card 1: Once upon a time there were three chicks eating porridge. *Anything else?* They were talking about their porridge, too. They said, "My porridge is too, too cold." (I repeat request for a "make pretend" story of her own, not something she heard, saw on TV, or read in a book). I don't have imagination. *Anything happen next in the story you started?* I don't know. Only how it goes in the story.

Comment

We see here lack of self-esteem in the comments, "I don't have imagination" and "I don't know." Tendency to give stereotype story she's heard or seen and tendency to describe in concrete terms only what is seen by her in the picture on the card are evident. Talking about their porridge suggests some ability to go beyond action itself and the idea of the porridge being too cold suggests feelings of being rejected or deprived.

Card 2: I know this one—"Goldilocks and the Three Bears." (I again explained the nature of the test, the direction to provide one's own fantasy from your own mind, your own imagination, a make-pretend story, pretend the picture you see is part of a bigger story you make up yourself, etc.) I can't think of anything. They're trying to, if somebody falls down the hill, the second one gets to win. They fall down and they hurt theirself.

Comment

Again we see the tendency to provide a stereotype tale and perhaps difficulty paying attention to the direction I gave her, as ADD children have difficulty paying attention to teachers in school. Low self-esteem is repeated in her comment "I can't think of anything." But then she manages to elaborate a fantasy of her own, which brings in a theme of trying to do things and failing (also her experience in school) and the theme of accident proneness (falling and getting hurt). There is also the theme of a chain reaction, if one falls down, the second one gets to win (is she the older of two siblings wherein she feels the younger, second born gets to win when she fails?), but at the end, "They fall down the hill and they hurt theirself." Presumably they all end falling down getting hurt. This could also suggest her perception of a divorce, since card 2 is often seen by children of separation and divorce as a struggle, tug-of-war between the two parents in which the child is asked to take sides. If so, does Lisa feel that when one parent left, the other won custody, but they all ended up losing? These are questions that could be explored in psychotherapy or verified from the social history. The C.A.T., like a dream, provides a way for children to express their feelings about their lives and then a way for us to hypothesize about what their feelings and perceptions might be about their lives.

Card 3: I don't know any of these. It's a lion, but I can't even talk about it. But he was make pretending he was Old King Cole . . . *What happens next?* I don't see Old King Cole on TV. I imagine it is on the TV. And he called for his pipe and his bowl to eat and three fiddlers. He has a cane, too There's a mice in the wall. Nothing else in the wall, either. Flowers are on the rug, too *Anything happen there?* I don't know. The mice is traveling around in the wall, putting his head out and back in, out and back in, back out and in again and again.

Comment

She again brings in a stereotyped story and describes the details of the picture before her. When she notices the mouse, she perseverates, the mouse coming out, going in, out, in, over and over, suggesting the perseverative, driven, repetitive actions typical of ADD children in life and seen in their C.A.T. stories. It also suggest an approach/avoidance style with regard to fear of a potentially predatory larger animal that could attack the mouse if he stays out. Anxiety and fear also may stimulate the hyperactive, frenetic activity. Instead of being able to tolerate anxiety, she may engage in sudden, impulsive actions over and over in this driven, compulsive manner.

Card 4: Two babies, one riding a bike and one in the mother's pouch. The mother's hopping with a picnic basket and pocket book and I see trees . . . *Next?* If she looks at her babies, lets go of her picnic basket, lets go of the baby in her pouch, all the food is going to be on the floor and cheese will be rotten. The baby lets go of the balloon and it flies away and the other one rides his bike and crashes into one of the trees there. The mother doesn't want that to happen.

Comment

She moves aways from a beginning concrete description of the picture before her to provide some action and fantasy elaboration on the theme of letting go (separation of the mother from the children) and letting go of impulses (when the children are deprived of mother's holding and nurturance—food that drops and becomes rotten), the child crashes into a tree (aggressive assault on the tree with also potential for serious harm by hitting the tree). The fact that she places this letting go in the hypothetical and adds at the end, "The mother doesn't want that to happen," suggests a desire to monitor impulsivity and develop signal anxiety (the ability to anticipate danger in the future), rather than react to danger with sudden panic, frenetic action, primitive impulsive outbursts, and feelings of being totally helpless, totally overwhelmed.

Card 5: A bed, two beds, floor, a lamp, windows, curtains are there. . . . *Anything happen next?* The rain and the thunder and the lightning broke the window. Nothing else happened. It's making noise in the house by the rain and thunder and everything was wet and the crib was wet, too.

Comment

Beginning with concrete description of the visual scene in the picture on the card, she moves into a theme of being overwhelmed by external danger. The storm outside intrudes and breaks into the house and overwhelms everything. This is a typical theme in C.A.T. stories of ADD children to experience the enviroment as impulsive and as dangerous as they feel their own feelings to be. On the one hand, this is an externalization of their own impulsivity onto the environment (they are not dangerously aggressive, it is the environment of the weather and big animals and adults that are aggressively threatening to them). On the other hand, this may be part of their actual experience. They act impulsively and the parents aggressively act out, which is modeled by the child in the child's hyperactivity. Usually, it is an interaction between the two participants, parent and child, and the two domains of physiologically increased activity level and that of emotional anxiety, lack of signal function, and lack of adequate defenses. The theme of everything wet at night also suggest the possibility of this child having encopresis, which is often seen in ADD children having very poor impulse control.

Card 6: Two mother bears and one momma bear and the other father bear and the baby bear in the cave. They think it's winter. Then the wind blew in the cave and they got chilly . . . *Anything else happen?* They had to sleep cuddling together and all that stuff, 'cause it was cold together and all that stuff like I said before.

Comment

The environment overwhelms again, comes into their home, which is defended against here by dependent clinging. While the previous story shows no defense against being overwhelmed, this story shows a step forward with the defensive coping mechanism of using another person as an auxiliary ego to cling to and to help one with ego control over one's own impulsivity. Separation anxiety is usually intensified in ADD children to some extent by the need for the adult figure as an auxiliary ego to monitor and control their impulsivity. It may also be increased due to the tendency of the parent to be somewhat rejecting of the ADD child.

Card 7: One tiger is chasing the monkey. A monkey got afraid. Then the monkey climbed up a tree. But the tiger catched him and killed him.

Comment

The fear of aggression from the environment continues in which the defensive reaction is the monkey climbing up a tree(the ego defense of avoidance or withdrawal symbolized by actively trying to escape external threat).

Card 8: One Papa monkey, one momma monkey, and one grandma monkey with a baby monkey. And they lived in a house and then they put on the stove with food and they didn't know the stove was burning and they smelled the smoke. They had to hurry out of the house. They had to pull down the alarm; if they don't put on the alarm, the firemen will not know where the house or where the fire is. Always when you have a fire, always put on the alarm.

Comment

This is a marvelous story illustrating the attempt to develop a signal function in a child with a *moderate* level of ADD. The danger is the burning stove. They smell the smoke (a signal of fire). They run out of the house (the ego defense of avoidance/withdrawal expressed again). Then they put on the alarm for the firemen to put out the fire (perhaps symbolizing her dependency upon a parent when she feels impulsively aggressive). The child with *severe* ADD would not be able to create a C.A.T. story such as this with the ego defenses and the symbolization of the need for signal function (the anticipation of danger and the ability to mobilized coping mechanisms to cope with it).

Card 9: A crib, a door, windows. The family is next door to the baby. The next neighbors—that's the father and the mother. Then they had thunder and lighting broke the baby's window. Then the room got all wet on the floor and then the baby fell on the floor and hurt his head.

Comment

She begins with concrete description of the picture and then again brings in the theme of the environment coming into the house and making everything wet, which leads to the baby falling and getting hurt. Encopresis, falling out of bed, and being let go of by the holding mother or father are all suggested in this story. The only defense is the statement that the parents are next door to the baby, so it may be that this is how she feels when separated or threatened with separation from one or both of the parents, She falls apart and is overwhelmed and lets go of her own impulses. This may also be why it is more scary for her at night, when she is sleeping by herself away from proximity to the auxiliary ego parent.

Card 10: Two dogs, one the momma and the papa died and there was a little puppy. Then the puppy, he had to vomit. And he stopped the vomiting; then the momma was standing up. Then the momma flushed the toilet and that's the end of this one.

Comment

Note that she used the word *mother* before in story 4 and now she regresses to the more infantile word *momma* for the parent in the story. Since the picture shows a bathroom scene, it may be that she has anxiety around the bathroom, perhaps related to some enuresis suggested by the previous stories of flooding by water. This

anxiety is responded to, then, by the ego defense of regression, going back to acting like a much younger child as if to say, "I'm just a baby, so how can I help myself?" The desire to externalize bad feelings is suggested by the child vomiting. The
mother flushing the toilet shows the ego defense of undoing, but it is the auxiliary
ego adult that does the undoing not the child figure himself.

Summary of C.A.T.

The C.A.T. suggests Lisa has fears of dangers in the environment, of storms,
of attacking animals, fear of the dark at night, separation fear, anxiety about falling
and getting hurt, fear of fire, and perhaps anxiety over the need for approval (the
bathroom story 10). To cope with these fears and anxieties, she uses defenses of dependent clinging, avoidance/withdrawal, denial ("I don't know" comments), regression to more infantile behavior, repetitive, ritualized action (motor intensity),
and acting out impulses (immediate discharge of anxiety in action that is maladaptive, rather that adaptive). She tends to give concrete descriptions of the picture or
to provide a stereotypic story she has heard or seen, rather than freely elaborate a
fantasy story of her own. The stories are short without much fantasy elaboration,
but she shows an ability to go beyond the visual data before her (which is another
reason she is of moderate ADD, rather than severe). There is a tendency not to finish stories similar to the tendency in schoolwork of ADD children to become distracted, not to stick with things, and not to finish what they started. But a few stories are given endings again suggesting a moderate rather than severe ADD
syndrome.

As with children with severe ADD, many Lisa's C.A.T. stories show smaller figures totally overwhelmed by storms or by larger threatening figures without much
evidence of any attempt to cope with these dangers, without really doing anything
to counteract these dangers. Then there are a few stories in which the smaller figure either tries to run away, climb a tree, or go back in his hole (which are indicators of the ego defense of avoidance/withdrawal) or the smaller figures regress to
infantile, dependent clinging to a more powerful adult figure(defenses of regression and dependent clinging).

The acting out in Lisa's stories rarely seems to be used defensively to counteract threat, but rather seems to be largely an intensification of her hyperactivity.
Similarly, the use of ritualization or preservation is sometimes thought of as an ego
defense, as it is part of undoing (doing and undoing over and over, for example),
but here it again seems to be for the most part an intensification of her driven, compulsive hyperactivity symptom. The final instance of her having moderate, rather
than severe, ADD and of moving in the direction of neurotic (higher ego structure)
are the two stories suggesting the beginning development of signal function. These
are the stories about what could happen if the mother lets go of food and of the
baby in her pouch (4) and the family that puts on the alarm to call the firemen to
put out the fire from the burning stove (8). A hallmark of the borderline child is
the absence of signal function. Anxiety and fear leads them to total panic, fragmentation of the self-structure, and impulsive acting out—often psychotic-like. The
neurotic child, however, can deal with anxiety and danger as a signal to mobilize
ego defenses and coping mechanisms. Lisa not only shows the ability to use ego de-

fenses of denial, avoidance, withdrawal, regression, dependent clinging, persevera-tion/ritualization, and some defensive acting out, she has also symbolized the idea of signal function in two stories, which may also be an example of the observing ego function.

T.A.T. Protocol Illustrating Attention Deficit Disorder

T.A.T. Protocol

Julie Sand, 24 years old, has suffered from a long history of dyslexia (reading problems), dyscalculia (arithmetic problems), and other school problems since her early childhood. Ms. Sand reported that she had a short attention span, was hyper-active, had difficulty sitting still, had physical coordination difficulties, and visual fo-cusing difficulties from her early childhood onwards through high school. This re-sulted in slow learning, feeling that she was "stupid" in some areas and "clumsy," and experiencing extreme headaches. Frequent earaches and inner-ear infections further complicated her social and academic adjustment in her early years. By third grade, the school psychologist felt she might be depressed because of her lack of reading ability, intense headaches, frequent falling, lack of close friends, stubborn behavior, and outbursts of bulliness.

Ritalin was tried for a while between the ages of 9 and 12 years, she remem-bers, which resulted in some improvement in her difficulties. Her early flair for vo-cabulary, for expressing complex issues, and for relating to adults when at her fa-ther's place of business provided a very confusing contrast to her and her parents (and probably also to her teachers) to the learning disabilities syndrome. It was un-clear why such a talented, indeed gifted and precocious, child, could have such ma-jor school learning difficulties. An intelligence test given toward the end of ele-mentary school showed around 139 IQ in the Verbal area, hence her parents were informed that she should be getting straight As. The conclusion tended to be that all her problems were emotional, that she was just lazy, unmotivated, and uninter-ested. Valium was started, which she feels she became addicted to by 14 years old of age. The school and behavior problems persisted, so that she ended up quitting high school.

Ms. Sand continued to do well in sales work, but has had a very erratic work history involving frequent job changes, mood swings from manicky and restless overactivity to withdrawal and depressive states often with suicidal ideation. In the attempt to get some release from these feelings of low self-esteem, labile mood swings, some explosive temper outbursts, restlessness, depression, feelings of scat-teredness or lack of integration, and frequently intense anxiety, Ms. Sand increas-ingly attempted to self-medicate herself with barbituates, diet pills, and marijuana. However, Ms. Sand reports that these drugs have little effect and that she feels that she has a high threshold for being affected by medication or drugs of almost any kind. She feels more prone to feelings of depression at night, becomes extremely agitated and hyperexcited during activities of social interaction, such as car auc-tions, and often experiences her mind racing with numerous fast-moving thought patterns in the evening, all of which she often attempts to "quiet" with drugs, but experiences little relief.

Recently, Ms. Sand has been attending a college, majoring in business administration and political science. Her parents have emphasized the value of gaining a marketable skill, such as computer programming or some other technical skill, and Ms. Sand is not sure she could manage such type of work due to her early history of learning disabilities, her restlessness, and pattern of changing jobs. She also feels that she may be capable of working towards a career that would capitalize more on her high verbal skills, such as in sales, politics, law, creative arts involving writing, advertising, or public relations work.

Ms. Sand has also been feeling very depressed, had suicidal thoughts, and has contacted a psychiatrist wondering if she should go into a hospital or if she should have a neurological work-up to determine if there could be some organic basis for her continued academic and social difficulties and unhappiness. Psychological testing was, therefore, requested in order to assist in the identification of these difficulties and to help Ms. Sand in her vocational decision making at present.

Card 1: Looks like he was practicing and just stopped with something. He laid his violin down and his music and he's looking at it. Looks like he's just trying to figure out how to do that, right? Something's not jogging. He's just staring at the music and trying to figure out how the music goes, so he can play it that way. Looks like he's saying, "This just doesn't sound right. How can this be?" Either that or just doesn't want to practice. You won't be a great violinist. I remember my sister had to practice the piano. She'd just sit there and look at the music. So you got two stories out of that one.

Comment

Here we have the theme of trying to play or learn the violin, not going it successfully, and wanting to withdraw and give up trying. She appears confused about the plot, should it be this or that? She asked the tester for approval at one point. The tendency to wander off with inattention is stated, "He's just staring at the music . . ." Then she swiched central characters to bring in her sister, but realized, "So you got two stories out of that one." This suggests the shifting of attention from one character to another. The story lacks a real ending.

Card 2: Hmmm . . . (long pause). This reminds me of an old farm family. Probably their daughter and she's holding books and seeing that's her way out of the fields. Those are her parents. Her parents are dressed in farm clothes and she is not, maybe she's in college and this is her way out. She looks like it's her reason, her way out. Looks like a far away look in her face, different dimensions than they are and she can feel it and see it. The books are the way out.

Comment

Punctuating pause is seen. She stays close to a concrete description of the picture. She does not go beyond the visual information given by the picture. No action is stated, except holding books and looking with a far away look in her eyes. The latter aspect restates the tendency of the mind to wander off in inattention, without specific focus. No ending is given. A personal dynamic or defensive withdrawal is suggested by the far away look at the theme of finding a "way out" of the farm life of her parents.

Card 3BM: Hmm. (Pause) This looks like she's got an anxiety attack or a depression attack and she's just gone limp. Keys are on the floor. Either they're crying or giving up for the moment. She's tired of it all. Like why ever more move, why pick up the car keys, and start going through everything again. Something activated some kind of emotional trauma and how it would end? I, it would end in many ways. It could pick up with the keys and go on, but if it's serious enough, she could take a bottle of pills and end it. It reminds me of being tired of it all. Either tired or go and get undressed and go back to bed and start all over again.

Comment

Confusion is seen in the plot probably related to depressive feelings she has within her. Depressive anxiety, in other words, intensifies the ADD characteristic of lack of focus, shifting theme, confusion of theme inability to finish plot with an ending. The breakthrough of primitive impulses appears to be just about to occur, in this story perhaps the suicidal impulse of taking pills. Defensive withdrawal and turning aggression against the self are present in this idea of taking pills to end her struggle.

Card 4: This looks like it should be at a 1930 movie. Um, there's a bad tragedy, something's wrong and she's asking him not to go, to stay, and he's going. So she's trying to hold onto him to reason with him. I think it was the type of fury that you see in many men, "Bam Bam!, I'll do it anyway!" (gestures angry movements in the air). It looks like there's anger in his eyes and she just looks like she's pleading with him to reason with him, and he's just about going to turn and go and she's going to end up crying. He goes off and has a big fight.

Comment

Breakthrough of primitive aggressive impulse is clear in this story, perhaps a turning outward of what she turned inward on the last story. The man has fury "Bam Bam!" and she gestures angry movements in the air. The female figure clings to him, bringing out a dependent clinging similar to ADD individuals. The story has a sequence of action and as ending, which suggests a mild-to-moderate rather than a severe level of ADD.

Card 6GF: It's an old Gary Cooper movie. He's come up behind her, startled her, and he may be saying something that got her off guard, maybe he caught her doing something or he's lecturing her and she's saying, "What the hell do you want?" Or she looks like she's a little stunned and taken aback and he looks like he's demonstrative, authoritative, like he thinks he's just giving advice and she should be taking it and looks half out of it and about to say, "You do it that way!"

Comment

The sudden outbreak of impulsivity is stated in the idea of the man startling the woman from behind, a typical theme of this card in ADD individuals. The swearing also suggests impulsivity. Again she "looks half out of it," further stating the wandering mind of inattention. Depressive, dependent withdrawal tendencies is a theme in this story.

Card 7GF: Ah. . . . (pause). The mother is reading a story to her daughter, again from back in the 30s or 40s time, like an old Jewish mother or Italian mother, and the young girl's just going off and she's the character in the story her mother's reading and she's holding a doll and kind of limp. She's listening to her mother, but she's kind of far off and her eyes are just (gestures) kind of going. She has a far away look also on her face. She's not turned towards her mother, listening and her mind is wandering. She's there, her spirit's in the story. Either that or she's thinking I want to go out to play.

Comment

Punctuating pause is seen. The girl listens, but her mind is wandering (a marked symptom of the ADD syndrome). The withdrawal is present in mind wandering, in the idea of wanting to go out to play, and in the reference to long ago in time (the 30s or 40s). References to earlier times are examples of the defense of regression as well, another frequent theme in this woman's TAT stories.

Card 8BM: Oooooh! (She puts the card down near the floor next to her side). It reminds me of what I would think of someone who's returned from war and would have to think back. Paramedics. It's a flashback. Seeing someone lying on a table, and yet all dressed up in suit. It looks like he's not part of the picture, like it's a flashback for him. What gives me that impression is the way the light comes into his head. It makes it seem like he's definitely separate from the scene and the vagueness of the scene makes it again seem like it's a flashback kind of thing.

Comment

Defensive avoidance and withdrawal is evident in putting the card down near her side (nonverbal proximity, distancing, biting, hitting, or other behavior with the TAT cards always need to be noted as they usually corroborate the content analysis of the stories, as is evident with this woman). She withdraws further by regressing in time ("It's a flashback"). Inattention is again restated in her separating the boy from the scene. She mainly describes the picture giving only one action of "doctors cutting him" and not providing an ending.

Card 9GF: This, I don't like this. The one girl is running away from something. Either she had a fight with her boyfriend or somebody assaulted her, something scared her and she's running away from it. I think it's like this other girl looks like she's sitting behind a tree, I don't know if she's trying to hear or not. . . . But she overhears and sees her running and she doesn't do anything to help her. She's hiding behind the tree just watching the other girl run, like she was eavesdropping, maybe not purposely, but was a witness to whatever has upset the other one.

Comment

Punctuating pauses, self-doubt, concrete description of the picture without fantasy elaboration of her own, and shifting aspects of the theme of confusion ("either this or that . . .") are ADD characteristics in this story. A defensive withdrawal of avoidance (hiding behind a tree) is also noted.

Card 10: It shows love, compassion. The other person on the right needs that physical reassurance and the other person seems to be kissing her on the forehead saying it will be all right with compassion. It's sensitive and yet her mother has darkened out, part of her forehead, her facial features are (gestures vagueness). But it looks like she's holding on or learning. That's about it.

Comment

Some dependency is stated, the concrete description of the picture, the few words, and the single action (kissing and reassuring) are notable. Depressive theme of the "mother darkened out" is suggested, as well as the ADD. symptom of part-object or vague visual perception.

Card 12M: . . . (Pause). It reminds me of a priest giving last rites. . . . The priest wouldn't be leaning with a foot on the bed (pause). . . It's really, I don't know. It's a weird picture. It could be an old man looking physically decrepit looking at a physically well boy and looking over him and thinking why isn't he like that. It's hard to tell if he's dead or alive. His legs are crossed, so he's alive, not dead. Either that or the priest. A very old man. It looks like his hand is closed and he's giving last rites or he has closed his eyes.

Comment

Punctuating pauses, the breakthrough of primitive impulses, self-doubt expressions ("I don't know"), confusion of plot ("either that or . . ."), and mind wandering (?) suggested by the eyes closed are further statements of ADD characteristics in this T.A.T. story.

Card 13MF: Hmmm! This could be many things. Either he just strangled her or she's laying there dead *or* they've just made love and she's laying there and he's just gotten up and gotten dressed. But it looks like he's sad, so he may have just done her in and he looks distraught in a way. But I prefer it was that they've just made love, but it looks like it was more violent. Like he's saying, "What have I done?," and turning away from it. The abuse a woman has to go through whether she's alive or dead.

Comment

Breakthrough of primitive aggressive and sexual impulse is very clear on this card with references to strangling, laying dead, making love, something "violent." Guilt and defensive withdrawal are displace onto the man figure, as she displaced the learning disability with the music lesson onto her sister on card 1. Defensive passivity is expressed in regard to the female in this story, who lays there dead and who has to go through abuse "whether she's alive or dead." She manages to go a little beyond the description of the picture, which again shows the mild-to-moderate rather than severe ADD, but she fails to provide a sequence to logical ending for the story.

Summary of T.A.T.

It is clear from the pattern analysis of Ms. Sand's psychological tests that there is a strong neurological underpinning to her academic, social, and emotional problems, which has recently been described as a general learning disability or Attention Deficit Disorder syndrome. This leads her into vulnerability to sensory overload, to desires to withdraw, restlessness, and to job changes. *Diagnostic impression* is, therefore, of ADD with depressive and obsessive features.

CHAPTER 14

THE C.A.T.

Nature and Purpose of the Test

The Children's Apperception Test (C.A.T.)[1] is a projective method or, as we prefer to call it, an apperceptive method of investigating personality by studying the dynamic meaningfulness of individual differences in the perception of standard stimuli (Abrams, 1993a, 1995; Bellak & Siegel, 1989; Boekholt, 1993).

The test is a direct descendant of the T.A.T., although it does not compete with or substitute for it. Unsurpassed as we believe the T.A.T. to be for adult personality investigation, it is nevertheless relatively unsuited for young children to the same degree that the C.A.T. is unsuited for adults. Kitron and Benziman (1990) have suggested that the C.A.T. may, in some circumstances, be utilized as an adjunct to the T.A.T. with adults, since it provides for the exploration of basic family relationships of childhood. Kitron and Benziman suggested that adults may be encouraged to "let go" more with the C.A.T., when they may have remained more contained and constricted in their stories to the T.A.T. Be that as it may, we should like to see the C.A.T. used for children from 3 to 10 years old, Symonds's Picture Story Test used for adolescents, and the T.A.T. used for adolescents and adults.

The C.A.T. was designed to facilitate understanding of a child's relationship to important figures and drives. The pictures (see Figure 14–1) were designed to elicit responses to feeding problems specifically, and to oral problems generally; to investigate problems of sibling rivalry; to illuminate the attitude toward parental figures and the way in which these figures are apperceived; and to learn about the child's relationship to the parents as a couple—technically referred to as the oedi-

---

[1] L. Bellak and S. S. Bellak (1949), C.P.S., Inc., P.O. Box 83, Larchmont, NY 10538. The test is also published in French by the Centre du Psychologie Appliquée, Paris, France; in Italian by the Organizzazione Speciali, Florence, Italy; in German by Verlag fuer Psychologie, Goettingen, Germany; in Spanish by Editorial Paidos, Buenos Aires, Argentina; in Portugese by Editorial Psy, Campinas, Brazil; and in Japanese by Nihon Bunka Kagakusha, Tokyo, Japan. An adaptation for India has been devised by Uma Chowdhury, with the help of B. S. Guha and L. Bellak, published by Manasayan, New Delhi, India. There are Polish, Philippine, Pakistani and Ukrainian versions. In past years, the test was published in Flemish and there was an Indonesian adaptation, as well. In Indonesia they now use the American version since the Indonesian adaptation did not fare as well.

The original C.A.T., consisting of 10 plates depicting animals in various situations, was published in 1949. It was followed in 1952 by the Children's Apperception Test, Supplement (C.A.T.-S), and in 1965 the Children's Apperception Test, Human (C.A.T.-H) was published, consisting of an exact substitution of human figures for the original animal ones. Most of the remarks in this chapter refer to the original C.A.T.—for convenience's sake, sometimes designated as C.A.T. A. For a discussion of the C.A.T.-H and the C.A.T.-S, see Chapters 15 and 17, respectively.

1

2

3

4   5

Figure 14–1   Pictures for Use with the C.A.T.

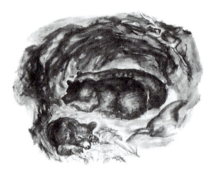

6

7

8

9

10

Figure 14–1   (continued)

pal complex and its culmination in the primal scene (i.e., the child's fantasies about seeing the parents in bed together). Related to this, we wish to elicit the child's fantasies about aggression, intra- and extra-, about acceptance by the adult world, and about his or her fear of being lonely at night with a possible relation to masturbation, toilet behavior, and the parents' handling of and response to it. We wish to learn about the child's structure, defenses, and dynamic ways of reacting to, and handling, his or her problems of growth.

This test, similar to the T.A.T., is primarily concerned with the *content* of productions. An analysis of apperceptive behavior is usually concerned with *what* one sees and thinks in distinction to an examination of expressive behavior, which is concerned with *how* one sees and thinks. We have previously discussed this relationship of adaptive, expressive, and apperceptive aspects of psychological productions in the previous section on the T.A.T., in which we pointed out that the Rorschach is primarily a study of the formal organization of expressive factors. As such, it is better qualified to facilitate diagnosis, if this is taken to mean identifying a given person with a nosological entity as set forth in an official manual on diagnosis. On the other hand, the C.A.T., like the T.A.T., is better able to reveal the dynamics of interpersonal relationships, of drive constellations, and the nature of defenses against them.

Thus, we believe that the C.A.T. may be clinically useful in determining what dynamic factors might be related to a child's behavior in a group, in school, or in kindergarten, or to events at home. The C.A.T. may be profitable in the hands of the psychoanalyst, the psychiatrist, the psychologist, the social worker, and the teacher, as well as the psychologically trained pediatrician. It may be used directly in therapy as a play technique. After the original responses have been given, one may wish to go over them with the child in the form of play and make appropriate interpretations.

Furthermore, the C.A.T. should lend itself particularly well to much-needed longitudinal research studies on child development; if the C.A.T. were administered to children at half-year intervals from the third year on, we might learn a good deal about the developmental fate of a number of psychological problems thus far studied only in psychoanalytic investigations or other crosssectional studies. The latter are, by necessity, reconstructions and inferences that need further confirmation and/or elaboration. In research studies and in clinical use alike, it should be helpful that the C.A.T. is relatively culture-free. Since we deal with animal pictures, the test can be used equally well with white, black, and other groups of children—except, of course, those groups who might be unfamiliar with some of the inanimate objects pictured, such as bicycles and the like.

Lack of familiarity with the animals depicted does not seem to constitute a problem, since the children simply substitute animals with which they are familiar. The test is published in 11 different countries and has become the thematic test of choice with children, particularly with young children. A long history of research studies has demonstrated its value in facilitating personality assessment and in the study of specific research variables, ranging from parental loss (Haworth, 1964) and linguistic articulation difficulties (Kagan & Kaufman, 1954; Porterfield, 1969) to effects of examiner attitudes on the projective test responses of children (Lyles,

1958), the longitudinal comparison of motives and fantasy change in children's fantasy stories (Nolan, 1959; Scheffler, 1975), and punishment and aggression in fantasy responses of boys with antisocial character traits (Schaefer & Norman, 1967).

Reviews of its research and clinical use with preschool and elementary school-aged children suggest that it is an extremely popular and relatively culture-free assessment instrument in the United States (Bellak & Siegel, 1989) and in other countries (Boekholt, 1993).

History of the C.A.T. and the C.A.T.-H.

The original idea of the C.A.T. came about as a result of the discussion between Ernst Kris and the senior author, concerning theoretical problems of projection and the T.A.T. Dr. Kris[2] pointed out that one could expect children to identify themselves much more readily with animals than with persons—a fact therapists have known ever since Freud wrote his story of little Hans in "The Phobia of a Five Year Old." After thinking the whole problem over for nearly a year, the senior author specified a number of situations fundamental to children that might conceivably be expected to expose the dynamic workings of a child's problems. It seemed that the T.A.T., a wonderful instrument for adults, could not entirely fulfill the needs with young children; similarly, Symonds could not recommend his Picture Story Test for use prior to adolescence. Theoretically, there was reason to assume that animals might be preferred identification figures from age 3 years up to possibly age 10, and thus we set out to create, pictorially, situations vital to this age range.

Violet Lamont, a professional illustrator of children's books, agreed to draw the pictures according to our suggestions, adding a few of her own liking. She presented us with 18 pictures, some of somewhat antropomorphized nature, some entirely in animal fashion. These we had photostated, used some sets ourselves, and distributed others to a number of psychologists working with small children. The senior author knew the majority of these psychologists in connection with T.A.T. courses and therefore knew that they had an acquaintance with projective procedures and their use. These colleagues were good enough to use the original picture of the C.A.T. and to send us protocols with additional information about the subjects' backgrounds, and so on, as well as their own impressions of the problems of the test.

On this basis, and on the basis of our own experience with records, we reduced the number of cards from 18 to the 10 most useful ones and developed the data described herein.

During the last 15 years, a number of studies have focused on a comparison of the relative merits of animal versus human figures. Despite the limitations of the studies purporting to show that human figures in the C.A.T. setting may have more

---

[2] We are extremely grateful to Dr. Ernst Kris for having provided the stimulus and inspiration for our own work.

stimulus value than the animal figures, it was decided to develop a human version for use in certain specific situations.[3]

Among the studies reviewed, those of Budoff (1960) and especially of Weisskopf-Joelson and Foster (1962) suggested that some children seem to do better with animal stimuli, and some with human stimuli, and that these preferences may be associated with specific personality variables. For instance, children having difficulty with producing responses seemed to do better with animal figures. Future exploration of relative preferences of some personality types, the relationship of defensive patterns, age, I.Q., and psychopathology is likely to be much more fruitful than the mechanical either/or propositions of many previous studies.

Another important reason for providing a human equivalent to the C.A.T. was found in the clinical fact that sometimes children between ages 7 and 10, especially if their I.Q.s were high, would consider animal stimuli beneath their intellectual dignity. Needless to say, many found them "childish" for purely defensive reasons. Nevertheless, it was felt that a human version would lend itself especially well to an upward extension of the usefulness of the C.A.T. and go further toward closing an age gap between the applicability of the C.A.T. and the T.A.T.

The changing of the animal figures to human figures presented a number of difficult problems. In fact, this process highlighted many of the advantages of the original choice of animals with regard to figures that were rather ambiguous as to age, sex, and many cultural attributes.

Three different artists tried their skill in portraying the regular C.A.T. in human form (C.A.T.-H), following the instruction of the senior author and Sonya Sorel Bellak—recreating the pictures of the C.A.T. as human presented varying degrees of difficulty. (See Figure 15–1, Chapter 15, for the final version of the C.A.T.-H. figures.)

In picture 1, for instance, the adult on the left was clothed in a shapeless garment, which could be a male or female in pajamas and robe. The hairdo and facial expression can, at best, be described as not necessarily of either sex. About as much can be said for the children's figures.

In picture 2, the adult human figure on the right was initially turned more sideways to avoid the problem of breasts, or their lack, as a defining characteristic, but we finally decided to reproduce this figure in the same position as the bear in the original. We experimented with a variety of garments and hairdos before arriving at the present version.

In picture 3, the lion was meant to be a father figure and was always seen that way, so we faced no problem of disguise of the sex of the figure. However, the representation of the mouse in a semblance of the relationship to the lion that was often ascribed to it by children was a difficult matter. There is simply no way in which a child could elicit stories either of outwitting the lion by disappearing into its hole (possibly with the lion bumping his head in pursuit), or of any version of the fable of the mouse helping the lion. However, the child was given a somewhat mischievous facial expression, and a child so inclined might still produce stories of similar

---

[3] The material from the following line through page 278 is reprinted (Bellak & Hurvich, 1966) by permission.

nature, by giving help to a man who needs a cane to walk, or by interpreting the shadow near the left knee as an object suitable for mischief.

Picture 4 presented relatively few problems except for the absence of tails, of course, and the fact that an infant in arms is not quite the same as an infant in the maternal pouch, alas.

Picture 5, with the anthropomorphic situation in the original, presented little difficulty.

Picture 6, however, was a different story. If one is interested in what Murray has called *press claustrum,* there just is no substitute for a cave. To preserve some of the possible stimulus value of the outdoor situation (in primitivity, in romance, in fear of animals, and the wild), the tent-like nature of the structure was emphasized by introducing the new features of trees. Undoubtedly, responses taking off from the story of the three bears will hardly continue to play a role.

Picture 7 was a real challenge. Fears of being devoured needed to be given a stimulus resembling the tiger threat. The grasping, evil-toothed, genii-like figure, supplemented by a steaming kettle (as seen in cartoons about cannibals), was introduced for that purpose. The way the child is depicted might result in chances of escape roughly equivalent to those of the monkey in the original.

Picture 8 presented the by now familiar problem of sexual identity. However, the adult figures were nearly always identified as female with the possible exception of the extreme left figure. Therefore, this one was dressed in slacks, rather than a dress, giving it still some ambiguity, at least in most of U.S. subcultures.

Picture 9, with its anthropomorphic setting and lack of determining characteristics, presented no adaptational problem.

Picture 10, however, was redrawn many times until we finally arrived at a version relatively ill defined with regard to sex and still leaving the most frequent two choices available—being dried and cared for or being spanked. In order to maintain more ambiguity, the child's face is seen in profile rather than full face, as the dog is seen in the original.

There is little doubt that the degree of ambiguity of the sex of the figures in the C.A.T.-H. will vary much more with different cultures and subcultures than the original animal figures. One of the reasons for choosing the animals at the time had been their relative freedom from cultural determinants, at least within the western world. (The furniture in some of the original C.A.T. pictures was redrawn in the Indian, Figure 14–2, and the Indonesian, Figure 14–3, versions.) However, in those instances in which the C.A.T.-H is preferred from the start, the advantages determining the choice will presumably outweigh the disadvantages of less ambiguity.

Theory of the C.A.T.

The theoretical considerations of the C.A.T. and the C.A.T. Supplement (presented later) do not differ basically from the theoretical problems and the frame of reference previously discussed for the T.A.T. However, there is one additional aspect to be considered in the C.A.T. and the C.A.T.-S.: the use of animals as stimuli. As has been noted earlier, on the basis of psychoanalytic experience with children,

1   **2**

3

4   **5**

Figure 14–2   Indian Adaptation of the C.A.T. by Uma Chowdhury,
Assisted by B. S. Guha and L. Bellak

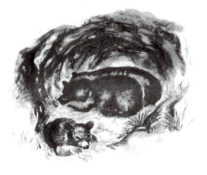

6

7

8

9

10

Figure 14–2   (continued)

1

2

3

4   5

Figure 14–3 Indonesian Adaptation of the C.A.T.

6

7

8

9

10

Figure 14–3   (continued)

it was expected that children would identify more readily with animal than human figures. This assumption was predicated on the fact that emotional relationships to animals are easier for children to handle, and that animals are usually smaller than adult humans and are "underdogs," like children. Animals play a prominent role in children's phobias and as identification figures in children's dreams; on a conscious level, they figure importantly as children's friends. The primitivity of animal drives of oral and anal nature also increase animals' symbolic proximity for children. From the technical standpoint of a projective test, it could also be assumed that the animals would offer some manifest disguise: aggressive and other negative sentiments could more easily be ascribed to a lion than to a human father figure, and the child's own unacceptable wishes could be more easily ascribed to the less transparent identification figure, as compared to human children.

The use of animals as identification figures by psychotics and in primitive cultures also tended to support the expectation of a high stimulus value for children. Furthermore, clinical experience with the Rorschach has empirically established the high animal percent and, even more striking, the relative absence of human figures in the Rorschach records of children, particularly with the younger age groups.

These theoretical expectations have been bolstered by an experiment made by Bills (1950), who tested 48 school children both with T.A.T. cards and with 10 pictures of animals engaged in various activities. Since his experiment was a preliminary investigation, Bills confined himself to comparing, in the two sets of stories, only word count, refusals, description, and coherency. He found that almost all the children told considerably longer stories to the animal pictures and that all the children seemed to find the task easier. Only 1 animal card was rejected, as compared to 18 T.A.T. cards. Two of the children rejected the entire test when first presented with the T.A.T. cards; none of the children rejected the test when the animal cards were presented first.

Vuyk (1954) has also reported work with the C.A.T. indicating that animals as stimuli produced richer stories than were obtained with the use of human figures with children.

There is a good deal of literature in support of the theory that children identify more readily with animals. Goldfarb (1945) expressed marked interest in the animal fantasy of children and found a close connection between the psychodynamics of the individual child and the kind of animal that predominated in the child's fantasy. Blum and Hunt (1952) believed in the superiority of animal over human figures because the latter might be "too close to home," and the use of animal figures overcomes the child's resistance. Bender and Rapaport (1944) supported this concept on the basis of clinical experience. Olney (1935) found that over 75 percent of children's picture books contained animal characters, while Spiegelman and colleagues (1935) reported that animals appear in 50 percent of all Sunday comic strips.

Biersdorf and Marcuse (1953) used six of the C.A.T. cards and had the same artist design six corresponding cards, substituting human figures for the animals. Otherwise, the two sets of cards were similar, though not identical. Some unnecessary differences (e.g., only one figure in the crib in picture 5, the kangaroo being carried in the arms rather than the pouch in card 4, ambiguity removed in card 1 where the figure is obviously female, etc.) make the results quite questionable. In administering the two sets of cards to 30 first-grade children ranging in age from approximately 6 to 8 years, no significant differences in the two sets of stories were found. However, it is extremely likely from empirical evidence with the Rorschach and in psychoanalytic practice that animal stimuli and animal identification figures may be of greater value with the younger children than with children aged 6 to 8 and older.

Furthermore, the usefulness of the C.A.T. does not depend on whether animal pictures produce better or only equally good stories. The C.A.T. and C.A.T.-S. pictures were carefully selected to elicit themes relevant to children's growth and emotional problems. There is considerable evidence thus far that the C.A.T. is clinically useful, and the question of animal versus human stimulus will probably remain a more or less theoretical issue.

Some Differences between C.A.T. and T.A.T. Responses

By virtue of the fact that the subjects of the C.A.T. are children below age 10, certain systematic differences exist between their responses and those of adults to the T.A.T. Specific differences from year to year, both in formal characteristics of language and thought processes, and dynamic differences in terms of psychoanalytic theory, are yet to be investigated.

By and large, stories to the C.A.T. and C.A.T.-S. are shorter and less complex than those of adults to the T.A.T. Very frequently, particularly in 3 and 4 year olds, the responses do not occur in clear-cut themes. Haphazard, sometimes descriptive remarks may be made to one or another of the pictures, and rejections are not infrequent. However, it should be emphasized that the majority of children, even in the younger age group, do tell proper stories, if not to all the pictures, at least to some.

The structure of children's stories is naturally poorer than those of adults. What would be considered a thought disturbance of major proportions in an adult is merely a reflection of appropriate immaturity in a child. If one is inexperienced with children's fantasies, one must be careful not to be misled by seemingly pathological productions. It must be kept in mind that what would have to be considered schizophrenic in an adult simply corresponds to an appropriate developmental expression in a child.

Symbolisms, as Freud (1900) reported, are much more abundant and much freer in children's dreams than in those of normal adults. This, of course, parallels the nature of stories. Simple wish fulfillment is quite frequently manifest.

Instead of revealing the entire character structure, C.A.T. stories may sometimes reflect transitory problems; developmental stages are shown, phases of socialization, of internalization of the superego, may clearly appear. Children often express a moral in their stories, when the internalization of mores and the superego formation become complex enough, beginning at around the age of 6. In essence, this is learning the "other side of the rule" as Susan Isaacs (1933) calls a child's growing awareness of "Do unto others as you would have others do unto you." Observations of the finer features of internalization are consistent with Van Ophuijsen's teaching—that, in essence, obsessive/compulsive neurosis first appears at the age of 7.

The observations of Piaget (1932) concerning the language and thought processes of children are amply illustrated in C.A.T. stories. While concretisms, syncretisms, and animistic notions abound, the most striking aspect is usually the specificity of the children's productions. Characters are usually given proper names, and events are placed in specific locations at precise times. A large field for exploration exists in attempts to codify these maturational aspects to provide normative data for the clinician.

C.A.T. stories of preschool children are also likely to reflect differences in perceptual style among the children that are related to each child's reactions in the test situation. Moriarty and Murphy (1960) have noted that the following devices are used in coping with the demands of the C.A.T. task: reduction in level of participation; resistance to further inquiry; positive efforts at problem solving; restructuring or reversing roles with the examiner; using a familiar story as a prop; being overprecise in small areas of the picture; the use of fantasy or magical processes; using humor; releasing tension through motor expressiveness; appealing for help from the examiner; and using defensive maneuvers such as regression, denial, avoidance, projection, and sublimation.

Administration of the C.A.T.

Administration of the C.A.T. must take into account the general problems of child testing. Good rapport must be established with the child. This will, in general, be considerably more difficult with the younger children as well as with the more disturbed ones. Whenever possible, the C.A.T. should be presented as a game, not as a test. In cases of children who are obviously aware that it is a test—whether from previous experience with such procedures or sophistication—it will be advisable to fully acknowledge this fact, but to explain most carefully that it is not a challenging kind of test in which the child must face approval, disapproval, competition, disciplinary action, and so on. In other words, it is important for the administrator to convey positive attitudes to the child. Not only does this situation aid in the establishment of good rapport but it also has other effects. Lyles (1958) has found that positive attitudes, compared to negative or neutral ones, on the part of the examiner elicit increased productiveness and an increased inclination to adaptation in the child. Negative attitudes lead to an increase in anxiety and aggression.

For the actual instruction, it may be best to tell the child that he or she and the therapist are going to engage in a game in which the child has to tell a story about pictures, and that he or she should tell what is going on, what the animals are doing now. At suitable points, the child may be asked what went on in the story before and what will happen later.

It will probably be found that much encouragement and prompting may be necessary; interruptions are permitted. One must be certain not to be suggestive in one's prompting. After all stories have been related, one may go over each of them, asking for elaboration on specific points such as why somebody was given a certain name, proper names of places, ages, and so on, and even questions regarding the particular type of outcome of a story. If a child's attention span does not permit this procedure, it would be well to attempt it at a date as soon after administration as possible.

Cain (1961) suggested a supplementary "dream technique" for use on cards 5, 6, and 9 especially, where the characters are often seen as being asleep. In these instances, the examiner's final question is: "What did X dream?" Dreams that children report have been found to contain more unconscious material than the original theme, and to be based more on fantasy.

All side remarks and activities should be noted, in relation to the story being told. Blatt and colleagues (1961) advised attending to physical activity, gestures, facial expressions, or posturing accompanying the responses; they viewed this "elaboration of the response" as equivalent to the adult's verbal productions. Bellak and Siegel (1985), Boekholt (1993), and Haworth (1966) reviewed all the relevant literature.

A difficult situation to deal with may arise if the child wants the examiner to tell a story; this is primarily a request to be given something rather than to have to give, and is best dealt with in that light. While it may help to explain that the therapist wants to hear what the particular child can make of the picture, it may be necessary to promise (and to adhere to it) to tell a story later, or to put off testing until one can ingratiate oneself with the child by a giving of one kind or another, then to resume again.

It is helpful to keep all the pictures out of sight except the one being dealt with, since younger children have a tendency to play with all pictures at once, choosing them at random for storytelling. These pictures have been numbered and arranged in a particular sequence for particular reasons and should therefore be administered in the order indicated.

If, however, a child is particularly restless and one has some indication as to what problems his current disturbance may be related to, one may restrict the test to those few cards that are likely to illuminate those specific problems. Thus, a child who apparently has sibling rivalry problems might be given cards 1 and 4 particularly.

Description of and Typical Responses to Pictures

The following are typical themes seen as responses to the various pictures.

Picture 1

Chicks seated around a table on which is a large bowl of food. Off to one side is a large chicken, dimly outlined.

Responses resolve around eating, being or not being sufficiently fed by either parent. Themes of sibling rivalry enter in around who gets more, who is well behaved and not, and so on. Food may be seen as a reward or, inversely, its withholding seen as punishment; general problems of orality are dealt with (i.e., satisfaction or frustration, feeding problems per se).

Picture 2

One bear pulling a rope on one side while another bear and a baby bear pull on the other side.

It is interesting to observe whether the baby here identifies the figure with whom he cooperates (if at all) as the father or the mother. It may be seen as a serious fight with accompanying fear of aggression, fulfillment of the child's own aggression or autonomy. More benignly, this picture may be seen as a game (tug-of-war, for example). Sometimes, the rope itself may be a source of concern (i.e., breakage of the rope as a toy and fear of subsequent punishment) or, again, purely as a symbol concerning masturbation with the rope breaking representing castration fears.

Picture 3

A lion with pipe and cane, sitting in a chair; in the lower right corner a little mouse appears in a hole.

This is usually seen as a father figure equipped with such symbols as pipe and cane. The latter may be seen either as an instrument of aggression or may be used to turn this paternal figure into an old, helpless figure of whom one need not be afraid. This is usually a defensive process. If the lion is seen as a strong paternal figure, it will be important to note whether he is a benign or a dangerous power.

The mouse is seen by many children as the identification figure. In such a case—by tricks and circumstance—the mouse may be turned into the more powerful one. On the other hand, the mouse may be totally in the power of the lion. Some children identify themselves with the lion, and there will be subjects who will switch identification one or more times, giving evidence of confusion about role, conflict between compliance and autonomy, and so on.

Picture 4

A kangaroo with a bonnet on her head, carrying a basket with a milk bottle; in her pouch is a baby kangaroo with a balloon; on a bicycle is a larger kangaroo child.

This usually elicits themes of sibling rivalry, or some concern with the origin of babies. In both cases, the relation to the mother is often an important feature. Sometimes, a child who is an older sibling will identify with the pouch baby, thus indicating a wish to regress in order to be nearer to the mother. On the other hand, a child who is in reality the younger may identify himself with the older one, thus signifying his or her wish for independence and mastery. The basket may give rise to themes of feeding. A theme of flight from danger may also occasionally be introduced.

Picture 5

A darkened room with a large bed in the background; a crib in the foreground in which are two baby bears.

Productions concerning primal scene in all variations are common here; the child is concerned with what goes on between the parents in bed. These stories reflect a good deal of conjecture, observation, confusion, and emotional involvement on the part of the children. The two children in the crib lend themselves to themes of mutual manipulation and exploration between children.

Picture 6

A darkened cave with two dimly outlined bear figures in the background; a baby bear lying in the foreground.

This, again, is a picture eliciting primarily stories concerning primal scene. It is used in addition to picture 5, since practical experience has shown that picture 6 will enlarge frequently and greatly upon whatever was held back in response to the previous picture. Plain jealousy in this triangle situation will at times be reflected. Problems of masturbation at bedtime may appear in response to either picture 5 or 6.

Picture 7

A tiger with bared fangs and claws leaping at a monkey which is also leaping through the air.

Fears of aggression and manners of dealing with them are here exposed. The degree of anxiety in the child often becomes apparent. It may be so great as to lead to rejection of the picture, or the defenses may be good enough (or unrealistic enough) to turn it into an innocuous story. The monkey may even outsmart the tiger. The tails of the animals lend themselves easily to the projection of fears or wishes of castration.

Picture 8

Two adult monkeys sitting on a sofa drinking from tea cups. One adult monkey in foreground sitting on a hassock talking to a baby monkey.

Here, one often sees the role in which the child places himself or herself within the family constellation. The child's interpretation of the dominant (foreground) monkey as either a father or mother figure becomes significant in relation to his or her perception of it as a benign monkey or as an admonishing, inhibiting one. The tea cups will, on occasion, give rise to themes of orality again.

Picture 9

A darkened room seen through an open door from a lighted room. In the darkened room there is a child's bed in which a rabbit sits up looking through the door.

Themes of fear of darkness, of being left alone, desertion by parents, significant curiosity as to what goes on in the next room, are all common responses to this picture.

Picture 10

A baby dog lying across the knees of an adult dog; both figures with a minimum of expression in their features. The figures are set in the foreground of a bathroom.

This leads to stories of "crime and punishment," revealing something about the child's moral conceptions. There are frequent stories about toilet training as well as masturbation. Regressive trends will be more clearly revealed in this picture than in some others.

Haworth (1966) noted that a blank card, an all black card, or a half-black and half-white card can be added. Her use of the half-and-half card has shown that it uncovers strong racial feelings in black children.

Influence of the Perceptual Aspects of the Stimulus on Responses

In the interpretation of thematic materials of children, it is important to remain aware of the perceptual inaccuracies that may exist for certain age groups and that may therefore affect the responses given. Boulanger-Balleyguier (1957) has found shifts in common reactions to some of the C.A.T. stimuli in a group of children 3 to 7 years old. Some of her findings follow:

Card 3: The pipe is not recognized well enough by children below 6 years to be mentioned. Only after age 6 do themes of conflict between the lion and mouse appear frequently. The perceptual accuracy of young children with respect to small details is questioned. This card does not yield data about father/child relationships until both figures are perceived.

Card 4: Children under age 6 do not recognize the animals as kangaroos, are not aware of the pouch, and often omit the baby figure. The card is not indicated for the study of sibling rivalry or birth themes.

Card 7: The common response is concerned with conflict. Nonperception of conflict on this card is significant for interpretive purposes.

Considering the high frequency of certain omissions for many of the stimuli and the regular decrease of such omissions with age, it is suggested that young children do not actually perceive these figures. Those omitted most often are either blurred or vague (hen on card 1, bear on card 6) or very small (mouse on card 3, baby on card 4). Where the incidence of omissions is different for boys and girls, or where the decline is not regular with age, the emotional significance of the omission is greater.

CHAPTER 15

THE C.A.T.-H.

Development of the C.A.T.-H.

After the creation of the C.A.T., many studies were reported that showed that some children responded better to animal stimuli and others to human figures. Bellak and Bellak (1965), partly in response to this new evidence, therefore developed a human modification of the C.A.T. (C.A.T.-H.). It was also believed that the human form would be more adequate to the intellectual development of some children between the ages of 10 and 12, especially those with high I.Q.'s.

Review of Studies Comparing Animal versus Human Pictures

The following studies are representative of the kinds that were conducted in the intervening period between the development of the C.A.T. and the creation of the C.A.T.-H. with the purpose of comparing responses obtained with different samples of children on animal and human forms of the C.A.T.

Budoff (1960) tested 4-year-old preschoolers with C.A.T. cards and an analogous human set. There were no statistically significant differences between picture sets on measures of productivity, story level, and transcendence index, although the general trend indicated higher scores for the human figures on story level and transcendence index. It was hypothesized that, where responses to human figures seemed especially threatening, animal figures elicited more productive stories possibly due to the increase of psychological distance.

Biersdorf and Marcuse (1953) tested first-grade children with animals and human pictures. No significant differences were obtained on the following measures: number of words, ideas, characters mentioned, characters introduced, and response-time indices.

Armstrong (1954) compared the responses of first-, second-, and third-grade children on five C.A.T. cards and a duplicate set with human figures. The mean I.Q. for each grade of children was in the superior range. Significantly higher transcendence index scores were found for the human figures, in that more subjective, personalized, and interpretive responses were obtained instead of mere description.

Boyd and Mandler (1955) studied third-grade children's reactions to human and animal stories and pictures. It was found that animal stimuli led to a greater degree of expression of ego involvement, particularly as manifested in the projection of negative affects. On the other hand, it was reported that the more significant effect of human stories on the production of imaginative material did not corroborate the hypothesis of children's primary identification with animals.

A study using animal and human figures with children aged 5½ to 7 years was conducted by Weisskopf-Joelson and Foster (1953). It was found that the mean transcendence index scores for all stories to human pictures compared with all stories to animal pictures did not differ significantly. A more detailed analysis of the results indicated, though, that the group of children with the lowest transcendence index scores were more productive when responding to animal pictures, suggesting to the authors that low scores are able to reveal themselves more easily when they believe that they are telling about animals rather than humans. It was inferred that personality differences among children are associated with greater productivity to either animal or human pictures, depending on the specific personality involved.

Bellak and Hurvich (1966) have considered the evidence obtained from several reports in the literature (see Table 15–1) concerning the superiority of either the animal or the human pictures, and have noted that the two most influential factors responsible for the conflicting evidence have been variations among the studies in stimulus cards used and in outcome measures employed. The sets of human drawings used have generally not been characterized by the ambiguity of age or sex that is achieved with the animal figures. As far as outcome measures are concerned, dynamic evaluation of the responses has been infrequent. However, Silva (1982, 1985) has done normative and sex-related differences in his work in Portugal.

Modification of the Pictures for Use in the C.A.T.-H.

The major difficulty in the creation of the human drawings for inclusion in the C.A.T.-H. derived from the effort to achieve at least some ambiguity with regard to some of the figures in terms of age, sex, and cultural attributes. Although the C.A.T.-H. figures are not as free from cultural determinants as are the original animal figures, the C.A.T.-H. has and will serve as a highly useful instrument for those purposes for which it was developed. The set of 10 pictures that were finally selected is shown in Figure 15–1.

Studies with the C.A.T.-H.

Haworth (1966) tested a clinic sample of children whose diagnoses ranged from neurotic difficulties to borderline psychoses with the C.A.T. and an experimental set of C.A.T.-H. provided by the senior author. All stories were scored for specific defense mechanisms, as assessed by Haworth's "A Schedule of Adaptive Mechanisms in C.A.T. Responses" (Figure 15–2) and for story content, assessed with the Haworth C.A.T. Story Dynamics for (Table 15–2). No significant differences were obtained between the animal and human forms on the total number of categories receiving critically high scores. However, a difference was found, for this group of children, between the two sets of stimuli concerning the elicitation of certain defense mechanisms. The largest difference in critical score incidence was in the projection/introjection category, with the greater number of such scores on the animal form. Children were most consistent between forms in the Identification category. The story content analysis enabled a card by card comparison of the two

TABLE 15–1 Studies of Animal vs. Human Figures*

Stimuli	Subjects	Response Measures	Results	Ref.
10 T.A.T. cards vs. 10 chromatic pics of rabbits in various activities	48 M and F, 5 to 10, normal school children	Story length, card rejections	Animals—significantly longer stories, fewer card rejections	49
Same as Bills (1950)	8 M and F, 3rd grade, normal school children	Comparison on 26 of Murray's manifest needs	Animals, seen as easier for children; correlation from a 0.09 to +0.58 (3 stat. sig.)	50
6 C.A.T. cards (1, 2, 4, 5, 8, and 10) vs. comparable human set	30 M and F, 1st grade, normal school children	Number of words, ideas, characters mentioned, characters introduced response-time indices	No significant differences	48
Same as Biersdorf and Marcuse (1953)	28 M and F, 5.4 to 8.5 emotionally disturbed	Similar to Biersdorf and Marcuse (1953) plus ratings of clinical usefulness	No significant differences; human judged more clinically useful	174
5 C.A.T. cards (1, 2, 4, 8, 10) vs. a comparable human set	60 M and F, 1st-3rd grade, superior, normal school children	Story length, number of nouns, verbs, ego words, transcendence scores, and reaction time	Human significantly higher transcendence index; other measures no difference	6
C.A.T. vs. T.A.T.	75 M and F, 9-10.6, normal school children	Amount and kinds of feelings, themes, conflicts, and definite outcomes	Human—all response criteria significantly higher except number of words	169
2 stories (with animal or human characters), each followed by 2 pics of animals or humans in ambiguous action	96 M and F mean age 8.5, mean I.Q. 101, normal school children	Story length, presence of original ideas, value judgments, punishment, reward, new themes, pronoun I, and formal features	Human for stimulus stories; animal for stimulus pics	56
Same as Biersdorf and Marcuse (1953)	72 Japanese, M and F, 6 to 12, normal school children	Definite outcomes, expression of feelings	Human—more definite outcomes and more expression of feelings and significant conflicts	103

(continued)

TABLE 15–1   (continued)

Stimuli	Subjects	Response Measures	Results	Ref.
C.A.T. vs. 28 German, Story length comparable human set	Human—8-9, 2nd grade normal	Story length, speed of verbalization, number of themes, reaction time	Human—superior on all the response measures	247
9 C.A.T. cards (6 omitted) vs. comparable human set	18 M and F, age 4, all I.Q.'s above 120, normal nursery school children	Productivity, story level, and transcendence index	No statistical difference; trend in favor of human	61
4. C.A.T. cards (3, 4, 9, 10) vs. comparable human set, color and black and white	40 M and F, 5.5 to 9, normal kindergarten	Transcendence index	No difference except by personality	277

See additional references.
*Reprinted from Bellak and Hurvich (1966) by permission.

versions. There was high agreement in the themes elicited by the two forms, although a greater degree of negative effect was expressed in responses to certain cards for the animal form.

Card 1. Oral gratification is the main theme for both animal and human forms. For those subjects not using this response on both forms, the trend favors the animal form, while more oral deprivation is used on the human form. The adult is most often seen as the mother on both forms, with only a few responses of "shadow" or figure other than father (who is seen one-third as often as mother). Few punishment themes are reported on either form.

Card 2. Predominantly seen as a game, rather than a fight, on both forms, with the pair most frequently seen as the winner, especially on the human card. The child is more often seen with either mother or father on the animal version and almost exclusively with a peer on the human form.

Card 3. No outstanding use of either the adult attacking the child or the child helping the adult on either form. The large figure is seen as powerful (or as king) only on the animal form, and is more often seen as old or tired on the human form. The child figure teases the adult only on the animal form.

Card 4. Most frequently seen as going to a picnic or to the store on both forms, and with very few disasters happening in either version. Only a few instances on either card of the child running over the adult's heel with his bike.

Card 5. Children are seen as playing, sleeping (most often), or being naughty equally on both cards; parents are mentioned equally on both forms.

Card 6. There is no difference between cards in terms of the child running away, fearing attack, or an attack taking place; none of these themes were used frequently.

Card 7. The smaller figure is frequently seen as being attacked on both versions, but with somewhat greater incidence on the animal form. The child escapes equally often on both cards and only infrequently turns to retaliate against the larger figure.

1

2

3

4   **5**

Figure 15–1   Pictures for Use with the C.A.T.-H.

6

7

8

9

10

Figure 15–1   (continued)

Name_____ Bd:_____ Date:_____ Age:_____

Critical Scores: _____

TOTALS   DEFENSE MECHANISMS

A. *Reaction-formation* (only one check per story)

‾‾‾‾‾   _____ 1. Exaggerated goodness or cleanliness
(A +   _____ 2. Oppositional attitudes, rebellion, stubbornness
B = 5)   _____ 3. Story tone opposed to picture content

B. *Undoing and Ambivalence* (only one check per story)

_____ 1. Undoing
_____ 2. Gives alternatives; balanced phrases (asleep–awake; hot–cold, etc.)
_____ 3. Indecision by *S* or story character
_____ 4. Restates (e.g., "that_____, no this_____;" "he was going to, but_____")

C. *Isolation*

‾‾‾‾‾   _____ 1. Detached attitude ("it couldn't happen," "it's a cartoon")
(6)   _____ 2. Literal ("it doesn't show, so I can't tell.")
_____ 3. Comments on story or picture ("That is hard"; "I told a good one.")
_____ 4. Laughs at card, exclamations
_____ 5. Use of fairy-tale, comic-book, or "olden times" themes or characters
_____ 6. Describes in detail, logical; "the end"; gives title to story
_____ 7. Specific details, names or quotes ("four hours"; she said, "   ")
_____ 8. Character gets lost
_____ 9. Character runs away due to anger
_____ 10. *S* aligns with parent against "naughty" child character; disapproves child's actions

D. *Repression and Denial*

‾‾‾‾‾   _____ 1. Child character waits, controls self, conforms, is good, learned lesson
(5)   _____ 2. Accepts fate, didn't want it anyway
_____ 3. Prolonged or remote punishments
_____ 4. ("It was just a dream")
_____ 5. Forgets, or loses something
_____ 6. Omits figures or objects from story (on #10 must omit mention of toilet *and* tub or washing)
_____ 7. Omits usual story content
_____ 8. No fantasy or story (describes card blandly)
_____ 9. Refuses card

E. *Deception*

‾‾‾‾‾   _____ 1. Child superior to adult, laughs at adult, is smarter, tricks adult, sneaks, pretends, hides
(3)*   from, steals from, peeks at or spies on adult (only one check per story)
_____ 2. Adult tricks child, is not what appears to be (only one check per story)

F. *Symbolization*

‾‾‾‾‾   _____ 1. Children play in bed
(4)   _____ 2. See parents in bed (#5)
_____ 3. Open window (#5, #9); Dig, or fall in, a hole
_____ 4. Babies born
_____ 5. Rope breaks (#2); chair or cane breaks (#3); balloon breaks (#4); tail pulled or bitten (#4, 7); crib broken (#9)
_____ 6. Rain, river, water, storms, cold
_____ 7. Fire, explosions, destruction
_____ 8. Sticks, knives, guns
_____ 9. Cuts, stings, injuries, actual killings (other than by eating)
_____ 10. Oral deprivation

G. *Projection and Introjection*

‾‾‾‾‾   _____ 1. Attacker is attacked, "eat and be eaten"
(4)   _____ 2. Innocent one is eaten or attacked
_____ 3. Child is active aggressor (bites, hits, throws; do not include verbal or teasing attacks)
_____ 4. Characters blame others
_____ 5. Others have secrets or make fun of somebody
_____ 6. *S* adds details, objects, characters, or oral themes
_____ 7. Magic or magical powers

(* or 2, if both are E-2 responses)

Figure 15–2   A Schedule of Adaptive Mechanisms in C.A.T. Responses, by Mary R. Haworth. Copyright C.P.S. Inc., Box 83, Larchmont, New York 10538.

PHOBIC, IMMATURE, OR DISORGANIZED

H. *Fear and Anxiety*

_____ (3) _____
 1. Child hides from danger, runs away due to fear
 2. Fears outside forces (wind, ghosts, hunters, wild animals, monsters)
 3. Dreams of danger
 4. Parent dead, goes away, or doesn't want child
 5. Slips of tongue by *S*

I. *Regression*

_____ (2) _____
 1. Much affect in telling story
 2. Personal references
 3. Food spilled
 4. Bed or pants wet, water splashed
 5. Dirty, messing, smelly; person or object falls in toilet
 6. Ghosts, witches, haunted house

J. *Controls weak or absent*

_____ (1) _____
 1. Bones, blood
 2. Poison
 3. Clang or nonsense words
 4. Perseveration of unusual content from a previous story
 5. Tangential thinking, loose associations
 6. Bizarre content

IDENTIFICATION

K. *Adequate, same-sex*

_____
(L = or > K) _____
 1. *S* identifies with same-sex parent or child character
 2. Child jealous of, scolded or punished by, same-sex parent
 3. Child loves, or is helped by, parent of opposite sex

L. *Confused, or opposite-sex*

_____ _____
 1. *S* identifies with opposite-sex parent or child character
 2. Child fears, or is scolded or punished by, opposite-sex parent
 3. Misrecognition by *S* of sex or species
 4. Slips of tongue with respect to sex of figures

   This checklist has been designed primarily as an aid in the qualitative evaluation of children's CAT stories; it can also be used to furnish a rough quantitative measure for making comparisons between subjects and groups. The Schedule provides a quick summary of the number and kinds of defenses employed as well as the content of items used most frequently. The categories are arranged as nearly as possible on a continuum from indicators of high control and constriction to suggestions of disorganization and loosening of ties to reality.

   Directions for Scoring: In the blank preceding each item, indicate with a check mark (or the card number, for future reference) any occurrence of such a response. A story may be "scored" in several categories and, except where indicated, a story may receive checks on more than one item under any one category.

   After all stories have been scored, record the total number of checks for each category in the blank provided. The number in parentheses under each of these blanks indicates the *minimum* number of checks regarded as a "critical score" for that category.

   For the Identification measure, the equivalent of a critical score is secured by comparing the relative number of checks for categories *K* and *L*. If the sum of checks for *L* is equal to or exceeds the sum for *K*, identification is considered to be "confused" and contributes one unit to the total of critical scores.

   The final quantitative measure consists of the number of categories receiving critical scores (and *not* the total number of checks for all categories).

   On the basis of research findings,* five or more critical scores would indicate enough disturbance to warrant clinical intervention.

---

*Mary R. Haworth, Ph.D., A Schedule for the Analysis of CAT Responses, *Journal of Projective Techniques & Personality Assessment*, Vol. 27, 1963, No. 2, 181–184.

Figure 15–2   (continued)

TABLE 15–2 C.A.T. Story Dynamics

Name: Sex: Form: A or H

1. Oral gratification _____   Deprivation _____
   Adult is Father, _____, Mother _____, Shadow _____, Other _____ *M & F _____
   Punishment theme _____

2. Game _____   Fight _____
   Winner: Pair _____   Single _____
   Child with: Parent of same sex _____ of opposite sex _____ Peer _____

3. Adult attacks or scolds child _____   Child helps adult _____
   Adult is king _____ old, tired, lonely, etc. _____
   Child teases or attacks adult _____

4. Picnic _____   Disaster, fire, etc. _____
   Bike runs over tail or leg _____

5. Parents in bed _____
   Children play in bed _____ Naughty _____ Sleep _____

6. Child runs away _____   *Camp (Hibernate) _____
   Attack from outside: feared _____   takes place _____

7. Child is: attacked _____ gets away _____ turns on large fig. _____ *Friends _____

8. Scolding, punishing _____   Child is helpful _____
   Mention of picture _____   Secret _____
   Male adult _____

9. Attack from outside: feared _____   takes place _____
   **Everyday event _____   Loneliness _____ *Naughty _____
   Parents in another rm. _____   *Sleep _____ *Sick _____

10. Naughtiness relates to toilet _____   Other _____
    Punisher is same sex _____   opposite sex _____
    Continues naughtiness _____   learned lesson _____

Cards rejected:
Unusual stories:

Reprinted from Bellak and Bellak (1965) by permission.

*Haworth included 48 items on her original story dynamics form. Lawton added 6 items when she employed the list. Additions of Lawton are identified by an asterisk.

**This item was deleted by Lawton in her study.

Card 8. Scoldings occur with equal frequency with both cards, and the child is rarely seen as being helpful. The picture on the wall is mentioned more frequently on the human form, and secrets are reported more often on the animal card. Male figures were seen only on the animal form and were mentioned in 10 of the 22 stories.

Card 9. Attacks are only infrequently reported as being feared or as taking place on either card. Rather, a preponderance of everyday events are mentioned (especially to the human form), and the parents are occasionally reported as being in the next room. Themes of loneliness occurred more often on the human form.

Card 10. Toilet naughtiness was reported with fair frequency on both forms, but with somewhat more on the human. Punishing parents are seen about equally as being of the same or the opposite sex, but with a trend for more same-sex parents on the animal form and more opposite-sex parents on the human form. In only a very few cases does the child "learn a lesson," and this tends to happen more often on the human form.[1]

Lawton (1966) conducted a study similar to Haworth's (1964). She tested school children with the C.A.T. and the same experimental set of the C.A.T.-H. used by Haworth (1964) and scored each form for the presence of 10 defense mechanisms. Analysis of the data showed no significant agreement between the two forms in eliciting or not eliciting the 4 defense mechanisms: reaction formation, isolation, symbolization, and identification. The one major exception was the result for projection, which showed significant agreement between forms. Lawton also compared the protocols for both forms with the expected themes and found considerable agreement between forms with a few exceptions, the principal one being the finding of more negative reactions on the animal form. Most of these thematic differences were deemed capable of resolution by slight modifications in the pictures, and not indicative of a theoretical difference between the forms.

Porterfield (1969) administered the C.A.T.-H. and the Bender Gestalt test to a group of African American preschool stutterers and to similar age and ability groups of nonstuttering classmates (adaptive group) and nonstutterers characterized by behavior problems (maladaptive group). C.A.T.-H. protocols were evaluated with Haworth's "A Schedule of Adaptive Mechanisms in C.A.T. Responses," and it was found that the categories of repression/denial, symbolization, and projection/introjection differentiated stutterers from nonstutterers. Significant differences were obtained between stutterer and adaptive nonstutterer groups on the three dimensions, with the stutterer group attaining higher scores on repression/denial and symbolization. Whereas no significant differences were found between stutterer and maladaptive nonstutterer groups on the C.A.T.-H. dimensions, differences were obtained between these groups on Bender Gestalt scores, the latter group performing on a lower level. These last findings were indicative both of the lesser relevance of the C.A.T.-H. to overt behavior, and of the relation of adaptive mechanisms to convert behavior.

In their study of second-grade girls, Neuringer and Livesay (1970) suggested that the C.A.T. and C.A.T.-H. are equivalent forms. Myler and colleagues (1972) agreed, and found in addition that the C.A.T. and C.A.T.-H. were more useful for second-grade girls than the T.A.T.

---

[1] Reprinted from Bellak and Bellak (1965) by permission.

CHAPTER 16

INTERPRETATION OF THE C.A.T.

When one approaches the interpretation of an apperceptive method such as the C.A.T., it is best to keep some basic principles firmly in mind. The subject is asked to apperceive—that is, to meaningfully interpret—a situation. The subject's interpretation of the stimulus in following our instruction to tell a story exceeds the minimal "objective" stimulus value. The subject does so, by necessity, in his or her own way, which must be a function of continually present psychological forces which, at that moment, manifest themselves in relation to the given stimulus material.

If one accepts a motivational continuity of the personality structure, one may use the following analogy for a testing procedure as well as psychotherapeutic free association. If a river is sampled at various relatively close intervals, the chemical analyses of the content will be highly similar. Any pailful will be representative of the total content. This procedure is commonly followed in public health assays.

Now, if a new tributary joins (as compared to a new situational factor in psychological sampling), it may, of course, add factors about which the assayer has to know in order to account for changes in content. A primary genetic theory of personality, like psychoanalysis, maintains that the main contents of the stream will remain the primary matrix, which, after a certain point, can only be modified by tributaries to a greater or lesser degree.

To leave the dangers of further analogies, we believe (and by now, ample experimental literature supports this belief) that interpretations of stimuli in our test material give us a valid sample of the subject's psychic continuum known as personality. Still in its formative stage, it is, of course, more changeable in childhood. We can learn about the motivational forces from the fact that any individual response is meaningful for that person; we can furthermore increase our insight by comparing one individual's responses to those of others. To that extent, we are really studying individual differences and making inferences about a given subject by this comparison.

To facilitate the interpretation analysis of the C.A.T., we are suggesting the study of the 10 variables as they are shown on the Bellak T.A.T. Short Form and C.A.T. Blank.

Ten Variables

1. The Main Theme

We are interested in what a child makes of our pictures and then we want to know *why* he or she responds with this particular story (or interpretation). Rather than judge by one story, we will be on safer ground if we can find a common denominator or trend in a number of stories. For example, if the main hero of several stories is hungry and resorts to stealing in order to satisfy himself or herself, it is not unreasonable to conclude that this child is preoccupied with thoughts of not getting enough—food literally, or gratification generally—and, in the child's fantasy, wishes to take it away from others. Interpretation, then, is concerned with the finding of common denominators in behavioral patterns. In this sense, we can speak of the theme of a story or of several stories. A theme may, of course, be more or less complex. We find that particularly in our younger subjects of age 3 or 4 it is usually very simple. In the case of S.Q. (p. 348), one may simply say that the theme in the lion story is "I do not want any clothes, and wish to be dirty and behave like a small child, because then apparently one gets more affection." On the other hand, themes may be more complex, as in subject M. I.'s (p. 351) "I'm powerful and dangerous but in order to be liked and to live in peace with myself, I must give up my aggressive and acquisitive wishes." The theme in such a case is simply a restatement of the moral of the story. A story may have more than one theme, however, and themes may sometimes be complexly interrelated.

2. The Main Hero

A basic assumption behind our reasoning thus far has been, of course, that the story our subject tells is, in essence, about himself or herself. Since there can be a number of people in a story, it becomes necessary to state that we speak of the figure with which our subject mainly identifies himself or herself as the hero. We will have to specify, for this purpose, some objective criteria for differentiating the hero from other figures—namely, that the hero is the figure about whom the story is woven primarily, that he or she resembles the subject most in age and sex, and that the story events are seen from the standpoint of the hero. While these statements hold true most of the time, they do not always do so. There may be more than one hero and our subject may identify with both, or first with one and then with another. There may be a deviation in that a subject may identify with a hero of a different sex; it is important to note such identifications. Sometimes, an identification figure secondary in importance in a story may represent more deeply repressed unconscious attitudes of the subject. Probably the interests, wishes, deficiencies, gifts, and abilities with which the hero is invested are those that the subject possesses, wants to possess, or fears he or she might have. It will be important to observe the adequacy of the hero—that is, the child's ability to deal with whatever circumstances may exist in a way considered adequate by the society to which he or she belongs. The adequacy of the hero serves as the best single measure of the ego strength—of the subject's own adequacy. An exception is, of course, the case of the story that is a blatant compensatory wish fulfillment. Careful scrutiny will usually reveal the real inadequacy. See, for example, story 3 of subject M. I. (p. 351) in which the hero is a mighty lion, who, however, does not like his body and in the end can be happy only by giving up his omnipotence.

Self-Image.   By self-image, we mean the conception the subject has of his or her body and of his or her entire self and social role. Schilder first described body image as the picture of one's own body in one's mind. In Case 3, M. I., for example (p. 351), tells us about his own body image in unusually overt terms when he says, "he didn't have a beautiful body," and then proceeds to tell us how he would like his body to be, what fantasy self-image he would like to have—namely, that of a big, powerful, all-possessing person.

3. Main Needs and Drives of the Hero

The story behavior of the hero may have one of a variety of relationships to the storyteller. The needs expressed may correspond directly to the needs of the patient. These needs may be, at least in part, expressed behaviorally in real life, or they may be the direct opposite of real-life expression and constitute the fantasy complement. In other words, very aggressive stories may be told sometimes by a very aggressive child, or by a rather meek, passive/aggressive one who has fantasies of aggression. At least to a certain extent, the needs of the hero may not reflect so much the needs of the storyteller as they do the drive quality that he or she perceives in other figures. In other words, the child may be describing the aggression feared from various objects or referring to idealized expectations, such as brilliance and fortitude, ascribed to significant figures in his or her life and only in part internalized in self. In short, the behavioral needs of the hero expressed in the story have to be examined and understood in the light of all the varieties and vicissitudes of drive modification and subsumed under the broader concepts of projection or apperceptive distortion.

It is the difficult task of the interpreter to determine to what extent the manifest needs of the hero correspond to various constituents of the storyteller's personality, and in addition what the relationship of these constituents is to the narrator's manifest behavior. It is here that comparison with the actual clinical history is most useful and entirely appropriate under clinical circumstances (as distinct from a research setting). If a child is reported to be particularly shy, passive, and withdrawn, and his C.A.T. stories overflow with aggression, the compensatory nature of the fantasy material is obvious. On the other hand, it must remain a goal of psychological science to develop more and more criteria for increasingly valid predictions—by relating the fantasy material to actual behavior and to discernible behavior patterns. The study of ego functions is particularly useful in this respect (Bellak et al., 1970, 1973). The relationship of drives expressed within the story, together with their vicissitudes, may often serve as one clue; that is, if the story sequence shows an initial aggressive response with this aggression becoming controlled by the end of the story, chances are that this is a person who does not translate fantasy or latent need into reality. This assumption may then be checked against available behavioral data. There are other criteria helpful in attempting predictions about what might be called "acting out." The high degree of detail and realism in the description of needs may suggest a direct likelihood of their expression in reality. Vaguely structured needs of the hero are less likely to be related to reality.

Figures, Objects, or Circumstances Introduced.   A child who introduces weapons of one sort or another in a number of stories (even without using them in context) or who has food as an integral part (even without eating it) may be tentatively judged on such evidence as having a need for aggression or oral gratification, respectively. And since the introduction of a figure or circumstance not pictorially represented is extremely significant, this should be noted, possibly by adding an exclamation mark to the analysis sheet. External circumstances such as injustice, severity, indifference, deprivation, and deception (included with the figures and objects introduced) help to indicate the nature of the world in which the child believes herself or himself to be living.

Figures, Objects, or Circumstances Omitted.   Similarly, if one or more figures in the picture are omitted or ignored in the story related, we must consider the possibility of dynamic significance. The simplest meaning is usually an expression of the wish that the figure or object were not there. This may mean plain hostility or that the figure or object is severely conflict arousing, possibly because of its positive value. Of course, this level of inference can only be tentative; at present we do not have a large enough sample of norms to provide expectations regarding objects themselves, introduced and/or omitted.

4. The Conception of the Environment (World)

This concept is, of course, a complex mixture of unconscious self-perception and apperceptive distortion of stimuli by memory images of the past. The more consistent a picture of the environment appearing in the C.A.T. stories, the more reason we have to consider it an important constituent of our subject's personality and a useful clue to his or her reactions in everyday life. Usually, two or three descriptive terms will suffice, such as *succorant, hostile, exploiting* or *exploitable, friendly, dangerous,* and so on.

Identification.   It is important to note with whom the child identifies in the family—namely, which sibling, which parent, and so on. It will also be most important to observe the role which each parent takes with regard to adequacy, and appropriateness, as an identification figure—for instance, whether a male child after the age of 5 identifies with the father, or an older brother, uncle (etc.), rather than with, say, the mother or a younger sister. Of course, the process of identification will not have been completed until the end of puberty, but the early history may be of great importance.

5. Figures Seen as . . .

Here, we are interested in the way the child sees the figures around him or her and how the child reacts to them. We know something about the quality of object relationships—symbiotic, analytic, oral dependent, ambivalent (etc.)—at different stages of development and in different personalities. However, in a broader scheme, we may descriptively speak of supportive, competitive, and other relationships.

6. Significant Conflicts

When we study the significant conflicts, we not only want to know the nature of the conflicts but also the defenses that the child uses against anxiety engendered by these conflicts. Here, we have an excellent opportunity to study the early character formation, and we may be able to derive ideas concerning prognosis.

There are those conflicts that all children experience as they grow from one phase to the next. Thus, beginning at about age 3, we ought not to be alarmed to find evidence of the oedipal struggle and defenses against the fantasied relationship. Some conflicts are part of normal growing up; others may have pathological significance.

7. Nature of Anxieties

The importance of determining the main anxieties of a child hardly needs emphasizing. Those related to physical harm, punishment, and the fear of lacking or losing love (disapproval) and of being deserted (loneliness, lack of support) are probably the most important. It will be valuable to note in the context the child's defenses against the fears that beset him or her. We will want to know the form the defense takes, whether it is flight, passivity, aggression, orality, acquisitiveness, renunciation, regression, and so on.

8. Main Defenses against Conflicts and Fears

Stories should not be studied exclusively for drive content, but should, in addition, be examined for the defenses against these drives. Not infrequently such a study of defenses will actually offer more information in that the drives themselves may appear less clearly than the defenses against them; on the other hand, the defensive structure may be more closely related to manifest behavior of the child. By means of studying drives and defenses, the C.A.T. often permits an appraisal of the character structure of the subject.

Aside from a search for the main defense mechanisms, it is also valuable to study the molar aspects of the stories. For instance, some subjects choose obsessive defenses against a picture of disturbing content. They may produce four or five themes, each very short and descriptive, manifestly different but dynamically similar. Sometimes, a succession of themes to one and the same picture shows the subject's attempts to deal with a disturbing conflict; successive stories may become more and more innocuous, showing an increase in defensive operation.

The concept of defense has to be understood in an increasingly broader sense, best discussed by Lois Murphy and associates in connection with coping (i.e., the person's general ability and mode of meeting external and internal stimuli). With the advance in ego psychology and a focus on the problems of adaptation, a study of these functions is likely to play an increasing role in the exploration of projective methods. We not only want to know the nature of the defensive maneuvers but also the success with which they are employed and/or rather the sacrifice such maneuvers demand from the functioning personality.

The concept of perceptual vigilance may be thought of in connection with projective methods. Various studies have suggested that not only is the defensive projective function of the ego increased in stress but also its cognitive acuity may be improved at the same time.

In the study of children's stories, it must be remembered that we view the nature and pathogenicity of defenses and other structural concepts in terms of age appropriateness. What may be quite normal at one age may be pathological at another age. In the absence of reliable data, not only in the projective literature but any literature at all, some very rough, fallible guidelines have to be adhered to.

9. Adequacy of Superego as Manifested by "Punishment" for "Crime"

The relationship of the chosen punishment to the nature of the offense gives us an insight into the severity of the superego; a psychopath's hero who murders may receive no punishment other than a slight suggestion that he or she may have learned a lesson for later life, while a neurotic may have stories in which the hero is accidentally or intentionally killed or mangled or dies of an illness following the slightest infraction or expression of aggression. On the other hand, a nonintegrated superego, sometimes too severe and sometimes too lenient, is also frequently met in neurotics. A formulation as to the circumstances under which a person's superego can be expected to be too severe, and under what other conditions it is likely to be too lenient, is, of course, related to the difficult problem of acting out. In addition, however, it is a generally valuable piece of information.

10. Integration of the Ego

This is, of course, an important variable to learn about, for in its many aspects it reveals the general level of functioning. To what extent is the child able to compromise between drives and the demands of reality on the one hand and the commands of his or her superego on the other? The adequacy of the hero in dealing with the problems the storyteller has confronted him or her with in the C.A.T. is an important aspect in this variable.

Here, we are interested also in formal characteristics. Is the subject able to tell appropriate stories that constitute a certain amount of cognizance of the stimuli, or does the subject leave the stimulus completely and tell a story with no manifest relation to the picture because he or she is not well enough, therefore, and too preoccupied with personal problems to perceive reality? Does he or she find comfort and salvation from anxiety stimulated by the test by giving very stereotyped responses, or is he or she well enough and intelligent enough to be creative and give more or less original stories? Having produced a plot, can the child attain a solution of the conflicts in the story and within himself or herself that is adequate, complete, and realistic; or do the thought processes become unstructured or even bizarre under the impact of the problem? Does the child have the ability to go from a past background of the story to a future resolution? This will depend on the age of the child as well as on his or her unique personality.

These observations, together with the dynamic diagnosis which the content variables supply—thus facilitating possible classifications of the patient in one of the nosological categories—are the main contributions of the C.A.T.

From a formal standpoint, it is useful to consider that telling stories to the pictures is a task which the subject must perform. We may judge the subject's adequacy and ego strength and other variables from the standpoint of his or her ability and way of meeting the task. Of course, the adequacy of the ego and its various functions has to be considered in relation to the specific age. Consideration should be given to a variety of ego functions such as drive control (related to the story sequence and outcome), frustration tolerance (related to adequacy of hero), anxiety tolerance, perceptual and motor adequacy, and others.[1]

Use of the Short Form T.A.T. and C.A.T. Blank

For the purpose of facilitating the analysis and recording of the stories, the senior author signed the Short Form T.A.T. and C.A.T. Blank. A similar blank designed for the T.A.T. alone served as a useful frame of reference, particularly in the beginning of one's experience and even for the experienced worker when a record seems unusually valueless. In the event of ordinary physical and mental strain, or of one's own emotional blind spots, such a schema will yield much better results.

Stories can be recorded individually. On the summary page, we recommend briefly noting the main data culled from every story in order to gain an impression of the whole. We recommend the final report be written in such a way that the most salient facets of the personality, as they appear, are summed up in the first large paragraph. In the second large paragraph, each general statement made in the first should be briefly supported by concrete references to the stories and details appearing in them. Or each abstract statement may be immediately supported by reference to the concrete story content upon which it is predicated.

Case Illustrations

The following three cases are presented in rank order of disturbance revealed. Each is an example of various specific disorders, although they all have certain features in common. They will be formally analyzed and interpreted in detail so that the reader may observe some of the subtler aspects of insight to be gained.

---

[1] The 1974 revision of the C.A.T. manual discusses ego functions depicted on page 5 of the Short Form in a way similar to that of the Long Form for the T.A.T.

Case 1 has been selected for its relative freedom from pathology. It demonstrates the developmental process of internalization of authority and social learning or socialization. These stories are classically illustrative of the "statement of a moral" so often found in children's stories. This child does it explicitly; it is more often implicit. The moral is so strongly and repetitively stated and reaction formation is so prominent that one wonders if the child is in the early stages of an obsessive/compulsive character disorder. The tentative appearance of this tendency would have to be investigated more carefully in a study of the behavioral aspects of his or her life and in the light of all other available data.

It will be particularly useful to compare stories 3, 4, and especially 5 in the three cases presented. While all three reveal primal scene fears, they are apparently of differing intensities and are handled in different ways.

Case 1[2]

The following C.A.T. stories are of a boy 7 years and 9 months old. His I.Q. was 133 on Form L of the Stanford-Binet. His father is an artist described as easygoing and apparently well adjusted, while the mother, although also gifted as well as warm and outgoing, appears somewhat more tense. There is a little sister four years younger.

John himself is an attractive youngster with considerable social poise and many friends. He is without specific difficulties except for the fact that his teachers report that he is somewhat troublesome in asking embarrassing questions, putting the teachers on the spot. At times, when his mother has been engaged in activities that took her away from home, John has been demanding and irritable. His relationship to the sister is said to be protective.

Summary
Record of Main Theme (Diagnostic) and Other Main Data

1. Need for autonomy; evidence of superego; compliance to authority figure; guilt feelings—superego. Conflicts: between superego and aggression and reacts with compliance, learning. Between autonomy and compliance. Some confusion of roles of mother and father.
2. Identifies with mother as the weaker one. Feels that aggressive contest may lead to damage. Fear of aggression? Fear of injury. Guilt feelings over aggression.
3. Need for intelligence and inquisitiveness as a form of protection against unpleasant surprises. Significant conflict: between activity and passivity.
4. Need for autonomy, aggression (riding fast). Guilt feelings. Compliance with maternal authority.
5. Fearful at night, probably related to primal scene noises. Mother seen as nonprotective and scolding. Probably suffers from a mild sleeping disturbance.

---

[2] The authors are indebted to Ms. Sadi Oppenheim for permission to use this case.

SHORT FORM
BELLAK T.A.T. and C.A.T. BLANK
For Recording and Analyzing Thematic Apperception Test and Children's Apperception Test

Name _____ John _____ Sex _M_ Age _7-9_ Date _____

(circle one)

Education _____ Occupation _____ , m. s. w. d.

Referred by_____ Analysis by _____

    After having obtained the stories analyze each story by using the variables on the left of Page 2. Not every story will furnish information regarding each variable: the variables are presented as a frame of reference to help avoid overlooking some dimension.

    When all ten stories have been analyzed it is easy to check each variable from left to right for all ten stories and record an integrated summary on page 4 under the appropriate headings. That way a final picture is obtained almost immediately.

    Then, keeping Page 4 folded out, the Final Report: Diagnostic Impressions and Recommendations can be written on Page 1 by reference to Page 4. Page 5 gives available space for any other notations. The stories then can be stapled inside the blank against page 5.

FINAL REPORT: Diagnostic Impressions and Recommendations

    These stories reveal a child of above average intelligence, verbally gifted, who is in the process of adjusting himself to the world, i.e., in the process of socialization and internalization of rules and regulations. This may be seen in the moral which sums up nearly every story. His main hero is a child striving for autonomy in stories 1 and 4, and a need for curiosity and participation in adult freedom of acquisition, sex, and general achievement in stories 6, 8, 9, and 10, where he variously wants to know what is going on at night, at adult parties, etc. However, his hero usually has to renounce his goals and learn that it is better to obey the parents' instructions not to go to the brook, as in story 1 (which one can fall into), not to be too anxious to get honey, as in story 6 (one gets stung), or not to ride a bicycle too wildly (or one falls off, as in story 4).

    He clearly has oedipal feelings, excluding father from the bedroom in story 5, and engaging in classical competition with him in story 7, where the monkey fighting with the mighty lion has his tail cut off, and expresses his resignation in the succinct, "If you want to keep your tail long, you don't want to fool around with the lion." Similarly, he is scared of nocturnal animals harming him. He identifies with mother in story 2, helping her pull the rope because father is stronger, but on other occasions, such as in stories 4 and 10, sees her as somewhat punishing and restricting.

    Much as he wants to be grown up, there is evidence in story 10 and possibly in story 4 that he may identify slightly regressively with the younger sister. He has a strong curiosity which is in the service of the defenses. He wants to know how to avoid possible harm or injury, for instance in story 3 where the lion has trouble because he doesn't know how to read, and sublimates his interest in magnifying glasses, fingerprints, etc.

    His anxieties center around fear of physical harm, sometimes obviously of a castration nature, for instance, the monkey with his tail cut off, being stung by a bee, and the breaking rope. His conflicts are characterized by a strong superego winning out over his need for aggression, autonomy, and sexual curiosity, to a point where he may possibly develop into a somewhat obsessive-compulsive character with some lack of spontaneity and a tendency to overcompliance. Reaction formation will undoubtedly figure prominently in his makeup. However, note should be taken of the realistic and usually happy outcome of the stories, and the lack of any viciousness in the superego. The punishments are always mild and sometimes considerate--for instance, in story 8 where the parents wait until the company is gone to spank him.

    There is considerable hope that the problem areas pointed out will become part of a sufficiently well-functioning character structure rather than a character disorder or psychoneurosis.

	Story No. 1	Story No. 2
1. Main Theme: (<u>diagnostic level</u>: if descriptive and interpretative levels are desired, use a scratch sheet or page 5)	Need for autonomy evidence of super-ego compliance to authority figures	Identifies with mother. Feels aggressive contest may lead to damage.
2. Main hero: age _7_ sex _M_ vocation _____ abilities _gifted_ verbally interests ____ traits ____ body image _____ adequacy (√, √√,√√√) and/or self-image _____	Children	Child helping mother
3. Main needs and drives of hero: a) behavioral needs of hero (as in story): _____ implying: _____	Child who has to learn	
b) figures, objects, or circumstances *introduced:* _____ implying need for or to: _____	Brook misfortune. Enuresis?	Breaking rope
c) figures, objects, or circumstances *omitted:* _____ implying need for or to: _____		Fear of damage due to aggression
4. Conception of environment (world) as: _____		
5. a) **Parental figures** (m ____, f √) are seen as _restricting_ and subject's reaction to a is _____	Both parents seen as in-structive and nurturant	Competitive
b) **Contemp. figures** (m ____, f ___) are seen as _____ and subject's reaction to b is _____		
c) **Junior figures** (m ____, f √) are seen as _____ and subject's reaction to c is _protective_		
6. Significant conflicts: _strong superego winning out over need for_ _aggression, autonomy, and sexual curiosity_	Between superego and aggression	Between superego and aggression
7. Nature of anxieties: (√) of physical harm and/or punishment ____ √ of disapproval _____ of lack or loss of love _____ of illness or injury _____ of being deserted _____ of deprivation _____ of being overpowered and helpless _____ of being devoured _____ other _____	Mild physical harm	Fear of damage resulting from aggressive competition.
8. Main defenses against conflicts and fears: (√) repression _____ reaction-formation ____ √ regression _____ denial _____ introjection _____ isolation _____ undoing _____ rationalization _____ other _intellectualization_ projective identification _____ splitting _____		
9. Adequacy of superego as manifested by "punishment" for "crime" being: ( ) appropriate ____ √ _____ inappropriate _____ too severe (also indicated by immediacy of punishment) _____ inconsistent _____ too lenient _____ also: _mild and considerate_ delayed initial response or pauses _____ stammer _____ other manifestations of superego interference _____		Too severe and immediate
10. Integration of the ego, manifesting itself in: (√, √√, √√√) Hero: adequate ___ √√√ _____ inadequate _____ outcome: happy ___ √√√ _____ unhappy _____ realistic _____ unrealistic _____ drive control _____ thought processes as revealed by plot being: (√, √√, √√√) stereotyped _____ original _____ appropriate _____ complete _____ incomplete _____ inappropriate _____ syncretic _____ concrete _____ contaminated _____ Intelligence: _above average_ Maturation level _high_	Happy Realistic	Happy Realistic

2

Story No. 3	Story No. 4	Story No. 5	Story No. 6	Story No. 7	Story No. 8
Need for intelligence and inquisitiveness as a form of protection against unpleasant surprises	Need for autonomy. Compliance with maternal authority.	Fearful at night. Non-protective and scolding mother	Guilt feelings over oral acquisition	Has competitive aggressive feelings toward father. Afraid of father's strength. Castration anxiety.	Feelings of competition with adults. Guilt feelings. Father seen as discreet.
Adult lion	Disobedient child	Two children	Punished child	Monkey	Child
Needs to be informed	Autonomy	For reassurance			
Crown, train, broken tracks, newspaper	Accident Compliance to avoid harm	Bats, birds, and insects	Punisher Food	Pencil sharpener Need for preparedness	Food, dancing, magnifying glass
Need to be grown up and adequate		Father To exclude father from bedroom			Implying inquisitiveness
	Mother seen as instructive and nurturant	Mother seen as punishing and rejecting		Father seen as aggressive, competitive	Punishing. Powerful. Rejecting
Activity-passivity	Autonomy-compliance	Fear of sexual desires	Between superego and acquisition	Between superego and aggression	Between superego and acquisition and sexual desires
Fear of inadequacy and surprise due to lack of information and attention.	Fear of physical harm.	Fear of physical harm and being overpowered and helpless.	Fear of physical harm or punishment by phallic injury?	Fear of physical harm and punishment, illness, or injury. Being overpowered and helpless.	Fear of being excluded from adult society. Being found out by parents.
Too severe.	Too severe and immediate		Too severe and immediate	Too severe? immediate	Just?
Happy Realistic	Happy Realistic	Unhappy Realistic	Unhappy Realistic	Unhappy Realistic	Unhappy Realistic

3

Story No. 9	Story No. 10	SUMMARY
Primal scene fears Uses sleep and withdrawal as avoidance of anxiety.	Competition with adults. Compliance with maternal authority.	**1–3. Unconscious structure and drives of subject (based on variables 1–3)** A need for autonomy, oedipal desires, aggression, and voyeurism are in conflict with a moderately severe, consistent ego syntonic superego.
Child	Small child	Result is adaptive striving and moderate anxiety--probably the part of developmental phase.
	To be adult	
Night, mother, strange noises	Pot, fingerprints, magnifying glass	
Implying curiosity concerning sexual events at night.	Implying need for regression, inquisitiveness	
		4. Conception of world: As firmly but fairly controlling and capable of being controlled by intelligent behavior.
	Mother seen as punishing, hostile, and domineering	**5. Relationship to others:** The relationship to parental figures is somewhat ambivalent. Nothing emerges about peer relations.
Between superego and sexual desires	Between superego and autonomy	**6. Significant conflicts:** Between superego and oedipal desires, etc. (See #1)
Fear of physical harm or punishment	Fear of disapproval	**7. Nature of anxieties:** Some fear of disapproval and castration.
Withdrawal		**8. Main defenses used:** Intellectualization, reaction-formation, healthy repression.
Too severe and immediate	Too severe and immediate	**9. Superego structure:** Consistent, somewhat too severe.
Unhappy Realistic	Unhappy Unrealistic?	**10. Integration and strength of ego:** Excellent integration, possible danger of somewhat obsessive formation later in life.

Ego function assessment from CAT data:

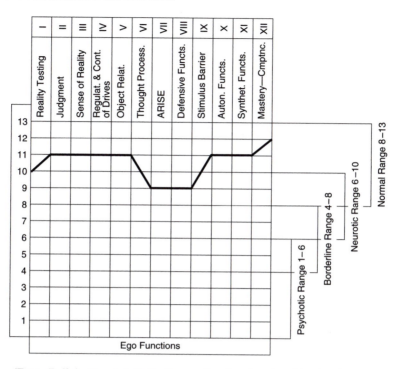

(From Bellak, Hurvich & Gediman, *Ego functions in schizophrenics, neurotics, and normals.* Copyright © 1973, by C. P. S., Inc. Reprinted by permission of John Wiley & Sons, Inc.)

Ego functions observed during test administration:

6. Guilt feelings over oral acquisition. Anxiety about physical harm—by phallic injury?
7. Has competitive aggressive feelings toward father. Afraid of father's strength. Castration anxiety. Need for preparedness.
8. Feelings of competition with adults. Need for oral acquisition. Guilt feelings. Superego. Sexual curiosity and guilt.
9. Strong interest in the primal scene. Primal scene fears. Uses sleep and withdrawal as an avoidance of anxiety.
10. Competition with the adults with regard to excretory functions. Strong superego. Mother seen as punishing. Anger at mother. Compliance with maternal authority. Self-image of younger child—regression.

Story 1

Story 1: Something funny about this—chickens don't eat at a table—the chickens were eating their breakfast one morning and they went out and there they saw the rooster, and Mr. Rooster said, "How are you today?" And they said, "We're fine," and they wanted to go to the brook, but their mother said, "You shouldn't go to the brook, you might fall in." They said, "We won't." And they didn't obey their mother and they did go and they fell in and then they went to their mother and started crying and mother said, "I told you you shouldn't go," and they never did. The rooster is the mother; well, the rooster is the father, you could say the chicken then . . . (end of story.)

Descriptive theme	Interpretive theme	Diagnostic level
Chickens go to the brook against mother's warning	If one disobeys mother,	Need for autonomy;
and fall in,	one gets into trouble	evidence of superego;
and then go crying to mother and never did this again.	and obeys thereafter.	compliance to authority figure; guilt feelings—superego.

Clinical Notes

This story shows a typical children's "moral"; note, however, that the calamity is minor and that punishment by the mother is absent save for simple repetition of the injunction. The only other point of interest is the indecision in the child's designation of the male and female roles to the rooster. If one had no data other than the stories, one would note this bit of possible significance and be on the lookout for a repetition in subsequent stories. As it happens, we do have a background on this child and we know that while both parents are benign, the father is particularly easygoing and that domestic management and decisions are thus relegated to the mother. So far, these observations are merely to be kept in mind without coming to any definite conclusions.

The introduction of water (especially getting accidentally wet) suggests the possibility of enuresis.

Story 2

Story 2: One day a couple of bears met each other and they said—one bear had a rope, and they said, "Let's play tug-of-war." The baby bear was helping the mother bear because the father bear was the strongest, and the rope broke and then they had no more rope to play tug-of-war. They feel sorry.

Descriptive theme	Interpretive theme	Diagnostic level
When playing tug-of-war, the baby bear helps mother bear because father is stronger.	If mother and father are engaged in a contest, the hero helps mother because father is stronger.	Identifies with mother as the weaker one.
Then the rope broke and they had to stop playing	An aggressive contest can lead to damage	Feels that aggressive contest may lead to damage. Fear of aggression? Fear of injury.
and feel sorry.	and one feels sorry.	Guilt feelings over aggression.

Clinical Notes

While the roles of father and mother were somewhat confused in story 1, here the father is clearly identified as the stronger one.

Again, there is evidence of the existence of a superego without any excess of severity.

Story 3

Story 3: Something wrong with this picture—the lion's not wearing the crown. Once there was a lion who was waiting for a train. He was a very nice-looking lion and he smoked a pipe and he had a cane and he waited but the train didn't come. All of a sudden he heard the train and it was on the other side, so he sat down again and he waited and waited and he sat there all day, 'cause the train track was broken and the train didn't go through. He said, "I'm getting tired," and he got up and found out in the newspaper that the train track was broken, and so he went down into his house and took a long snooze on the chair like he is doing here, and then he had his supper and had to wait for his train till the next day. Darn old train. I'll make a moral for it: You can't tell if it's coming if you don't read.

Descriptive theme	Interpretive theme	Diagnostic level
A lion waits in vain all day for a train until he finds out that the track is broken and therefore has to wait another day.	Mishaps occur.	Fear of damage?

| If one doesn't read, one can't tell what is coming. | If one is not intelligent and inquisitive, one may have trouble. | Need for intelligence and inquisitiveness as a form of protection against unpleasant surprises. |

Clinical Notes

Again, a moral is expressed, making a virtue of the acquisition of learning.

In this boy's first story, the mention of "Something funny about this—chickens don't eat at a table," was not significant by itself; however, in the preceding story, there is a similar kind of expression in the first sentence, and we must begin to take note of the "stickler for actuality" quality and to look for any signs of repetitiveness in subsequent stories. The lion's not wearing a crown is certainly a threat of continuity through these first three stories: the indecision in story 1 over whether mother or father is the "rooster"; the definite relegation of superior strength to the father in story 2, with identification with the mother; and the reference in this last story to the lack of crown on the lion—crown being a literal expression of who's "king."

The reference to hearing the train and its appearance "on the other side" could be merely a biographical reference to the child's experience on some suburban railroad or city subway, and is not meaningful by itself. The reference to the broken track adds up with the broken rope in story 2 to at least a raising of the question of possible symbolic fear of genital harm. The history did reveal a recent increase in masturbation. Neither of these references suggests a problem of any clinical proportions. This may possibly be just a developmental factor related to the younger sister's being "different," may be related to his being a stickler for facts in these stories and correlate with the teachers' complaint of putting them on the spot, and suggests an aggressive or obsessive connotation.

Story 4

Story 4: Once a mother kangaroo and her baby kangaroo went to the store. The baby kangaroo had a bicycle. There were three kangaroos. One was in the mother's pocket. The baby in the pocket was holding a balloon. The next day they went to the market again and when they were coming home the baby kangaroo said "I want to ride the bicycle very fast," and the mother said, "Don't ride fast or you'll fall off." But he didn't listen and fell off and mother said, "Serves you right." Whoever doesn't listen had a fall, the moral.

Descriptive theme	Interpretive theme	Diagnostic level
A little kangaroo wants to ride his bicycle fast		Need for autonomy; aggression (riding fast).
against mother's warning	If one doesn't listen to one's mother	
and promptly falls.	one gets into trouble.	Guilt feelings; compliance with maternal authority.

Clinical Notes

At first, only one child is mentioned, suggesting some sibling rivalry. While there may be some question as to whether the baby on the bicycle now refers to the baby sister or to himself, it is not unreasonable to assume that it probably refers more directly to the hero. The theme is really a repetition of story 1.

Here, there is no mention at all of the food in the picture, and it is only casually referred to in story 1, whereas usually it is the theme. This may indicate little oral interest.

Story 5

Story 5: What's in the bed? They look like bears to me but bears don't sleep in a cradle. Well, one night two bears went to sleep, two baby bears, and mother bear was sleeping right next to them, and they heard an owl and they got scared, and they woke the mother bear and she said, "That's just an owl." So the baby bears went to bed and they heard a bee, and they woke up again, and the mother said, "That's just a bee." And they heard a bat, and the mother said, "If you don't stop waking me up I'll have to sleep in another room." So the next morning the mother said, "What's the idea of making all that noise—you made more noise than the owl and the bat and the bee did." They felt scared. "I don't like sleeping." The babies stayed up all night looking out the window and mother was in another room.

Descriptive theme	*Interpretive theme*	*Diagnostic level*
Two children sleeping with their mother were scared repeatedly by noises at night.	If one hears noises at night, one wakes up scared.	Fearful at night, probably related to primal scene noises.
and woke the mother who finally threatened to sleep in another room, scolding them.	If one wakes mother, she is annoyed and threatens to leave one,	Mother seen as nonprotective and scolding.
The children are scared and don't like sleeping and stay up all night watching.	whereupon one doesn't like sleeping and stays up all night watchfully.	Probably suffers from a mild sleeping disturbance.

Clinical Notes

The first sentence is a repetition of this child's characteristic literalness. It is very unusual for children to remark on the anthropomorphic aspects of the pictures. He did this in stories 1, 3, and 5, but not in stories 2 and 4. We should then take special cognizance of the kind of stories that evoke this characteristic and see what conclusions we may be justified in drawing. Thus far, we might tentatively say that stories 3 and 5 have one feature in common with reference to their calculated stimulus value: 3 is intended to arouse (among other things) phallic concern, whereas 5 is intended to elicit primal scene fears, and there is, of course, a close relation between the two. We might therefore say tentatively that when the boy is confronted with sexual considerations, one of his defenses is to become concerned with "factual" and familiar realisms, or, on another level, we might say that a certain constriction sets in. Now we must ask ourselves why story 1 was prefaced in the same way when there is certainly nothing in the stimulus to cause sexual concern. To this, one could only hazard a guess, and suppose that *any* anxiety-arousing situation—whether sexual, sibling rivalry, or whatever—provokes this special response in this boy. What can be considered anxiety producing in picture 1 can only be the fact that it is the *first* picture so that his frame of reference has not yet been sufficiently secured. For other children, of course, the picture more often has its emphasis on oral problems.

As to the primal scene per se, the main feature of his story is his omission of the usually seen second figure vaguely indicated in the large bed. Many children omit mention of figures altogether; some omit one parent or the other. We would expect this boy to omit the father, since it has become quite apparent that his relationship to his mother is stronger.

As to the specificity of the references to the various animal and insect noises, specificity is a characteristic of this child and he is merely being consistent. However, the animals he does mention, bats, birds, and insects, are phallic symbols not infrequently seen clinically as phobias. Children's fears of "noises in the night" very often refer to the sounds of the parents having intercourse.

The reference to "another room" is as yet obscure. Perhaps it is factually biographical; we do not know. In any case, when the mother does remove herself to another room on the following night, the babies' anxiety is apparently increased, since they stay up all night. All this tells us is that the subject does not benefit by closing his eyes to the bigger bed.

Story 6

Story 6: One day two bears had a big supper and they felt so tired they couldn't even move from all the meal, so they fell asleep. Next morning when they woke up they went hunting for honey. The baby bear was first one to find it, and the baby bear looked in the honey tree hive and she grabbed some honey and the bees came zooming after her and she got stung on the nose, and she had a big bandage on her nose all night, and she went to sleep. Moral is: Don't hunt for honey if you don't want to get stung.

Descriptive theme	*Interpretive theme*	*Diagnostic level*
Bears are looking for honey and are stung on the nose. One shouldn't hunt for honey if one doesn't want to be hurt.	If one has (oral) acquisitive desires one may get hurt.	Guilt feelings over oral acquisition.

Clinical Notes

Here again, as in story 4, one wonders if misbehavior is ascribed to the younger sibling, or the hero, or both. The child identifies again with the parent, moralizing as usual. There is the introduction of food in a stimulus where none appears. The child has omitted one figure that is present. This picture is generally perceived as comprising two large bears and one small one, which is actually the case. It is generally evocative of additional primal scene stories, either more intensely or less intensely described, because of its position in following up an earlier one, depending on the particular child's modes of defense. The total omission of a more realistic mention of the figures involved, and the story of stealing forbidden food, can be tentatively considered as a most remote allusion to the sexual connotations of the story and is consistent with the child's strict sense of being "a good boy."

The nose as a choice of organ to be punished, having phallic significance, supports the notion of a sexual meaning to the story.

Story 7

Story 7: The name of this story is "The Monkey and the Lion." One day the monkey was standing up on the tree and he saw a lion—I forgot, it was a tiger—for a moment, and the lion—the tiger is next to the king of beasts. "I want to show the lion that I could be next to the king of the beasts too. I'll fight the lion and win." (Monkey says this.) So the monkey sharpened up his nails with a pencil sharpener and tried to scratch the lion on the neck to kill him, but the lion jumped up and pushed him over and lion got the monkey by the tail, rather, the tiger, and the monkey had his tail shortened. And the moral is: If you want to keep your tail long, you don't want to fool around with the lion.

Descriptive theme	Interpretive theme	Diagnostic level
A monkey tries to compete with a lion	If one competes with authority figures	Has competitive aggressive feelings toward father.
but the lion overpowers him and cuts his tail off.	one gets hurt—cut down to size.	Afraid of father's strength. Castration anxiety.

Clinical Notes

This story is classic in its demonstration of castration. It is so clearly stated that explanation or interpretation would be redundant. However, two additional items are also worthy of notice. First, the consistent specificity in the phrase "The monkey sharpened his nails with a *pencil sharpener.*" Second, it is interesting that while the picture clearly shows the tiger attacking the monkey, the boy make no mention of this fact and starts with an expression of his desire to show the tiger that he, the monkey, can also be "next to the king of beasts"—not quite the king. The earlier confusion between lion and tiger is quite clear and is also consistent with the subject's insistence on facts being facts. He knows that the lion is the king of beasts. The aggressive figure of the tiger urges him to acknowledge the unarguable superiority of the "king" (father). He makes his peace with the discrepancy with which he is faced (tigers are not lions) by admitting him the second most important position—next to the king—and then prepares to prove that he can compete with a secondary superiority. But he is merely paying lip service (as he has done all along with his moralizing) and is defeated.

Story 5, where the stimulus-implied father figure is omitted, corroborates the reflection of the sexual competition seen in this story.

Story 8

Story 8: Once a monkey had a party and he invited a lot of people, but the little boy had to go to sleep because it was late, but the little boy didn't want to. He said, "I want to stay up for the party too," a dancing party and ice cream, and the father said no. But the monkey stayed up in his room and listened to the party and when they went dancing he snuck some ice cream, and his father, when he went to the ice cream with a magnifying glass, saw the monkey had had it so he called the mother in. But the monkey didn't come and pretended to be asleep but the father shook him. "What is the idea of stealing the ice cream?" Because of the company he didn't spank him, but the next day he did. No moral!

Descriptive theme	Interpretive theme	Diagnostic level
The parents had guests in. The child wanted to participate	If one wants to do things which the adults do	Feelings of competition with adults.
and have some ice cream	and permits oneself oral acquisition.	Need for oral acquisition.
against father's orders. Father discovers this and spanks him privately.	one is discovered by father and punished privately.	Guilt feelings. Superego. Father seen as discreet.

Clinical Notes

Again, oral acquisition seems forbidden, possibly more than is quite reasonable, since ice cream is usually permitted to children, but again, as in the honey story (6), oral acquisition is associated with the prerogatives of the adults and their (sexual) dancing preoccupations.

The mother being called in emphasizes her role as the authority figure. The punishing being postponed until there are no strange witnesses suggests a level of discreet discourse in the family.

Story 9

Story 9: Once there was a little bunny. He went out with his mother, and his name was Bunny Cottontail, and he always used to sing a song about himself: "Here comes Bunny Cottontail hoppin' down the bunny bunny trail, hippety hop." That night he stayed up, he wanted to stay up, he wanted to see what it was like in the nighttime and he heard strange noises and he got scared and from then on he never stayed up because he didn't want to get scared. And the moral is: Stay asleep if you don't want to get scared.

Descriptive theme	*Interpretive theme*	*Diagnostic level*
A little bunny wants to stay up to see what happens at night	If one wants to find out what is going on at night,	Strong interest in the primal scene.
and is scared by strange noises	one may hear frightening noises	Primal scene fears.
and chooses to stay asleep to avoid anxiety.	and renounce one's curiosity and choose flight into sleep.	Uses sleep and withdrawal as an avoidance of anxiety.

Clinical Notes

This story is a direct supplement and counterpart to story 5. This time, he chooses denial and avoidance as a way of dealing with the anxiety, which is strong though not overwhelming in story 5. The chances are that his defensive behavior in the present story presents the behavioral status consistent with the strong defenses in this child.

Story 10

Story 10: One day a baby dog—his mother bought him a little pot that little dogs are supposed to make in but the little dog didn't want to make it in there. He said, "I want to make it in the big toilet." But his mother said not to or he'll get a spanking. But he didn't obey her and he did go on the big toilet and he got spanked the next day 'cause she found out somehow (took a magnifying glass and saw fingerprints). Then he got a spanking and he was crying and he promised never to do it again. It hurted him very much, the spanking, 'cause he was such a little baby, he felt mad to his mother.

Descriptive theme	*Interpretive theme*	*Diagnostic level*
A little dog wants to use the grown-up toilet, not his little one.	If one is little and one wants to use the big toilet (instead of the little one)	Competition with adults with regard to excretory functions.
His mother forbade it, but he did it against her orders	against mother's orders,	
and got spanked and cried and was angry and hurt	one is found out and spanked, is hurt and angry at mother	Strong superego. Mother seen as punishing. Anger at mother.
and promised never to do it again.	and promises to be good.	Compliance with maternal authority.

Clinical Notes

The feature emerging most strongly here is the use of baby talk as an identification with the baby. That this regression takes place in response to a picture evoking images of excretory functions is particularly neat. Obviously, the boy identifies strongly with his younger sibling, for the first time in any of these stories, and empathizes with the baby quite thoroughly. He also acknowledges that spanking hurts little babies (more than older children?). Perhaps he is recalling his own earlier experiences with toilet training and the identification is with himself. Certainly he has never been this sympathetic to his sibling before. It is interesting also, although it tells us nothing conclusive, that he feels that babies can feel angry with their mothers. He has not previously expressed any anger toward punishing figures in his other stories.

Case 2

The second case is that of an 8-year-old boy whose C.A.T. was analyzed blindly in the course of a class on projective techniques. The C.A.T. record was obtained by Dr. Bela Mittelman, to whom we are very grateful, both for the record and for permission to use the case of the little boy who was in psychoanalytic treatment.

As it happens, we did not become familiar with the clinical data until four or five years after the initial interpretation of the C.A.T., which is presented here. While such a blind method is not recommended, it happened to have been a part of a teaching program.

The clinical facts are as follows: This 8-year-old boy was brought for psychoanalytic treatment because he had suffered from eczema since his fifth month of life. He had been restless and cranky since the age of 2½ years, when he sustained a severe burn of the right thigh. He had been doing poor work in school and was a disciplinary problem because of minor but continuous infractions of rules, such as talking, giggling, and fighting. He was unpopular with the children, got into frequent scraps, and threw stones at others, or hit them.

His behavior toward his brother, 13 months his junior, became very aggressive after his mother became more affectionate toward the younger one, about a year before. He frequently refused food, and he would not bathe himself or wash or clean his face, hands, or teeth unless there were constant reminders from his mother.

The mother had given him little intimate contact, adhered strictly to a feeding schedule, and was generally excitable. The child's hands had been tied for several weeks to prevent his scratching (when he was age 2 and was hospitalized). The father and mother were divorced when the child was in the fifth month of analysis. The father is described as close to the children but less assertive than the mother. The parental divorce is reported to have renewed his mistrust of the world and endangered anew the boy's confidence in the analyst's ability to help him (he had stoutly maintained that what he needed and expected was physical treatment). He saw the world as full of hostile forces and suffered an increase in his oedipal conflict and in his fear of retribution from his father.

It is easy to correlate the facts unearthed in the C.A.T. with the psychodynamics consistent with the boy's history: The feeling of hostility and hopelessness consequent to his traumatic infancy appears clinically and in the C.A.T., and so does his secondary regression to dirtiness and the jungle and his anger toward mother and brother. No sleeping disorder was reported clinically, and we do not know whether this means that it did not exist or whether it was minor enough to be lost in the multitude of complaints.

It must be remembered that projective techniques may point up problems that are not clinically manifest but that may become so, under stress or when therapy interferes with the defenses; we have frequently seen this (e.g., in relation to impotence inferred correctly from Rorschach signs in adult male patients several months before they really become impotent in the course of psychoanalytic treatment). Also, curiously enough, we had no inkling of the eczema from the C.A.T. record. This coincides with observations that the T.A.T. may present a complete personality picture without permitting one to infer the chief complaint. All the component parts of the psychodynamics (of eczema, in this case) are present (lack of oral gratification, hostility due to very disturbed early mother/child relationship) but no specific reference to or indication of a skin disorder. Theoretically, this is a problem in need of further investigation. Practically, it is simple enough to see the skin disorder or elicit other chief complaints as part of the history taking; indication of this disorder need not be expected from the projective methods.

Summary
Record of Main Theme (Diagnostic) and Other Main Data

1.
2.
3. Subject feels troubled by small sibling. Feels unsuccessful in aggression toward sibling; subject tries to enlist help of someone, probably therapist, whose role he sees as helping do away with sibling. Therapist considered useless. Sibling seen as outsmarting subject. He sees his extra-aggression as boomerang. He attempts withdrawal (or other modes of behavior), finds these measures useless, regresses to more primitive behavior. Conflict between superego and aggression, reacts with intra-aggression.
4.
5.
6. Night noises are troubling subject: primal scene disturbances? Subject hopes expert will do away with these troubles. Subject disturbed by therapist to a greater degree than by the primal noises, and refuses help of therapist.
7.
8. Mother seen as coercive, child complies manifestly. Subject resents mother's pleasure in house, considers her a braggart. Subject feels explosive anger in himself and wants to destroy mother's pleasure. Angry feelings against mother. Exclusion of father. Conflict between superego and aggression, reacts with manifest compliance.

SHORT FORM
BELLAK T.A.T. and C.A.T. BLANK
For Recording and Analyzing Thematic Apperception Test and Children's Apperception Test

Name _____ Sex __M__ Age __8__ Date _____
                                                                    (circle one)
Education _____ Occupation _____ , m. s. w. d.

Referred by_____ Analysis by _____

After having obtained the stories analyze each story by using the variables on the left of Page 2. Not every story will furnish information regarding each variable: the variables are presented as a frame of reference to help avoid overlooking some dimension.

When all ten stories have been analyzed it is easy to check each variable from left to right for all ten stories and record an integrated summary on page 4 under the appropriate headings. That way a final picture is obtained almost immediately.

Then, keeping Page 4 folded out, the Final Report: Diagnostic Impressions and Recommendations can be written on Page 1 by reference to Page 4. Page 5 gives available space for any other notations. The stories then can be stapled inside the blank against page 5.

FINAL REPORT: Diagnostic Impressions and Recommendations

This report is predicated only on the four stories analyzed in detail. In these stories our patient seems preoccupied particularly with the problem of aggression and counteraggression. Most of the aggression seems to be directed toward the younger brother, as for instance story 3, where the brother appears as vermin which the patient tries to exterminate, or on story 9, where rabbits (brother) are being hunted. In these two stories, as well as in story 8, which shows aggression toward the mother, the aggression seems to be of a very explosive, superficially strongly controlled nature. Because of an extremely severe though not integrated superego, the hostile wishes are usually turned into violent intra-aggression, and our patient himself comes to harm. The brother is seen as a nuisance and the mother as a braggart and somewhat coercive. The father figure does not emerge clearly in these stories except possibly as an accomplice and helper in story 9.

The patient perceives himself as rather helpless in coping with his problems and uses withdrawal and regression as defensive measures, as for instance in story 3, where he returns to the jungle, or in story 6, where he sees himself as troubled, suggesting that he suffers from insomnia because of nocturnal fears (probably concerning primal scene noises).

The treatment situation and transference relationship are reflected in story 3 and in story 6, where the boy seems to see the therapist as a fellow-conspirator against the brother (exterminator of the vermin), who is as useless as the carpenter called in to do away with the nocturnal disturbances. In fact, in the latter story, there is a suggestion that he conceives of therapy as a further unloosing of anxiety, and wishes to leave.

In summary, one may say that this is a fairly neurotic child with severe problems in his relationship to his younger sibling and to his mother, an inability to handle his repressed explosive hostility, and a potentiality for sleeping disturbances.

Published by
C.P.S. Inc.
P.O. Box 83
Larchmont, N.Y. 10538

Printed in U.S.A.

	Story No. 1	Story No. 2
1. Main Theme: (<u>diagnostic level</u>: if descriptive and interpretative levels are desired, use a scratch sheet or page 5)		
2. Main hero: age ___8___ sex ___M___ vocation_____ abilities_____ interests_____ traits_____ body image _rather helpless_ adequacy ($\checkmark$, $\checkmark\checkmark$, $\checkmark\checkmark\checkmark$) and/or self-image_____		
3. Main needs and drives of hero: a) behavioral needs of hero (as in story): _____ implying: _____ b) figures, objects, or circumstances *introduced*:_____ implying need for or to:_____ c) figures, objects, or circumstances *omitted*:_____ implying need for or to:_____		
4. Conception of environment (world) as: _full of hostile forces_		
5. a) **Parental figures** (m___, f $\checkmark$) are seen as _braggart_ and subject's reaction to a is_____ b) **Contemp. figures** (m $\checkmark$, f___) are seen as_therapist seen as_ and subject's reaction to b is_____ _fellow conspirator_ c) **Junior figures** (m $\checkmark$, f___) are seen as _nuisance_ and subject's reaction to c is_____		
6. Significant conflicts: _between superego and aggression and counteraggression_		
7. Nature of anxieties: ($\checkmark$) of physical harm and/or punishment ____$\checkmark$____ of disapproval_____ of lack or loss of love_____of illness or injury_____ of being deserted____$\checkmark$____of deprivation_____ of being overpowered and helpless____$\checkmark$____ of being devoured_____other_____		
8. Main defenses against conflicts and fears: ($\checkmark$) repression_____ reaction-formation_____ regression____$\checkmark$____ denial_____introjection_____ isolation_____ undoing_____ rationalization_____ other_withdrawal_ projective identification_____ splitting_____		
9. Adequacy of superego as manifested by "punishment" for "crime" being: ( ) appropriate_____ inappropriate_____ too severe (also indicated by immediacy of punishment)_$\checkmark$____ inconsistent_____ too lenient_____ also:_____ delayed initial response or pauses_____ stammer_____other manifestations of superego interference_____		
10. Integration of the ego, manifesting itself in: ($\checkmark$, $\checkmark\checkmark$, $\checkmark\checkmark\checkmark$) Hero: adequate_____inadequate_____ $\checkmark\checkmark\checkmark$ outcome: happy_____unhappy_____ realistic_____unrealistic_____ drive control_____ thought processes as revealed by plot being: ($\checkmark$, $\checkmark\checkmark$, $\checkmark\checkmark\checkmark$) stereotyped_____ original_____appropriate_____ complete_____ incomplete_____ inappropriate_____ syncretic_____ concrete_____ contaminated_____ Intelligence:_____ Maturation level_____		

2

Story No. 3	Story No. 4	Story No. 5	Story No. 6	Story No. 7	Story No. 8
Subject feels troubled by and unsuccessful in aggression toward small sibling			Night noises are troubling subject. Hopes expert will do away with trouble		Mother seen as coercive. Subject resents mother's pleasure. Angry feelings toward mother.
Adult, male lion			Very troubled child		Male child
To get rid of vermin					Manifest compliance
Worms, exterminator, traps, poison, jungle, Florida			Carpenter Noise Falling rocks		Explosion. Crooks.
Implying need for aggression, withdrawal, regression			One adult parent. Anxiety over night noise.		Father. Implying aggressive wishes toward mother and exclusion of father
			Wants something done about them		
Father seen as friendly and powerless					Mother seen as domineering, exhibitionistic
Between superego and aggression					Between superego and aggression
Of being ineffective, defenseless, and helpless			Anxiety at night concerning noises		
Resignation					Manifest compliance
			None		None
Realistic and unhappy			Realistic and unhappy		Wishful and unrealistic

Story No. 9	Story No. 10	SUMMARY
Aggression toward brother seen as dirty. Severe superego and intra-ggression		**1–3. Unconscious structure and drives of subject (based on variables 1–3)** Aggression is felt generally and specifically against mother and brother. Feels helpless against their annoyance, ridden by nocturnal anxiety especially, and rather guilty over his nearly murderous anger.
Male child		
Aggression. Intra-aggression		
Hunters, father, squirrels, dynamite		
Implying need for aggression		
		4. Conception of world: As dangerous, annoying. He is nearly helpless against it.
		5. Relationship to others: Father and therapist are seen as friends but rather helpless. Mother is seen as coercive braggart, and younger sibling as a nuisance.
Between superego and aggression		**6. Significant conflicts:** Between superego and aggression.
		7. Nature of anxieties: Of being coerced, annoyed, frightened at night.
Displacement Projection?		**8. Main defenses used:** Resignation. Displacement. Projection. Regression.
Severe		**9. Superego structure:** Inconsistent, too little and too severe.
		10. Integration and strength of ego: Not very well able to deal with aggression or the world around him.
Wishful, unhappy, unrealistic		

Ego function assessment from TAT data:

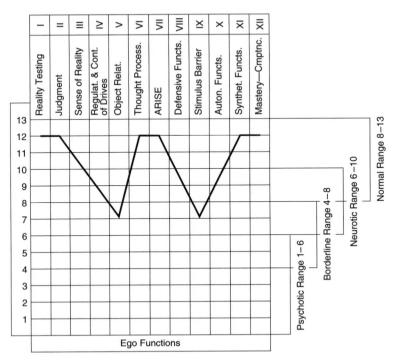

(From Bellak, Hurvich & Gediman, *Ego functions in schizophrenics, neu-rotics, and normals.* Copyright © 1973, by C. P. S., Inc. Reprinted by per-mission of John Wiley & Sons, Inc.)

Ego functions observed during test administration:

9. Strong need for aggression toward brother. Severe superego. Severe intra-aggression. Anal character?

10.

Story 3

Story 3: Well, this lion is troubled by mice, and he's sitting there and doesn't know what to do about the mice. He's tried everything, so he calls the exterminator, and the exterminator says, "The only thing to do is to blow the mice out." But the lion says, "I've tried that and lost three houses." "Why not make traps?" "But the mice have certain things that disconnect the traps and they always get the cheese." "Why not try poison, then?" "But that's impossible because the mice know it's poison and they'll never come out." Finally the lion decides he will move to Florida, but when he gets there he sees now . . . he's being troubled by worms coming through the floor. So finally he says, "I'll go back and live in the jungle where I belong."

Descriptive theme	Interpretive theme	Diagnostic level
A lion is troubled by mice; has tried everything;	If one is troubled by small things, and one tries in vain to be rid of them,	Subject feels troubled by small sibling. Feels unsuccessful in aggression toward sibling.
calls in an exterminator	one calls in powerful (lethal) helper	Subject tries to enlist help of someone, probably therapist, whose role he sees as helping do away with sibling.
who makes suggestions already tried and found useless and/or harmful to oneself.	who makes suggestions already found useless (because one is outsmarted) or harmful to oneself.	Therapist is considered useless. Sibling is seen as out-smarting subject. He sees his extra-aggression as boomerang.
Then the lion decides to move away.	Thereupon one moves to a new field	He attempts withdrawal (or other modes of behavior).
only to be troubled by worms,	only to be troubled by little things there too,	Finds these measures useless.
and finally returns to the jungle where he feels he belongs.	and finally regresses to more primitive conditions.	Regresses to more primitive forms of behavior.

Clinical Notes

In this story, the mice and the worms probably represent the younger sibling. The story is particularly interesting, since we can see elements of the transference relationship. This child sees his psychotherapist in the role of an exterminator (who should exterminate the brother as a way of helping the patient). Apparently, however, he is thus far dissatisfied with the psychotherapist, feeling that therapy does not offer him any better solutions than he had already tried; for instance, permitting himself some extra-aggression seems to have boomeranged. His return to the jungle implies not only regression but also withdrawal. Inasmuch as this withdrawal is the result of a difficult reality situation, we are probably justified in thinking of it as secondary withdrawal, more comparable to a phobic situation (rather than of a primary withdrawal of object cathexis, as is seen in narcissistic disorders). However, the indications are not quite clear, and skin conditions are frequently consistent with severely narcissistic disorders.

Story 6

Story 6: They're in the cave and they've been very disturbed by falling rock. And the bear goes to the bear carpenter and says, "Now you be sure no more rocks fall from my cave; my baby is very troubled." The bear carpenter comes and goes bang, bang, Later, he goes bang, bang every night. Finally the baby says, "This keeps me awake more than the falling rocks. Never mind."

Descriptive theme	*Interpretive theme*	*Diagnostic level*
Bears are in a cave and are disturbed by falling rock.	If one is troubled by falling rock noises in the night,	Night noises are troubling subject; primal scene disturbances?
Mamma bear asks bear carpenter to end this situation.	one enlists aid of carpenter	Subject hopes expert will do away with these troubles.
Bear makes noise himself.	who makes noises also,	Subject is disturbed by therapist
Baby is more disturbed by carpenter's noise (at night) than by falling rock	more troublesome than falling rock;	to a greater degree than by the primal noises,
and says, never mind.	one tells the carpenter to forget it— never mind helping.	and refuses help of therapist.

Clinical Notes

Here, we have a clear reference to noises in the night that are generally of a primal scene nature. The fact that the bear carpenter goes "bang, bang" confirms the nature of the disturbance and adds to it the possibility that the noises are inner ones of the subject's, as well as the usual environmental ones. The child is saying "The doctor disturbs me more than my family; I'll ask him to leave me alone after all." (The cure is worse than the disease.) We could then say about the therapy situation that the child is resisting because the treatment is too disturbing to him.

Story 8

Story 8: Well, mother monkey and baby monkey are having company. Grandma and uncle come, and there's a picture of grandma monkey hanging on the ceiling. Mamma monkey says, "Now mind your manners, child, we're going to have a lot of company today." And the child says, "All right." Grandma monkey says, "What a beautiful house you have." And the mother is a big bragger. She says, "Oh yes, I have a beautiful house, and you should see my kitchen. It's so nice; everything is so nice." Just then a few crooks who were outside blew up the house, and the mother never bragged again.

Descriptive theme	*Interpretive theme*	*Diagnostic level*
Mother and baby are having company; grandma and uncle.	If one is having company,	
Mamma monkey tells baby to behave and baby agrees.	mamma wants one to behave and one does.	Mother seen as coercive, child complies manifestly.
Grandma compliments mother on beauty of house and mamma brags.	Grandma compliments mamma on beauty of house, and mamma brags.	Subject resents mother's pleasure in house, considers her a braggart.
Crooks outside then blow up house,	Crooks blow up house,	Subject feels explosive anger in himself and wants to destroy mother's pleasure.
and mother never brags again.	and mother never brags again.	Angry feelings against mother.

Clinical Notes

This story again reflects the social level in the child's home. We have had glimpses on other occasions—the mention of Florida, and the ease with which this child procures paid professional help (the exterminator and the carpenter)—and now we get a realistic picture of the polite company manners observed in the home and the child's negative conception of his mother. The explosion already mentioned in story 3 again indicates the strong aggressive feelings bottled up in this child, here clearly directed to the mother.

On the one hand, we see a very strict superego which makes him comply manifestly; on the other hand, he permits himself rather vicious retribution when the house and, presumably, mother and the company (but perhaps himself too) are blown up. This is a good example of lack of integration of the superego constituting at the same time too much and too little control.

Story 9

Story 9: My brother likes rabbits but I hate them, and I like squirrels but he hates them. I'll make up a bad story about him—I hate him! Rabbits are very troublesome; they smell a lot. Well, a rabbit is lying in bed and papa rabbit says, "I've heard that hunters are on the trail." The baby says, "Well, I have a smart idea. Since those hunters like to hunt, we'll give them something to hunt." And the father says, "What?" And the baby says, "Fetch me a lot of pillows." And they draw a lot of rabbits and they look real, and in each rabbit is a piece of dynamite; so when the hunters come they shoot at the rabbit and those hunters flew into China and said, "I'm never going rabbit hunting again."

Descriptive theme	*Interpretive theme*	*Diagnostic level*
My brother likes rabbits but I hate them. I like squirrels but he hates them. I'll make up a bad story about him; I hate him.	Temperamental differences with brother.	Aggression toward brother.
Rabbits are a nuisance; they smell a lot.	Brother is a nuisance, smelly.	Aggression toward brother, seen as dirty.
There are hunters, and the child fools them and punishes them by putting dynamite into rabbit decoys, and the hunters are blown all the way to China when they try to shoot the rabbits. They say they'll never hunt rabbits again.	If one wants to kill, one is killed oneself.	Strong need for aggression. Severe superego. Severe intra-aggression.

Clinical Notes

This is a very complex story. At first, the difference in sentiments between the brothers and their dislike of each other is clearly set forth. The sentence, "I'll make up a bad story about him—I hate him" may either refer manifestly to the rabbit in the picture or to the brother, although dynamically there is probably no difference. Under the impact of his emotions, this story is less well structured in that there is a transition from the stimulus of a picture of a rabbit in bed to hunters. Apparently the direct expression of aggression against the brother is interfered with and instead of the real rabbit, he uses decoys. The next twist of the story brings about a switch of identification figures, where the hunters are being punished for their aggression. This is probably where the intra-aggression again appears; as in story 3, the aggressor himself gets into trouble and forswears aggression forever.

The complaint about the rabbits being not only troublesome but also smelling a lot may, on the one hand, refer to the younger brother's original lack of toilet training; on the other hand, preoccupation with smells may point toward an anal character structure in our patient.

Case 3[3]

Kenneth was 8 years and 5 months old at the time of testing, with an I.Q. of 89 on the Stanford-Binet. Entered in a parochial school before he was 5 years old, he proved to be so severe a behavior problem that the sisters refused to keep him. Things were no better in public school, where he proved to be an academic problem as well, in his inability to learn to read.

Kenneth is tall for his age, thin, and undernourished. He wears glasses. The mother appears to be a heavy, ignorant, placid woman who does not want her placidity disturbed. She apparently rejects Kenneth, preferring the younger child, a girl about 4 years old. The father, high-strung and unstable, expects his son to be perfect, and believes that perfection in children is attained by beating them. He also openly shows his preference for the younger child.

The boy's behavior at school is markedly aggressive; he has assaulted several children quite severely, stole from the girls' pocketbooks, removed articles from the teacher's desk, is constantly noisy and restless.

Kenneth does not come home for lunch as the other children do—his mother finds it too much trouble to fix lunch for him.

Kenneth loses bladder control by night or day and soils himself occasionally at school.

Summary
Record of Main Theme (Diagnostic) and Other Main Data

1. Mother seen as depriving children of basic needs, food (love). Patient feels unhappy. Mother seen as responding to crying. Subject feels especially deprived in relation to others (sister? mother?). Subject clearly identifies with deprived child in stimulus (chick minus bib).
2. Child and mother are aligned against father. Father doesn't quite manage (wishful?). Contest is between father and child alone? (Mother is no help or hindrance.) Subject finally feels defeated (without ever acknowledging that father wins; mother has a completely passive role in this story, but somewhat allied with child). Fear of being weak.

---

[3] We are indebted to Ms. Greta Freyd for permission to use this case and for the data on Kenneth.

3. Subject feels small and in danger. Fear of being devoured by father. Subject withdraws rapidly into small dark place; uses tricks for indirect aggression against father. Poor self-image.

4. Tremendous need for aggression towards mother, some of it possibly sexually fused (crashing into her). Tremendous hostility manifesting itself in destruction of objects, including food, which he probably identifies with mother. Urethral problems.

5. Fear of his own aggressive wishes and of aggression against him at night. Identifies mother with dirt, garbage. Strong oral-incorporative wishes and fears (if ghost is the father). Bizarre story. Nocturnal fears.

6. Again subject expresses oral incorporation and aggression, this time in the night. Aggression against sibling or self. Since mother has previously been described as a repulsive figure, one might assume she is the one now described. Father and mother seen as wanting to revenge themselves upon the evildoer and are poisoned by the bones, which are more powerful than they; that is, our subject is so inherently evil and omnipotent that he is able to kill the parents merely by contact. Sibling (or self) suffers same fate. Bizarre story.

7. Repetition of oral aggression and incorporation. Identity of hero not clear. Perserveration of theme to extent of leaving stimulus. Assumes garb of king (father), wanting to supplant him after vanquishing him, and going further to notions of grandeur.

8. Sees great-grandmother as a domineering figure. Sees mother as "telling on him" to father (and thereupon?) he goes to get supplies and makes himself useful. Feels forced into servitude. Matches suggest urethral complex.

9. Extreme aggression against the mother, the younger sibling, the father, and great intra-aggression. Ignores stimulus entirely in perseveration of intra-psychic stimuli concerned with aggression.

10. Sees mother as coercive, punishing. Regressive resistance and fear of bath. Intra-aggression (flight *into* tub). Identifies food and love. Associates food and bed. Running water shows urethral preoccupation.

Story 1

Story 1: She's going to eat the food up (pointing to big one), then the little ones won't have any. Then they're going to start crying. Then she's going to make some more . . . (*Prompted*). The mother will give him some food when it's cooked (pointing to chick without bib). (*Prompted*) . . . They all had their food already—all the others.

Descriptive theme	Interpretive theme	Diagnostic level
The mother will eat all the food, depriving the little ones.	If there is food, the mother eats it all up,	Mother seen as depriving children of basic needs, food (love).

SHORT FORM
BELLAK T.A.T. and C.A.T. BLANK
For Recording and Analyzing Thematic Apperception Test and Children's Apperception Test

Name _____ Kenneth _____ Sex _M_ Age _8.5_ Date _____

(circle one)

Education _____ Occupation _____ , m. s. w. d

Referred by_____ Analysis by _____

After having obtained the stories analyze each story by using the variables on the left of Page 2. Not every story will furnish information regarding each variable: the variables are presented as a frame of reference to help avoid overlooking some dimension.

When all ten stories have been analyzed it is easy to check each variable from left to right for all ten stories and record an integrated summary on page 4 under the appropriate headings. That way a final picture is obtained almost immediately.

Then, keeping Page 4 folded out, the Final Report: Diagnostic Impressions and Recommendations can be written on Page 1 by reference to Page 4. Page 5 gives available space for any other notations. The stories then can be stapled inside the blank against page 5.

FINAL REPORT: Diagnostic Impressions and Recommendations

These are stories of an exceedingly disturbed boy, as can be seen from the first story to the last. The themes deal throughout with deprivation and bizarre, diffuse, all-around hostility and destructiveness, particularly in stories 4 and 5. The hero as an identification figure is either a rat or a ghost, and the vile object of deadly aggression by incorporation (story 6). The father is seen as unremittingly aggressive, the mother mostly as depriving and punishing, as for instance in stories 1 and 10. The subject shows a great deal of hostility toward her when he specifies that she is put in the garbage pail head down in story 5 and has her head hurt repeatedly in story 4, as well as toward his baby sister.

The superego, though vicious in its intra-agression, as in stories 6 and 9, is also inconsistent. There is no evidence of any successful defenses.

Although some degree of magical thinking is not unusual in children of this age level, story 6, which deals with the poisoned bones which are able to kill merely by contact, transcends the bounds of expectancy for this age. The malevolence and omnipotence which this child ascribes to himself are distinctly pathological.

There are two suggestions in the stories that this child is probably enuritic: the matches which are introduced into story 8 and the running water in story 10.

In view of the general lack of structure of the stories, the lack of control and tendency to bizarreness, the oral features of devouring, being devoured, and going to sleep (Lewin's oral triad), it is very likely that this boy will develop into an adult psychotic with schizophrenic and manic depressive features.

	Story No. 1	Story No. 2
1. Main Theme: (<u>diagnostic level</u>: if descriptive and interpretative levels are desired, use a scratch sheet or page 5)	Mother seen as depriving children of basic needs and responding to crying.	Child and mother seen as aligned against father not powerful enough (wishful?). Subject finally feels defeated
2. Main hero: age _child_ sex _M_ vocation_____ abilities_____ interests_____ traits_____ body image_____ adequacy (√, √√,√√√) and/or self-image___rejected_	Child	Child
3. Main needs and drives of hero: a) behavioral needs of hero (as in story):_____ implying:_____	Food	falling down fear of weakness
b) figures, objects, or circumstances *introduced:*_____ implying need for or to:_____	Crying Appeal by crying	
c) figures, objects, or circumstances *omitted:*_____ implying need for or to:_____		
4. Conception of environment (world) as:_____	Depriving	Aggressive
5. a) **Parental figures** (m___, f___) are seen as _father, aggressive and_ and subject's reaction to a is_____mother depriving_	Mother seen as hostile, acquisitive and rejecting	father-aggressive mother-passive
b) **Contemp. figures** (m___, f___) are seen as____and punishing_ and subject's reaction to b is_____		
c) **Junior figures** (m___, f___) are seen as_____ and subject's reaction to c is_____		
6. Significant conflicts:_____	None	Between superego and aggression
7. Nature of anxieties: (√) of physical harm and/or punishment_____ of disapproval_____ of lack or loss of love_____of illness or injury_____ of being deserted_____of deprivation___√___ of being overpowered and helpless_____ of being devoured___√___other_____	Deprivation. Lack or loss of love.	
8. Main defenses against conflicts and fears: (√) repression_____reaction-formation_____ regression_____denial_____introjection_____ isolation_____undoing_____ rationalization_____other_____ projective identification_____splitting_____		
9. Adequacy of superego as manifested by "punishment" for "crime" being: ( ) appropriate_____inappropriate_____ too severe (also indicated by immediacy of punishment)___√___ inconsistent_____too lenient_____ also:_____ delayed initial response or pauses_____ stammer_____other manifestations of superego interference_____		
10. Integration of the ego, manifesting itself in: (√, √√, √√√) Hero: adequate_____inadequate___√√√ outcome: happy_____unhappy___√√√ realistic_____unrealistic___√√√ drive control_____ thought processes as revealed by plot being: (√, √√, √√√) stereotyped_____original_____appropriate_____ complete_____incomplete_____inappropriate_____ syncretic_____concrete_____contaminated_____ Intelligence:_____ Maturation level __low_	Happy, realistic, wishful	Realistic Unhappy

2

Story No. 3	Story No. 4	Story No. 5	Story No. 6	Story No. 7	Story No. 8
Subject feels small and in danger. Fear of being devoured by father. Withdraws rapidly into small dark place. Uses trucks for indirect aggression against father.	Tremendous need for aggression toward mother. Enuresis.	Fear of his own aggressive wishes and of aggression against him at night.	Oral incorporation and aggression in the night.	Oral incorporation and aggression. Wants to supplant king. Notions of grandeur.	Sees great-grandmother as domineering. Mother telling on him to father. Enuresis.
Rat	Child	Ghost		Monkey and lion	Child
For aggression	For aggression	Aggression			
Mouse seen as rat. Feels dirty, aggressive		Ghost, rats, garbage pail Preoccupation with dirt	Lion. Poisoned bones	People, clothes. King	Birthday cake matches lit candles
		Bizarreness	Fear of father. Fiery death. Tremendous aggression	Acquisition. Desire to be king.	Urethral complex
Depriving	Full of aggression	Devouring	Bizarre	Devouring	Oral
Father seen as aggressive and hostile			Father seen as hostile and powerful	Father seen as hostile, powerful, and aggressive	Mother seen as domineering, hostile, and untrustworthy
None					
Being devoured		Nocturnal fears	Being devoured, overpowered, and helpless	Being devoured, overpowered, and helpless	
	None	None		None	
Happy Wishful	Wishful	Wishful ✓✓✓ Bizarre ✓✓✓	Unhappy ✓✓✓ Bizarre ✓✓✓	Wishful ✓✓✓ Unrealistic ✓✓✓	Wishful Happy

3

Story No. 9	Story No. 10	SUMMARY
Extreme aggression against mother, father, and younger sibling and great intra-aggression	Sees mother as coercive. Fear of bath. Identifies food and love. Associates food and bed.	**1–3. Unconscious structure and drives of subject (based on variables 1–3)** Strong, primitive, oral, devouring needs, with generalized great and nearly bizarre aggression.
Ghost	Child	Urethral fixation (fire, water), with anal as well as acquisitive desires.
Aggression		
Cops, electric chair	Food, tub, running water	
Entire stimulus implying punishment perseveration of intra-psychic stimuli concerned with aggression	Implying oral needs. Urethral occupation	
Dangerous	Hostile	**4. Conception of world:** As depriving, dirty, hostile, dangerous, devouring
	Mother seen as aggressive and nurturant	**5. Relationship to others:** Full of wild aggression and afraid of theirs.
		6. Significant conflicts: Full of uncontrolled aggression.
Physical harm and punishment	Physical harm and punishment	**7. Nature of anxieties:** Some conflict over aggression.
Between superego and aggression	Between autonomy and compliance	**8. Main defenses used:** Inadequate defenses throughout.
	Too severe	**9. Superego structure:** Inadequate.
		10. Integration and strength of ego: Poor in nearly every respect.
Unhappy ✓✓✓ Unrealistic ✓✓✓	Happy ✓✓✓ Wishful ✓✓✓	

Ego function assessment from TAT data:

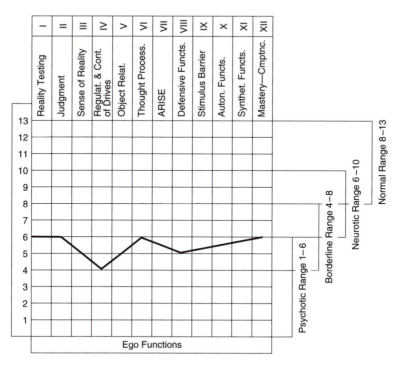

(From Bellak, Hurvich & Gediman, *Ego functions in schizophrenics, neurotics, and normals.* Copyright © 1973, by C. P. S., Inc. Reprinted by permission of John Wiley & Sons, Inc.)

Ego functions observed during test administration:

They will cry.	and children cry.	Patient feels unhappy.
She will relent and make more and give bibless chick food.	Mother relents and cooks more for one,	Mother seen as responding to crying.
All the others already had some.	the others having already received theirs.	Subject feels especially deprived in relation to others (sisters? mother?). Subject clearly identifies with deprived child in stimulus (chick minus bib).

Clinical Notes

The first story already suggests an atmosphere of deprivation and unhappiness, the subject feeling especially neglected.

Story 2

Story 2: The daddy bear is trying to pull the rope away from the mamma and the baby bear. The father bear wants to win, and the little one wants to win. The father pulls and pulls and can't get it away. So the baby is losing. (*Prompted*) . . . The baby will fall down. (*Prompted*) . . . The mamma will fall down too.

Descriptive theme	*Interpretive theme*	*Diagnostic level*
A papa bear is trying to take a rope away from the mamma and the baby.	If there is a contest between papa and mamma and baby,	Child and mother are aligned against father.
Father and baby are trying to win. Father can't succeed.	fathers tries but can't win.	Father seen as not powerful enough (wishful?).
Baby can't succeed. Baby loses.	Baby is losing.	Contest is between father and child alone? (mother is no help or hindrance).
Falls down, as does mamma.		Subject finally feels defeated (without ever acknowledging that father wins; Mother has a completely passive role in this story, but somewhat allied with child).

Clinical Notes

There are some inconsistencies in this story. The father cannot get the rope away, yet, in the next sentence, the subject states that the baby is losing.

Story 3

Story 3: (Sits up straight, big smug grin) The lion is waiting for the rat to come out of the hole so he can eat him up—eat him for his dinner. He's resting. The rat is coming out. The lion don't know the rat is coming out. (*Prompted*) . . . The lion will chase the rat, and the rat will run into the hole, and the lion will run into the wall and get a bump on his head (big smile).

Descriptive theme	Interpretive theme	Diagnostic level
A lion is biding his time awaiting the rat's emergence from his hole, whereupon	If one is small,	Subject feels small and in danger.
the lion intends to eat the rat for his dinner.	one is in danger of being eaten by big ones.	Fear of being devoured by father.
The rat outsmarts the lion,	One runs back into hole and escapes big ones.	Subject withdraws rapidly into small dark place,
and the lion is punished by a bump on the head from the wall of the rat's hole.	and the big one is hurt himself.	uses tricks for indirect aggression against father.

Clinical Notes

This story continues the struggle between the father and the boy. This time, the boy wishfully outwits the father. It must be considered significant that he identifies himself with a rat rather than the little mouse that is usually seen. The rat constitutes a more aggressive, more dangerous, and, at the same time, a socially much less acceptable, dirty self-image.

The theme of devouring is worth noting but may not be given too much pathological significance here since the stimulus tends to suggest this theme. However, we will see that the theme recurs in later stories in a much more clearly pathological form.

Story 4

Story 4: (Big smile at examiner) He's going to crash right into the mamma with his bike. The mamma will get hurt. Then he's going to run over her. The balloon will bust and he'll run over the milk and stuff and they'll spill all over the place. . . . Then she'll get up and run into the tree 'cause her hat's over her head and she can't see and she'll bump on her head again.

Descriptive theme	Interpretive theme	Diagnostic level
The boy will crash into the mother with his bike and hurt her, then run over her in addition; will break balloon, spill milk and food all over. Mother will run into tree because hat is blinding her and will bump her head again.	If one gets a chance, one hurts mother repeatedly; one also breaks and spills things.	Tremendous need for aggression toward mother, some of it possibly sexually fused (crashing into her). Tremendous hostility manifesting itself in destruction of objects, including food. Enuresis (spilled fluid).

Clinical Notes

Judging by the smile at the examiner, the subject feels happy at releasing aggression, of which he apparently cannot get enough. If this story is compared with the one told to the same picture in case 1, the severe pathology in the present case is dramatically revealed. The way he destroys the food suggests that the food itself is a frequent source of frustration, probably also identified with the mother.

Story 5

Story 5: The mamma bear is under the covers so she's afraid there might be a ghost around the house. The baby sticks its head out and screams. Then the rats came out under the bed and pushed the bed up near the window. The ghost puts its hand in and grabs the mamma bear and puts the mamma in the garbage pail, with her head first, and then the ghost takes the baby bears and takes them home and eats them. Then the ghost goes to bed—he's too full.

Descriptive theme	Interpretive theme	Diagnostic level
A mamma is under bed covers afraid of ghost around house. Baby is screaming in fear. Rats come out from under bed, are strong enough to push bed near window where	If one is in bed, there are rats and a ghost to threaten one.	Fear of his own aggressive wishes and of aggression him at night.
ghost can get at the mother and dispose of her in garbage pail, head first.	Rats and ghost put mother in garbage pail, head first.	Identifies mother with dirt, garbage.

Ghost eats babies, goes to bed too full.	Ghost eats babies, goes to bed full.	Strong oral-incorporative wishes and fears (if ghost is the father).

Clinical Notes

This must be considered a rather bizarre story even for an 8½-year-old boy. We seem to deal with multiple identification in this story, in that the rat in story 3 suggests that the rats in the present story who are so hostile to the mother also represent the subject. Probably the ghost is also an identification figure, further disguised for defensive displacement from consciousness.

The tremendous amount of hostility again becomes apparent in his refinement of detail, specifying, "with her head first." Probably the baby bears are here identified with the baby sister, if the ghost is our hero; but the possibility of another shift of identification, where the aggressor also becomes the victim, cannot be excluded. This story suggests an extreme of nocturnal anxiety, among other things, by a projection of his own aggressive impulses. Again, incorporation plays a clearly pathological role. This theme is illustrative of Bertram Lewin's (1950) oral triad: the wish to devour, to be devoured, and to sleep. This suggests that the subject is likely to develop a severe affective disorder of a manic-depressive nature. Hand in hand with the bizarreness of the story, one would be inclined to predict that this boy might well go on to an adult psychosis which may at first appear of a manic-depressive variety and later become a schizophrenic disorder with affective features (schizoaffective disorder.)

Story 6

Story 6: The baby bear's asleep in a cave and the lion's going to come in and eat him up. The lion came in and took the baby bear far away in the forest and ate him up and left the bones there. Then the lion came and took the other baby bear and took him to the forest and ate him up and left the bones there too. There's one there, asleep and fat. The father woke up and saw the two babies gone and he saw the bones walking around and he jumped on the bones and they died 'cause they were poison bones. Just the father and mother jumped. The bones came near the baby and he died and the bones died too. (*Note:* Questioning caused resentment, but examiner is certain that the "they died" referred to father and mother.)

Descriptive theme	*Interpretive theme*	*Diagnostic level*
A baby bear asleep in a cave is going to be eaten by a lion except for the bones.	If one is asleep, a lion comes and takes one away into forest and eats one, leaving only bones.	Again subject expresses oral incorporation and aggression, this time in the night.
The lion eats other baby bear in same way.	Lion returns for other baby, meting out same fate.	Sibling or self this time being devoured.

One figure is fat and asleep in cave.	One figure is asleep and fat.	Since mother has previously been described as a repulsive figure, one might assume she is the one now described.
Father awakens, sees bones walking around, jumps on bones.	Father awakens, perceives children missing and bones walking around, and wishes to destroy them—mother does this too.	Father and mother are seen as wanting to revenge themselves upon the evildoer,
Father and mother both jump (and die?) because bones are poison.		and are poisoned by the bones, which are more powerful than they, that is, our subject is so inherently evil and omnipotent that he is able to kill the parents merely by contact.
Bones approach baby, who also dies.	Bones approach baby, who also dies merely by the contact.	Sibling (or self) suffers same fate.

Clinical Notes

This must also be considered a rather bizarre story even for the subject's age level, in view of the fact that it is a very unusual story to this or any other C.A.T. picture and so little suggested in its details by the stimulus. In a continuation of the theme of oral incorporation, the father figure is again seen as orally aggressive, although the latter part of the story shows some defensive switching with the father in a somewhat protective role; at the same time, the father is a victim, as are the mother and the baby sister. Earlier in the story, our hero himself also has to die. In other words, we deal with an abundance and diffusion of hostility and aggression and intra-aggression.

The walking bones are probably the most bizarre feature of the story, the idea of poison occurring often enough in children without clear-cut or serious pathological implications, connoting fears of orally incorporating harmful objects related both to the mother's milk and fantasies of oral impregnation.

Story 7

Story 7: A lion is chasing a monkey and the monkey is climbing up the tree and the lion breaks down the tree. The monkey jumps to the next tree and the lion grabs him by the tail and eats him up and only the bones are left. Then the tiger goes to one of the houses and eats the people and takes the clothes and said (voice pitched high and dramatic), "I'm the greatest king in the whole jungle." The end.

Descriptive theme	Interpretive theme	Diagnostic level
A lion chasing a monkey catches him by the tail and eats him up.	If a lion chases a monkey, he catches him and eats him up.	Repetition of oral aggression and incorporation. Identity of hero not yet clear.
The lion (tiger) goes to a house and eats the people,	Lion (tiger) goes to a house and eats the people,	Perseveration of theme to extent of leaving the stimulus (introduces people not existing in picture).
and takes the clothes of a king who was there, puts them on, and proclaims himself the greatest king in the whole jungle.	takes the clothes of a king and puts them on, proclaiming himself the greatest king in the whole jungle.	Assumes the garb of the king (father), wanting to supplant him after vanquishing him, and going further to notions of grandeur in being the *greatest* king in the *whole* jungle (the usual phrase being king of the jungle).

Clinical Notes

Here, we see a further perseveration of the theme of eating up people (or animals) with a reference to remaining bones. Again, this is mainly directed against the father figure (king) and all father figures (greatest king) in the whole jungle— a wild and primitive place in which this boy seems really to be living. The references to bones, particularly as in story 6 (poisoned bones of malevolent power) is the kind of literal organic concept seen in the Rorschach and in Figure Drawing responses also, and consistent with psychosis.

Story 8

Story 8: They're having a party. The mother bear's grandma says, "You go get the lunch." He don't want to. The mamma tells secrets to the father about the baby and he don't like it. He got breakfast, dinner, and lunch and went out to get candles for the birthday cake. It was his birthday, and he got matches too and lighted the candles and blew them out. Then he cut the cake for the grandma, mother, and father. Then he ate and went to bed and the grandma went home and to bed.

Descriptive theme	Interpretive theme	Diagnostic level
There is a party and mother's grandma says, "Go get the lunch." He doesn't want to,	If there is a party, great-grandma asks him to get lunch. He doesn't want to.	Sees great-grandmother as a domineering figure.
but mother tells secrets to father about the baby and he doesn't like it.	But mother tells secrets to father which he doesn't like	Sees mother as "telling on him" to father;
He gets breakfast, dinner and lunch and goes to get candles for his birthday cake (and matches). Lights candles, blows them out, serves cake to grandma, mother, father. Eats some himself,	He gets a great deal to eat, there is fire,	(and thereupon?) he goes to get supplies and makes himself useful. Feels forced into servitude, into passivity. Enuresis (reference to fire).
goes to bed. Grandma goes home to bed.	and he goes to bed.	

Clinical Notes

This story appears extremely innocuous after the previous ones. The introduction of matches to light the candles suggests the possibility of a urethral complex, since fire, as well as water, has this diagnostic significance in T.A.T. and C.A.T. stories.

Story 9

Story 9: The mamma bear came out of bed and made supper for the baby. The baby's looking and the mamma's dead, and the ghost came in and killed the baby. The papa came in and saw it and he took a bottle out. The ghost saw it and shot the father. Then the cops came and saw it and sent the ghost to the electric chair.

Descriptive theme	Interpretive theme	Diagnostic level
Mother makes supper for the baby and dies,	If mother dies	Extreme aggression against the mother,
and a ghost comes and kills the baby	and the baby dies	the younger sibling,
and later the father.	and father dies,	and the father,
And then the cops kill the ghost.	the ghost dies.	and great intra-aggression.

Clinical Notes

This is a very disturbed story. It does not consider the stimulus at all, and diffuse, uncontrolled hostility abounds.

Story 10

Story 10: The little doggie don't want to get hit. He's crying 'cause he don't want to get in the tub. The mother sits down and hits and hits and he barks and barks. He starts to run away into the tub. He turns the water on and takes a bath and she'll pet him and give him dessert, breakfast, and dinner, and supper, and pet him and put him to bed.

Descriptive theme	*Interpretive theme*	*Diagnostic level*
A doggie doesn't want to get hit and is crying because he doesn't want to have a bath. Mother hits him and he barks (cries).	If one doesn't want to take a bath, one gets hit by mother, cries,	Sees mother as coercive, punishing. Reaggressive resistance and fear of bath. Water suggests urethral problems.
He runs away—into the tub and takes a bath	and runs into tub,	Intra-aggression (flight *into* tub).
and is rewarded by being given a great deal of food and being personally put to bed by her.	and is rewarded by much food and personal attention (again, the very meaning of love to him).	Identifies food and love. Associates food and bed.

Clinical Notes

In this story, the hostile and fearful relationship between mother and child clearly emerges. Remarkable is his running *into* the tub. Food obviously plays a tremendous role in gratification. While it is only reasonable to point out that children generally go to bed after having eaten, the frequent association of the two in this subject's stories suggests that it is also part of the oral triad.

Postscript to Case 3

Kenneth was never known to either of the authors. The C.A.T. record and other information printed verbatim above was kindly made available by Miss Freyd, when she took a course in the C.A.T. As an afterthought, having brought the rest of this book up to date, it occurred to us to try to check on the dire prognosis, so we got in touch with Ms. Freyd. It is due to her strenuous efforts to trace this boy's subsequent career that the following tragic history can be made available.

Kenneth moved from his hometown. After a few years, a social worker from the new domicile requested information on him because at about age 13, he assaulted his sister sexually, threatened to kill her if she told anyone, and, when discovered in the act by his mother at one time, almost strangled the mother. The father, who previously had told the school's social worker to mind her own business, that he knew how to handle the boy, then told the social worker she should take care of him—"he is all yours."

Ken was then sent to a state school. He ran away several times. At some later time, according to a relative, he seemed to adjust better for several years, worked, got married, and had a daughter. After about three years of marriage, he met another young woman who became pregnant by him. Meeting her in a park near his childhood home, he strangled her to death. He was executed at age 28, just about 20 years after taking the test reported here.

The C.A.T. report that he was an exceedingly disturbed boy was hardly overstated. Extreme aggression and hostility are noted throughout. The report failed to predict overt mayhem, though the fact was obvious from the behavioral report. What the C.A.T. supplies is the bizarreness of the aggression and the general severe pathology. It has been impossible to obtain institutional records to ascertain whether a psychosis was diagnosed at any point. The crime Ken was executed for certainly sounds like a direct repetition of his earlier tendencies to choke someone to death, and most likely was the result of sudden loss of control rather than premeditation. This makes the sentence a puzzling one. It is unlikely that any amount of therapy at that late date would really have made him a safe person to have around, but at the same time it is very unlikely that he could have been a person of sound mind who was aware of the consequences of his act while engaged in it. It is probably a reflection on the nature of our criminal justice that this man was executed rather than hospitalized.

This whole story underlines points made elsewhere (Bellak & Barton, 1969): Not only is it necessary to screen children psychologically at school entrance, but one must have the legal right to insist on treatment, removal from a pathological home, and/or treatment of the parents, if necessary without their voluntary consent. Like the mother of Lee Harvey Oswald, the boy's father rejected professional help until it was clearly too late. Society can ill afford the burden of criminal psychosis, nor is it fair to innocent children to insist on their parents' right to mistreat and cripple them.

Further Examples

Here, we present a number of parts of more sample records to illustrate a variety of responses to the C.A.T. They are not particularly selected for success, but rather in order to show difficulties and subtleties of interpretation.

Case 1

S. Q., aged 3 years, 11 months, male, African American, poor socioeconomic situation. Subject was easily approached in nursery with an offer to help him dress for out-of-doors period. Later brought cut cheek to be cared for and accepted offer to play game (C.A.T.). Seemed a little indecisive about going out or coming with examiner. Short period observed in outdoor playground showed him to feel ill at ease, although not shy. Three stories of his record will be presented.

Picture 2: Bear, kitty cat, and rope man . . . A big, big bear . . . and he gets *so big*. (*What is he doing?*) He came to visit the people.

Picture 3: A pipe man that lives in the house. He's taking his clothes off. (*Why?*) Because he has no clothes. He threw all his clothes away. He don't want no clothes. (singsong). No pants, no socks, no shoes. (*What does he want?*) He wants to have a lot of hair around him. (*What's he doing?*) He's sitting in a dirty chair with no clothes on.

Picture 9: Bunny rabbit. You see this bunny? He's in his bed. And the other bunny rabbit is way upstairs. He took the stuff and come home and said he may put another bunny up the house. He ran upstairs and come right back down (*singsong*) and the father bear come out from the basement (dark left corner) and saw a rabbit—run upstairs—got upstairs to your bed!

Story 2 is certainly a very meager one. All that attracts attention is, "the big bear who got so big"—which by itself surely barely deserves any speculation. Story 3, however, demonstrates repeatedly that the subject rejects the clothing, wants to "sit in a dirty chair with no clothes on." This would indicate a wish to regress to an earlier stage. Still, we have no idea why. Then, in picture 9, the most manifest clue is contained in the fact that the bunny "may put another bunny up the house." This definitely sounds as though the subject is preoccupied with another baby coming into the house. Those psychoanalytically trained will be able to see a symbolic restatement of this thought in the running upstairs and the father bear coming out from the basement coupled with an apparent memory of being told to go to bed perhaps in connection with some sexual activity. Our assumption now may find some corroboration in the brief reference in story 2, "the big bear who got so big," which may refer to the mother's pregnancy. Then we can understand his regressive pattern in story 3 in relation to the arrival of the rival. These were the conclusions we arrived at on blind analysis of these stories.

A check with data from the social worker showed that it was not actually a sibling, but a little cousin that had arrived in the home. Since the aunt and the rival (her son) lived in the same household with the subject, the psychological significance was the same. The kindergarten teacher was replete with confirmation of the subject's behavioral problems. We had occasion to consider further the subject's statement that the hero "wants to have a lot of hair around him." The interference one could make is that he has compared himself to the father and wants to have hair on the chest and in the pubic area also. Outstanding among the behavioral problems as reported by the teacher was the fact that the subject explored his little girl playmates with a great deal of interest.

This record can serve as an example of relatively poor returns in a small child wherein each story by itself is quite disappointing unless and until one can bring each story in meaningful relation to the others. Nevertheless, the usefulness of the C.A.T., in this case, becomes quite clear. The teacher and social worker knew that he was a behavioral problem with excessive sexual interest in little girls. Our test relates his behavioral difficulties to rivalry with a sibling-like figure, and a preoccupation with procreation. Having established these relationships, it should be relatively simple to discuss this with the child apropos of his stories: that he must be angry about the new arrival; must wonder where babies come from; and so on. At the same time, the social worker might attempt to decrease his sexual stimulation by whatever means the circumstances might permit, and instruct the mother about handling him.

Case 2

K. S., aged 6 years, 4 months, female, white, upper middle-class socioeconomic situation. We are presenting only the response to picture 3. In this, the lion becomes the father figure for this very bright girl, and the oedipal situation is clearly revealed.

This will be a good one. King Lion, that's what I'll call it. Now, I guess I'll make a name for these, O.K.? There was a lion and he said to the king: "I have heard your stories and I hear you are very tired and you are looking for another lion to put in your place." This I don't want you to write—I just want to tell you (to examiner). You see, the other lion was the king of all the lions and was getting tired, so he said to the other lion, "If you will do all these hard tasks, if you can do them all, you will become king. The first task is that you must go and find a princess—a queen—no, a princess, to marry. If you don't find one who will be right for you—off with your head." "Ah!" thought this lion, "if I could only find my dear, dear daughter." Because he was a king of the lions also, but he never mentioned it, see. "Now, I can go and look for my daughter." This I just want to tell you, but don't write it.

The story was then considered finished but the subject took it up again, later:

Now I don't want you to write this one, I just want to tell you about it. The king wanted to find his daughter. He had sent her out to seek the world and so he called her up at the first place she was supposed to be and they told him she had left. Then he called at the second place she was supposed to be and she wasn't their either. So he called her at the third hotel and they got her on the phone and she said she would be right there—in four minutes and they were married and then they played a joke on the other king. You know, this king was really the king of lions but hadn't told anyone. So now they went before the other king and he said, "What are you doing here? Get out of here!" But they said they were married and that this king was the real king; so the other king had to go away.

Unabashed by cultural taboos as yet, the king (father) marries his daughter though some of the story becomes quite confused. There is clear evidence of identification—switching, as well. There is some subliminal awareness of the forbiddenness of it all in the fact that the little girl asks the examiner not to write the story down.[4] Aside from the dynamic aspects, the concreteness and specificity of the childish thought processes deserve note: "*in four minutes* and they were married."

---

[4] Investigation revealed beyond doubt that this little girl was in marked conflict and rivalry with her mother.

Case 3

M. I., aged 10 years, 4 months, white male, poor socioeconomic situation. We are presenting the following story to picture 3 to demonstrate how extensive and rife with material a response may be.

Once upon a time there was a lion who lived in the forest. He was very mad and he didn't like anybody but himself, and he was very proud of himself and he didn't like no one but himself, and everyone was afraid of him because he was very strong and he could break anything, like trees that were 60 or 70 feet high and three feet thick, and he just pushed them like rope and they were nothing. One day, he thought that he was going to hypnotize all the people and animals so that he could rule over them. First, he went to one of the homes of the fox and he looked at them and looked at them until they were hypnotized and the whole family came running to him. Then he went to the chipmunks' place; he hypnotized their whole family and all the chipmunks that were around. He lived in a great big home and he had everything he wanted. After he hypnotized everybody and he had a great big chair and a nice pipe and he had a storage room full of tobacco and he had a dungeon and he had another one full of canes; but there was one thing he didn't have—he didn't have a beautiful body. He wanted to have yellow hair—yellow and brown together, blue eyes and his hair combed out nice and straight. He wanted all of his things shiny and he didn't have enough people to polish his canes and things. The next day he went into the forest again and he didn't see anyone, so he kept walking until he came to a big city and he did not see anyone there because it was dark, not even a light was shining, so he kept on walking until he came to a big, big castle. He was very jealous of it because it had a great big steeple and on the top was a great big diamond that he wanted and there was also a great big courtyard; on the other end was another part of the castle that had three steeples, a big courtyard; on the other end was another part of the castle that had three steeples; a great big one in the middle and a smaller one on each side and they all had diamonds on them; and on the door there was a big ruby and the other door on the other side had one, too—a blue ruby and he was so jealous that he was running around in circles. And he roared very loud and it reflected on all the building around and it hit him in his ears and he got quiet because it hurt him. He had never known how strong his voice was. Then he was sneaking up into the castle, then he got near the door and he saw a bell and he didn't know what it was, so he pressed it and it made so much noise it scared him; then a little while no one answered it. so he saw the door knob and he opened it and saw that it was pitch black, so he was walking around in circles and finally he hit something—so he fell down, and found it was a door, so he opened it and found there was a bed with a beautiful princess on the bed and he saw it and he didn't like to see her having a good time when he wasn't, so he went over and gulped her down in one mouthful and after he was walking and when he got back to his castle he felt very funny. So he sat down and was thinking and got very mad at himself cause it was the girl—she was a very good girl and she loved everybody—and he went over to his place where he had lots and lots of food; so he got chickens, pigs (animals that were already killed) all food that the animals liked and then he went to another room and got wood. Then he was getting all the wood and food and everybody was watching him—even the mouse in the house. Then he went in another storage and he got tons and tons of cheese and made a big hole and the mouse made his home in the cheese. He was very hungry cause he was very thin and by the time he finished he couldn't get back in his hole. Then the lion went outside and gave everyone everything and he was very happy. The next day everyone liked him but he still didn't like himself because he forgot to unhypnotize beavers so he went over and unhypnotized the beavers and everybody liked him.

M. I. identifies himself with the lion in a story that is apparently to a large extent a wish-fulfilling fantasy. Frequently, however, self-criticism and awareness of self-deficiency stand side by side, with overcompensation. "He didn't like anybody but himself and he was very proud of himself and everybody was afraid of him and he could break anything like . . ." Then, after equipping himself with a beautiful home and a nice pipe, he suddenly shows us that he feels his body is inadequate. This is followed by a symbolic story of jealousy of a "great, big steeple" . . . "with two smaller ones on each side," probably a symbolic representation of a big genital. Subsequently, he finds a beautiful princess in bed. He then gives us a perfectly primitive oral fantasy of acquisition (probably of the mother): "he gulps the princess down in one mouthful." Having committed this crime, he shows his conscience (superego) as a form of reaction formation to his drives. He procures tons of food for all the animals including the mouse and "gave everyone everything . . . then he was very happy." In the course of this story, he makes certain, in a parenthetical remark, that all the chickens and pigs, which he is now feeding to the other animals, were already dead. That is, he lets us know that he did not commit any further killing. Later, he finds the reward for renunciation of his acquisitive and aggressive drives in being liked by everyone, that is, we clearly find a picture of socialization. He still disapproves of himself until he recalls and undoes his earliest act and unhypnotizes the beavers.

This is the story of an apparently fairly disturbed child who feels that his body is inadequate, who has strong acquisitive and aggressive drives that he considers very evil, and who is developing an excessive superego to deal with these drives. The severity of the disorder and the full extent of it became clearer in a number of other stories not reproduced here. Examination of the reality situation revealed that this child lived in a very disturbed home, the father having deserted, and the mother being suspected of gross promiscuity. The boy actually was physically undersized and frequently did not have enough to eat. This latter information highlights his (the lion's) dissatisfaction with his body and his great need for acquisition and oral incorporation.

This story and several others of this subject show an excellent vocabulary, and an organizing ability consistent with intelligence considerably higher than average. The C.A.T. proves most helpful in this respect since formal intelligence testing has resulted in an I.Q. of only 103. The C.A.T. shows us that his true intellectual level must be considerably higher and that probably the emotional disturbance of this child is responsible for his poor functioning.

Special Clinical Problems

Here, we present a few highlights of special problems.

The following stories[5] are those of a boy of 7 years, 11 months, whose mother has been separated from his father since the boy was 4 years old. He was referred for consultation because he never defended himself when attacked by other children. He frequently asked his mother to get married and wants her to have a baby.

His first story is an excellent illustration of his pregnancy fantasies concern-

---

[5] We are indebted to Dr. C. Lealtad for permission to reproduce these stories.

ing oral incorporation and birth from the stomach by bursting. Also apparent is a fear of being devoured.

Story 1: Once upon a time there were three little chickens. All of a sudden they saw a ghost rooster. All got scared. The ghost rooster said, "I want to eat you," and they all threw their mush in his face and the rooster threw the bowls back at them, and they ran and called the papa rooster. And the ghost said, "I'd like to eat you." "Gobble, gobble, gobble," said the turkey. "I'll eat you, ghost rooster," and he chopped off his head. And the ghost turned into a man and he turned on the chickens and said, "Ah, nice chickens to eat," and they chopped off the man's head and he turned into a chicken and ate the mush until it was all gone and mush went into his stomach and came out through his eyes, and he ate more mush and more mush from the bowl but the bowl was magic and mush bowl kept giving more mush. Suddenly it gave sugar and more sugar, then fruit and fruit and fruit, and he ate it all and ate and ate and ate. And suddenly his stomach popped and he changed into a prince.

Story 3 shows a repetition of the theme in the eating of the tail and the cane. It also illustrates his preoccupation with the role of the phallus and castration.

Story 3: Once there was a lion, and he was king of the lions. "I'm getting so old a mouse could eat me up—guess I'll smoke my pipe." A little mouse was looking and he said, "Guess I'll try it," and he sneaked up and began eating a little of his tail and a little of his mane. But it was tough. And then he came up and tried eating a little of his cane and the cane popped. And the old lion sent for other lions to get the mouse, and another cane. But the mouse ran into the hole and one lion ran after him and ran in flat and his nose came out of the hole square. And the mouse said, "Hee, hee, hee," saw he had a new cane, and he gnawed and gnawed and gnawed and tried and tried and tried, but this cane was steel and he could only make teeth marks. And the lion walked and walked and walked and met an old man, and he said, "May I have your cane?" And took his cane. And then he met a bachelor, and he said, "May I have your pipe?" And the lion said, "Yes, you may. I can get another." And then he walked and walked and walked to the barber shop. And the barber said, "Can I have your mane to make wigs?" And he said, "Sure, cut all you want—I can grow more hair." Barber then cut mane and the mane grew and grew and grew and he stepped on his mane and tripped and fell and then the mouse killed him.

Story 5 explicitly reveals this child's pregnancy fantasies when he says that the stomach got so high and then burst open. The wish for the baby is actually expressed here.

Story 5: There was a little baby and father and mother and a crib with one baby. Every night they sat down and said a prayer, "How we wish we had two babies." And said maybe at Christmas maybe we'll get a baby. One night they looked in and saw two babies. "Oh, it must be a magic cradle. Oh, no. Make another wish for a flounder." The husband caught a giant flounder and opened him and ate him. "Here's another giant flounder—maybe the babies would like to eat it themselves." The babies' stomach almost burst—stomach growled. Stomach got so high, couldn't get the cover over them. "Oh, I don't know what I should do." The stomach weighed over fifty pounds—then bang! There was lots of noise and the stomach burst open and the mother and father fell in and said. "What is this—a firecracker?" Other baby's stomach went up and stomach opened and it died. Maybe if we eat flounder and ate and ate and ate and ate—then they fell flat and everything goes BOOM and everything splits—even the earth split.

Story 6 repeats the theme, showing that any part of the body can be used in pregnancy fantasies—in this case, the nose, whereas it is the mouth in story 7.

Story 6: Once there were two bears and they slept all day and all night, and if they hear of work they say. "We'll do it tomorrow." Would you like to eat tomorrow? Then they got hungrier and hungrier. Then they ate dirt. "Oh, what can we eat? Poison ivy?" Then they began scratching. Then papa bear said. "I know what to eat, honey from the pear tree." But there were bees and hornets who stung him, and he said. "Ouch!" And his nose got bigger and bigger and finally his nose broke open. Then two bulls came running out and ran into his stomach and there was noise louder than an atom bomb and he died. And he shouldn't have said, "We'll do it tomorrow."

Story 7: Once there was a tiger and he ate everything in sight—lucky his paws were not in sight. Tarzan ran into the tree and a cheetah ran behind him. Tarzan jumped on him and the tiger said, "Try to kill me." Tarzan said, "I will. Don't eat everything in sight." The tiger ran to eat a tree one day and the tree fell and honey ran out. And the bees swooped into his mouth and into his stomach and the tiger tried to roar but all he could say was a buzzing sound from the bees. He got Tarzan to open his stomach but the lion fell dead. Tarzan saw him alive again and he said, "I'll never eat a person again, only honey." But he had not learned his lesson from the bees. So he reached for honey and the bee said, "I'll sting." The tiger screamed and fell back and the monkey tickled him in the stomach. The bees took the honey back but the tiger growled and the bees came down but ran back because they did not like to be in the tiger's stomach. Then the queen bee said, "I'll show him my beauty." She came down but the tiger ate her. Then the whole squad swarmed into his mouth and he chewed them. Then a big hornet came in and stung him on the tongue but his fangs chewed him. But one day the tiger ate poison ivy and died.

Story 7 also shows suggestions that the child takes the passive role ("Try to kill me"), that he has tremendous incorporative needs; he is invariably being visually overstimulated (the queen bee showing her beauty, and the tickling).

The next case, a 5-year-old boy,[6] was actually referred to a medical clinic for chronic constipation for which he had been receiving enemas, laxatives, and an emphasis on eating foods that would promote intestinal activity. When the physical findings were entirely negative, he was referred to the Mental Hygiene Clinic.

The C.A.T. stories show that the child is concerned with fantasies of pregnancy—that is, conception and delivery. He is afraid that dangerous, explosive poisons get into him in stories 1 and 8, although the rabbit in story 9 and the mouse in stories 3 and 6 are also being eaten. The monkey in story 7 and the puppy in story 10 are also being devoured. On the other hand, the open window in stories 9 and 10 is connected with danger, suggesting that this little boy associates body openings with the entrance of danger. Story 1 also suggests that bowel movements are associated with exploding—probably a fantasy of giving birth by explosion.

The constipation started two and one-half to three years before, at a time when his mother had been pregnant with a baby girl who died a few weeks after birth. It seems likely that medical help for the constipation was precipitated by an exacerbation of his condition, since at the time of his examination another baby sister was born. The patient shared his parents' bedroom at the time of both pregnancies.

A recent dream that the boy related was as follows: "I was in a car and it drove over the side into the river. My daddy was driving us across the bridge and my mommy and I were sitting in the back seat. It crashed into the water." This dream

---

[6] We are indebted to Miss J. Schoelkopf for permission to reproduce these stories.

also suggests a concern with the parental relations and injury that might come to him as well as to his mother.

While playing after the administration of the C.A.T., he devoted himself to loading and piling blocks into trucks which he hauled across the floor, unloaded and piled up again, making such statements as, "Boy, I sure have got a heavy load this time!" This play too suggests the concern with carrying a burden with which he probably equates both pregnancy and feces inside him.

Story 1: What is they eating—poison. They would eat poison and they'd explode. Their heads would bust on the ceiling. (*What's that?*) It's a big old rooster standing and talking. (*Where did the poison come from?*) They bought the poison and thought it was cereal.

Story 2: I know what's going to happen. The rope's gonna break and they're gonna go ker-plonk on their seats. The little bear will go ker-plonk and the daddy'll fall on the baby. The mommy will fall on her seat. It's the mommy's rope and she doesn't want the daddy to pull on it.

Story 3: I know what's gonna happen. The mouse is going to come out of the hole. The lion is gonna eat the mouse. The lion is smoking a cigar with a cane. He should be smoking a pipe. (*Why did the mouse come out?*) Mouse doesn't know lion is there!

Story 4: I know what's gonna happen. The little mouse is going to run right under the kangaroo's legs and knock the mother down. She's carrying the purse, baby, and basket. He wants to get the baby out of there so he knocks her out and gets in.

Story 5: Where's the baby? Where's the mommy and daddy? Where's their beds? Something must have happened. He threw the baby and mommy and daddy out and then he had the whole house to himself.

Story 6: I know what's gonna happen. Mouse (baby bear) is sleeping in big bear's cage. In the morning the bears will see the mouse and eat him up.

Story 7: I know what this is gonna be: Lion is going to eat the monkey because the monkey's dropping from the trees. The lion doesn't like the monkey because monkeys eat lion's dads up. Baby tiger is gonna get the monkey.

Story 8: I know what's gonna happen. They're drinking poison. They think it's coffee. It's the mommy and daddy. Relation and little boy are talking. (*Who put the poison in?*) Cowboy didn't like monkeys eating up lion dads.

Story 9: I know what's gonna happen. If the lion came in the rabbit will get eaten up. The window is open (*What does the rabbit dream?*) He dreams he's upside down; then the lion can't get him.

Story 10: Nothing's gonna happen! (emphatically). (*It looks like something is happening.*) There's a window open and if the lions come, they will eat up the puppy. (*What's happening right now?*) Dog petting little dog because he likes him.

Illustration of Longitudinal Clinical Data[7]

Following are shown, side by side, the responses of a boy who at the time of first testing was 6 years, 10 months, and at the time of the second testing was 8 years, 5 months. Timothy was originally referred to the school psychologist because he was extremely immature, showed off constantly, wanted to be different and get attention, pushed other children, and was frequently inattentive. At the time of first

[7] From L. Bellak and C. Adelman, the Children's Apperception Test (CAT). In A. I. Rabin and M. R. Haworth (Eds.): *Projective Techniques with Children*. New York, Grune & Stratton, 1960.

testing, his Stanford-Binet I.Q. was 124. The reason for the second test was that he created classroom disturbance; he didn't conform, hit other children, and looked unhappy. The teacher thought he probably had an I.Q. of about 140.

Stories

Age 6 years, 10 months
1. What are these, chickens? This chicken was eating badly and spilling and making work for the big chicken, and the big chicken has to spank them and send them back to their grandfather.

Age 8 years, 5 months
1. I wonder what it is. I know! The hen and the naughty little people, when the fox fell in the river! There were three and they were bad and they didn't want to help and they spilled crumbs.

And one day the fox came and ate the mother hen up, and then he fell asleep and they put rocks in him and he drowned. (*Mother hen was out when they put rocks in?*) Which would you rather have, four days of rain, fog, or snow? (*Which would you?*) Snow, then we could have snowball fights. Which would you rather have, three days hot or three days of cold? (*You*) Cold because I don't like short-sleeved shirts (*Want to look at the next one?*) O.K.

3. You wouldn't be able to get near that, would you? Would he eat a mouse? (*Do you think so?*) Yes, I think so, but I don't know if the lion will find him or not. He's waiting for someone to come along that isn't looking what he's doing and he'll eat him.

3. (Timothy voluntarily picked up card 3, looked at it and said:) No, I don't want that; I feel like scaling it out of the window. A lion pooing on his chair. Somebody stole something of his and he was thinking what to do, and there was a little mouse there and he bit his tail and the lion put dynamite in the hole and blew him up. Which would you rather have, calm or a hurricane? (*Calm, and you?*) I don't know, hurricane, maybe.

5. I guess it's the nighttime and someone must be away and it's just getting black and I don't know what this is. I'll call this smoke, and there is a fire outside and when they come back they find their house is all burned down. That would make you cry, wouldn't it?

5. The mother bear and the daddy bear were out and two little bears came in and slept in this crib. And it was dark and father came home it was dark and ran out the back door and when mother and father, came home it was dark and they didn't know what was wrong and they never found 'em. Now, I have 32–38, here comes the kind of flag you have for 39–46. I like a fast wind

6. What is those, those swimming? Oh, a bear in his cave and the baby bear is with him. What eats bears, can you think of anything? (*Can you?*) No.

that blows trees down, do you? (*Not very much.*) (Timothy picked up the next card.)

6. What's this! There's three bears and they have no house and they slept in a cave, and one night someone put some mud over it and when they woke up they had to claw their way out. And the next night the same thing happened, and the next night the little bear didn't go to sleep he saw a man there. And the next day he told his mother and daddy and that night they ate the man up. 65, next is, no, 55–65, no that isn't right. I'm the best in numbers in my class. (Timothy continued to write and say aloud, wind speeds to above 75.) Which would you rather have, above 75 with 10 below zero and cloud, or 8 to 12 with 70 and clear? (*I'll take 10 below.*) Once it was zero and I ran all around, I am just about done, now I want to play a game with you.

Brief Analysis

In both card 1 stories, the children eat badly, are naughty, and antagonize the big chicken, who punishes them and sends them away. In the second testing, an aggressive animal is introduced, a fox, who eats up the mother and is, in turn, drowned for his misdeeds, whereupon the child reverts to an obsessive preoccupation with the weather, which went on all through the testing. In the story to card 3, in the first session, he is anxiously concerned with the idea that one has to be careful or else one is devoured. In the second session, he wants to do away with the card altogether by scaling it out the window. There is much more evidence of violence and anal regression here, with the lion "pooing" on his chair. The aggressive orality now relates specifically to the castrating notion of biting off the tail. There is also the suggestive evidence of explosive emotional tension in connection with the dynamite and the wish for a hurricane. In story 5, in the first testing, the reference to smoke and fire suggest a great deal of aggressive urethral sexual preoccupation, as does the reference to crying. This would be most suggestive of a history of enuresis (which we were unable to check on) but is certainly consistent with the aggressive behavior, including the aggressive need to show off. The second testing gives a much less clear-cut story, except that the little bears run out when the parents come home and are never discovered. This is followed by some reference to figures and the discussion again of violent weather, in this case a fast wind. Story 6 in the first session introduces water, supporting the notion expressed in story 5, and again a preoccupation with oral incorporation. Story 6 in the second session has to do with being walled up with mud and watchful nighttime observations. This is suggestive of insomnia, perhaps associated with oral incorporation fantasies, and then comes the preoccupation with numbers, windspeeds, and the weather—his restlessness is also indicated by the reference to running.

An examination of test material suggests not only the marked pathology consistent with the clinical report of aggression and showing off but also that the process is worsening. Judging by the leaving of the stimulus, the inappropriate material, and very poor drive control, this boy is probably on the way towards a psychotic condition. Obsessive preoccupation and acting out have so far served as brakes on the ego disintegration. A school psychiatrist who saw the child suspected that he might be schizophrenic.

CHAPTER 17

A SUPPLEMENT TO
THE C.A.T.[1]

Purpose of the C.A.T.-S.

The C.A.T. Supplement (C.A.T.-S.) was designed to supply pictures that might illuminate situations not *necessarily pertaining to universal problems,* but that occur often enough to make it desirable to learn more about them as they exist in a good many children.

Ten pictures have been designed (see Figure 17–1), any single one of which may be presented to children *in addition* to the regular C.A.T. For instance, C.A.T.-S. picture 5 may be given to children with a temporary or permanent physical disability or with a history of disability. It might permit one to learn about the psychological effects of this somatic problem upon the specific child. Or children with any kind of psychosomatic disorder or hypochondriasis might project these onto the stimulus. Picture 10 may permit us to learn what fantasies a boy or girl may have about the mother's pregnancy. If, for example, a child is brought to a clinic with a number of behavioral problems, and the history shows that the mother is currently pregnant or has delivered relatively recently, then this picture may permit one to learn about the possible relationship between the behavior problems and the fantasies concerning the family event.

In short, the C.A.T.-S. may be used in specific situations for the purpose of eliciting specific themes—as seem indicated (and as discussed below).

A further use of the C.A.T.-S. may lie in its usefulness as material for play techniques. Even though establishing proper rapport will obtain longer and better stories from children than the beginner is likely to think, there remain children severely enough disturbed to be unable to relate stories. For such subjects it may be expedient to make all the pictures of the C.A.T.-S. available at once, upon a table (arranged from 1 to 10, in three rows, the last row having 4 pictures), and to let them see them, handle them, arrange, and talk about them as they will. All of the child's remarks and behavior should be carefully recorded. Also, such use of the pictures may encourage storytelling in children less able to comply immediately with instructions. It should be mentioned, however, that this

---

[1] This material was presented as a paper at the 1953 Annual Meeting of the American Orthopsychiatric Association in Atlantic City, N.J., and is published here independently with the permission of the Editors of the *American Journal of Orthopsychiatry.* We are indebted to L.J. Stone, Professor of Child Study at Vassar College, and C. Fear for supplying data for the CAT-S.

Figure 17–1.   Pictures for Use with the C.A.T.-S.

method is not the most desirable procedure if the stories can be obtained in the regular manner.

By such means one may derive material less reliable for inferences than the regular stories, but more reliable than usual play situations permit; at least we know something empirically about these pictures and will have some norms concerning responses to them. Thus, we may be able to make clinical inferences with some semblance of experimental validity.

For the purpose of adapting to this kind of play technique, the C.A.T.-S. has been constructed from washable material not too easily marred or destroyed.

Administration

The problems of administering the C.A.T.-S. are not different from those of the C.A.T. (and will be only summarized here) except for its special uses, as just discussed.

Proper rapport between child and administrator is most important. It is best to get to know the child before administration, to play games first so as to let him or her become accustomed to the examiner and to the situation and to reduce anxiety to a minimum.

To younger children particularly, the C.A.T. or the C.A.T.-S. may best be presented as a storytelling game. By far the most successful technique has been to make the test administration *part of a group situation* as often as possible. In a nursery, for example, one may choose the most fear-free and friendly child first, allowing it to appear that this is something of a distinction and something pleasant and interesting. If the first is thus successfully carried off, the rest of the children will compete about who may be next and will be cooperative and interested.

Children usually do not mind at all when recordings are made either by hand or by instrument. It is simple to flatter their narcissism by telling them that one will be able thus to read or play the stories back to them (should they inquire about the recording.)

Again, it is important not to permit a child to see more than one picture at a time (unless the play technique is being used) and to conceal (in a desk drawer, for instance) the others, lest the child be impatient to cut short the current story in his or her eagerness to see the next picture.

When the C.A.T.-S. is used as an instrument of play technique, all pictures of the Supplement—and possibly also those of the regular C.A.T.—are exposed simultaneously and, as previously stated, all remarks, manipulations, picture constellations, and combinations are recorded.

Inquiry

Special attention needs to be directed to the importance of knowing the behavioral conditions and the real-life situation of the subject. It is entirely true that "blind" interpretations of stories (i.e., interpretations of stories without knowledge of any other data) may lead to impressive and startlingly accurate insights. Nevertheless, *for clinical use it is important that the projective data be seen in conjunction with as much information about the reality situation as possible.*

The inquiry should be directed toward that part of the reality most closely linked with the stories. One should ascertain as often as possible where specific names, places, and other precise references in a story come from. If a plot is taken from TV, radio, films, fairytales, comic strips, or other sources, it is important for the examiner to know it. This does not mean that the story is useless—on the contrary—there will doubtless be individual distortions of the original source which will be particularly illuminating. Even if the story should be a faithful reproduction of the original source (TV, etc.), it will nevertheless be subjectively indicative that this specific story was elicited by the stimulus card.

Of particular importance for the inquiry is that attempts be made to discover whether a given story or certain details of one reflect a factual or a wishful state of affairs. For instance, if a father figure is seen as especially patient, nurturant, and protective, it should be a simple matter to establish whether this reflects the child's actual conception of the father or whether the father is the opposite in reality and the stories thus primarily reflect a wish.

Description of and Typical Responses to Pictures

Picture 1

This picture shows four mice children on a slide. One is just sliding down, one about to start the slide, and two are climbing up the ladder. Numbers one and three suggest males; two and four suggest females (skirts, bows in hair).

A play situation, this picture permits expression of fears of physical activity, of physical harm, and problems in social (play) activities with other children generally, and with the opposite sex specifically. The children may be seen as happy, as fighting, as pushing, frightened, and so on.

Picture 2

A classroom situation with three little monkeys, two sitting at typical school desks, one standing with a book in hand, and one of the seated monkeys holding his tail.[2]

This picture lends itself to a projection of problems with the teacher, schoolmates, and other classroom situations (learning, reciting, etc.). It leaves ample play for ascription of various characteristics to the unseen teacher, and a number of predicaments of the pupil reciting as well as possibilities of wanting to show off knowledge, of relating fears of inadequacy, stagefright, and the like. The monkey holding his tail in his hand may give rise to stories concerning masturbation.

Picture 3

This picture shows children "playing house." Father mouse, with eyeglasses much too big for him and obviously belonging to an adult, is receiving a beverage from "Mother mouse" while toys and a baby doll in a carriage are dispersed about them.

Here, children may have a chance to relate their wishful fantasies about being grown up and doing what seems to them desirable and possibly forbidden. The apperceived, imagined relationships in the family will be clearly depicted. Because this picture encourages particular identification with adults, it is more likely to prompt wishful fantasy rather than biographical data. Thus, it is especially necessary to conduct an inquiry at the end of the test to determine—as much as possible—the level from which this story comes.

Picture 4

A big bear sits crouched forward, holding a baby bear on its lap and in its arms.

This picture may elicit themes of wishes of oral nature, sentiments against infant siblings, regressive tendencies, and so on. Light will also be shed on the con-

---

[2] The situation is frequently not recognized as pertaining to a classroom by preschool children.

flict between remaining (and wanting) to be dependent and independent, as well as the general relationship to parents.

Picture 5

This picture depicts a kangaroo on crutches and with a bandaged tail and foot.

It prompts stories of fear of injury and castration. It may elicit feelings about a physical handicap or feeling of general inadequacy, as well as illuminating for us something about the subject's body image (see picture 7). Social rejection related to physical handicap may also be touched on.

Picture 6

A group of four foxes—two male and two female—are in a race with the goal in sight and one male closest to it.

Competition between siblings and playmates and the accompanying feelings may be dealt with here, as well as themes of success or failure.

Picture 7

A cat stands before a mirror looking at its image.

This should elicit ideas of body image—as Schilder described it: "The image of the human body means the picture of our own body which we form in our mind . . . the way in which the body appears to ourselves." Picture 7 may tell us the ideas the growing child has about himself and his body, the shortcomings, pride. The tail may have phallic significance in the card particularly, and children may express their notions about some people being "so plain" and some "so fancy," as well as their ideas concerning sexual differences, exhibitions, and so on.

Picture 8

A rabbit doctor is examining a rabbit child with a stethoscope; some bottles of medicine are visible in the background.

Here, we may be told stories of fears and traumata connected with physical illness, operations, doctors, and hospitals. An impending or past tonsillectomy or some such illness may be clearly revealed in its more or less traumatic and more or less specific meaning for the individual child. We may also obtain biographical or fantasy detail concerning illness of a family member.

Picture 9

A grown deer is taking a shower and is half hidden by a shower curtain. A small deer is looking towards the larger figure. An enema bag hangs against the wall.

Here, we hope to learn more about the subject's ideas of sexual differences, nudity, voyeurism, the family bathroom habits; whether or not a child is being over-stimulated, what disturbances there may be in this area; the child's handling of the situation, if any. The enema bag may give us biographical data concerning his feelings about enemas. Stories illuminating masturbation practices may appear.

Picture 10

An obviously pregnant cat, standing upright, with large belly, and apron askew.

This is designed to bring out ideas about where a baby comes from and fantasies and/or fear about this. It should be particularly useful with children who are expecting a sibling or who have recently had one and seem to have special problems with the situation.[3]

Interpretation

The basic principles of interpretation need not be discussed here again.

The recording and analysis booklet for the C.A.T. is applicable to the pictures of the C.A.T.-S. without any changes.

The interpretation of the C.A.T.-S. as an instrument of play technique must be predicted on general clinical experience and theoretical knowledge of psychodynamics. Extreme caution must be preserved, lest one read into random behavior or remarks significance that exists only in the examiner's mind and that cannot be clinically and/or historically substantiated.

It has been pointed out (Bellak & Brower, 1951) that projective techniques make use of several dimensions: content analysis, formal analysis, Gestalt functioning, body image or self-image, and the analysis of choices. Among the techniques using inferences on the basis of choices and preferences are, notably, the Szondi as well as finger painting (choice of colors); in the Rorschach, judgments are made on the basis of rejection of cards and that portion of the inquiry concerning the choices of the best and the least liked pictures. The C.A.T.-S. as a play technique may employ this dimension. For example, say a child has refused to tell stories to any of the 10 C.A.T. cards. When the C.A.T.-S. is placed before the child, he or she reaches for the mother bear with the cub; and if—when the C.A.T. pictures are also made available for manipulation—he or she chooses the first picture and the 4 card and will evince interest in the baby kangaroo in the pouch as well, a tentative inference that this child has oral problems and wants to be cuddled and taken care of is probably safe.

Norms

It has been said that the validity of inferences from projective techniques is based on three factors:

---

[3] Ideas about the necklace (e.g., its being torn) may well refer to notions about the body.

1. A study of the individual differences and forms of apperceptive distortion by finding repetitive patterns throughout the record: *intra-test data*. If there is a theme of lack of support and love and food in nearly every story, we may make the inference that the subject has a strong oral need apparently related to a feeling of deprivation. Similarly, if most stories end upon a hapless note implying that the odds are against one and are just too much, we may again make the inference that this subject feels hopeless and overwhelmed.

2. One may compare the fantasy behavior, as revealed in the test, with manifest behavior and make inferences on this basis: on *intra-individual data*. For instance, if most stories drip with gore as the result of the hero's aggression, and the subject is referred for timidity and shyness, we may make the inference that this child is so full of aggression that he projects it onto other people, and also that he dare not associate socially lest it break through (that is, if other data support this connotation—namely, indication of lack of control, fear of losing control, etc.).

On the basis of these two levels of interpretation we have remarked that norms and normative studies—as is customary with intelligence tests and other quantitative samples of performance—are not a necessity with projective tests despite much academic complaint. Actually, each person and each record constitutes a sample population of needs and behavioral variables which may be studied as mentioned above.

Nevertheless, it is useful—and, in the long run, desirable—to establish norms of apperception concerning our standard stimuli and to be able to make certain quantitative inferences from comparisons of each individual record with a large sample. We speak then, of:

3. A *normative-statistical* approach to the validity of inference on the basis of *inter-individual* differences in apperception. For example, if we should find that 80 percent of all children tested express fear of falling off the slide, we would consider such a reference in a newly tested child as not of pathological significance. If, on the other hand, a little boy says that the girl on top of the slide has just kicked the little boy below her in the head, and only 5 out of a sample of 100 children has ever seen some aggression between the two, we may be inclined to infer that this child has a particular fear of aggression from girls.

In a pilot study, Fear and Stone (1957) presented the supplement pictures to 40 children of Poughkeepsie schools: 10 girls of 6 years of age, 10 boys of 6 years of age, and 10 boys and girls each aged 7. The stories were told consecutively to each picture.[4] They tabulated the frequency of themes for each picture, the description of attitudes expressed, and outcomes of the stories. Their structural analysis was concerned with the settings for the scene, children departing from the scene, figures used and figures imported, and total story time and wordage per picture (see Table 17–1).

---

[4] A tenth picture—the pregnant cat—was added later to the set and three of the pictures had some features added: an enema bag was added to picture 9; the last monkey in 2 was made to play with his tail; the kangaroo in picture 5 had its tail bandaged.

TABLE 17–1   Tabulation of Responses of 40 School Children to the C.A.T.-S.

	Total	Boys	Girls
Frequency of Themes for Picture 1:			
Expected themes			
Peers sliding	29	15	14
Siblings sliding	6	1	5
Having fun	15	7	8
Playing other things, too	9	5	4
Concern with fair play	7	1	6
Other "problems"	20	8	12
Imported themes			
Sibling rivalry	2	1	1
Concern with injury, death	5	3	2
Dangers encountered but children succeed	2	2	—
Interventions but children not successful	2	2	—
Sliding when should be doing something else; being bad	4	1	3
Real parental involvement	4	—	4
Concern for acceptance vs. rejection by peers	1	—	1
Concern for selfish vs. kind children	1	—	1
Birth	1	1	—
Running away	1	1	—
Imported themes only (from responses that did not relate to the stimulus of sliding or playing)			
Concern with danger, death	4	2	2
Self-assertion	2	1	1
Concern with failure, inferiority	1	—	1

Total Wordage for Each Picture:
1, ranged from 13–528 words, average 98
2, ranged from 21–388 words, average 80
3, ranged from 9–476 words, average 83
4, ranged from 9–234 words, average 68
5, ranged from 10–306 words, average 68
6, ranged from 12–227 words, average 81
7, ranged from 12–348 words, average 76
8, ranged from 9–288 words, average 74
9, ranged from 6–346 words, average 88
Average 79 words

Fear, C., and Stone, L. J.: Table from C. Fear's B.A. Thesis, Vassar, 1951, reproduced by permission of the authors.

In their study of the 40 children, only a few variables of the many included yielded suggestive differences between boys and girls, and between the ages of 6 and 7. This is not surprising in view of the relative similarity of age and background. Even from the small sample of 40, we can arrive at some notion of what may constitute popular responses, and the like. But because of the small numbers involved, it is safe to say only that trends are in the direction expected rather than to consider the data as statistically soundly significant. It is for this reason, too, that we mention only a very few of the more important variables.

To picture 1, 31 of the 40 children responded with stories directly concerning the stimulus situation (of a playground with slide). Eleven of this total sample spoke of gaiety, while 10 mentioned apprehensiveness.

To picture 2, 38 responded with stories of a schoolroom. We shall return to speak of the two who did not in greater detail. Twenty-five children introduced a teacher into the story (none being present in the picture).

To picture 3, only 23 children plainly referred to playing house, while 17 introduced themes of their own (27 and 28 respectively identified the male and female figures in the picture correctly); recognition of the stimulus increased with age.

To picture 4, 27 responded strictly to the presented stimulus, while 27 introduced or added stimuli of their own.

To picture 5, 30 children responded with characterization of the kangaroo as hurt, while 10 spoke of it as sick.

To 6, 21 children spoke of the race as dangerous, 12 felt happy, and 13 were apprehensive.

In 7, 23 children referred to the mirror manifestly; the 7 year olds of both sexes did so about twice as much as the 6 year olds.

To 8, 21 spoke of the child as sick, and 22 children introduced the mother as a figure.

To 9, more girls spoke of washing and dressing than did boys, and more so at age 7 than at age 6. Thirty-three children, in all, speak of it manifestly as a bathroom scene.

Thus, such data, when based upon large enough numbers, may permit us to deal with a record in terms of how it meets certain norms and will help us identify a deviation (also such a normative scheme may be useful to demonstrate developmental trends).

For instance, if more than half of our sample introduce the mother in picture 8, it would not be reasonable to infer from such an introduction in any individual record that there is a clinically significantly greater dependence upon the mother than in most children of this age. On the other hand, if 38 out of 40 children speak of picture 2 as a schoolroom situation, any child who does not do so merits special attention. Sure enough, the records of our two deviants are very informative. One of them says this:

Three little monkeys were reading very good. Suddenly a fourth one came in. It said, "Oh, they are reading. What dopes they are. They never knew how to fight teachers." The teacher said, "You must not disturb them." They fought and fought with the teacher and she said, "You must go to the cellar and be drowned." They cried and cried. The three little monkeys had finished their books. She said, "You bad, bad children. You must come to be drowned." So she drowned them (the bad ones). The good monkeys finished another book in a minute. Another and another, seconds and minutes, halves of second, fourths of seconds. Finally they read all the books in the world and she said, "What wonderful children you are."

Although implicitly this story refers to a school situation, it does not do so explicitly. At any rate, even without norms, a clinician would have considered this story as indicative of special problems of aggression and fear and compliance.

Case Illustrations

The following C.A.T.-S. stories were obtained in a normal sampling of school children.[5]

Case 1: Jim, 6 Years

Story 1: They went up the slide, and the last one doesn't think the one on top is going fast enough so when they get down the next time she is the first one up the slide. Then she goes down the slide and she can't get off, so the others start to come down and they try to push her off. And then they finally get her off and they get up again and go down, and the first gets stuck again. And they try to push and when the last one comes down the first one goes off. And then the first one goes up again and they go down and they go back up. They can't go down the slide because on gets stuck in the middle and one goes at the bottom and tries to push him up and then goes in the back and tries to push him down. And then they finally get him off and then they go around and play a little and then they try to go up the slide and then go down the stairs. (*Why did they get stuck?*) Because there probably was a little paste on the slide.

Story 2: Here looks like one can't figure out what the word is (points to one on right) and the other one is standing up reading and then the one behind him is looking out the window with his pencil in his hands. And then the teacher tells him something else to do. And then it is time to go out for recess, and then they have about a half an hour out in the morning and then they come in and take a little rest and then they do some more work in their workbooks and then they read in their reading books and then they go down for lunch. They have 15 minutes for lunch, I think, and then they have 10 more minutes until it is time to go home. Then it is time to go home, and then they get in the buses. The bus skids. (*Then what happens?*) It gets going.

Story 5: (Laughs) Mother kangaroo when she was hopping hurt her foot. And then they had to take her to the hospital and then they give her some crutches and then they (mother and father) get home and then they eat their supper and then they go to bed and then that night they had a baby—the baby was born. Then the next morning they get up and eat. Then the mother goes shopping and then the bear asks her what happened to her foot. And she said when she was hopping she broke her leg. And then the bear goes on and then she meets the wolf, and the wolf buys some more food at the grocery store and then she goes home. When she gets home she feeds the baby. Then she goes over to see her neighbor. And then the doctor calls her on the phone and then tells her she has to go to the hospital again to have an operation. Then she sleeps there overnight. (*Then what happens?*) Then she goes home and goes to bed.

Story 8: Well, the mother rabbit has a little baby rabbit that goes to school in first grade and the baby has to have an operation at the doctor's. Then that day they go to the doctor's and then it is time for them to go back to their home. Then when they get home they eat their lunch and then the doctor gave them some medicine that the baby should take. Then they take the medicine. Then it's time for the baby to go to bed. And she calls the mother because she feels a little sick to her stomach. (*Then what happens?*) Then she throws up and then the doctor thinks that it is okay for the baby to go to school today. And then when the baby gets to school she feels okay and then she does some work. (*Operation?*) On her stomach—that's why she threw up.

---

[5] We are indebted to Ms. Clara Fear and Dr. L. J. Stone for permission to reproduce the following C.A.T.-S. stories.

In both stories 1 and 2, there is some disturbance of control; in story 1, the child gets stuck on the slide, and in story 2, the bus skids, suggesting considerable anxiety. This is borne out by the peculiarly hurried tempo of all the stories. Stories 5 and 8 suggest concern with pregnancy.

Case 2: Burton, 6 Years

Story 1: The little foxes are sliding down the sliding board and they're having fun (pause). (*What happens then?*) They went down and up. The mother snugged them nice and warm when they was in the house (*Anything else?*) They played. (*What?*) Games.

Story 2: They are in school reading and writing and the teacher is teaching the other kids to learn. The kids are good. They are monkeys. They have a blackboard. They are thinking. They are sitting down. They have lots of kids.

Story 3: The mouses are playing doctor and house. They are having fun. They have a doll carriage. They're playing lady and man. They have a pretty home. They are eating. They are playing. They are pretty. They have coffee pots and spoons and plates. They have clothes. They have two blocks and one ball. They have big ears and pretty chairs. They are nice mouses.

Story 9: The father is getting washed to go out for a big hunt with his little boy. They will have fun. The father is scrubbing and scrubbing and scrubbing. He will get nice and clean. And they are going to stay out nice and late and he doesn't want to get too dirty. The little boy is getting his shoes on. He will tighten them very very tight. They are getting their clothes on and then they will go out and hunt and when they get done they will eat. Now the father is getting out of the bathtub to get on his nice shiny clothes. They are going to have a party out there for every kangaroo. They will have their food—their deer and their wolf food and their tiger food. They will have an awful lot of food. The little boy is not afraid because his father is going to be with him. They have an awful long, long trip for they have good feet and do not get tired for a long while. His father likes his little boy and the little boy likes his father because the father helps the little boy. They are healthy. The eat an awful lot of carrots, cabbage, and lettuce and lots of food. He was a very good little boy and his father is a very good little father. The father is cleaning out the bathtub and then they are going for their trip. The little boy sees a little wolf. The father is shooting the wolf. Then they go on hunting. They see a big moose. The father says, "Here, little boy, you can shoot him." The little boy shot and he missed him. The moose started running. The father took the bow away from the little boy and shot the moose, and the father was very proud. And they went on hunting and got all they could. They got a deer, a rat, a mouse, a tiger, and an elephant, and black bear. They had a very good feast. Everyone caught 20 things. The little boy only caught five. It was a little mouse, a little rat, and a little bear, and a little elephant, and a rabbit. And then they had a very good time and then they lived happily ever after.

These stories are typical of the purely descriptive responses of an apparently rather frightened child. The examiner reports that he seemed very timid in the testing situation and was being cooperative because it was the thing to do. Toward the middle of the administration, Burton became interested in the length of his stories in relation to the rest of the group and in relation to his first few stories. After each story he counted the lines, and seemed proud of his achievement.

Case 3: Clark, 7 Years

Story 4: Once upon a time there was a mother and father and little bear—Jim, Fuzzy, and Andrea (mother's name). They lived happily but one day a mean hunter came along.

Fortunately there was a big wise elephant. They all liked him and he liked them. He snatched the gun out of the hunter's hand. "You aren't going to be any more trouble to animals so I'm going to put you in a real strong jail with big double bars." The animals learned how to make guns. After they made guns they caught all hunters that came in the jungle. After that people made pets of elephants and were nice to them and fed them in winter, and didn't hurt them. They lived happily ever after. A mean man came in and tried to kill nice people but all the elephants came up and grabbed the guns and hid them four miles down into the ground. They dug for one year. They hid everything they had in tunnels in the rock.

Story 5: Once upon a time a sad kangaroo had a broken leg. He broke it by having a fight with an ostrich. The ostrich was mean and started the fight. Ostrich didn't like anyone on his land and nobody liked him. He was mean to every animal that passed his home. Kangaroo had a hard time walking 'cause he wasn't a human being. One day his leg healed and he decided to get all the animals and have them break the ostrich's leg so he wouldn't break their legs any more. "Ha, ha, shows what happens to you when you cross my house." Ostrich cried when his leg was broken by the others. He saw how mean he'd been. He was a nice ostrich ever after. He knew he should never fight or same thing would happen to him.

The outstanding feature of these stories is this child's concern with aggression and his use of reaction formation against the aggression. In essence, these stories reflect socialization and internalization of the superego.

Case 4: Myra, 10 Years

The following two stories were told by a 10-year-old girl who was in psychotherapy for nausea and vomiting apparently related to unconscious pregnancy fantasies. She was also suffering from a great many fears.

Story 5: I can't think of what kind of an animal this is supposed to be. I know the name of it but I can't remember it. Anyway, the animal broke its leg and it was very hard for it to get about. It can't go any place because of the broken leg and it's always left behind. He doesn't mind; he feels that when his leg is better he'll get along just as well as anyone else.

Story 8: The little rabbit is sick. The doctor is examining it. He tells the rabbit he's got the grippe and he has to stay in bed. The rabbit doesn't want to stay in bed; he wants to go out and play and as a result of that he gets very sick and has to stay in bed for a month. As a result of that, he gets a heart condition and has to be very careful and can't run around like all the other rabbits.

In story 5, she tells, in essence, her own feelings of bodily inadequacy. She responds with a typical defense of denial, minimizing the emotional implications. Her associations, however, showed her real concern when she told of a man she knew who had had his leg cut off (apparently because of gangrene) and of another man who had both legs cut off in an accident.

Story 8 also shows her fear of illness and the phobic limitations she imposes on herself (having to be very careful).

CHAPTER 18

REVIEW OF LITERATURE RELEVANT TO INTERPRETATION OF THE C.A.T.

Use of the C.A.T. in Developmental Assessments of Normal Children

Normative data are crucial for the understanding and interpretation of thematic protocols of children, since the C.A.T. may be administered to children who have obtained any of several developmental levels. Responses can only be judged "normal" or "disturbed" in terms of the outstanding needs, drives, and abilities that are typical of the child's age level. Many of the recent normative studies using the C.A.T. in the personality evaluation of normal children have been concerned with the assessment of ego functions, their development, and their strength as seen in the C.A.T. (Bellak & Siegel, 1989; Boekholt, 1993).

Byrd and Witherspoon (1954) conducted a 10-year longitudinal study with preschool children aged from 2 years, 8 months, to 6 years, 5 months, at the first testing. The conclusions were:

1. Responses to the C.A.T. are largely apperceptive in nature. The frequency of nonapperceptive responses decreases with age and is minimal by age 8.
2. Sex differences in the nature of responses, with the possible exception of those at 3 and 4 years, are very small.
3. Judged by frequency and intensity, the dynamics of parental identification, aggression, and orality are best elicited by the C.A.T., whereas responses concerned with fears, sibling rivalry, the oedipal situation, toileting, cleanliness, and sexuality are infrequent.

Moriarty (1968, 1972) studied normal preschoolers' reactions to the C.A.T.; prominent perceptual responses suggested the following hypotheses. Misperception is related to sex role confusion and/or feelings of maternal deprivation. Habitual omissions reflect distorted mother/child relationships and/or denial and inhibition of aggressive impulses. Staying concrete in the C.A.T. may be an effective avoidance device, or it may represent a generally passive orientation. Finally, adding ideas beyond those typically given to the objective perceptual stimulus is characteristic of children with high potential for imagination and creativity. Moriarty noted that all the children used maneuvers such as denial, repression, avoidance, and projection of hostility in order to cope with the potentially stressful content. The defenses varied in intensity and effectiveness among the children who employed them.

Rosenblatt (1958) examined C.A.T. responses of children in the phallic phase (aged 3–6) and in the latency period (aged 6–10) in an effort to test the effectiveness of the C.A.T. in revealing personality dynamics from the psychoanalytic viewpoint. The younger age group indicated less interaction with threatening figures; children in the latency period indicated more cooperative activities between family members and more independence functions.

It has been demonstrated by Nolan (1959) that the motives of achievement, affiliation, and power are expressed in young children's responses. There was a statistically significant increase by age 8–10 for achievement and affiliation, and by age 6–10 for the power motive. Sex differences were not found. Interestingly, the stimulus value of certain cards was much greater than that of others: 65 percent of the achievement responses were to card 2; cards 3, 5, 8, and 9 elicited 72.5 percent of the affiliation responses. Similar results were found by Schroth (1979, 1985).

Finally, Witherspoon (1968) has classified C.A.T. protocols into categories on the basis of content. The nine scoring categories then being studied were: schizothymia, emotionality, character-integrity, basic needs, sex role, activity, description, self-reference, and evasion. The protocols studied were of children aged 3–11 years. Responses scored as schizothymia, emotionality, character-integrity, and basic needs were infrequent at all ages. A continuous increasing trend with increasing age was noted in sex role and activity responses, while with greater age there was also less description, self-reference, and evasion.

Sample Variables and Sociocultural Studies

Intelligence level and socioeconomic level are two important variables that must be considered in evaluation of thematic protocols. Kaake (1963) studied the relationship between intellectual level and maturity of responses among children 6 years, 3 months, and 7 years of age with slow, average, and superior I.Q.s. The proportions of interpretive and identification responses increased as intelligence increased, while proportions of enumeration and description decreased. Ginsparg (1957) also has concluded that children of lower intelligence have limited ability to express their ideas dynamically.

C.A.T. responses of four socioeconomic groups of Canadian kindergarten children were studied by Lehmann (1957); the groups were low intact, low broken home, average, and high. Differences were obtained on five dynamic themes:

1. *Aggression.* No significant differences, but low-broken groups used the fewest aggressive themes.
2. *Fear.* High group had significantly more fear responses than the low-broken group, but total frequency was low for all groups.
3. *Toileting and cleanliness.* High group mentioned toileting the least and cleanliness the most frequently.

4. *Punishment.* Such themes were most frequently given by high and average groups.
5. *Orality.* Oral themes constituted over half the responses. No significant differences were obtained, although the average group showed the most orality.

A number of sociocultural studies include both normative comparisons of responses of children from two different cultures and comparisons of the responses of children from one culture. Rabin (1968) tested 5- and 6-year-old *Kibbutz* and non-*Kibbutz* children with the C.A.T. Differences in concern with parental figures, as noted in the responses of these children reared in different family settings, were of interest. *Kibbutz* boys and girls both produced more evaluative responses of parents and higher proportions of positive, evaluative responses, compared to non-*Kibbutz* children. This finding was related to the relatively lower oedipal intensity and lower ambivalence in the attitude of *Kibbutz* children to parental figures. Booth (1953) compared the C.A.T. responses of 9-year-old Latin American (LA) and Anglo American (AA) boys. Differences between the groups, as noted from their responses, were as follows: LA boys are more dependent and less in conflict with parental authority; they have clearer male identification, which may be related to their view of the father as the more frequent punisher. AA boys have less respect for adults, they regard the mother as the more frequent punisher, and they are more goal-directed and striving.

Chowdhury (1960) administered the C.A.T. to children in India and found that some city children could handle the environmental details in the pictures, but that other city children could not, as demonstrated by the fact that their responses did not reflect the problem situations indicated in the cards and did not point to identification with the characters. In her revision for the Indian culture, Chowdhury adapted the original C.A.T. by creating new cards that were more appropriate to the social and environmental situations of the Indian culture specific to it, keeping the additions as close as possible to the original. It is suggested that this technique be followed whenever the pictures must be adapted to another culture (Dana, 1993, 1996; French, 1993; Chapter 20 of this text).

Children of Rakau, a Maori community in New Zealand, ages 6 to 13, were studied by Earle (1958). She found that they responded to the C.A.T. quite differently, judging by the reported typical responses of Americans, and interpreted the results in terms of aspects of the Maori culture. When results of the C.A.T. studies of the middle years were compared with doll-play responses of 5-year-olds and with T.A.T. and Rorschach responses of adolescents, high agreement was noted with respect to modal personality patterns in the culture.

Diagnostic Studies

Many diagnostic groups have been studied with the C.A.T. with the purpose of determining any differences in thematic responses obtained from such groups, compared with those found with a normal sample. Bennett and Johannsen (1954) have studied the effects of diabetes on the child's personality with the C.A.T., and have found that children who had diabetes the longest had more active and more withdrawing fantasy heroes and fewer heroes who were punished. Katzenstein (1957) used the C.A.T. in evaluating children with polio and other physical disabilities, and found that children's reactions to their disabilities were reflected in test responses. Bose (1972; Bose & Benerjee, 1969) also studied children with disabilities.

The possible relationships between functional speech disorders and emotional problems were studied by Kagan and Kaufman (1954). First-grade children were given the C.A.T., and the children with articulation problems were compared with children with normal speech. The articulation group gave a much lower overall mean number of words per story, significantly more oral aggressive responses, and significantly more themes indicating perception of parental hostility directed toward the child. Porterfield (1969) also studied children with functional articulation disturbance and obtained similar results with the C.A.T.

C.A.T. studies with children who are mentally retarded and brain damaged have led to essentially similar conclusions in regard to the usefulness of the test with samples such as these. Butler (1958) gave the C.A.T. to institutionalized mental retardates whose I.Q.s ranged from 30 to 77. Butler stated that, compared to "normal" children, the retardates' responses were most often just descriptive of the card stimuli, contained fewer words per story, and included little expression of feelings or conflicts. The usefulness of thematic techniques with children of such low intelligence is questioned. Boulanger-Balleyguier (1960) administered the C.A.T. to children who are retarded and obtained these results: A large number of omissions, strong perseverative trends for all picture stimuli, characters were neither named nor described when indicated, and few typical responses expected for the child's chronological age were found. Children with cerebral palsy have also been studied with the C.A.T. Holden (1956) observed that they tended to get overly involved in the enumeration of small details and that their responses were typically closely bound to the stimuli presented. It was concluded that the brain-injured are unable to assume that the abstract attitude necessary to tell a story.

DeSousa (1952) administered the C.A.T. to a group of children with emotional disturbances characterized as having behavior problems, and found several differences between their responses and those of a well-adjusted group. Maladjusted children more frequently viewed the identification figure as inferior and rejected, more often identified with the character seen as aggressive, viewed the environment as more threatening, and more frequently expressed antagonism to the mother figure. There was also greater occurrence of the following concepts in the stories of maladjusted children: punishment, violence, accidents, aggression, friends, enemies, injustice, deception, stealing, and weapons. Boulanger-Balleyguier (1960) compared 6- and 7-year-old "normal" and disturbed children using the C.A.T. The disturbed were subdivided into two groups of children whose most characteristic behavioral reactions were, respectively, aggression and anxiety. "Normal" children showed better perception of the stimulus in their stories, and had fewer depressing themes. Aggressives gave stories with little imagination, and indicated emotional immaturity, egocentrism, and retarded conscience development. Anxious children used their imagination freely, reflected high anxiety concerning their own identification, and depicted the hero egocentrically as participating in much aggressive activity. Beller and Haeberle (1959) studied the C.A.T.

responses of emotionally disturbed preschool children. Children high in dependency motivation responded with more dependent fantasies, more themes of direct need gratification, and tended to deny any threatening characteristics of parental figures. Children with high dependency conflict reacted more frequently with fantasies of threat, pain, and punishment to situations that implied dependency, stressed aggressive features of the parents, and did not adequately differentiate between aggressive and dependent stimuli.

Gurevitz and Kapper (1957) administered the C.A.T. to schizophrenic children aged 5 to 12 years. The following was the description of the responses obtained: "Hostility and anxiety were predominant in the responses of this group of children; this could be observed in the content of their stories, the nature of their outcomes, the qualities attributed to the characters, and in the interpersonal relationships, particularly those involving child and adult." The stories were frequently bizarre and the responses dramatized.

Children who have experienced parental loss have also been studied with the C.A.T., with the aim of further clarifying the personality dynamics involved. Stevenson (1952) compared the responses of 8- and 9-year-old orphanage children to those of control subjects. Twice as many orphanage children felt inadequate; they manifested less aggression, due to repression rather than to lack of hostile feelings. Guilt, especially for aggression, was highest for orphanage children; sex typing was not as clearly defined for orphanage children; and orphanage children showed more intense fears. Haworth (1964) tested children between the ages of 6 and 14, who had lost one or both parents before age 6, with the Rorschach, the T.A.T., and the C.A.T. These children responded much more frequently than a group of control children with themes of damage, contrasts, separations, successive attacks, and death. The themes used most often by the loss group indicated the depressive aspects of the fantasies of these children, and suggested an unusual amount of concern with matters of hostility, ambivalence, sexuality, origins, and death. The degree of deviation from typical responses for children in the loss group varied, depending on factors such as whether one or both parents had been lost, sex of the child, and sex of the parent lost.

In a study of sex differences in childrens' perceptions of their parents as inferred from the C.A.T. and Rorschach, Zimmerman and colleagues presented responses of 200 "normal" 6-year-old Caucasian boys and girls to the Rorschach cards frequently considered to evoke parental images (cards 3 and 4). They compared these with responses to C.A.T. cards (1, 2, 5, 6 and 9), which clinical judgment suggests are likely to elicit specific themes or support or nurturance from parental figures. Responses were scored for parent mentioned as negative, positive, or not identified, and scores on the C.A.T. and Rorschard were combined for each parent to produce an overall score for each, designated as negative (nonsupportive), positive (supportive), or both (ambivalent).

When responses given to the C.A.T. and Rorschach were summed, to check on the consistency of perception from one measure to another, both parents were seen positively or negatively to a similar extent: fathers 27 percent positive, 22 percent negative, mothers 31 percent positive, 24 percent negative. Examined for differences attributable to sex, both boys and girls perceived the father similarly.

However, the perception of the mother figure differed between boys and girls, with 43 percent of the girls reporting a positive figure, only 20 percent of the boys.

From a psychoanalytic viewpoint, at this age level, boys could be seen as rejecting the mother, as a resolution of the Oedipal strivings, while girls turn back to the mother as an identification figure. "More pragmatically, Maccoby and Jacklin (1974), in their review of sex differences, noted that boys are punished more frequently and harshly than girls, while girls are given more maternal affection. Perhaps this helps explain why girls respond more favorably to the maternal figure."

Bases for Interpretations

Haworth (1966) has noted three major bases for interpretations made from C.A.T. data:

1. *Recurrent themes.*
2. *Sequence analysis.* Haworth (1962), for example, has found a sequential pattern from card 6 to card 9. Neither card portrays aggression (both suggest sleep), but she obtained the following results in studying a group of neurotic and control children. Neurotics all told attack stories to both cards, with stories to card 6 generally indicating fears that an attack was imminent, while all stories to card 9 described an actual attack occurring. For control children, an attack theme was rarely given to card 6, and any fantasy attacks given for card 9 did not actually take place. Examination of stories to these cards is suggested as a possible indicator of phobic or panic reactions.
3. *Use of case history information.* It is advisable to be aware of the child's home situation and any recent or impending crisis events before one undertakes interpretation of the C.A.T., since such information can frequently alter the meanings attributed to test responses.

Assessment of Identification Patterns

The assessment of identification from child/parent situations depicted in C.A.T. themes requires more than naming of the parent figure. Haworth (1966) has stated that other factors to be considered are: sex of the child in relation to sex of the parent, the role function portrayed in the specific situation, the affects by which each figure in the card is characterized, and the sex ascribed by the child to child characters in the stories. The last method is probably better for assessing identification patterns of boys as compared to girls, due to the cultural stereotype of characterizing figures whose sex is ambiguous as masculine. King and King (1964) also questioned the validity of feminine identification on verbal tests such as the C.A.T. since girls' responses would be more likely to contain more cross-sex identifications than boys' stories on the basis of cultural and linguistic factors. Haworth (1966) stated that, in regard to child characters, the main significance is in the attribution of feminine characteristics, with opposite-sex identification indicated when given by a boy and same-sex identification when supplied by a girl. Because of the tendency to see child figures as males, and because of the child's limited abstracting abilities, it is suggested that expressed attitudes and activities of parent figures be interpreted in relation to the actual sex of the child instead of in relation to the sex attributed to the child figure. Mengarda (1983) and Simmonnet (1988) had similar findings.

Overt versus Fantasy Behavior

Lindzey (1952) proposed that thematic content that can be directly connected to elements in the presented stimulus is less likely to be significant in interpretation than that which has been added or is only indirectly related to the stimulus. This statement implies that thematic material not closely tied to the stimulus is more likely to be relevant to overt behavior.

Kagan (1956) investigated the problem of manifest versus latent levels of fantasy, and presented groups of aggressive and nonaggressive boys with pictures ambiguous for aggression and pictures that implied aggressive actions. Ambiguous pictures did not differentiate between groups, whereas aggressive children responded to aggressive stimuli with significantly more aggressive stories. It would seem that aggressive boys had less anxiety about telling aggressive stories to aggressive stimuli.

Lesser (1957) presented children with aggressive and nonaggressive pictures. It was found that, for boys whose mothers encouraged aggression, there was a positive correlation between overt and fantasy aggression; for those whose mothers discouraged aggression, the correlation was negative.

It has been concluded (Kagan, 1960) from these findings and others that, in predicting overt aggression in children, the following should be attended to: fantasy content that indicates anxiety over aggression, and distortions and sudden changes in fantasy responses to stimuli that suggest aggressive behavior. Kagan (1960) believes that these statements about aggression are relevant to other areas of conflict.

Kenny (1959) has suggested that the C.A.T. is best used now as a source of hypotheses to be checked against other clinical procedures. More information is needed about how much the thematic content reflects the conditions immediately preceding the testing, the atmosphere of the test administration itself, and the thematic stimuli. Once this has been obtained, those aspects of the story content which actually reflect the underlying structure of the child will be susceptible to clearer delineation.

Interpretive Outlines

There are two interpretive outlines that are relevant to the C.A.T. They are Bellak's T.A.T. and C.A.T. Blank (Short Form), which was outlined in Chapter 8, and Haworth's "A Schedule of Adaptive Mechanisms in C.A.T. Responses" (Figure 15–2). Others are Schroth (1979) and Chandler and associates (1989).

The Schedule of Adaptive Mechanisms was developed by Haworth (1963, 1965) mainly for the purpose of delineating defense mechanisms and assessing identification patterns, as manifested in C.A.T. themes. The schedule basically provides a foundation for qualitative evaluation of the stories, and secondarily affords a way of obtaining rough quantitative scores which can be used for comparisons between children and groups.

Haworth (1966) describes the schedule in this way:

> The schedule provides a quick summary of the number and kinds of defenses employed as well as the content of items frequently used. The categories are arranged as nearly as possible on a continuum from measures indicating a high degree of control and constriction to indicators of disorganization and loosening of reality ties. In individual qualitative assessment, the total number of responses within a category and their distribution among the various subitems provide a meaningful summary picture when making personality evaluations. However, for research purposes, the quantitative measure used consists of the number of categories "receiving critical scores." The latter are determined by comparing the number of responses checked under each category with a pre-established cut-off point for the category. If the number of responses exceeds the cut-off point, a "critical score" is assigned to that category.

It is suggested that 5 or more critical scores indicate some degree of emotional disturbance; 8 to 10 such scores imply that the child uses various defenses in attempts to control his or her anxiety, but that these defenses are not working successfully.

Schroth's (1979, 1985) method for scoring motives and the need-threat scoring system of Chandler and colleagues (1989) are interesting updates of Murray's (1943a) need-press system for scoring the C.A.T. Both schemes outline motives or needs and threats specific to the C.A.T. pictures. A drawback of the Chandler and colleagues' approach is that it becomes increasingly more complicated to score, when it comes to scoring different needs in relation to specific threats (not unlike the increasing complexity of Murray's hierarchy of needs). The Bellak system, on the other hand, begins by scoring the various needs of the hero in a story, anxieties, insecurities, and fears, and conflicts. Then one considers the defenses available to deal with the above needs, anxieties, and conflicts. This is a simpler relationship to consider, because we want to know *what* the individual is concerned about and *how* she or he is attempting to manage these anxieties, conflicts, and concerns. In this sense, the delineation of motives and needs by Schroth and Chandler and colleagues fits into the first part of Bellak's system, just as Haworth's (1963) inventory of adaptational mechanisms and Cramer's (1991a) clarification of defenses fit into his next category of "Main Defenses."

CHAPTER 19

THE S.A.T.

The Senior Apperception Technique (S.A.T.)[1] is an extension of the T.A.T. designed to elucidate the problems of elderly individuals. When the S.A.T. was designed in 1973, 10 percent of the population in the United States was over 65 years of age. Medical advances and an overall increase in physical health through better nutrition, less smoking and alcohol consumption, and other factors have led to an average increase in the percentage of elderly Americans of over 1 percent increase every two years. Between the year 2010 and 2030, the number of people in the United States over age 65 will grow from what is now one in eight to one in five (Gatz, 1995). Similar increases in health care and in the standard of living in other countries have increased the number of individuals over 65 years of age throughout the world. But the world has been no better prepared for the population explosion of the aged than it has been for the ecological effects of population growth, the development of atomic power, or any of the other changes in geometric proportions so typical of this era.

Shortly after developing the S.A.T., Bellak (1975) published one of the first general handbooks on aging, outlining typical life tasks and problems of the elderly and practical recommendations for addressing them. A main point is that age and physical health may not be as significant a factor as the diminishing economic status of an individual as she or he reaches retirement age. It is difficult to describe *the aged,* even as defined for people above 65 years old. Average life expectancy has increased to about 78 years for women and about 71 years for men, these numbers increasing every year. The increase in health and life expectancy has brought about a change in people's conceptions of the elderly and of retirement in general. An individual of 65 years may still be very productive and healthy with the capability of working well into his or her 70s, as opposed to the earlier pattern of people retiring at 65 years of age. Therefore, even if subdivided, as has been suggested, into "young," "old," and "old-old," a more relevant complicating factor concerning a general statement of the aged may be the economic factor.

Largely it seems to hold true that the relatively better off someone is economically, the relatively more benign is their aging. The blue-collar person, often having lived a harder life, is less able to be concerned with an often more expensive diet, is generally living under less favorable circumstances, and is likely to be significantly worse off than a well-to-do person. Also, the blue-collar, lower middle-

---

[1] Originally published in 1973 by L. Bellak, M.D., and S. S. Bellak, C.P.S., Inc., P.O. Box 83, Larchmont, New York, 10538, telephone (914) 833-1633; revised edition published in 1996 with the assistance of Violet Lamont and Marina Livshits.

class, and lower-class aged population has developed fewer resources, having usually come home from a day of labor and not finding more energy than for talking with friends, playing sports, or television watching. Such a person may have done little networking and perhaps may not have developed many leisure-time activities, such as photography, reading books, playing a musical instrument, or going to concerts or the theater. The individual may not have learned to play chess or have had an opportunity to develop an enjoyment in literature. The net result is a person with few resources for leisure-time activities, with a higher incidence of illness, and generally finding aging a much more vexing problem. In distinction, a middle-class or upper middle-class person of age 70 may still play tennis, go skiing, and travel. That does not keep this person free of physical complaints, problems of loneliness, and fear of debilitating illness and death, but it does ameliorate and alleviate some of the problems of aging.

In constructing the Senior Apperception Technique (S.A.T.), this differentiating role of economic factors was very much kept in mind. For example, picture 2, showing an elderly couple downcast, looking at the wares in the window of a butcher shop, tends to elicit specific individual concerns about having enough money to survive, which would not be as much an issue for an individual who is well-to-do. On the other hand, a fear of loss of motor control, as depicted in picture 8, could be a more common problem for elderly individuals.

"It is therefore important to use a basic set of 8 to 10 cards and to supplement others of the 16 S.A.T. cards selectively. *A good basic set of 8 cards that can be administered to all individuals in the same order is cards 1, 2, 3, 6, 8, 9, 10, and 12.* This can be administered in one session of 30 to 45 minutes; the other cards can be administered in a second session, since elderly patients are likely to become fatigued and impatient with too long an administration.

Nature and Purpose of the Technique

The concerns of the aged frequently are thought to be centered around loneliness, uselessness, illness, helplessness, and lowered self-esteem (Baltes & Baltes, 1990; Bellak, 1975; Knight et al., 1995; La Rue, 1992). Many of the infirmities associated with old age may be alleviated or eliminated by advances in medicine, and many of the social, economic, and psychological problems of the aged are consequences of social policies that could be altered.

In providing apperceptive stimuli to reflect the problems of old age, we could not be utopian. We had to design pictures that, though ambiguous enough to give individual leeway, were likely to reflect such situations and problems as exist for the aged. Although this means that we provide stimuli that permit ascription of themes of loneliness, illness, and other vicissitudes, we also provide pictures that lend themselves to the reflection of happy sentiments, such as joy in grandchildren, pleasures of a social dance, and social interaction game playing (Bellak, 1973, 1975). Five pictures are ambiguous enough to lend themselves either to happy themes or some reflection of difficulties (Ackerly, 1973; Bellak, 1954, 1967, 1965; Foote & Kahn, 1979); a family setting and a scene in a Senior Citizens Center fall into this group.

Compared with the T.A.T. and the C.A.T., we see the use of the S.A.T. as both broader and narrower. We see its applicability *broader* than the other two, as we believe that certain relatively superficial problems revealed through the S.A.T. may be useful to professionals, such as physicians, social workers, and nurses, not specifically trained in clinical psychology. As a prelude to counseling with an elderly individual or a part of an ongoing counseling, a social worker, nurse, or recreation therapist might administer the S.A.T. to elicit themes and issues useful for further discussion with the individual in contrast to a psychologist administering the S.A.T. as part of a psychological test battery.

The stories told in response to the S.A.T. are often a good concrete guide to manifest concerns about getting along with peers and juniors, about health, or about entering a home for the aged. More often than young adults, and more than some young children, the aged give relatively concrete stories with a great deal of self-reference, thus lending themselves to that level of inference. In that sense, utilization of the S.A.T. is *narrower* than the use of the T.A.T. and C.A.T. for insight into general personality dynamics.

This view is, for instance, in accordance with those enumerated by more general texts on psychological assessment of the elderly by Albert and Moss (1988), Birren and Schaie (1990), La Rue (1992), and Busse and Pfeiffer (1973), who point out that:

> The psychological disturbances which occur commonly in old age tend to be rather simple direct reactions to stressful circumstances, making use of relatively simple, even primitive psychological defense mechanisms. Thus, the defenses seen most prominently in this age group are withdrawal, denial, projection, and somatization; all of them mechanisms for dealing with anxiety that become available early in life. Sometimes not even these simple mechanisms are used by older persons, and the anxiety evoked by adverse circumstances is experienced in totally unmodified form. It is the use of these relatively simple defenses, or no defenses, which shapes the clinical manifestations of psychiatric disorders in old age, and which dictates modifications in diagnostic and therapeutic technique. These modifications . . . seek to take into account the special needs, limitations, and circumstances of older persons. (p. 124)

At the same time, of course, many stories are amenable to the type of sophisticated interpretation of unconscious drive representation, conflicts, anxieties, and ego functioning for which the T.A.T and C.A.T. are useful.

The aims of the S.A.T. are modest to the same extent that they are also specific. In most instances, it does not need a great deal of clinical acumen, and surely no test, to discover that an aged person suffers from depression or loneliness or rage. What the S.A.T. may be able to add in information are the specific forms that these general states may take or be caused by in a given individual. Is the aged woman depressed because she specifically feels deserted by her oldest daughter, rather than because she feels let down by the other daughter, or the son? Or is she depressed because she is acutely aware of some loss of her faculties, or because of injury to her pride over the loss of her desirability as a sexual object? And what defenses and other drives does her story suggest? Often, the stories reflect problems the patient cannot verbalize directly.

One may not be able to do anything about the chronological facts of age, or the disease processes responsible for what is often wrongly considered aging, or the current social burdens imposed on the elderly. There is something that can be done about the specific meaning of various emotional states if one understands the specific set of circumstances that precedes or precipitates them (Knight et al., 1995).

In this respect, the afflictions of old age do not represent different therapeutic problems from those conditions at any other age that have a more or less precipitating factor. Earlier, it was noted that heart disease (Bellak, 1956) or tuberculosis (Bellak, 1950) has specific meanings for those afflicted, as do other illnesses (Bellak, 1950). As suggested, particularly in volumes on emergency and brief psychotherapy (Bellak, 1965; Bellak, Abrams, & Ackermann-Engel, 1992), it is essential that the unique and specific causes and precipitating factors of panic, depression, and others to be understood and dynamically formulated before intervention takes place. *Brief, limited intervention is often all that is needed,* as Aiken (1995), Berezin (1963), Goldfarb (1945), Knight and associates (1995), and Woodward and Wallston (1987) also emphasize.

Again, following the general principles of psychotherapy, it is important to understand and place in sequence a current chief complaint in terms of the preexisting personality. People react differently to fire, rape, the loss of a loved one, retirement, removal—and so they do to aging. Very often, a person who had a great deal of body narcissism and vanity in earlier life will react with excessive narcissistic injury to aging. A man whose main defense against anxiety and depression lay in his pride of masculine prowess will suffer more from infirmity than another man.

To the extent, then, to which life history and S.A.T. data give a general picture of personality structure and dynamics, they furnish the specific data concerning the acute upset; it can be seen in perspective of the larger picture. In this way, the S.A.T. may also be used for effective therapeutic intervention and/or restructuring of the situation.

The history of dynamic psychotherapy, even for the dying, is fairly old. Sigmund Freud treated a Hungarian baron during his terminal illness so successfully that the grateful patient, Anton von Freund, endowed what was to become the International Psychoanalytic Publishing Company.

One can only hope that the S.A.T. will be used by psychologists, physicians, psychiatrists, rehabilitation workers, nurses, therapists, and other professionals concerned with the care of the aged. It is designed to help them reduce for the aged the irrational overlay of unrelenting facts of their existence in order to make their lives, as well as the lives of those concerned with them, more comfortable and bearable.

Construction of the Senior Apperception Technique

Historical accounts of the development of the T.A.T. in biographical accounts of the pioneering psychologist, Henry Murray (Anderson, 1990; Robinson, 1992), and of his assistant, Christiana Morgan (Douglas, 1993), and research on the origin and history of the T.A.T. images (Morgan, 1995) underscore the value of a collaboration between a specialist in personality assessment (Murray) and a visual artist

(Morgan). The C.A.T. was similarly devised through the collaboration of Leopold Bellak, his artist wife, Sonya Sorel Bellak, and the artist Violet Lamont. The process involves thinking of pictorial situations that will be most expressive of basic life tasks and issues of a particular age group, drawing pictures of these situations, trying the pictures out with different groups of people, and then narrowing the group of pictures down to a manageable basic set. Normative studies of at least 100 participants of the same age group and of large groups of "normal" individuals of different cultural groups should be conducted in order to know what is typical on this test for these populations. Validity studies need to be done to compare individuals with different psychiatric disorders on the test. Convergent validity studies of the projective test should be done to compare it with similar tests that are presumed to measure the same variables, as well as test-retest reliability to see if the test measures the same variables at two different points in time, and cross-cultural comparisons.

We had to start with some working notions concerning those themes we wanted to highlight. In addition to personal clinical experience, themes discussed in the gerontological psychology literature are relevant (Abeles, 1994; Albert & Moss, 1988; Cummings, 1961; Eisdorker, 1973; La Rue, 1992; McIntosh et al., 1994).

We set out to design pictures that were likely to pull themes we had learned are of significance for the aged, as seen in private practice, clinics, and other settings. Sonya Sorel Bellak drew a successive series of 44 pictures that were photocopied and administered to a stratified sampling of the aged—some working, some retired, some institutionalized, some living at home, and so on.

In the course of story collecting (almost all were taped), it became obvious that some of the pictures rarely elicited good stories, while others stimulated stories very limited in variety. Out of 44 pictures, we rejected or modified 30 to arrive at the current set of 16.

By clinical inspection, some pictures failed to have a pull due to insufficient ambiguity as well as lack of interest in the particular theme. To the latter belonged, surprisingly, the picture of a mourning family behind a casket in a funeral home. The lack of rich stories in response to this picture may be consistent with the widespread clinical impression that the elderly tend to feel very matter-of-fact about death, or simply avoid concern with it, except in the case of suicidal older adults (McIntosh et al., 1994).

In other instances, pictures were redrawn or dropped because they failed to produce expected results. We thought that the problem of motor control and its loss would be an outstanding concern of the aged. We presented the picture of an elderly person dropping one of two crutches, expecting to elicit such themes, but found little response; the stories showed no specific attempt to deal with loss, or fear of loss of control and generally did not rouse much interest in terms of length of stories or liveliness of themes.

We attempted to approach this problem with a different picture—an elderly person stands at the curb while a young boy runs across the street filled with trucks and cars. A situation frequent in urban settings, we thought, would lead to generalized reflections on loss of speed and agility and the resulting dangers for the elderly. It also seemed likely that stories noting the ease with which the youth could cross the street, in contrast to the difficulties facing the old person, would result in various individual features: anger, self-pity, adaptation, fear of injury, withdrawal, and envy of the young. However, even when the picture was twice redrawn to emphasize the problem, most responses simply dealt with the boy and did not mention the street-crossing problem at all. Even after removing the boy, no stories concerned with the traffic problem materialized, so we dropped the picture from the series.

Another picture showing the checkout counter of a supermarket was meant to produce responses about economic concerns (thought to be such a common problem of the aged), and possibly to reflect individual and even irrational anxieties above and beyond the ordinary concerns. It, too, was not productive and was dropped.

We decided to have most figures ambiguous for sex. We designed the cards in a slightly larger format than the C.A.T. or T.A.T. pictures, as poor eyesight is a frequent problem of the aged.

The mood of the pictures was a special problem. These stimuli are designed to elicit possible psychological problems. By that definition, they cannot be expected to be pictures of gaiety, just as the T.A.T., and to a certain extent the C.A.T., are not cheerful. Some attempt was made to keep them from being too depressing or wholly gloomy in order not to discourage the individuals more than may be unavoidable for this sort of task. Also, a good deal of thought was given to attempts to make the settings suitable for various socioeconomic, ethnic, and personal life situations.

Anyone who has had dealings with the elderly at all will have experienced the fact that an 80-year-old is likely to speak of another 80-year-old as "that old man" or "that old woman"; a certain degree of denial of one's own age seems very common. From that standpoint, some resistance to relating to clearly aged figures in the pictures seemed almost unavoidable. (One is reminded of the Thompson modification of the T.A.T. for African Americans which, at the time it was published, was found less acceptable to African Americans than the regular T.A.T.)

No statistically sophisticated claims for validity and reliability are being made for this technique, except for the fact that the pictures represent situations frequently met in everyday life and are therefore likely to elicit typical responses, feelings, and thoughts about such situations.

The present information on the S.A.T. is predicated on our preliminary normative study of responses from 100 people (not counting previously discarded ones), the four pilot studies discussed next, a growing body of research studies (Dalakishvili et al., 1989; Foote & Kahn, 1979; Kahana et al., 1995; Kornfied & Marshall, 1987; Maddox, 1994; Rajagopalan, 1990; Schaie, 1978; Schroth, 1978; Stock & Kantner, 1980; Swartz, 1985), and clinical data since obtained.

In our preliminary normative study, there were 46 males and 54 females between the ages of 65 and 84 years of age. We tried to have a socioeconomic cross-section. It is doubtful that we succeeded in drawing equally from all of the classes, for instance, of the Hollingshead Index. We did administer the S.A.T. in a variety of settings. Among the stories from these 100 people, the average length in terms of word count was 112, with the mean 138 and the mode of 280. The average length of time for administration of 10 pictures ranged from 20 to 30 minutes.

Four Pilot Studies Based on the S.A.T.[2]

Four background studies with consultation by Bellak were conducted at a local university in the 1970s subsequent to the development of the S.A.T. The thesis by Nancy Altobello (1973) studied hope and despair by utilizing the S.A.T. It produced interesting results contradicting Neugarten's (1972) hypotheses of disengagement that elderly persons, if given a relatively supporting social environment, will choose personal involvement.

The *disengagement theory,* originally stated by Cummings and Henry (1961), was investigated and later propounded by Neugarten (Neugarten & Gutmann, 1968). She originally proposed that elderly persons experience a decrease in emotional involvement during the aging process and therefore withdraw from those activities that once characterized their lives; these disengaged persons, she hypothesized, maintained a sense of psychological well-being and of life satisfaction. In a later study, however, Neugarten (1972) found that those aged persons who were socially active and involved, rather than the uninvolved, retained a high degree of life satisfaction.

Altobello set out not only to test hypotheses that elderly people convey more experience of despair, death, and a feeling of struggling than a control group of students, but also to explore whether the disengagement theory held. She attempted to estimate involvement by word count, made estimates of degree of involvement, and compared the kinds of hope and despair experienced by the elderly as compared with young people. In the process, she also compared the S.A.T. with the T.A.T. For the elderly participants, she used 3 T.A.T. cards and 20 S.A.T. cards, some of which have been modified or dropped from the present series. The younger participants were given the same set of S.A.T. cards in the same way, but because of time limitations, they were not given the T.A.T. cards. Each story was evaluated with regard to kinds of activity, degree of interpersonal involvement, themes of despair, outcome, and word count. Each scoring category was examined with regard to age and sex differences between the S.A.T. and the T.A.T.

In terms of the five subcategories of *activities* (daydreaming, daily routine, passivity, conflict, and affiliation), there were no sex differences for the elderly participants nor for the students. It also is striking that the main activities for the students were the same as those for the elderly, with the exception of daily routine that was slightly higher for the students.

In terms of the five subcategories of *hope* for S.A.T. (happiness, optimism, effort to maintain self, meaningful kinship, and interest in people), there was no difference between the age groups.

The degrees of *social involvement* also showed no differences between the students and elderly. The men in both groups seem to have more scores of moderate involvement, while the women in both groups had more scores of low involvement.

---

[2] We would like to express our appreciation to Dr. Bernard Landis, professor at the State University of New York College at Purchase, for his counsel and for supervision of these studies, which are on file at the library, SUNY College at Purchase.

In accordance with Prola's (1972) findings, the categories of *word count* and *involvement* seem to be related. Participants with higher word counts tend to have more scores for high degree of involvement.

With regard to the three T.A.T. cards, administered to see what might be elicited from pictures of younger people, the activities scored were consistent with the S.A.T. results, showing similar rankings for affiliation, daily routine, and passivity. Although too small a number of T.A.T. cards was used to draw conclusions, it is significant that quite different stimuli resulted in similar thematic contents. The hypothesis that the T.A.T. cards would elicit more responses of hope and fewer of despair, in comparison with the S.A.T. cards, was not supported in this study. The T.A.T. outcomes were actually more despairing than the S.A.T. outcomes, and the S.A.T. cards did not produce the grimness that might have been expected.

The prediction that elderly people would overwhelmingly respond with images of despair and death was not supported by this study. The stories elicited by the S.A.T. showed a yearning for connectedness and activity in the elderly. Despite the fear of infirmity and death, these stimuli elicited aspects of hope, indicating that aging need not be viewed as depressing, unhopeful, and isolating. Overall, the control group of students did not differ substantially from the elderly. The only notable differences were between the two sexes.

In an investigation of the elderly's psychosexual concerns and the effects that aging may have on their sexual ideation, Lynette Ackerly used the S.A.T. as well at the T.A.T. and Rorschach (Ackerly, 1973). Ackerly's hypotheses were that older people will reveal their interest in sex through stories they will tell to various picture stimuli; that the T.A.T. would elicit a higher rate of sexual imagery than the S.A.T. because of stereotyped attitudes about sexual feelings in older people; that there would be a higher percentage of sexual images in the elderly as compensation for unfulfilled sexual longings; and that individual differences, more than age differences, should be reflected in the degrees of sexual responsiveness to the projective materials.

Ackerly's 15 participants ranged from 65 to 86 years, with an average of 75.6 years. Of the seven men, two were single, three widowed, and two presently married. Among the eight women, one was single, four widowed, and three presently married. She studied the frequency of seven themes: depression and loneliness; competition, antagonism, and aggression; discouragement and disappointment; security and health concerns; needs for nurturance; affiliation and compassion; and sexuality.

Participants were given 21 S.A.T. cards, 4 T.A.T. cards, and the 10 Rorschach cards. Seven of the participants were given the S.A.T. first, whereas eight were given the T.A.T. and Rorschach first.

The most striking finding was that sexuality did not disappear as people age; among the seven themes, it was the fifth in prevalence on the S.A.T., but second highest on the T.A.T. Generally, the older half of the participants showed as much interest in sexual subjects as the younger half. No significant difference was found between the level of sexual interest in men and women. There were marked individual differences.

Deanna Toone investigated whether old age is accompanied by a constricted world view. She considered the degree and breadth of responses to S.A.T. pictures as an indication of the respondents' engagement in the external world and hypothesized that older subjects would score lower on all measures than the younger group.

In her review of the literature, she calls attention to the importance of individual personality characteristics and to the concept of stages of development during adulthood as factors affecting engagement, as noted in studies that tend to support the theory of disengagement during old age (Cummings & Henry, 1961), persistence of lifestyle, and isolation (Toone, 1974).

Toone administered a questionnaire and 10 S.A.T. pictures to a group of 15 healthy African American women aged 60 to 81 years. Responses were scored for mentioning the physical setting, describing a person, describing interaction between characters, and introducing content not specifically present in the picture. Word count was employed as an additional measure of involvement and stories were also scored for positive, negative, or neutral outcome.

The disengagement theory did not hold for Toone's sample. In fact, the older participants scored higher on measures of involvement and introduction of new ideas, although none of the scores was significant. The mean number of words was very close between the two groups, the measure for the younger women being slightly higher. Finally, the older respondents told more stories with positive or neutral outcomes, while the outcomes of the younger groups' stories were more often neutral and negative than positive. Toone suggested the possibility that the high involvement of the older subjects was due, in part, to the particular relevance of the stimuli to them, and also that her sample, as members of a senior citizens club, was predisposed to social interaction.

Finally, Toone pointed to the limited attention to women in the literature on aging, and especially to the virtual absence of studies of African American women. She sees a need for studies comparing the adjustment of women who have been employed with those who have been "housewives."

Clio Garland used the S.A.T. to study the degree and kinds of dependency that may accompany old age. She hypothesized that there will be a significant increase in overall dependency among the aged, but "it remains an open question as to whether there will be different kinds of dependency manifested by elderly and young people." She believes that the impairments that accompany old age and individual personality characteristics, rather than age itself, are important factors affecting dependency.

Garland administered a questionnaire and 10 S.A.T. plates to two groups of 15 white women. The older group ranged in age from 65 to 81 with various marital histories; the younger, mostly unmarried college students, were aged 20 to 25 years. Each participant was scored for the number and categories of themes of dependency they mentioned as follows: passive orientation, need for proximity, inability to make decisions, reliance on others or on institutions, feelings of rejection, exaggerated need for attachment, regressive imagery, and inability to function alone.

There were no significant differences between the two age groups as far as the kinds of dependency themes mentioned. In keeping with a view that regression is typical of old age, older respondents had three regressive responses and the younger women had none. Surprisingly, younger participants more frequently mentioned themes of rejection, and the kind of rejection they conveyed was more general than was the case for the older women. Educational level and health were not related to dependency; it was unclear from this sample whether marital status might be related to dependency. Garland also divided her older participants into two age groups: those over 70 and those younger. The older women averaged less themes of dependency than the younger ones.

Since the S.A.T. was established in 1973, it has proven itself clinically useful in the assessment of elderly individuals. Research studies in the United States (Foote & Kahn, 1979; Hayslip, 1986; Henry & Cumming, 1992; Kahana et al., 1995; Kornfield & Marshall, 1987; Panet et al., 1983; Schroth, 1978; Stock & Kantner, 1980) and in other countries, such as India (Rajagopalan, 1990) and Russia (Dalakishvili et al., 1989), have also shown that the S.A.T. is an excellent research instrument in differentiating the psychological concerns of the elderly from younger age groups.

One drawback of the original S.A.T. has been that the pictures have few details, as compared to the more detailed, evocative pictures for the C.A.T. and the T.A.T. This relatively simple style was intentional in order to have pictures of elderly individuals that could not be easily identified with specific ethnic groups or identified as to economic level (through the absence of wearing jewelry or wearing shabby clothes, etc.). However, clinicians have frequently pointed out that people tend to provide more responses when the pictures are more complex and artistic. This leads to richer, more revealing, and clinically useful scoring variables for the S.A.T. (Schaie, 1978; Swartz, 1985).

Therefore, the original pictures were redrawn by Violet Lamont with more detail in keeping with the style of the C.A.T. and T.A.T. Violet Lamont was enlisted for this task, since she had been the artist who drew the pictures for the C.A.T. During the development of the S.A.T. revision and in subsequent clinical work with this instrument, we have found that participants immediately respond to these pictures, appear more comfortable in creating stories to them, and appear to reveal their conflicts, feelings, and anxieties with more elaboration and detail than when responding to the original S.A.T. pictures.

Figure 19–1 shows the original set of S.A.T. pictures and Figure 19–2 shows the new, revised pictures.

Administration

The S.A.T. is a technique that lends itself to many different uses. Therefore, the qualifications of people administering this technique (as well as interpreting it) depends on the use to which it is put. If a general practitioner of medicine or a social worker without specific psychiatric or psychological training merely wishes to enlarge her or his ordinary questioning by getting some responses to these pictures as additional information virtually on the conscious level, no further qualifications for administration or interpretation are indicated—that is, none with regard to ad-

1

2

3

4

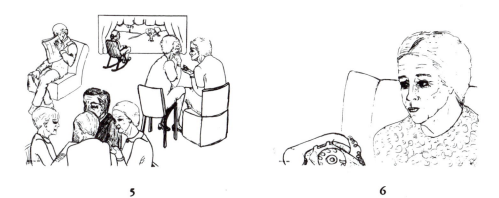

5

6

Figure 19–1.   Pictures for Use with the S.A.T.

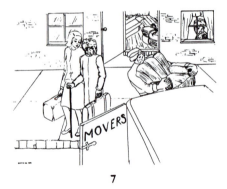

7

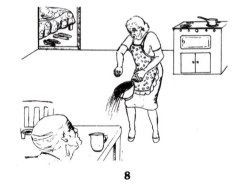

8

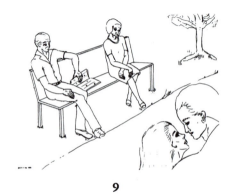

9

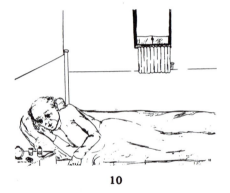

10

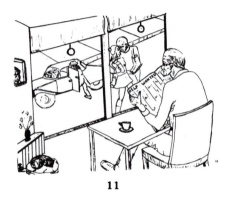

11

Figure 19–1.   (continued)

12

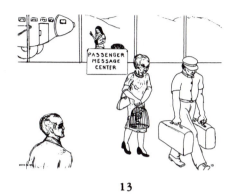

13

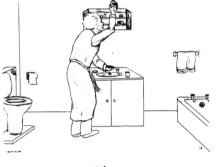

14

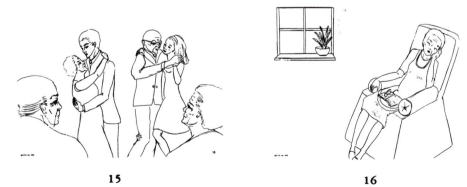

15

16

Figure 19–1.   (continued)

1

2

3

4

5

6

Figure 19–2.   Revised Pictures for Use with the S.A.T.

7

8

9

10

11

12

Figure 19–2.   (continued)
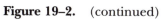

13

14

15

16

17

Figure 19–2.   (continued)

ministration beyond ordinary clinical prudence in showing the pictures with tact and with the words recommended here.

In administering the S.A.T., the general principles of establishing psychological rapport and a general working alliance must be kept in mind. In addition, some factors that might be specific for the age group over 65 years old also have to be remembered.

Among the general factors are that the patient be comfortably seated, that a friendly atmosphere be established, and that some ordinary human interest be exhibited. This should, under no circumstances, involve a condescending attitude, such as referring to a patient as "Pop" or "Grandma." Elderly patients may claim to be too tired, not to be alert enough, or not able to see well. (This may be true; on the other hand, this may often turn out to be wrong. Occasionally, it may be found that small objects are seen quite well while large objects are not seen at all.)

Elderly people, indeed, often have a limited attention span, tend to be more concrete than younger adults, and tend to lack distance to the picture. They are likely to refer the content to themselves. "Leaving stimulus" is also more frequent in this age group, and attempts to lead them back to the stimulus picture may have to be made gently while keeping a record of their spontaneous productions. An interruption of the story telling with a drink of water for the participant may be necessary or appropriate.

As already mentioned, we recommend administration of a basic set of 8 cards that can be administered in a 30- or 45-minute session to all individuals in the same order: *cards 1, 2, 3, 6, 8, 9, 10, and 12.* If one wishes to administer the remainder of the S.A.T. or selective cards after this basic set, we recommend scheduling the second administration on another day in order to test the individual when she or he is most relaxed and most rested. As with the C.A.T. and the T.A T., after presentation of the pictures has been completed, one may go back and ask specific questions on different aspects of the responses.

Instructions

1. Each interview should last, at most, half an hour, depending on the responsiveness of the participant and how easily he or she tires. Allow no more than five minutes per picture, unless you are getting a lot of rejections; in that case, allow more time to pictures with which the participant is willing to deal. If there is no response to a given picture, say, "Maybe we will come back to this one."

2. Keep the microphone out of reach of the individual, using the mike stand. (If you tape the stories, it must be with the patient's permission.)

3. The 16 pictures of the S.A.T. provide for a good basic set of 8 to 10 pictures, especially if the individual is likely to be easily fatigued or to have a brief attention span. The pictures should be administered in the order in which they are arranged (e.g., pictures 5, 7, 8, 9), clearly recording which pictures were used. If the individual is not fatigued at the end of this series and there is some use for further information, then more pictures can be shown.

Most of the pictures of the S.A.T. are left ambiguous with regard to sex. However, even the two clearly identified as females and the one as a male could be given to the opposite sex. Although the obvious identification may not be as clear for the like-sexed figures as for the ambiguous figures, the participant may be all the readier to reflect on some deeper lying problem. This tendency to ascribe problems to other than immediate identification figures has been spoken of by Murray (1951b) as "object needs" (i.e., needs [of the subject] ascribed to other objects). It has been suggested that such needs or problems are often of the kind especially unacceptable to the participant and therefore rather removed one step—that is, permitted to be expressed because they seem removed from him or her by obvious identification.

In Chapter 11 on object relations assessment with thematic tests, it was pointed out that all the characters in a story may be considered as "representations" of the storyteller. The character that is most similar to the storyteller in gender, body build, and age may represent a more conscious, manifest side of the storyteller. The characters least similar to the storyteller may represent less conscious, more latent sides of the storyteller's personality. It is possible, then, to present a balanced presentation of cards of featuring males and featuring females to both male and female participants. However, it is expected that female participants will tend to be more comfortable relating stories to pictures in which the protagonist is female and elderly individuals will tend to be more comfortable relating stories to the S.A.T. than to the T.A.T.

This point is relevant for *picture 16*, for which there are *special instructions*. When this is the last picture presented, the test administrator should say: *"Here is a picture of a sleeping person having a dream.* Tell me in some detail what the dream might be about—make it a lively dream." This picture, though of a woman, should also elicit very useful information from men, possibly even somewhat less guarded material.

4. Keep all pictures face down both before and after showing. Keep the pictures out of reach of the individual until ready to show the next one. Hand each picture to the individual for viewing. If necessary, place the next picture over the one being viewed, gently remove the previous picture and place it down on the side.

Description of and Typical Responses to Pictures

As noted earlier, the S.A.T. pictures are designed to reflect common thoughts and feelings of elderly individuals. Beginning with a rather bland picture followed by one relating to a concrete problem of economic nature because its very concreteness, as with the blandness of the first one, helps to ease the person into the task.

Next, we present typical themes seen as responses to the various pictures. The 1996 cards have the following changes from the original set of S.A.T. pictures: Card 11 in the 1996 revision is of a large family gathering at dinner, rather than the earlier card 11 showing a man with the "Help Wanted" section of the newspaper. Card 13 in the new revision shows a man and a woman sitting at a table in a restaurant reading the menus, rather than the earlier card 13 showing an airport scene with an elderly woman carring a bird in a cage and a porter carrying hand luggage. Card 16 showed a woman sleeping, whereas the new card 13 shows a homeless man sleeping on a sidewalk, which we have found elicits deeper psychological feelings and conflicts. The 1996 revision adds a new card, 17, showing three people on a golf course.

Picture 1

Three elderly figures in discussion. The middle one may be seen as female or male. This picture was chosen as the first shown because it is innocuous and some kind of social relations can be easily related to it.

Themes elicited often revolve around social interaction—two women competing for the middle person's attention, arguments, or references to social arrangements. They often show clearly how the participant relates to her or his peers, whether she or he is actively involved, somewhat withdrawn, critical, bides her or his time, whatever. There have also been introduced themes of sex, adultery, and rivalry—rivalry between older people for a son or a daughter, or of a mother in relation to the daughter where men were concerned.

Doctors may be introduced. There are also themes of two of the figures giving advice to the third who may be in trouble or ill.

Picture 2

An elderly couple looking through a store window containing a display of food, with the prices conspicuously marked.

This picture especially elicits concerns of a financial nature and oral themes, as well as reflections on the relationship between the two figures.

Picture 3

A small boy is in the center between his grandfather to the left and grandmother to the right. Each person is extending an arm to each other in a warm, happy manner.

This picture typically elicits themes of a young child visiting with grandparents. It is commonly seen as a happy picture with the grandchild cheering up the grandparents.

Picture 4

At the right foreground, an elderly woman; on the left a somewhat nondescript figure holding a small child; a teenager sprawled on the floor using the telephone with a display of mini-skirt and thighs, and the partially visible figure of a presumable middle-aged woman at the kitchen range; in the background, a table with chairs.

Themes elicited are those of family relations, possible competitive ones to-ward grandchildren, attitudes toward adolescents and sex, living and/or visiting in the home of the family presumably by the grandmother.

The elderly woman at the right is identified with the male on the left (the young man) as her spouse; occasionally, he is seen as the son, and the baby thus becomes the grandchild. There is a confusion of identity, the male seen as grandfather as well as father.

The figure in the background has been made into a servant by some. By others, she is seen as the mother of the teenager and the baby, and thus the young man's wife, too busy to participate in the family activities because she is providing the evening meal. There has been evidence of rivalry between the elderly female and this younger woman in disguised form, mainly when the young man is seen as the spouse of the older female rather than as her son. The wish to take the younger woman's place becomes very clear again and again in the misinterpretation of the male figure, who is obviously young compared with the woman in the foreground. It is the only consistent way in which rivalry for a son's favors emerges.

The teenager is often patronizingly referred to as "a teenager on the phone—of course, aren't they all?" She is occasionally referred to as being "spread out." Indirect allusion to the sexuality implied in the drawing emerges.

Picture 5

Eight figures, grouped and individual, in a setting that could be a comfortable home for the aged or a private home. A large picture window; a small old lady looking out of it with her back to the room; four card players in the foreground; two ladies on the right gossiping; a man on the left reading a newspaper.

This picture lends itself to elucidation of social feelings and needs, especially in an institutional setting. The old lady in the background is pictured as a great-grandmother, and the bridge foursome as perhaps cronies either enjoying their game or in keen competition. Grandfather, the figure on the left, is often spoken of either as relaxed or disengaged, and the "two gossips on the right" are talking about members of their family or what they disapprove of in an institutional social room.

The two ladies on the right are seen as envious of the females in the foreground because they have a man with them. The woman looking out of the window has been seen as not caring about cards or gossip; she is watching the road, perhaps waiting for someone to visit her.

Picture 6

An elderly woman staring at the telephone.

Reactions to this picture deal mainly with loneliness, neglect, and distress. It also brings out themes of anxiety—waiting for a phone call that may or may not come, or that will bring bad news. Feelings of neglect, feelings of anger at family mistreatment of the participant, and contemplation by the participant of making a phone call to air her complaint are seen.

Another theme is that of a woman waiting for her husband—an overdue husband—to come home. There are stories in which the participant wonders why she is neglected; she has done her best and will do her best to try not to make demands.

Picture 7

A moving van. A mover carries an armchair while an elderly woman and a younger woman carry hand luggage.

This scene is likely to bring out themes rather typical for aged people—either leaving a home of their own to join someone else's or going to an institution. Though the two female figures are facing away from the house, there are occasional stories of moving in rather than out, frequently defensive in nature.

The old figure is ambiguous and is seen just as often as an old man as an old woman. A daughter is seen taking the parent to live with her, or to an institution or other living situation, or to a hospital. The young woman is seen as benign more often than not.

The figure in the window is often described as a nosy neighbor, sometimes as the spouse of the elderly figure in the street. When seen as a spouse, he or she is left behind and does not know, the stories go, whether she will remain there, join her husband, or go elsewhere, to live in a home or with another child. Almost invariably there is grief about breaking up the home; the armchair is sometimes seen as a prized possession, going with them or, less happily, being given away. All regret leaving the home, or wish they did not have to go.

Some participants actually make the pair on the sidewalk a contemporary couple. Even in otherwise intact protocols, they are sometimes perceived as a young married couple.

Sometimes, it is the figure in the window who is moving and is watching her belongings being removed. The elderly person on the sidewalk has been seen as helping with the young woman's moving. Some participants turn the picture into something relatively innocuous, such as the elderly person going on a trip with the daughter. Peeping Tommery was also introduced.

There is fear of the furniture being mishandled or stolen. Attitudes by women in relation to men's ineptitude appear in this context.

Varying degrees in attitudes emerge about being moved into an old age home—from attempts to be understanding and to take it gracefully, to rage at being "shoved off" because children do not want parents to be a burden. Younger people are seen as not really interested in the elderly, while the older people are interested only in themselves. Old age is seen as not being needed any more and being disposed of, however kindly. This picture elicits or engenders more confusion in otherwise fairly intact protocols than do any of the others.

Picture 8

A woman carrying a deep bowl and dropping it on her way to the table at which an elderly man is seated. Through a doorway, two pairs of slippers are seen next to a bed.

This picture lends itself to surfacing of feelings about loss of bodily control and attitudes toward that phenomenon, towards one's own body, and to aging in that context. In some people, it brings out aggression, remarks that the spilled matter is scalding hot and spills all over, or that the person at the table will not (or refuses to) help.

Picture 9

An elderly couple seated at opposite corners of a bench, facing a young couple in embrace.

This picture is likely to lend itself to feelings of companionship and sex among the aged, as well as to sentiments about the younger generation. Among the most common responses are: nostalgia, estrangement, wish for companionship, envy, and disapproval. Clear indications of coping mechanisms and reality testing emerge.

Picture 10

A lone figure is in bed in a sparsely furnished room with a spoon, a glass, a clock, and a bottle on the night chest beside him.

This picture suggests stories of loneliness, illness, and feelings of isolation and poverty. Suicidal thoughts may be elicited by the medicine.

We hear occasional stories in which merely the facts were related: Someone who is ill will take his medicine, get a good night's rest, and recover; a woman is crying or merely being awakened too early by the staff and would like to sleep longer; a poor old man is waiting for the time when he can take his medicine—he is trying to stay awake, he looks pretty sick, even the doctor cannot tell if he will die. Hangover is another suggested theme.

Picture 11 (Original Set)

A man with the "Help Wanted" section of the newspaper in his hands. From his window, a man getting into a car and a young couple carrying ice skates can be seen.

This picture is likely to elicit themes concerned with envy of those better off and themes about the young. Mainly, we have stories indicating envy both of the youths and of the man getting into his own auto while he himself has to look for a job and cannot enjoy himself. Feelings of depression emerge and hopelessness is mentioned in connection with the job hunting. The cozy cat is noticed, as well as the other objects.

Picture 11 (1996 Revision)

A large, multigeneration family gathering at a dinner table. At the head of the table, a grandfather serves a grandson surrounded by the rest of the family looking on, each awaiting their turn to be served.

This picture is similar to card 1 on the C.A.T. in which three chicks are sitting at a table waiting to be served by a parent figure behind them. Both pictures bring out oral themes of nurturance and envy issues of the others feeling the "head of the family" may prefer this young boy over other grandchildren, even perhaps over the grandfather's own children. Another common theme is the gradual shift in power roles in a family, when the "grandparent generation" has to step back and allow the "parent of the grandchildren generation" to "sit at the head of the table" in terms of making the major decisions with their own children and later making major decisions about the care of the grandparents, as they become less independent themselves.

Picture 12

A woman deep in thought. A picture to the right shows a younger couple, which may lead to reverie about her own life in younger days with her husband and mate, and a smaller picture of two children may bring out stories relating to her own offspring, when they were children.

Themes revolve around the "all-too-quick passage of time" with everyone growing older, the children are no longer little children, one's spouse may have died, there may have been serious illness, bad news, a runaway or philandering husband, problems with children, and so on. Grief may be attributed to an overwhelming feeling of helplessness, to loss of a pocketbook with all her money, bereavement, or fear of the future. A mother's grief for her children often emerges stronger than that for her husband.

Picture 13 (Original Set)

An airport scene showing an elderly woman carrying a bird in a cage and a porter carrying hand luggage. A man is off to the left.

This picture lends itself to many interpretations: themes of leaving someplace or joining someone, or going on a trip (less likely because of the bird). Display of the passenger message center lends itself to feelings of disappointment at not being met and to feelings of being lost.

Stories range from an innocuous lady who has been away and is returning home or an old man who is also coming home to taking a trip to visit a child, carrying candy for someone, going to visit some member of the family because of being unhappy alone, leaving home possibly after a fight with her husband. There are stories of jealousy and separation, and remarks about a busy, busy world in which no one is concerned with anyone but themselves. Feelings of anxiety over reception at destination were expressed.

Picture 13 (1996 revision)

A man and a woman sitting at a table in a restaurant reading the menus. The woman is speaking to the man, who is looking in another direction.

This card elicits themes relating to having limited money to eat in restaurants, the elderly often feeling ignored by much of the world, such as waiters and waitresses waiting on tables with people who are younger, who have more money for larger tips, and so on. The man looking away may also bring out themes of the woman feeling unattended to by the man, whom she is afraid may prefer to look at younger woman rather than at her.

Picture 14

A bathroom scene showing a person getting a medicine bottle from the top of the chest.

This frequently produces a measure of shock, and then elicits stories mainly concerned with physical ailments, medicine, hypochondriacal thoughts, or suicidal thoughts. Most references are fairly innocuous: mention of indigestion, sleeping tablets to help through the night, constipation, cleaning the bathroom, and so on. A number of protocols produced references, both overt and covert, to suicide and to alcoholism or secret tippling. There are also frequent references to being old and of trying to manage as best one can.

Picture 15

A relief from the previous pictures. An older man dancing with a younger woman and an older woman with a younger man; two older figures are off in the corners.

This lends itself to a variety of themes—the relations between the generations on a social and sexual level, sexual feelings of elderly people toward much younger men and women, competitiveness, impotence, jealousy, resentment, anger, and disapproval. We also had benign stories of young people dancing with older ones, pleased to be making the old people happy, as perhaps at a family function. It frequently illuminates the intactness or failure of reality testing.

Picture 16

The figure of a homeless man sleeping on a sidewalk

For this picture, we give specific instructions: "This is a person having a dream. I would like you to tell me what the dream is about in as much detail as possible and as lively as possible." People who have had difficulty in relating specific content before may be able to do it with these specific instructions and be somewhat less guarded in reporting a dream. The situation of the homeless man sleeping in the street with the morning sun coming down on his head may bring out fears of becoming destitute, of being alone, of having no place of one's own in which to live, and so on. The morning sun often brings out a theme of some area in the person's life bringing a ray of hope.

Picture 17

A picture of two men and a women on a golf course. One man is teeing off, while the other man watches him. The woman is walking toward the golf clubs.

This picture, as in picture 15, brings relief from the darker themes of the previous stories. Issues of retirement bringing opportunities for pleasant past-times, sports, time to visit with friends, and time for relaxing from the areas of younger life that may have been filled with intense tension. Other themes may be whether the elderly individual feels physically fit enough to enjoy forms of physical exercise, the woman walking toward the golf clubs may suggest an issue of a woman leaving a man through divorce or death, and the issue of elderly individuals often feeling ignored by younger, more physically fit and working individuals.

Interpretation

As mentioned earlier, we prefer to think of S.A.T. as a *technique* rather than as a test. It is only a slight variation on the clinical technique of asking people to tell us what ails them. It does not make more claims than to facilitate the process of communicating one's feelings and thoughts by responding to standard stimuli, rather than to standard clinical questions. Interpretation of the S.A.T. can be done by the identical technique previously described for the C.A.T. and the T.A.T.

Case Example

The following protocol[3] illustrates the 1996 revised S.A.T. in clinical assessment of elderly individuals. This is a S.A.T. protocol of a woman of 74 years of age, who lives alone:

Story 1: This is a picture of three women of different ages meeting together. One has good news, and she talks about it. The two others are doubtful. The one who is older does not believe it is happy news. She is tough. The other woman talks to the younger one gently, talking her out of whatever it is. The younger one is happy. She does not want any criticism. She looks into herself. Perhaps she is making a mistake. (*How does the story end?*) I think the other two would be right. The younger one is mistaken and can't judge that well. She is too emotional.

The three women in the picture could either be of similar age or of different ages. That this woman sees them as being of different ages may express some of her

---

[3] We are indebted to Marina Livshits of Yeshiva University's Doctoral Program in Clinical Psychology for contributing the case study.

conflicts around aging. She sees the "happy" one (who can't judge that well, as too emotional, and does not want any criticism) as younger, while the other two are doubtful. Specifically, the "older" one is the one she sees as "tough" and who "does not believe it is happy news." Therefore, a hypothesis is that she may view being younger as a happy, emotional, care-free time, while growing older is identified with being "tough," negative, and depressed.

The story could also point to some conflict she herself experienced with her own mother, when she was younger. She may, then, be expressing a feeling that her own mother was hard and critical and viewed her as "too emotional" and lacking in good judgment. If she has a child, she may also be expressing a conflict she experiences between herself as the "older" critical one in relationship to her child, whom she sees as happy but somewhat irresponsible.

Story 2: Sad story. Two lonely people stand by each other. They don't know each other. They have financial problems. The man is hungry. They stand in front of a deli and look at it. The woman is unhappy, hopeless, and helpless. Maybe she was kicked out of her apartment. The man is used to being poor. She is not. They can't buy any of the things in the store. Look! Only ½ pound is $3.87. These are hard times for both of them. The woman is more intelligent. She may commit suicide; he would not.

The negative, "tough," unhappy theme of being "older" in card 1 is repeated in this story in which the "more intelligent" woman is described as "unhappy, hopeless, and helpless" and who contemplates committing suicide because she cannot tolerate being poor. The other person in the picture is seen as a man who can better tolerate being poor and hungry because he is "used to being poor."

It may be significant that this woman does not see these two people as a married couple or even as speaking to each other. Her loneliness seems to be underscored by the fact that she sees this picture as two people who are total strangers and do not interact with each other.

Story 3: It's a happy family. Finally, the dream of the older people came true. They either adopted this young child or they are the grandparents. No, those are grandparents. They are happy. The grandpa wants to teach him how to play tennis or golf. They are well off people with a loving family. The grandma is coquettish. (*How does the story end?*) O.K. He will come home. They will wait for another visit. They will be fine. Not to worry. Grandma looks well bred.

The picture's scene of two older people with a little boy seems to cheer up the storyteller, who sees it as grandparents having a visit with their grandson. The association of happiness with having more money from card 2 is repeated here. But there is a deeper issue in her statement that "finally, the dream of the older people came true" when they adopted the child or saw their grandson. This woman may have never had a child, so never had her dream of having one come true. Now that she is elderly, she may feel even more alone because of this fact. The statement that "the grandma is coquettish" is confusing, since this word would appear to associate the idea of flirtation by the grandma during a visit with her grandson. Perhaps she feels she has to go out of her way to appear cheerful and "coquettish" in order to have relatives or others visit her?

Story 6: "Please call me, please call me." A single, lonely woman beyond 30 years of age. A professional but not wealthy, maybe a clerk. She looks pretty, but loses hope to find somebody. She is waiting for a very important call. Most probably a man will never call. She is wearing earrings and has a hairdo. She is wearing a robe to be more casual. It does not look like a happy ending. He won't call. (*Her?*) She will watch TV, take off her earrings, go to work, and so on.

The subject seems to be a lonely woman who wants to meet a man. The progression of the story suggests that she is hopeful on some level, so she tries to look attractive with jewelry and her hairdo. But in the end, nothing happens, the man never calls her, so she just goes through her routine without a happy ending.

Story 8: What's the big deal? This is a family who does not have enough money. The kitchen and dining room are the same area. The bedroom is there. It's a small apartment. Her husband was hungry. She was rushing. She could not carry the food. She is horrified that the food fell on the floor. Maybe she burnt herself. Maybe they don't have anything else to eat. She is neat and clean, but they are poor. He is afraid she hurt herself. He cares for her. (*How will the story end?*) She will scrape around for more. She will use a home remedy for her burn. Empty table, empty stove. Bare table. It's a good, loving family. They never had much money, close to the poverty line. This is like O'Henry's story in which the woman cut her hair to buy her loved one a present.

The theme of having financial difficulties is repeated. But in this story, there is an expression of caring for another person and a reciprocal, loving relationship. The man is hungry, but he is more worried if the woman burnt herself while trying to cook food for him. The woman is willing to self-sacrifice in order to provide for the man, as the subject associates to the O'Henry story at the end. The story suggests that this woman may have been married and at one time experienced a loving, reciprocal relationship. Perhaps now she is widowed or divorced, lives alone, and is hoping to meet someone else with whom to love again.

Story 9: Two young people in love. Full of health and hope. They are fine financially, they don't see anyone else. The old man stopped reading, watching the young couple. He has a kind expression on his face. The woman, on the other hand, is a snake. She is not kind. Two old people, lonely. One is sympathetic to young love, another one is feeding the birds, and is not so kind . She likes animals better. Everything will be fine. The young couple will be happy.

This story repeats the earlier theme from card 1 of an association of being elderly with being "tough" and "unhappy" in contrast to younger people being happier. The "young people" in this story are the ones who are "full of health and hope" and are "fine financially." The older man is seen as "kind" and "sympathetic to young love," while the woman is seen as "a snake" and "not kind." This may express two different feelings in this woman who is creating the stories. While she herself is "sympathetic to young love," as we saw in card 8, she may feel that she is also becoming angry, "tough," and "not kind" as she grows older and fails to meet another man with whom to live and love.

Story 10: It's a terminally ill woman; no, a man. It takes place in a hospital. The man is very ill and lonely. He looks at the clock waiting for a visit. He can't even read, he is so distressed. He is terminally ill. (*How does the story end?*) He will die eventually.

This story brings out this woman's loneliness and fear of dying. The abrupt change of the "terminally ill woman" to a terminally ill "man" at the beginning of the story suggests a defense of displacement to attempt to deal with these fears. The story suggests that this woman is "emotional" in a positive sense of being able to express a deep fear in an open, direct manner, which other people are often unable to do without a significant amount of psychotherapy.

Story 12: A woman who is 50 or 60 or older who has lived a good happy life. It's a happy, loving family. She looks at the picture. Now she is distressed. She lost her husband whom she loved. She is alone now. Her children are all grown up. She takes care of herself. She has a nice hairdo and neat clothes. She is distressed about the loss. She doesn't know what will happen. (*How would the story end?*) If others like her friends and family wouldn't intervene, she will not endure for long. She may not be able to overcome the loss and will become ill and die. She is used to being loved and admired.

This last story further expresses the underlying strengths in this woman. It would appear that she was once married in a loving, reciprocal, caring relationship. After her husband died and her children grew up, she still tries to dress attractively. But she despairs of meeting another man and of becoming ill and dying alone.

Summary of S.A.T. protocol

The S.A.T. brings out the basic issues of elderly individuals that this woman, at age 74 years, is experiencing. It would appear that she has less money than she did previously and that she is worried about having enough money to eat and dress properly. It would appear that she once experienced a loving marriage but is now either widowed or divorced. She is facing much loneliness. But she may become cheered up when her children or grandchildren visit, and she has some hope of still being able to meet another man to love.

She has the psychological health of being able to express her conflicts, feeling, and anxieties openly and directly without much defensive displacement, distancing, or denial. She struggles to dress attractively and perhaps to appear "happier" on the surface than she may feel underneath. Fear of poverty, loneliness, illness, and death give her depressive feelings of unhappiness, even perhaps some suicidal ideation. The mention of suicide is of concern and should warrant referral for psychotherapy. However, it would appear that the balance of healthy adaptation and hopefulness in a woman who expresses her feelings rather directly suggests that she is not clinically depressed or at risk of suicide.

The overall conclusion is that this woman is a relatively well-adjusted individual who is facing the life tasks of old age, but who feels more lonely and depressed because she does not have a husband and she is at an age when she is more alone. An intervention might be to help her connect to a program for elderly individuals—perhaps volunteer to work with young children; do arts and crafts, music, or recreation with other individuals in a community center; or join some clubs related to her areas of special interest.

Future Use of the Senior Apperception Technique

By tradition, the S.A.T. falls into the class of projective techniques—a stimulus is presented to a participant whose responses in the form of stories, words, and behavior are scrutinized for whatever they may reveal about that participant. In 1950,

Bellak introduced the study of the defenses in projective techniques (1950), enlarged on the application of ego psychology to them in a later paper (1954), and further extended the concept in extensive research studies (Bellak & Goldsmith, 1984; Bellak, Hurvich, & Gediman, 1973) and in this current book. The S.A.T. provides a document that expresses an elderly individual's personal identity, as an autobiography provides a narrative of the individual's life story (Cohler, 1993).

Cognitive style is the term now generally used to comprise the totality of responses, somewhat anticipated in the preceding references. To the extent that a therapist studies each person as an individual, idiosyncratic ideographic ways of dealing with a particular stimulus situation affect the process the therapist is studying. For this reason, Herman Rorschach's term for his inkblot inquiry was a "Versuch," an experiment, and it is still by far the best term and much to be preferred to "test," with its normative connotations in U.S. psychology. For this reason, the title Senior Apperception *Technique* may be preferable to Senior Apperception Test. This is also true for the T.A.T. and C.A.T. In responses to these picture stimuli, we are dealing with the unique Gestalt of thought processes, of structure as well as content.

To the extent to which inferences about a person are made from comparisons of one person's responses to a group of other people's responses, certain norms are indicated and useful. The American Psychological Association (1985) publication on test standards goes into a great deal of detail on these points.

What are the basic data that should be available for a technique such as the S.A.T.?

1. Some assurances are needed that people will, indeed, tell stories of some length and meaningful content. In the present cases, it means that the pictures should elicit stories that reveal something about the personalities and problems of people in the target population of above 65 years of age. (By our procedure, starting experimentally with a large number of pictures and finding some of them useless, we did something akin to proving the null hypothesis: Some pictures [28 out of 44] had to be dropped because the stories were short, banal, or not reflective of the problem we wanted illuminated.)

2. The length of stories related to the picture themselves seems highly correlated to the Ambiguity Index, according to Prola (1972), and therefore it is a measure of the usefulness of a picture by this generally accepted criterion.

3. An account of themes and a study of the frequency of themes is another empirical approach; yet another is face validity by consistency with—and by internally consistent amplification of—clinical information. Even though face validity is not highly thought of in tests of skill and intelligence, the internal consistency with sets of dynamic data and reality obtained from interview and history give it greater value here.

4. There should be enough of a general idea about "popular" themes—that is, themes frequently elicited by the stimuli. On the one hand, this justifies and provides the basis for selection of certain pictures generally, and selection of some of them for some people specifically. Also, the establishment of some popular themes should make it possible to make some tentative inferences when individual responses deviate significantly from the expected norm.

As a further generalization, it can be said that the aged seem to tell more concrete stories than either children in response to the C.A.T. or adults of 18 to 65 years to the T.A.T. This observation is by no means established beyond mere clinical impressions. But it is consistent with a widely held assumption that there is a tendency toward disengagement and constriction of the field of interest among many aged people (Maddox, 1994).

Researchers in the future may be interested in a comparative analysis of overall "word count" as a rough measure of cognitive complexity between younger and older age groups and "idea counts" for personality variables—for example, by counting the number of words relating to hope, despair, affiliative tendencies, and sex. One might also count words relating to death and aggression, and the number of affective adjectives and adverbs.

Future research might include a variety of content analytic studies by word count. A content analytic study (by word count) of love and death in the short stories of Somerset Maugham by Judson (1963) led to results remarkably similar to those obtained by Bellak (1963). It may be of interest to see if such divergent approaches to S.A.T. stories in the future will bring a similar convergence of data. A comparison of this kind between the group over age 65 and those of younger adults should be of additional interest. (See the books of Gottschalk & Glesser [1969], Hall & Van de Castle [1966], and Smith [1992] for such word count content analysis approaches).

It should be possible to define other criterion words of depression, disorientation, deterioration (in terms of the organic brain syndrome), or evidence of a thought disorder. It should be entirely possible to define criteria in responses to the S.A.T. and to correlate them with criteria of established tests on thought disorder, deterioration, or depression scales and to get measures of validity.

Other studies might rate patients for their social relations in an old-age home on behavioral rating scales, and get correlation coefficients on measures of sociability derived from the S.A.T. Convergent validity studies—such as that of Fitzgerald and colleagues (1974), who compared the responses of an elderly sample on the Gerontological Apperception Test (G.A.T.) of Wolk and Wolk [1971] with responses on the T.A.T.—could also be done among the S.A.T., G.A.T., T.A.T., Rorschach, and other personality tests. This, however, is likely to be an exercise of limited value, since even these old and well-established techniques in turn have never fulfilled criteria of validity, such as are required by their very nature for intelligence tests of ability tests.

One way to approach this problem is do take a small number of specific quantifiable variables that can easily be scored on two or three different projective tests, such as the total number of words (word count) or number of people introduced (transcendence index) on the S.A.T. and the T.A.T. to determine which of the two tests is more revealing for an elderly population or to determine to what extent the two tests are measures of the same variable (convergent validity). Kornfield and Marshall (1987) conducted such a study of the time perspective variable in institutionalized and community-based senior adults using the S.A.T. and the T.A.T.

Neugarten's (1978) disengagement construct could be investigated by defining it carefully for a sample population, establishing content variables of social relations or disengagement on the S.A.T., and computing correlations between a rating scale of disengagement from self-reporting or some form of observed behavior and the one reflected in the S.A.T. Kahana and associates (1995) carried out a superb test-retest study of disengagement and other variables that compared 161 "old-old" (age 75+) individuals living in a retirement community on the S.A.T. in 1991 and then again in 1993. They scored the protocols for cognitive variables (word count, story complexity, story integration, and creativity) and emotional/personality variables (disengagement, anxiety, loneliness, pessimism/optimism). This research team found that the S.A.T. had fairly good test-retest reliability over these two points in time for most all variables. However, the most significant change was a decline in word count over time, which supports the concept of disengagement or diminished expansiveness in the elderly with increased age. This is consistent with Lieberman's (1965) findings of constriction on Bender Gestalt tests and Human Figure Drawings as respondents got closer to death.

Kahana and colleagues (1995) and Baltes and Baltes (1990) stressed that the original theory of progressive disengagement in the elderly was confounded with other variables, such as physical and psychological well-being or whether the individual was currently employed or had retired. Baltes and Baltes (1990) reported consistent but small declines in several areas of cognitive functioning during the elderly years, but suggested that what may appear as a type of depressive withdrawal from areas of former activity may be a form of selective optimization in order to conserve energy. In other words, the elderly may take more naps and do fewer different activities than when they were younger in order to save their energy for doing activities that claim their highest priority of interest and importance. If they are divorced or widowed, they may have to do different activities as before and perhaps develop new activities. As we suggested at the beginning of this chapter, one of the most important factors is the elderly person's financial status. It is a simple fact that when people have money, they can do more. Similarly, if an elderly person has less money available for leisure activities than when he or she was working, it may well be a responsible adaptation to selectively "disengage" from areas of expense that are not critical to financial survival. More studies in this important field of social gerontology that began with the use of thematic apperceptive tests (Neugarten & Gutmann, 1968; Maddox, 1994) need to consider the critical economic change that affects older people when they retire and have diminishing financial resources.

Another important area of future research that is very much needed is that of cross-cultural S.A.T. studies in order to develop norms and guidelines for the use of the S.A.T. in clinical assessment of individuals of different cultural groups. This is especially true for groups in multicultural society who are increasingly being evaluated by psychologists and neuropsychologists in nursing homes, on neurology services in hospitals and clinics, and as preludes to treatment planning and psychotherapy. Comparisons could be done of elderly individuals of different cultures within the same country, within several different countries, comparing individuals of the same age who are working with those who are retired, those of different socioeconomic levels, and those living in rural areas or urban areas.

CHAPTER 20

GENDER AND MULTICULTURAL ASSESSMENT WITH THEMATIC TESTS

Domains of Cross-Cultural Inquiry

Psychological tests—such as the T.A.T., Rorschach, intelligence, and other personality and cognitive tests—have been utilized by psychologists and anthropologists in order to study the relationship of culture and behavior, which has developed into an interdisciplinary field known as *psychological anthropology* (Hsu, 1972) or *cross-cultural psychology* (Brislin, 1990). Four domains of inquiry have been addressed:

1. A major focus is the *search for psychological universals,* as in the landmark studies of Otto Rank's (1990) *The Myth of the Birth of the Hero* and Joseph Campbell's (1971) *The Hero with a Thousand Faces.* These identify a common plot for hero narratives in literature, folklore, and myth throughout the world, which serves to communicate an idealized sequence of life tasks for those in each culture to emulate (Gilgamesh, Jesus, Buddha, etc.). Other identifications of basic elements that appear to be universal in the narratives of world literature, folklore, myth, and many other domains are discussed in several books, papers, and in the interdisciplinary field of narrative's major organ of communication, the *Journal of Narrative and Life History* (Cortazzi, 1993; Griffin, 1992; Mishler, 1995; Polkinghorne, 1988; Rosenwald & Ochberg, 1992; Sarbin, 1986; Toolan, 1988; Young, 1987).

However, an important gap in the thematic test literature is the absence of cross-cultural T.A.T., C.A.T., or S.A.T. studies that identify thematic test characteristics independent of cultural differences. Thematic tests would appear to be a natural choice for the cross-cultural study of narrative universals, since the research can employ the same test stimulus in contrast to cross-cultural comparisons of other forms of narrative that are not created to standard stimuli (Child et al., 1958; McClelland, 1961). The disadvantage is that the T.A.T. was developed in U.S. mainstream culture and may not be culturally familiar enough to be used with individuals of widely differing cultures.

Draguns (1990) argued that cross-cultural research with projective tests has not been pursued to a great extent because of premature assumptions that such instruments are based too much in Western culture, such as the T.A.T.'s original basis in European psychoanalytic personality theory, the Rorschach's original basis in the European Gestalt school of perceptual psychology, or the Kinetic-Family-Drawing Test in U.S. family systems theory. DeVos (1976) provided the counterargument that such instruments are very useful because they measure cultural universals, such as the organic basis for mental illness that is manifest in cognitive processes, social and cognitive maturational processes, and the universality of altered states of consciousness.

2. Another focus is *culture-specific research* employing cognitive psychological tests to study how members of a specific culture solve typical problems (Cole et al., 1968) or comparative research employing personality and projective tests to determine if members of particular cultures share common personality characteristics that differ from those of other cultures (Barnouw, 1985; De Ridder, 1961; Goldstine & Gutmann, 1972; Kaplan, 1956; Kluckholn et al., 1953; MacGregor, 1946; Mussen, 1953; Scheper-Hughes, 1979; Singh & Kaur, 1987; Suarez-Orozco, 1987, 1989; Wagasuma & DeVos, 1984; Zhang et al., 1993). In order to test an hypothesis that a southern Mediterranean culture tends to express emotions more directly and openly than a northern European culture, for example, one might administer a standard sequence of T.A.T. cards and rate each story for level of direct affect verbs, or administer the Rorschach and measure the number of Color and ColorForm responses.

3. A third focus is to develop *norms for psychological tests for different cultures,* so that these instruments may be utilized for psychological evaluation in those different cultures. The majority of thematic test studies in non-Western cultures start by adapting the T.A.T. pictures to a specific culture, but then they rarely take the next step to provide adequate norms with the particular culture for these T.A.T. adaptations (Dana, 1996).

4. A fourth focus of cross-cultural research is the process of individuals from one culture adapting to life in a different culture, referred to as *acculturation.* The world is rapidly becoming smaller, with many forms of instantaneous communication beyond the telephone (e.g., fax machines, teleconferencing, satellite television providing local television programming from one country to nearly any other area of the world, and the international network of computer communication through the Internet). Cultures today rarely exist in isolation from each other. Travel from one country to another is becoming easier and faster than ever before, with increasing numbers of people moving and setting up permanent residences in new countries, all of which leads to more inter-marriages across cultures.

When evaluating an individual from a minority culture, it is important to consider the possible influence of degree of exposure to the mainstream culture on the individual's test performance. Since the tests employed in psychological test evaluations were developed for mainstream culture, often the more acculturated a minority individual is to the mainstream culture, the better the individual's test performance. Therefore, one should be careful not to confuse lower performance on a mainstream-oriented test by an individual who is not very acculturated to main-stream culture, with lower intelligence.

In this chapter, we will present the argument for a standard battery of six or seven main psychological tests and the development of cross-cultural norms for these same six or seven psychological tests across the wide array of different sub-cultures in the United States and in different cultures throughout the world. This has the purpose of searching for psychological universals on these tests that may be independent of cultural differences and it has the purpose of establishing cultural norms to assist psychologists who test individuals from many different cultures. We will then examine attempts to adapt the T.A.T. and C.A.T. pictures to specific cultures, discuss some of the test characteristics for thematic tests in different cultures, and look at the contribution of thematic tests in studies of the acculturation process of one culture adjusting to life within a new culture. Finally, we will discuss the problem of gender, culture, and power bias in psychological testing and recommend a 12-step program for gender and multicultural thematic test assessment for the contemporary clinician.

A Standard Battery with Adequate Test Norms

When a consumer requests a psychological evaluation from a psychologist, it is important that the tests administered consist of the variety of tests that are considered by the psychological profession to be the best at addressing the basic areas of intellectual functioning, screening for academic achievement, neuropsychological or learning disability screening, and personality assessment. The American Psychological Association outlines standards for a basic grouping of psychological tests employed in mental health clinics, schools, hospitals, and by private practitioners, which all psychologists are expected to be competent in administering and interpreting (A.P.A., 1985). This "standard battery" typically consists of a Wechsler intelligence test, the Wide Range Achievement Test, the Bender Gestalt, the Draw-a-Person, the House-Tree-Person, the Kinetic-Family-Drawing, the T.A.T. or C.A.T., and the Rorschach. Other tests are often added to this basic group—particularly by school psychologists attempting to evaluate learning disabilities and neuropsychologists evaluating specific areas of cognitive deficits—but the majority of all psychological test evaluations tend to include this grouping.

At the present, the Wechsler intelligence tests set the highest standard of test construction, since they are normed on a very large sample of individuals of different gender, age, socioeconomic status, and culture within the United States. There are Wechsler versions with excellent norms in many other countries and cultures throughout the world, such as American Hispanic, French Canada, France, Germany, and so forth. The Wide Range Achievement Test and the Rorschach have very good norms. The Bender Gestalt test only has norms for children from 5 to 9 years of age (Koppitz, 1964) and the only drawing test with adequate norms is the Goodenough Draw-a-Person Test for children and adolescents from 3 to 15 years of age (Harris, 1963). However, these sets of age norms are basically employed only for a rough estimate of the developmental maturity of an individual on these tests, since norms for other types of scoring (such as neuropsychological or emotional indicators) have not been established.

The clinician has available norms for typical themes on the T.A.T. and the C.A.T., and for varying scoring variables within the United States (Bellak et al., 1947; Booth, 1953; Eron, 1950; Holt, 1978; Murstein, 1972; Neman et al., 1973, 1974; Rosenblatt, 1958, Veroff, 1961). However, the T.A.T. does not always utilize the same T.A.T. card sequences. The various adaptations of thematic tests to specific cultures rarely provide age, gender, socioeconomic, or other norms, except for the notable normative studies of Avila Espada (1983) on the T.A.T. for the Spanish population and that of Rodrigues Silva (1982) on the C.A.T.-H. for Brazil.

Therefore, if a psychologist is attempting to evaluate an individual from a culture for which there are not adequate test norms and the psychologist is not fluent in the language of the individual or knowledgeable about the individual's cultural frame of reference, there is likely to be an inhibition in test responses called *reticence* (Snowden & Todman, 1982) and a cultural bias in the psychologist's manner of interpreting the test results. (These are discussed in detail later in the chapter.) At the end of this chapter, we list some guidelines for researchers and test developers who wish to adapt thematic tests to specific groups and for the psychologist to keep in mind in conducting test evaluations with individuals of gender, culture, and other variables different from that of the psychologist.

Development of Culture-Specific T.A.T. Cards

There were many early attempts to develop culture-specific T.A.T. cards (Alexander & Anderson, 1957; Caudill, 1949, 1952; Geertz, 1957; Gladwin, 1953; Gladwin & Sarason, 1953; Hanks, 1956; Henry, 1947; Kaplan, 1956; Lessa & Spiegelman, 1954; MacGregor, 1946; Parker, 1964; Preston, 1964; Thompson & Joseph, 1944; Thompson, 1949; Vogt, 1951). The main approach is to follow some of Murray's (1943) T.A.T. cards, while changing the features and often the skin color of the people, clothing, backgrounds, and situations to make them culturally familiar to the particular culture being studied. The most important are those with American Indians, African Americans, and the Turkese of Micronesia, because they highlight many of the strengths and weaknesses inherent in the effort to adapt Murray's cards for specific subgroups in U.S. society and elsewhere.

Thematic Test Adaptations with American Indians

One of the earliest and most extensive research programs to develop a culture-specific T.A.T. is a collaboration between the Indian Education Research Project of the United States Bureau of Indian Affairs and the Committee on Human Development of the University of Chicago. Lessa (Lessa & Spiegelman, 1954) developed a T.A.T. adaptation for the research program consisting of 2 of Murray's cards and 10 original cards of everyday situations of American Indian children drawn by an American Indian artist. Over 100 children between the ages of 6 and 18 from five American Indian tribes—Hopi, Navaho, Papago, Sioux, and Zuni—were administered the T.A.T., Rorschach, projective drawings, and a few other personality measures.

The first report of this research is by Thompson and Joseph (1944) in their book, *The Hopi Way*, who find that the T.A.T.s of the Hopi children tend to support anthropological assumptions about the Hopi culture, such as the heroes in the stories tend to be less important than the group and there tends to be more careful control of impulses, rather than themes of direct aggression and of other strong emotional expression. The authors also report that many of the children's T.A.T. stories contain variations of the Spider Woman, a very powerful and malignant figure in Hopi folklore, which the authors suggest gives evidence of a defensive retreat into covert aggressive fantasizing. The T.A.T. protocols show a need for self-control with respect to the outer world in the careful and cautious attention to environmental story details, contrasted with the covert aggressive images. The authors interpret this as supporting the Hopi culture's value on a defensive displacement of aggressive feelings into the subjective, inner world of fantasy.

The Hopi Way is very well written, interesting, and charming in many respects, but it does not publish any strong concurrent validity measures, such as other tests showing the same findings and behavioral rating scale measures or other measures of outer behavior. Publication of such data would place the interpretations of Hopi culture and personality on a firmer, more empirical, quantitative basis.

MacGregor's (1946) *Warriors Without Weapons*—a study of 200 Pine Ridge Sioux children from 6 to 18 years of age using the same projective and other personality tests as used with the Hopi—reaches a similar conclusion. The overall personality pattern on these tests presents a picture of viewing the outside world as hostile and dangerous with strong emotional constriction, lack of spontaneity, and inhibited expression of aggressive impulses and a heavy stress on defensive fantasy. MacGregor finds these children more restrained than either the white or Navaho children in the large, interdisciplinary research program. However, his results suggest an inhibition in both outer and inner expressiveness. A major difference between MacGregor's and the earlier report of Thompson and Joseph with Hopi children is that MacGregor has 10 full-length case histories by William Henry—a very competent T.A.T. interpreter. The case studies present the test protocols together with observational and other supportive data, which provide a better way for the reader to evaluate the author's conclusions.

Leighton and Kluckholn's (1947) report on Navaho children presents a roughly similar personality picture of emotional inhibition. Both the Rorschach and T.A.T. protocols "tend to be short, literal, commonplace descriptions with little elaboration or imaginative detail" (p. 176). They find the children are "quite restrained" on the whole and "a little anxious in a general way and feel subject to their parents' authority" (p. 178). There are 16 brief case histories with statements about the personalities of the individual cases, but without any guidelines as to how the T.A.T. in particular was interpreted.

The fourth volume on the Papago Indians (Joseph et al., 1949) is similarly flawed by lack of detail in methods of scoring the projective tests. The results of the T.A.T. are not really reported at all, except for brief comments on the T.A.T. in the series of case histories provided at the end of the publication. Of note, however, is the authors' conclusion that the Papago Indians differ from the other American Indian tribes studied in having an "intensity of emotions, a relatively precarious control and discipline, and a peculiar swing between realistic participation in the life about them and extreme withdrawal. Against outer and inner conflicts, they seem to defend themselves essentially by evasion and by subjective interpretation of facts and feelings . . . [and] their intellectual approach seems to be largely subjective interpretation instead of objective and analytical" (pp. 215–216).

It is clear that this type of personality interpretation of a particular cultural group based on what appears to be very loose and subjective projective test analyses is not only scientifically unfounded but also prejudicial and potentially harmful to a cultural group. It appears to report the results of a "scientific study using standard research stimuli," but in the end, it serves only to support uninformed and largely prejudicial views of a minority culture in U.S. society. Some political policymakers might want to cite such poorly done research in order to justify cutting down on funds for educational, vocational, and other programs on the basis that the Papago culture does not value objective, intellectual thinking.

By contrast, Henry's (1947) report on the results of the large-scale study of southwestern American Indian children is distinguished by the number of different areas of test scoring, the high level of his T.A.T. interpretations, and the inclusion of independent information available for validation, such as comparisons with the Rorschach, other tests, and behavioral observations. Different examiners administered the tests to the children, occasionally using an interpreter when necessary. Henry included a measure of acculturation by comparing the amount of contact each child had had with whites. Age differences and differences between Hopi and Navajo children were found.

Kluckhold and Rosenzweig (1949) conducted a very interesting longitudinal study of two Navaho children who were given repeated psychological testing with the T.A.T., Rorschach, and other tests over a five-year-period with independent interpretation of the psychological tests by different individuals. The first administration was in 1942, when the children were 6 and 7 years of age, with later testing in 1946, and 1947. The major focus is on the Rorschach. However, an important finding with the T.A.T. was that when it was later administered to one of the children in the Navaho language, rather than in English, the protocol was more than five times as long. Other studies of North American Indians employing Murray's T.A.T. cards are those of Caudill (1949), who used Henry's (1947) interpretative systems to the score the T.A.T.'s of Ojibwa Indians in Wisconsin; Bigart (1971) with the Flathead tribe; and Preston (1964) with Eskimos. Goldstine and Gutmann (1972) used a mixture of the Murray T.A.T. cards and culture-specific T.A.T. adaptations with Navajo men, while only culture-specific T.A.T. adaptations were employed in studies of northern Cheyenne children (Alexander & Anderson, 1957), Eskimos (Parker, 1964), and Sioux adults (Dana, 1982).

African American Adaptations

Thompson (1949) modified Murray's cards primarily by darkening the skin color to make the figures in the pictures appear to be African Americans. Both Murray's T.A.T. and Thompson's modification are published by Harvard University Press in exactly the same format. Thompson's modification is an excellent vehicle for research on the independent variable of skin color, since the researcher is able to control for card size, background, situation, and all the other variables of Murray's pictures.

Thompson followed Murray's assumption that people will create better and more psychologically revealing stories if it is easier for them to identify with the protagonists featured in the T.A.T. cards. Murray reasoned that it is easier to identify with the "hero" of a T.A.T. picture if the central person portrayed is of the same gender and general age of the test taker. Hence, Murray has specific cards for women, for men, for boys, and for girls. Thompson set out to test this hypothesis by comparing stories of a sample of African American college students in a southern university told to his T.A.T. adaptations with stories told to Murray's T.A.T. cards. He scored the stories for number of words, verbs, and nouns, excluding pronouns and modifiers. He found that the African American college students tended to give more words, nouns, verbs, and modifiers to the T.A.T. pictures of African Americans than they did to Murray's T.A.T. cards.

Riess and colleagues (1950) compared African American and white women attending a northern university with the Thompson and Murray T.A.T. cards, as well as with cards administered by an African American to those administered by a white psychologist. There were basically no appreciable differences among the African American and white college students with either Thompson's or Murray's T.A.T. cards. When the stories in this study were compared with those in Thompson's study, it was found that the stories of both African American and white northern college students in the Reiss and colleagues' (1950) study were longer than those in the Thompson (1949) study, whether the test administrator was African American or white. The overall conclusion from this study was that it did not appear that African Americans will create more productive stories to pictures that feature African Americans than to Murray's original T.A.T. cards.

A further study by Swartz and associates (1951) came to the same conclusion that it does not appear to make a difference whether the administrator is white or African American and whether the T.A.T. pictures depict African Americans (the Thompson modification) or whites (the Murray cards). Korchin and colleagues (1950) compared the stories of African American and white men, half of each group were middle-class and the other half lower-class men, using four of Murray's cards (1BM, 2, 6BM, 7BM). There were not any differences in number of words between the two racial groups, but there was a significant difference between middle-class and lower-class men for both ethnic groups.

Cook (1953) compared the Murray and Thompson T.A.T. cards with a group of African American and a group of white college students, using cards 4, 6BM, 13MF, 18GF, and 18BM for both versions of the T.A.T. He divided the two ethnic groups and gave one group of African Americans the Murray cards and another group of African Americans the Thompson cards. Similarly, one group of white college students were given the Murray cards and another group of whites the Thompson cards. He asked each student to write out stories to each of the five cards and, at the end, he asked each student whether he or she had thought of the people seen on the cards as "blacks, whites, or just as people." Both the group of African Americans who viewed the Murray cards and the group of African Americans who viewed the Thompson cards reported that they viewed the figures in the cards as "just people," rather than as black or white. However, the white group who created stories to the Thompson cards reported that they were aware that the figures in the pictures were African Americans. This study raises several questions regarding the basic assumptions of thematic tests:

1. Does an individual identify more with a T.A.T. that features individuals of similar gender, age, and ethnicity, or is it more useful to utilize T.A.T. cards that feature individuals slightly different from the test taker? Cook's results point to the possibility that the African Americans in his study might have been just as likely to identify with "white" T.A.T. figures, as with the "African American" T.A.T. cards, while the whites did not appear to do so with African American T.A.T. figures. On the other hand, the results could mean that the African Americans were more sensitive to the question of ethnicity and more committed to getting past racial identifications of people, whereas the whites tended more to support racial boundaries.

2. Could Cook's question for the students to choose among only three descriptions—"blacks, whites, or just people"—have been viewed by the African American college students as too simplistic, since the majority of African Americans in the United States have at least some white ancestry and many presumably "white" individuals are similarly of mixed heritage? If so, the "white" students may have given a less informed and perhaps more racially prejudiced answer, while the "African American" students being more sensitive to racial identifications may have given a more accurate answer in keeping with the reality of a multicultural society.

3. It is possible that the use of culture-specific T.A.T. cards could actually have the opposite effect of making the test taker more defensive? Could presenting an individual with T.A.T. cards that feature individuals of similar age, gender, and culture make the test taker more resistant to revealing personal feelings and conflicts? Or do T.A.T. cards with some ambiguity and distance in the figures to the test taker provide for a freer stimulus with which to explore, express, and elaborate personally revealing feelings and conflicts?

One of the main powers of the Rorschach inkblots is precisely their vagueness and dissimilarity to the world of everyday reality. The majority of the inkblots do not resemble people, animals, or any distinct objects. Instead, they lead to numerous "approximations" to people, animals, and objects in the real world. This facilitates the psychological process of projection, whereby the lack of clarity and very dissimilarity of the test stimuli to the test taker allows him or her to "read into" or "project himself or herself into" the inkblots in attempting to make structure, order, and meaning out of the designs.

The only significant difference between the African American and white college students on the Murray or Thompson T.A.T. cards was: The stories told by the group of white students to the Thompson cards were longer than those of the African American group who told stories to the Thompson cards. This was the group of white students who reported at the end of the storytelling that they were aware that the figures in the cards represented African Americans. Therefore, Cook's study suggests that it may actually facilitate T.A.T. story creating if the cards have a little "psychological distance" in identification from the test taker, which is in keeping with the projective hypothesis underlying the great success of the Rorschach to tap and usually reveal deeper psychological dynamics than any other projective test. Cook's study concluded that it did not appear to be necessary to adapt the Murray T.A.T. cards for use with African Americans, in agreement with the other studies of Korchin and colleagues (1950), Riess and colleagues (1950) and Schwartz and colleagues (1951).

Mussen (1953) criticized these comparisons of African Americans and whites on the Thompson and Murray T.A.T. cards, because they used only story productivity measures, rather than measures that might tap more important cultural differences in personality, such as Murray's (1943) "needs and presses of the hero." When Mussen scored T.A.T. protocols of 50 African American and 50 lower socioeconomic white boys, he found that the African American children appeared to feel more insecure and tended to see the environment as more hostile; the white children felt more secure and viewed the environment as friendlier. In a comparison of white and African American juvenile delinquents on Murray's T.A.T., Megaree (1966) found similar cultural differences.

Others have criticized the early comparative studies using the Thompson T.A.T. cards for singling out the racial criterion of skin color, rather than developing a T.A.T. for African Americans that also adapted the pictures for background (Kagan & Lesser, 1961) and a more cultural perspective (Bailey et al., 1977; Snowden & Todman, 1982).

An important step in this direction is the Themes Concerning Blacks (T.C.B.) test of Williams (1972), who developed 20 drawings in charcoal similar to the style of Murray's T.A.T. drawings, but portraying African Americans in different urban and rural settings (Williams & Johnson, 1981). The scoring incorporates the emotional tone rating of Eron and associates (1950) as well as other categories developed by Williams to score internal control, goal setting, instrumental activity, reality perception, personal responsibility, and self-confidence. Published case studies of the T.C.B. with African American individuals suggests that it presents a culturally relevant test stimulus and a contextual grounding for clinical interpretations (Petty & Robinson, 1982; Terrell, 1982). However, there are not yet any norms for the T.C.B. to be used with the scoring system of Williams (1972).

The African Continent

Thematic test studies on the African continent include Arab university studies by Melikian (1964) and notable studies of black South Africans by Lee (1953), Biesheuvel (1958), DeRidder (1961) (who constructed a culture-specific T.A.T. for this population), and Baran (1971) (with Bantu-speaking South Africans). One of the most important papers in the field of culture-specific T.A.T. adaptations is by Sherwood (1957), who outlined what he felt are the most psychologically important characteristics of the T.A.T. that should be incorporated in any attempt to adapt them to another culture or group. These include the dimensions of sharpness/vagueness, incompleteness, compression or adequacy/relevance (card pull), symbolism, contrast in visual impact, number/appropriateness of figures/objects/physical environments presented, familiarity with human figures, appropriateness and range of relationships portrayed (including basic family relationships), and range of emotional tone.

Asian Americans

The relatively few thematic test studies of Asian Americans have all employed Murray's T.A.T. cards: Caudill (1952), Caudill and De Vos (1956), and Vaughn (1988) with Japanese Americans; Watrous and Hsu (1972) with students from Hong Kong and Taiwan; and De Vos (1983) with Korean Americans.

The Asian Continent

The earliest attempt to develop a culture-specific T.A.T. for an Asian culture is that of Lessa and Spiegelman (1954), who developed a series of 18 pictures to be used in a study of the Ulithian people of the Caroline Islands in Micronesia. In a landmark cross-cultural classic, *Truk: Man in Paradise,* Gladwin and Sarason (1953) utilized Lessa's T.A.T. adaptation, the Kohs Block Test, and the Rorschach in their very creative study of the stages of personality development of 12 Trukese men ranging in age from 13 to 56 and 13 women from 14 to 50 years of age. The study is an unusual collaboration of an outstanding anthropologist, Gladwin, and an outstanding psychologist, Sarason, who provided the very detailed and excellent projective test interpretations. Considerable information is given for each of the research participants, whose psychological test results are reported in 23 detailed case histories that are presented individually in the book.

This book is an important paradigm in cross-cultural research methodology, since it demonstrates how an ethnological study of a culture by an anthropologist conducting intensive interviews with key informants can be significantly enhanced through the use of psychological tests, which can be administered and scored in a standardized manner. The authors emphasized that the independent scoring and interpretation of the psychological tests in this study provided "a number of hypothesis and made evident several relationships within ethnographic data which were not apparent during the initial 'anthropological' analysis" (p. 460). As Gladwin (1953) also emphasized in a separate paper, when he returned home after four years of work with these people, he had been convinced that men were dominant and more secure and women were more insecure and subservient. Sarason's independent interpretations of the test protocols administered by Gladwin and colleagues in the field suggested, on the other hand, that the men were actually more anxious than the women and appeared to be less competent in dealing with ambiguous or conflictual situations. This led Gladwin to take a closer look at his field data, such as number of suicide attempts, male versus female role in adulterous relations, the treatment of brother and sister at puberty when children must be separated by cultural decree, and so on, which supported Sarason's test interpretations and convinced Gladwin to revise his earlier anthropological understanding of the Turkese culture.

Other studies in Polynesia are those of Hanks (1967), who developed a culture-specific T.A.T. for Thailand; Kline and Svaste-Xuto (1981), who compared British and Thai children on Bellak's C.A.T.; and Lagmay (1964, 1975), who adapted the C.A.T. for the Philippines. Rao and Ramadevi (1958a, 1958b) used the T.A.T. with individuals in India, and Chowdhury (1960a, 1960b) developed T.A.T. and C.A.T. adaptations for India, which are commercially available. In Japan, Fujita (1956) used the T.A.T. with delinquents, Marui (1960) conducted a normative T.A.T. study, and De Vos (1960, 1973), De Vos and Vaughn (1992), and Wagatsuma and De Vos (1984) have done T.A.T. studies of Japanese expressive and instrumental social role behavior. Hwang (1975) compared Chinese and Scottish adolescents on the T.A.T., and De Vos and associates (1979) compared Chinese and Japanese adults on the T.A.T. A large-scale adaptation of the T.A.T. to mainland Chinese culture with reported norms was done by Zhang and colleagues (1993).

Hispanic Americans

An attempt to develop a culture-specific thematic test for Hispanic American children ages 5 to 18 years of age is the TEMAS, which in Spanish means "themes" (Costantino et al., 1988b). In contrast to the C.A.T.'s black-and-white pictures of animals, the TEMAS consists of chromatic, culturally specific, and gender-balanced pictures of Hispanic American children in different situations. The pictures also attempt to depict conflictual interpersonal situations requiring solutions, which the test developers maintain provide a way to score the child's maladaptive as opposed to adaptive responses. An inquiry may be employed, if necessary, and there is also a short form available. The scoring system consists of many of the personality variables of Bellak's scoring system—such as self-conflict, sexual identity, interpersonal relations, anxiety/depression, delay of gratification, moral judgment, and reality testing—and adds those of aggression and achievement motivation. The cognitive scoring variables expand on Bellak's scoring variables of main conflict, omissions (a total number, as well as omissions of main character, secondary character, event, and setting), introductions (a total number, as well as introductions of main character, secondary character, event, and setting), and add cognitive scoring variables of reaction time, total time, fluency, sequencing, imagination, relationship, and inquiries. The authors provide some tentative norms to be employed with Anglo Americans, African Americans, Puerto Ricans, and other Hispanic Americans. Alpha, inter-rater, and test-retest reliabilities are reported to be highly satisfactory, and content, construct, and criterion validation studies suggest that the test is a good measure of personality constructs and prediction of psychotherapy outcomes. A parallel group of TEMAS pictures has been developed for use with mainstream Anglo American children (Costantino et al., 1988a; Costantino et al., 1991).

However, the long tradition of research with the C.A.T. and C.A.T.-H. in the United States and in other cultures and the C.A.T.'s publication and active clinical use for psychological testing in 11 other countries suggest that these tests are preferable to the TEMAS. Moreover, Chapter 15 discusses the rationale and research tradition for the value of utilizing animal pictures in the C.A.T., particularly for young, preschool aged children, as opposed to pictures of children (Biersdorf & Marcuse, 1953; Blum, 1956; Byrd & Witherspoon, 1954; Furyua, 1957; Light, 1954; Moriarty, 1972; Myer et al., 1972; Scheffler, 1975; Witherspoon, 1968).

Cross-cultural research with the C.A.T. includes the comparison of Latin American and Anglo American children by Booth (1953) in Texas; Chowdhury's (1960b) slight modification of the C.A.T. with children of India; Lagmay's (1964, 1975; Ilan & Resurreccion, 1971) C.A.T. adaptation for Philippine culture; Earle's (1968) C.A.T. study of Rakau children in New Zealand; Berman and Seward's (1958) with Israeli children; and Rabin's (1972) with *Kibbutz* and non-*Kibbutz* children in Israel.

Since the C.A.T.-H. was developed for children between the ages of 10 and 12 to whom the C.A.T. animal pictures might appear as too "immature" for their current preadolescent concerns, this may be the most applicable age group for both the Hispanic American and the Anglo American TEMAS. The charm of the animal pictures of the C.A.T., the overall test construction of psychologically meaningful situations, and the research history make the C.A.T. especially useful with young children—particularly those of 3 or 4 years up through children of 10 or 11—who are just becoming preadolescents, when the T.A.T. is more appropriate. The use of animal pictures on the C.A.T. makes it useful across a number of different cultures and countries in which it is published and has been the major thematic test for children. However, an older child of differing culture, who might be given the C.A.T.-H., should be given a more culturally relevant thematic test, such as the Hispanic American TEMAS.

Other thematic test studies of Hispanic American culture are those of Johnson and Sikes (1965) and Doane and associates (1989) comparing Mexican American and Anglo Americans and Urrabazo's (1986) study of Machismo in Mexican American men on the T.A.T. and the Kinetic-Family-Drawing Test. Suarez-Orozco (1987, 1989, 1990) utilizes the T.A.T. in his research on acculturation of Central American immigrants in the United States. In South America, there are T.A.T. studies of Mayan culture by Guttmann (1966) and Press (1987). In Spain, there is the extensive normative T.A.T. research of Avila Espada (1983, 1985, 1990).

Socioeconomic Status

T.A.T. studies of socioeconomic status include Ehrenreich (1990), Korchin and associates (1950), Mason and Ammons (1956), McArthur (1955), Minuchin and associates (1967), Mitchel (1951), Levy (1970), Riessman and Miller (1958), and Veroff (1961). Mitchel (1951) and McArthur (1955) found a tendency to describe father figures more warmly in the T.A.T. stories of middle-class individuals and for lower-class individuals to introduce more family figures into their stories, and Korchin and colleagues (1950) report a tendency for lower-class individuals to give shorter stories than middle-class individuals. As the many different cultures within the United States and throughout the world become increasingly intermixed through intermarriage, instantaneous forms of international communication, and other factors, the specificity of cultural difference may not be as important a variable in psychological test performance as differences in socioeconomic status. Therefore, more research needs to be done in this important area for the future.

The Question of Gender, Cultural, and Power Bias

There is a very lively debate in the field of psychological testing on the question whether it is possible for a psychologist to evaluate objectively the psychological testing of an individual of a different gender and culture without introducing gender and cultural bias. There is an example of the Wechsler intelligence tests that have excellent age and gender norms for the United States, for Hispanic American culture, French Canada, France, Germany, and elsewhere. The test questions and testing materials are culture specific and the test questions are given in the language of each culture.

The U.S. version of the Wechsler intelligence tests sets the standard for test construction, the establishment of representative norms, and the interpretation of test results. This is done through the use of a very clear and specific test administration and age norms based on very large stratified random sampling according to the different ethnic, cultural, and socioeconomic urban and rural groups of the United States census. The psychologist is then able to compare an individual's test results with well-developed norms for all individuals within the same small age group in the United States on the same tests.

However, while the main socioeconomic and cultural subgroups in the United States census were employed in order to develop age norms for the United States Wechsler intelligence tests, there continues to be very important questions raised as to the appropriateness of this test for specific cultures. For example, Helms (1992) argues that it is biased toward African American minorities, since the test items themselves were developed primarily in Europe and the United States within predominantly white, mainstream culture. Therefore, the test may be said to measure only the African American individual's *degree of acculturation and knowledge of white, mainstream culture,* rather than reflecting the individual's *true intellectual functioning.*

The history of U.S. psychology has the unfortunate dark shadow of Jensen's (1969) well-known paper on the so-called "genetic inferiority of blacks in intelligence," which was given the appearance of "scientific" credibility with its many statistical references and its publication in the prestigious *Harvard Educational Review.* Later expanded into a full-length book, *Genetics and Education,* Jensen's (1972) argument essentially is that efforts to boost the I.Q. scores of African American children through government-funded preschool early intervention programs, such as Head Start, are not likely to result in helping African American children "catch up" to the educational level of their white peers due to this fundamental difference in basic intelligence.

Ryan's (1971) sociological classic, *Blaming the Victim,* on the other hand, suggested that the actual *inferiority* is not in the African American child, but in the educational environment. Ryan pointed out that in such comparisons of intelligence of African American and white children,

> no one remembers to ask questions about the collapsing buildings and torn textbooks, the frightening, insensitive teachers, the six additional desks in the room, the blustering, frightened principals, the relentless segregation, the callous administrator, the irrelevant curriculum, the bigoted or cowardly members of the school board, the insulting history book, the stingy taxpayers, the fairy-tale readers, or the self-serving faculty of the local teachers' college. We are encouraged to confine our attention to the child and to dwell on all his alleged deficits. (p. 4)

The majority of African American children in the studies cited by Jensen (1969, 1972) were growing up in *an inferior environment* of extreme poverty, in which they are frequently exposed to lead poisoning and rarely have enough food to eat. Baghurst (1992) found lower I.Q. scores in children exposed to lead poisoning prior to 7 years of age. Extensive reviews by Lynn (1990) and Ricciuti (1993) support the obvious fact that adequate food results in children having increases in height, head circumference, brain size, improved neurological development, and functioning of the brain, measured in part on I.Q. tests.

Labov (1973), a pioneer in the field of sociolinguistics, also provided a powerful critique of Jensen in his important paper, "The Logic of Nonstandard English." Labov explained that most African Americans grow up in the bilingual environment of the standard English of the Anglo American mainstream culture school system and their own "nonstandard Black English." He outlined how several aspects of the grammar and vocabulary of Black English that often appear as "ungrammatical" to standard English dominant Anglo Americans are, on the contrary, absolutely logical and rule-based within this system of nonstandard Black English.

This relates directly to the situation when an African American is tested by a white psychologist with the standard English-based I.Q. tests developed for white Americans, and the African American individual is found to perform at a lower intellectual level. Labov reported that his African American research assistant audiotaped the language of African American gang leaders, many of whom had dropped out of public school and were thought to use ungrammatical language. The corpus of language obtained and analyzed according to the rules of nonstandard Black English revealed, however, that they are actually highly intelligent, with a wealth of vocabulary and a highly playful and creative linguistic expression. Labov's work underscores the importance for cross-cultural researchers using psychological tests to be thoroughly conversant with the language of the culture studied and its cultural frame of reference, and to make sure the test items are culturally appropriate.

Snowden and Todman (1982) further pointed out that when an Anglo American administers a psychological test, particularly if the Anglo American is not known to an African American test taker, a culture-specific response called *reticence* is likely to occur. This response is characterized by cautiousness, vagueness, and inhibition in storytelling, which stand in direct contrast to the rich, vital, and elaborate storytelling tradition in African-based culture. When the white supervisors of black South Africans coerced them into taking the Seven Squares Test, for example, the black South Africans did as little as possible. Dana (1965; Dana & Voigt, 1962) found that a similar type of reticence in the test behavior of African Americans on I.Q. tests was erroneously interpreted as a racial difference in intelligence.

Gender bias is also very likely to be introduced if the test taker is a woman and the psychologist a man from a culture in which men actively oppress women. If women are considered second-class citizens, who are viewed as less capable of important decision making in the society and less intelligent, overall, than the men of that culture, such a male psychologist from that particular culture is not likely to be able to make an objective assessment of such a woman's true intellectual functioning. Although some other countries in the world have had women leaders, the United States—a modern, progressive world leader in the area of human rights and equal opportunity—has never had a woman president. Hence, it is obvious that some gender bias is likely to be a factor in intelligent testing of women by male psychologists in our culture and elsewhere.

Sexism is a term that has come to mean the attribution of certain attitudes, traits, and characteristics by one gender to that of another. Women and men and boys and girls are each capable of attributing gender bias to the other gender. *Prejudice* is similarly defined as making usually negative but occasionally positive assumptions about characteristics of an individual's identity and functioning, primarily based on the individual's gender, age, race, culture, religion, socioeconomic status, physical handicap, or other such factors, rather than on a more informed and objective assessment. Prejudice can stem from one's attempt to bolster one's own self-esteem by viewing others as inferior to oneself in some superficial manner, such as the simple color of their skin.

Sexism, cultural bias, and all forms of prejudice tend to be supported and tolerated by the typical power relationships of the particular society. If men have more power in a society to run the government, make the laws, and run the largest companies, the women of the society tend to be viewed as less important and less powerful. As women and minorities obtain increased leadership roles in the United States, and as labor laws of equal opportunity, laws against discrimination and sexual harrassment in the workplace, Civil Rights, Americans with Disabilities, and other legislation are enacted and enforced, there is a chance that the amount of sexism, cultural bias, and other forms of prejudice in U.S. society will diminish.

But what about a woman whose children were removed due to child neglect, and who is later ordered by the court to have a psychological evaluation to assess whether she is psychologically healthy enough to have the children returned to her? Or what about two divorcing parents in a custody battle over which parent should have primary custody of their children? Are the test responses of these parents likely to be influenced by the particular test situation? Forensic psychological evaluation brings in a power relationship between the test takers who are usually very fearful of being seen as less capable, less intelligent, and less psychologically healthy than they are in reality and the psychologist, who would appear to have been given too much power by the court to decide their fate, in the parents' view.

In such circumstances, parents often believe they will not be awarded the care of their children if they are not good at drawing pictures of houses, trees, and people or at making up good stories on the T.A.T. Psychologists conducting test evaluations in such forensic cases need to pay close attention to the very powerful influence of the legal context (Ackerman & Kane, 1993; Shapiro, 1991; Ziskin, 1995).

A powerful relationship is also involved when an adult psychologist evaluates a child. The test situation is relevant in terms of whether the psychologist is going to recommend the child for placement in a special education class, which the child believes is seen by other children as the class for dumb children. The child is being tested by an adult psychologist in a society in which children are considered weak and powerless, compared to adults. In such a situation, the child's responses will be influenced by the test situation of the dreaded special education placement recommendation and the basic power difference between adults and children in the society.

The psychologist testing in these different situations must be very careful in considering the possibility of gender, cultural, and power bias in the test responses and the scoring and evaluation of the test results. More research is needed to establish typical patterns of response, social desirability factors, and other test characteristics in forensic settings and in situations where a psychologist is from a very different culture and background from the person being tested. The development of standards for the choice of which tests to employ and for establishing adequate test norms are important steps in this direction.

It is important to try to learn as much as possible about the background and culture of an individual prior to making a clinical assessment and recommendations for intervention. Schwartzman (1983) suggested following the model of the anthropological ethnographer, who goes to another culture and locates an "expert informant" from whom to learn as much as possible about the culture from an "inside perspective." In a good psychological testing evaluation, there needs to be a balance in the power relationship between the "expert" psychologist who evaluates and the individual being tested, who is the "expert informant." Falicov (1988) pointed out that mainstream, white, middle-class U.S. society tends to value disengagement and independence from the nuclear family in young adulthood, marital unity, parental distance from young adult children, self-assertion, and low reliance on social institutions, which are synonymous with psychological adjustment and mental health. Mexican individuals she has studied tend to grow up in large families, place a higher value on interdependence within the extended family, and place a higher value on hierarchical authority within the family and within the larger social institutions, particularly the church. It would be misleading, then, to assess a young adult Mexican American, who is still very closely involved in the nuclear family, as being overly passive and dependent, rather than having a healthy adjustment for this stage of development.

Another contrast is the importance of the husband/wife *dominant dyad* in mainstream U.S. culture compared to the more central father/son dyad in Chinese and Middle Eastern families, the mother/son dyad in Hindu society, or the brother/brother dyad in some African societies (Hsu, 1971). When an individual migrates from one of these more traditional cultures to mainstream U.S. culture, there is likely to be a culture shock in the period of adjusting to the new culture and a major clash between the traditional culture and that of the new culture. Sluzki (1979) provides an excellent model for this conflict typically experienced by families during different stages of migration and acculturation.

Conclusion

Clinical, counseling, and school psychologists in today's society need to be aware of the possibility of different forms of bias that can result from a lack of adequate knowledge about age, gender, ethnic, religious, socioeconomic, cultural, and other important areas of differences among people. This chapter has presented the history of cross-cultural research and clinical use of thematic tests with individuals of different backgrounds within the United States and other countries. Increased legislation in the United States on human rights, affirmative action, and equal opportunity have helped to sensitize the field of cross-cultural psychological research and contemporary clinical practice to the importance of these issues when using psychological tests.

This tradition emphasizes the paramount importance of *the rights of all individuals to be evaluated and assessed in their own terms within the framework of their own cultural framework and often in their own native languages, as opposed to being tested with gender and/or culturally biased materials and tested by mainstream middle-class professionals who do not speak their language or understand their basic cultural assumptions.* This should be one of the "patient rights" in mental health law and one of the rights of students being evaluated by psychological tests in education law, and it should be clearly stated in all psychology ethics codes.

The T.A.T. has never been considered to be gender biased, since it has the option of a specific sequence for males and a specific sequence for females. Chapter 4 provides a rationale for a standard T.A.T. sequence for men and women with gender-balanced T.A.T. cards with adequate norms. The animal pictures of the C.A.T. are basically independent of specific gender and culture identification. However, the T.A.T.'s primary portrayal of white, middle-class individuals is likely to bias the protocols of individuals who are not from white, middle-class backgrounds.

Therefore, we presented the long tradition of attempts to develop culturally specific T.A.T., C.A.T., and S.A.T. cards for different cultural groups and the use of the T.A.T. in the field of anthropology and psychology dating back to the 1940s. A fundamental assumption of the T.A.T., beginning with Murray, is that an individual will be more comfortable in revealing oneself on T.A.T. stories if he or she is shown pictures in which the central hero resembles the individual's same age, sex, and cultural background. This gave rise to Thompson's (1949) T.A.T. modification for African Americans that depicts African Americans in different situations. The majority of research with this instrument found that African American participants are just as comfortable with the regular T.A.T. as they are with the ethnically specific T.A.T. modification.

What about the C.A.T. that depicts young animals being a more successful projective test with children than the C.A.T.-H that shows human children in different situations? Which version of the test is more likely to reveal the child's true feelings, anxieties, and conflicts?

Object relations theory suggests that a man's story about a hero who is a woman or a child's story about a young animal may be both expressions of the individual's own feelings and conflicts on some level, since it is the individual's own story. It is not someone else's story. Since Murray's T.A.T. is based on powerfully evocative situations, it has become a more popular assessment instrument for people of different ages, gender, and cultural groups than was originally intended. For example, many school psychologists find the T.A.T. to be clinically useful with very young children and many psychologists find that Murray's T.A.T. cards originally designed only for women are valuable to use with men and vice versa. Similarly, the C.A.T. has been utilized with good results as an additional assessment instrument with adults (Kitron & Benziman, 1990). Many of the attempts to develop different thematic test cards for individuals of different cultural groups have not been as successful as the T.A.T. or C.A.T., because either the drawings are not of equal artistic quality or the situations depicted are not as evocative as the standard thematic test instruments.

The more important issue is for the psychologist to be aware that if a man is testing a woman, a woman testing a man, a white person testing an Asian American, or a Hispanic American testing a white person, this very gender or cultural difference is likely to influence the test results. Since the testing situation is usually a power relationship, the individual being tested may create stories that communicate what the individual believes are most acceptable to the tester. It is preferable for an individual to be tested by another individual who speaks the same language and who comes from the same cultural group. The production of test responses may be influenced by gender and cultural factors and the interpretation of the test results must be considered in light of the storyteller's cultural frame of reference. What is considered to be a religious belief in one culture may be misinterpreted as a form of psychopathology by another individual, as in the example of a belief in the spirit world or in ghosts in some American Indian or some South American cultures, which a white, mainstream professional psychologist might misinterpret as an instance of a lack of healthy reality testing.

This fascinating area brings us back to the very beginning of this book in the fundamental assumption of thematic apperception test assessment—the *projective hypothesis*. Clearly, an individual of particular gender and a particular cultural group may be more comfortable being tested by an individual of the same gender and cultural group. But how is one to interpret the various heroes and protagonists in the individual's T.A.T. stories? Is the central hero who most resembles the storyteller in age and sex the closest expression of the storyteller's own personality, desires, and conflicts? Or are figures that least resemble the storyteller in a story expressions of deeper, more dissociated aspects of the storyteller's personality that the storyteller wishes to keep hidden or deny? A man who relates a story of a woman beating up a man may be expressing a reality he has experienced at the hands of an abusive woman. However, another possibility is that on some level he may wish to be able to express angry, aggressive feelings toward someone. So, he displaces and projects these socially unacceptable feelings onto a figure in a story of the opposite sex and makes himself the victim at the same time in order to punish himself for giving expression in his story to these unacceptable aggressive feelings.

These subtle and deep issues of power relationships, gender and cultural differences, and levels of conscious and unconscious meanings of different characters in thematic test stories underscore the serious responsibility of contemporary clinicians in administering and interpreting psychological tests. The best way to become sensitive to these gender and cultural issues is to increase one's understanding of the multiplicity of possible meanings of T.A.T. stories and the social and specific cultural setting of the testing situation (Dana, 1996).

If a psychologist understands the typical normative responses to the T.A.T. for individuals of different ages, sexes, and cultural groups, and for those who have different types of personality orientation or psychiatric disorders, the psychologist is able to come to the best possible diagnostic conclusion and treatment recommendation. If a psychologist understands how different levels of consciousness may be represented by different protagonists in a T.A.T. story and how the reality of a past trauma can be symbolically communicated in a highly atypical element in one story or in repeated elements in several different stories, the psychologist is better able to see beneath the most obvious surface meaning to help the individual become aware of and work through the reality of a past trauma and to identify, express, and work through other significant issues and conflicts.

In sum, clinicians and researchers employing thematic tests in their work should consider the following criteria for gender-specific and culture-specific thematic test assessment:

1. If the T.A.T., C.A.T.-H., or S.A.T. are being adapted for use with a specific culture, it is important to depict individuals of a particular ethnicity of that culture, as in Thompson's (1949) modification of the T.A.T. for African Americans by redrawing the T.A.T. with pictures of African Americans. *A culture-specific T.A.T. adaptation should have pictures of individuals of the same ethnicity of the culture as well as culturally familiar situations, backgrounds, and situations that are powerful elicitors of projective information about the individuals in that culture,* as in Lessa's (Lessa & Spiegelman, 1954) American Indian T.A.T. adaptation and William's (1972) Themes Concerning Blacks Test (T.C.B.).

2. Murray's (1943a) T.A.T. cards were developed over a period of eight years (1935–1943), during which hundreds of different pictures were trial tested in order to derive the final set of those that were found to stimulate the basic range of human emotions and the basic conflictual situations of interpersonal relations. Similarly, Bellak's (1949) C.A.T. pictures show animals in basic conflictual situations typical of childhood, such as little chicks waiting for their parent to feed them, sibling rivalry, being awake and alone at night, a toilet-training situation, and so on. The success of the C.A.T. as a projective instrument for young children is based on these fundamental situations of childhood, family and peer relationships, and sources of pleasure, anxiety, and fear, along with artistically interesting and involving pictures with sufficient detail, occasional ambiguity, contrast, and visual impact.

Sherwood (1957) published a set of criteria that have been researched in Murray's T.A.T. cards and Bellak's C.A.T. cards that one should follow when attempting to adapt these tests to specific cultures. These are the dimensions of *sharpness/vagueness, incompleteness, compression or adequacy/relevance (card pull), symbolism, contrast in visual impact, number/appropriateness of figures/objects/physical environments presented, familiarity with human figures, appropriateness and range of relationships portrayed (including basic family relationships), and range of emotional tone.*

3. *Culture-specific T.A.T. adaptations* should adapt the T.A.T. cards showing familiar everyday situations to situations that are culturally familiar to the specific culture of the individual being evaluated. T.A.T. cards that are designed to be ambiguous or to allow for some psychological distance for the test taker to project personal thoughts, feelings, and conflicts should be based on what is ambiguous or psychologically distancing for the culture of the person being evaluated.

4. *The method of test scoring should be based on or at least take into consideration the test taker's cultural belief system.* The psychologist should not evaluate the individual with a European scoring system such as psychoanalysis or an American system such as family systems theory or behaviorism if that does not fit with the client's cultural belief system. We give the example of misdiagnosing an individual's belief in ghosts as a lack of adequate "reality testing," when this belief in many South American cultures is held by all normal and adjusted individuals in the culture. Therefore, those who wish to conduct a T.A.T. or other projective test study of an individual or individuals from a culture foreign to their own should become knowledgeable about the life and literature, folklore, religion, mythology, and histories of the particular group. This may be done by reading autobiographies, histories, novels, and poetry written by the members of the particular culture, as well as any material available on the history of contact of that culture with other cultures (acculturation).

5. In testing individuals who are not from a mainstream Western culture, the method of test scoring needs to be based on *variables that tap the specific culture's established views of "intelligent" problem solving and decision making, psychological health, psychopathology, adjustment difficulty, and typical types of personality orientation.* Western culture-bound psychologists who assess individuals of differing culture need to be careful not to adhere too rigidly to Western standards of mental health—such as putting a high value on independence from the nuclear family at young adulthood, emotional expressiveness, and open communication styles—or assuming that acculturation to Western culture is synonymous with healthy overall psychological adjustment.

6. The test scoring system should be based on *statistical norms* as to what is typical on the test for individuals of the same age, gender, culture, personality orientation, or psychiatric disorder. Dana (1993) pointed out that none of the normative studies of any projective tests have included minority groups in their standardization efforts. We would add to this criterion that, if the psychologist and test taker are from different cultures, it is also valuable for the psychologist to have norms from the psychologist's own culture to compare with norms for the test taker's culture, as a control against the psychologist introducing cultural bias into the psychological test evaluation.

7. Lindzey (1961) emphasized that cross-cultural studies of projective tests need to provide *full-length case studies that clearly detail the inference process the psychologist employs in going from the specific test data to the summary interpretations.* We described the excellent projective test case studies with American Indians by Henry (1947), Trukese individuals of Micronesia by Gladwin and Sarason (1953), and the case studies of African Americans with the Themes Concerning Blacks test (Petty & Robinson, 1982; Terrell, 1982) that provide a clear understanding of how the particular responses on the tests were interpreted. However, there is a major need in the T.A.T. literature for more case studies of culture-specific T.A.T. adaptations as well as for case studies of individuals of different age, gender, socioeconomic status, culture, clinical disorder, and personality orientation on Murray's T.A.T. cards.

8. *Gender bias* is likely to be introduced whenever the psychologist is male and the test taker female, particularly within societies where males actively discriminate against females. On the T.A.T., one way to control for gender bias in test administration and test interpretation is to utilize Murray's specific card sequence for males with a male test taker or the female card sequence if the test taker is female. As we recommend in Chapter 4, another method is to *utilize a gender-balanced standard T.A.T. sequence.* The additional attempt to control against gender bias by having the psychologist and test taker be of the same gender should not be necessary if the psychologist takes into account the possibility of gender bias and power relationship components being introduced into the responses and test interpretation.

9. *Cultural bias* is likely to be introduced if the psychologist is from the mainstream culture and the test taker is from a minority culture, particularly if the psychologist is from a cultural or ethnic group that actively discriminates against the culture and ethnic group of the individual being evaluated. We presented the test behavior response pattern Snowden and Todman (1982) identified as *reticence* that is likely to occur when the psychologist is from white, U.S. mainstream culture and is evaluating an individual from African American minority culture. Particularly, when the psychologist is also not known to the test taker, the testing situation is likely to provoke inhibition, vagueness, uncertainty, and caution in responses. Again, it should not be necessary to attempt to control against cultural bias by having the psychologist and test taker be from exactly the same gender and culture, providing the psychologist is careful to evaluate the possibility of gender, culture, and power difference components in the test taker's responses and in the psychologist's own test interpretations.

10. *Socioeconomic bias* is likely when a middle-class psychologist evaluates an impoverished individual and the psychologist has theoretical bias and stereotyping on the basis of a belief in a syndrome of personality characteristics produced by the so-called "culture of poverty" (Dana, 1993, p. 152). Many African American and Hispanic American parents emphasize that a similar "socioeconomic bias" can exist when the psychologist is from the same ethnicity and culture but is middle class and the test taker is poor. In the future, there should be more research on this important variable of socioeconomic status in projective tests and thematic tests in particular.

11. The testing situation always involves a *power relationship* of the psychologist being the one to administer and "evaluate" the test taker and the test taker not knowing exactly what test answers are considered "intelligent, psychologically healthy, and adjusted." Therefore, the psychologist needs to evaluate the relative impact of this power difference in each case of psychological testing.

12. When testing an individual from a different gender and culture, the psychologist should approach the situation similar to an anthropologist, whose chief method of learning about a different culture is to interview an "expert informant" from within the culture (Schwartzman, 1983). The psychological testing situation should be considered one in which it is the test taker who informs and teaches the psychologist, rather than the psychologist being the only "expert" who evaluates, diagnoses, and recommends. This approach helps balance the power situation in psychological test evaluations and increases sensitivity to these gender, cultural, socioeconomic, and power differences.

CHAPTER 21

THE PSYCHODIAGNOSTIC TEST REPORT BLANK

Figure 21–1 shows the Report Blank that is a logical extension of the forms developed for T.A.T. and the C.A.T. It permits recording not only of these tests but also of the basic data of an entire test battery. The emphasis is again on the practicality of an overview and the provision of a systematic framework for the formulation of diagnostic inferences.

The Report Blank is meant primarily to be used by the psychologist for imparting information derived from a detailed study of the tests to the referring psychiatrist, psychologist, or social worker. Some psychologists might also want to use it as a worksheet, supplemented by scratch paper and necessary modifications, though it is not specifically designed for this purpose. However, the Report Blank should lend itself especially well to teaching and training purposes. It was designed with the following goals:

1. Test reporting will be less of a chore. A frame of reference and a set of variables are provided that, in part, need only to be check rated (rather than requiring a lengthy written essay).
2. A somewhat standardized basis for test reporting is provided. The problems of test reporting are numerous. One of the most frequent problems is that the peruser of the report does not get enough of an idea of the test reporter's progression from raw data to inference.
3. A more orderly form is provided in which to submit the report than the frequently used personal stationery or blank pieces of paper. It will make individual test reports comparable to others.

For the purpose of providing an overall view of the data, the fold-out style (which has been found helpful in the Bellak Short Form T.A.T. and C.A.T. Blank) of the actual form is arranged so that the summary and the final report can be in simultaneous view, both for test reporter and test user.

Designed by
Leopold Bellak, M.D.

© C.P.S. Inc 1965
Box 83, Larchmont, N.Y.
Revised 1974

PSYCHODIAGNOSTIC TEST REPORT BLANK

Grade_____

Name_____ Age_____ Birthdate_____ Sex_____ Education_____ Occupation_____

Married_____ Single_____ Divorced_____ Widowed_____

Tests administered:

WISC	☐	Rorschach	☐	Figure Drawing	☐
WAIS	☐	TAT	☐	Bender Gestalt	☐
Stanford Binet	☐	CAT-A-H-S	☐	Other	☐
School Achievement	☐	SAT	☐	Other	☐

FINAL REPORT
(See Summary page for details)

Test Behavior:

Diagnostically, the findings are consistent with:

Dynamically:

Therapeutically:

Recommendations:

Tested by: _____

Signature

Figure 21–1.   The Psychodiagnostic Test Report Blank

WECHSLER INTELLIGENCE SCALE

	Weighted Score	Selected Illustrative Responses	Inference or Conclusion
1. Information			
2. Comprehension			
3. Digit Span			
4. Arithmetic			
5. Similarities			
6. (Vocabulary)			
Verbal Score			
7. P. Arrangement			
8. P. Completion			
9. Block Design			
10. Object Assembly			
11. Digit Symbol			
Performance Score			
Total Score			
I.Q. Verbal Scale			
I.Q. Perfrom Scale			
I.Q. Full Scale			

Functioning Intellectually:

    At optimum: ☐

☐ Below optimum because of:

    Anxieties ☐

    Constriction ☐

    Deterioration ☐

    Organic factors ☐

    Other ☐

Functioning Psychodynamically:

Test Behavior and
Other:

Figure 21–1.   (continued)

RORSCHACH

Card	Selected Illustrative Responses	Inference or Conclusion
1.		
2.		
3.		
4.		
5.		
6.		
7.		
8.		
9.		
10.		

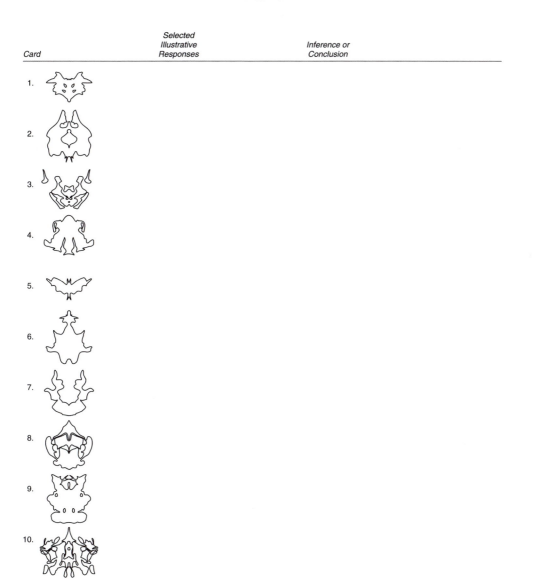

Test Behavior:

Figure 21–1.   (continued)

T.A.T. or C.A.T. or S.A.T.

Card TAT ☐ SAT ☐	CAT-A CAT-H ☐ CAT-S ☐	Selected Illustrative Responses	Inference or Conclusion

1.

2.

3.

4.

5.

6.

7.

8.

9.

10.

Other:

Figure 21–1.   (continued)

Illustrative Data	Inference or Conclusion

Bender Gestalt:

Figure Drawing:

Other:

Figure 21–1.   (continued)

SUMMARY

1. Intellectual functioning

2. Significant drives and conflicts

3. Nature of anxieties

4. Ego functions

      a) reality testing

      b) judgment

      c) sense of reality and of self

      d) regulation and control of drives

      e) object relations

      f) thought processes

      g) ARISE (adaptive regression in the service of the ego)

      h) defensive functioning

      i) stimulus barrier

      j) autonomous functioning

      k) synthetic–integrating functioning

      l) mastery–competence

5. Superego function

6. Organic disturbances

Other:

Figure 21–1.   (continued)

Ego function assessment from test data:

	I	II	III	IV	V	VI	VII	VIII	IX	X	XI	XII
	Reality Testing	Judgment	Sense of Reality	Regulat. & Cont. of Drives	Object Relat.	Thought Process.	ARISE	Defensive Functs.	Stimulus Barrier	Auton. Functs.	Synthet. Functs.	Mastery—Cmptnc.

Scale (vertical axis): 13, 12, 11, 10, 9, 8, 7, 6, 5, 4, 3, 2, 1

Ego Functions

Psychotic Range 1–6
Borderline Range 4–8
Neurotic Range 6–10
Normal Range 8–13

(From Bellak, Hurvich & Gediman, *Ego functions in schizophrenics, neurotics, and normals.* Copyright © 1973, by C. P. S., Inc. Reprinted by permission of John Wiley & Sons, Inc.)

You may decide to record only current overall ego functions or may draw in graphs indicating what you consider optimal, minimal or characteristic levels for any or all ego functions.

Ego functions observed during test behavior:

Figure 21–1 (continued)

REFERENCES

Aaron, N. (1967). Some personality differences between asthmatic, allergic, and normal children. *Journal of Clinical Psychology, 3,* 336–340.

Abel. T. M. (1945). Responses of Negro and White morons to the Thematic Apperception Test. *American Journal of Mental Deficiency, 49,* 463–468.

Abel, T. M. (1973). *Psychological testing in cultural contexts.* New Haven, CT: College & University Press.

Abeles, R. (1994). *Aging and quality of life.* New York: Springer.

Abend, S. M. Porter, M. S. & Willick, M. S. (1983). *Borderline patients: Psychoanalytic perspectives.* New York: International Universities Press.

Abrams, D. M. (1977). *Conflict resolution in children's fantasy storytelling: A test of Erikson's theory and of the culture-enculturation hypothesis.* Unpublished doctoral dissertation, Columbia University, NY.

Abrams, D. M. (1991). Looking at and looking away: Etiology of preoedipal splitting in a deaf girl. *Psychoanalytic Study of the Child, 46,* 277–304.

Abrams, D. M. (1992). The dream's mirror of reality. *Contemporary Psychoanalysis, 28,* 50–71.

Abrams, D. M. (1993a). Pathological narcissism in an eight-year-old boy: An example of Bellak's T.A.T. and C.A.T. diagnostic system. *Psychoanalytic Psychology, 10,* 573–591.

Abrams, D. M. (1993b). Freud and Max Graf: On the psychoanalysis of music. In S. Feder, R. Karmel, & G. H. Pollock (Eds.), *Psychoanalytic explorations in music: Vol. 2* (pp. 279–307). Madison, CT: International Universities Press.

Abrams, D. M. (1994). Review of Charles Ives: My father's song: A psychoanalytic biography by Stuart Feder. *Psychoanalytic Books: A Quarterly Review, 5,* 86–92.

Abrams, D. M. (1995). Narcissisme pathologique chez un garçon de huit ans: Une exemple du système diagnostique du CAT et du TAT de Bellak [French translation of Abrams, 1993a]. *Psychologie Clinique et Projective, 1,* 245–267.

Abrams, D. M. (in press). Narrative fantasy of children and adolescents with narcissistic pathology. In P. Berran (Ed.) *Narcissism in children and adolescents.* New York: Jason Aronson.

Abrams, D. M., & Bellak, L. (1986). Object relations assessment with the T.A.T., C.A.T. and S.A.T. In L. Bellak (Ed.), *The T.A.T., C.A.T., and S.A.T. in clinical use* (4th ed.) (pp. 190–198). Boston: Allyn and Bacon.

Abrams, K. (1991). Hearing the call of stories. *California Law Review, 79,* 971–1052.

Abt, L. E., & Bellak, L. (1950). *Projective psychology: Clinical approaches to the total personality.* New York: Knopf.

Ackerly, L. (1973). *Sexual fantasies of elderly people.* Unpublished bachelor's thesis, State University of New York College, Purchase, NY.

Ackerman, M. J. & Kane, A. W. (1993). *Psychological experts in divorce, personal injury, and other civil actions.* New York: Wiley Law Publications.

Aiken, L. R. (1995). *Aging: An introduction to geropsychology.* Thousand Oaks, CA: Sage.

Albert, M. S., & Moss, M. B. (Eds.) (1988). *Geriatric neuropsychology.* New York: Guilford.

Alexander, T., & Anderson, R. (1957). Children in a society under stress. *Behavior Science, 2,* 46–55.

Alkire, A. A., Brunse, A. J., & Houlihan, J. P. (1974). Avoidance of nuclear family relationships in schizophrenia. *Journal of Clinical Psychology, 30,* 398–400.

Allport, G., & Vernon, F. (1933). *Studies in expressive movement.* New York: Macmillan.

Allport, G., & Vernon F. (1937). *Personality: A psychological interpretation.* New York: Holt, Rinehart and Winston.

Allport, G., & Vernon, F. (1942). The use of personal documents in psychological science. *Social Science Research Council Bulletin, 49.*

Altobello, N. (1973). *Hope and despair in old age.* Unpublished bachelor's thesis, State University of New York, Purchase, NY.

American Psychiatric Association (1994). *DSM-IV.* Washington, DC: Author.

American Psychological Association. (1985). *Standards for educational and psychological testing.* Washington, DC: American Psychological Association Press.

Ames, L. B. (1961). *Child rorschach responses*. New York: Hoeber.

Ames, L. B., Metraux, R. W., & Walker, R. N. (1961). *Adolescent rorschach responses*. New York: Hoeber.

Anderson, H. H., & Anderson, G. L. (Eds.) (1951). *An introduction to projective techniques*. New York: Prentice-Hall.

Anderson, J. W. (1990). The life of Henry A. Murray: 1893–1988. In A. I. Rabin, R. A. Zucker, R. A. Emmons, & S. Frank (Eds.), *Studying persons and lives* (pp. 304–333). New York: Springer.

Anzieu, D., & Chabert, C. (1983). *Les méthodes projectives*. Paris: Presses Universitaires de France.

Araoz, D. L. (1972). The Thematic Apperception Test in marital therapy. *Journal of Contemporary Psychotherapy, 5,* 41–48.

Araujo, M. G., & Araujo, P. G. (1986). A funcao de narrativa na elaboracao dos conflitos infantis: Estudo comparativo de dois grupos de diferentes condicoes socio-economicas [The function of narrative in the elaboration of children's conflicts: Comparative study of two socioeconomic groups]. *Arquivos Brasileiros de Psicologia, 38,* 140–157.

Archer, R. P., Maruish, M., Imhof, E. A., & Piotrowski, C. (1991). Psychological test usage with adolescent clients: 1990 survey findings. *Professional Psychology: Research and Practice, 22,* 247–252.

Armstrong, M. (1954). Children's responses to animal and human figures in thematic pictures. *Journal of Consulting Psychology, 18,* 67–70.

Arnaud, P. (1987) Expression of aggressivity and its mental elaboration through projective tests in children: Rorschach and C.A.T. *Psychologie Medicale, 19,* 519–521.

Arnold, M. (1951). In E. S. Shneidman (Ed.), *Thematic test analysis*. New York: Grune & Stratton.

Arnold, M. B. (1962). *Story sequence analysis*. New York: Columbia University Press.

Aron, B. (1949). *A manual for analysis of the Thematic Apperception Test*. Berkeley, CA: Willis E. Berg.

Aron, B. (1950). The Thematic Apperception Test in the study of prejudiced and unprejudiced individuals. In T. W. Adorno, E. Frenkel-Brunswick, D. Levinson, & R. N. Sanford, (Eds.), *The authoritarian personality* (pp. 489–544). New York: Harper & Brothers.

Aron, B. (1951. In E. S. Shneidman (Ed.), *Thematic test analysis*. New York: Grune & Stratton.

Atkinson, J. W. (1950). *Studies in projective measurement of achievement motivation*. Unpublished doctoral dissertation, University of Michigan.

Atkinson, J. W. (1958). *Motives in fantasy, action and society*. Princeton, NJ: D. Van Nostrand.

Atkinson, J. W. (1964). *An introduction to motivation*. Princeton, NJ: Van Nostrand.

Atkinson, J. W., Bastian, J. R, Earl, R. W., & Litwin, G. H. (1960). The achievement motive, goal setting and probability preferences. *Journal of Abnormal and Social Psychology, 60,* 27–36.

Atkinson, J. W., & Feather, N. T. (Eds.). (1966). *A theory of achievement motivation*. New York: John Wiley.

Atkinson, J. W., Hyns, R. W., & Veroff, J. (1954). The effect of experimental arousal of the affiliative motive in thematic apperception. *Journal of Abnormal and Social Psychology, 49,* 405–410.

Atkinson, J. W., & Litwin, G. H. (1960). Achievement motive and test anxiety conceived as motive to approach success and motive to avoid failure. *Journal of Abnormal and Social Psychology, 60,* 52–63.

Atkinson, J. W., & McClelland, D. C. (1948). The projective expression of needs II. The effect of different intensities of the hunger drive on thematic apperception. *Journal of Experimental Psychology, 38,* 643–658.

Auld, F. (1954). Contributions of behavior therapy to projective testing. *Journal of Projective Techniques, 18,* 421–426.

Auld, F., Eron, L. D., & Laffal, J. (1954). Application of Guttman's scaling method to the T.A.T. *Educational and Psychological Measurement, 15,* 596–616.

Avila Espada, A. (1983). *El Test de Apercepcion Tematica de H. A. Murray en la poblacion española: Estudio normativo y analisis para una adaptacion* (Vols. 1–2). Madrid: Editorial de la Universidad Complutense.

Avila Espada, A. (1985). Investigacion normativa con el T.A.T. de H. A. Murray en la poblacion española [Normative investigation of H. A. Murray s T.A.T. in the population of Spain]. *Revista de Psicologia General y Aplicada, 40,* 277–316.

Avila Espada, A. (1986). *Manual Operativo del T.A.T.* [Operational T.A.T. manual]. Madrid: Editorial Piramide.

Avila Espada, A. (1990a, July). *Un système integratif pour le TAT: Quelques considerations théorétiques et empiriques*. Unpublished paper presented at the 13th International Congress of Rorschach and Projective Techniques, Paris.

Avila Espada, A. (1990b). *Fundamentos empiricos del Test de Apercepcion Tematica* [Empirical foundations of the Thematic Apperception Test]. Madrid: Editorial Piramide.

Avila Espada, A., Jimenez Gomez, F., Ortiz Quintana, P., & Rodriguez Sutil, C. (1992). *Evaluacion en psicologia clinica. Proceso, methodo y estrategias psicometricas* (Vol. 1). [Evaluation in clinical psychology. Process, method, and psychometric strategies (Vol. 1)]. Salamanca: Amar.

Avila Espada, A., & Rubi, M. L. (1990, July). *Revision de l'étude normative espagnole pour le TAT dans son utilisation avec le système integratif du TAT* [Revised Spanish normative study of the T.A.T. using the integrative T.A.T. system]. Unpublished paper presented at the 13th International Congress of Rorschach and Projective Techniques, Paris.

Bachrach, R., & Peterson, R. A. (1976). Test-retest reliability among three locus of control measures for children. *Perceptual and Motor Skills, 43,* 260–262.

Bachtold, L. M. (1977). Perceptions of emotionally disturbed male adolescents on the Thematic Apperception Test. *Perceptual and Motor Skills, 40,* 867–871.

Bacque, M. (1990, July). *Mental organization through Rorschach and TAT of 10 acute leukemia patients.* Unpublished paper presented at the 13th International Congress of Rorschach and Projective Techniques, Paris.

Baily, B. E., Bruce, E., & Green, J. (1977). Black Thematic Apperception Test stimulus material. *Journal of Personality Assessment, 4*(1), 1.

Bailey, B. E., & Green, J. (1979). Black Thematic Apperception Test stimulus material. *Journal of Personality Assessment, 41,* 25–30.

Bakker, D. I., & Satz, P. (Eds.). (1970). *Specific reading disability.* Lisse: Swets & Zeithnger.

Balier, C. (1987). Les comportements psychiques des personnes agées [Psychological behaviors of elderly individuals]. Reprint from *Évolutions Medicales,* No. 5, Tome 13, 417-21. Paris: Les Imprimeries Reunies Moulins.

Balken, E. R., & Masserman, J. H. (1940). The language of phantasy III. The language of the phantasies of patients with conversion hysteria, anxiety and obsessive compulsive neuroses. *Journal of Psychology, 10,* 75–86.

Baltes, P. B., & Baltes, M. M. (Eds.). (1990). *Successful aging: Perspectives from the behavioral sciences.* New York: Cambridge University Press.

Baran, S. (1971). *Development and validation of a T.A.T.-type projective test for use among Bantu-speaking people.* (CSIR Special Report 138). Johannesburg, South Africa: National Institute for Personnel Research Council for Scientific and Industrial Research.

Barclay, A. M. (1969). The effect of hostility on physiological and fantasy responses. *Journal of Personality, 37,* 651–667.

Barclay, A. M. (1970). The effect of female aggressiveness on aggressive and sexual fantasies. *Journal of Projective Techniques and Personality Assessment, 34,* 19–26.

Barnouw, V. (1963). *Culture and personality.* Homewood, IL: Dorsey.

Barrios, B. A., & Hartman, D. P. (1989). The contributions of traditional assessment: Concepts, issues, and methodologies. In R. O. Nelson & S. C. Hayes (Eds.), *Conceptual foundations of behavioral assessment* (pp. 81–110). New York: Guilford.

Bateson, G., Jackson, D., Haley, J., & Weakland, J. (1956). Toward a theory of schizophrenia. *Behavioral Science, 1,* 251–264.

Battaglia, A. R., Graziano, M. R., & Scafidi, M. G. (1983). Experimental research onto the changes in the way sexuality is experienced by the infertile woman. *Acta Euro. Fertility 14*(1), 67–73.

Baty, M., & Dreger, R. (1975). A comparison of three methods to record T.A.T. protocols. *Journal of Clinical Psychology, 31,* 348.

Becache, S. (1987). Reflections of a psychologist-psychoanalyst on her use of the T.A.T. *Psychologie Française, 32,* 145–149.

Bedford, V. H. (1986). Themes of affiliation, conflict, and separation in adults T.A.T. stories about siblings at two life periods. *Dissertation Abstracts International, 47* (3-B), 1271.

Bedford, V. H. (1989). A comparison of thematic apperceptions of sibling affiliation, conflict, and separation at two periods of adulthood. *International Journal of Aging and Human Development, 28,* 53–66.

Behar-Azoulay, C. (1990, July). *Changing process in the TAT in young schizophrenic patients.* Unpublished paper presented at the 13th International Congress of Rorschach and Projective Techniques, Paris.

Bell, J. E. (1948). *Projective techniques: A dynamic approach to the study of personality.* New York: Longmans & Green.

Bellak, L. (1942). A note about the Adam's apple. *Psychoanalysis Review, 29*(3).

Bellak, L. (I944). The concept of projection: An experimental investigation and study of the concept. *Psychiatry, 7,* 353–370.

Bellak, L. (1947, revised in 1951). *A guide to the interpretation of the Thematic Apperception Test.* New York: The Psychological Corporation.

Bellak, L. (1948). A note on some basic concepts of psychotherapy. *Journal of Nervous and Mental Disorders, 108,* 137–141.

Bellak, L. (1950a). Thematic apperception: Failures and the defenses. *Transactions of the New York Academy of Science Series II, 12,* 112–126.

Bellak, L. (1950b). On the problems of the concept of projection. In L. Abt, & L. Bellak (Eds.), *Projective psychology* (pp. 7–33). New York: Knopf.

Bellak, L. (1950c). Projection and the Thematic Apperception Test. In L. W. Crafts, T. C. Schneirla, E. E. Robinson, & R. W. Gilbert (Eds.), *Recent experiments in psychology*. New York: McGraw-Hill.

Bellak, L. (1950d). A further experimental investigation of projection by means of hypnosis. In L. W. Crafts, T. C. Schneiria, E. E. Robinson, & R. W. Gilbert (Eds.), *Recent experiments in psychology*. New York: McGraw-Hill.

Bellak, L. (1950e, May). Psychiatric aspects of tuberculosis. *Social Casework*.

Bellak, L. (1952a). The emergency psychotherapy of depression. In G. Bychowski & J. L. Despert (Eds.), *Specialized techniques in psychotherapy*. New York: Basic Books.

Bellak, L. (1952b). *Manic-depressive psychosis and allied disorders*. New York: Grune & Stratton.

Bellak, L. (1952c). *Psychology of physical illness: Psychiatry applied to medicine, surgery, and the specialties*. New York: Grune & Stratton.

Bellak, L. (1952d). *The psychology of physical illness*. New York: Grune & Stratton.

Bellak, L. (1952e). *Revised manual for the TAT*. New York: Psychological Corporation.

Bellak, L. (1954a). A study of limitations and "failures": Toward an ego psychology of projective techniques. *Journal of Projective Techniques, 18*, 279–293.

Bellak, L. (1954b). *The T.A.T. and the C.A.T. in clinical use*. New York: Grune & Stratton. Grune & Stratton: 2nd edition (1971) and 3rd edition (1975). Allyn and Bacon: 4th edition (1986) and 5th edition (1993). (Spanish translation: Bellak L. (1996). *T.A.T., C.A.T. y S.A.T.: Uso clínico*. Ed. El Manual Moderno, S.A. Mexico).

Bellak, L. (1955). An ego-psychological theory of hypnosis. *International Journal of Psychoanalysis, 36*, 375–378.

Bellak, L. (1956). Psychiatric aspects of cardiac illness and rehabilitation. *Social Casework, 37*, 482–489.

Bellak, L. (1958). Creativity: Some random notes to a systematic consideration. *Journal of Projective Techniques, 22*(4).

Bellak, L. (1959). The unconscious. *Annuals of the New York Academy of Sciences, 76*, 1066–1081.

Bellak, L. (1961). Free association. *International Journal of Psychoanalysis, 42*, 9–20.

Bellak, L. (1963). A psychological study of the stories of Somerset Maugham: A profile of a creative personality. In R. White (Ed.), *The study of lives*. New York, Atherton Press, 1963; and In D. P. Spence (Ed.), *The broad scope of psychoanalysis: Selected papers of Leopold Bellak*. New York: Grune & Stratton.

Bellak, L. (1964). Depersonalization as a variant of self-awareness. In A. Abrams (Ed.), *Unfinished tasks in the behavioral sciences*. Baltimore: Williams & Wilkins.

Bellak, L. (1970). A study of ego functions in the schizophrenic syndrome. *Archives of General Psychiatry, 23*.

Bellak, L. (1975). *The best years of your life: A guide to the art and science of aging*. New York: Atheneum.

Bellak, L. (1979). *Psychiatric aspects of minimal brain dysfunction in adults*. New York: Grune & Stratton.

Bellak, L. (1982a). Current status of classical Freudian psychoanalysis, Part I. *Directions in Psychiatry, 2*(9).

Bellak, L. (1982b). Current status of classical Freudian psychoanalysis, Part II. *Directions in Psychiatry, 2*(10).

Bellak, L. (1982c). Current status of classical Freudian psychoanalysis, Part III. *Directions in Psychiatry, 2*(11).

Bellak, L. (1983) Psychoanalysis in the 1980s. *American Journal of Psychotherapy, 37*(4).

Bellak, L. (1985a). *My first fifty years with psychoanalysis*. Unpublished manuscript.

Bellak, L. (1985b). A.D.D. Psychosis: A Separate Entity. *Schizophrenia Bulletin, 11*(4).

Bellak, L. (1992). Projective Techniques in the Computer Age (Bruno Klopfer Award). *Journal of Personality Assessment, 58*(3), 445–453.

Bellak, L. (1993a). *Psychoanalysis as a science*. Boston: Allyn and Bacon.

Bellak, L. (1993b). *Confrontation in Vienna*, Larchmont, NY: C.P.S., Inc.

Bellak, L. (1994). The schizophrenic syndrome and attention deficit disorder: Thesis, antithesis, and synthesis? *American Psychologist, 49*, 25–29.

Bellak, L., Abrams, D. M., & Ackermann-Engel, R. (1992). *Handbook of intensive brief and emergency psychotherapy*. Larchmont, NY: C.P.S., Inc.

Bellak, L., & Antell, M. (1974). An intercultural study of aggressive behavior on children's playgrounds. *American Journal of Orthopsychiatry, 44*, 503–511.

Bellak, L., & Barten, H. (1969). *Progress in community mental health: Vol. 1*. New York: Grune & Stratton.

Bellak, L., & Barten, H. (1970). The validity and usefulness of the concept of the schizophrenic syndrome. In R. Cancro (Ed.), *The schizophrenic reactions*. New York: Brunner/Mazel.

Bellak, L., & Bellak, S. (1949). *The Children's Apperception Test*. Larchmont, NY: C.P.S., Inc.

Bellak, L., & Bellak, S. (1965). *The C.A.T.-H.—A human modification*. Larchmont, NY: C.P.S., Inc.

Bellak, L., & Bellak, S. (1973, 1996). *The Senior Apperception Technique*. Larchmont, NY: C.P.S., Inc.

Bellak, L., & Brower, D. (1951). Projective methods. In *Progress in neurology and psychiatry* (Vol. 6). New York: Grune & Stratton.

Bellak, L., & Chassan, J. (1964). An approach to the evaluation of drug effect during psychotherapy: A double blind study of a single case. *Journal of Nervous and Mental Diseases, 39,* 20–30.

Bellak, L., Ekstein, R., & Braverman, S. (1947). A preliminary study of norms for the Thematic Apperception Test. *American Psychologist, 2,* 271.

Bellak., & Goldsmith, L. A. (1984). *The broad scope of ego function assessment.* New York: Wiley.

Bellak, L., & Hurvich, M. (1966). A human modification of the Children's Apperception Test. *Journal of Projective Techniques, 30,* 228–242.

Bellak, L., Hurvich, M., & Crawford, P. (1970). Psychotic egos. *Psychoanalytic Review, 56*(4).

Bellak, L., Hurvich, M., & Gediman, H. (1973). *Ego functions in schizophrenics, neurotics, and normals.* New York: Wiley.

Bellak. L., Hurvich, M., Gediman, H., & Crawford, P. (1969, October). The systematic diagnosis of the schizophrenic syndrome. *Dynamic Psychiatry.*

Bellak, L., & Karasu, T. (1976). *Geriatric psychiatry: A handbook for psychiatrists and primary care physicians.* New York: Grune & Stratton.

Bellak, L., Levinger, L., & Lipsky, E. (1950). An adolescent problem reflected in the TAT. *Journal of Clinical Psychology, 6,* 295–297.

Bellak, L., & Loeb, L. (1969). *The schizophrenic syndrome.* New York: Grune & Stratton.

Bellak, L., & Murray, H. A. (1941). *Thematic Apperception Test Blank.* Unpublished.

Bellak, L., Pasquarelli, B., & Braverman, S. (1949). The use of the Thematic Apperception Test in psychotherapy. *Journal of Nervous and Mental Disease, 110,* 51–65.

Bellak, L., & Siegel, H. (1989). The Children's Apperception Test (CAT). In C. S. Newmark (Ed.), *Major psychological assessment instruments: Vol. 2* (pp. 99–132). Boston: Allyn and Bacon.

Bellak, L., & Small, L. (1965). *Emergency psychotherapy and brief psychotherapy.* New York: Grune & Stratton.

Bellak, L., et al. (1949). The use of the TAT in psychotherapy. *Journal of Nervous and Mental Diseases, 110,* 51–65.

Bellak, L., et al. (1959). Psychological test reporting. A problem in communication between psychologists and psychiatrist. *Journal of Nervous and Mental Diseases, 129,* 76–91.

Beller, E., & Haeberle, A. (1969, March). *Motivation and conflict in relation to phantasy responses of young children.* Unpublished paper presented at the meeting of the Society for Research in Child Development, Bethesda, MD.

Beltran Yguino, J. (1981). *La proyeccian en la percepcion* [Projection in perception]. Cordoba: Exca Diputacion Provincial.

Bender, L., & Rapaport, J. (1944). Animal drawings of children. *American Journal of Orthopsychiatry, 14,* 521–527.

Bennett, E., & Johannsen, D. (1954). Psychodynamics in the diabetic child. *Psychological Monograph, 68*(11).

Benton, C. J., Hernandez, A. C. R., Schmidt, A., Schmitz, M. D., Stone, A. J., & Weiner, B. (1983). Is hostility linked with affiliation among males and with achievement among females? A critique of Pollak and Gilligan. *Journal of Personality and Social Psychology, 45,* 1167–1178.

Berends, A., Westen, D., Leigh, J., & Silbert, D. (1990). Assessing affect-tone of relationship paradigms from TAT and interview data. *Psychological Assessment, 2,* 329–332.

Berezin, M. A. (1963). Some intrapsychic aspects of aging. In N. E. Zinberg & I. Kaufman (Eds.), *Normal psychology of the aging process.* New York: International Universities Press.

Berman, I., & Seward, G. (1958). A little Jewish boy under pressure of orthodoxy. In G. Seward (Ed.), *Clinical studies in culture conflict* (pp. 455–477). New York: Ronald Press.

Bernstein, L. (1956). The examiner as an inhibiting factor in clinical testing. *Journal of Consulting Psychology, 20,* 287–290.

Bettelheim, B. (1947). Self interpretation of fantasy: The Thematic Apperception Test as an educational and therapeutic device. *American Journal of Orthopsychiatry, 17,* 80–100.

Bexton, W., Heron W., & Scott, T. (1954). Effects of decreased variation in the sensory environment. *Canadian Journal of Psychology, 8,* 70–76.

Biersdorf, K. R., & Marcuse, F. L. (1953). Responses of children to human and animal pictures. *Journal of Projective Techniques, 17,* 455–459.

Biesheuvel, S. (1958). Methodology in the study of attitudes of Africans. *Journal of Social Psychology, 47,* 169–184.

Bijou, S. W., & Kenny, D. T. (1951). The ambiguity values of TAT cards. *Journal of Consulting Psychology, 15,* 203–209.

Bills, R. (1950). Animal pictures for obtaining children's projections. *Journal of Clinical Psychology, 6,* 291–293.

Bills, R., Leiman, C., & Thomas, R. (1950). A study of the validity of the T.A.T. and a set of animal pictures. *Journal of Clinical Psychology, 6,* 293–295.

Birney, R. C. (1959). The reliability of the achievement motive. *Journal of Abnormal and Social Psychology, 58,* 266–267.

Birren, J. E., & Schaie, K. W. (Eds.). (1990). *Handbook of the psychology of aging.* San Diego, CA: Academic Press.

Blatt, S. J. (1975). The validity of projective techniques and their research and clinical contribution. *Journal of Personality Assessment, 39,* 327–343.

Blatt, S. J. (1992). The Rorschach: A test of perception or an evaluation of representation. In E. I. Megaree & C. D. Speilberger (Eds.), *Personality assessment in America: A retrospective on the occasion of the fiftieth anniversary of the Society for Personality Assessment* (pp. 160–169). Hillsdate, NJ: Erlbaum.

Blatt, S., Engel, M., & Mirmow, E. (1961). When inquiry fails. *Journal of Projective Techniques, 25,* 32–37.

Blum, G. S. (1950). *The Blacky pictures: A technique for the exploration of personality dynamics.* New York: The Psychological Corporation.

Blum, G. S. (1962). A guide for research of the Blacky pictures. *Journal of Projective Techniques, 26,* 3–29.

Blum, G. S. (1964). Defense preferences among university students in Denmark, France, Germany and Israel. *Journal of Projective Techniques and Personality Assessment, 28,* 13–19.

Blum, G., & Hunt, H. F. (1952). The validity of the Blacky pictures. *Psychological Bulletin, 49,* 238–250.

Blumenthal, J. A., Lane, J. D., & Williams, R. B., Jr. (1985). The inhibited power motive, type A behavior, and patterns of cardiovascular response during the structured interview and Thematic Apperception Test. *Journal of Human Stress, 11*(2), 82–92.

Boekholt, M. (1987). Level of conflicts and depression: Their expression to picture 12BG of the T.A.T. in adolescents and adults. *Psychologie Française, 32,* 169–174.

Boekholt, M. (1993). *Épreuves thématiques en clinique infantile: Approche psychanalytique* [Thematic tests in clinical work with children: Psychoanalytic approach]. Paris: Dunod.

Bogen, T. M. (1982). *Patterns of developmental change in formal characteristics of stories children tell.* Unpublished doctoral dissertation, University of Michigan, Ann Arbor.

Booth, L.. (1953). *A normative comparison of the responses of Latin-American and Anglo-American children to the Children's Apperception Test.* Unpublished doctoral dissertation, Texas Technological College, Lubbock.

Born, M. (1975). [Attempts at a quantitative approach to ego functions in the TAT]. *Revue de Psychologie et des Sciences de l' Éducation, 10,* 435–444.

Bornstein, B. M. (1987). Comparative diagnostic validity of the Thematic Apperception Test and a revision designed to eliminate negative pull. *Dissertation Abstracts International, 48*(12A), 112.

Bose, S. (1972). A study on the social world of some physically handicapped children. *Indian Journal of Applied Psychology, 9,* 20–23.

Bose, S., & Benerjee, S. N. (1969). A resolution on the personality make-up of some institutionalized physically-handicapped children by the Children's Apperception Test. *Journal of Psychological Research, 13,* 32–36.

Bose, S., & Biswas, C. (1972). A study on the social world of some physically handicapped children. *Indian Journal of Applied Psychology, 9,* 20–23.

Bouchard, C. (1990, July). *Suite et séquence dans l'épreuve T.A.T. de Henry Murray.* Unpublished paper presented at 13th International Congress of Rorschach and Projective Techniques, Paris.

Boulanger-Balleyguier, G. (1957). Etudes sur le C.A.T.: Influence du stimulus sur les récits d'enfants de 3 a 8 ans [C.A.T. studies: The influence of the stimulus on children's stories from 3–8 years]. *Revue de Psychologie Appliquée, 7,* 128.

Boulanger-Balleyguier, G. (1960). La personalité des enfants normaux et caractériels à travers le test d'apperception C.A.T. [The personality of normal and conduct disordered children with the C.A.T.]. *Monographe Française de Psychologie, 40.*

Boyd, N., & Mandler, G. (1955). Children's responses to human and animal stories and pictures. *Journal of Consulting Psychology, 19,* 367–371.

Breger, L. (1963). Conformity as a function of the ability to express hostility. *Journal of Personality, 31,* 247–257.

Brelet, F. (1981). A propos du narcissisme dans le T.A.T. [On narcissism in the T.A.T.]. *Psychologie Française, 26,* 24–37.

Brelet, F. (1983). T.A.T. et narcissisme: Perspectives dynamiques et économiques [T.A.T. and narcissism: Dynamic and economic perspectives]. *Psychologie Française, 28,* 119–123.

Brelet, F. (1986). *Le T.A.T.: Fantasme et situation projective: Narcissisme, fonctionnement limite, depression* [The T.A.T.: Fantasy and the projective situation: Narcissism, borderline functioning, depression]. Paris: Dunod.

Brelet, F. (1987). Wanted, a producer. *Psychologie Française, 32,* 137–140.

Brelet, F. (1988). *Le T.A.T.: Fantasme et situation projective: Une application clinique: Le T.A.T. chez l'alcoolique*

[The T.A.T.: Fantasy and the projective situation: A clinical application of the T.A.T. with the alcoholic]. Unpublished doctoral dissertation, University of Paris X, Nanterre.

Brelet-Foulard, F. (1986). The TAT and narcissism: Some comments on the relations between the narcissistic organization of the phantasmic world and the elaboration of the patient's history on the TAT. *Bulletin de la Societé Française du Rorschach et des Méthodes Projectifs, 33,* 67–72.

Brelet-Foulard, F. (1990, July). *TAT: Fantisizing and thinking.* Unpublished paper presented at the 13th International Congress of Rorschach and Projective Techniques, Paris.

Brelet-Foulard, F. (1994). Expression of narcissistic fantasy in the T.A.T. *Rorschachiana, 19,* 97–112.

Brelet-Foulard, F. (1995). En echo: Réponse à l'article de David M. Abrams. *Psychologie Clinique et Projective, 1,* 269–274.

Brislin, R. W. (Ed.). (1990). *Applied cross-cultural psychology.* Newbury Park, CA: Sage.

Brittain, H. L. (1907). A study in imagination. *Pediatric Seminars, 14,* 137–207.

Britton, B. K., & Pellegrini, D. (Eds.). (1990) *Narrative thought and narrative language.* Hillsdale, NJ: Erlbaum.

Brody, S., & Siegel, M.G. (1992). *The evolution of character: Birth to 18 years: A longitudinal study.* Madison, CT: International Universities Press.

Broverman, D., Jordan, E., & Phillips, L. (1960). Achievement motivation in fantasy and behavior. *Journal of Abnormal Social Psychology, 60,* 374–378.

Brown, F. (1965). The Bender Gestalt and acting out. In L. E. Abt & S. L. Weissman (Eds.) *Acting out* (pp. 320–332.). New York: Grune & Stratton.

Bruner, J. S., & Goodman, C. (1947). Value and need as organizing factors in perception. *Journal of Abnormal Social Psychology, 42,* 33–44.

Bruner, J. S., & Postman, L. (1954). Tension and tension-release as organizing factors in perception. *Journal of Personality, 15,* 300–308.

Budoff, M. (1960). The relative utility of animal and human figures in a picture story test for young children. *Journal of Projective Techniques, 42,* 347–352.

Buehier, C. (1949). *Development of basic Rorschach scores with manual for directions, No. I of Rorschach Standardization Studies.* Los Angeles.

Bush, M., Hatcher, R., & Mayman, M. (1969). Reality attentiveness-inattentiveness and externalization-internalization in defensive style. *Journal of Consulting and Clinical Psychology, 33,* 343–350.

Buss, A. H. (1961). *The psychology of aggression.* New York: Wiley.

Busse, E., & Pfeiffer, E. (1973). *Mental illness in late life.* Washington, DC: American Psychiatric Press.

Butler, R. (1961). Responses of institutionalized mentally retarded children to human and to animal pictures. *American Journal of Mental Deficiency, 65,* 620–622.

Byrd, E., & Witherspoon, R. (1954). Responses of preschool children to the Children's Apperception Test. *Child Development, 25,* 35–44.

Byrne, D., McDonald, R. D., & Mikawa, J. (1963). Approach and avoidance affiliation motives. *Journal of Personality, 31,* 1–20.

Cabal Bravo, J. C., Bobes Garcia, J., Vazquez Fernandez, A. Gonzalez-Quiros Corujo, P., Bousono Garcia, M., Garcia Prieto, A., & Garcia-Portilla, P. (1990). TAT: Psicodiagnostico en pacientes heroinomanos [Thematic Apperception Test: Psychodiagnosis in heroin-dependent patients]. *Actas Luso-Españolas de Neurologia, Psiquiatria y Ciencias Afines, 18,* 1–6.

Cabras, P. L., Benvenuti, P., Marchetti, G., & Asti, N. (1983). La rinuncia al fantastico: Studio mediante il Thematic Apperception Test di un gruppo di pazienti con reltocolite ulcerosa [The renunciation of the fantastic: A study of the Thematic Apperception Test of a group of patients with ulcerative colitis]. *Medicina-Psicosomatica, 28,* 149–161.

Cain, A. (1961). A supplementary dream technique with the Children's Apperception Test. *Journal of Clinical Psychology, 17,* 181–184.

Cain, C. (1991). Personal stories: Identity acquisition and self-understanding in Alcoholics Anonymous. *Ethos, 19,* 210–253.

Campell, J. (1971), *The hero of a thousand faces.* Princeton, NJ: Princeton University Press.

Campus, N. (1976). A measure of needs to assess the stimulus characteristics of TAT cards. *Journal of Personality Assessment, 40,* 248–258.

Cann, A. (1977). *The effects of the attitudes of Whites toward Blacks on thematic apperception of racial stimuli.* Unpublished doctoral dissertation. New York University, New York.

Carey, J. L. (1988). Assessing the relevency of the Thematic Apperception Test: A contemporary alternative. *Dissertation Abstracts International, 48* (12-A), 3072.

Carliez, L. (1973). T.A.T. et théories psychoanalytiques: Aperçus bibliographique [The T.A.T. and psychoanalytic theories: Annotated bibliography]. *Revue de psychologie et des sciences de l'éducation, 8,* 467–489.

Carlile, S. St. H. (1952). The Thematic Apperception Test applied to neurotic and normal adolescent girls. *British Journal of Medical Psychology, 25,* 244–248.

Carr, A. C. (1956). The relation of certain Rorschach variables to the expression of affects in the T.A.T. and S.C.T. *Journal of Projective Techniques, 20,* 137–142.

Carrigan, W. C., & Julian, J. W. (1966). Sex and birth-order differences in conformity as a function of need affiliation arousal. *Journal of Personality and Social Psychology, 3,* 479–482.

Castro, D. (1990, July). *Étude psychopathologique du sujet glaucomateux à travers le Rorschach et le TAT* [Psychopathological study of glaucoma patients with the Rorschach and the T.A.T.]. Unpublished paper presented at the 13th International Congress of Rorschach and Projective Techniques, Paris.

Cattell, R. B. (1951). Principles of designs in "projective" or misperception tests of personality. In H. H. Anderson & G. L. Anderson (Eds.), *An introduction to projective psychology.* New York: Prentice-Hall.

Caudill, W. (1949). Psychological characteristics of acculturated Wisconsin Ojibwa children. *American Anthropologist, 51,* 409–427.

Caudill, W. (1952). Japanese-American personality and acculturation. *Genetic Psychology Monographs, 45,* 3–102.

Caudill, W., & De Vos, G. (1956). Achievement culture and personality: The case of the Japanese-Americans. *American Anthropologist, 58,* 1102–1126.

Cerutti, P. (1990, July). *Le profil de personnalité du sujet avec syndrome de l'articulation tempe-mandibulaire (S.A.D.A.T.M.) sur la base du réactif de Rorschach et de TAT.* Unpublished paper presented at the 13th International Congress of Rorschach and Projective Techniques, Paris.

Chabert, C. (1980). Manifest and latent content in the Children's Apperception Test. *Psychologie Française, 25*(2), 115–124.

Chabert, C. (1987). Rorschach and TAT: Antinomy or complimentarity. *Psychologie Française, 32*(3), 141–144.

Chamson, S. F. (1983). *An investigation of T.A.T. responses as a function of figure-ground deficits.* Unpublished docotoral dissertation, School of Professional Psychology, Florida Institute of Technology.

Chandler, L. A., Shermis, M. D., & Lempert, M. E. (1989). The need-threat analysis: A scoring system for the C.A.T. *Psychology in the Schools, 26,* 47–54.

Chapin, N. (1953). A dynamic approach to the T.A.T. *Psychiatric Quarterly Supplement, 27,* 62–89.

Chauhan, N., & Dhar, U. (1981). The psychodynamic side of leprosy: A Children's Apperception Test (CAT) study. *Leprosy India, 53*(3), 379–384.

Child, I. L., Storm, T., & Veroff, J. (1958). Achievement themes in folktales related to socialization practice. In J. W. Atkinson (Ed.), *Motives in fantasy, action and society* (pp. 479–492). Princeton, NJ: D. Van Nostrand.

Chin, J. L. (1983). Diagnostic considerations in working with Asian Americans. *American Journal of Orthopsychiatry, 7,* 263–278.

Chowdhury, U. (1960a). An Indian modification of the Thematic Apperception Test. *Journal of Social Psychology, 51,* 245–263.

Chowdhury, U. (1960b). *An Indian adaptation of the Children's Apperception Test.* Delhi, India: Manasayan.

Chusmir, L. H. (1983). Male-oriented versus balanced-as-to-sex Thematic Apperception Test. *Journal of Personality Assessment, 47,* 29–35.

Chusmir, L. H. (1985). Short-form scoring for McClelland's version of the TAT. *Perceptual and Motor Skills, 61,* 1047–1052.

Clark, R. A. (1944). A method of administering and evaluating the Thematic Apperception Test in group situations. *Genetic Psychology Monographs, 30,* 3–55.

Clark, R. A. (1952). The projective measurement of experimentally induced levels of sexual motivation. *Journal of Experimental Psychology, 44,* 391–399.

Clark, R. A., & Sensibar, M. R. (1955). The relationship between symbolic and manifest projections of sexuality with some incidental correlates. *Journal of Abnormal and Social Psychology, 50,* 327–334.

Clifford, J., & Marcus, G. E. (Eds.). (1986). *Writing culture: The politics and poetics of ethnography.* Berkeley, CA: University of California Press.

Coche, E., & Sillitti, J. A. (1983). The Thematic Apperception Test as an outcome measure in psychotherapy research. *Psychotherapy Theory, Research and Practice, 20,* 41–46.

Cohen, R. J., & Horstron, D. R. (1975). Fear of failure and rigidity in problem-solving. *Perceptual and Motor Skills, 40,* 930.

Cohler, B. J. (1993). Aging, morale, and meaning: The nexus of narrative. In T. R. Cole, W. A. Achenbaum, P. L. Jakobi, & R. Kastenbaum (Eds.), *Voices and visions of aging: Toward a critical gerontology.* New York: Springer.

Cole, M., Gay, J., Glick, J., & Sharp, D. (1971). *The cultural contest of learning and thinking.* New York: Basic Books.

Coleman, W. (1947). The Thematic Apperception Test. I. Effect of recent experience. II. Some quantitative observations. *Journal of Clinical Psychology, 3,* 257–264.

Combs, A. (1946). The use of personal experience in Thematic Apperception Test story plots. *Journal of Clinical Psychology, 2,* 357–363.

Conant, J. A. (1950). *A comparison of thematic fantasy among normals, neurotics, and schizophrenics.* Unpublished doctoral dissertation, University of Southern California.

Condrell, C. (1989). Comparison of fantasy production on the Thematic Apperception Test (TAT) and the Apperceptive Personality Test (APT). *Dissertation Abstracts International, 49* (12-A, Pt 1), 3670.

Cook, R. A. (1953). Identification and ego defensiveness in Thematic Apperception. *Journal of Projective Techniques, 17,* 312–319.

Cooper, A. (1977). Adolescent T.A.T. responses: Normative and developmental approaches. *Dissertation Abstracts International, 38* (4-B), 1873.

Cooper, A. (1981). A basic set for adolescent males. *Journal of Clinical Psychology, 37,* 411–414.

Corsaro, W. A., & Heise, D. R. (1990). Event structure models from ethnographic data. In C. Clogg (Ed.), *Sociological methodology* (pp. 205–241). New York: Academic.

Cortazzi, M. (1993). *Narrative analysis.* Washington, DC: Falmer.

Costantino, G. (1990a, July). *Assessment of attention deficit disorder using a Thematic Apperception Technique.* Unpublished paper presented at the 13th International Congress of Rorschach and Projective Techniques, Paris.

Costantino, G. (1990b, July). *Cross-cultural standardization of TEMAS in four different Hispanic subcultures.* Unpublished paper presented at the 13th International Congress of Rorschach and Projective Techniques, Paris.

Costantino, G., Malgady, R., Rogler, L., & Tsui, E. (1988a). Discriminant analysis of clinical outpatients and public school children by TEMAS: A thematic apperception test for Hispanics and Blacks. *Journal of Personality Assessment, 4,* 670–678.

Costantino, G., Malgady, R., & Rogler, L. H. (1988b). *Tell-Me-A-Story TEMAS manual.* Los Angeles, CA: Western Psychological Services.

Costantino, G., Malgady, R. G., & Vazquez, C. (1981). Verbal fluency of Hispanic, Black, and White children on T.A.T. and TEMAS: A new thematic apperception test. *Hispanic Journal of Behavioral Sciences, 3,* 291–300.

Costantino, G., Colon-Malgady, G., Malgady, R. G., & Perez, A. (1991) Assessment of attention deficit disorder using a thematic apperceptive technique. *Journal of Personality Assessment, 57,* 87–95.

Costello, R. M., & Wicoff, K. A. (1984). Impression management and testing for control locus in an alcoholic sample. *International Journal of the Addictions, 19,* 45–56.

Couchard, F. (1990, July). *TAT of women of muslim culture: Influence of socio-cultural variables.* Unpublished paper presented at the 13th International Congress of Rorschach and Project Techniqnies, Paris.

Cowan, G. (1971). Achievement motivation in lower class negro females as a function of the race and sex of the figure. *Representative Research in Social Psychology, 21,* 42–46.

Cowan, G., & Goldberg, F. (1967). Need achievement as a function of the race and sex of figures of selected T.A.T. cards. *Journal of Personality, 5,* 245–249.

Craig, R. J., & Horowitz, M. (1990). Current utilization of psychological tests at diagnostic practicum sites. *The Clinical Psychologist, 43,* 29–36.

Cramer, P. (1979). Defense mechanisms in adolescence. *Developmental Psychology, 15,* 476–477.

Cramer, P. (1983). Children's use of defense mechanisms in reaction to displeasure caused by others. *Journal of Personality, 51,* 78–94.

Cramer, P. (1987). The development of defense mechanisms. *Journal of Personality, 55,* 597–614.

Cramer, P. (1988). The Defense Mechanism Inventory: A review of research and discussion of the scales. *Journal of Personality Assessment, 52,* 142–164.

Cramer, P. (1991a). *The development of defense mechanisms: Theory, research, and assessment.* New York: Springer-Verlag.

Cramer, P. (1991b). Anger and the use of defense mechanisms in college students. *Journal of Personality, 59,* 39–55.

Cramer, P., & Blatt, S. J. (1990). Use of the T.A.T. to measure change in defense mechanisms following intensive psychotherapy. *Journal of Personality Assessment, 54,* 236–251.

Cramer, P., Blatt, S. J., & Ford, R. Q. (1988). Defense mechanisms in the anaclitic and introjective personality configuration. *Journal of Consulting and Clinical Psychology, 56,* 610–616.

Cramer, P., & Carter, T. (1978). the relationship between sexual identification and the use of defense mechanisms. *Journal of Personality Assessment, 42,* 63–73.

Crenshaw, D. A., Bohn, S., Hoffman, M., Mathews, J. M., & Offenbach, S. G. (1968). The use of projective methods in research 1947–1965. *Journal of Projective Techniques and Personality Assessment, 32,* 3–9.

Cuenca, C., & Salvatierra, V. (1981). T.A.T. de Murray y comportamiento sexual [Murray's TAT and sexual behavior]. *Revista de Psiquiatria y Psicologia Medica de Europa y America Latinas, 25,* 49–64.

Cummings, E., & Henry, W. E. (1961). *Growing old.* New York: Basic Books.

Cusack, G. P. (1977). The effects of story writing instructions and openness to experience on the production of achievement and playful fantasy content on the T.A.T. *Dissertation Abstracts International, 37* (9-B), 4643.

Dalakishvili, S. M., Bakhtadze, N. A., & Nikuradze, M. D. (1989). A study of personality traits in longevity [Russian]. *Psikologicheskii Zhurnal, 10,* 94–103.

Dana, R. H. (1949). *The Thematic Apperception Test applied to an experiment in perception personality.* Unpublished doctoral dissertation, Princeton University, Princeton, NJ.

Dana, R. H. (1955). Clinical diagnosis and objective T.A.T. scoring. *Journal of Abnormal and Social Psychology, 50,* 19–25.

Dana, R. H. (1956a). Cross validation of objective T.A.T. scoring. *Journal of Consulting Psychology, 20,* 33–36.

Dana, R. H. (1956b). Selection of abbreviated T.A.T. sets. *Journal of Clinical Psychology, 12,* 36–40.

Dana, R. H. (1959a). Proposal for objective scoring of the T.A.T. *Perceptual and Motor Skills, 9,* 99–112.

Dana, R. H. (1959b). The perceptual organization T.A.T. score: Number, order and frequency components. *Journal of Projective Techniques, 23,* 307–310.

Dana, R. H. (1968). Thematic techniques and clinical practice. *Journal of Projective Techniques and Personality Assessment, 32,* 204–214.

Dana, R. H. (1972). Review of Thematic Apperception Test. In O. K. Buros (Ed.), *The seventh mental measurements yearbook: Vol. 1* (pp. 45–47). Highland Park, MD: Gryphon Press.

Dana, R. H. (1985). Thematic Apperception Test. In C. S. Newmark (Ed.), *Major psychological assessment instruments* (pp. 89–134). Boston: Allyn and Bacon.

Dana, R. H. (1986). Thematic Apperception Test used with adolescents. In A. I. Rabin (Ed.), *Projective techniques for adolescents and children* (pp. 14–36). New York: Springer.

Dana, R. H. (1993). *Multicultural assessment for professional psychology.* Boston: Allyn and Bacon.

Dana, R. H. (1996). Culturally competent assessment practice in the United States. *Journal of Personality Assessment, 66,* 472–487.

Dana, R. H., & Cunningham, K. M. (1983). Convergent validity of Rorschach and Thematic Apperception Test ego strength measures. *Perceptual and Motor Skills, 57,* 1101–1102.

Davids, A. & Devault, S. (1960). Use of the T.A.T. and Human Figure Drawings in research on personality, pregnancy, and perception. *Journal of Projective Techniques, 24*(4), 362–365.

Davison, A. H. (1953). A comparison of fantasy productions on the T.A.T. of 60 hospitalized psychoneurotic and psychotic patients. *Journal of Projective Techniques, 17,* 20–33.

Deabler, H. L. (1947). The psychotherapeutic use of the Thematic Apperception Test. *Journal of Clinical Psychology, 3,* 246–252.

Debray, R. (1987). How significant is the TAT for a 6-year-old child? *Psychologie Française, 32*(3), 157–159.

Debray, R. (1990, July). *Contribution of Rorschach and TAT in psychosomatic research.* Unpublished paper presented at the 13th International Congress of Rorschach and Projective Techniques, Paris.

De Ridder, J. C. (1961). *The personality of the urban African in South Africa: A Thematic Apperception Test study.* London: Routledge.

De Sousa, T. (1952). A comparison of the responses of adjusted and maladjusted children on a Thematic Apperception Test. Unpublished master's thesis, Loyola University, Chicago. *Dissertation Abstracts International, 47*(1-B), 435.

De Vos, G. (1960). The relation of guilt toward parents to achievement and arranged marriage among the Japanese. *Psychiatry, 23,* 287–301.

De Vos, G. A. (1973). *Socialization for achievement: Essays on the cultural psychology of the Japanese.* Berkeley, CA: University of California Press.

De Vos, G. A. (1976). The interrelationship of social and psychological structures in transcultural psychology. In W. P. Lebra (Ed.), *Culture-bound syndromes, ethnopsychiatry, and alternate therapies* (pp. 278–298). Honolulu: University Press of Hawaii.

De Vos, G. A. (1983). Achievement motivation and intra-family attitudes in immigrant Koreans. *Journal of Psychoanalytic Anthropology, 6,* 25–71.

De Vos, G. A. (1990, July). *Cross-cultural comparisons with the TAT: Quantifications of scoring of interpersonal concerns.* Unpublished paper presented at the 13th International Congress of Rorschach and Projective Techniques, Paris.

De Vos, G. A., Hauswald, L., & Borders, O. (1979). Cultural differences in family socialization: A psychocultural comparison of Chinese and Japanese. In A Craig (Ed.), *Japan: A comparative view.* Princeton, NJ: Princeton University Press.

De Vos, G. A., & Murakami, E. (1974). Violence and aggression in fantasy: A comparison of American and Japanese lower-class youth. In W. Lebra (Ed.), *Youth, socialization and mental health* (pp. 153–177). Honolulu: University of Hawaii Press.

De Vos, G. A., & Vaughn, C. A. (1992). The interpersonal self: A level of psychocultural analysis. In L. B. Boyer, R. M. Boyer, & S. M. Sonnenberg (Eds.), *The psychoanalytic study of society.* (Vol. 17) (pp. 95–142). Hillsdale, NJ: Analytic Press.

Dias, B. (1976). *Les mécanismes de défense dans la genèse des normes de conduite: Étude experimentale basée sur le Thematic Apperception Test (TAT)* [Defense mechanisms in the etiology of behavioral norms: Experimental study based on the T.A.T.]. Fribourg, Suisse: Editions Universitaires.

Dies, R. R. (1968). Development of a projective measure of perceived locus of control. *Journal of Projective Techniques and Personality Assessment, 32,* 487–490.

Doane, J. A., Miklowitz, D. J., Oranchak, E., & Flores de Apodaca, R. (1989). Parental communication deviance and schizophrenia: A cross-cultural comparison of Mexican and Anglo-Americans. *Journal of Abnormal Psychology, 98,* 487–490.

Doane, J. A., & Mintz, J. (1987). Communication deviance in adolescence and adulthood: A longitudinal study. *Psychiatry, 50,* 5–13.

Dobson, K. S., & Block, L. (1988). Historical and philosophical basis of the cognitive-behavioral therapies. In K. S. Dobson (Ed.), *Handbook of cognitive-behavioral therapies* (pp. 3–38). New York: Guilford.

Dollin, A. P. (1960). *The effect of order of presentation on perception of TAT pictures.* Unpublished doctoral dissertation, University of Connecticut.

Dollinger, S. J., & Cramer, P. (1990). Children's defensive responses and emotional upset following a disaster: A projective assessment. *Journal of Personality Assessment, 54,* 116–121.

Dorr, D. (1990, July). *Rorschach patterns in psychiatric inpatients diagnosed as borderline personality disorder.* Unpublished paper presented at the 13th International Congress of Rorschach and Projective Techniques, Paris.

Douglas, C. (1993). *Translate this darkness: The life of Christiana Morgan.* New York: Simon & Schuster.

Douville, O. (1987). The TAT in adolescence. *Psychologie Française, 32*(3), 162–167.

Draguns, J. G. (1990). Applications of cross-cultural psychology in the field of mental health. In R. W. Brislin (Ed.), *Applied cross-cultural psychology.* Newbury Park, CA: Sage.

Dreyfus, A., Husain, O., & Rousselle, I. (1987). Schizophrenia and the Thematic Apperception Test: Some reflections on its formal aspects. *Psychologie Française, 32*(3), 181–186.

Dudek, S. Z. (1975). Regression in the service of the ego in young children. *Journal of Personality Assessment, 39,* 369–376.

Dungan, D. S., & Holmes, C. B. (1982). Factors determining gender of the figure in TAT Card 3BM. *Perceptual and Motor Skills, 55,* 1209–1210.

Dunlevy, G. P., Jr. (1953). *Intentional modification of Thematic Apperception Test stories as a function of adjustment.* Unpublished doctoral dissertation, Purdue University, IN.

Dymond, R. F. (1954). Adjustment changes over therapy from Thematic Apperception Test ratings. In C. R. Rogers & R. F. Dymond (Eds.), *Psychotherapy and personality change* (pp. 76–84). Chicago: University of Chicago Press.

D'Zurilla T. J. (1988). Problem-solving therapies. In K. S. Dobson (Ed.), *Handbook of cognitive-behavioral therapies* (pp. 85–135). New York: Guilford.

D'Zurilla, T. J., & Goldfried, M. R. (1971). Problem solving and behavioral modification. *Journal of Abnormal Psychology, 78,* 107–126.

D'Zurilla, T. J., & Nezu, A. M. (1990). Development and preliminary evaluation of the social problem-solving inventory. *Psychological Assessment: A Journal of Consulting and Clinical Psychology, 2,* 156–163.

Eagle, C. (1964). *An investigation of individual consistencies in the manifestations of primary process.* Unpublished doctoral dissertation, New York University, New York.

Earle, M. (1958). *Rakau children: From six to thirteen years.* Wellington, New Zealand: Victoria University Publications in Psychology, No. 11 (*Monographs on Maori Social Life and Personality,* No. 4).

Easter, L. V., & Murstein, B. I. (1964). Achievement fantasy as a function of probability of success. *Journal of Consulting Psychology, 28,* 154–159.

Edgerton, R. B. (1971). *The individual and cultural adaptation.* Berkeley, CA: University of California Press.

Ehrenreich, J. H. (1990). Effect of social class of subjects on normative responses to TAT cards. *Journal of Clinical Psychology, 46,* 467–471.

Eisdorfer, C., & Lawton, M. P. (1973). *The psychology of adult development and aging.* Washington, DC: American Psychiatric Press.

Eisner, D. A., & Maibaum, M. (1987). Determining psychosis in retarded adults through psychological tests. *Psychological Reports, 61*(3), 789–790.

Eissler, K. (1954). Notes upon defects of ego structure in schizophrenia. *International Journal of Psychoanalysis, 35,* 141.

Emmanuelli, M. (1990, July). *Study of thought mechanisms in adolescence through Rorschach and TAT.* Unpublished paper presented at the 13th International Congress of Rorschach and Projective Techniques, Paris.

Epley, D., & Ricks, D. R. (1963). Foresight and hindsight in the TAT. *Journal of Projective Techniques, 17,* 51–59.

Epstein, S. (1962). The measurement of drive and conflict in humans: Theory and experiment. In M. Jones (Ed.), *Nebraska symposium on motivation.* Lincoln: University of Nebraska Press.

Epstein, S. (1966). Some theoretical considerations on the nature of ambiguity and the use of stimulus dimensions in projective techniques. *Journal of Consulting Psychology, 30,* 183–192.

Epstein, S., & Smith, R. (1956). Thematic Apperception as a measure of the hunger drive. *Journal of Projective Techniques, 20,* 376–384.

Epstein, S., & Smith, R. (1957). Thematic apperception, Rorschach content, and ratings of sexual attractiveness of women as measures of the sex drive. *Journal of Consulting Psychology, 21,* 473–478.

Erasmus, P. F., & Minaar, G. G. (1978). *The discriminative ability of the TAT-Z with regard to hospitalised and non-hospitalised groups of black men: Validity study.* Pretoria: Human Sciences Research Council.

Eriksen, C. W. (1951). Some implications for T.A.T. interpretations arising from need and perception experiments. *Journal of Personality, 19,* 282–288.

Erikson, E. H. (1950). *Childhood and society.* New York: W. W. Norton.

Eriksson, H. E. (1979). An alternative way of administering CAT. *Tidsskrift for Norsk Psykologforening, 16*(11), 484–492.

Eron, L. D. (1948). Frequencies of themes and identifications in the stories of schizophrenics and non-hospitalized college students. *Journal of Consulting Psychology, 12,* 387–395.

Eron, L. D. (1950). A normative study of the Thematic Apperception Test. *Psychological Monographs, 64*(9).

Eron, L. D. (1953). Responses of women to the Thematic Apperception Test. *Journal of Consulting Psychology, 17,* 269–282.

Eron, L. D. (1972). Review of the Thematic Apperception Test. In D. K. Buros (Ed.), *The seventh mental measurement yearbook* (Vol. 1) (pp. 181–182). Highland Park, MD: Gryphon Press.

Eron, L. D., Auld, F., & Laffal, J. (1955). Application of Guttman's scaling method to the TAT. *Educational and Psychological Measurement, 15,* 422–435.

Eron, L. D., & Jake, D. T. (1950). Psychometric approach to the evaluation of the Thematic Apperception Test. In J. Zubin (Ed.), *Quantitative techniques and methods in abnormal psychology* (pp. 1–14). New York: Columbia University Press.

Eron, L. D., & Ritter, A. M. (1951a). A comparison of two methods of administration of the Thematic Apperception Test. *Journal of Consulting and Clinical Psychology, 15,* 55–61.

Eron, L. D., & Ritter, A. M. (1951b). In E. S. Shneidman (Ed.), *Thematic test analysis* (p. 55). New York: Grune & Stratton.

Eron, L. D., Terry, D., & Callahan, R. (1950). The use of rating scales for emotional tone. *Monographs, 64*(9).

Ervin, S. M. (1964). Language and TAT content in bilinguals. *Journal of Abnormal and Social Psychology, 68,* 500–507.

Evans, E. (1990, July). *Omens of future ills: The prognostic value of the TAT among African youth in Kenya.* Unpublished paper presented at the 13th International Congress of Roschach and Projective Techniques, Paris.

Exner, J. E. (1974, 1986, 1994). *The Rorschach: A comprehensive system* (Vol. I). New York: Wiley.

Exner, J. E. (1976). Projective techniques. In I. B. Weiner (Ed.), *Clinical Methods in psychology* (pp. 61–121). New York: Wiley.

Fabian, J. (1983). *Time and the other: How anthropology makes its object.* New York: Columbia University Press.

Fagiani, M. B., et al. (1989). The elderly and their existence model: A study with projective techniques. *Minerva. Psichiatr., 30*(2), 6975.

Fairbairn, W. R. D. (1954). *An object relations theory of the personality.* New York: Basic Books.

Fairweather, G., Simon, R., Gebhard, M., Weingarten, E., Holland, J., Sanders, R., Stone, G., & Reahl, J. (1960). Relative effectiveness of psychotherapeutic programs: A multicriteria comparison of four programs for three different patient groups. *Psychology Monographs, 74*(5).

Falicov, C. J. (1988). Learning to think culturally. In H. A. Liddle, D. C. Breunlin, & R. C. Schwartz (Eds.), *Handbook of family therapy and supervision* (pp. 335–357). New York: Guilford.

Fassino, S., Scarso, G., Barbero, L., Taylor, J., Pezzini, F., & Furian, P. M. (1992). The image of self and of the environment in drug abusers: A comparative study using the TAT. *Drug and Alcohol Dependence, 30,* 253–261.

Fear, C., & Stone, L. J. (1951). *A study of 40 school children with the C.A.T.-S.* Unpublished thesis, Vassar College, Poughkeepsie, NY.

Feifel, H. (1959, July). Psychological test report: A communication between psychologist and psychiatrist (L. Bellak, Chairman). *Journal of Nervous and Mental Diseases, 129*(1), 76–91.

Fenichel, O. (1945). *The psychoanalytic theory of neurosis.* New York: Norton.

Fernandes, I. (1990, July). *Étude comparative de la projection au Rorschach et au TAT avec un groupe de sujets schizophreniques.* Unpublished paper presented at the 13th International Congress of Rorschach and Projective Techniques, Paris.

Fernandez Ballesteros, R. (1973). Ensayo de sistematizacion de los resultados del T.A.T. [Systematization study of T.A.T. results] *Revista de Psicologia General y Aplicada, 123–125,* 1017–1023.

Ferreria, A. J., & Winter, W. D. (1965). Family interaction and decision-making. *Archives of General Psychiatry, 13,* 214–223.

Ferreira, A. J., Winter, W. D., & Poindexter, E. (1966). Some interactional variables in normal and abnormal families. *Family Process, 5,* 60–75.

Feshbach, S. (1961). The influence of drive arousal and conflict upon fantasy behavior. In J. Kagan & G. Lesser (Eds.), *Contemporary issues in Thematic Apperception methods* (pp. 119–138). Springfield, IL: Charles C. Thomas.

Festinger, L. (1957). *The theory of cognitive dissonance.* New York: Harper.

Fiester, S. & Siipola, E. (1972). Effects of time pressure on the management of aggression in T.A.T. stories. *Journal of Personality Assessment, 36,* 230–240.

Fine, R. (1951). In E. S. Shneidman (Ed.), *Thematic test analysis* (p. 64). New York: Grune & Stratton.

Fine, R. (1955a). A scoring scheme for the T.A.T. and other verbal projective techniques. *Journal of Projective Techniques, 19,* 306–309.

Fine, R. (1955b). Manual for a scoring scheme for verbal projective techniques. *Journal of Projective Techniques, 19,* 310–316.

Finn, M. (1951). *An investigation of apperceptive distortion in the obsessive-compulsive character structure by three methods: Verbal, graphic-emotional, and graphic-geometric.* Unpublished doctoral dissertation, New York University, New York.

Fisher, C. (1954). Dreams and perception: The role of preconscious and primary modes of perception in dream formation. *Journal of the American Psychoanalytic Association, 11,* 389–445.

Fisher, S., & Fisher, R. L. (1960). A projective test analysis of ethnic subculture themes in families. *Journal of Projective Techniques, 24,* 366–369.

Fiske, D. W., & Pearson, P. H. (1970). Theory and techniques of personality measurement. *Annual Review of Psychology, 21,* 49–86.

Fitzgerald, B. (1958). Some relationships among projective test, interview, and sociometric measures of dependent behavior. *Journal of Abnormal and Social Psychology, 56,* 199–203.

Fitzgerald, B. J., Pasewark, R. A., & Fleisher, S. (1974). Responses of an aged population on the Gerontological and Thematic Apperception Tests. *Journal of Personality Assessment, 38,* 234–235.

Fitzsimons, R. (1958). Developmental, psychosocial, and educational factors in children with non-organic articulation problems. *Child Development, 29,* 481–489.

Fleming, E. (1946). *A descriptive analysis of responses in the Thematic Apperception Test.* Unpublished master's thesis, University of Pittsburgh, PA.

Fogel, M. L. (1967). Picture description and interpretation in brain-damaged patients. *Cortex, 3,* 443–448.

Fogelgren, L. A. (1974). Comparison of two objective scoring systems for the T.A.T. *Perceptual and Motor Skills, 39,* 255–260.

Foote, J., & Kahn, M. W. (1979). Discriminative effectiveness of the Senior Apperception Test with impaired and nonimpaired elderly persons. *Journal of Personality Assessment, 43,* 360–364.

Foulds, G. (1953). A method of scoring the T.A.T. applied to psychoneurotics. *Journal of Mental Science, 99,* 235–246.

Frank, A. F., & Gunderson, J. G. (1990). The role of the therapeutic alliance in the treatment of schizophrenia: Relationship to course and outcome. *Archives of General Psychiatry, 47,* 228–236.

Frank, L. K. (1939). Projective methods for the study of personality. *Journal of Psychology, 8,* 343–389.

Franz, C. E. (1994). Does thought content change as individuals age? A longitudinal study of midlife adults. In T. F. Heatherton & J. L. Weinberger (Eds.), *Can personality change?* (pp. 227–249). Washington, DC: American Psychological Association.

Freeman, A., Pretzer, J., Fleming, B., & Simon, K. M. (1990). *Clinical applications of cognitive therapy.* New York: Plenum.

French, E. G., & Lesser, G. S. (1964). Some characteristics of the achievement motive in women. *Journal of Abnormal and Social Psychology, 68,* 119–128.

French, L. A. (1993). Adapting projective tests for minority children. *Psychological Reports, 72,* 15–18.

Freud, A. (1936). *The ego and the mechanisms of defense.* New York: International Universities Press.

Freud, A. (1965). *Normality and pathology of childhood.* New York: International Universities Press.

Freud, S. (1900). Interpretation of dreams. *Standard Edition* (Vols. 4 & 5). London: Hogarth Press.

Freud, S. (1909). The analysis of a phobia in a five-year-old boy. *Standard Edition* (Vol. 10) (pp. 5–149). London: Hogarth Press.

Freud, S. (1915). Instincts and their vicissitudes. *Standard Edition* (Vol. 14) (pp. 117–140). London: Hogarth Press.

Freud, S. (1920). Beyond the pleasure principle. *Standard Edition* (Vol. 18) (pp. 7–64). London: Hogarth Press.

Freud, S. (1923). The ego and the id. *Standard Edition* (Vol. 19) (pp. 12–66). London: Hogarth Press.

Freud, S. (1938). Totem and taboo. In A. A. Brill (Ed.), *Basic writings of Sigmund Freud.* New York: Modern Library.

Freud, S. (1940a). The anxiety neurosis. *International Psychoanalytic Library* (No. 1). London: Hogarth Press.

Freud, S. (1940b). The future of an illusion. *International Psychoanalytic Library* (No. 15). Hogarth Press.

Freud S. (1940c). Group psychology and the analysis of the ego. *International Psychoanalytic Library* (No. 6). London: Hogarth Press.

Freud, S. (1940d). Neuropsychoses. *International Psychoanalytic Library* (No. 1). London: Hogarth Press.

Freud, S. (1943). Psychoanalytic notes on an autobiographical account of a case of paranoia (dementia paranoides). *International Psychoanalytic Library* (No. 3). London: Hogarth Press.

Freidman, I. (1957a). Objectifying the subjective: A methodological approach to the T.A.T. *Journal of Projective Techniques, 21,* 243–247.

Freidman, I. (1957b). Characteristics of the Thematic Apperception Test heroes of normal, psychoneurotic, and paranoid schizophrenic subjects. *Journal of Projective Techniques, 21,* 372–376.

Friedmann, E., & Lockwood, R. (1991). Validation and use of the Animal Thematic Apperception Test (ATAT). *Anthrozoos, 4,* 174–183.

Fry, F. D. (1953). Manual for scoring the T.A.T. *Journal of Psychology, 35,* 181–195.

Fujita, S. (1959). T.A.T. with delinquents. *Psychological Diagnosis Series* (Vol. 3) (pp. 255–267). Tokyo: Nakayama Books (in Japanese).

Furyua, K. (1957). Responses of school children to human and animal pictures. *Journal of Projective Techniques, 21,* 248–252.

Gardner, R., & Lohrenz, L. (1960). Leveling-sharpening and serial reproduction of a story. *Bulletin of the Menninger Clinic, 24,* 295–304.

Garfield, S. L., Blek, L., & Melker, F. (1952). The influence of method of administration and sex differences on selected aspects of T.A.T. stories. *Journal of Consulting Psychology, 16,* 140-146.

Garfield, S. L., & Eron, L. D. (1948). Interpreting mood and activity in T.A.T. stories. *Journal of Abnormal and Social Psychology, 43,* 338–345.

Garland, C. (1974). *The experience of dependency in the elderly.* Unpublished bachelor's thesis, State University of New York College, Purchase, NY.

Gartner, J., Hurt, S. W., & Gartner, A. (1989). Psychological test signs of borderline personality disorder: A review of the empirical literature. *Journal of Personality Assessment, 53,* 423–441.

Gatz, M. (Ed.). (1995). *Emerging issues in mental health and aging.* Washington, DC: American Psychological Association Press.

Geertz, C. (1988). *Works and lives: The anthropologist as author.* Stanford, CA: Stanford University Press.

Geist, H. (1968). *The psychological aspects of the aging process.* St Louis, MO: Warren H. Green.

Gergen, M. M. (1988). *Narrative structure in social explanation.* London: Sage.

Geriatrics. (1972). In *Medical World News.* New York: McGraw Hill.

Gerver, J. M. (1946). *Level of interpretation of children on the Thematic Apperception Test.* Unpublished master's thesis, Ohio State University.

Gilbert, G. M. (1947). *The Nuremberg diary.* New York: Prentice-Hall.

Ginsparg, H. (1957). *A study of the Children's Apperception Test.* Unpublished doctoral dissertation, Washington University, Seattle.

Gladwin, T. (1953). The role of man and woman on Truk: A problem in personality and culture. *Transactions of the New York Academy of Science* (Series 2), *15,* 305–309.

Gladwin, T., & Sarason, S. B. (1953). *Truk: Man in paradise.* New York: Wenner Gren Foundation.

Gluck, M. R. (1955). Relationship between hostility in the T.A.T. and behavioral hostility. *Journal of Projective Techniques, 19,* 21–26.

Goh, D. S., Teslow, C. J., & Fuller, G. B. (1981). The practice of psychological assessment among school psychologists. *Professional Psychology: Research and Practice, 12,* 696–706.

Golden, C. J. (1978). *Learning disabilities and brain dysfunction.* Springfield, IL: Charles C. Thomas.

Golden, C. J. (1979). *Clinical interpretation of objective psychological tests.* New York: Grune & Stratton.

Goldfarb, A. (1973, April 6). How to stay young: Probing the mysteries of aging. *Newsweek.*

Goldfarb, W. (1945). The animal symbol in the Rorschach test and in animal association test. *Rorschach Research Exchange Projective Techniques, 9,* 8–22.

Goldfried, M., & Zax, M. (1965). The stimulus value of the T.A.T. *Journal of Projective Techniques, 29,* 46–57.

Goldman, R., & Greenblatt, M. (1955). Changes in Thematic Apperception Test stories paralleling changes in clinical status of schizophrenic patients. *Journal of Nervous and Mental Diseases, 121,* 243–249.

Goldstein, M. J. (1985). Family factors that antedate the onset of schizophrenia and related disorders: The results of a fifteen-year prospective longitudinal study. *Acta Psychiatrica Scandinavica, 71,* 7–18.

Goldstine, T., & Gutman, D. (1972). A TAT study of Navajo aging. *Psychiatry, 35,* 373–384.

Gordon, H. L. (1953). A comparative study of dreams and responses to the Thematic Apperception Test. *Journal of Personality, 22,* 234–254.

Gori, R. C., & Poinso, V. (1970–1971). Projet d'une approche psycholinguistique du T.A.T. *Bulletin de Psychologique, 24,* 713–717.

Gottschalk, L. A., & Glesser, G. C. (1969). *The measurement of psychological states through content analysis of verbal behavior.* Berkeley, CA: University of California Press.

Greenacre, P. (1952). *Trauma, growth, and personality.* New York: International Universities Press.

Greenbaum, M., Qualtere, T., Carrouth, B., & Cruickshank, W. (1953). Evaluation of a modification of the T.A.T. for use with physically handicapped children. *Journal of Clinical Psychology, 9,* 40–41.

Griffin, L. J. (1993). Narrative, event structure analysis, and causal interpretation in historical sociology. *American Journal of Sociology, 98,* 1094–1133.

Grzesiak, R. C., Kegerreis, J. P., & Miller, G. D. (1973). A comparison of thematic content on selected Rorschach and T.A.T. cards. *British Journal of Projective Psychology and Personality Study, 18,* 31–35.

Gurel, L., & Ullmann, L. P. (1958).Quantitative differences in response to T.A.T. cards: The relationship between transcendence score and number of emotional words. *Journal of Projective Techniques, 22,* 399–401.

Gurevitz, S., & Kapper, Z. (1951). Techniques for and evaluation of the responses of schizophrenic and cerebral palsied children to the Children's Apperception Test (C.A.T.). *Quarterly Journal of Child Behavior, 3,* 38–65.

Guthrie, E. R., & Horton, G. P. (1946). *Cats in a puzzle hox.* New York: Rinehart.

Gutmann, D. L. (1964). An exploration of ego configurations in middle and later life. In B. Neugarten et al. (Eds.), *Personality in middle and late life* (pp. 14–148). New York: Atherton Press.

Gutmann, D. L. (1966). Mayan aging—A comparative TAT study. *Psychiatry, 29,* 246–259.

Haber, R. N., & Alpert, R. (1958). The role of situation and picture cues in projective measurement of the achievement motive. In J. W. Atkinson (Ed.), *Motives in fantasy, action, and society.* Princeton, NJ: D. Van Nostrand.

Hafner, J., & Kaplan, A. (1960). Hostility content analysis of the Rorschach and T.A.T. *Journal of Projective Techniques, 24,* 137–143.

Haley, J. (1967). Cross-cultural experimentation: An initial attempt. *Human Organization, 26,* 110–117.

Hall, C. S., & Lindzey, G. (1978). *Theories of personality* (3rd ed.). New York: Wiley.

Hall, C. S., & Van de Castle, R. L. (1966). *The content analysis of dreams.* New York: Appleton-Century-Crofts.

Hanks, L. M., Jr. (1956). Modified T.A.T.s of 47 Thai children and adults. In B. Kaplan (Ed.), *Primary records in culture and personality* (Vol. 1). Madison: The Microcard Foundation.

Harder, D. W. (1979). The assessment of ambitious-narcissistic character style with three projective tests: The Early Memories, TAT, and Rorschach. *Journal of Personality Assessment, 43,* 23–32.

Harris, D. B. (1963). *Children's drawings as measures of intellectual maturity: A revision and extension of the Goodenough Draw-a-Man Test.* New York: Harcourt, Brace & World.

Harrison, R. (1965). Thematic apperceptive methods. In B. Wolman (Ed.), *Handbook of clinical psychology* (pp. 562–620). New York: McGraw Hill.

Harrison, R., & Rotter, J. B. (1945). A note on the reliability of the T.A.T. *Journal of Abnormal and Social Psychology, 40,* 97–99.

Harrower, M. (1950). Group techniques for the Rorschach protocol. In L. Abt & L. Bellak (Eds.), *Projective psychology.* New York: Knopf.

Harrower, M. (1968). *Appraising personality: An introduction to the projective techniques.* New York: Simon & Schuster.

Hart, B., & Hilton, I. (1988). Dimensions of personality organization as predictors of teenage pregnancy risk. *Journal of Personality Assessment, 53*(1), 116–132.

Hartman, A. A. (1949). An experimental examination of the Thematic Apperception Test in clinical diagnosis. *Psychological Monographs, 63*(303).

Hartman, A. A. (1951). In E. S. Shneidman (Ed.), *Thematic test analysis* (p. 83). New York: Grune & Stratton.

Hartman, A. H. (1970). A basic T.A.T. set. *Journal of Projective Techniques, 34,* 391–396.

Hartmann, H. (1950). Comments on the psychoanalytic theory of the ego. *Psychoanalytic Study of the Child, 5,* 75–96.

Hartmann, H. (1951). Ego psychology and the problems of adaptation. In D. Rapaport (Ed.), *Organization and pathology of thought.* New York: Columbia University Press.

Haworth, M. (1962). Responses of children to a group projective film and to the Rorschach, C.A.T., Despert Fables, and D-A-P. *Journal of Projective Techniques, 26,* 47–60.

Haworth, M. (1963). A schedule for the analysis of C.A.T. responses. *Journal of Projective Techniques and Personality Assessment, 27,* 181–184.

Haworth, M. (1964a). *C.A.T. vs. C.A.T.-H. with a clinic sample.* Unpublished manuscript.

Haworth, M. (1964b). Parental loss in children as reflected in projected responses. *Journal of Projective Techniques, 28,* 31–45.

Haworth, M. (1965). A *schedule of adaptive mechanisms in C.A.T. responses.* Larchmont, NY: C.P.S., Inc.

Haworth, M. (1966). *The C.A.T.: Facts about fantasy.* New York: Grune & Stratton.

Haworth, M. (1968). Symposium: The Children's Apperception Test: Its use in developmental assessment of normal children. Introduction. *Journal of Projective Techniques and Personality Assessment, 32*(5), 405.

Haworth, M. (1986). Children Apperception Test. In A. I. Rabin (Ed), *Projective techniques for adolescents and children* (pp. 37–72). New York: Springer.

Hayslip, B. (1986). The clinical use of projective techniques with the aged: A critical review and synthesis. *Clinical Gerontologist, 5,* 63–64.

Healy, W. A., Bronner, A. F., & Bowers, A. M. (1930). *The structure and meaning of psychoanalysis.* New York: Knopf.

Heath, D. H. (1958). Projective tests as measures of defensive activity. *Journal of Projective Techniques, 22,* 284–292.

Heckausen, H. (1967). *The anatomy of achievement motivation.* New York: Academic.

Heilbrun, A. B. (1977). The influence of defensive styles upon the predictive validity of the Thematic Apperception Test. *Journal of Personality Assessment, 41,* 486–491.

Heilman, K. M., & Valenstein, E. (Eds.). (1985). *Clinical neuropsychology* (2nd ed.). New York: Oxford University Press.

Helms, J. E. (1992). Why is there no study of cultural equivalence in standardized cognitive ability testing? *American Psychologist, 9,* 1083–1101.

Henderson, O. (1990). The object relations of sexually abused girls. *Melanie Klein and Object Relations, 8,* 63–76.

Henry, W. E. (1947). The Thematic Apperception Test in the study of culture personality relations. *Genetic Psychology Monographs, 35.*

Henry, W. E. (1956). *The analysis of fantasy: The Thematic Apperception Technique in the study of personality.* New York: John Wiley & Sons (Republished 1973, Huntingon, NY: Krieger).

Henry, W. E., & Cumming, E. (1992). Personality development in adulthood and old age. In E. I. Megargee & C. D. Speilberger (Eds.), *Personality assessment in America: A retrospective on the occasion of the fiftieth anniversary of the Society for Personality Assessment* (pp. 78–86). Hillsboro, NJ: Erlbaum.

Henry, W. E., & Farley, J. (1959a). The validity for the Thematic Apperception Test in the study of adolescent personality. *Psychology Monographs, 73* (Series no. 17).

Henry, W. E., & Farley, J. (1959b). Symposium on current aspects of the problems of validity: A study in validation of the Thematic Apperception Test. *Journal of Projective Techniques, 23,* 273–277.

Henry, W. E., & Guetzkow, H. (1947). In F. Wyatt (Ed.), The scoring and analysis of the Thematic Apperception Test. *Journal of Psychology, 24,* 319–330.

Henry, W. E., & Guetzkow, H. (1951). Group projection sketches for the study of small groups, Publication 4 of the Conference Research Project at the University of Michigan. *Journal of Social Psychology, 3*(3), 77–102.

Heppner, P. P. (1988). *Manual for the Personal Problem Solving Inventory.* Palo Alto, CA: Consulting Psychologist Press.

Herron, J. (Ed.). (1980). *Neuropsychology of left-handedness.* New York: Academic.

Hertz, M. R. (1939). A further study of suicidal configurations in Rorschach records. Rorschach Research Exchange. *Journal of Projective Techniques, 13,* 1.

Hertz, M. R. (1970). *Frequency tables for scoring Rorschach responses* (5th ed.). Cleveland: The Press of Case Western Reserve University.

Hibbard, S., Farmer, L., Wells, C., Difillipo, E., Barry, W., Korman, R., & Sloan, P. (1994). Validation of Cramer's Defense Mechanism Manual for the T.A.T. *Journal of Personality Assessment, 63,* 197–210.

Hilgard, E. R. (1948). *Theories of learning.* New York: Appleton-Century-Crofts.

Hoar, M. W., & Faust, W. L. (1973). The Children's Apperception Test: Puzzle and regular form. *Journal of Personality Assessment, 37,* 244–247.

Hofer, P. W. (1987). Psychopathic, thematic apperceptive responses of two groups. *Dissertation Abstracts International, 48* (3-B), 877.

Hoffman, S., & Kuperman, N. (1990). Indirect treatment of traumatic psychological experiences: The use of TAT cards. *American Journal of Psychotherapy, 44,* 107–115.

Holden, R. (1956). The Children's Apperception Test with cerebral palsied and normal children. *Child Development, 27,* 3–8.

Holmes, C. B., & Dungan, D. S. (1981). Gender of Thematic Apperception Card 3BM figure. *Perceptual and Motor Skills, 53,* 897–898.

Holmes, D. S. (1974). The conscious control of thematic projection. *Journal of Consulting and Clinical Psychology, 42,* 323–329.

Holmstrom, R. W., Karp, S. A., & Silber, D. E. (1992). Factor structure of the Apperception Picture Test (APT). *Journal of Clinical Psychology, 48,* 207–210.

Holmstrom, R. W., Karp, S. A., & Silber, D. E. (1994). Prediction of depression with the Apperception Picture Test. *Journal of Clinical Psychology, 50,* 234–237.

Holt, R. (1951). In E. S. Shneidman (Ed.), *Thematic test analysis* (p. 1010). New York: Grune & Stratton.

Holt, R. (1956). Gauging primary and secondary processes in Rorschach responses. *Journal of Projective Techniques, 20,* 14–25.

Holt, R. R. (1951). The Thematic Apperception Test. In H. H. Anderson & G. L. Anderson (Eds.). *An introduction to projective techniques* (pp. 181–229). Englewood Cliffs, NJ: Prentice Hall.

Holt, R. R. (1958). Formal aspects of the T.A.T.: A neglected resource. *Journal of Projective Techniques, 22,* 163–172.

Holt, R. R. (1961). The nature of T.A.T. stories as a cognitive product. In J. Kagan & G. Lesser (Eds.), *Contemporary issues in apperceptive methods* (pp. 3–44). Springfield, IL: Charles C. Thomas.

Holt, R. R. (1971). *Assessing personality.* New York: Harcourt Brace Jovanovich.

Holt, R. R. (1978). *Methods in clinical psychology: Projective assessments* (Vol.1). New York: Plenum.

Holt, R. R. (1992). Formal aspects of the TAT: A neglected resource. In E. I. Megargee & C. D. Speilberger (Eds.), *Personality assessment in America: A retrospective on the occasion of the fiftieth anniversary of the Society for Personality Assessment* (pp. 70–78). Hillsdale, NJ: Erlbaum.

Holt, R. R., & Luborsky, L. (1958a). *Personality patterns of psychiatrists: A study of methods for selecting residents* (Vol. 1). New York: Basic Books.

Holt, R. R., & Luborsky, L. (1958b). *Personality patterns of psychiatrists: Supplementary and supporting data* (Vol. 2). Topeka, KA: Menninger Foundation.

Holzberg, J. (1963). Projective techniques and resistance to change in psychotherapy as viewed through a communications model. *Journal of Projective Techniques, 27,* 430–435.

Holzman, P., & Klein, G. (1954). Cognitive system-principles of leveling and sharpening: Individual differences in assimilation effects in visual time-error. *Journal of Psychology, 37,* 105–122.

Holzman, P., & Klein, G. (1969, April). Highlights: The Menninger Foundation Conference on the schizophrenic syndrome, Topeka, KS.

Horn, D. (1943). *An experimental study of the diagnostic process in the clinical investigation of personality.* Unpublished doctoral dissertation, Harvard University, Cambridge, MA.

Horwitz, M., & Cartwright, D. (1951). A projective method for the diagnosis of groups. *Human Relations.*

Howard, K. G. (1952). *Certain variables in the T.A.T.* Unpublished master's thesis, University of Western Ontario, ON, Canada.

Hsu, F. I. (Ed.). (1971). *Kinship and culture.* Chicago: Aldine.

Hsu, F. I. (Ed.). (1972). *Psychological anthropology.* Cambridge, MA: Schenkman.

Huebner, D. A. (1988). Assessing psychological mindedness: The TAT self-interpretation technique. *Dissertation Abstracts International, 48*(11-B), 3416.

Hunt, R. G., & Smith, M. E. (1966). Cultural symbols and response to Thematic Test materials. *Journal of Projective Techniques and Personality Assessment, 30,* 587–590.

Hurley, A. D., & Sovner, R. (1985). The use of the Thematic Apperception Test in mentally retarded persons. *Psychiatric Aspects of Mental Retardation Reviews, 4,* 9–12.

Hurley, J. R. (1955). The Iowa Picture Interpretation Test: A multiple-choice variation of the T.A.T. *Journal of Consulting Psychology, 19,* 372–376.

Hurt, S. W., Reznikoff, M., & Clarkin, J. F. (1991). *Psychological assessment, psychiatric diagnosis, and treatment planning.* New York: Brunner/Mazel.

Hurtig, A. L., & Rosenthal, I. M. (1987). Psychological findings in early treated cases of female pseudohermaphroditism caused by virilizing congenital adrenal hyperplasia. *Archives of Sexual Behavior, 16,*(3), 209–223.

Husain, O., Rossel, F., & Merceron, C. (1988). "Or" responses on the Rorschach and the T.A.T.: The logic of alternative and its pschopathological aspects. *British Journal of Projective Psychology, 33*(2), 18–30.

Hutt, M. L. (1969). *The Hutt adaptation of the Bender Gestalt test* (2nd ed.). New York: Grune & Stratton.

Hwang, Chien-hou. (1975). A follow-up study on social attitudes of Chinese and Scottish adolescents. *Bulletin of Educational Psychology, 8,* 95–106.

Hynd, G., & Cohen, M. (1983). *Dyslexia: Neuropsychology, theory, research, and clinical differentiation.* New York: Grune & Stratton.

Ichheiser, G. (1947). Projection and the mote-beam mechanism. *Journal of Abnormal Social Psychology, 42,* 131–133.

Ilan, L. C., & Resurreccion, V. E. (1971). Responses of preschool children to the Philippine Children's Apperception Test (PCAT): A preliminary study. *Philippine Journal of Psychology, 4*(1): 44–52.

Irvin, F. S., & Woude, K. (1971). Empirical support for a basic T.A.T. set. *Journal of Clinical Psychology, 27,* 514–516.

Isaacs, S. (1933). *Social development in young children.* London: Routledge & Kegan Paul.

Isakower, O. (1938). A contribution to the pathopsychology of phenomena associated with falling asleep. *International Journal of Psychoanalysis, 19,* 331–345.

Jackson, L. (1950). Emotional attitudes towards the family of normal, neurotic, and delinquent children. *British Journal of Psychology, 41,* 35–51, 173–185.

Jackson, R. J. (1988). Behavioral confirmation in the assessment process: The effects of clinicians' expectancies on TAT card selection and perceptions of TAT protocols. *Dissertation Abstracts International, 49*(2-B), 544.

Jacobs, B. (1958). A method for investigating the cue characteristics of pictures. In J. W. Atkinson (Ed.), *Motives in fantasy, action, and society* (pp. 108–136). Princeton, NJ: Van Nostrand.

Jacobson, E. (1964). *The self and the object world.* New York: International Universities Press.

Jacquemin, A. (1988). Le Thematic Apperception Test—T.A.T. dans la pratique clinique [The Thematic Apperception Test (T.A.T.) in clinical practice]. *Bulletin de Psychologie Scolaire et d'Orientation, 30,* 25–31.

James, P. B., & Mosher, D. L. (1967). Thematic aggression, hostility-guilt, and aggressive behavior. *Journal of Projective Techniques and Personality Assessment, 31*(1), 61–67.

Jeammet, N. (1983). Un parti-pris diagnostique face á un Rorschach et un T.A.T. apparement non congruents [A set purpose diagnosis with regard to the Rorschach and the TAT which are apparently not congruent]. *Psychologie Française, 28,* 129–140.

Jensen, A. R. (1959). The reliability of projective techniques: Review of the literature. *Acta Psychologica Scandinavica, 16,* 108–136.

Jensen, A. R. (1969). How much can we boost IQ and scholastic achievement? *Harvard Educational Review, 39,* 1–123.

Jensen, A. R. (1972). *Genetics and education.* New York: Harper & Row.

Joel, W., & Shapiro, D. (1951). In E. S. Shneidman (Ed.), *Thematic test analysis* (p. 119). New York: Grune & Stratton.

John-Steiner, V. (1992). Narrative competence: Cross-cultural comparisons. *Journal of Narrative and Life History, 2,* 219–233.

Johnson, B. L., & Kilmann, P. B. (1975). Prediction of locus of control orientation from the Thematic Apperception Test. *Journal of Clinical Psychology, 31,* 547–548.

Johnson, D., & Sikes, M. (1965). Rorschach and T.A.T. responses of Negro, Mexican-American, and Anglo psychiatric patients. *Journal of Projective Techniques, 29,* 183–188.

Johnson, J. L. (1994). The Thematic Apperception Test and Alzheimer's disease. *Journal of Personality Assessment, 62,* 314–319.

Johnston, R. A. (1957). A methodological analysis of several revised forms of the Iowa Picture Interpretation Test. *Journal of Personality, 25,* 283–293.

Jones, J. E. (1977). Patterns of transactional style deviance in the TAT's of parents of schizophrenics. *Family Process, 16,* 327–337.

Jones, R. M. (1956). The negation T.A.T., a projective method for eliciting repressed thought content. *Journal of Projective Techniques, 20,* 297–303.

Josselson, R., & Lieblich, A. (Ed.). (1993). *The narrative study of lives.* Newbury Park, CA: Sage.

Judson, A. (1963). Love and death in the short stories of W. Somerset Maugham: A psychological analysis. *Psychiatric Quarterly, 37,* 250–262.

Kaarke, N. (1951). *The relationship between intelligence level and responses to the Children's Apperception Test.* Unpublished master's thesis, Cornell University, Ithaca, NY.

Kagan, J. (1956). The measurement of overt aggression from fantasy. *Journal of Abnormal and Social Psychology, 52,* 390–393.

Kagan, J. (1958). Socialization of aggression and the perception of parents in fantasy. *Child Development, 29,* 311–320.

Kagan, J. (1959). The stability of TAT fantasy and stimulus ambiguity. *Journal of Consulting Psychology, 23,* 266–271.

Kagan, J. (1960). Thematic apperceptive techniques with children. In A. I. Rabin & M. R. Haworth (Eds.), *Projective techniques with children*. New York: Grune & Stratton.

Kagan, J., & Lesser, G. S. (1961). *Contemporary issues in thematic apperceptive methods*. Springfield, IL.: Charles C. Thomas (Republished 1976, Westport, CT: Greenwood Press).

Kagan, J., & Moss, H. A. (1959). Stability and validity of achievement fantasy. *Journal of Abnormal and Social Psychology, 58*, 357–363.

Kagan, J., & Mussen, P. H. (1956). Dependency themes on the T.A.T. and group conformity. *Journal of Consulting Psychology, 20*, 29–32.

Kagan, M., & Kaufman, M. (1954). *A preliminary investigation of some relationships between functional articulation disorders and responses to the Children's Apperception Test*. Unpublished master's thesis, Boston University, Boston.

Kahana, B. (1978). The use of projective techniques in personality assessment of the aged. In M. Storandt, I. C. Siegler, & M. Elias (Eds.), *The clinical psychology of aging*. New York: Plenum.

Kahana, E., Kahana, B., McCrone, N., Kelly, J., Thomas, W., & Kercher, K. (1995). *Age and gender effects on projective test responses: A longitudinal analysis of the Senior Apperception Technique*. Paper presented at the American Gerontological Society Annual Meeting, Los Angeles.

Kahn, S. (1961). *T.A.T. and understanding people*. New York: Vantage Press.

Kalaita, T. A. (1980). *The expression of attachment and separation anxiety in abused and neglected adolescents*. Unpublished doctoral dissertation. California School of Professional Psychology, Los Angeles.

Kalliopuska, M. (1982). Empathy measured by Rorschach and TAT. *British Journal of Projective Techniques and Personality Study, 27*, 5–11.

Kane, A. C., & Hogan, J. D. (1985). Death anxiety in physicians: Defensive style, medical specialty, and exposure to death. *Omega Journal of Death and Dying, 86*, 11–22.

Kaplan, B. (1956). (Ed.). *Primary records in culture and personality* (Vol. 1). Madison: The Microcard Foundation.

Kaplan, B. (1961). Cross cultural use of projective techniques in psychological anthropology. In F. L. K. Hsu (Ed.), *Approaches to culture and personality*. Homewood, IL.: Dorsey.

Kaplan, M. F. (1967). The effect of cue relevance, ambiguity, and self-reported hostility on TAT responses. *Journal of Projective and Personality Assessment, 31*, 45–50.

Kaplan, M. F. (1969). The ambiguity of TAT ambiguity. *Journal of Projective and Personality Assessment, 33*, 25–29.

Kaplan, M. F. (1970). A note on the stability of interjudge and intrajudge ambiguity scores. *Journal of Projective and Personality Assessment, 34*, 201–203.

Kardiner, E. T. (1951). *A comparison of T.A.T. readings with psychoanalytic findings*. Unpublished master's thesis, The City College, New York.

Karon, B. (1963). The resolution of acute schizophrenic reactions: A contribution to the development of non-classical psychotherapeutic techniques. *Psychotherapy, 1*, 27–43.

Karon, B. P. (1981). The Thematic Apperception Test (T.A.T.). In A. I. Rabin (Ed.), *Assessment with projective techniques* (pp. 85–120). New York: Springer.

Karon, B. P., & Widener, A. J. (1994). Is there really a schizophrenic parent? *Psychoanalytic Psychology, 11*, 47–61.

Katzenstein, B. (1957). Estudos individuals e orientacao psico-pedagogica de criancas acornetidas de poliomielite [Case studies and psychopedagogical guidance of children attacked by poliomyelitis]. *Rev. Psicol. Norm. Patol., 3*, 77–85.

Kazdin, A. E., Matson, J. L., & Senatore, V. (1983). Assessment of depression in mentally retarded adults. *American Journal of Psychiatry, 140*(8), 1040–1043.

Keiser, R. E., & Prather, E. N. (1990). What is the T.A.T.? A review of ten years of research. *Journal of Personality Assessment, 55*, 800–803.

Kenny, D. (1959). The Children's Apperception Test. In O. K. Buros (Ed.), *The fifth mental measurements yearbook*. Highland Park, NJ: Gryphon.

Kenny, D. T. (1954). Transcendence indices, extent of personality factors in fantasy responses. *Journal of Consulting Psychology, 18*, 345–348.

Kenny, D. T. (1961). A theoretical and research reappraisal of stimulus factors in the TAT. In J. Kagan & G. S. Lesser (Eds.), *Contemporary issues in thematic apperception methods* (pp. 288–310). Springfield, IL: Charles C. Thomas.

Kenny, D. T., & Bijou, S. W. (1953). Ambiguity of pictures and extent of personality factors in fantasy responses. *Journal of Consulting Psychology, 17*, 283–288.

Kernberg, O. (1975). *Borderline conditions and pathological narcissism*. New York: Jason Aronson.

Kernberg, O. (1976). *Object relations theory and clinical psychoanalysis*. New York: Jason Aronson.

Kernberg, O. (1980). *Internal world and external reality*. New York: Jason Aronson.

Kerner, O. J. (1956). Stress, fantasy, and schizophrenia: A study of the adaptive processes. *Genetic Psychology Monographs, 53*, 189–281.

Kimura, N. (1983). A study of the repression-sensitization dimension in the Thematic Apperception Test. *The Japanese Journal of Psychology, 54,* 95–101.

King, F., & King, D. (1964). The projective assessment of the female's sexual identification, with special reference to the Blacky pictures. *Journal of Projective Techniques, 28,* 293–299.

Kirk, U. (Ed.). (1983). *Neuropsychology of language, reading, and spelling.* New York: Academic.

Kitron, D. G., & Benziman, H. (1990). The Children's Apperception Test: Possible applications for adults. *Israel Journal of Psychiatry and Related Sciences, 27,* 29–47.

Klebanoff, S. (1947). Personality factors in symptomatic chronic alcoholism as indicated by the Thematic Apperception Test. *Journal of Consulting Psychology, 11,* 111–119.

Klebanoff, S. (1951). In E. S. Shneidman (Ed.), *Thematic test analysis* (p. 126). New York: Grune & Stratton.

Klein, G. (1954). Need and regulation. In M. Jones (Ed.), *Current theory and research in motivation: A symposium.* Lincoln: University of Nebraska Press.

Klein, M. (1948). *Contributions to psychoanalysis, 1921–1945.* London: Hogarth Press.

Klein, R. G. (1987). Questioning the clinical usefulness of projective psychological tests for children. *Developmental and Behavioral Pediatrics, 7,* 378–382.

Kline, P., & Svaste-Xuto, B. (1981). The responses of Thai and British children to the Children's Apperception Test. *Journal of Social Psychology, 113,* 137–138.

Klopfer, B., & Kelly, D. (1942). *The Rorschach technique.* Yonkers-on-Hudson, NY: World Book.

Kluckholn, C., Murray, H. A., & Schneider, D. (1953). *Personality in nature, society and culture.* New York: Knopf.

Knight, B. C., Teri, L., Wohlford, P., & Santos, J. (Eds.). (1995). *Mental health services for older adults: Implications for training and practice in geropsychology.* Washington, DC: American Psychological Association Press.

Knights, R. M., & Bakker, D. J. (Eds.). (1976). *The neuropsychology of learning disorders.* Baltimore, MD: University Park Press.

Kohlberg, L. (1969). *Stages in the development of moral thought and action.* New York: Holt.

Kohut, H. (1971). *The analysis of the self.* New York: International Universities Press.

Kohut, H. (1977). *The restoration of the self.* New York: International Universities Press.

Kohut, H. (1984). *How does analysis cure?* Chicago: University of Chicago Press.

Kolb, B., & Whishaw, I. Q. (1980). *Fundamentals of human neuropsychology.* San Francisco: Freeman.

Kolter, N. (1970). Self-selection of TAT cards: A technique for assessing test-resistant children. *Journal of Projective Techniques and Personality Assessment, 34,* 324–327.

Koppitz, E. M. (1963). *The Bender Gestalt test for young children.* New York: Grune & Stratton.

Korchin, S. (1951). In E. S. Shneidman (Ed.), *Thematic test analysis* (p. 132). New York: Grune & Stratton.

Korchin, S., Mitchell, H., & Meltzoff, F. (1950). A critical evaluation of the Thompson Thematic Apperception Test. *Journal of Projective Techniques, 14,* 445–452.

Kornadt, H-J. (1982). *Aggressionsmotiv und aggressionschemmung.* Bern: H. Huber.

Kornfield, A. D., & Marshall, P. E. (1987). S.A.T. and T.A.T. scores as measures of time perspective in institutionalized and community-based senior adults. *International Journal of Psychosomatics, 34,* 11–13.

Krahn, G. L. (1985). The use of projective assessment techniques in pediatric settings. *Journal of Pediatric Psychology, 10,* 179–193.

Kraiger, K., Milton, D., & Cornelius, E. T. (1984). Exploring fantasies of TAT reliability. *Journal of Personality Assessment, 48,* 365–370.

Kris, E. (1950). On preconscious mental processes. *Psychoanalytic Quarterly, 19,* 540–560.

Kutash, S. B. (1943). Performance of psychopathic defective criminals on the Thematic Apperception Test. *Journal of Criminal Psychopathology, 5,* 319–340.

Labov, W. (1973). The logic of nonstandard English. In N. Keddie (Ed.), *The myth of cultural deprivation* (pp. 21–66). London: Penguin.

Lagmay, A. V. (1964). *Preliminary report: Development and construction of the Philippine Thematic Apperception Test.* Article presented at the Annual Convention of the Psychological Association of the Philippines.

Lagmay, A. V. (1975). Studies on a Philippine Children's Apperception Test: (PCAT) 1. Construction and development administration. *Philippine Journal of Mental Health, 6*(1), 18–25.

Lambert, W. E., Havalka, J., & Crosby, C. (1958). The influence of language acquisition on texts on bilingualism. *Journal of Abnormal and Social Psychology, 56,* 239–244.

La Rue, A. (1992). *Aging and neuropsychological assessment.* New York: Plenum.

Lasaga, J. I. (1951). In E. S. Shneidman (Ed.), *Thematic test analysis* (p. 144). New York: Grune & Stratton.

Laskowitz, D. (1959). *The effect of varied degrees of pictorial ambiguity on fantasy evocation.* Unpublished doctoral dissertation, New York University, New York.

Lawton, M. (1966). Animal and human C.A.T.'s with a school sample. *Journal of Projective Techniques, 30*(3), 243–246.

Lazarus, R. (1953). Ambiguity and nonambiguity in projective testing. *Journal of Abnormal Social Psychology, 17.*

Lazarus, R. S. (1949). The influence of color on the protocol of the Rorschach Test. *Journal of Abnormal Social Psychology, 4,* 506.

Lazarus, R. S. (1961). A substitutive-defense conception of apperceptive fantasy. In J. Kagan & G. Lesser (Eds.), *Contemporary issues in thematic apperceptive methods* (pp. 51–77). Springfield, IL: Charles C. Thomas.

Lazarus, R. S. (1966). Storytelling and the measurement of motivation: The direct versus substitutive controversy. *Journal of Consulting Psychology, 30,* 483–487.

Lee, P. W., et al. (1983–1984). Death anxiety in leukemic Chinese children. *International Psychiatry and Medicine, 13*(4), 281–289.

Lee, S. G. (1953). *Manual of a Thematic Apperception Test for African subjects: Set of 22 pictures.* Pietermarizburg, South Africa: University of Natal Press.

Lefebvre, A. (1990, July). *Differential study of mental process in mentally retarded and character disorder children and adolescents.* Unpublished paper presented at the 13th International Congress of Rorschach and Projective Techniques, Paris.

Lefebvre, A., & Vercruysse, N. (1987). Contribution of the TAT to the clinical treatment of depression. *Psychologie Française, 32*(3), 175–179.

Lehmann, I. (1959). Responses of kindergarten children to the Children's Apperception Test. *Journal of Clinical Psychology, 15,* 60–63.

Leigh, J. (1992). The assessment of complexity of representations of people using TAT and interview data. *Journal of Personality, 60,* 809–837.

Leitch, M., & Schaeffer, S. (1947). A study of the Thematic Apperception Test of psychotic children. *American Journal of Orthopsychiatry, 17,* 337–342.

Lennerlof, L. (1967). *ITAT: Studies performed with a version of TAT intended for use in industrial psychology.* Stockholm: PA-radet.

Lessa, W. A., & Spiegelmann, M. (1954). Ulithian personality as seen through ethnological materials and thematic test analysis. *Publications in culture and society* (Vol. 2) (pp. 243–301), University of California.

Lesser, G. S. (1957). The relationship between overt and fantasy aggression as a function of maternal response to aggression. *Journal of Abnormal and Social Psychology, 55,* 218–221.

Levine, F. (1969). Thematic drive expression in three occupational groups. *Journal of Projective Techniques, 33,* 357–364.

Levine, R., Chein, I., & Murphy, G. (1943). The relationship of the intensity of a need to the amount of perceptual distortion. A preliminary report. *Journal of Psychology, 13,* 283–293.

Levy, M. R. (1970). Issues in the personality assessment of lower-class patients. *Journal of Projective Techniques and Personality Assessment, 34,* 6–9.

Lewin, B. (1946). Sleep, the mouth and the dream screen. *Psychiatric Quarterly, 15.*

Lewin, B. (1950). *Psychoanalysis of elation.* New York: Norton.

Lezak, M. D. (1983). *Neuropsychological assessment* (2nd ed.). New York: Oxford University Press.

Lezak, M. D. (1987). Norms for growing older. *Developmental neuropsychology, 3,* 1–12.

Libby, W. (1908). The imagination of adolescents. *American Journal of Psychology, 19,* 249–252.

Lieberman, M. (1965). Psychological correlates of impending death: Some preliminary observations. *Journal of Gerontology, 20,* 182–190.

Lievens, S., & Mouton, R. (1973). Vergelijkend onderzoek van methodes van ambiguiteits berekening bij de Murray-T.A.T. *Psychologica Belgica, 13,* 25–36.

Light, B. H. (1954). Comparative study of a series of T.A.T. and C.A.T. cards. *Journal of Clinical Psychology, 10,* 179–181.

Light, B. H. (1955). A further test of the Thompson T.A.T. rationale. *Journal of Abnormal and Social Psychology, 51,* 148–150.

Lilio de, R., & Januszka, S. (1969). Factor analysis of measures of divergent thinking obtained from the Children's Apperception Test and measures of intelligence obtained from the Wechsler Intelligence Scale for Children. *Dissertation Abstracts International, 30*(2-B), 831.

Lindgren, H. C., et al. (1986). Validity studies of three measures of achievement motivation. *Psychological Reports, 59*(1), 123–136.

Lindzey, G. (1951). *Projective techniques and cross-cultural research.* New York: Appleton-Century-Crofts.

Lindzey, G. (1952). Thematic Apperception Test: Interpretive assumptions and related empirical evidence. *Psychological Bulletin, 49,* 1–25.

Lindzey, G., Bradford, J., Tejessy, C., & Davids, A. (1959). The Thematic Apperception Test: An interpretive lexicon. *Journal of Clinical Psychology* (monograph supplement, No. 12).

Lindzey, G., & Heinemann, S. H. (1955). Thematic Apperception Test indices of aggression in relation to measures of overt and covert behavior. *American Journal of Orthopsychiatry, 26,* 567–576.

Lindzey, G., & Herman, P. S. (1955). Thematic Apperception Test: A note on reliability and situational validity. *Journal of Projective Techniques, 19,* 36–42.

Lindzey, G., & Kalnins, D. (1958). Thematic Apperception Test: Some evidence bearing on the hero assumption. *Journal of Anormal and Social Psychology, 57,* 76–83.

Lindzey, G., & Newburg, A. S. (1954). Thematic Apperception Test: A tentative appraisal of some signs of anxiety. *Journal of Consulting Psychology, 18,* 389–395.

Lindzey, G., & Silverman, M. (1959). Thematic Apperception Test: Techniques of group administration, sex differences, and the role of verbal productivity. *Journal of Personality, 27,* 311–323.

Lipgar, R. M. (1969). Treatment of time in the TAT. *Journal of Personality Assessment, 33,* 219–229.

Little, K. B., & Shneidman, E. S. (1955). The validity of thematic projective technique interpretations. *Journal of Personality, 23,* 285–294.

Lolas, F., & Von Rad, M. (1977). Conducta verbal de pacientes psicosomaticos y psiconeuroticos: Un estudio comparativo. *Acta Psiquiatrica y Psicologica de America Latina, 23,* 110–117.

Lonner, W. J. (1985). Issues in testing and assessment in cross-cultural counseling. *Counseling Psychologist, 13,* 599–614.

Loreto, D. (1974). [TAT and schizophrenia]. *Revista Sperimentale di Freniatria e Medicina Legale delle Alienazioni Mentali, 98,* 635–668.

Lubin, B. (1960). Some effects of set and stimulus properties on T.A.T. stories. *Journal of Projective Techniques, 24,* 11–16.

Lubin, B., & Larsen, R. M. (1984). Patterns of psychological test usage in the United States: 1935–1982. *American Psychologist, 39,* 451–454.

Luborsky, L. (1953). Self interpretation of the T.A.T. as a clinical technique. *Journal of Projective Techniques, 17,* 217–223.

Lunazzi de Jubany, H. (1990, July). *Some observations in borderline production on the O.R.T.* Unpublished paper presented at the 13th International Congress of Rorschach and Projective Techniques. Paris.

Lundy, A. (1985). The reliability of the Thematic Apperception Test. *Journal of Personality Assessment, 49,* 141–145.

Lundy, A. (1988). Instructional set and Thematic Apperception Test validity. *Journal of Personality Assessment, 52*(2), 309–320.

Luria, A. R. (1973). *The working brain: An introduction to neuropsychology.* New York: Basic Books.

Lyle, J. G., Gilchrist, A. A., & Groh, L. (1958). Three blind interpretations of a T.A.T. record. *Journal of Projective Techniques, 22,* 82–96.

Lyes, W. (1958). *The effects of examiner attitudes on the projective test responses of children.* Unpublished doctoral dissertation, New York University, New York.

MacBrayer, C. T. (1959). Relationship between story length and situational validity of the T.A.T. *Journal of Projective Techniques, 23,* 345–350.

MacGregor, G. (1946). *Warriors without weapons: A study of the society and personality development of the Pine Ridge Sioux.* Chicago: University of Chicago Press.

Mccoby, E. E., & Jacklin, C. N. (1974). *The psychology of sex differences.* Stanford, CA: Stanford University Press.

Maddi, S. R., Propst, B. S., & Feldinger, I. (1965). Three expressions of the need for variety. *Journal of Personality, 33,* 82–98.

Maddox, G. L. (1994). Lives through the years revisited. *The Gerontologist, 34* (6), 764–767.

Mahler, M. (1968). *On human symbiosis and the vicissitudes of individuation.* New York: International Universities Press.

Mahler, M., Pine, F., & Bergman, A. (1975). *The psychological birth of the human infant.* New York: Basic Books.

Mainford, F., & Marcuse, F. (1954). Responses of disturbed children to human and animal pictures. *Journals of Projective Techniques, 18,* 475–477.

Maitra, A. K. (1987). Thematic phantasy differentials of the delinquents. *Psychological Research, 11*(1), 1–10.

Mandler, G., Lindzey, G., & Crouch, R. G. (1957). Thematic Apperception Test: Indices of anxiety in relation to test anxiety. *Educational Psychological Measurements, 17,* 466–474.

Markmann, R. (1943). *Predictions of manifest personality trends by a thematic analysis of three pictures of the Thematic Apperception Test.* Unpublished doctoral dissertation, Radcliffe College, Cambridge, MA.

Martin, B. (1964). Expression and inhibition of sex motive arousal in college males. *Journal of Abnormal and Social Psychology, 68,* 307–312.

Marui, F. (1960). A normative study of T.A.T.: Chiefly on emotional tone, outcome, and shift. *Japanese Journal of Psychology, 31,* 83–92.

Masling, J. M. (1960). The influence of situational and inter-personal variables in projective testing. *Psychological Bulletin, 57,* 65–85.

Masling, J. M., & Harris, S. (1969). Sexual aspects of TAT administration. *Journal of Consulting and Clinical Psychology, 33,* 166–169.

Mason, S., & Ammons, R. B. (1956). Note on social class and the Thematic Apperception Test. *Perceptual and Motor Skills, 6,* 88.

Matranga, J. T. (1976). The relationship between behavioral indices of aggression and hostile content on the TAT. *Journal of Personality Assessment, 40,* 130–133.

Maugham, M. S. (1953). *Complete short stories* (Vols. 1–2). New York: Doubleday.

May, R. (1966). Sex differences in fantasy patterns. *Journal of Projective Techniques, 30*(6), 576–586.

May, R. (1975). Further studies on deprivation/enhancement patterns. *Journal of Personality Assessment, 39,* 116–122.

Mazumdar Sen, D. P. (1979). A comparative study of emotionally disturbed and normal children on selected criteria of projective apperception tests (TAT/CAT). *Indian Journal of Clinical Psychology, 6*(2), 115–117.

McAdams, D. P. (1980). A thematic coding system for the intimacy motive. *Journal of Research in Personality, 14,* 413–432.

McAdams, D. P., & Bryant, F. B. (1987). Intimacy motivation and subjective mental health in a nationwide sample. *Journal of Personality, 55*(3), 395–413.

McAdams, D. P., Lester, R. M., Brand, P. A., McNamara, W. J. & Lensky, D. B. (1988). Sex and the TAT: Are women more intimate than men? Do men fear intimacy? *Journal of Personality Assessment, 52*(3), 397–409.

McArthur, C. (1953). The effects of need achievement on the content of T.A.T. stories: A reexamination. *Journal of Abnormal and Social Psychology, 45.*

McArthur, C. (1955). Personality differences between middle and upper classes. *Journal of Abnormal Social Psychology, 50,* 247–254.

McClelland, D. C. (1955). *Studies in motivation.* New York: Appleton-Century-Crofts.

McClelland, D. C. (1961). *The achieving society.* New York: D. Van Nostrand Co.

McClelland, D. C., Atkinson, J. E., Clark, R. A., & Lowel, E. L. (1953). *The achievement motive.* New York: Irvington.

McClelland, D. C., & Atkinson, J. W. (1948). The projective expression of needs. The effect of different intensities of the hunger drive on perception. *Journal of Psychology, 27,* 311–330.

McClelland, D. C., Clark, R. A., Roby, T., & Atkinson, J. W. (1949). The projective expression of needs, IV: The effect of the need for achievement on thematic apperception. *Journal of Experimental Psychology, 39,* 242–255.

McClelland, D. C., & Liberman, A. M. (1949). The effect of need for achievement on recognition of need related words. *Journal of Personality, 18,* 236–251.

McClelland, D. C., & Steele, R. S. (1973). *Human motivation.* General Learning Press.

McCully, R. S. (1965). Current attitudes about projective techniques in APA approved internship centers. *Journal of Projective Techniques and Personality Assessment, 27,* 271–280.

McGrew, M. W. (1988). The TAT responses of disturbed and normal boys using an integrated scoring system. *Dissertation Abstracts International, 48*(10-A), 2583.

McGrew, M. W., & Teglasi, H. (1990). Formal characteristics of Thematic Apperception Test stories as indices of emotional disturbance in children. *Journal of Personality Assessment, 54,* 639–655.

McInerney, I. F. (1976). Sex role typed content in the T.A.T. responses of normal children of two generations. *Dissertation Abstracts International, 36* (11-B), 5808.

McIntosh, J. L., Santos, J. F., Hubbard, R. W., & Overholser, J. L. (1994). *Elder suicide: Research, theory, and treatment.* Washington, DC: American Psychological Association Press.

McKay, J. R. (1991). Assessing aspects of object relations associated with immune function: Development of the affiliative trust-mistrust coding system. *Psychological Assessment, 3,* 641–647.

McPherson, S. R. (1974). Parental interactions at various levels. *Journal of Nervous and Mental Disease, 158,* 424–431.

Megargee, E. I. (1966a). A comparison of the scores of white and Negro male juvenile delinquents on three projective tests. *Journal of Projective Techniques, 30,* 530–535.

Megargee, E. I. (Ed.). (1966b). *Research in clinical assessment.* New York: Harper & Row.

Megargee, E. I. (1967). Hostility on the T.A.T. as a function of defensive inhibition and stimulus situation. *Journal of Projective Techniques, 31,* 73–79.

Megargee, E. I. (1970). The prediction of violence with psychological tests. In C. Spielberger (Ed.), *Current trends in clinical and community psychology* (Vol. 2) (pp. 97–156). New York: Academic.

Megargee, E. I. & Cook, P. E. (1967). The relation of TAT and inkblot aggressive content scales with each other and with criteria or overt aggression in juvenile delinquents. *Journal of Projective Techniques and Personality Assessment, 31,* 48–60.

Megargee, E. I., & Hokanson, J. E. (Eds.). (1970). *The dynamics of aggression: Individual, group, and international analyses.* New York: Harper & Row.

Megargee, E. I., & Parker, G. V. C. (1968). An exploration of Murrayan needs as assessed by the adjective checklist, the TAT, and the Edwards Personal Preference Schedule. *Journal of Clinical Psychology, 24,* 47–51.

Melikian, L. H. (1964). The use of selected T.A.T. cards among Arab university students: A cross cultural study. *Journal of Social Psychology, 62,* 3–19.

Meltzoff, J. (1951). The effect of mental set and item structure upon response to a projective test. *Journal of Abnormal Social Psychology, 46,* 177.

Mengarda, C. F. (1983). Projection of significant items in previous history in responses to illustrations used in the CAT. *Psico. 6*(2), 27–41.

Menke, H. (1989). Identifications in several young alcoholics. *Psychiatrie de l'Enfant, 32*(1), 209–248.

Menninger, K. (1954). Psychological aspects of the organism under stress, Parts I and II. *Journal of the American Psychoanalytic Association, 2.*

Mercer, M. (1973). Review of Gerontological Apperception Test by R. L. Wolk & R. B. Wolk. *Journal of Personality Assessment, 37,* 395–397.

Meyer, B. T. (1951). An investigation of color shock in the Rorschach Test. *Journal of Clinical Psychology, 7,* 367.

Meyer, M. M. (1951). The direct use of projective techniques in psychotherapy. *Journal of Projective Techniques, 15.*

Meyer, M. M., & Tolman, R. S. (1955). Parental figures in sentence completion test, T.A.T., and in therapeutic interviews. *Journal of Consulting Psychology, 19,* 170.

Miklowitz, D. J., Strachan, A. M., Goldstein, M. J., Doane, J. A., Snyder, K. S., Hogarty, G. E., & Falloon, I. R. (1986). Expression emotion and communication deviance in the families of schizophrenics. *Journal of Abnormal Psychology, 95,* 60–66.

Miklowitz, D. J., Velligan, D. I., Goldstein, M. J., & Neuchterlein, K. H. (1991). Communication deviance in families of schizophrenic and manic patients. *Journal of Abnormal Psychology, 100,* 163–173.

Milam, J. R. (1954). Examiner influence on T.A.T. stories. *Journal of Projective Techniques, 18,* 221–226.

Miller, J. S., & Scodel, A. (1955). The diagnostic significance of usual T.A.T. stories. *Journal of Consulting Psychology, 19,* 91–95.

Miller, P. J., & Moore, B. B. (1989). Narrative conjunctions of caregiver and child: A comparative perspective on socialization through stories. *Ethos, 17,* 428–449.

Miller, P. J., Potts, R., Fung, H., Hoogstra, L., & Mintz, J. (1990). Narrative practices and the social construction of self in childhood. *American Ethnologist, 17,* 292–311.

Miller, T. W., & Veltkamp, L. J. (1989). Assessment of child sexual abuse: Clinical use of fables. *Child Psychiatry and Human Development, 20,* 123–133.

Mills, H. D. (1965). The research use of projective techniques: A seventeen year survey. *Journal of Projective Techniques and Personality Assessment, 29,* 513–515.

Minuchin, S., et al. (1967). *Families of the slums—An exploration of their structure and treatment.* New York: Basic Books.

Mira, E. (1940). Myokinetic psychodiagnosis. *Proceedings of the Royal Society of Medicine.*

Mishler, E. G., (1995). Models of narrative analysis: A typology. *Journal of Narrative and Life History, 5,* 87–123.

Mitchell, H. E. (1951). Social class and race as factors affecting the role of the family in Thematic Apperception Test stories. *American Psychologist, 5,* 299–300.

Mitchell, K. (1968). An analysis of the schizophrenic mother concept by means of the Thematic Apperception Test. *Journal of Abnormal and Social Psychology, 6,* 571–574.

Molish, H. B. (1969). The quest for charisma. *Journal of Projective Techniques, 33*(2).

Molish, H. B. (1972). Projective methodologies. *Annual Review of Psychology, 23,* 577–614.

Montague, J. C., Jensen, P. J., & Wepman, J. M. (1973). Lexical analysis of institutionalized versus non-institutionalized mentally retarded. *Training School Bulletin, 70,* 160–166.

Morales, M. (1986). Projective tests carried out on young referred drug addicts. *Psychiatrie de l'Enfant, 9*(2), 421–467.

Morgan, C. D., & Murray, H. A. (1935). A method for investigating fantasies: The Thematic Apperception Test. *Achives of Neurological Psychiatry, 34,* 289–306.

Morgan, H. H. (1952). A psychometric comparison of achieving and nonachieving college students of high ability. *Journal of Consulting Psychology, 16,* 292–298.

Morgan, W. (1995). Origin and history of the Thematic Apperception Test images. *Journal of Personality Assessment, 65*, 237–254.

Moriarty, A. (1972). Normal preschoolers reactions to the C.A.T.: Some implications for later development. *Journal of Projective Techniques, 36*, 413–419.

Moriarty, A., & Murphy, L. (1960). Observations of patterns in perception related to basic motivations of children. Unpublished manuscript, Menninger Foundation, Topeka, KS.

Moriarty, A., & Murphy, L. (1968). Normal preschoolers' reactions to the C.A.T.: Some implications for later development. *Journal of Projective Techniques, 32*(5), 413–419.

Mormont, D. (1988). Methodes projectives et dangerosité [Projective methods and dangerousness]. *Acta Psychiatrica Belgica, 88*, 52–59.

Morval, M. (1977). *Le T.A.T. et les fonctions de moi* [The T.A.T. and ego functions]. Montréal: Presses de l'Université de Montréal.

Morval, M. (1990, July). *TAT and ego function.* Unpublished paper presented at the 13th International Congress of Rorschach and Projective Techniques, Paris.

Moss, H. A., & Kagan, J. (1961). Stability of achievement-and recognition-seeking behavior from early childhood through adulthood. *Journal of Abnormal and Social Psychology, 62*, 504–513.

Mowrer, O. J. (1940). An experimental analogue of "regression" with incidental observations on "reaction-formation." *Journal of Abnormal Social Psychology, 35*, 56–87.

Munroe, R. (1951). *The administration of projective tests* [Film]. Pennsylvania State College, Psychological Cinema Register.

Murray, H. A. (1938). *Explorations in personality.* New York: Oxford University Press.

Murray, H. A. (1940). What should psychologists do about psychoanalysis? *Journal of Abnormal and Social Psychology, 35*, 150–156.

Murray, H. A. (1943a). *Thematic Apperception Test Manual.* Cambridge, MA: Harvard University Press.

Murray, H. A. (1943b). Note on the selection of combat officers. *Psychosomatic Medicine, 5*, 386–391.

Murray, H. A. (1951a). Toward a classification of interaction. In T. Parsons & E. A. Shils (Eds.), *Towards a general theory of action* (pp. 433–464). Cambridge, MA: Harvard University Press.

Murray, H. A. (1951b). Foreword. In H. H. Anderson & G. L. Anderson (Eds.), *An introduction to projective techniques.* New York: Prentice Hall.

Murray, H. A. (1951c). Uses of the Thematic Apperception Test. *American Journal of Psychiatry, 107*, 577–581.

Murray, H. A. (1959). Preparations for the scaffold of a comprehensive system. In *Psychology: A study of science* (Vol. 3) (pp. 17–37). New York: McGraw-Hill.

Murray, H. A., & Stein, M. I. (1943). *Assessment of men.* New York: Rinehart.

Murstein, B. I. (1959). A conceptual model of projective tecniques applied to simulus variations with thematic techniques. *Journal of Consulting Psychology, 23*, 3–14.

Murstein, B. I. (1961). *A caution regarding the levels hypothesis and the use of psychological tests.* Unpublished manuscript, Interfaith Counseling Center, Portland, OR.

Murstein, B. I. (1962). *The projection of hostility on the T.A.T. as a function of stimulus, background, and personality variables.* Unpublished manuscript, Interfaith Counseling Center, Portland, OR.

Murstein, B. I. (1963a). The relationship of expectancy of reward to achievement performance on an arithmetic and thematic test. *Journal of Consulting Psychology, 27*, 394–399.

Murstein, B. I. (1963b). *Theory and research in projective techniques.* New York: Wiley.

Murstein, B. I. (1964). A normative study of T.A.T. ambiguity. *Journal of Projective Techniques, 28*, 210–218.

Murstein, B. I. (Ed.). (1965a). *Handbook of projective techniques.* New York: Basic Books.

Murstein, B. I. (1965b). New thoughts about ambiguity and the T.A.T. *Journal of Projective Techniques, 29*, 219–226.

Murstein, B. I. (1965c). Projection of hostility on the TAT as a function of stimulus, background, and personality variables. *Journal of Consulting Psychology, 29*, 43–48.

Murstein, B. I. (1965d). The scaling of the T.A.T. for N-ach. *Journal of Consulting Psychology, 29*, 286.

Murstein, B. I. (1968). Effect of stimulus, background, personality, and scoring system on the manifestation of hostility on the T.A.T. *Journal of Consulting and Clinical Psychology, 32*, 355–365.

Murstein, B. I. (1972). Normative written T.A.T. responses for a college sample. *Journal of Personality Assessment, 36*, 109–147.

Murstein, B. I., & Collier, H. L. (1962). The role of the TAT in the measurement of achievement as a function of expectancy. *Journal of Projective Techniques, 26*, 96–101.

Murstein, B. I., David, C., Fisher, D., & Furth, H. G. (1961). The scaling of the TAT for hostility by a variety of scaling methods. *Journal of Consulting Psychology, 25*, 497–504.

Mussen, P. (1953). Differences between the T.A.T. responses of Negro and white boys. *Journal of Consulting Psychology, 17*, 373–376.

Mussen, P., & Naylor, H. (1954). The relationships between overt and fantasy aggression. *Journal of Abnormal and Social Psychology, 49*, 235–240.

Myer, B., Rosenkrantz, A., & Holmes, G. A. (1972). Comparison of the T.A.T., C.A.T. and C.A.T.-H among second grade girls. *Journal of Personality Assessment, 36,* 440–444.

Myler, B., Roenkrantz, A., & Holmes, G. (1972). A comparison of the TAT, CAT and CAT-H among second grade girls. *Journal of Personality Assessment, 36*(5), 440–444.

Nathan, R. (1966). *Manuel du Test de Nathan et Mauco, planches de situation scolaire complémentaires au T.A.T.* [Manual for the Nathan and Mauco Test: School situation cards to augment the T.A.T.]. Paris: Éditions du Centre de Psychologie Appliqueé.

Nelson, J. T., & Epstein, S. (1962). Relationships among three measures of conflict over hostility. *Journal of Consulting Psychology, 26,* 345–350.

Neman, R. S., Brown, T. S., & Sells, S. B. (1973). Language and adjustment scales for the thematic apperception test for children 6–11 years: A report on the development and standardization of objective scoring procedures for five cards of the TAT used in the Health Examination Survey of children 6–11 years of age. *Vital and Health Statistics* (series 2), No. 58.

Neman, R. S., Neman, J. F., & Sells, S. B. (1974). Language and adjustment scales for the Thematic Apperception Test for youths 12–17 years. *Vital and Health Statistics, Series 2,* No. 62.

Neugarten, B. (1972). Personality and the aging process. *Gerontologist, 12,* 9–15.

Neugarten, B. L., & Guttmann, D. L. (1958). Age-sex roles and personality in middle age: A thematic apperception study. *Psychology Monographs, 72* (Serial No. 470), 1–33.

Neugarten, B. L., & Gutmann, D. L. (1968). *Middle age and aging: A reader in social psychology.* Chicago: University of Chicago Press.

Neuringer, C. (1968). A variety of thematic methods. In A. I. Rabin (Ed.), *Projective techniques in personality assessment* (pp. 222–261). New York: Springer.

Neuringer, C., & Livesay, R. C. (1970). Projective fantasy on the C.A.T. and C.A.T.-H. *Journal of Projective Techniques and Personality Assessment, 34,* 487–491.

Newbigging, P. L. (1955). Influence of a stimulus variable on stories told to certain T.A.T. pictures. *Canadian Journal of Psychology, 9,* 195–206.

Newmark, C. S. (1975). Test anxiety and children. *Journal of Personality Assessment, 39*(4), 409–413.

Newmark, C. S., & Flouranzano, R. (1973). Replication of an empirically derived T.A.T. set with hospitalized psychiatric patients. *Journal of Personality Assessment, 37,* 340–341.

Nezu, A. M., & Ronan, G. F. (1985). Life stress, current problems, problem-solving, and depressive symptoms: An integrative model. *Journal of Consulting and Clinical Psychology, 53,* 693–697.

Nezu, A. M., & Ronan, G. F. (1988). Social problem-solving as a moderator of stress-related depressive symptoms: A prospective analysis. *Journal of Counseling Psychology, 35,* 134–138.

Nigg, J., Silk, K., Westen, D., Lohr, N. Gold, L., Goodrich, S., & Ogata, S. (1991). Object representations in the early memories of sexually abused borderline patients. *American Journal of Psychiatry, 148,* 864–869.

Nolan, R. (1959). *A longitudinal comparison of motives in chidren's fantasy stories as revealed by the Children's Apperception Test.* Unpublished doctoral dissertation, The Florida State University, Tallahassee.

Nuttall, R. (1964). Some correlates of high need for achievement among urban northern Negroes. *Journal of Abnormal Social Psychology, 68,* 593–600.

Ober, W. (1969, October). A few kind words about W. Somerset Maugham (1874–1965). *New York Journal of Medicine.*

Obrzut, J. E., & Boliek, C. A. (1986). Thematic approaches to personality assessment with children and adolescents. In H. M. Knoff (Ed.), *The assessment of child and adolescent personality* (pp. 183–198). New York: Guilford.

Obrzut, J. E., & Cummings, J. A. (1983). The projective approach to personality assessment: An analysis of thematic picture techniques. *School Psychology Review, 12,* 414–420.

Obrzut, J. E., & Zucker, S. (1983). Projective personality assessment techniques. In G. W. Hynd (Ed.), *The school psychologist* (pp. 195–229). Syracuse, NY: Syracuse University Press.

Ochs, E., Smith, R., & Taylor, C. (1989). Dinner narratives as detective stories. *Cultural Dynamics, 2,* 238–257.

O'Gorman, J. G., & Stair, L. H. (1977). Perception of hostility in the TAT as a function of defensive style. *Journal of Personality Assessment, 41,* 591–594.

O'Kelly, E. (1956). The O.R.T. test: Some quantitative findings to early separation from the mother. *Bulletin of the Psychological Society,* 24–29.

Olney, E. E., & Cursing, H. M. (1935). A brief report of the responses of preschool children to commercially available pictorial material. *Child Development, 6,* 52–55.

Ombredane, A., & Anzieu, D. (1969). *Exploration de la mentalité des noirs* [Explorative study of the intelligence of blacks]. Paris: Presses Universitaires de France.

Orbach, C. E. (1952), *The perception of meaning in schizophrenia.* Unpublished doctoral dissertation, Teacher's College, Columbia University, New York.

Ornduff, S. R., Freedenfeld, R. N., Kelsey, R. M., & Critelli, J. W. (1994). Object relations of sexually abused female subjects: A T.A.T. analysis. *Journal of Personality Assessment, 63,* 223–238.

Ornduff, S. R., & Kelsey, R. M. (1996). Object relations of sexually and physically abused female children: A T.A.T. analysis. *Journal of Personality Assessment, 66,* 91–105.

Orpen, C. (1978). Conscious control of projection in the Thematic Apperception Test. *Psychology, 15,* 67–75.

Orsillo, D. G. (1973). A comparative analysis of formal education as an operative determinant of the Thematic Apperception Test. *Disseration Abstracts International, 34*(3-B), 1280–1281.

Orso, D. (1969). Comparison of achievement and affiliation arousal of n-Ach. *Journal of Projective Techniques, 33,* 230–233.

Oz, S., Tari, A., & Fine, M. (1992). A comparison of psychological profiles of teenage mothers and their nonmother peers: II: Responses to a set of TAT cards. *Adolescence, 27,* 357–367.

Palmer, J. O. (1952). A note on the intercard reliability of the T.A.T. *Journal of Consulting Psychology, 16,* 473–474.

Pam, A., & Rivera, J. (1995). Sexual pathology and dangerousness from a Thematic Apperception Test. *Professional Psychology, 26,* 72–77.

Panek, P. E., Wagner, E. E., & Kennedy-Zwergel, K. (1983). A review of projective test findings with older adults. *Journal of Personality Assessment, 40,* 588–591.

Pasewark, R. A., Fritzgerald, B. J., Dexter, V., & Cangemi, A. (1976). Responses of adolescent, middle-aged, and aged females on the Gerontological and Thematic Apperception Test. *Journal of Personality Assessment, 40,* 588–591.

Passman, R. H., & Lautmann, L. A. (1982). Fathers, mothers, and security blankets: Effects on the responsiveness of young children during projective testing. *Journal of Consulting & Clinical Psychology, 50*(2), 310–312.

Patalano, F. (1986). Drug abusers and card 3BM of the TAT. *Psychology: A Quarterly Journal of Human Behavior, 23*(2–3), 34–36.

Perret-Catipovic, M. (1990, July 26). *Analysis of formal aspects of the TAT: Contribution to the differentiation of psychotic and prepsychotic diagnosis.* Unpublished paper presented at the 13th International Congress of Rorschach and Projective Techniques, Paris.

Peruchon, M. (1990, July). *Travail du négatif dans le vieillessment à travers les Rorschach et le T.A.T.* Unpublished paper presented to the 13th International Congress of Rorschach and Project Techniques, Paris.

Peterson, C.A. (1990). Administration of the Thematic Apperception Test: Contributions of psychoanalytic psychotherapy. *Journal of Comtemporary Psychotherapy, 20,* 191–200.

Phelps, S. L. (1976). The effect of equalized sex roles in a modification of the Thematic Apperception Test. *Dissertation Abstracts International, 40*(6), 588–591.

Pheulpin, M. (1990, July). *Caracteristiques des protocoles Rorschach et T.A.T. de personalités allergiques essentielles* [Characteristics of Rorschach and T.A.T. protocols of allergy patients]. Unpublished paper presented at the 13th International Congress of Rorschach and Projective Techniques, Paris.

Phillipson, H. (1955). *The object relations technique.* Chicago: Free Press.

Piaget, J. (1932). *The language and thought of the child.* London: Routledge & Kegan Paul.

Pine, F. (1959). Thematic drive content and creativity. *Journal of Personality, 27,* 136–151.

Pine, F. (1960). A manual for rating drive content in the Thematic Apperception Test. *Journal of Projective Techniques, 24,* 32–45.

Pine, F. (1962). Creativity and primary process: Sample variations. *Journal of Nervous and Mental Diseases, 134,* 506–511.

Pine, F., & Holt, R. R. (1960). Creativity and primary process: A study of adaptive regression. *Journal of Abnormal and Social Psychology, 61,* 370–379.

Piotrowski, C. (1937). The Rorschach inkblot method in organic disturbances of the central nervous system. *Journal of Nervous and Mental Diseases, 86,* 525–537.

Piotrowski, C. (1950). A new evaluation of the Thematic Apperception Test. *Psychoanalytic Review, 37,* 101–127.

Piotrowski, C. (1952). A TAT of a schizophrenic interpreted according to new rules. *Psychoanalytic Review, 39,* 230–249.

Piotrowski, C., & Keller, J. W. (1984). Psychodiagnostic testing in APA-approved clinical psychology programs. *Professional Psychology: Research and Practice, 3,* 450–456.

Piotrowski, C., Sherry, D., & Keller, J. W. (1985). Psychodiagnostic test usage: A survey of the society for personality assessment. *Journal of Personality Assessment, 49*(2), 115–119.

Pirozzolo, F. J. (1979). *The neuropsychology of developmental reading disorders.* New York: Praeger.

Pistole, D. R., & Ornduff, S. R. (1994). T.A.T. assessment of sexually abused girls: An analysis of manifest content. *Journal of Personality Assessment, 63,* 211–222.

Pittluck, P. (1950). *The relation between aggressive fantasy and overt behavior.* Unpublished doctoral dissertation, Yale University, New Haven, CT.

Poe, W. (1969). *The old person in your home.* New York: Charles Scribners & Sons.

Polkinghorne, D. E. (1988). *Narrative knowing and the human sciences.* Albany: State University of New York Press.

Pollack, S., & Gilligan, C. (1982). Images of violence in Thematic Apperception Test stories. *Journal of Personality and Social Psychology, 42,* 159–167.

Pollak, S. M. (1986). A study of gender differences in violent Thematic Apperception Test stories. *Dissertation Abstracts International, 47*(2-A), 476.

Polyson, J., Norris, D., & Ott, E. (1985). The recent decline in T.A.T. research. *Professional Psychology: Research and Practice, 16,* 26–28.

Porcerelli, J. H., & Dietrich, D. R. (1994). Dietrich Object Relations and Object Representations Scale: Convergent and discriminant validity and factor structure. *Psychoanalytic Psychology, 11,* 101–113.

Porter, S. (1990). Adolescent sex offenders: A study of the relationship between self-concept and sexual behavior in adolescent males. *American Journal of Forensic Psychology, 8,* 61–73.

Porterfield, C. (1969). Adaptive mechanisms of young disadvantaged stutterers and nonstutterers. *Journal of Projective Techniques, 33,* 371–376.

Poster, E. C. (1989). The use of projective assessment techniques in pediatric research. *Journal of Pediatric Nursing, 4*(1), 26–35.

Postman, L., Bruner, J. S., & McGinnies, E. (1948). Personal values as selective factors in perception. *Journal of Abnormal Social Psychology, 43,* 142–154.

Press, I. (1967). Maya aging: Cross-cultural projective techniques and the dilemma of interpretation. *Psychiatry, 30,* 197–202.

Prola, M. (1972a). A review of the transcendence index. *Journal of Personality Assessment, 36,* 8–12.

Prola, M. (1972b). Verbal productivity and transcendence. *Journal of Personality Assessment, 36,* 445–456.

Purcell, K. (1956). The T.A.T. and antisocial behavior. *Journal of Consulting Psychology, 20,* 449–456.

Pytkowicz, A. R., Wagner, N., & Sarason, G. (1967). An experimental study of the reduction of hostility through fantasy. *Journal of Personality and Social Psychology, 5,* 295–303.

Rabin, A. I. (1961). Culture components as a significant factor in child development: A. Kibbutz adolescents. *American Journal of Orthopsychiatry, 49,* 3–12.

Rabin, A. I. (1968). Children's Apperception Test findings with Kibbutz and non-Kibbutz preschoolers. *Journal of Projective Techniques and Personality Assessment, 32*(5), 420–424.

Rajagopalan, I. (1990). A study of intergenerational attitudes on the Senior Apperception Test. *Indian Journal of Applied Psychology, 27,* 15–19.

Rank, O. (1990). *In quest of the hero.* Princeton, NJ: Princeton University Press.

Rao, S. K., & Ramadevi, T. (1958a). An experiment in the analysis of T.A.T. responses. *Journal of All India Institute of Mental Health, 1,* 42–50.

Rao, S. K., & Ramadevi, T. (1958b). Situational analysis of the T.A.T. responses. *Journal of All India Institute of Mental Health, 1,* 18–25.

Rapaport, D. (1943). The clinical application of the Thematic Apperception Test. *Bulletin of the Menninger Clinic, 7,* 106–113.

Rapaport, D., (1946). *Diagnostic psychological testing.* Chicago: Yearbook.

Rapaport, D. (1947). In F. Wyatt (Ed.), The scoring and analysis of the Thematic Apperception Test. *Journal of Psychology, 24,* 319–330.

Rapaport, D. (Ed.). (1951). *Organization and pathology of thought.* New York: Columbia University Press.

Rapaport, D. (1952). Projective techniques and the theory of thinking. *Journal of Projective Techniques, 16*(3), 269–275.

Rapaport, D., Gill, M., & Schafer, R. (1946). *Diagnostic psychological testing.* Chicago: Yearbook.

Rapaport, D., Gill, M. M., & Schafer, R. (1970). *Diagnostic psychological testing.* New York: International Universities Press.

Rauchfleisch, U. (1986). Use of the Thematic Apperception Test in the psychotherapy of delinquents. *Psyche (Stuttgart), 40*(8), 735–754.

Rauchfleisch, U. (1989). *Der thematische apperzeptionstest (T.A.T.) in diagnostik und therapie: Eine psychoanalytische interpretationsmethode* [The T.A.T. in diagnosis and treatment: A psychoanalytic interpretative method]. Stuttgart: Enke.

Reitman, W. R., & Atkinson, J. W. (1958). Some methodological problems in the use of thematic apperceptive measures of human motives. In J. E. Atkinson (Ed.), *Motives in fantasy, action, and society* (pp. 664–683). Princeton, NJ: Van Nostrand.

Renaud, H. (1946). Group differences in fantasies: Head injuries, psychoneurotics and brain diseases. *Journal of Psychology, 21,* 327–346.

Reteif, A. I. (1987). Thematic Apperception Test across cultures: Selection versus tests of inclusion. *South Africa Journal of Psychology, 17*(2), 47–55.

Revers, W. J., & Allesch, C. G. (1985a). From the Thematic Apperception Test (TAT) to the Salzburg Thematic Construction Test: Remarks on an overdue test revision. *Klin. Psychol. Psychopathol. Psychother., 33*(4), 305–312.

Revers, W. J., & Allesch, C. G. (1985b). *Handbuch zum thematischen gestaltungs-test (Salzburg)* [Handbook for the Salzburg Thematic Gestalt Test]. Weinheim/Basel: Beltz Verlag.

Reynolds, D. (1964). Social desirability in the T.A.T.: A replication and extension of Reznikoff's study. *Journal of Projective Techniques, 28,* 78–80.

Reznikoff, M. (1961). Social desirability in T.A.T. themes. *Journal of Projective Techniques.*

Reznikoff, M., & Dollin, A. (1961). Social desirability and the type of hostility expressed on the T.A.T. *Journal of Clinical Psychology, 17,* 315–317.

Richardson, V., & Partridge, S. (1982). Construct validation of imaginative assessment of family orientation and status perception: Theoretical and methodological implications for the Thematic Apperception Test. *Educational and Psychological Measurement, 42,* 1243–1251.

Ricoeur, P. (1984–1988). *Time and narrative* (Vols. 1–3). Chicago: University of Chicago Press.

Riess, B., Schwartz, E., & Cottingham, A. (1950). An experimental critique of assumptions underlying the Negro version of the T.A.T. *Journal of Abnormal and Social Psychology, 45,* 700–709.

Riessman, C. K. (1993). *Narrative analysis.* Newbury, CA: Sage.

Riessman, F., & Miller, S. M. (1958). Social class and projective tests. *Journal of Projective Techniques, 22,* 432–439.

Ritter, A. M., & Eron, L. D. (1952). The use of the Thematic Apperception Test to differentiate normal from abnormal groups. *Journal of Abnormal and Social Psychology, 45,* 147–158.

Roazen, P. (1996). Review of Confrontation in Vienna by Leopold Bellak. *Psychoanalytic Books, 7,* 19–20.

Robinson, F. G. (1992). *Love's story told: A life of Henry A. Murray.* Cambridge, MA: Harvard University Press.

Roby, T. B. (1948). *Effect of need for security on thematic apperception.* Unpublished master's thesis, Wesleyan University, Middleton, CT.

Rock, M. H. (1975). *Self-reflection and ego development.* Unpublished doctoral dissertation, New York University, New York.

Rockwell, F. V., et al. (1948). Changes in palmar skin resistance during the Rorschach Test. II. The effect of repetition with color removed. *Mschr. Psychiat. Neurol. 116,* 321.

Rodgers, C. W. (1973). Relationship of projective to direct expression of selected needs for nonpsychotic subjects. *Perceptual and Motor Skills, 36,* 571–578.

Rodrigues Silva, D. (1982) *O teste de apercepcao para criancas (figuras humanas). CAT-H* [On the C.A.T.-H: A normative study]. Lisboa: Instituto Nacional de Investigacao Cientifica.

Rodrigues Silva, D. (1990, July). *Comparative study through Rorschach and TAT of two groups of ulcerous patients.* Unpublished paper presented at the 13th International Congress of Rorschach and Projective Techniques, Paris.

Roe, A. (1952). *The making of a scientist.* New York: Dodd Mead.

Rogoff, T. L. (1985). T.A.T. disturbances of thinking in borderline personality disorder: Differential diagnosis of inpatient borderlines from schizophrenics, schizotypals, and other personality disorders. *Dissertaiton Abstracts International, 46*(2-B), 658–659.

Ronan, G. F., Colavito, V. A., & Hammontree, S. R. (1993). Personal problem-solving system for scoring T.A.T. responses: Preliminary validity and reliability data. *Journal of Personality Assessment, 61,* 28–40.

Ronan, G. F., Date, A. L., & Weisbrod, M. (1995). Personal problem-solving scoring of the T.A.T.: Sensitivity to training. *Journal of Personality Assessment, 64,* 119–131.

Rosen, B. (1954). The achievement syndrome and economic growth in Brazil. *Social Forces, 42,* 341–354.

Rosen, B. (1958). The achievement syndrome: A psychocultural dimension of social stratification. In J. Atkinson (Ed.), *Motives in fantasy action and society.* Princeton, NJ: Van Nostrand.

Rosen, B. (1961). Family structure and achievement motivations. *American Sociological Review, 26,* 574–585.

Rosen, J. L., & Neugarten, B. L. (1964). Ego functions in the middle and later years. A Thematic Apperception study of normal adults. In B. L. Neugarten & Associates, *Personality in middle and late life.* New York: Atherton.

Rosegrant, J. (1995). Borderline diagnosis in projective assessment. *Pschoanalytic Psychology, 12,* 407–428.

Rosenblatt, M. (1958). *The development of norms for the Children's Apperception Test.* Unpublished doctoral dissertation, Florida State University.

Rosenfeld, H. M., & Franklin, S. S. (1966). Arousal need for affiliation in women. *Journal of Personality and Social Psychology,* 245–248.

Rosenwald, G. C. (1968). The Thematic Apperception Test. In A. I. Rabin (Ed.), *Projective techniques in personality assessment* (pp. 172–221). New York: Springer.

Rosenzweig, S. H. (1948). The Thematic Apperception Test in diagnosis and therapy. *Journal of Personality, 16,* 437–444.

Rosenzweig, S. H. (1949). Apperceptive norms for the Thematic Apperception Test: The problem of norms in projective methods. *Journal of Personality, 17,* 475–483.

Rosenzweig, S. H., & Fleming, E. (1949). Apperceptive norms for the Thematic Apperception Test II: An empirical investigation. *Journal of Personality, 17,* 483–503.

Rosoff, A. L. (1988). Thematic Apperception Test characteristic and the psychotherapy of schizophrenic patients: A study of pretreatment patient *variables* and psychotherapy process. *Dissertation Abstracts International, 48*(2-B), 2108.

Rossman, I. (Ed.). (1971). *Clinical geriatrics.* Philadelphia: Lippincott.

Rothstein, A., Benjamin, L., Crosby, M., & Eisenstadt, K. (1988). *Learning disorders: An integration of neuropsychological and psychoanalytic considerations.* Madison, CT: International Universities Press.

Rotter, J. (1960) Some implications of a social learning theory for the prediction of goal-directed behavior from testing procedures. *Psychology Review, 67,* 301–316.

Rotter, J. B. (1946). Thematic apperception test: Suggestions for administration and interpretation. *Character and Personality, 9,* 18–34.

Rotter, J. B. (1947). In F. Wyatt: The scoring and analysis of the Thematic Apperception Test. *Journal of Psychology, 24,* 319–330.

Rotter, J. B., & Jessor, S. (1951). In E. S. Schneidman (Ed.), *Thematic test analysis* (p. 163). New York: Grune & Stratton.

Rourke, B. P., Bakker, D. J., Fisk, J. L., & Strang, J. D. (1983). *Child neuropsychology: An introduction to theory, research, and clinical practice.* New York: Guilford.

Rubin, S. (1964). A comparison of the Thematic Apperception Test stories of two I.Q. groups. *Journal of Projective Techniques, 28,* 81–85.

Rund, B. R. (1989). Communication deviances in parents of schizophrenics. *Family Process, 25,* 133–147.

Rund, B. R., & Blakar, R. M. (1986). Schizophrenic patients and their parents: A multimethod design and the findings from an illustrative empirical study of cognitive disorders and communication deviances. *Acta Psychiatrica Scandinavica, 74*(4), 396–408.

Runes, D. (Ed.). (1955). *Dictionary of philosophy.* Patterson, NJ: Littlefield.

Russell, E. W., Neuringer, C., & Goldstein, G. (1970). *Assessment of brain damage: A neuropsychological key approach.* New York: Wiley-Interscience.

Ruth, W. J., & Mosatche, H. S. (1985). A projective assessment of the effects of Freudian sexual symbolism in liquor advertisements. *Psychological Reports, 56,* 183–188.

Rutter, M. (Ed.). (1983). *Development neuropsychiatry.* New York: Guilford.

Ryan, W. (1971). *Blaming the victim.* New York: Vintage Books.

Saltz, G., & Epstein, S. (1963). Thematic hostility and guilt responses as related to self-reported hostility, guilt, and conflict. *Journal of Abnormal and Social Psychology, 67,* 469–479.

Salvini, A. (1983). *Interpersonalita: Strumenti per l indagine clinica dei processi interpersonali.* Milano: Unicopli.

Sampson, E. (1963). Achievement in conflict. *Journal of Personality, 31,* 510–516.

Samuels, H. (1952). The validity of personality-trait rating based on projective techniques. *Psychology Monographs 66,* No. 5.

Sandler, J. (1985). *The analysis of defense: The ego and the mechanisms of the ego revisited.* New York: International Universities Press.

Sandler, J., & Rosenblatt, B. (1962). The concept of the representational world. *Psychoanalytic Study of the Child, 17.*

Sanford, R. N. (1936). The effects of abstinence from food upon imaginal processes: A further experiment. *Journal of Psychology, 3,* 145–159.

Sanford, R. N., et al. (1943). *Physique, personality and scholarship.* Washington, DC: Society for Research in Child Development.

Santostefano, S. (1978). *A biodevelopmental approach to clinical child psychology.* New York: Wiley.

Sarason, B. R., & Sarason, I. C. (1958). The effect of type of administration and sex of subject on emotional tone and outcome ratings of T.A.T. stories. *Journal of Projective Techniques, 22,* 333–337.

Sarason, S. B. (1948). The T.A.T. and subjective interpretation. *Journal of Consulting Psychology, 12,* 285–299.

Sarbin, T. R. (Ed.). (1986). *Narrative psychology: The storied nature of human conduct.* New York: Praeger.

Sargent, H. (1951). In E. S. Schneidman (Ed.), *Thematic test analysis* (p. 180). New York: Grune & Stratton.

Sargent, H. (1953). *The insight test.* New York: Grune & Stratton.

Saxe, C. H. (1950). A quantitative comparison of psychodiagnostic formulations from the T.A.T. and therapeutic contacts. *Journal of Consulting Psychology, 14,* 116–127.

Schaefer, J. B. (1962). *Stability and change in Thematic Apperception Test response from adolescence to adulthood.* Unpublished doctoral dissertation, University of Chicago.

Schaefer, J. B., & Norman, M. (1967). Punishment and aggression in fantasy responses of boys with antisocial character traits. *Journal of Personality and Social Psychology, 4,* 237–240.

Schafer, R. (1948). *The clinical application of psychological tests.* New York: International Universities Press.

Schafer, R. (1954). *Psychoanalytic interpretation of Rorschach testing.* New York: Grune & Stratton.

Schafer, R. (1958). How was the story told? *Journal of Projective Techniques, 22,* 181–210.

Schaible, M. (1975). An analysis of noncontent T.A.T. variables in a longitudinal sample. *Journal of Personality Assessment, 39,* 480–485.

Schaie, K. W. (1978). The Senior Apperception Technique. In O. K. Buros (Ed.), *The eighth mental measurements yearbook.* Highland Park, NJ: Gryphon.

Scheffler, R. Z. (1975). The child from five to six: A longitudinal study of fantasy change. *Genetic Psychology Monographs, 92,* 19–56.

Scheper-Hughes, N. (1979). *Saints, scholars and schizophrenics: Mental illness in rural Ireland.* Berkeley, CA: University of California Press.

Schiff, B. B., & Lamon, M. (1994). Inducing emotion by unilateral contraction of hand muscles. *Cortex, 30,* 247–254.

Schilder, P. (1925). Entwurf zu einer Psychiatrie auf Psychoanalytischer Grundiage, Leipzig, Wien, Zurich. *Int. Psychoanalytische Bibliothek., 17.*

Schneider, S. (1988). Attitudes toward death in adolescent offspring of Holocaust survivors: A comparison of Israeli and American adolescents. *Adolescence, 23*(91), 703–710.

Schroth, M. L. (1977). The use of the associative elaboration and integration scales for evaluating C.A.T. protocols. *Journal of Psychology, 97,* 29–35.

Schroth, M. L. (1978). Sex and generational differences in Senior Apperception Technique projections. *Perceptual and Motor Skills, 47,* 1299–1304.

Schroth, M. L. (1979). The relationships between motives on the Children's Apperception Test. *Journal of Genetic Psychology, 134*(2), 219–224.

Schroth, M. L. (1985). The effect of differing measuring methods on the relationship of motives. *Journal of Psychology, 119*(3), 213–218.

Schwartz, E. K., Riess, B. F., & Cuttingham, A. (1951). A further critical evaluation of the negro version of the T.A.T. *Journal of Projective Techniques, 15,* 394–400.

Schwartz, L. A. (1932). Social-situation pictures in the psychiatric interview. *American Journal of Orthopsychiatry, 2,* 124–132.

Schwartz, S., & Giacoman, S. (1972). Convergent and discriminant validity of three measures of adjustment and three measures of social desirability. *Journal of Consulting and Clinical Psychology, 39,* 239–242.

Schwartzman, J. (1983). Family ethnography: A tool for clinicians. *Family Therapy Collections, 6,* 137–149.

Schweitzer, J. J. (1978). Sex-typing in the T.A.T. stimulus. *Dissertation Abstracts International, 39*(4-A), 2157.

Scodel, A., & Lipetz, M. E. (1957). T.A.T. hostility and psychopathology. *Journal of Projective Techniques, 21,* 161–165.

Sears, R. R. (1943). Survey of objective studies of psychoanalytic concepts. *Social Science Research Council Bulletin, 5,* 1.

Seifert, W. (1984). *Der charakter und seine geschichten psychodiagnostik mit dem thematischen apperzeptions-test (T.A.T.)* [Character and its psychodiagnostic history with the T.A.T.]. Munich/Basel: Ernst Reinhardt Verlag.

Seifert, W. (1986). Projection or development: A conflict of semantics or chance for a new paradigmatic orientation in personality diagnosis. *Klin. Psychol. Psychopathol. Psychother., 34*(4), 335–350.

Seiter, A. A. (1985). The influence of the examiner's method of inquiry upon the productivity of clinical material on the Thematic Apperception Test. *Dissertation Abstracts International, 45*(10B), 3346.

Sells, S. B., Cox, S. H., & Chatman, L. R. (1967). Scales of language development for the T.A.T. *Psychological Association, 2,* 171–172.

Semeonoff, B. (1976a). The effect of colour on T.A.T. responses. *British Journal of Projective Psychology and Personality Study, 21,* 31–38.

Semeonoff, B. (1976b). *Projective techniques.* New York: Wiley.

Sen, A. (1953). A preliminary study of the Thematic Apperception Test. *British Journal of Statistical Psychology, 6,* 91–100.

Shabad, P. Worland, J., Lander, H., & Dietrich, D. (1979). A retrospective analysis of the TAT's of children at risk who subsequently broke down. *Child Psychiatry and Human Development, 10,* 49–59.

Shalit, B. (1970). Environmental hostility and hostility in fantasy. *Journal of Personality and Social Psychology, 15,* 171–174.

Shapiro, D. L. (1991). *Forensic psychological assessment: An integrative approach.* Boston: Allyn and Bacon

Sharav, D. (1991). Assessing adoptive parents using a combined individual and interaction procedure. In E. D. Hibbs (Ed.), *Adoption: International perspectives* (pp. 73–89). Madison, CT: International Universities Press.

Sharkey, K. J., & Ritzler, B. A. (1985). Comparing diagnostic validity of the TAT and a New Picture projective test. *Journal of Personality Assessment, 49*(4), 406–412.

Shatin, L. (1955). Relationship between the Rorschach test and the Thematic Apperception Test. *Journal of Projective Techniques, 17,* 92–101.

Shatin, L. (1958). The constriction-dilation dimension in Rorschach and T.A.T. *Journal of Clinical Psychology, 14,* 150–154.

Sheikh, A. A., & Twerski, M. (1974). Future-time perspective in Negro and White adolescents. *Perceptual and Motor Skills, 39,* 308.

Shentoub, V. (1972–1973). Introduction théorétiques du processus—T.A.T. *Bulletin de Psychologie, 26,* 305, 10–11, 582–602.

Shentoub, V. (1973). Approaches projectives en France. *Revue de Psychologie Appliqueé, 26,* 359–400.

Shentoub, V. (1981). T.A.T., test de creativite. *Psychologie Française, 26,* 66–70.

Shentoub, V. (1986). Presentation of the method of interpreting the T.A.T. *Bulletin de la Société Française du Rorschach et des Methodes Projectifs, 33,* 59–65.

Shentoub, V. (1987). Thematic Apperception Test (TAT): Theory and methodology. *Psychologie Française, 32*(3), 117–126.

Shentoub, V., Azoulay, C., Bailly-Salin, M-J., Benfredj, K., Boekholt, M., Brelet, F., Chabert, C., Chretien, M. Emmanuelli, M., Martin, M., Monin, E., Peruchon, M., & Serviere, A. (1990). *Manual d' utilisation du T.A.T. (approche psychanalytique)* [Manual for the use of the T.A.T.: (Psychoanalytic approach)]. Paris: Dunod.

Shentoub, V., & Debray, R. (1969). Contribution du T.A.T. au diagnostic differential entre le normal et le pathologique chez l'enfant [Contribution of the T.A.T. to differential diagnosis of normal and emotionally disturbed children]. *Psychiatrie de l'Enfant, 12,* 241–266.

Sherwood, E. T. (1957). On the designing of T.A.T. pictures with special reference to a set for an African people assimilating western culture. *Journal of Social Psychology, 45,* 161–190.

Sherwood, J. V., & Potash, H. M. (1988). Induced anxiety, defensive style, and performance on the TAT. *Journal of Clinical Psychology, 44,* 817–820.

Shill, M. (1981). T.A.T. measures of gender identity (castration anxiety) in father-absent males. *Journal of Personality Assessment, 45,* 136–146.

Shipley, T., & Veroff, J. (1952). A projective measure of need for affiliation. *Journal of Experimental Psychology, 43,* 349–356.

Shneidman, E. S. (1952). *The Make a Picture Story Test (MAPS).* New York: Psychological Corporation.

Shneidman, E. S. (1956). Some relationships between the Rorschach technique and other psychodiagnostic test. In B. Klopfer (Ed.), *Developments in the Rorschach technique* (pp. 595–642). New York: World Book.

Shneidman, E. S., & Farberom, N. I. (1958). T.A.T. heroes of suicidal and non-suicidal subjects. *Journal of Projective Techniques, 22,* 211–228.

Shnneidman, E. S., Joel, W., & Little, K. B. (1951). *Thematic test analysis.* New York: Grune & Stratton.

Shore, M. F., Massimo, J. L., & Mack, R. (1964). The relationship between levels of guilt in thematic stories and unsocialized behavior. *Journal of Projective and Personality Assessment, 28,* 346–349.

Shulman, D. G., & Ferguson, G. R. (1988). Two methods of assessing narcissism: Comparison of the Narcissism-Projective (N-P) and the Narcissistic Personality Inventory (NPI). *Journal of Clinical Psychology, 44,* 857–866.

Shulman, D. G., McGarthy, E. C., & Ferguson, G. R. (1988). The projective assessment of narcissism: Development, reliability, and validity of the N-P. *Psychoanalytic Psychology, 5,* 285–297.

Siguan, M. (1988). Formulario para la interpretacion y registro de los datos del T.A.T. *Revista de Psicologia General y Aplicada, 9,* 305–312.

Siipola, E. M. (1950). Influence of color on reactions to ink-blots. *Journal of Personality, 18,* 358.

Silberer, H. (1951). Report on a method of eliciting and observing certain symbolic hallucination phenomena. In D. Rapaport (Ed.), *Organization and pathology of thought.* New York: Columbia University Press.

Silva, D. (1982). *Teste de Apercepao para Criancas (figuras, humanas-CAT-H.) Un Estudio de Normals.* Lisbon, Portugal.

Silva, D. (1985). Algunas caracteristicas de resposta de rapazes e raparigas ao C.A.T.-H. *Revista Portuguesa de Psicologia, 20/21,* 7–34.

Silverman, L. H. (1959). A Q-sort study of the validity of evaluations made from projective techniques. *Psychological Monographs, 73* (Series No. 7).

Silverstein, A. B. (1959). Identification with same-sex and opposite-sex figures in thematic apperception. *Journal of Projective Techniques, 23,* 73–75.

Simmonnet, P. (1988). Identification on the Bellak Children's Apperception Test (CAT): A new approach. *Perspectives Psychiatriques, 27*(12, pt. 2), 146–149.

Si Moussi, A. (1990). Le T.A.T. aujourd'hui en algerie [The T.A.T. today in Algeria]. *Revue Officielle de la Societé Algérienne de Recherche en Psychologie.* (No. 1).

Simson, E. (1959). Vergleich von C.A.T. und einer inhaltsanalogen Mensch-Bilderserie. *Sonderdr. Diagnost., 5,* 54–62.

Singer, J. L., & Herman, J. L. (1954). Motor and fantasy correlates of the Rorschach human movement response. *Journal of Consulting Psychology, 18,* 325–331.

Singer, M., & Wynne, L. (1966). Principles for scoring communication deviances in parents of schizophrenics: Rorschach and T.A.T. scoring manuals. *Psychiatry, 29,* 260–288.

Singer, R. (1963). A cognitive view of rationalized projection. *Journal of Projective Techniques, 27,* 235–243.

Singh, S., & Kaur, J. (1987). Motive to avoid and approach success: Two dimensions of the same motive. *Asian Journal of Psychology and Education, 19,* 1–7.

Singh, U. P., & Akhtar, S. N. (1970). The Children's Apperception Test in the study of orphans. *Psychology Annual, 4,* 1–6.

Sjoback, H. (1973). *The psychoanalytic theory of defensive processes.* New York: Wiley.

Sklover, T. G. (1989). Gender differences in TAT-like themes of violence, achievement, affiliation and intimacy. *Dissertation Abstracts International, 49*(8-B), 3424.

Skolnik, A. (1966). Motivational imagery and behavior over twenty years. *Journal of Consulting Psychology, 30,* 463–478.

Slemon, A. G., Holwartz, E. J., Lewis, J., & Sitko, M. (1976). Associative elaboration and integration scales for evaluating T.A.T. protocols. *Journal of Personality Assessment, 40,* 365–369.

Sloate, N. (1974). Aging and community health problems. In L. Bellak (Ed.), *A concise handbook of community psychiatry and community mental health.* New York: Grune & Stratton.

Sluzki, C. (1979). Migration and family conflict. *Family Process, 18,* 379–390.

Smith, C. P. (Ed.). (1992). *Motivation and personality: Handbook of thematic content analysis.* New York: Cambridge University Press.

Smith, K. (1983). Using a battery of tests to predict suicide in a long term hospital: A clinical analysis. *Omega Journal of Death and Dying, 13,* 261–275.

Smith, M. S. (1968). The computer and the TAT. *Journal of School Psychology, 6,* 206–214.

Smythe, L. D. (1982). Psychopathology as a function of neuroticism and a hypnotically implanted aggressive conflict. *Journal of Personality and Social Psychology, 43*(3), 555–564.

Snyders, G. (1966). Y a-t-il un bon usage du T.A.T.? [Is there a good use for the T.A.T.?] *Enfance, 19,* 49–69.

Sobel, H. J. (1981). Projective methods of cognitive analysis. In T. V. Merluzzi, C. R. Glass, & M. Genest (Eds.), *Cognitive assessment* (pp. 127–148). New York: Guilford.

Solomon, I. L., & Starr, B. D. (1968). *School Apperception Test: SAM.* New York: Springer.

Spain, D. H. (1972a). On the use of projective tests for research in psychological anthropology. In F. I. Hsu (Ed.), *Psychological anthropology* (pp. 267–308). Cambridge, MA: Schenkman.

Spain, D. H. (1972b). A supplemental bibliography on projective testing. *Psychological Anthropology,* 609–623.

Spangler, W. D. (1992). Validity of questionnaire and TAT measures of need for achievement: Two meta-analyses. *Psychological Bulletin, 112,* 140–154.

Spence, D. P. (1982). *Narrative truth and historical truth: Meaning and interpretation in psychoanalysis.* New York: Norton.

Spiegelman, M., Terwilliger, C., & Fearing, F. (1952). The content of comic strips: A study of a mass medium of communication. *Journal of Social Psychology, 35,* 37–57.

Spitz, R. (1955). The primal cavity: A contribution to the genesis of perception and its role for psychoanalytic theory. *Psychoanalytic Study of the Child, 10.*

Spivack, G., Platt, J., & Shure, M. (1976). *The problem-solving approach to adjustment.* San Francisco: Jossey-Bass.

Squire, L. H. (1985). Race differences in response to Thematic Apperception Test stimulus material. *Dissertation Abstracts International, 46*(4-B), 1347–1348.

Squyres, E. M. (1981). Guidelines for use in scoring TAT stories for time-span. *Perceptual and Motor Skills, 52*, 333–334.

Squyres, E. M., & Craddick, R. A. (1982). A measure of time perspective with the T.A.T. and some issues of reliability. *Journal of Personality Assessment, 46*, 257–259.

Stabenau, J., Turpin, J., Werner, M., & Pollin, W. (1965). A comparative study of families of schizophrenics, delinquents, and normals. *Psychiatry, 28*(1).

Stamps, L. W., & Teevan, R. C. (1974). Fear of failure of conformity in the Asch and Crutchfield situations. *Psychological Reports, 34,* 1327–1330.

Starr, S. (1960). *The relationship between hostility-ambiguity of the T.A.T. cards, hostile fantasy and hostile behavior.* Unpublished doctoral dissertation, Washington State University.

Stein, M. I. (1949). Personality factors involved in the temporal development of Rorschach responses. *Rorschach Research Exchange Journal of Projective Techniques, 13*, 355–414.

Stein, M. I. (1955). *The Thematic Apperception Test: An introductory manual for its clinical use with adult males.* Cambridge, MA: Addison-Wesley.

Stein, M. I. (1978). Thematic Apperception Test and related methods. In B. B. Wolman (Ed.), *Clinical diagnosis of mental disorders* (pp. 179–235). New York: Plenum.

Stephenson, W. (1953). *The study of behavior: Q technique and its methodology.* Chicago: University of Chicago Press.

Stern, E. (1950). *Le test d'aperception thematique de Murray (TAT)* [The Thematic Apperception Test of Murray (TAT)]. Neuchatel: Delachaux Niestle.

Stern, E. (1952). *Experimentelle personlichkeitsanalyse nach dem Murray test (TAT)* [Experimental personality analysis with the Murray test (TAT)]. Zurich: Rascher.

Stern, E. (1953). Contribution a l'interpretation formelle du Thematic Apperception Test. *Archives Internationales de Neurologie, 72*, 73–86.

Stevenson, M. (1952). Some emotional problems of orphanage children. *Canadian Journal of Psychology, 6*, 179–182.

Stewart, A. J. (1978). A longitudinal study of coping styles in self-defining and socially defined women. *Journal of Consulting and Clinical Psychology, 46*, 1079–1084.

Stewart, A. J., & Winter, D. G. (1974). Self-definition and social definition in women. *Journal of Personality, 42*, 238–259.

Stewart, T. D., & Golding, E. R. (1985). Use of projective testing on a consultation-liaison service. *Psychotherapy of Psychosomatics, 43*(3), 151–155.

Stock, N. A., & Kantner, J. E. (1980). Themes elicited by the Senior Apperception Test in institutionalized older adults. *Journal of Personality Assessment, 44*, 600–602.

Stolorow, R. D. (1973). T.A.T. coding system for the theme of voluntary control. *Catalog of Selected Documents in Psychology, 3*(51).

Stone, D. R. (1953). *The auditory apperception test (AAT) manual.* Beverly Hills: Western Psychological Services.

Stone, H. (1956). The T.A.T. aggressive content scale. *Journal of Projective Techniques, 20*, 445–452.

Stone, H., & Dellis, N. (1960). An exploratory investigation into the levels hypothesis. *Journal of Projective Techniques, 24*, 333–340.

Stovall, G., & Craig, R. J. (1990). Mental represensations of physically and sexually abused latency-aged females. *Child Abuse and Neglect, 14*, 233–342.

Strachey, J. (Ed.). (1953). *The standard edition of the complete psychological works of Sigmund Freud.* London: Hogarth.

Strivzer, G. L. (1961). *Thematic sexual and guilt responses as related to stimulus-relevance and experimentally induced drive and inhibition.* Unpublished doctoral dissertation, University of Massachusetts, Amherst.

Strnadova, M., & Bos, P. (1977). A semiprojective test for the assessment of interpersonal relations in the child's family and his social environment. *Psychologia a Patapsychologia Dietata, 12*(5), 449–457.

Strober, M. (1979). The structuring of interpersonal relations in schizophrenic adolescents: A decentering analysis of Thematic Apperception Test stories. *Journal of Abnormal Child Psychology, 7*, 309–316.

Suarez-Orozco, M. M. (1987). Becoming somebody: Central American immigrants in U.S. inner-city schools. *Anthropology and Education Quarterly, 18*, 287–299.

Suarez-Orozco, M. M. (1989). *Central American refugees and U.S. high schools: A psychological study of motivation and achievement.* Stanford, CA: Stanford University Press.

Suarez-Orozco, M. M. (1990a, July). *Achievement culture and personality revisited: The case of the Japanese-Argentines.* Unpublished paper presented at the 13th International Congress of Rorschach and Projective Techniques, Paris.

Suarez-Orozco, M. M. (1990b). Speaking of the unspeakable: Toward a psychosocial understanding of responses to terror. *Ethos, 18*, 353–383.

Suinn, R. M., & Oskamp, S. (1969). *The predictive validity of projective techniques*. Springfield, IL: Charles C. Thomas.

Sullivan, H. S. (1940). Conceptions of modern psychiatry. *Psychiatry, 3,* 147.

Sutcliffe, G. J. (1989). A comparison of story organization on the Thematic Apperception Test and the Robert's Apperception Test for children with emotionally disturbed parents. *Dissertation Abstracts International, 49* (12-A), 3670 (5th ed.: *49*(10-A), 2980).

Sutton, P. M., & Swensen, C. H. (1983). The reliability and concurrent validity of alternative methods for assessing ego development. *Journal of Personality Assessment, 47,* 468–475.

Sutton-Smith, B., Abrams, D. M., Botvin, G. J., Caring, M., Gildesgame, D. P., Mahony, D. H., & Stevens, T. R. (1981). *The folkstories of children*. Philadelphia: University of Pennsylvania Press.

Swartz, J. D. (1985). Senior Apperception Technique. In D. J. Kuper & R. C. Sweetland (Eds.), *Test Critiques: Vol. 4*. Test Corporation of America.

Symonds, P. M. (1948). *Manual for Symond's Picture-Story Test*. New York: Columbia University Press.

Symonds, P. M. (1949). *Adolescent fantasy*. New York: Columbia University Press.

Symonds, P. M. (1951). In E. S. Shneidman (Ed.), *Thematic test analysis* (p. 185). New York: Grune & Stratton.

T.A.T. Newsletter. (1953). *Journal of Projective Techniques, 17*(1).

Tachibana, Y., Ohgishi, M., Monden, K., & Gifu, U. (1984). Experimental study of aggression and catharsis in Japanese. *Perceptual and Motor Skills, 58,* 207–212.

Tappan, M. B. (1991). *Narrative and storytelling: Implications for understanding of moral development*. San Francisco: Jossey-Bass.

Taylor, G. J., & Doody, K. (1985). Verbal measures of alexithymia: What do they measure? *Psychotherapy of Psychosomatics, 43*(1), 32–37.

Teglasi, H. (1993). *Clinical use of storytelling: Emphasizing the TAT with children and adolescents*. Boston: Allyn and Bacon.

Temple, R., & Amen, C. W. (1959). A study of anxiety reactions in young children by means of a projective test. *General Psychology Monographs, 30,* 59–144.

Terry, D. (1952). The use of a rating scale of level of response in T.A.T. stories. *Journal of Abnormal and Social Psychology, 47,* 507–511.

Theiner, E. (1962). Experimental needs are expressed by projective techniques. *Journal of Projective Techniques, 26,* 354–363.

Thelan, M. H., Varble, D. L., & Johnson, J. (1968). Attitudes of academic clinical psychologists toward projective techniques. *American Psychologist, 23,* 517–521.

Thomas, A. D., & Dudeck, S. Z. (1985). Interpersonal affect in Thematic Apperception Test responses: A scoring system. *Journal of Personality Assessment, 49,* 30–36.

Thompson, A. E. (1981). *The theory of affect development and maturity: Applications to the TAT*. Unpublished doctoral dissertation, University of Michigan.

Thompson, C. E. (1949). *Thematic Apperception Test: Thompson modification*. Cambridge, MA: Harvard University Press.

Thompson, C. E., & Bachrach, A. J. (1949). The Thompson modification of the Thematic Apperception Test. *Journal of Projective Techniques, 13,* 173–184.

Thompson, C. E., & Bachrach, A. J. (1951). The use of color in the Thematic Apperception Test. *Journal of Projective Techniques, 15,* 173–184.

Tomkins, S. S., & Miner, J. B. (1957). *The Tomkins-Horn picture arrangement test*. New York: Springer.

Tomkins, S. S., & Tomkins, E. J. (1947). *The Thematic Apperception Test: The theory and technique of interpretation*. New York: Grune & Stratton.

Toolan, M. J. (1988). *Narrative: A critical linguistic introduction*. London: Routledge.

Tooley, K. (1967). Expressive style as a developmental index in late adolescence. *Journal of Projective Techniques, 31,* 51–60.

Toone, D. (1974). *Is old age accompanied by a constricted view of the world?* Unpublished bachelor's thesis, State University of New York College, Purchase, NY.

Traue, H. C., Gottwald, A., Henderson, P. R., & Bakal, D. A. (1985). Nonverbal expressiveness and EMG activity in tension headache sufferers and controls. *Journal of Psychosomatic Research, 29,* 375–381.

Truckenmiller, J. L., & Schai, K. W. (1979). Multi-level structural validation of Leary's interpersonal diagnosis system. *Journal of Consulting and Clinical Psychology, 47,* 1030–1045.

Turner, G. C., & Coleman, J. C. (1962). Examiner influence on Thematic Apperception Test responses. *Journal of Projective Techniques, 26,* 478–486.

U.S. Bureau of the Census. (1990). *Statistical abstracts of the United States: 1990* (110th ed.). Washington, DC.

Ullmann, L. (1957). Selection of neuropsychiatric patients for group psychotherapy. *Journal of Consulting Psychology, 21,* 277–280.

Ullmann, L. P., & McFarland, R. L. (1957). Productivity as a variable in T.A.T. protocols: A methodological study. *Journal of Projective Techniques, 21,* 80–87.

Upadhyaya, S., & Sinha, A. K. (1974). Some findings on psychodiagnostic tests with young retarded adults. *Indian Journal of Clinical Psychology, 1,* 74–79.

Urrabazo, R. (1986). Machismo: Mexican-American male self-concept: An interpretation and reflection on Thematic Apperception Test and Kinetic Family Drawing. *Dissertation Abstracts International, 47*(1-B), 435.

Vahn, C. (1990, July). *Japan vs. U.S.: Cross-cultural differences in student apperceptions of authority, competence, and responsibility.* Unpublished paper presented at the 13th International Congress of Rorschach and Projective Techniques, Paris.

Vaillant, G. E. (1971). Theoretical hierarchy of adaptive ego mechanisms. *Archives of General Psychiatry, 24,* 107–118.

Vaillant, G. E. (1977). *Adaptation to life.* Boston: Little, Brown.

Vaillant, G. E., & Drake, R. E. (1985). Maturity of ego defenses in relation to DSM III Axis II personality disorder. *Archives of General Psychiatry, 42,* 597–601.

Valentine, M., & Robin, A. A. (1950a). Aspects of thematic apperception testing: Paranoid schizophrenia. *Journal of Mental Sciences, 96,* 869–888.

Valentine, M., & Robin, A. A. (1950b). Aspects of thematic apperception testing: Depression. *Journal of Mental Sciences, 96,* 435–447.

van Lennep, A. J., & Houwink, R. H. (1948). *Four Picture Test.* Utrecht.

Vane, J. R. (1981). The Thematic Apperception Test: A review. *Clinical Psychology Review, 1,* 319–336.

Varble, D. L. (1971). The present status of the Thematic Apperception Test. In P. McReynolds (Ed.), *Advances in psychological assessment* (Vol. 2) (pp. 216–235). Palo Alto, CA: Science & Behavior Books.

Varendonck, J. (1931). *The psychology of daydreams.* New York: Macmillan.

Varendonck, J., Atkinson, J., Feld, S., & Gurin, S. (1960). The use of thematic apperception to assess motivation in a nationwide interview study. *Psychology Monographs, 12,* 74.

Varendonck, J., Feld, S., & Crockett, H. (1966). Explorations into the effects of picture cues on thematic apperceptive expression of achievement motivation. *Journal of Personality, 3,* 171–1816.

Varendonck, J., Feld, S., & Gurin, G. (1962). Achievement motivation and religious background. *American Sociology Review, 27,* 205–217.

Vaughan, C. (1988). *Field independency and school achievement: A comparative inquiry.* Unpublished doctoral dissertation, School of Education, University of California at Berkeley.

Vaz, E. C. (1990, July). *A comparison of the TAT of Tukuna Indians and settlers in the Amazon.* Unpublished paper presented at the 13th International Congress of Rorschach and Projective Techniques, Paris.

Velligan, D. I., Goldstein, M. J., Nuechterlein, K. H., Miklowitz, D. J., & Ranlett, G. (1990). Can communication deviance be measured in a family problem-solving interaction? *Family Process, 29,* 213–226.

Veroff, J. (1957). Development and validation of a projective measure of power motivation. *Journal of Abnormal and Social Psychology, 54,* 1–8.

Veroff, J. (1958). A scoring manual for the power motive. In J. W. Atkinson (Ed.), *Motives in fantasy, action, and society.* Princeton, NJ: D. Van Nostrand.

Veroff, J. (1961). Thematic apperception in a nationwide sample survey. In J. Kagan & G. Lesser (Eds.), *Contemporary issues in thematic apperceptive methods* (pp. 83–110). Springfield, IL: Charles C. Thomas.

Veroff, J., Atkinson, J., Feld, S., & Gurin, S. (1960). The use of thematic apperception to assess motivation in a nationwide interview study. *Psychological Monographs, 12*(74), 36.

Veroff, J., Chadiha, L., Leber, D., & Sutherland, L. (1993). Affects and interactions in newlyweds' narratives: Black and White couples compared. *Journal of Narrative and Life History, 3,* 361–390.

Veroff, J., Feld, S., & Crockett, H. (1966). Explorations into the effects of picture cues on thematic apperceptive expression of achievement motivation. *Journal of Personality, 3,* 171–181.

Veroff, J., Feld, S., & Gurin, S. (1962). Achievement motivation and religious background. *American Sociological Review, 27,* 205–217.

Veroff, J., Wilcox, S., & Atkinson, J. W. (1953). The achievement motive in high school and college-age women. *Journal of Abnormal and Social Psychology, 48,* 108–119.

Vestiwig, R. E., & Paradise, C. A. (1977). Multidimensional scaling of the TAT and the measurement of achievement motivation. *Journal of Personality Assessment, 41,* 595–603.

Viberg, M., Blennow, G., & Polski, B. (1987). Epilepsy in adolescence: Implications for the development of personality. *Epilepsia, 28,* 542–546.

Volkan, V. D. (1976). *Primitive internalized object relations.* New York: International Universities Press.

Vollhardt, B. R., Ackerman, S. H., & Shindledecker, R. D. (1986). Verbal expression of affect in rheumatoid arthritis patients: A blind, controlled test for alexithymia. *Acta Psychiatrica Scandinavica, 74,* 73–79.

Vuyk, R. (1954). *Plaatjes als hulpmiddel bij het kinderpsychologisch onderzoek.* Leiden: H. E. Stenfert Korese N.V.

Wagatsuma, H., & De Vos, G. A. (1984). *Heritage of endurance: Family patterns and delinquency formation in urban Japan.* Berkeley, CA: University of California Press.

Wakefield, J. F. (1986). Creativity and the TAT blank card. *Journal of Creative Behavior, 20*(2), 127–133.

Wanamaker, C. E., & Reznikoff, M. (1989). Effects of aggressive and nonaggressive rock songs on projective and structured tests. *Journal of Psychology, 123*(6), 561–570.

Warren, M. (1989). Achievement and power motivation of inmates on the Thematic Apperception Test. *Dissertation Abstracts International, 49*(10-A), 2980.

Waxenberg, S. E. (1955). Psychosomatic patients and other physically ill persons: A comparative study. *Journal of Consulting Psychology, 10,* 183–196.

Webster, H. (1952). Rao's multiple discriminant technique applied to three T.A.T. variables. *Journal of Abnormal and Social Psychology, 47,* 641–648.

Weiner, I. B. (1966). *Psychodiagnosis of schizophrenia.* New York: Wiley.

Weiner, N. (1948). *Cybernetics.* New York: Wiley.

Weisskopf, E. A. (1950a). A transcendence index as a proposed measure in the T.A.T. *Journal of Psychology, 29,* 379–390.

Weisskopf, E. A. (1950b). A experimental study of the effect of brightness and ambiguity on projection in the TAT. *Journal of Psychology, 29,* 407–416.

Weisskopf, E. A., & Dieppa, J. J. (1951). Experimentally induced faking of TAT responses. *Journal of Consulting Psychology, 15,* 469–474.

Weisskopf, E. A., & Dunleavy, G. P. (1952). Bodily similarity between subject and central figure in the TAT as an influence on projection. *Journal of Abnormal and Social Psychology, 47,* 441–445.

Weisskopf-Joelson, E. A., & Foster, H. C. (1962). An experimental study of stimulus variation upon projection. *Journal of Projective Techniques, 26,* 366–370.

Weisskopf-Joelson, E. A., & Lynn, D. B. (1953). The effect of variations in ambiguity on projection in the Children's Apperception Test. *Journal of Consulting Psychology, 17,* 67–70.

Weisskopf-Joelson, E. A., & Money, L. (1958). Facial similarity betwen subject and central figure in the TAT as an influence on projection. *Journal of Abnormal Psychology, 48,* 341–344.

Weisskopf-Joelson, E. A., Zimmerman, J., & McDaniel, M. (1970). Similarity between subject and stimulus as an influence on projection. *Journal of Projective Techniques and Personality Assessment, 34,* 328–331.

Weissman, S. (1964). Some indicators of acting out behavior from the Thematic Apperception Test. *Journal of Projective Techniques, 28,* 366–375.

Wender, P. H., & Klein, D. F. (1981). *Mind, mood, and medicine: A guide to the new biopsychiatry.* New York: Farrar, Straus, & Giroux.

Werner, H. (1950). The acquisition of word meanings: A developmental study. *Society for Research in Child Development, 15*(1).

Werner, M., Stabenau, J. R., & Pollin, W. (1970). Thematic Apperception Test Method for the differentiation of families of schizophrenics, delinquents, and normals. *Journal of Abnormal and Social Psychology, 75,* 139–145.

West, A., et al. (1983). Marijuana-induced primary process content in the TAT. *Journal of Personality Assessment, 47*(5), 466–467.

Westen, D. (1991a). Social cognition and object relations. *Psychological Bulletin, 109,* 429–455.

Westen, D. (1991b). Clinical assessment of object relations using the T.A.T. *Journal of Personality Assessment, 56,* 127–133.

Westen, D., Lohr, N., Silk, K. R., Gold, L., & Kerber, K. (1990a). Object relations and social cognition in borderlines, major depressives, and normals: A thematic apperception test analysis. *Psychological Assessment, 2,* 355–364.

Westen, D., Ludolph, P., Block, M. J., Wixom, J., & Wiss, F. C. (1991b). Developmental history and object relations in psychiatrically disturbed adolescent girls. *American Journal of Psychiatry, 148,* 1419–1420.

Westen, D., Ludolph, P., Lerner, H., Ruffins, S., & Wiss, C. (1990b). Object relations in borderline adolescents. *Journal of the American Academy of Child and Adolescent Psychiatry, 29,* 338–348.

Westen, D., Klepser, J., Ruffins, S. A., Silverman, M., Lifton, M., & Boekamp, J. (1991a). Object relations in children and adolescents: The development of working representations. *Journal of Consulting and Clinical Psychology, 59,* 400–409.

White, M., & Epston, D. (1990). *Narrative means to therapeutic ends.* New York: Norton.

White, R. K. (1944). Value-analysis: A quantitative method for describing qualitative data. *Journal of Social Psychology, 19,* 351–358.

White, R. K. (1951). *Value analysis: The nature and use of the method.* New York: Society for the Psychological Study of Social Issues.

White, R. W. (1951). In E. S. Shneidman (Ed.), *Thematic test analysis* (p. 188). New York: Grune & Stratton.

White, R. W., & Sanford, R. N. (1941). *Thematic Apperception Test Manual.* Unpublished report. Harvard Psychological Clinic, Cambridge, MA.

Wiener, N. (1948). *Cybernetics.* New York: Wiley.

Williams, E. L. (1986). Early recollection and Thematic Apperception Test responses of restricted anorexic, bulimic anorexic, and bulimic women. *Dissertation Abstracts International, 47*(2-B), 810.

Wilson, A., Passik, S. D., Faude, J., Abrams, J., & Gordon, E. (1989). A hierarchical model of opiate addiction: Failures of self-regulation as a central aspect of substance abuse. *Journal of Nervous and Mental Diseases, 177,* 390–399.

Winchester, T. H. (1948). *A study of differences between written and oral protocols from the Thematic Apperception Test.* Unpublished master's thesis, University of Denver.

Windleband, W. (1904). *Geschichte und Naturwissenschaft, 3.*

Winget, C. N., Gleser, G. C., & Clements, W. H. (1969). A method for quantifying human relations, hostility, and anxiety applied to TAT productions. *Journal of Projective Techniques and Personality Assessment, 33,* 433–437.

Winnicott, D. W. (1965). *The maturational process and the facilitating environment.* New York: International Universities Press.

Winter, D. G. (1973). *The power motive.* New York: Free Press.

Winter, W. D., & Ferreira, A. J. (1969). *Research in family interaction: Readings and commentary.* Palo Alto, CA: Science & Behavior Books.

Winter, W. D., & Ferreira, A. J. (1970). A factor analysis of family interaction measures. *Journal of Projective Techniques and Personality Assessment, 34,* 55–63.

Winter, W. D., Ferreira, A. J., & Olson, J. L. (1965). Story sequence analysis of a family TAT. *Journal of Projective Techniques and Personality Assessment, 29,* 392–397.

Winter, W. D., Ferreira, A. J., & Olson, J. L. (1966). Hostility themes in the family TAT. *Journal of Projective Techniques and Personality Assessment, 30,* 270–274.

Witherspoon, R. (1968). Development of objective scoring methods for longitudinal C.A.T. data. *Journal of Projective Techniques, 32,* 406–412.

Wittenborn, J. R. (1949). Thematic Apperception Test. In O. K. Buros (Ed.), *The third mental measurements yearbook* (pp. 206–207). Highland Park, NJ: Gryphon Press.

Wohlford, P. (1968). Extension of personal time in TAT and story completion stories. *Journal of Projective Techniques and Personality Assessment, 32,* 267–280.

Wohlford, P., & Herrera, J. H. (1970). TAT stimulus-cues and extension of personal time. *Journal of Projective Techniques and Personality Assessment, 34,* 31–37.

Wolk, R. L., Rustin, S. L., & Seiden, R. (1966). A custom-made projective technique for the aged: The Gerontological Appercepion Test. *Journal of the Long Island Consultation Center, 4,* 8–21.

Wolk, R. L., & Wolk, R. B. (1971). *Gerontological Apperception Test.* New York: Behavioral Publications.

Wolowitz, H., & Shorkey, C. (1966). Power themes in the T.A.T. stories of paranoid and schizophrenic males. *Journal of Projective Techniques, 30*(6), 591–596.

Woodward, N. J., & Wallston, B. S. (1987). Age and health care beliefs: Self-efficacy as a mediator of low desire for control. *Psychology and Aging, 2,* 3–8.

Worchel, F. F., & Dupress, J. L. (1990). Projective storytelling techniques. In C. R. Reynolds & R. W. Kamphaus (Eds.), *Handbook of psychological and educational assessment of children* (pp. 70–88). New York: Guilford.

Wyatt, F. (1947). The scoring and analysis of the Thematic Apperception Test. *Journal of Psychology, 24,* 319–330.

Wyatt, F. (1958). A principle for the interpretation of fantasy. *Journal of Projective Techniques, 22,* 173–180.

Wyatt, J., & Veroff, J. B. (1956). Thematic apperception and fantasy tests. In D. Brower & L. E. Abt (Eds.), *Progress in clinical psychology* (pp. 32–57). New York: Grune & Stratton.

Yanovski, A., & Fogel, M. L. (1988). Effects of instructions for visual imagery on Thematic Apperception Test responses. *Psychological Reports, 60*(3), 779–789.

Young, F. M. (1956). Responses of juvenile delinquents to the Thematic Apperception Test. *Journal of Genetic Psychology, 88,* 251–259.

Young, K. G. (1987). *Taleworlds and storyrealms: The phenomenology of narrative.* Dordrecht, Holland: Martinus Nijhoff.

Young, R. D. (1953). *The effect of the interpreter's personality on the interpretation of T.A.T. protocols.* Unpublished doctoral dissertation, University of Texas.

Zhang, T., Xu, S., Cai, Z., & Chen, Z. (1993). Research on the Thematic Apperception Test: Chinese revision and its norm. *Acta Psychologica Scandinavica, 25,* 314–323.

Zimmerman, I. L., & Woo-Sam, J. M. (1973). *Clinical interpretation of the Wechsler Adult Intelligence Scale.* New York: Grune & Stratton.

Ziskin, J. (1995). *Coping with psychiatric and psychological testimony.* Los Angeles: Law and Psychology Press.

Zubin, J., Eron, L. D., & Schumer, F. (1965). *An experimental approach to projective techniques.* New York: Wiley.

Zubiri, M. (1990, July), *TAT and psychosomatic classification in melanoma patients.* Unpublished paper presented at the 13th International Congress of Rorschach and Projective Techniques, Paris.

Name Index

Subject Index

Acculturation, 411, 422
Achievement:
    imagery in thematic stories, 192
    motivation in stories, scoring subcate-
        gories, 83–84
    and T.A.T. picture 1, 61–62
Acting in T.A.T. stories, 238
Acting-out test takers, 190–191
Adaptive behavior, 39
Adaptive regression in the service of the
    ego (ARISE), 102, 106
Adolescents:
    developmental differences in, 186
    and T.A.T. stories, 161–164
    as test takers, 190–191
Affect states in T.A.T. stories, 237–238
Affiliation imagery in thematic stories, 192
African Americans:
    adaptations for thematic tests, 416–418
    and T.A.T., 187
Africans, thematic test adaptations for,
    418–419
Aggression/hostility, 39, 188–191
    and T.A.T. picture 1, 61
    and T.A.T. picture 8BM, 65
    and T.A.T. picture 3BM, 63
    and T.A.T. picture 18GF, 72
Agoraphobics and the T.A.T., 154
Ambition and T.A.T. picture 8BM, 65
Ambivalence in T.A.T. stories, 236
American Indians, thematic test adaptations
    for, 414–416
Anhedonia, 199
Anorexia, predicting, 154
Anticipation as coping mechanism, 204
Anxieties:
    in C.A.T. stories, 305
    defense against, 32
    in T.A.T. stories, 99
Apperceptive distortion, 18–19, 31–40, 177
    forms of, 34–40
Apperception Picture Test (APT), 50
Asian Americans, thematic test adaptations
    for, 419

Asians, thematic test adaptations for,
    419–420
Attack, fear of:
    and T.A.T. picture 5, 67
    and T.A.T. picture 11, 68
    and T.A.T. picture 18BM, 71
Attention deficit disorder (ADD), 50
    C.A.T. protocol illustrating, 262–267
    T.A.T. protocol illustrating, 267–271
Auditory Apperception Test (AAT), 50
Authority figures, 53
Autism, 37, 86–87
Autonomous functioning and T.A.T. stories,
    103, 106
Auxiliary ego, 259
Avoidance as defense mechanism, 153,
    196
Avoidant personality disorder, 196

Barren records, problem of, 26–27
    ways to alleviate, 29–31
Beery Test of Visual Integration, 255
Behavioral needs of the story's hero, 97
Bellak Scoring System, 89–151
    case illustrations, 106–151
    the blank, 92–94
    observation-near and observation-distant,
        90–91
    scoring categories, 94–103
    short form of blank, 104–106
    summary and final report, 103–104
Bender Gestalt Test, 14, 19, 25, 48, 49, 60,
    75, 255, 412
Benton Test of Visual Retention, 255
Bias in thematic tests, 422–426
Blacky Pictures test, 3, 50
Body image:
    in C.A.T. stories, 303
    in C.A.T.-S. picture 7
    in T.A.T. picture 1, 61
    in T.A.T. picture 3BM, 64
    in T.A.T. picture 17BM, 71
    in T.A.T. pictures, 96

DATE DUE

DEMCO 38-297